The English ~~for~~ English

Uncle Tungsten, Dr Sacks

The Myth that Changed the World

Simon Winchester

THE METAPHYSICAL CLUB

Wilky James recovering from wounds received in the attack on
Fort Wagner, 1863. (Drawing by William James.)

THE METAPHYSICAL CLUB

LOUIS MENAND

Flamingo
An Imprint of HarperCollins*Publishers*

Flamingo
An imprint of HarperCollins*Publishers*
77–85 Fulham Palace Road,
Hammersmith, London W6 8JB

Flamingo is a registered trademark of
HarperCollins*Publishers* Ltd

www.**fire**and**water**.com

Published by HarperCollins*Publishers* 2001
1 3 5 7 9 8 6 4 2

Copyright © Louis Menand 2001

Louis Menand asserts the moral right to
be identified as the author of this work

A catalogue record for this book
is available from the British Library

ISBN 0 00 712689 1

Printed and bound in Great Britain by
Omnia Books Limited, Glasgow

Illustration and text credits appear on pp. 545–6

To my parents

and to Gilda

CONTENTS

Contents

PREFACE

It is a remarkable fact about the United States that it fought a civil war without undergoing a change in its form of government. The Constitution was not abandoned during the American Civil War; elections were not suspended; there was no coup d'état. The war was fought to preserve the system of government that had been established at the nation's founding—to prove, in fact, that the system was worth preserving, that the idea of democracy had not failed. This is the meaning of the Gettysburg Address and of the great fighting cry of the North: "Union." And the system was preserved; the union did survive. But in almost every other respect, the United States became a different country. The war alone did not make America modern, but the war marks the birth of modern America.

As a political and economic event, the transformation is not hard to see or difficult to explain. Secession allowed the North, for four years, to set the terms for national expansion without interference from the South, and the wartime Congress did not let the opportunity slip. That Congress was one of the most active in American history. It supported scientific training and research; it established the first system of national taxation and created the first significant national currency; it made possible the construction of public universities and the completion of the transcontinental railway. It turned the federal government into the legislative engine of social and economic progress. And it helped to win a war. The military defeat of the Confederacy made the Republican Party the dominant force in national politics after 1865, and the Republican Party was the champion of business. For more than thirty years, a strong central government protected and promoted the ascendance of industrial capitalism and the way of life associated with it—the way of life we call "modern."

To this extent, the outcome of the Civil War was a validation, as Lincoln had hoped it would be, of the American experiment. Except for one thing, which is that people who live in democratic societies are not supposed to settle their disagreements by killing one another. For the generation that lived through it, the Civil War was a terrible and traumatic experience. It tore a hole in their lives. To some of them, the war seemed not just a failure of democracy, but a failure of culture, a failure of ideas. As traumatic wars do—as the First World War would do for many Europeans sixty years later, and as the Vietnam War would do for many Americans a hundred years later—the Civil War discredited the beliefs and assumptions of the era that preceded it. Those beliefs had not prevented the country from going to war; they had not prepared it for the astonishing violence the war unleashed; they seemed absurdly obsolete in the new, postwar world. The Civil War swept away the slave civilization of the South, but it swept away almost the whole intellectual culture of the North along with it. It took nearly half a century for the United States to develop a culture to replace it, to find a set of ideas, and a way of thinking, that would help people cope with the conditions of modern life. That struggle is the subject of this book.

There are many paths through this story. The one that is followed here runs through the lives of four people: Oliver Wendell Holmes, William James, Charles S. Peirce, and John Dewey. These people had highly distinctive personalities, and they did not always agree with one another, but their careers intersected at many points, and together they were more responsible than any other group for moving

American thought into the modern world. They not only had an unparalleled influence on other writers and thinkers; they had an enormous influence on American life. Their ideas changed the way Americans thought—and continue to think—about education, democracy, liberty, justice, and tolerance. And as a consequence, they changed the way Americans live—the way they learn, the way they express their views, the way they understand themselves, and the way they treat people who are different from themselves. We are still living, to a great extent, in a country these thinkers helped to make.[1]

Within this claim for the importance of Holmes, James, Peirce, and Dewey and the work they did, there is a point about the nature of intellectual culture. It is a point, in fact, which is very much a part of their legacy. There is a difference between an idea and an ideology. The suggestion that Holmes, James, Peirce, and Dewey were the first modern thinkers in the United States—that they helped put Americans into a better relation with the conditions of modern life—does not mean that their thought constituted a justification of those conditions. It did not. But it cannot be said that their thought stands in radical opposition to those conditions, either. If we are looking for alternative visions of American life in the decades following the Civil War, Holmes, James, Peirce, and Dewey are not the figures we would turn to. This has something to do, no doubt, with their temperaments and their politics, but it is also a consequence of their attitude toward ideas.

What was that attitude? If we strain out the differences, personal and philosophical, they had with one another, we can say that what these four thinkers had in common was not a group of ideas, but a single idea—an idea about ideas. They all believed that ideas are not "out there" waiting to be discovered, but are tools—like forks and knives and microchips—that people devise to cope with the world in which they find themselves. They believed that ideas are produced not by individuals, but by groups of individuals—that ideas are social. They believed that ideas do not develop according to some inner logic of their own, but are entirely dependent, like germs, on their human carriers and the environment. And they believed that since

ideas are provisional responses to particular and unreproducible circumstances, their survival depends not on their immutability but on
their adaptability.

The belief that ideas should never become ideologies—either justifying the status quo, or dictating some transcendent imperative for
renouncing it—was the essence of what they taught. In many ways
this was a liberating attitude, and it accounts for the popularity
Holmes, James, and Dewey (Peirce is a special case) enjoyed in their
lifetimes, and for the effect they had on a whole generation of
judges, teachers, journalists, philosophers, psychologists, social scientists, law professors, and even poets. They taught a kind of skepticism that helped people cope with life in a heterogeneous,
industrialized, mass-market society, a society in which older human
bonds of custom and community seemed to have become attenuated, and to have been replaced by more impersonal networks of
obligation and authority. But skepticism is also one of the qualities
that make societies like that work. It is what permits the continual
state of upheaval that capitalism thrives on. Holmes, James, Peirce,
and Dewey helped to free thought from thralldom to official ideologies, of the church or the state or even the academy. There is also,
though, implicit in what they wrote, a recognition of the limits of
what thought can do in the struggle to increase human happiness.

This book is an effort to write about these ideas in their own
spirit—that is, to try to see ideas as always soaked through by the
personal and social situations in which we find them. Holmes,
James, Peirce, and Dewey were philosophers, and their work is part
of the history of abstract thought. Its philosophical merits were contested in its own time, and they are contested today. This book is not
a work of philosophical argument, though; it is a work of historical
interpretation. It describes a change in American life by looking at a
change in its intellectual assumptions. Those assumptions changed
because the country became a different place. As with every change,
there was gain and there was loss. This story, if it has been told in the
right way, should help make possible a better measure of both.

PART ONE

The first known photograph of John Brown, taken in Osawatomie, Kansas, in 1856, the year he and his sons abducted five proslavery settlers in Pottawatomie and split their skulls open with cutlasses.

ONE

THE POLITICS OF SLAVERY

I

OLIVER WENDELL HOLMES, JR., was an officer in the Union Army. He stood six feet three inches tall and had a soldierly bearing. In later life, he loved to use military metaphors in his speeches and his conversation; he didn't mind being referred to good-naturedly as Captain Holmes; and he wore his enormous military mustaches until his death, in 1935, at the age of ninety-three. The war was the central experience of his life, and he kept its memory alive. Every year he drank a glass of wine in observance of the anniversary of the battle of Antietam, where he had been shot in the neck and left, briefly behind enemy lines, for dead.

But Holmes hated the war. He was twenty years old and weighed just 136 pounds at the time of his first battle, at Ball's Bluff, where he was shot through the chest. He fought bravely and he was resilient, but he was not strong in a brute sense, and as the war went on the physical ordeal was punishing. He was wounded three times in all, the third time in an engagement leading up to the battle of Chancellorsville, when he was shot in the foot. He hoped the foot would have to be amputated so he could be discharged, but it was spared, and he served out his commission. Many of his friends were killed in battle, some of them in front of his eyes. Those glasses of wine were toasts to pain.

Holmes recovered from the wounds. The effects of the mental ordeal were permanent. He had gone off to fight because of his moral beliefs, which he held with singular fervor. The war did more than make him lose those beliefs. It made him lose his belief in beliefs. It impressed on his mind, in the most graphic and indelible way, a certain idea about the limits of ideas. *This* idea he stuck to, with a grimness and, at times, a cynicism that have occasionally repelled people who have studied his life and thought. But it is the idea that underlies many of the opinions he wrote, long after the war ended, as an associate justice on the United States Supreme Court. To understand the road Holmes had to travel in order to write those opinions, we have to go back to one of the worlds the Civil War made obsolete, the world of prewar Boston.

2

We think of the Civil War as a war to save the union and to abolish slavery, but before the fighting began most people regarded these as incompatible ideals. Northerners who wanted to preserve the union did not wish to see slavery extended into the territories; some of them hoped it would wither away in the states where it persisted. But many Northern businessmen believed that losing the South would mean economic catastrophe, and many of their employees believed that freeing the slaves would mean lower wages. They feared secession far more than they disliked slavery, and they were unwilling to risk the former by trying to pressure the South into giving up the latter.

The abolitionists were careless of the future of the union. "If thy right hand offend thee, cut it off" was the text they preached. They despised the unionists as people who put self-interest ahead of righteousness, and they considered any measure short of abolition or partition to be a bargain with evil. They baited the unionists with

Dr. Oliver Wendell Holmes, poet, novelist, and dean of the Harvard Medical School, the man who named Boston "the Hub."

charges of hypocrisy and greed; the unionists responded by accusing the abolitionists of goading the South into secession, and by trying to run them out of town and sometimes to kill them. Before there was a war against the South, there was a war within the North.

Holmes's father, Dr. Oliver Wendell Holmes, Sr., was a unionist. The Holmeses were related to families that had prospered in New England since the time of the Puritans—the Olivers, the Wendells, the Quincys, the Bradstreets, the Cabots, the Jacksons, and the Lees—but they were not exceptionally wealthy. Dr. Holmes was a professor; his father, Abiel, had been a minister. He regarded himself as a New England Brahmin (a term he coined),[1] by which he meant not merely a person of good family, but a scholar, or what we would call an intellectual. His own mind was a mixture of enlightenment and conformity: he combined largeness of intellect with narrowness of culture.

Dr. Holmes had become famous in 1830, the year after he graduated from Harvard, when he wrote a popular poem protesting the breakup of the U.S.S. *Constitution*, "Old Ironsides." After college he tried the law but quickly switched to medicine. He studied in Paris, and in 1843, when he was thirty-four, published a paper on the causes of puerperal (or childbed) fever that turned out to be a landmark work in the germ theory of disease. (He showed that the disease was carried from childbirth to childbirth by the attending physician; it was a controversial paper among the medical establishment.) He joined the faculty of the Harvard Medical School, where he eventually served as dean. But his celebrity came from his activities as a belletrist. He was one of the first members of the Saturday Club, a literary dining and conversation society whose participants included Emerson, Hawthorne, Longfellow, Richard Henry Dana, Jr., James Russell Lowell, and Charles Eliot Norton. He was a founder of the *Atlantic Monthly*, whose name he invented and in whose pages he published his popular column of aperçus, "The Autocrat of the Breakfast-Table" (followed by "The Professor at the Breakfast-Table" and "The Poet at the Breakfast-Table"). He wrote hundreds of verses and three novels. Many people, and not only Bostonians, believed him to be the greatest talker they had ever heard.

Yet he was unabashedly provincial. His chief ambition was to represent the Boston point of view in all things. (He also suffered from asthma, which made travel uncomfortable.) On the other hand, he regarded the Boston point of view as pretty much the only point of view worth representing. He considered Boston "the thinking centre of the continent, and therefore of the planet."[2] Or as he also put it, in a phrase that became the city's nickname for itself: "Boston State-House is the hub of the solar system."[3] He was an enemy of Calvinism (which had been his father's religion) and a rationalist, but his faith in good breeding was nearly atavistic, and he saw no reason to challenge the premises of a social dispensation that had, over the course of two centuries, contrived to produce a man as genial and accomplished as himself.

Dr. Holmes's views on political issues therefore tended to be reflexive: he took his cues from his own instincts and the prevailing tendencies, and where these conflicted, he went with the tendencies. In 1850, for example, while he was serving as dean of the Medical School, he was approached by a black man named Martin Delany who requested admission. Delany was an exceptional character. He had, with Frederick Douglass, helped to found the leading black newspaper in the United States, the *North Star*; he later wrote a novel in answer to *Uncle Tom's Cabin*, called *Blake; Or, the Huts of America*, and served as a major in the Union Army, the highest rank achieved by an African-American during the Civil War. He was already thirty-eight years old in 1850, and his credentials for admission to medical school were unimpeachable, although he had been turned down by four schools, including the University of Pennsylvania, before he tried Harvard.

As it happened, two other black candidates, Daniel Laing, Jr., and Isaac H. Snowden, both from Massachusetts, had applied for admission in the same year. Laing and Snowden were sponsored by the American Colonization Society, a group that advocated resettling African-Americans in Liberia as a solution to the problem of slavery. They promised to emigrate as soon as they received their degrees; Delany made it clear that he intended to practice in the United States. Holmes could see no reason not to admit all three. He also arranged to admit (on the understanding that she would not sit in the regular anatomy class) the first woman to attend Harvard Medical School, Harriet Hunt, another Bostonian—though it was his view that for the most part the education of women was a wasteful practice. (There were a few women who had the capacity to profit from education, he once conceded—Madame de Staël, for example—but "[a] natural law is not disproved by a pickled monster.")[4]

The medical students revolted. They notified the faculty of their objection to the presence of a woman at the lectures, and Delany, Laing, and Snowden were ostracized. In December sixty students, a majority of the student body, met and approved a petition resolving that "we cannot consent to be identified as fellow students with blacks, whose company we would not keep in the streets, and whose Society as associates we would not tolerate in our houses," and that "we feel our grievances to be but the beginning of an evil, which, if not checked will increase, and that the number of respectable *white* students will, in future, be in an inverse ratio to that of *blacks*." A slightly smaller group, of forty-eight students, submitted a dissenting petition, noting that as unpleasant as the situation was, "they would feel it a far greater evil, if, in the present state of public feeling, a medical college in Boston could refuse to this unfortunate class any privileges of education, which it is in the power of the profession to bestow."

The faculty met for two evenings at Holmes's house. At first it held firm, but after it received notice from some of the white students of their intention to transfer, it capitulated, and directed Holmes to inform the American Colonization Society that "the result of this experiment has satisfied [the Medical School faculty] that the intermixing of races is distasteful to a large portion of the class, & injurious to the interests of the school," and that no applications from black candidates would be accepted in the future. Delany, Laing, and Snowden were not permitted to register for the following term. Harriet Hunt had already withdrawn her application on the advice of the faculty.[5] Holmes had seen nothing wrong with admitting these new students, but when the consensus of his colleagues moved in the other direction, he seems to have seen nothing wrong with changing his course.

Laing ended up at Dartmouth, where he received his degree; Snowden returned to study privately with a surgeon at Massachusetts General Hospital. (In 1853, he reapplied to Harvard and was rejected.)[6] Delany stuck around. He expected his cause to be taken up by the Boston abolitionists, who were then embattled in a series of highly publicized efforts on behalf of escaped slaves being hunted down under the Fugitive Slave Law of 1850. In October, a few weeks before Delany arrived in Cambridge, a Boston vigilance committee, led by the minister Theodore Parker, had run out of town two agents who were trying to hunt down William and Ellen Craft, a black couple who had escaped from Georgia disguised as a white gentleman and his manservant. In February 1851, after a black waiter and former slave known as Shadrach was seized by slave catchers in a Boston coffeehouse, an antislavery posse stormed the federal courthouse where he was being held, overwhelmed the marshals, and got him safely onto the underground railroad to Canada (where he eventually opened his own restaurant). In April, 300 soldiers and armed deputies, marching in the dead of night, succeeded in escorting a third fugitive, seventeen-year-old Thomas Sims of Georgia, to the ship in Boston Harbor waiting to return him to slavery.[7]

But no abolitionist protested the expulsion of Laing, Snowden, and Delany from the Harvard Medical School. (No one seems to have complained about the fate of Harriet Hunt, either. Harvard Medical School did not admit a woman until 1945.) Part of the reason was that the abolitionists disapproved of the meliorist policies of the American Colonization Society, and were not disposed to enter into a grievance on their behalf. But Delany concluded that the antislavery activists were more offended by the notion of Southerners presuming to send their agents into Northern cities to retrieve their "property" than they were by discrimination against any particular black man already in their midst. And he was not wrong. For the politics of slavery in antebellum Boston was a complicated business.

3

The mill towns that sprang up in the Merrimack Valley north of Boston around 1820—Haverhill, Lawrence, Lowell—were heavily dependent on Southern cotton, which they made into finished goods and then sold, along with footwear, machine parts, rubber goods, and other manufactured products, back to the South. The dependency ran in both directions, for the South had no real industrial base of its own: there were more cotton spindles in Lowell, Massachusetts, in 1860 than in all eleven of the states that eventually made up the Confederacy combined.[8] The city of Boston, by the middle of the nineteenth century, had become a financial service center with a large stake in this peculiar domestic economy. The state's business leaders and most of its political leaders had no interest in antagonizing the South; and for antislavery campaigners, State Street, which was the main address of the Boston banking industry, became a synonym for appeasement.

The hero of State Street was Daniel Webster, whose "Seventh of March Speech" in the United States Senate, invoking the principle of union above section, had cleared the way for the Compromise of 1850. That act—really a series of acts—dealt with the status of slavery in the new territories and in California in a manner satisfactory to the South. It also responded to Southern demands for reinforcement of the fugitive slave laws. Laws affirming the property rights of slaveholders in former slaves who had escaped across state lines had been on the books since 1793; under the terms of the Compromise, their enforcement became for the first time a federal responsibility, which meant that Southern slaveholders could enlist federal marshals and magistrates in their efforts to hunt down and retrieve refugees in the North—thereby trumping the authority of local officials and state "liberty laws."

The new Fugitive Slave Law was the least-debated item in the Compromise of 1850, but it radicalized the North. It pushed many previously passive unionists into active animosity toward the South —not because they considered the law an encroachment on the

liberties of black Americans, but because they considered it an encroachment on the liberties of Northern whites. It was "a degradation which the North would not permit," wrote Ulysses S. Grant near
the end of his life, and he regarded it as the prime instigator of the
war: "[T]he great majority of the people of the North had no particular quarrel with slavery, so long as they were not forced to have it
themselves. But they were not willing to play the rôle of police for
the South in the protection of this particular institution."[9]

A Northerner might therefore resent and resist the mandates of
the Fugitive Slave Law without being an advocate of abolition.
Richard Henry Dana, for example, considered himself a political
conservative; but he risked his life representing fugitives and their
protectors in federal court in Boston. He was not only attacked in the
streets for his efforts; he was snubbed socially, as was his friend
Charles Sumner, who had denounced the Compromise, in a speech
at Faneuil Hall, as belonging to "the immortal catalogue of national
crimes" dating back to ancient Rome.[10] George Ticknor, the cynosure
of Boston high society, sent Dana a note after he appeared as counsel in the Sims case informing him that they would never meet again.
The year before, he had rented Dana his summer home.[11]

Ticknor is a representative figure of the prewar Boston establishment. He occupies the place where its business, legal, and academic
interests intersected. He was the son of a fairly successful merchant;
he married a daughter of Samuel Eliot, an extremely successful merchant. His mother's grandson by her first marriage was George Ticknor Curtis, a lawyer who became the United States commissioner
charged with overseeing the enforcement of the Fugitive Slave Law;
he facilitated the return to slavery of Thomas Sims. George Curtis's
brother, Benjamin, was the judge at the trial at which the rescuers of
Shadrach were convicted; he soon after became, on Webster's recommendation, an associate justice of the United States Supreme
Court. All three were close friends of Daniel Webster. But Ticknor
was not a businessman or a lawyer himself. He was a former Harvard
professor who had been educated at Dartmouth and then in Europe.
He was an academic reformer, a scholar of Spanish literature, and a
philanthropist, one of the founders of the Boston Public Library. His

views on slavery were dictated in part by family connections and by the social circles in which he moved, but they were also the views of a Harvard Unitarian.

Unitarianism, to which Harvard College essentially converted following the appointment of Henry Ware as Hollis Professor of Divinity in 1805, was a creed founded on a belief in the innate moral goodness of the individual (in reaction to Calvinism, which was a creed founded on a belief in the innate moral depravity of the individual). It was in many ways a religion that led its followers naturally to oppose slavery. The leaders of the antislavery posses that stormed the federal courthouse to rescue captured fugitives—Theodore Parker and Thomas Wentworth Higginson—were graduates of the Unitarian Harvard Divinity School. But many Harvard professors were Unitarians of a different stripe. They were social conservatives. They believed in law and order and the sanctity of property.

The ministerial spokesman for Boston Unitarianism, William Ellery Channing, was connected by birth and marriage to the New England mercantile elite. His parents had owned slaves; his father-in-law, George Gibbs (who was also his uncle), had made part of his fortune operating a distillery that sold rum to the slave traders.[12] In 1835, the year a Boston mob attempted to drag the abolitionist William Lloyd Garrison through the streets at the end of a rope, Channing published a pamphlet called *Slavery*, in which he condemned both the slaveowners and the abolitionists, and in which he advocated a policy of moral suasion, rather than political coercion, as the proper means for inducing the South to give up slavery.

And this was, for many years, the *liberal* Unitarian position, not only at places like Harvard, but in Channing's own ministry, on Federal Street in Boston, as well. Channing's close friend Charles Follen, a German scholar, was dismissed from the Harvard faculty in part because of his antislavery activities (he was also an irritant to the administration on the issue of faculty free speech). After Follen's death in a steamboat fire in 1840, the laymen refused to permit Channing to hold a memorial service for his friend in his own church.[13] Cornelius Conway Felton, a professor of Greek at Harvard (and member of the Saturday Club) who later became president of

Harvard College, was proslavery and an opponent of antislavery agitation. He broke with Sumner, who had been a close friend, over Sumner's views on the Compromise of 1850.[14] Only one member of the Harvard faculty enlisted to fight in the Civil War. He was a German émigré.[15]

Though they were shunned on State Street, Dana and Sumner did have political allies in Boston, notably the Adamses. John Quincy Adams, in his postpresidential career as a Congressman, had been a stalwart and often lonely opponent of the slave interests. He spoke out so long and so fervently against the so-called petition gag rule, which, beginning in 1834, tabled without debate all antislavery petitions sent to Congress, that an attempt was made to censure him by his House colleagues. (It failed.) Both he and his father, John Adams, had been defeated in their presidential campaigns for second terms by the Southern vote, and his son Charles Francis Adams had run for vice-president on the Free Soil ticket in 1848.

Dana, Sumner, and Charles Francis Adams were antislavery, but they were not abolitionists. They were Conscience Whigs. They believed in using the political system to resist the spread of slavery to the new states and the territories and to oppose what they regarded as the South's political blackmail. The abolitionists, by contrast, did not believe in using the political system to resist slavery, because they did not believe in systems. It can sometimes seem as though they didn't believe in politics, either, but that is not quite true, for abolitionism was, in the end, and with a few adjustments to its platform, politically triumphant. The abolitionists were not apolitical. The renunciation of politics was the secret of their politics.

Abolitionism arose out of the Second Great Awakening, the evangelical revival that swept through New England and then upstate New York between 1800 and 1840, and that also spawned temperance, women's rights, and other social reform movements, along with a number of utopian and religious sects, most famously the Mormons. The foundations of the abolitionist movement were therefore spiritual and anti-institutional. Abolitionism was a party for people who did not believe in parties—a paradoxical law of attraction that turned out to be ideally suited to a Unitarian, Transcendentalist, and generally post-Calvinist culture like New England, a culture that was increasingly obsessed with the moral authority of the individual conscience. The American Anti-Slavery Society, the movement's organizational arm, had relatively few members, membership in an organization being the sort of thing that tends to compromise the inner vision. But it had many fellow travelers.

Holding that any system that countenanced slavery was evil, the most extreme abolitionists refused to help circulate the antislavery petitions that poured into Congress from the North in response to the petition gag rule.[16] Their nominal leader, William Lloyd Garrison, was a pacifist who believed that no abolitionist should hold political office. He printed the motto "The United States Constitution is a covenant with death and an agreement with hell" on the front page of his newspaper, the *Liberator*, and he made a practice of burning copies of the Constitution at his public appearances. His political text was the Declaration of Independence, since it asserts that people have a natural right to resist the state for reasons of conscience. (The Declaration of Independence was also, of course, on a somewhat different reading, the political text of the Southern secessionists.) And he preached an otherworldly indifference to the consequences of his platform. "If the State cannot survive the anti-slavery agitation, then let the State perish," he announced in an address called "No Compromise with Slavery." "If the American Union cannot be maintained, except by immolating human freedom on the altar of tyranny, then let the American Union be consumed by a living thunderbolt, and no tear be shed over its ashes."[17]

The abolitionists were not interested in reform. They were interested in conversion. Any "political reformation," Garrison wrote in a stern reply to a fellow abolitionist (and former slaveholder) who had ventured to suggest that people hoping to end slavery might have an obligation to vote for antislavery candidates, "is to be effected solely by a change in the moral vision of the people;—not by attempting to prove, that it is the duty of every abolitionist to be a voter, but that it is the duty of every voter to be an abolitionist."[18] "Genuine abolitionism," he said elsewhere, ". . . is of heaven, not of men. . . . [I]t is a life, not an impulse."[19]

This contempt for ordinary politics made the abolitionists the enemies even of their antislavery allies. They had no more patience with the Conscience Whigs and the American Colonization Society, groups that advocated tactical or gradualist approaches to the eradication of slavery, than they had with slaveholders and their apologists—since, said Garrison, as "the experience of two centuries [has] shown, . . . gradualism in theory, is perpetuity in practice."[20] Garrison's associate Wendell Phillips was disgusted when, in 1852, Conscience Whigs who had opposed Daniel Webster when he was alive showed up for his funeral. No abolitionist would have made such a concession to decorum. "We do not *play* politics," Phillips said.[21]

Garrison was originally a poor boy from Newburyport whose father had abandoned the family. Phillips's father was mayor of Boston, a wealthy lawyer who did business with the mercantile interests. Phillips started out in the law as well, but he gave it up in 1837, after an abolitionist printer named Elijah Lovejoy was shot and killed by a unionist mob in Illinois. At a meeting in Faneuil Hall in Boston following the murder, the attorney general of Massachusetts, James T. Austin, spoke in defense of Lovejoy's killers, comparing them to the patriots who had participated in the Boston Tea Party. Phillips rose from the audience and delivered an extemporaneous denunciation of Austin. The speech was probably not as unpremeditated as it was made to appear, but it was enthusiastically received, and it launched Phillips on his career as the "Golden Trumpet of Abolition." His family thought he had gone insane, and considered putting him in an asylum.[22]

As the Martin Delany case suggests, there were antislavery activists—Theodore Parker himself, for example[23]—whose belief that slavery was wicked did not entail a belief that the races were equal, or that African-Americans should be admitted to the Harvard Medical School. Wendell Phillips was not one of these. He preached a doctrine of pluralism, a vision of an America in which "all races, all customs, all religions, all languages, all literature, and all ideas" enjoyed the protection of "noble, just, and equal laws."[24] He was as outspoken on the social equality of women as he was on the social equality of black people; when conservative newspapers got tired of ridiculing his racial egalitarianism, they ridiculed his sexual egalitarianism. But although Phillips talked like a utopian, he had an astute understanding of the political uses of an absolutist refusal to "play politics." "Republics exist," he believed, "only on the tenure of being constantly agitated. . . . There is no republican road to safety but in constant distrust."[25] He was willing to say the unspeakable on any occasion (and at any length); and he made the degree of outrage he was able to rouse in his opponents the measure of his success.

Wendell Phillips was a cousin of Dr. Holmes's. As a unionist, Holmes was a staunch supporter of Webster. More than that, he had (as he confessed many years later) picked up a racial prejudice from his father, Abiel, who had lived briefly in Georgia and had known several "enlightened" slaveholders. Abiel had owned a copy of a pamphlet, written to alarm whites, about a slave insurrection in New York City in 1741,[26] which had made an impression on Holmes when he was young. Holmes was one of the signatories on a public letter of congratulations to Webster, orchestrated by Benjamin Curtis, after the Seventh of March speech in 1850; and five years later, in a lecture in New York City, he attacked the abolitionists—or as he called them, in one of the unhappier inspirations of his genius for phrasemaking, the "ultra melanophiles"—and dilated on the natural superiority of the white race. "The Creator has hung out the colors that form the two rallying points, so that they shall be unmistakable, eternal," he explained. "The white man must be the master in effect, whatever he is in name."[27] His remarks got picked up in the press. He was criticized in Horace Greeley's *New York Tribune*; the *Boston Advertiser*, a unionist paper, wrote that Holmes had called the abolitionists "traitors to the union."[28] These reports upset a number of Holmes's literary acquaintances, particularly Ralph Waldo Emerson.

4

Emerson's name, after his death, became linked with Holmes's, in part because Holmes wrote a popular book on Emerson in 1884. They had had cordial relations; but they were cordial men, and they were often thrown together by common interests. Holmes was in the audience (along with Wendell Phillips) when Emerson gave his celebrated Phi Beta Kappa address on "The American Scholar" at Harvard in 1837; Emerson worked with Holmes on the founding of the *Atlantic Monthly* and in organizing the business of the Saturday Club, where they dined together regularly. Holmes was often invited to recite his poems in venues where Emerson was invited to deliver his lectures, and Emerson acquired from these occasions a kind of backhanded admiration for Holmes's facility. "He could always write or speak *to order*," he noted in his journal, "partly from the abundance of the stream, which can fill indifferently any provided channel."[29]

But the notion that Holmes was the person to write the life of Emerson struck most of the people who knew them as absurd. When Holmes's friend Henry Bowditch heard the news, he laughed out loud. He could not conceive, he said, "of two men more diametrically opposed in their natural traits."[30] Their common ground was professional, not personal. Emerson believed in communing with the like-minded, but solitude, a kind of selfless self-absorption, was the essence of his thought and his personality. Dr. Holmes radiated gregariousness. He was not afraid, in conversation, to flirt with taboos, but it was the flirtation he cared about, not the suggestion that there was anything wrong with propriety. He had all the equipment for debunking convention and, for the most part, no impulse to use it.

Emerson's impulses were completely different. Emerson's standing in the culture of midcentury New England tells us something about the culture of midcentury New England and something about Emerson. Emerson worked out most of his ideas in the form of public lectures. Unsympathetic listeners sometimes thought them dreamy and diffuse; sympathetic ones frequently found them galvanizing. "An event without any former parallel in our literary annals, a scene to be always treasured in the memory for its picturesqueness and inspiration," remembered James Russell Lowell about listening to Emerson's lecture on "The American Scholar." "What crowded and breathless aisles, what windows clustering with eager heads, what enthusiasm of approval."[31] "An apparently incoherent and unintelligible address," was the reaction of the aged Reverend John Pierce to the same speech. "He professed to have a method; but I could not trace it."[32]

It was a generational difference, but it was not only a generational difference. For there is a division within Emerson's thought itself. Nothing sounds more uplifting, for example, than Emerson's key term "self-reliance," and so it was understood by many of his contemporaries. But the term describes a paradox—a matchstick propped up by leaning against . . . itself. What is the "I" that is being urged to rely on this "self"? Emerson's thought plays continually with the limits of thought, and his greatest essays are efforts to get at the way life is held up, in the end, by nothing. Except in the mingled intensity and detachment of their unfolding, those essays are deeply unconsoling. But many of his readers and listeners received them as affirmations.

Another way to put it is to say that Emerson was a genuine moralist whose mistrust of moralism led him continually to complicate and deflect his own formulations. He was a preacher whose message was: Don't listen to preachers. "I like the silent church before the service begins, better than any preaching,"[33] as he put it in the essay on "Self-Reliance." We are still going to church, in other words, but we're no longer there to hear someone else tell us what to do. Emerson represented the tradition of the New England churchman, which is one reason he became an honored and respected figure despite his anti-institutionalism; and, at the same time, he represented that tradition's final displacement. Unitarianism had rescued the integrity of the individual conscience from Calvinism. Emerson rescued it from Unitarianism—which is why after his famous address to the Harvard Divinity School in 1838, in which he scandalized the Unitarians by renouncing organized Christianity in favor of personal revelation, he was not invited to speak at Harvard again for thirty years.[34] By the time he returned, religion was no longer an issue most people in Cambridge cared to fight about; the last of the anti-Darwinists were just going under. "I regard it as the irresistible effect of the Copernican astronomy to have made the theological *scheme of Redemption* absolutely incredible," Emerson announced in 1832, in a sermon in which he also announced his disbelief in a supernatural Jesus.[35] He had, as usual, gotten there about a generation ahead of schedule.

When Dr. Holmes learned of Emerson's distress over the reports of his attack on the abolitionists, he wrote to explain that he had been misrepresented by the press. It was only technically so: he had not called the abolitionists traitors, but he had come close enough. "I am relieved to know that they misreported you," Emerson wrote back, "and the more they misreported or the wider you are from their notion of you, the better I shall be pleased." Still, he went on,

> the cant of Union . . . is too transparent [for] its most impudent re-peater to hope to deceive you[.] And for the Union with Slavery no manly person will suffer a day to go by without discrediting disinte-grating & finally exploding it. The "union" they talk of, is dead & rot-ten, the real union, that is, the will to keep & renew union, is like the will to keep & renew life, & this alone gives any tension to the dead letter & if when we have broken every several inch of the old wooden hoop will still hold us staunch.[36]

This was abolitionist talk. Emerson had been slow to warm to the abolitionist cause. He distrusted anything so collective and so fo-cused on conditions remote from his own experience. From the be-ginning of his career he had made a point of distancing himself from the controversy over slavery. "Is it not the chief disgrace of the world," he asked in the lecture on "The American Scholar," ". . . to be reckoned in the gross, in the hundred, or the thousand, of the party, the section, to which we belong; and our opinion predicted geo-graphically, as the north, or the south?"[37] "North" and "south" were obvious codes for positions in the quarrel over the spread of slavery. Emerson was not discounting the moral significance of the issue of slavery in "The American Scholar"; but he was not making it simple, either.

Emerson was, after all, fundamentally a lapsed Unitarian. He ad-mired Channing and had been impressed by Channing's pamphlet on *Slavery*; and he subscribed to Channing's general view that "[o]ur danger is, that we shall substitute the consciences of others for our own, that we shall paralyze our faculties through dependence on foreign guides, that we shall be moulded from abroad instead of determining ourselves."[38] Like Channing, he rated the work of "self-culture" far above the work of social improvement—or what he called, referring to one of his own rare early interventions in a political controversy, the forcible resettlement of the Cherokees to the west bank of the Mississippi in 1838, "this stirring in the philanthropic mud." "I will let the republic alone," he vowed then, "until the republic comes to me."[39]

But unlike Channing and the Harvard Unitarians, Emerson's suspicion of social activism had nothing to do with a respect for the status quo. On the contrary: it was precisely his distrust of established institutions that led him to avoid reform movements, and to regard them as crampers and perverters of individual integrity. He saw, in the beginning, no difference between abolitionism and the institutionalized religion he had rejected in the Divinity School address. They were both ways of discouraging people from thinking for themselves. "Each 'Cause,' as it is called," he wrote in 1842, explaining why the Transcendentalists were not a "party," "—say Abolition, Temperance, say Calvinism, or Unitarianism,—becomes speedily a little shop, where the article, let it have been at first never so subtle and ethereal, is now made up into portable and convenient cakes, and retailed in small quantities to suit purchasers."[40] Even Phillips struck him as less a radical than a puppet. "He had only a *platform-*existence, & no personality," he noted in his journal. "Mere mouthpieces of a party, take away the party & they shrivel & vanish."[41]

This was, of course, exactly the sort of person the antipolitics of abolitionism was designed to attract. Like many New Englanders, Emerson was radicalized by events. And as his consciousness of Southern perfidy rose, his identification with the abolitionists grew stronger. He had been disturbed by the murder of Lovejoy in 1837, but in a talk on the incident he treated the issue as one of free speech (Lovejoy had been a printer) rather than of slavery—much to the exasperation of his abolitionist friends. His reaction to the Compromise of 1850 was far more pointed. He thought Webster, whom he had once admired, had sold his soul to get the Compromise passed—"The word *liberty* in the mouth of Mr Webster sounds like the word *love* in the mouth of a courtezan,"[42] he wrote—and he pronounced the Fugitive Slave Law a "filthy law."[43] That law's local consequences, culminating in the return to slavery of Thomas Sims in April 1851, inspired Emerson to announce, in a speech in Concord a month later, that "[t]he last year has forced us all into politics, and made it a paramount duty to seek what it is often a duty to shun."[44]

This struck the properly *ultra* abolitionist note: it expressed the imperative of social obligation in the language of personal conscience. Many years later, in his book on Emerson, Dr. Holmes would claim that Emerson was never "hand in hand with the Abolitionists. . . . He seems to have formed a party by himself."[45] But this was plainly untrue, and Holmes probably knew it.[46] In any case, forming "a party of oneself" was perfectly consistent with joining the abolitionists. By the time of Holmes's New York speech, in 1855, Emerson had come to see the abolitionists not (as he had in his earlier writings) as ideologues and party men, but as versions of himself—versions, he tried to suggest, of Holmes, too, if Holmes would only be true to his identity as a scholar.

"A scholar need not be cynical," Emerson explained in his letter to Holmes,

> to feel that the vast multitude are almost on all fours; that the rich always vote after their fears that cities churches colleges all go for the quadruped interest, and it is against this coalition that the pathetically small minority of disengaged or thinking men stand for the ideal right, for man as he should be, & (what is essential to any sane maintenance of his own right) for the right of every other as for his own.[47]

In writing about the abolitionists as loners and nonconformists ("the pathetically small minority of disengaged or thinking men"), Emerson was assigning them a role in the quarrel over slavery and, at the same time, he was elevating them above the fray. "The world of any moment is the merest appearance," he had explained eighteen years earlier in "The American Scholar."

Some great decorum, some fetish of a government, some ephemeral trade, or war, or man, is cried up by half mankind and cried down by the other half, as if all depended on this particular up or down. The odds are that the whole question is not worth the poorest thought which the scholar has lost in listening to the controversy. Let him not quit his belief that a popgun is a popgun, though the ancient and honorable of the earth affirm it to be the crack of doom.[48]

It was not a matter of choosing sides. It was a matter of rising above the whole concept of sidedness.

Dr. Holmes was unpersuaded. The abolitionists, he wrote back to Emerson, "have used every form of language calculated to inflame the evil passions and the consequence is that growing sectional hostility, the nature of which is the disruption of the government which Mr. Parker thinks is near at hand."[49] It was a point. For despite the way Emerson preferred to imagine them, the abolitionists were distinctly a "side": they had an agenda, and the agenda had political consequences. To Theodore Parker himself, Holmes wrote that he stood by his statement that, come what may, the white race must always have the upper hand.[50] (It was, of course, a view that Parker shared.)

Despite their disagreement about the abolitionists, though, Dr. Holmes's relations with Emerson continued to be friendly enough, and he seems to have maintained his regard for Emerson's work; for in 1858, he and his wife gave five volumes of Emerson's writings as a birthday present to their son Wendell.

TWO

THE ABOLITIONIST

I

IN 1858 WENDELL HOLMES WAS seventeen and a freshman at Harvard College. Emerson, he said many years later,
"set me on fire."[1] In December, nine months after his birthday present, he published an essay in the *Harvard Magazine* entitled "Books."
It was his first publication, and its indebtedness is plain and sweetly
acknowledged. It is an Emersonian tribute to Emerson. Emerson,
young Holmes explains, is a person "who probably takes about as
large a view of men and events as any one we could point out now
living in America." He is also, Holmes goes on, the model reader. For
he reads freely, and without regard to conventional notions of what is
proper and what is not. He reads to satisfy himself: "he studies all
the great inspired books of all the great literatures . . . [many of]
which we contemn on the authority of others, without ever having
looked into them ourselves, and some of which . . . teach us lessons
of love and forbearance, that, after eighteen hundred years have gone
by, we have not yet granted the New Testament to inculcate."[2]

A month later, Holmes happened to pass Emerson and his daugh-

Oliver Wendell Holmes in March 1861, a month before he dropped
out of Harvard to join the Union Army.

ter Ellen on the street. He turned back and ran after them. "Wendell Holmes, Dr. Holmes's son, he thought he ought not to pass Mr. E. without paying his respects," Ellen reported to her sister Edith. " 'He was a handsome stately fellow,' said Father, 'it was pleasant to see him.' "[3] Holmes's own memory of the encounter, more than fifty years later, was that he told Emerson: "If I ever do anything, I shall owe a great deal of it to you."[4] If he did make such a remark, Ellen Emerson did not record it (and it is the kind of remark she tended to record). But it is clear that Holmes had adopted Emerson as his special inspiration. A few years later, he wrote an essay on Plato expressly for Emerson's approval. (Holmes found Plato outdated on one or two points. Emerson's reaction, when Holmes showed him the essay, is choice: "When you strike at a king," he said, "you must *kill* him.")[5]

Holmes's remark in his essay on "Books" about the "lessons of love and forbearance" which Christians have yet to learn is an oblique reference to slavery. "Do men own other men by God's law?" he asks elsewhere in the essay. "[W]hen we, almost the first of young men who have been brought up in an atmosphere of investigation, instead of having every doubt answered, It is written,—when we begin to enter the fight, can we help feeling it is a tragedy? Can we help going to our rooms and crying that we might not think?"[6] This is not just the language of abolitionism; it is the language of Emersonian abolitionism, for it associates the tolerance of slavery with the conformist mentality of institutionalized religion.

"[D]uty is not less binding had the Bible never been written, or if we were to perish utterly tomorrow," Holmes wrote two years later, in another essay in the *Harvard Magazine*.[7] This remark was not so oblique, and it provoked a classmate to publish an angry rebuttal, in which he accused Holmes of imitating Emerson and of flippancy toward Jesus. Holmes was by then one of the editors of the *Harvard Magazine*, which was running articles supporting abolition, the admission of women to Harvard, and curricular reform. In January 1861 the magazine printed an editorial by one of Holmes's classmates, Wendell Phillips Garrison, the son of the abolitionist leader, attacking the retiring Professor of Christian Morals, Frederic Dan Huntington, and demanding "free will in matters of religion."[8] This was too much for President Felton, who wrote to Dr. Holmes objecting to the disrespectful tone of the magazine his son was editing. In April 1861, in Holmes's senior year, the faculty voted to admonish Holmes and another student for "repeated and gross indecorum" in the classroom of Francis Bowen, a defender of Unitarian orthodoxy and an outspoken critic of Emerson.

The discipline of the apostate is often stricter than the observance of the faithful, and Emerson is a case in point. There was a chastity about his intellectual style, and Holmes emulated it. This is a side of the young Holmes's personality it has proved easy to miss. Wendell Holmes was, of course, a child of privilege, and he was not a prig. He was sociable and well connected; he liked to banter; in later life, he made much of his taste for pretty women and for drink. But it is a mistake to discount—even when he was still a student—the severity of his character as an intellectual. Holmes was an unusually compartmentalized personality. He knew when to work and when to play, and he never mixed his occasions. Socially, he exhibited the gregariousness of his father; in thought, he cultivated the solitariness of his hero. Even at seventeen he was a bookish young man who wrote poetry, collected prints, and debated philosophical issues with his father at the dinner table. And he treated those issues with a rare gravity. He thought his father much too disposed to split the difference between opposing views, or to fall back on conventional wisdom; he considered most of his teachers hidebound traditionalists. He was, in the context of his times, a student radical.

As the phrase in "Books" about "love and forbearance" suggests, Holmes was highly sensitive to cruelty, and he had inherited none of his father's racial prejudice. He disliked *The Pickwick Papers*, a novel that has fun with West Indians and temperance societies, because he thought it morally coarse; minstrel shows upset him because he thought they demeaned black people.[9] He joined the campus Christian Union, but only, he said, "because I wished to bear witness in favor of a Religious society founded on liberal principles in distinction to the more 'orthodox' & sectarian platform of the 'Xtian Brethren' "[10] (the other student religious group). He believed, like Emerson, that a scientific view of the world was not incompatible with moral beliefs, and that a finer morality was possible outside organized religion than inside it. His best friend at Harvard was Norwood Penrose Hallowell, a Quaker from Philadelphia whose older brother Richard lived near Boston and supplied protection to the abolitionists. In January 1861 Richard Hallowell recruited Holmes to serve in the bodyguard of Wendell Phillips.

The post was not merely honorific. By the winter of 1860–61, Holmes's senior year at Harvard, the political war over slavery had reached its endgame. Events, and the South's intransigence, had battered convictions across the entire spectrum of opinion in the North. As it had been all along, the issue for most Northerners was not the morality of slavery; it was the balance of power between the North and the South. But the more the South intervened in the North's affairs and frustrated the North's political will, the more corrupt the institution of slavery began to seem. When it was relatively out of sight, slavery could be kept relatively out of mind. The more belligerently the South thrust its business in Northern faces, the more distasteful that business became.

In 1854 a fugitive named Anthony Burns had been captured in Boston and, thanks to the intervention of President Franklin Pierce, successfully returned to slavery. An attempt by an antislavery posse to rescue Burns à la Shadrach turned out badly. A deputy marshal was killed, and Higginson, Parker, Phillips, and four other militants were indicted. The spectacle of the national government backing slaveholders in a bloody raid on a Northern city converted many unionists into antislavery activists. "We went to bed one night old fashioned, conservative, Compromise Union Whigs," wrote Amos Adams Lawrence, the son of the textile manufacturer for whom the Massachusetts mill town is named, "& waked up stark mad Abolitionists."[11] Amos Lawrence became a financial backer of the free-soil settlers in Kansas.

The nearly fatal caning of Charles Sumner by Preston Brooks of South Carolina on the Senate floor in 1856 persuaded proslavery unionists like Cornelius Felton that the South no longer deserved their sympathies; Felton turned antislavery. A year later, the Supreme

Court handed down its opinion in the Dred Scott case, affirming the South's position that Congress had no right to outlaw slavery in the territories, on the theory that such an act constituted an unconstitutional deprivation of property. Even free blacks, the Court concluded, had no standing in federal court: the framers, Chief Justice Roger B. Taney remarked, had regarded blacks as "a subordinate and inferior class of beings, who . . . had no rights or privileges but such as those who held the power and the Government might choose to grant them."[12] This was the same logic that had underlain the Fugitive Slave Law of 1850, which treated escaped slaves as chattel. But by 1857 Northern opinion had been transformed. The black man Dred Scott was represented before the Court by George Ticknor Curtis, the former United States commissioner charged with enforcement of the Fugitive Slave Law in Boston; George's older brother, Benjamin, once the champion of Daniel Webster and now an associate justice on the Court, filed one of the two dissents. He resigned in disgust soon afterward. (No one seems to have complained about the conflict of interest, presumably because the brothers were on the losing side anyway.)

The turning point, though, was reached not by words but by blood. Dred Scott and Bleeding Kansas transformed conservatives into activists; John Brown transformed pacifists into warriors. In 1856 Brown had abducted five proslavery settlers in Pottawatomie, Kansas, and split their skulls with cutlasses. In October 1859, at Harpers Ferry, Virginia, he tried to invade the South with an army of twenty-one men and almost no clue about how to proceed once he got started. The first person his troops managed to kill was a free black man who worked for the railroad. Brown's apotheosis marked the final stage in the radicalization of Northern opinion. He became, for many Americans in both the North and the South, a human omen—"the meteor of the war,"[13] Melville called him. Brown was the South's worst nightmare: a white man fomenting black insurrection inside the South itself, the fear exploited by the anonymous pamphlet that had implanted a racial prejudice in Dr. Holmes when he was a boy, Negro Plot. To many Northerners, including antislavery Republicans who were quick to dissociate themselves from him,

Brown was an inflammatory and a madman. But to the abolitionists, he achieved, after his execution in Virginia in December 1859, a kind of divinity.

"Brown will die . . . like a martyr and also a SAINT,"[14] proclaimed Theodore Parker, who was then dying of tuberculosis in Italy but who had been, along with Higginson and the physician Samuel Gridley Howe (Julia Ward Howe's husband), one of the so-called Secret Six, the men who provided Brown with the weapons used for the Harpers Ferry raid. Brown made "the gallows glorious like the cross,"[15] exclaimed Emerson—a simile used by many others. Amos Lawrence helped to pay for Brown's defense, and Wendell Phillips and Richard Hallowell were members of the party that retrieved the body after Brown's hanging in Virginia and escorted it back to Brown's home in northern New York State for burial. Phillips delivered a eulogy over the grave. Brown gave the abolitionists a taste of blood, and they found it thrilling. An Old Testament figure, a pure atavism, threw what for thirty years had been a distinctively liberal, New Testament–style movement back to the spiritual world of Oliver Cromwell. Emerson tried out the argument that Brown was really a Transcendentalist: he "was an idealist," he explained in a speech after Brown's conviction. "He saw how deceptive the forms are."[16] But he was also a kamikaze and a killer, and with his execution the antislavery movement, which had been associated from the beginning with pacifism, began to tilt toward violence.[17]

After the election of Lincoln in 1860, Northerners who favored appeasement found themselves facing the abyss they had long predicted. Anticipating secession, Southerners began canceling orders for Northern goods. Wages were cut; shoemakers in Haverhill, Marblehead, and Lynn went out on strike.[18] The abolitionists continued to call for partition, and violent mobs of unionists gathered to threaten them and to shout them down. Unionists attempted to kidnap Phillips on Staten Island after he returned from Brown's funeral; he began to carry a gun whenever he left his house in Boston. When he gave a speech with the deliberately taunting title "The Mob and Education" at the Boston Music Hall on December 16, more than three thousand people turned up. Twenty armed volunteers sat be-

hind Phillips on the platform while he spoke, and when he finished
two hundred policemen were needed to convey him safely through
the crowd in the streets outside.[19]

Four days later, South Carolina seceded, followed by Mississippi
on January 9, Florida on the 10th, Alabama on the 11th, and Georgia
on the 19th. On January 20, with half the South gone, Phillips spoke
at the Music Hall on the topic—calculated, as always, to incite—
"Disunion." A huge mob convened outside. Samuel Gridley Howe
was one of Phillips's bodyguards; in a letter to Charles Sumner, he
described the scene afterward:

> About fifty hard-fisted and resolute Germans went ahead and
> pushed the mob to the right and left. Then followed some fourty or
> fifty determined antislavery Yankees, who arm in arm and close ranks
> preceded and followed Phillips. . . . It was a hard struggle down
> Winter St. & through Washington St. as far as the corner of Bedford
> St. The mob pushed against us, howling & swearing & clamour-
> ing,—a few resolute fellows pushing us against the wall, & evidently
> longing for a stop or melee in which they could get a lick at Phillips;
> who however bore himself very resolutely & bravely. . . . At the cor-
> ner of Bedford St. there was some obstacle, & a sudden stop; & you
> may judge of the purpose when I tell you that I came near being
> thrust into Browns windows & one man near me was actually
> pushed & jammed against the huge plate glass so hard that it was
> smashed in. At last we got to Phillips' door & way was made for him
> to get in. Then there was groaning & hooting & other disgraceful
> acts, before the crowd dispersed.[20]

Such were the duties nineteen-year-old Wendell Holmes agreed
to perform. On January 23, three days after Phillips's Music Hall
speech, Holmes attended a fund-raising event for the Anti-Slavery
Society, to which he contributed a small sum. On the evening of January 24, he was scheduled to serve in Phillips's bodyguard following a
scheduled speech at Tremont Temple, and was issued a billy club by
Hallowell for the occasion. "I do hope you will not receive personal
injury," Hallowell wrote to Holmes, ". . . and trust you will not use a

weapon except as a last resort."[21] (Hallowell was, after all, still a Quaker.)

In a meeting at the Temple on the afternoon of the 23rd, Phillips managed to quiet the unionist hecklers in the hall for thirty minutes by the force of his oratory. But Emerson, who followed him on the platform, was able to utter only a few sentences against the union and the Constitution ("the monstrous concession made at formation of the Constitution . . . has blocked the civilization and humanity of the times up to this day,"[22] he said, echoing Garrison's standard line) before being hooted off the stage. After the meeting, Phillips went to the governor to demand the protection of the state militia. The governor refused, and when Phillips returned to the Temple for the evening meeting, he found himself locked out. The mayor had closed the building. Wendell Holmes's riot control skills were not tested. Still he had, at the highest pitch of prewar contention, aligned himself with the most radical abolitionist in the country, a man intimately identified with John Brown and an advocate of no compromise with the South.

The argument of Phillips and the rest of the abolitionists—the argument that so infuriated the unionists—was that if the Southern states wished to secede, the North's attitude should be, good riddance. Then, on April 12, Southern batteries opened fire on Fort Sumter in Charleston harbor, and with one stroke the South accomplished what no Northerner had been able to do since the Missouri Compromise of 1820: it unified the North. "The heather is on fire," wrote George Ticknor to an English friend. "The whole population, men, women, and children, seem to be in the streets with Union favours and flags. . . . Civil war is freely accepted everywhere . . . by all as inevitable, by all as the least of the evils among which we are permitted to choose, anarchy being the obvious, and perhaps the only alternative."[23] Abolitionists like Phillips switched from pacifism to militarism overnight. Quakers like Wendell Holmes's friends the Hallowells rushed to enlist. Unionists like Dr. Holmes became abolitionists and champions of war against the South. It was as though all the floors of the intellectual house of antislavery had given way at once, and everyone found themselves sitting on the ground together. Overnight, the one solution no one had advocated became the one solution everyone agreed on: the North must go to war. Politics could at last be pursued by other means. Shortly after the fall of Fort Sumter, Emerson, once almost the incarnation of post-Christian nonviolence, paid a visit to Charlestown Navy Yard near Boston. "Sometimes gunpowder smells good,"[24] he said.

Fort Sumter surrendered on April 14. On the 15th, Lincoln issued his first call for volunteers. By the 25th, Wendell Holmes had dropped out of Harvard to enlist. A number of other students left as well (the Southern students had gone home during the winter, as their states seceded), but Holmes was the only one who didn't bother to notify the college authorities. Dr. Holmes had to go to President Felton himself to explain what had happened. Holmes knew that he was forfeiting his chance for a degree, and he seems not to have cared. When it turned out that the battalion he had joined was not being sent south, he applied for a commission in one of the volunteer regiments being formed by the governor of Massachusetts. By then Harvard had agreed to take back everyone who had dropped out after Fort Sumter; but by June 10 Holmes still had not returned to the college. The only other student who seems to have ignored the offer of amnesty was his friend Pen Hallowell. Felton wrote to Dr. Holmes to explain that the faculty had ruled that his son would not be given his degree unless he returned. "Not knowing where he is at present," Felton pointed out, "I must rely on you to communicate this notice to him."[25]

This appeal succeeded. Holmes came back and took his examinations. On Class Day, June 21, he was Class Poet; Hallowell was Class Orator. They graduated with their class on July 17, in a ceremony at which an honorary degree was awarded to General Winfield Scott, the hero of the Mexican War, the war whose territorial acquisitions set off the quarrel over the spread of slavery that had now split the nation. On July 23, Holmes and Hallowell were commissioned as officers in the Twentieth Regiment of Massachusetts Volunteers.

The Harvard faculty had seen fit to penalize Holmes for his absence from classes during the spring, and the deduction from his

point total (the peculiar system by which students were then evaluated at Harvard) put him in the lower half of his class. He was not
distressed, but Dr. Holmes was. "He left college suddenly, no doubt,
but if he did not stop to kiss his Alma Mater, neither did many other
volunteers stop to kiss their mothers and wives and sweethearts," he
complained in a letter to Felton.

> His case was entirely exceptional. Revolutions do not follow prece-
> dents nor furnish them. The enforcement of the scholastic rule in
> this instance seems to me harsh and unworthy of the occasion. If a
> great General receives an LL.D. for military services, it seems hard
> that a poor private or Lieutenant should be publicly humiliated,—or
> his friends through him,—for being too prompt in answering the call
> of the Commander in Chief.[26]

"Revolutions do not follow precedents nor furnish them": Dr.
Holmes was starting to sound like Emerson. For some of the Northerners who stayed home, the suggestion that in the new state of
emergency the old decorums might no longer apply carried a certain
existentialist frisson.

2

Wendell Holmes felt no such frisson. He accepted his commission in
a spirit of moral obligation, and if he ever entertained a notion of war
as a kind of heroic adventure, the experience of his first battle, at
Ball's Bluff on October 21, 1861, snuffed it out. Ball's Bluff was a very
minor engagement, but what it lacked in strategic significance it
more than made up for in intensity and horror. Even more vividly
than the notorious Union rout at Bull Run three months earlier, it
dramatized the difficulties under which the Union armies operated
in the early years of the war.

One of these difficulties was the tension between the armies' political leadership and their military leadership. General George B.
McClellan, who assumed command of the Army of the Potomac after Bull Run, was not an admirer of Lincoln, whom he referred to as
a "well meaning baboon,"[27] or of the politics of the Republican Party.

He was an admirer principally of George B. McClellan; and although he was an excellent organizer and motivator of troops, he was reluctant to send his men into engagements where he could not be certain that the outcome would redound to the glory of their commander. He had, as a consequence, a tendency that amounted almost to a phobia to overestimate the strength of enemy forces. Yet he was also aware that if he wanted to keep his job, he needed to provide Washington with regular and palpable military results.

In October 1861 Confederate forces were assembled in the town of Leesburg, Virginia, forty miles up the Potomac from Washington. Under pressure from Lincoln to do something, McClellan ordered General Charles P. Stone to make a "slight demonstration" from the Maryland side of the river while he advanced a larger force against the Confederate flank. Stone gave the assignment to conduct this mission to Colonel Edward Baker. Baker was not a military man. Until the outbreak of the war, he had been senator from Oregon, and he was one of Lincoln's closest friends: Lincoln had named his second son after him. Baker chose a steep and rocky cliff about a hundred feet high on the Virginia shore—Ball's Bluff—for his assault. The Potomac had risen, and Baker had available only three boats, capable of carrying between thirty and forty men each, and a small launch, but he managed to ferry about 1,700 men and three artillery pieces across to the bluff from an island in the river known as Harrison's Island. In selecting a cliff for his route of entry, Butler evidently had not stopped to figure out how, in the event of a retreat, everyone would get safely back down it. He also was unaware (thanks in part to poor Union scouting) that a substantial Confederate force was waiting for him in the woods just beyond the top of the bluff.[28]

Holmes's regiment, the Twentieth Massachusetts, was in the Union force. The fighting began sometime after two o'clock in the afternoon. At four o'clock, Baker was shot through the head and killed, but by then the outcome was no longer in doubt. The Union soldiers had had no space in which to deploy their troops for an organized assault on Confederate positions and nowhere to fall back when their advances were repulsed. As the sun went down, they were driven over the edge of the cliff and into the river. "All retreat was now cut off," as the scene is described in one of the earliest histories of the war.

> Only a handful of men continued to offer any resistance at the top of the acclivity, which their comrades were descending in great haste. A final charge of the Eighth Virginia [under the command of Colonel Nathan Evans, one of the Confederate heroes of Bull Run] drove them, in turn, into that abyss, where further struggle was impossible. One of the cannon, which was flung from the summit of the cliff, rolled down to the water's edge and was broken in pieces. The battle was ended. The Confederates had nothing to do but to complete their victory by firing upon opponents who were no longer able to retaliate. The crowd of fugitives clung to the brushwood which covered the acclivities of Ball's Bluff, and, finding no shelter, sought their last chance of safety in the only boat which remained moored to the shore. The other two, which were filled with wounded men, were already far off, and being overloaded, as is always the case under such circumstances, soon sank with all those who were congratulating themselves upon having been able to get on board. A large number of officers and soldiers threw themselves into the river to cross by swimming. Most of these drowned, and a few were killed by the balls of the enemy, who pursued them without mercy. . . . At last darkness came to put an end to the scene of horror.[29]

Of the 1,700 Union soldiers who crossed the river to Ball's Bluff, only 800 made it back.

One of them, of course, was Wendell Holmes, but it was a close thing. The Twentieth Massachusetts had been stationed near the center of the Union position in a small field at the crest of the bluff, and Holmes, leading his company, was hit by a minié ball—a rifle bullet—just above the heart. He was dragged from the field and carried to the bottom of the cliff, where he was placed not in the large scow being used as a ferry, which later sank, but in the launch. This managed the crossing to Harrison's Island successfully, and Holmes was carried to a house that was being used for a hospital, where he was informed that he might die.

Pen Hallowell had led a line of skirmishers halfway up the bluff, holding off the Confederates while the Union troops evacuated. He then swam across the Potomac with his sword hanging from his neck, organized the construction of a makeshift raft, and made several trips to rescue Union soldiers trapped on the Virginia bank before the raft came apart in midstream. Two men drowned, but Hallowell got to shore safely.[30] He went to the hospital building to see his friend; Holmes remembered being kissed by him as he lay wounded. It was feared that the Confederates would begin shelling Harrison's Island, so later that night, Holmes was transported to the regimental hospital in a broken-down two-wheeled ambulance, where he was seated next to a man who had been shot in the head and was unconscious. There he finally learned that he would live.[31]

Ball's Bluff was a nightmare for everyone on the Union side who played a part in it. When he was told that his friend Baker was dead, Lincoln wept. A Congressional committee was convened to look into the conduct of the war, and General Stone was arrested and imprisoned without charges at Fort Lafayette in New York Harbor. He was released, still uncharged, after 189 days; eventually he returned to the army, but his career was ruined.[32] Thirty-eight men in the Twentieth Massachusetts, Holmes's regiment, were killed.[33] Holmes later remembered looking down, as he was being dragged from the field, and seeing one of his sergeants lying on the ground, shot through the head and covered with blood. One of his first sights when he was carried into the makeshift hospital on Harrison's Island was an amputated arm lying in a pool of blood on a blanket. It belonged to his friend John Putnam. Putnam's brother Willy lay wounded nearby; he died during the night. When Holmes reached the regimental hospital and the sun rose, he could see for the first time the head of the wounded man, Captain Ferdinand Dreher, who had been placed next to him in the ambulance: "a ghastly spectacle—," as he later described it. "Two black cavities seemed all that there was left for eyes—his whiskers & beard matted with blood which still poured black, from his mouth—and a most horrible stench—."[34]

In the midst of this mutilation and mayhem, Holmes did an extraordinary thing: he road tested his beliefs. Lying in the hospital on Harrison's Island, watching his comrades dying around him and lis-

tening to rumors that the building was about to be shelled, he inter-
rogated his philosophical convictions in order to discover whether
there were any he now might wish to revise. He was undergoing an
experience of terror that nothing in his life had prepared him for, and
he decided to solicit his own reactions to it. He thought the results
interesting enough to record them later in a notebook. "I always
wanted to have a memorandum of this experience—," as he put it,
"so novel at that time to all & especially so to me from the novelty of
the service and my youth."[35]

"When I thought I was dying," he wrote,

> the reflection that the majority vote of the civilized world declared
> that with my opinions I was *en route* for Hell came up with painful
> distinctness—Perhaps the first impulse was tremulous—but then
> I said—by Jove, I die like a soldier anyhow—I was shot in the breast
> doing my duty up to the hub—afraid? No, I am proud—then I
> thought I couldn't be guilty of a deathbed recantation—father and I
> had talked of that and were agreed that it generally meant nothing
> but a cowardly giving way to fear—Besides, thought I, can I recant if
> I want to, has the approach of death changed my beliefs much? & at
> this I answered—No—Then came in my Philosophy—I am to take a
> leap in the dark—but now as ever I believe that whatever shall hap-
> pen is best—for it is in accordance with a general law—and *good &
> universal* (or *general law*) are synonymous terms in the universe. . . .
> Would the complex forces which made a still more complex unit in
> *Me* resolve themselves back into simpler forms or would my angel be
> still winging his way onward when eternities had passed? I could not
> tell—But all was doubtless well—and so with a "God forgive me if
> I'm wrong" I slept—.[36]

He had found that he did not require a religious faith. Uncertainty—
"I am to take a leap in the dark"—turned out to be all the certainty
he needed. The assurance that he had done his duty was a wholly adequate consolation.

At the end of these recollections, he adds a note. "It is curious
how rapidly the mind adjusts itself under some circumstances to entirely new relations—," he writes. "I thought for awhile that I was dying, and it seemed the most natural thing in the world—The moment

the hope of life returned it seemed as abhorrent to nature as ever that I should die—."[37] "How rapidly the mind adjusts itself": the test of a belief is not immutability, but adaptability. Our reasons for needing reasons are always changing.

Holmes's account of his first wound was written, probably two years after the battle in which it occurred,[38] in a diary he kept during the war. At some point Holmes destroyed the rest of the diary, preserving only these recollections of Ball's Bluff, a list of regimental casualties, and a section covering his last three months of service, from May to July 1864. He also destroyed many of his own letters home from the front and all of the letters his family sent to him. A note by Holmes on one of the remaining envelopes gives a clue to what he chose to suppress: "letter referred to within destroyed," it says, "—rather pompous."[39] The letters to his family that survive never refer explicitly to the beliefs that led Holmes to go to war in the first place; and although Holmes expresses pride in his sense of duty and in his own actions when they demonstrated courage, the cause for which he is fighting is virtually unmentioned. Holmes carefully erased every connection between his experiences as a soldier and his views as an abolitionist. This is not because he changed those views. It is because he changed his view of the nature of views. It was the great lesson he thought the war had taught him, and he took pains, in later life, to make sure the record reflected it.

3

The suspicion that not every officer in the Union Army was committed to the political goals of the Lincoln administration dogged Northern efforts throughout the early years of the war, and it is another of the difficulties dramatized by the events at Ball's Bluff. The arrest of General Stone after the debacle there did not reflect Washington's estimation of his competence. It reflected Washington's estimation of his loyalty. Suspicion tended to focus on the professional military men, and it extended all the way to McClellan at the top (which is probably why McClellan was happy to throw Stone to the Republican wolves). That suspicion was not entirely unfounded: McClellan, after all, ended up running for president against Lincoln in 1864. Concern about political sympathies extended down the chain of command as well. Despite the presence of officers like Holmes and Hallowell, the dominant sentiment in the Twentieth Massachusetts was by no means abolitionist, or even Republican.

After the battle at Ball's Bluff, General Stone had ordered his troops to round up any slaves who had taken refuge behind Union lines and to return them to their owners. The order infuriated Pen Hallowell, who wrote to his brother Richard that the men of the Twentieth "have not only caught supposed fugitives but actually *hunted up* their masters & to them escorted the slaves—yes, by God! New England soldiers have done this detestable work, acting to be sure under orders from Stone, but not only without *protest*, but with a fawning, toadying eagerness."[40] Richard passed this letter along to Wendell Phillips, but Pen had written to Phillips already, explaining that many of the casualties in the Twentieth, including John and Willy Putnam, along with two officers who had been killed while trying to swim across the Potomac, had been abolitionists. "[T]here are several vacancies to be filled," he warned. "If you have anything to do with the State House see that good anti-slavery men are appointed. Else the 20th, *your* 20th will no longer be what it is—the most radical Mass. regiment in the field."[41] A month later, the Hallowells began to regard the Twentieth as politically a lost cause. "I wish my brother was in some position where he would not be sacrificed as he must be, where he is, to proslavery aristocracy,"[42] Richard complained to Phillips. He was referring to the Copperheads—the name for Northerners who opposed the war and sympathized with the South.

Holmes himself had little respect for Lincoln, but this was a common enough Northern attitude early in the war. Some Northerners considered Lincoln an extremist, but many thought him not forceful enough. Holmes once recalled a conversation in the trenches with some of his Harvard classmates about whether the Civil War had produced a great man. Someone timidly suggested Lincoln, and the others laughed him down. (Holmes later revised his estimation of Lincoln considerably upward.)[43] But as the Hallowells had discovered, many of Holmes's comrades in the Twentieth despised the abolitionists and thought the war was a mistake. One of the leaders of this faction was Henry Abbott, who was known in the regiment as "Little" Abbott.

Abbott became an important figure in Holmes's personal mythology, and it is therefore easy to get the wrong idea of his character. He came from a relatively well-off family, and entered Harvard at fourteen. His career there was distinguished principally by minor disciplinary infractions; he graduated a year ahead of Holmes. When the war broke out, he was reluctant to enlist, since he was uncertain of his capacity for martial valor. But after two of his brothers enlisted, he got himself commissioned a second lieutenant in the Twentieth Massachusetts. His company was in the thick of the fighting at Ball's Bluff, and it was there that he astonished himself by his own coolness under fire. It was a talent he had had no idea he possessed, and in every engagement afterward he seems to have gone out of his way to place himself in the position of greatest possible danger.

But he was contemptuous of the cause for which he fought. He admired McClellan as a military professional and a Democrat, and complained continually of the political generals in the army. When the Emancipation Proclamation went into effect, on January 1, 1863, Abbott wrote from the front to his aunt to explain that "[t]he president's proclamation is of course received with universal disgust, particularly the part which enjoins officers to see that it is carried out. You may be sure that we shan't see to any thing of the kind, having decidedly too much reverence for the constitution."[44]

These were the politics of the family. Henry's father, Josiah, a Boston judge, had already played a prominent role in the so-called People's Convention, held at Faneuil Hall on October 7, 1862, to protest the Emancipation Proclamation and to nominate a Democrat to run against the Republican governor of Massachusetts, John Andrew. The Abbotts detested Dr. Holmes, who had become a prominent Republican cheerleader in Boston. "As for Holmes senior," Henry wrote to his father, "I agree with you fully, that he is a miserable little mannekin, dried up morally & physically, & there is certainly nothing more aggravating than to have such a little fool make orations & talk about traitors & the 'man who quarrels with the pilot when the ship is in danger' &c, &c."[45]

But Henry Abbott and Wendell Holmes became close friends. "His father of course one can't help despising," Abbott explained to his father, who had evidently expressed some doubts.

> But Oliver Junior, though you have an instinctive dislike to his spec-
> ulative nature, is infinitely more manly than the little conceited doc-
> tor. . . . I am very confident that he is worthy of your friendship,
> because a man here in the hardships & dangers of the field can eas-
> ily detect what is base in a man's character, & it is particularly trying
> to Holmes, who is a student rather than a man of action.[46]

On September 17, 1862, Holmes was shot in the neck at the battle of Antietam, where Union troops suffered thirteen thousand casualties. Pen Hallowell had his arm shattered by a bullet in the same engagement. He and Holmes took refuge in a farmhouse, known as the Nicodemus House, which fell briefly into enemy hands. Afraid he would lose consciousness and be taken prisoner, Holmes wrote on a slip of paper, "I am Capt. O. W. Holmes 20th Mass. Son of Oliver Wendell Holmes, M.D. Boston."[47] Union troops eventually regained the ground around the house, and Holmes and Hallowell were evacuated safely. Holmes wrote to his parents that he would probably not end up paralyzed, and that he was returning home to recover. He asked not to be met, but Dr. Holmes was already on the way, and later published an account of his journey (probably to the chagrin of his son) in the *Atlantic Monthly*.[48] Wendell Holmes brought the scrap of paper with his name scribbled on it home with him. He preserved it for the rest of his life.

On November 7, when Lincoln finally relieved McClellan of command, Holmes was still in Boston recovering from his wound. He voted for John Andrew and the Union Republicans—who were running against Josiah Abbott's People's Convention ticket—in the Massachusetts elections (the Republicans won),[49] and then set out to rejoin his regiment. He was accompanied by Henry Abbott. The two men spent a week together on the road, and enjoyed it. "Have been more or less blue of course but Abbott has made the journey easier & pleasanter," Holmes wrote to his parents en route from Washington. "Keep your spirits up for 'I love you still the same' A. and I shall sleep out side the bed tonight for fear of bugs—. . . . Wash^n stinks of meanness—it's absolutely loathesome—Abbott & I are both of good cheer—."[50]

In a letter to his sister a few days later he ends by explaining that

> I've pretty much made up my mind that the South have achieved their independence & I am almost ready to hope spring will see an end—I prefer intervention to save our credit but believe me, we shall never lick 'em—The Army is tired with its hard, & its terrible experience & still more with its mismanagement & I think before long the majority will say that we are vainly working to effect what never happens—the subjugation (for that is it) of a great civilized nation. We shan't do it—at least the Army can't—.[51]

The tone of this letter is high-handed, and clearly intended to shock a little the pieties of the home front. But the sentences about the futility of fighting are serious enough, and they are the first signal of Holmes's disillusion with the war effort. They certainly show the effects of a week with Henry Abbott. Still, it's important to distinguish the complaint Holmes is making from sympathy toward the South.

The late summer and fall of 1862 was the most discouraging period of the war for the Union side. At Antietam more than twice as many Americans were killed in a single day than in every other nineteenth-century American war—the War of 1812, the Mexican War, and the Spanish-American War—combined.[52] The struggle began to seem to many Northerners a suicide mission. Mixed with this frustration was the suspicion that Northern lives were being wasted because of mismanagement and political meddling, a suspicion reinforced by Lincoln's firing of McClellan, who, despite his poor showing in the field, was widely respected as a military professional. These are the views reflected in Holmes's letter. They were Copperhead views, but one did not need to be a Democrat in the fall of 1862 to share them.

It got worse before it got better. At Fredericksburg, on December 13, almost 13,000 Union soldiers were killed or wounded, this time against fewer than 5,000 Confederate casualties, and no ground was gained. "If there is a worse place than Hell, I am in it," Lincoln said afterward.[53] Holmes did not fight at Fredericksburg because he was sick with dysentery, a battlefield disease that was often fatal: it killed more than 44,000 men in the course of the war.[54] A man who had just died of it was being carried out of the hospital as Holmes was being brought in, and another died while he was there. The Confederates had occupied Fredericksburg, and a pontoon bridge was set up by Union forces across the Rappahannock. Holmes's company was ordered to cross and, without covering fire, to enter the city. Holmes's absence meant that his men were commanded by Henry Abbott. In obedience to orders, and carrying only a sword, Abbott marched at the head of a platoon into the first semicircle of houses. His men were promptly wiped out by enemy fire. He returned and, without hesitation, ordered a second platoon forward— "to certain and useless death,"[55] as Holmes later wrote—when the order to advance was countermanded. Abbott survived Fredericksburg, but his second lieutenant was killed. The Twentieth Massachusetts lost forty-eight men, more than in any other engagement of the war.[56]

The disaster made a deep impression on Holmes. He wept, he told his parents, at not being able to be with his comrades.[57] Abbott's comportment seemed to him the acme of heroism. The story of the advance into Fredericksburg later became the centerpiece of one of Holmes's most famous orations, the Memorial Day Address at Harvard in 1884. Holmes did not, out of respect for the occasion, make a point of it in that address, but what had struck him was not that Abbott had exposed himself so cavalierly to danger. It was that he had done so despite knowing that the order to advance was stupid, and despite a complete antipathy toward the cause in whose name he was, for all he knew, about to die. The spectacle did not persuade Holmes that Abbott's political views were correct. It did persuade him that war, in which the boldest are the likeliest to die, was a hideous human waste. And he began, after Fredericksburg, to rate the professionalism and discipline of the soldier higher than the merits of any particular cause—to admire success more than purity of faith.

There is little doubt of Abbott's exceptional physical courage; many stories attest to it. There is also little doubt that his courage became, once he had discovered it, the organizing principle of Abbott's self-conception. He was modest about it, and he made a point of judging other soldiers by their bravery rather than their politics, as when, for example, he praised Pen Hallowell for his efforts at Ball's Bluff,[58] or when he defended Wendell Holmes in his letters to his parents.

But Abbott was also obsessed with the subject of promotion. His letters home are filled with diatribes against men who have been promoted on grounds other than professional merit, and with speculations about future recognition for himself and the fellow officers he admired. He was quick to suspect the resentment of other men in his regiment, particularly the amputees, such as the abolitionist John Putnam: he referred to them as "the cripples."[59] And he frequently denounced the superiors whose orders he executed in such exemplary fashion as butchers and dunces. "I firmly believe that . . . the men who ordered the crossing of the river are responsible to God for murder,"[60] he wrote to his sister after Fredericksburg. He made a fetish of self-sacrifice, and the less he respected the cause for which he risked his life, the more valiantly he acted.

Back in Boston, Dr. Holmes remained a voluble champion of the Republican faith, and he seems to have indulged in some armchair generalship in his letters to the front, for about a week after the battle at Fredericksburg, he received an irritated letter from his son. Fredericksburg, Wendell informed his father, amounted to "an infamous butchery in a ridiculous attempt." "I never I believe have shown, as you seemed to hint, any wavering in my belief in the right of our cause," he goes on, evidently in response to something his father has written.

> But I see no farther progress—I don't think either of you [he is referring to Dr. Holmes's friend the historian John Lothrop Motley] realize the unity or the determination of the South. I think you are hopeful

because (excuse me) you are ignorant. But if it is true that we represent civilization wh. is in its nature, as well as slavery, diffusive & aggressive, and if civ^n & progress are the better things why they will conquer in the long run, we may be sure, and will stand a better chance in their proper province—peace—than in war, the brother of slavery—brother—it is slavery's parent, child and sustainer at once.[61]

This is not a political judgment. It is a moral judgment. It is a rebuke to people (like Dr. Holmes and John Motley) who believe that their idea of civilization is a justification for killing those who decline to share it. Of course civilizations are aggressive, Holmes says, but when they take up arms in order to impose their conception of civility on others, they sacrifice their moral advantage. Organized violence, at bottom, is just another form of oppression. Embarked upon to abolish slavery, war reveals itself to be slavery's twin—"parent, child and sustainer all at once."

After Fredericksburg, Holmes, still suffering from dysentery, went on sick leave to Philadelphia, where he stayed with the Hallowells. (His parents came down from Boston to visit him. On the train they ran into Emerson. "I found Dr & Mrs Holmes in the cars at Boston," Emerson reported to his daughter, "& had the Doctor all the way to Springfield. . . . [He] talked steadily twenty miles.")[62] Wendell returned to the front in January 1863. At the end of that month, Governor Andrew announced the formation of the Fifty-Fourth Massachusetts, the regiment of black volunteers that would be led by Colonel Robert Gould Shaw. Pen Hallowell (now eager to get out of the Twentieth) was made lieutenant colonel, and on February 7, he invited Holmes to apply for the position of major. Holmes declined. His reasons are unknown, since his reply to Hallowell is lost. But the Hallowells evidently thought Holmes still sufficiently committed to abolitionism to join a black regiment. (The majority went to another Hallowell brother, Edward, known as Ned. Pen was eventually transferred to a second Massachusetts black regiment, the Fifty-Fifth, and was made a colonel.)[63]

For his part, Dr. Holmes continued to rattle Republican sabers. In the spring of 1863 General Benjamin Butler was honored at a dinner in Boston. As military governor of New Orleans, Butler had acquired such a reputation for anti-Southern virulence that many Northerners—for example, the Adamses—regarded him as an embarrassment and a political liability. But Dr. Holmes read a commendatory poem he had composed for the occasion, which included the couplet (forever remembered by Butler):

> The mower mows on, though the adder may writhe,
> And the copperhead curl round the blade of the scythe.[64]

In March Wendell, now in Virginia, wrote to his father in a conciliatory mood: "I had my blowoff in one of my last and now let bygones be bygones—if *you* will." But he remained proud of the professionalism of his regiment. He reports with satisfaction the remark of a senior officer that the Twentieth "have no poetry in a fight"—that is, they don't romanticize the business of war. "It's very well to recommend theoretical porings over Bible & Homer—," Wendell goes on to explain to his father. "One's time is better spent with Regulations & the like."[65]

Two months later, in May 1863, Holmes was shot in the foot in an engagement known as Second Fredericksburg, shortly after Union soldiers had retaken the city. He returned again to Boston, and this time he stayed home for nine months. "I envy my white Othello," Dr. Holmes wrote to Motley, "with a semi-circle of young Desdemonas about him listening to the often told story which they will have over again."[66] (A "white Othello" seems to have been Dr. Holmes's term for an abolitionist.)

But there was plenty, even in Boston, to remind Wendell Holmes of the war. The battle of Gettysburg began on July 1; forty-four men from the Twentieth died in action. One of these was Henry Ropes. Ropes was the brother of John Ropes, a lawyer who, soon after the war, founded the Boston firm Ropes & Gray with his friend John Chipman Gray; both were close friends of Holmes. John Ropes suffered from curvature of the spine and was ineligible to serve in the Twentieth, but he was in consequence one of its most ardent followers, and in order to contribute something to the cause for which his brother fought, he acted as its official historian. Henry Ropes was killed, inadvertently, by Union guns. On July 7, his brother wrote to Holmes:

> My dear Wendell,
> The body arrived this morning. It is, I am grieved to say, not in a state to be seen. It would not do to open the coffin. All that can be seen through the glass-plate is the breast, which is bare, and in which is a fearful wound in the region of the heart, which must have caused instant death. I think I can discern a fragment of shell imbedded in the breast. It is a sad & shocking sight. Nothing of the face can be seen but the chin, round which is a handkerchief.
> If you would take any satisfaction in seeing what can be seen of poor Henry's mortal remains, you can do so by coming at 10 a.m. at the house of Lewis Jones, undertaker, rear of St. Paul's Church.

He begged Holmes to serve as one of the pallbearers.[67]

Eleven days later, on the evening of July 18, the Fifty-Fourth Massachusetts made its famous assault on Fort Wagner, outside Charleston, South Carolina—the charge in which Shaw was killed with a bullet through the heart, and his body was thrown afterward into a ditch by the enemy. Ned Hallowell was badly wounded in the attack. In August he wrote to Holmes from Philadelphia, where he had gone to recover. "What an awful month July has been for us," he told Holmes. "I mean you & me. I feel at least one year older since I left Boston. Do you ever see John Ropes? How completely broken he must be. He and Henry loved each other not like brothers but like friends." Hallowell had shaken hands with Shaw just before the charge, and had last seen him as he was about to jump into the dike in front of the fort. "[B]ut it became so very dark I could distinguish no one after that. My friends I suppose thought me so badly wounded they were affraid to tell me the whole truth at first, so told me he was wounded and a prisoner. It did shock me when the *truth* was told me."[68]

The defeat at Fort Wagner had depleted the officer corps of the Fifty-Fourth, and on August 12, Hallowell wrote Holmes again, pleading with him to suggest some young Bostonian who might be willing to serve. He did not renew the invitation to Holmes, but the implication must have been clear enough. Henry Abbott had heard that Holmes might leave the regiment, and wrote several letters begging him not to. He reminded Holmes of their trip back to the front the previous year. "That was after all a devilish pleasant journey to look back on," he wrote in September. "I have felt a sort of brotherhood ever since. However that sort of talk is spooney. . . ."[69] Holmes eventually did decide to stay with the Twentieth; and Abbott, when he learned the news, was relieved. "I haven't time to tell you how much I am delighted at your decision to stick to the old mother," he wrote to Holmes. "I believe you have done not only what is agreeable to yourself & us, but what is thoroughly right and proper, instead of absurdly wasting yourself before the shrine of the great nigger."[70]

In the event, Holmes did not return to action until January 1864, and then he was quickly transferred out of the Twentieth to a staff position in the Sixth Corps. This took him off the front line, but by no means out of danger. The final months of Holmes's service were, in fact, the most terrible.

THREE

THE WILDERNESS
AND AFTER

I

THE CIVIL WAR WAS FOUGHT with modern weapons and premodern tactics. The close-order infantry charge, a method of attack developed in the era of the musket, a gun with an effective range of about 80 yards, was used against defenders armed with rifles, a far deadlier weapon with a range of 400 yards.[1] The mismatch was responsible for some of the most spectacular carnage of the war. In Pickett's charge at Gettysburg, whose failure broke the back of Lee's army, 14,000 Confederate soldiers advanced in a line a mile wide across open fields against Union guns, and only half came back. But the tactic was responsible for a lot of unspectacular carnage as well, and one of the reasons the North finally triumphed was that it found in Grant a commander unafraid to throw wave after wave of troops at entrenched Confederate positions. The North had the bigger army, but the South, for the most part, defended, and in most battles the advantage was with the defense.

The Civil War was therefore an unusually dangerous war for every

Henry L. Abbott of the Twentieth Regiment of
Massachusetts Volunteers.

soldier who fought in it. Holmes's exposure was exceptional, though, because his regiment participated in some of the bloodiest fighting. The reason Holmes was transferred to the general staff when he returned to the army in January 1864 was that there were not enough soldiers left in his regiment to accommodate all its officers. By the time Holmes left the service, the Twentieth Massachusetts had lost more men—killed, wounded, dead of disease, and taken prisoner—than had made up its original number. There were almost two thousand regiments in the Union Army. Only four suffered a higher number of battle deaths.[2]

So that even before the spring and summer of 1864, when Grant began his costly advance on Richmond, Holmes had had a grisly war. He was exhausted, but he was not prepared to quit. In April he read, in the *North American Review*, an article on the Crusades by Charles Eliot Norton. Norton was the son of Andrews Norton, a Harvard professor, popularly known as the Unitarian pope, who had been Emerson's fiercest theological opponent. Charles Norton was fourteen years older than Holmes, and although he later became a renowned Harvard professor, in the field of art history, he was then working as a journalist. (He became co-editor, with James Russell Lowell, of the *North American Review* that fall.)

Norton was a staunch antislavery spokesman—he served during the war as editor of the New England Loyal Publication Society, a group founded to oppose Copperheads like the Abbotts—but he did not believe in racial equality, and his social views were deeply conservative. His take on the war was Spartan: he regarded it as an opportunity to toughen up an elite class of young men who had been made effete by too much prosperity.[3] Two months after the Union disaster at Bull Run, he published an article in the *Atlantic Monthly* called "The Advantages of Defeat." The North, he explained, was simply too fond of life: "We have thought it braver to save than to spend it." All-out war would cure that. "We may well be grateful and glad for our defeat of the 21st of July," he suggested, "if we wrest from it the secrets of our weakness. . . . But if not, then let us be ready for another and another defeat, till our souls shall be tempered and our forces disciplined for the worthy attainment of victory."[4] "[P]ray that we may have suffering enough to make us as a nation nobler & worthier than we have been," he wrote to a friend on October 2, 1861.[5] Ball's Bluff took place three weeks later. It was only a taste of the suffering to come.

This was exactly the kind of high-minded satisfaction in agonies actually being sustained by other people that Holmes found so exasperating in his father. But he sat down and wrote Norton a letter praising his article on the Crusades, "now when we need all the examples of chivalry to help us bind our rebellious desires to steadfastness in the Christian Crusade of the 19th century. If one didn't believe that this war was such a crusade, in the cause of the future of the whole civilized world," Holmes went on,

> it would be hard indeed to keep the hand to the sword; and one who is rather compelled unwillingly to the work by abstract conviction than borne along on the flood of some passionate enthuasism, must feel his ardor rekindled by stories like this. . . . In all probability, from what I hear of the filling up of the Regt. I shall soon be mustered in for a new term of service as Lt. Col. of the 20th [he got the promotion, but was unable to accept it] and so with double reason I am thankful to read of the great dead who have "stood in the evil day." No—it will not do to leave Palestine yet.[6]

This is the only surviving letter of Holmes's from the front that expresses a strong political conviction, probably because it is a letter Holmes could not later get his hands on to destroy. The language may have been calculated to suit the prejudices of the correspondent, but the idea to write it was Holmes's own, and the contents express a continued commitment to the antislavery cause.

The tone is quite different from the letter Holmes had written his sister a year and a half earlier, before the battle of Fredericksburg, and it reflects a change in the mood of the army as well as the mood of the author. Abolitionist sentiment had increased among Northern troops after Gettysburg—partly as a backlash against the racist New York draft riots in the summer of 1863, partly in response to the bravery demonstrated at Fort Wagner by the black soldiers of the Fifty-Fourth Massachusetts, partly because of a reversal of fortunes in the war itself. For many Northerners, oddly, the Civil War became much more of a moral crusade in its final years than it had been at the start, and Holmes's letter reflects this. But Holmes also remained— and it is important to see that these attitudes lay side by side, so to speak, in his mind—a devotee of military professionalism. About the same time as his letter to Norton, he reported with pride to Emerson that "the Army of the Potomac is acquiring a professional feeling, & that they have neither panics nor excitements, but more self-reliance."[7]

A month later, on the night of May 3, Holmes wrote to his parents from northern Virginia. In anticipation of a battle, he says, he has sent his diary home. (This is the diary that was later destroyed.) "This is only a parting word of love to all at home—," he adds. "I suppose we fight in a day or two."[8] They did. It was the battle of the Wilderness, the beginning of a campaign that would last forty days.

2

"More desperate fighting has not been witnessed on this continent than that of the 5th and 6th of May," Grant wrote many years later.[9] Lee had decided to meet the advance of the Army of the Potomac through northern Virginia by attacking it as it passed through a scruffy, overgrown area south of the Rapidan River known as the Wilderness. This gave the Confederates, though outnumbered by nearly two to one, the advantage of fighting on a difficult terrain which they knew far better than the enemy did, and which provided ample opportunity for cover. Holmes had been assigned to the staff of General Horatio G. Wright. Soon after daybreak on the 5th, Wright's headquarters was shelled. "[O]ne [shell] struck within a yard of quite a number of us who were sitting on horseback & bounced under the horses—," Holmes recorded in his diary. "Others threw fragments round constantly for a few minutes & as a Regt. was filing by to the right a shell or roundshot striking in it covered many of the staff with brains."[10]

The next day, May 6, Abbott was shot. "Abbott wounded *severely* don't know where,"[11] Holmes wrote to his parents. Abbott was in charge of what was left of the Twentieth Massachusetts when he was ordered to hold off a Confederate force threatening a weakened Union position. He told his men to drop to the ground and a firefight began. To direct his own soldiers' fire, Abbott remained standing until he was struck by the bullet that killed him. Despite his Copperhead views, which he does not seem to have made a secret of, Abbott had acquired a reputation as one of the most valiant officers in the army. General Meade had intended to promote him; after his death, his brigade commander wrote that "his merit was so peculiar and his worth so well known to all the officers of the corps and to the general commanding, that it is not necessary for me to attempt to do him justice. My brigade lost in him its best soldier."[12]

To Holmes, of course, Abbott had been much more. That a man widely recognized as the most distinguished soldier in his unit had continually singled him out as a worthy comrade was a source of self-esteem for which he could feel grateful. But Abbott had also impressed on Holmes, possibly by his conversation but certainly by his example, the belief that nobility of character consists in doing one's job with indifference to ends, and his death seems to have set the seal on this belief. After that single sentence in his letter home from the Wilderness, Holmes never mentions Abbott again in any of the war correspondence or the diaries that survive. But after the war, Abbott's death became a touchstone in his thought.

Grant's forces did ultimately advance, and converged on Spotsylvania Courthouse, south of Chancellorsville. "Just think of it—," Holmes wrote to his mother on May 11. "Today is the 7th day we have fought, not pitched battles all the time of course, but averaging a loss I guess of 3000 (three thousand) a day at least—."[13] It was raining. The battle began the following morning at 4:30. At midday, Holmes was sent with a dispatch to "a point of woods in front of [General] Hancock's H.Q.," where unusually stubborn fighting was under way, but he couldn't find the officer to whom he was to report, and returned. When he went to sleep that night at 2 a.m., the sound of firing had not stopped.[14]

The next day, Holmes learned that the "point of woods" had been the scene of the most brutal fighting of the war, the so-called Bloody

Angle of Spotsylvania. In a small space along the breastworks of Confederate trenches, in the pouring rain, the two sides had fought hand to hand continuously for eighteen hours in a kind of blood frenzy. Men thrust bayonets through the logs or jumped onto the barricade and fired into the mass of soldiers below until they were themselves shot down.[15] A tree eighteen inches thick was completely severed by bullets.[16] "At 'the angle' in a space of 12 by 15 ft between two traverses," Holmes wrote in his diary, "Col. Penrose told Kent he counted 150 bodies—." The next morning Holmes rode to the spot himself. Not everyone was dead yet. "In the corner of woods referred to yesterday the dead of both sides lay piled in the trenches 5 or 6 deep—wounded often writhing under superincumbent dead—The trees were in slivers from the constant peppering of bullets."[17]

There is a neurochemistry of battle. For the men who fought at the Bloody Angle the universe must have reduced itself that day to a place in which killing and being killed were the only things that made sense, a world in which any other kind of behavior lay outside the boundaries of the thinkable. "I thought for awhile that I was dying, and it seemed the most natural thing in the world," Holmes had written about his wound at Ball's Bluff. But at Spotsylvania, he was on the outside. He did not know the fever. He only saw the horror.

By the 16th, he had had enough. "Before you get this you will know how immense the butchers bill has been—," he wrote to his parents. "[T]hese nearly two weeks have contained all of fatigue & horror that war can furnish—. . . . [N]early every Regimental off— I knew or cared for is dead or wounded—I have made up my mind to stay on the staff if possible till the end of the campaign & then if I am alive, I shall resign—I have felt for sometime that I didn't any longer believe in this being a duty." Then (as he often does in his war letters) he apologized for his grimness. "The duties & thoughts of the field are of such a nature that one cannot at the same time keep home, parents and such thoughts as they suggest in his mind at the same time as a reality—Can hardly indeed remember their existence—. . . . Still your letters are the one pleasure & you know my love."[18]

This confession of exhaustion dismayed Dr. Holmes, who evi-

dently wrote his son a patriotic rebuke. "[R]ec^d y'r letters of 21st 22^d,"
Holmes answered coldly on May 30,

> the latter fr. dad, stupid—I wish you'd take the trouble to read my
> letters before answering—I am sure I cannot have conveyed the
> idea, rightfully, that I intended resigning before the campaign was
> over. . . . I must say I dislike such a misunderstanding, so discred-
> itable to my feeling of soldierly honor, when I don't believe there was
> a necessity for it. . . . I am convinced from my late experience that if
> I can stand the wear & tear (body & mind) of regimental duty that it
> is a greater strain on both than I am called on to endure—If I am
> satisfied I don't really see that anyone else has a call to be other-
> wise—. . . . I am not the same man (may not have quite the same
> ideas) & certainly am not so elastic as I was and I *will not acknowl-
> edge the same claims upon me under those circumstances* that existed
> formerly.[19]

He went on to tell his parents the story of a recent adventure: while
carrying a dispatch, he had been ambushed by a band of Confederates and had escaped by riding his horse "Comanche fashion" as they
fired on him at close range. On the back of the envelope, he scribbled two sentences. "Write as often as poss.," he begs. And then: "It
is still kill—kill—all the time."[20] Four days later, at Cold Harbor,
Grant's army suffered seven thousand casualties in a single morning.

By June 7, the fighting had wound down temporarily, and Holmes
was in better spirits. But he had not changed his mind about resigning. "I started in this thing a boy I am now a man," he wrote to his
mother (whose views, in contrast to her husband's, had been stead-
fastly antislavery from the beginning, and whose opinion on this issue of his duty therefore mattered more to her son),

> and I have been coming to the conclusion for the last six months
> [that is, ever since he had returned from his foot injury] that my
> duty has changed—
>   I can do a disagreeable thing or face a great danger coolly enough
> when I *know* it is a duty—but a doubt demoralizes me as it does any
> nervous man—and now I honestly think the duty of fighting has
> ceased for me—ceased because I have laboriously and with much

suffering of mind and body *earned* the right which I denied Willy Everett [a classmate who spent the war as a student in England] to decide for myself how I can best do my duty to myself to the country and, if you choose, to God—.

"I hope that this will meet your approbation—," he says at the end, "you are so sure to be right."[21]

By the end of the month Grant had laid siege to Petersburg. In forty days, his army had lost sixty thousand men. Dr. Holmes continued to supply free military advice from Boston, but by now his son was accustomed to it. "Father'd better not talk to me about opinions at home & here," he writes tersely to his parents on June 24. "These last few days have been very bad. . . . I tell you many a man has gone crazy since this campaign begun from the terrible pressure on mind & body—I think the Army feels better than it might but theres no use in disguising that the feeling for McClellan has grown this campaign."[22] A few weeks later he writes to his mother that he is being discharged at last. If he were to reenlist, he explains, he would risk being reassigned as a captain of infantry and serving once again on the line. "If it should be necessary to go into the service again I should try for a commission from the Presd' but I shan't bother myself ab' that for the pres'," he wrote. "Do you think I could get a place for my nagur boy if I brought him with me?"[23]

3

Holmes arrived in Boston on July 19, 1864, a little less than three years after he had accepted his commission. A few weeks after his return, he went out to Concord to visit Emerson. He apparently (as he told the story many years later) wanted to see whether he should try to make a career like Emerson's, as a writer of philosophy. He concluded that he should not, and that fall he enrolled at Harvard Law School.[24] But he had not given up the idea of doing philosophy. He had only given up the idea of doing it in the way Emerson and his father had done it—by synthesis and introspection. He thought it could be done better by scholarship and analysis.

Dr. Holmes was a confirmed generalist. He was a professor of medicine who wrote poetry and delivered political orations, and he regarded his eclecticism as a mark of intellectual superiority. "It is strange, very strange to me, that many men should devote themselves so exclusively to the study of their own particular callings," he wrote in 1832. "It seems as if they thought a mind must grow narrow before it can come to a focus. . . . [But t]he knowledge of a man, who confines himself to one object, bears the same relation to that of the liberal scholar, that the red or violet ray of a prism does to the blended light of a sunbeam."[25] His attitude even toward his own profession was slightly unprofessional. The sight of blood made him sick.[26] His patients found his flippancy irritating ("The smallest fevers gratefully received," was a favorite pun)[27] and his practice was consequently short-lived. He was skeptical of some of the claims of medical science anyway, and took the view that "a very large proportion of diseases get well of themselves, without any special medication."[28]

The jesting manner makes Dr. Holmes's generalism seem frivolous; but it belonged to an era that took generalism extremely seriously. Emerson's own method (as the young Wendell Holmes had noted admiringly in his undergraduate essay on "Books") was to skim works of literature and philosophy, of all types and from all cultures, with an eye to ideas and phrases he could appropriate for his own use. This was his notion of research. It was based on the conviction that organized study deadens the mind, and that genuine insight arises spontaneously from the individual soul. "To believe your own thought," as he put it in a well-known passage in "Self-Reliance," "to believe that what is true for you in your private heart is true for all men,—that is genius."[29]

To the Wendell Holmes who returned from the war, generalism was the enemy of seriousness. War had made him appreciate the value of expertise: soldiers who understood the mechanics of battle fought better—more effectively, but also more bravely—than soldiers who were motivated chiefly by enthusiasm for a cause. When he had written his letter to Charles Norton comparing the Civil War to the Crusades, Holmes was still attempting to inspire himself by his feeling for the cause. When he emerged from the Wilderness three months later, that feeling seemed to him only an emotion people used to destroy themselves.

Holmes's rejection of the intellectual style of prewar Boston mirrored a generational shift. To many of the men who had been through the war, the values of professionalism and expertise were attractive; they implied impersonality, respect for institutions as efficient organizers of enterprise, and a modern and scientific attitude—the opposites of the individualism, humanitarianism, and moralism that characterized Northern intellectual life before the war.[30] For Holmes, though, the shift to professionalism was not quite so reductive. He shared his generation's faith in science. He also shared its indisposition to unsettle the status quo. He had been shell-shocked once, and he did not wish to repeat the experience. But he had not given up the hope of (as he liked, a little grandiosely, to put it) a glimpse of the infinite. He narrowed himself in order better to expand.

Twelve years after he entered law school, in 1876, Holmes sent a letter to Emerson, now in his dotage, explaining that he was mailing him a copy of one of his first law review articles, called "Primitive Notions in Modern Law," which had just been published. Holmes was working as an attorney, but he devoted all his spare time to legal scholarship. "If the clothing of detail does not stand in the way I hope the ideas may not be uninteresting to you," he wrote to Emerson.

> It seems to me that I have learned, after a laborious and somewhat painful period of probation that the law opens a way to philosophy as well as anything else, if pursued far enough, and I hope to prove it before I die. Accept this little piece as written in that faith, and as a slight mark of the gratitude and respect I feel for you who more than anyone else first started the philosophical ferment in my mind.[31]

The idea that disinterested inquiry is the best way to crack the world's nut was Holmes's message to his generation. He became, in effect, the Emerson of professionalism—or as he sometimes called it, "jobbism." "If one does one's job as well as one can one achieves a practical altruism, and . . . it doesn't matter so much how one feels about it,"[32] he explained to one of his regular correspondents, the diplomat Lewis Einstein, and he repeated the theme many times. "A man may live greatly in the law as well as elsewhere," he announced in a speech at Harvard in 1886 on "The Profession of the Law." (By then, he was a justice on the Supreme Judicial Court of Massachusetts, a position he would hold until 1902.) "If this universe is one universe, if it is so far thinkable that you can pass in reason from one part of it to another, it does not matter very much what that fact is. For every fact leads to every other by the path of the air."[33] Holmes is echoing "The American Scholar." "There is no trifle," Emerson wrote, "there is no puzzle; but one design unites and animates the farthest pinnacle and the lowest trench."[34]

But Holmes went on to create his own image of intellectual heroism:

> No man has earned the right to intellectual ambition until he has learned to lay his course by a star which he has never seen—to dig by the divining rod for springs which he may never reach. In saying this, I point to that which will make your study heroic. For I say to you in all sadness of conviction, that to think great thoughts you must be heroes as well as idealists. Only when you have worked alone—when you have felt around you a black gulf of solitude more isolating than that which surrounds the dying man, and in hope and in despair have trusted to your own unshaken will—then only will you have achieved. Thus only can you gain the secret isolated joy of the thinker, who knows that, a hundred years after he is dead and forgotten, men who never heard of him will be moving to the measure of his thought—the subtile rapture of a postponed power, which the world knows not because it has no external trappings, but which to his prophetic vision is more real than that which commands an army.[35]

The analogy to war is deliberate, for the whole passage is built from language Holmes had used more than twenty years earlier, in the fall of 1864, when he published anonymously, in the Boston *Evening Transcript*, a sonnet in memory of Henry Abbott:

He steered unquestioning nor turning back
Into the darkness and the unknown sea;
He vanished in the starless night, and we
Saw but the shining of his luminous wake.
Thou sawest light, but ah, our sky seemed black,
All too hard the inscrutable decree,
Yet, noble heart, full soon we follow thee
Lit by the deeds that flamed along thy track.[36]

In their dedication to the task at hand, human beings make, by their deeds, tracks in the wilderness. The wilderness itself is trackless.

4

The moment Holmes returned from the war, he seems to have fast-frozen his experience, and to have sealed its meaning off from future revision. He told the stories of his wounds for the rest of his life, he recalled former comrades with emotion, and he alluded frequently to the experience of battle in his writings and speeches. But although he read almost every other kind of book imaginable, he could not bear to read histories of the Civil War. He rarely mentioned the issues that had been the reason for the fighting or expressed a political opinion about the outcome. The war had burned a hole, so to speak, in his life. It was a hole he had paid a high price for, and he had no interest in rethinking its significance. For seventy years, he cherished it as protectively as the slip of paper he had carried away with him from the Nicodemus House.

The lesson Holmes took from the war can be put in a sentence. It is that certitude leads to violence. This is a proposition that has an easy application and a difficult one. The easy application is to ideologues, dogmatists, and bullies—people who think that their rightness justifies them in imposing on anyone who does not happen to subscribe to their particular ideology, dogma, or notion of turf. If the conviction of rightness is powerful enough, resistance to it will be met, sooner or later, by force. There are people like this in every sphere of life, and it is natural to feel that the world would be a better place without them.

But this is not quite what Holmes felt. He did have an intense dislike of people who presented themselves as instruments of some higher power. "I detest a man who knows that he knows,"[37] as he wrote, late in life, to his friend Harold Laski. And he had a knee-jerk suspicion of causes. He regarded them as attempts to compel one group of human beings to conform to some other group's idea of the good, and he could see no authority for such attempts greater than the other group's certainty that it knew what was best. "Some kind of despotism is at the bottom of seeking for change," he wrote to Laski. "I don't care to boss my neighbors and to require them to want something different from what they do—even when, as frequently, I think their wishes more or less suicidal."[38]

His standard example in criticizing the reformist mentality was the abolitionists. "The abolitionists had a stock phrase that a man was either a knave or a fool who did not act as they (the abolitionists) *knew* to be right," he wrote to another old friend, the British jurist Frederick Pollock, in 1929. "So Calvin thought of the Catholics and the Catholics of Calvin. So I don't doubt do the more convinced prohibitionists think of their opponents today. When you know that you know persecution comes easy. It is as well that some of us don't know that we know anything."[39] Holmes acknowledged that there were skeptics among the abolitionists he had known in Boston before the war (he was thinking of his mother and, possibly, of Emerson), and that his own skepticism was learned partly from them.[40] But abolitionism came to stand in his thought for the kind of superior certitude that drives men (frequently men other than the ones who are certain) to kill one another.

Still, Holmes did not think that the world would be better off without people like this, because he thought that *everyone* was like this—and this is the difficult part of his belief about certitude and violence. It is easy to condemn unwarranted certainty in others; we are always confident that people we disagree with would be improved by a little self-doubt. We even remind ourselves, in our better moments, to be skeptical of our own convictions. In the end, though, there just are some things that we are certain about. We have beliefs we cannot help feeling are valid—the belief, for instance, that slavery is wrong.

And when push comes to shove over those beliefs, we are prepared to shove back.

Holmes admitted that he, too, was capable of taking up arms in the name of what he thought was right. When that day came, nothing could save him from the resort to violence, not even the knowledge that what he was fighting for was, in the end, just his preference. "You respect the rights of man—," he wrote to Laski. "I don't, except those things a given crowd will fight for—which vary from religion to the price of a glass of beer. I also would fight for some things—but instead of saying that they ought to be I merely say they are part of the kind of world that I like—or should like."[41]

"Men to a great extent believe what they want to," Holmes wrote in 1918, when he had been sitting on the Supreme Court for sixteen years.[42] But he did not think that the absence of a higher authority made it pointless to talk of beliefs as good or bad, true or false, right or wrong. He only thought that rightness and wrongness are functions of the circumstances in which our lives happen to be embedded. Since we cannot (except at the margin) change the circumstances, it makes sense for us to talk of right and wrong without mental quotation marks. In the long view of human affairs custom and habit may be contingent, but in the short view they are often as good as necessity. "Man is like any other organism, shaping himself to his environment so wholly that after he has taken the shape if you try to change it you alter his life," Holmes told Einstein. "All of which is all right and fully justifies us in doing what we can't help doing and trying to make the world into the kind of world that we think we should like; but it hardly warrants our talking much about absolute truth."[43] Truth, Holmes said many times, is just the name for what it is impossible for a person to doubt. "All I mean by truth is the path I have to travel," as he explained to his friend Alice Green.[44]

This is an argument that splits in two directions, and understanding Holmes's work as a judge requires keeping both tracks of the argument simultaneously in mind. The assumption that people are justified in defending what they have become accustomed to is obviously an assumption heavily biased toward the status quo. There will naturally be people who want to change the way things are, but on Holmes's theory these people are simply attempting to shift some part of the aggregate social burden from one set of shoulders to another. "Justice" and "fairness" are slogans propping up particular struggles, not eternal principles, and reform is a zero-sum game. But if we flip Holmes's theory over onto its back, so to speak, the implications are reversed. For the friends of the status quo have no greater claim to the principles of justice and fairness than its enemies do. And if the enemies can muster sufficient support, the presumption of rightness will slide over to their side of the scale. In 1850 the abolitionists seemed, to most Northerners, dangerous subversives. Less than fifteen years later, they were patriots. There is no one way that life must be.

What prevents the friction between competing conceptions of the way life should be from overheating and leading to violence is democracy. In the seventy years that Holmes lived after the war, the chief struggle in America was the struggle between capital and labor. Nearly every judicial opinion for which he became known constituted an intervention in that struggle, and his fundamental concern was almost always to permit all parties the democratic means to attempt to make their interests prevail. The life struggle is mitigated, he argued in one of his first law review articles, a commentary on the legal consequences of a British work stoppage in 1872, by

> sympathy, prudence, and all the social and moral qualities. But in the last resort a man rightly prefers his own interest to that of his neighbors. And this is as true in legislation as in any other form of corporate action. All that can be expected from modern improvements is that legislation should easily and quickly, yet not too quickly, modify itself in accordance with the will of the de facto supreme power in the community, and that the spread of an educated sympathy should reduce the sacrifice of minorities to a minimum.[45]

He repeated the formula in his principal work of jurisprudence, *The Common Law*, published in 1881. "It seems to me clear," he wrote there, "that the *ultima ratio*, not only *regum*, but of private persons, is force, and that at the bottom of all private relations, however tempered by sympathy and all the social feelings, is a justifiable self-preference."[46] (Holmes later contemplated a new edition of *The Common Law*, and considered changing the phrase "all private relations," which is a little drastic and Nietzschean, to "all mere social relations."[47] The revised edition never appeared.)

It is easy to see Holmes's concern for allowing democracy to work its way, without peremptory restriction by courts, in his opinions in cases involving economic issues, such as the Massachusetts case of *Commonwealth v. Perry* (1891) and the U.S. Supreme Court case of *Lochner v. New York* (1905)—cases in which he supported, against a majority of his colleagues, the right of legislatures to regulate contractual relations between business owners and their employees. But that concern is also at the bottom of his opinions in the civil liberties cases, such as *Abrams v. United States* (1919), *Gitlow v. New York* (1925), and *United States v. Schwimmer* (1929). Those were ostensibly First Amendment disputes; but their real grounds were economic. For in every case, the defendant was some kind of socialist.

Holmes thought that socialism was a silly doctrine. He believed that most measures on behalf of labor were futile, since (as he explained privately) "the crowd now has substantially all there is."[48] And he regarded the ideas whose expression he was celebrated for protecting in his judicial opinions as fatuous and immature. His personal sympathies were entirely with the capitalists. He not only considered them virtuous engines of social wealth; he had a kind of schoolboy's respect for their energy and willpower. "If they could make a case for putting Rockefeller in prison I should do my part," he told Einstein; "but if they left it to me I should put up a bronze statue to him."[49] Holmes's first notable dissent as a U.S. Supreme Court justice, in *Northern Securities Co. v. United States* (1904), was a defense of J. P. Morgan and James T. Hill against the antitrust laws—an opinion that infuriated the trustbuster who had appointed him to the Court two years earlier, Theodore Roosevelt.

The key to Holmes's civil liberties opinions is the key to all his jurisprudence: it is that he thought only in terms of aggregate social forces; he had no concern for the individual. The spectacle of individuals falling victim to dominant political or economic tendencies, when those tendencies had been instantiated in duly enacted laws, gave him a kind of chilly satisfaction. It struck him as analogous to the death of soldiers in a battlefield victory, and justified on the same grounds—that for the group to move ahead, some people must inevitably fall by the wayside. "Every society rests on the death of men,"[50] he liked to provoke his friends by saying. He had, consequently, virtually no faith in the notion of individual human agency. On his view, successful people, like Morgan and Rockefeller, just had a better grasp of social tendencies than unsuccessful people did. Everyone is simply riding the wave chance has put them on. Some people know how to surf; some people drown.

Holmes's defense of civil liberties had nothing to do, in other words, with the notion that such liberties were owed to people merely by the fact of their being human—a belief he held in conspicuous contempt. He could defend the right of socialists and pacifists to express their views on grounds that those views represented a legitimate social interest, and at the same time exhibit indifference to the suffering of, for example, Southern blacks victimized by de facto discrimination.[51] In his most notorious opinion, in the case of *Buck v. Bell* (1927), he voted, in language evoking the Civil War, to uphold a Virginia law permitting the involuntary sterilization of mentally incompetent persons. "We have seen more than once that the public welfare may call upon the best citizens for their lives," he wrote. "It would be strange if it could not call upon those who already sap the strength of the State for these lesser sacrifices."[52] He disliked the self-righteous, but he had no sympathy for the weak. He reversed, in effect, the priorities of his youth: he took the Constitution for his text and rejected the Declaration of Independence.

When Holmes emerged as a consistent judicial defender of economic reform and of free speech, he became a hero to progressives and civil libertarians—to people like Louis Brandeis, Learned Hand, Walter Lippmann, and Herbert Croly. Holmes did not share the politics of these people, but he did not think it was his business as a judge to have a politics, and he did nothing to discourage their admiration. It suited his conception of heroic disinterestedness to serve as their Abbott—privately denouncing the stupidity of the views he strove, often boldly and alone, to defend. "It has given me great pleasure to sustain the Constitutionality of laws that I believe to be as bad as possible, because I thereby helped to mark the difference between what I would forbid and what the Constitution permits," as he explained to his cousin John T. Morse.[53] Holmes did not defend the interests of labor because he wished to see those interests prevail. He defended them because he believed that every social interest should have its chance. He believed in experiment. He knew what the alternative was.

5

Holmes once remarked to Lewis Einstein that the war had made him realize that Boston was just one American city.[54] He had not fought for Boston; he had fought for the United States, and the experience taught him that the two were not the same. Boston was not, as his father had loved to proclaim, the measure of all things. ("We all carry the Common in our heads as the unit of space, the State House as the standard of architecture, and measure off men in Edward Everetts as with a yard-stick,"[55] Dr. Holmes once proudly proclaimed to his friend Motley.) The views of a Bostonian, insofar as they were Bostonian views, were partial and provincial. This realization was liberating, but it was also alienating. It inspired Holmes, in his mature thought, to attempt to transcend the prejudices of his own time and place. On the other hand, it left him at home in the habits of no time or place.

One of the effects the Civil War had on American culture was to replace the sentiment of section with the sentiment of nation, and Holmes's self-conscious transformation from provincial to cosmopolite was of a piece with this larger development. But it gave him an aloofness that sometimes amounted to a blindness to the local, the practical, and the particular—things that are important enough, most of the time, to the rest of us. The need to uproot himself was so strong in Holmes that he developed an aversion almost to the very idea of soil. In his work as a judge, he took delight in exposing prejudices that masqueraded as timeless truths. In his personal life, he accumulated acquaintances but tended to avoid intimacy. He had no children. "This is not the kind of world I want to bring anyone else into," he confided to Learned Hand.[56]

The aloofness, the single-mindedness, and the contempt for other people's ideals make the older Holmes seem a cold figure, and there is no doubt that he plumed himself a little on his detachment from ordinary sentiment. He had set out to separate himself from the insular culture of his youth, and in many respects he succeeded. When, in 1928, he read V. L. Parrington's judgment on his father in Parrington's literary and intellectual history *Main Currents in American Thought*—"He was always an amateur," Parrington wrote; "life was too agreeable for him to take the trouble to become an artist"[57] —his reaction was mild. "I am not surprised at what he said about my father," he told Laski, "nor at his having missed what I think true, that although my father did not concentrate in his later days as he did when he wrote on puerperal fever, still he had in him a capacity for profound insight—that occasionally flashed out as I saw him." Parrington's sympathy with the Transcendentalist belief in the infinite value of every human soul, Holmes added, "got my hair up."[58]

Holmes believed that it was no longer possible to think the way he had as a young man before the war, that the world was more resistant than he had imagined. But he did not forget what it felt like to *be* a young man before the war. "Through our great good fortune," he said in the speech in which he memorialized Abbott's advance into Fredericksburg, "in our youth our hearts were touched with fire"[59]—a sentence that both ennobles the antislavery cause and removes it to an irretrievable past. When Pen Hallowell died, in 1914, Holmes told Einstein that although their paths had diverged, Hallowell had been "my oldest friend. . . . I don't know but the greatest soul I ever knew. . . . [H]e gave the first adult impulse to my youth."[60] And his enthusiasm for Emerson never faded. Holmes's posture of intellectual isolation was, after all, essentially Emersonian. "The only firebrand of my youth that burns to me as brightly as ever," he wrote to Pollock in 1930, when he was nearly ninety, "is Emerson."[61]

In 1932, after he had retired from the Court and was nearing the end, Holmes tried to read aloud to Marion Frankfurter, Felix Frankfurter's wife, a poem he liked about the Civil War, but he broke down in tears before he could finish it.[62] They were not tears for the war. They were tears for what the war had destroyed. Holmes had grown up in a highly cultivated, homogeneous world, a world of which he was, in many ways, the consummate product: idealistic, artistic, and socially committed. And then he had watched that world bleed to death at Fredericksburg and Antietam, in a war that learning and brilliance had been powerless to prevent. When he returned, Boston had changed, and so had American life. Holmes had changed too, but he never forgot what he had lost. "He told me," Einstein reported, "that after the Civil War the world never seemed quite right again."[63]

PART TWO

William James, self-portrait, made around 1866,
when he was a student at Harvard Medical School.

FOUR

THE MAN OF TWO MINDS

I

WILLIAM JAMES DID NOT FIGHT in the Civil War. He was nineteen years old when Fort Sumter surrendered, and his educational career, which had been episodic anyway, had reached an impasse. There was not much to keep him from signing up. But he remained behind the lines.

It is not as though he was isolated from the passions of the anti-slavery movement. His family was intimate with the Emersons, and two of his younger brothers, Garth Wilkinson (known as Wilky) and Robertson (called Bob), were students at a school in Concord run by Franklin Sanborn, who had been one of the abolitionist backers of John Brown's Harpers Ferry adventure—the so-called Secret Six. (Sanborn had fled briefly to Canada after Brown's capture, much to the disgust of his fellow Secret-Sixer Thomas Higginson.) Two of John Brown's daughters attended the school. Wilky and Bob both enlisted (Bob lied about his age), and they eventually served in black regiments, the Fifty-Fourth and Fifty-Fifth Massachusetts. Wilky was Robert Gould Shaw's adjutant in the Fifty-Fourth and was badly wounded in the assault on Fort Wagner. He was brought home to Newport, where the Jameses were living, and William, who was a talented artist, made a sketch of him recovering from his wounds. It was as close as William James ever got to a battlefield.

It has become customary to assume that William and his third brother, Henry, were prevented from enlisting by their father, Henry James, Sr., who, although willing to send his less promising sons off to war, was anxious to protect the investment he had made in William, the oldest and the most obviously gifted of the five James children. The relations between William and Henry Senior were complicated, and no doubt the father preferred to keep his oldest son out of danger. Still, William does not seem to have pulled very hard at the leash. He joined the Newport Artillery Company as a ninety-day volunteer on April 22, 1861, shortly after the fall of Fort Sumter; but this was a standard response for Northerners who had not made up their minds to fight, and it entailed no serious military obligation. In the fall, James enrolled in the Lawrence Scientific School at Harvard, and he spent the rest of war as a student.

But he was sensitive about his absence from the defining experience of his generation, and in the few places in which he mentions it, he attributes his failure to enlist not to his father's restraint, but to his own pusillanimity. He remembered, many years later, standing in the crowd as the newly formed Fifty-Fourth marched through Boston in the spring of 1863, and watching Charles Russell Lowell, Shaw's lieutenant and future brother-in-law, ride up on horseback with his fiancée: "I looked back and saw their faces and figures against the evening sky, and they looked so young and victorious, that I, much gnawed by questions as to my own duty of enlisting or not, shrank back—they had not seen me—from being recognized. I shall never forget the impression they made."[1]

It was a telling contrast. Charles Lowell, the "Beau Sabreur," was one of the most glamorous figures in wartime Boston; his marriage to the famously spirited Josephine Shaw, as her brother's Fifty-Fourth was going off to battle, embodied the convergence of Brahminism and abolitionism in the most romantic style. Charles's only sibling, James Jackson Lowell, had been mortally wounded, virtually in front of Wendell Holmes's eyes, in the battle of Glendale a year earlier, and had died a Confederate prisoner. Charles himself would be killed, in 1864, at Cedar Creek. Charles Lowell's public image was the reverse of William James's private image. He was heroic, decisive, and socially assured. William James was fragile; he was socially insecure; and he could never make up his mind.

That James was still fretting two years into the war about whether or not to enlist is typical of his capacity for decision. Many biographers have blamed William's indecisiveness on mixed signals from Henry Senior. Henry Senior was certainly a dizzy enough role model for anybody; but his oldest son had an aversion to making up his mind that was all his own. He worked most of his life to defend simultaneously held worldviews—modern science and religious faith—that most people regard as mutually exclusive, and he ended up inventing a philosophy, pragmatism, that is supposed to enable people to make good choices among philosophical options. James believed that a risk-assuming decisiveness—betting on an alternative even before all the evidence is in—was the supreme mark of character. He thought that the universe would meet such a person halfway. But he also thought that certainty was moral death, and he hated to foreclose anything.

His solution to this problem in his own life was to cultivate a self-conscious impulsivity. He would act decisively, and then, just as decisively, change his mind. He spent fifteen years trying to settle on an occupation, switching from science to painting to science to painting again, then to chemistry, anatomy, natural history, and finally medicine. Medicine was the only course of study he ever completed: he received an M.D. from Harvard in 1869 and never practiced or taught medicine for the rest of his life. He began teaching physiology at Harvard in 1872, but switched fields, first to experimental psychology and then to philosophy (though the boundaries between those fields were much less rigid than they are today). In 1903 he began the process of trying to decide whether to retire. His diary for the fall of 1905 reads: October 26, "Resign!"; October 28, "Resign!!!"; November 4, "Resign?"; November 7, "Resign!"; November 8, "Don't resign"; November 9, "Resign!"; November 16, "*Don't* resign!"; November 23,

"Resign"; December 7, "Don't resign"; December 9, "Teach here next year."[2] He retired in 1907.

He devoted two years to the courtship of the woman he married, Alice Howe Gibbens (who was perfectly willing to marry him)—starting out, in 1876, with the assumption that he would marry her, and then working his way around the compass until he arrived at the beginning again. Within that circle many smaller circles were nested. At one point, about a year into the courtship, the possibility arose that Alice might go to England without him. On a Monday evening, James wrote to approve the plan: "You must go to England. And with a view to all sorts of eventualities we must avoid the appearance of being in a peculiar relation to each other." On Tuesday morning, he sent another letter: "I have come to see that my saying you must go to England is pedantic folly. . . . I am an idiot, unfit to advise you." Six days later, he had some advice: "The thought of all this," he wrote, "has made me during the last twenty four hours wonder whether it be well for you to give up your english plan."[3] She didn't go to England; but she did go, somewhat later, to Canada. That seemed to work. They were finally married in 1878.

They had six children. William named the youngest son Francis; when the child seemed to dislike the name, he called him John; when the boy was seven, he officially changed the name to Alexander. When his family irritated him—as it frequently did: one of their children later described terrific shouting matches between William and Alice—he would sometimes go off alone to his country house in New Hampshire. As soon as he arrived, he began sending love letters back home. Whenever he was in Europe (it was his habit to be out of town when there were newborns in the house) he announced his distaste for European life and his preference for everything American. When he returned, he complained about America and longed to be in Europe. "He's just like a blob of mercury," his sister, Alice, wrote near the end of her life, after William had paid her a flying visit in London; "you cannot put a mental finger upon him."[4]

Yet everyone adored him. One of the few people whose feelings about him were even ambivalent was George Santayana, his student and then colleague in the Harvard philosophy department, and Santayana's characteristically mordant assessment gives a good idea of what it was that other people found so charismatic: "He was so extremely natural that there was no knowing what his nature was, or what to expect next; so that one was driven to behave and talk conventionally, as in the most artificial society."[5] James's version of this was that he believed (as he once told Bernard Berenson) "that every gush of feeling should be followed by adequate action."[6] And he was a person who had many gushes. That they sometimes conflicted with one another did not, in his view, lessen his obligation to respect each one.

Another way to put it is to say that James converted his weakness into a strength. This caused him an enormous amount of frustration: he spent most of the 1860s trying to manage it. Along the way, he did serve, in a sense, in the Civil War—or rather in the larger conflict of which the Civil War was a part. This was the conflict over the future of racial relations in the United States. The peculiar thing about James's role was that he served on the wrong side. But this was consistent with the general haphazardness of his early life.

2

The Jameses were not Brahmins. They were not even New Englanders. They were descended on both sides from Irish immigrants, and although the Jameses now seem as American as the Emersons or the Holmeses, to people like the Emersons and the Holmeses they seemed rather distinctively Irish. To understand Henry or William James, Holmes once explained to his English friend Frederick Pollock, "one must remember their Irish blood."[7] "In their speech, singularly mature and picturesque, as well as vehement, the Gaelic (Irish) element in their descent always showed," is the way Emerson's son Edward remembered the family.[8] The Jameses enjoyed great social success, but they knew themselves to be, subtly but irreducibly, outsiders—even, in their charming fashion, upstarts. For the most part, they liked it that way. It gave them their edge.

The first James in America was William, the grandfather of the philosopher. He was an Irish Protestant who came to the United

Henry James, Sr., and his son Henry in New York City in 1854, the
year before the family embarked on its transatlantic odyssey in search
of the perfect education. (From a daguerreotype by Mathew Brady.)

States in 1789, when he was eighteen, and settled in Albany. Without material or social advantages of any kind—he began his career as a clerk in a dry goods business—he eventually acquired a fortune, much of it through his involvement in the construction of the Erie Canal. At the time of his death, in 1832, he was said to be the second wealthiest man, after John Jacob Astor, in the state of New York. Among his holdings was a large portion of the village of Syracuse, which he purchased in 1824.

William James had three wives (two died in childbirth) and eleven children (two died in infancy). The second surviving child of his third wife, Catharine Barber James (also of Irish descent), was called Henry. He was a prodigal. He began as a rebel against his father's Calvinism—he made a habit, as a boy, of stopping off at the shoemaker's on the way to school for a nip of gin; as a young man, he ran up bills for clothing and cigars on his father's credit and then dropped out of college—but he turned into a classic product of the Second Great Awakening.

The central event of Henry's life (apart from the amputation of much of his right leg after it was burned in an accident when he was thirteen) was his disinheritance. None of William James's sheep was terribly white, but the truant Henry was the blackest of the flock. He became in consequence the most severely punished legatee in his Calvinist father's highly punitive will. William James died in 1832, leaving an estate whose value is estimated (depending on the estimator) to have been between $1.2 and 3 million. The will delayed final distribution of the assets for twenty years, and then denied bequests to any heir judged by the executors to have led a "grossly immoral, idle or dishonorable life."[9] Henry's initial allotment, $1,250 a year, was far smaller than any of his siblings'. So he did the American thing: he sued, twice—jointly, with the other disappointed relations, and again on his own behalf—and in 1836 the will was legally voided. William was declared to have died intestate, and Henry was granted his full share of the inheritance under the laws of descent. This gave him leisure for life, and thereby made possible the unusual educations of his sons.

Though the letter of William's will was effectively broken, its spirit triumphed anyway. For during the years the dispute was in court, Henry was roaming around upstate New York, where he devoted himself to drinking and gambling. At some point, probably when he was living in Buffalo, he was reborn.[10] Thus, when the will was finally thrown out and the money began coming in, Henry was in a position to put it to good use rather than bad. If the money had got into his pockets in 1832, the story of the James family would probably be quite different. It needed four years, not twenty, but William's scheme to deprive his son of his inheritance until he could be certain not to waste it bore its intended fruit after all.

"There is no country in the world where the Christian religion retains greater influence over the souls of men than in America,"[11] wrote Alexis de Tocqueville, and the remark has been cited many times since as a rebuke to people who prefer to see a secular morality prevail in American public life. It's true that the role of faith in the formation of American values can be underestimated by nonbelievers. But it's also the case that when Tocqueville visited the United States, in 1831 and 1832, religious exuberance was at an unusual pitch. Even if Tocqueville had not been the amazingly quick study he was, he could scarcely have missed it.

The Second Great Awakening, which had begun in New England at the turn of the century, had spread westward, spinning off denominations as it went. Between 1776 and 1845, the number of preachers per capita in the United States tripled.[12] Methodism, in the eighteenth century an insignificant offshoot of Anglicanism, grew to become the largest church in the nation; Mormonism, the Disciples of Christ, Universalism, Adventism, Unitarianism, the many Baptist churches, and the African-American church—along with Transcendentalism and a number of spiritually based humanitarian movements, including abolitionism—all emerged in the same period. It was a sectarian frenzy.

It was also, taken as a whole, a mass movement, and its tenor was populist. As Protestant revivalisms tend to be, it was pointedly anticlerical, and it therefore mixed a great deal of popular superstition and folk therapeutics with traditional Christian mythology.[13] From one point of view, the Second Great Awakening, which lasted from

1800 to the eve of the Civil War, was, as Tocqueville interpreted it, a kind of democratization of European Christianity, a massive absorption into American popular culture of the Protestant spiritual impulse, stripped of most of its traditional hierarchies and formalities. But from another point of view, it was the last blast of supernaturalism before science superseded theology as the dominant discourse in American intellectual life.

For a dissolute young man looking to be struck by evangelical lightning in the 1830s, western New York State was the place to be. The spirit of revivalism had arrived there in the 1820s, and it persisted for so long and generated so many diverse sectarian waves that the region began to be called the "Burned-over District," or, sometimes, the "Infectious District." Which teachings and tendencies Henry James was exposed to after his spiritual rebirth (which seems to have taken place through the agency of a temperance movement) is unclear. But he carried away from the experience two things: an infatuation with the religious impulse and a deep aversion to religious institutions. He was an orthodox apostate: he found wanting every organized faith he tried, and he ended as a convert to a religion largely of his own invention.

When Henry returned to Albany, in 1835, he was admitted into the Presbyterian church, and in the fall he enrolled at the Princeton Theological Seminary, a conservative Calvinist institution. But on a trip to Great Britain in 1837 (right after the money from his inheritance began coming in), he was introduced by the physicist Michael Faraday to Sandemanism, a sect named for an eighteenth-century Scotsman, Robert Sandeman, who had revolted against the Protestant churches in general, and the Presbyterian church in particular, on grounds that they corrupted Christian teaching by making salvation dependent on works rather than faith. Sandeman's cure for Protestantism would become James's own: more Protestantism. Close reading of the New Testament, Sandeman maintained, without the interposition of clergy, was the only form that worship need take.

When Henry got back to America, in 1838, he brought out at his expense an edition of Sandeman's principal work (first published in

1757), *Letters on Theron and Aspasio*, with a preface of his own attacking the Presbyterian clergy. This effectively severed his relations with Princeton. The following year, he traveled again to Great Britain, where he seems to have got involved with a group of Scottish Baptists. In 1839, he settled in New York City and joined a church on Canal Street listed, in the municipal guidebook, as the "Primitive Christians."[14] And he began to court the woman he eventually married, Mary Walsh (another descendant of successful Irish immigrants), by holding forth, as he paced her drawing room floor, on her duty to resign her membership in the local Presbyterian church, on grounds that true religion is unmediated by institutions.

James's final conversion was to Swedenborgianism, following a nervous breakdown he suffered in 1844, while living outside London with his new family (William was born in 1842, Henry in 1843). Sitting alone after dinner, he had an intuition of "some damnèd shape squatting invisible to me within the precincts of the room, and raying out from his fetid personality influences fatal to life."[15] The apparition (as he reported it later) completely undid his sense of self-possession; several weeks later, at a spa to which he had gone to recover, he met a Mrs. Chichester, who explained to him that he had suffered what Swedenborg called a "vastation." James took up Swedenborg as a result, and was forever afterward identified with him. But his career as a Swedenborgian consisted in large part of attacks on the New Church, the official church of Swedenborg's followers, which he accused (he was consistent in this, anyway) of betraying the master's teaching by institutionalizing it. The title of James's 1854 broadside against the Swedenborgian establishment summarizes his view of all establishments: *The Church of Christ Not an Ecclesiasticism*. James saw in Swedenborg's writings what he saw in every religious teaching he was influenced by: an injunction to eschew the forms.

A man who was drawn to this lesson was a man who would naturally be drawn to Emerson. They met in 1842, in New York City, where Emerson was on a lecture tour, and Emerson is supposed to have visited the James home and blessed the infant William in his cradle—a legend given special portentousness by the circumstance that Emerson's favorite child, his son Waldo, had died of scarlet fever only a few months before. Emerson seems to have made a point of staying with the Jameses whenever he was in New York; Henry James, the novelist, recalled that when he was growing up one of the rooms in the house was referred to as "Mr. Emerson's room."[16]

The relations between Emerson and Henry James, Sr., were characterized on Emerson's side by his customary kindly aloofness and on James's side by his customary ardent impetuousness. James in the beginning had some idea that the Transcendentalists had a philosophical "system," and he was exasperated by Emerson's elusiveness on the subject—"Oh you man without a handle!" he once addressed him.[17] But he came to realize what is obvious enough from their earliest correspondence, which is that his attraction to Emerson was, fundamentally, not philosophical at all. "I tried assiduously during the early days of our intimacy to solve intellectually the mystery of his immense fascination," James wrote about Emerson many years later. "But what the magic actually *was*, I could not at all divine, save that it was intensely personal, attaching much more to what he was in himself or by nature, than to what he was in aspiration or by culture. I often found myself in fact thinking: if this man were a woman, I should be sure to fall in love with him."[18]

Emerson liked James and was unfailingly considerate toward him. He introduced James to the lecture circuit; he also introduced him to the Transcendentalist circle, where he was regarded, for the most part, with condescension. "[A] little fat, rosy Swedenborgian amateur, with the look of a broker, & the brains & heart of a Pascal," the poet Ellery Channing described him.[19] Channing's friend Henry Thoreau met James through Emerson and was touched by his sincerity and generosity, but he grew impatient with James's views. "He utters *quasi* philanthropic dogmas in a metaphysic dress," Thoreau complained;

> but they are for all practical purposes very crude. He charges society with all the crime committed, and praises the criminal for committing it. But I think that all the remedies he suggests out of his head—for he goes no farther, hearty as he is—would leave us about

where we are now. For, of course, it is not by a gift of turkeys on Thanksgiving Day that he proposes to convert the criminal, but by a true sympathy with each one.[20]

Thoreau had known a few criminals, and he felt fairly certain that sympathy would not do the trick. Bronson Alcott, whose theological standards were a lot stricter than almost anyone's, had no use for James at all, and once referred to him, to his face, as "damaged goods."[21] He intended the metaphor spiritually, but it was a sharp thing to say to a man with a wooden leg.

3

Though he generally had to subsidize his own publications—he was given space to write in certain newspapers in return for the occasional "donation"—Henry James, Sr., was a prolific author. He was also an effervescent and gregarious man who was an active participant in transatlantic intellectual life and who enjoyed (this is perhaps what the remarks about his Irishness were meant to signify) mixing it up. He gave as good as he got from the likes of Bronson Alcott. He changed course frequently and abruptly, but, unlike his oldest son, he was never paralyzed by doubt. On the contrary: "A skeptical state," he once said, ". . . I have never known for a moment."[22]

James was an idiosyncratic religious thinker at a time—the decades before the Civil War—when the landscape swarmed with idiosyncratic religious movements. He belonged to a way of life, and a way of thinking about life, that the war and modern science rendered essentially obsolete; and this makes the question of his influence on members of the postwar, post-Darwinian generation of American thinkers, such as his son William, a little difficult. The usual biographical practice has been to assume continuity, but the social history suggests rupture.

"All my intellectual life I derive from you,"[23] William, then working in London, wrote to his father as he lay dying in Cambridge in 1882; and he repeated the general note of obligation many times. Specific notes of obligation, though, are hard to find, for in the details their views are not so much opposed as incommensurable. They arose out of divergent discursive systems. "I am going slowly through his other books," William wrote to his brother Henry shortly after the publication of their father's *The Secret of Swedenborg*, in 1869 (a book to which William Dean Howells's reaction is famous: "He kept it").[24] "I will write you more when I have read more. Suffice it that many points which before were incomprehensible to me because doubtfully fallacious—I now definitely believe to be entirely fallacious. . . . [H]is ignorance of the way of thinking of other men, and his cool neglect of their difficulties is fabulous in a writer on such subjects."[25]

Henry James, Sr., was a Platonist. He believed (following Swedenborg) that there are two realms, a visible and an invisible, and that the invisible realm, which he named the realm of Divine Love, is the real one. From this premise, the usual conclusions follow: humankind is now separated from the true and the real; its destiny is to arrive at the consummation intended for it by God; philosophers are here to help the rest of us understand what that consummation is. James's particular conception of it was derived in part from his reading of Swedenborg and in part from a writer with whom Swedenborg was often paired in the nineteenth century, the French socialist Charles Fourier: "Man's destiny on earth," as James expressed it in *Substance and Shadow* (1863), ". . . consists in the realization of a perfect society, fellowship, or brotherhood among men."[26]

The chief impediment to arriving at this redeemed state was belief in an independent selfhood (what Swedenborg called the "proprium"). James considered this belief "the great parental fount of all the evils that desolate humanity."[27] Belief in selfhood was bad because it led some people to regard themselves as superior to other people. Its basis was self-love, or egotism, a sin James continually preached against—to the public, to his friends, and to his family. (He deeply annoyed his very willful niece Minny Temple by pontificating to her on the importance of submissiveness.) James therefore claimed to have no use for morality, a concept he regarded as bound up with the pernicious belief that people are responsible for the good or evil of their actions. People who believe this are people who think they can make themselves worthier than other people by their own exertions. But this is to worship the false god of selfhood. "All conscious virtue is spurious,"[28] James insisted; genuine goodness comes only from God. Thus James's children "had ever the amusement," as his son Henry put it many years later, ". . . of hearing morality, or moralism, as it was more invidiously worded, made hay of in the very interest of character and conduct."[29]

The applications of such a cosmology are not self-evident. At the beginning of his career, James thought his views required him to become an advocate of free love. "If society left its subject free to follow the divine afflatus of his passion whithersoever it carried him," he wrote in the Fourierist journal the *Harbinger*, "we should never hear of such a thing as sexual promiscuity or fornication, never dream of a merely natural ultimation of the passions. The natural appetite in each case would be infallibly subject to the personal sentiment, and would thus always be elevated into celestial purity."[30] He believed that "a day will come when the sexual relations will be regulated in every case by the private will of the parties. The public sentiment, then, or law, . . . will declare the entire freedom of every man or woman to follow the bent of their private affections, will justify every alliance sanctioned by these affections."[31]

But several years later he found himself cited as an ally by Marx Edgeworth Lazarus in *Love vs. Marriage* (1852), an argument for sexual promiscuity, and he started furiously to backpedal. It was precisely its suppression of the male sexual impulse, he now explained, in a review of Lazarus's book in Horace Greeley's *New York Tribune*, that made marriage a divine state. Although the married woman will always disappoint "the promise which the unappropriated woman held out" (as he suavely put it), it is man's duty to overcome this frustration of his sexual urge and to realize his own divinity in his wife's "downcast eyes."[32]

This conformed a little better to James's general position on the difference between the sexes, which was that woman is "by nature inferior to man. She is man's inferior in passion, his inferior in intellect, and his inferior in physical strength"; she is, very properly, her husband's "patient and unrepining drudge, his beast of burden, his toilsome ox, his dejected ass, his cook, his tailor, his own cheerful nurse and the sleepless guardian of his children." But their inferiority, James thought, is precisely what makes women attractive to men, so that any "great development of passion or intellect in woman is sure to prejudice" male attention. "Would any man fancy a woman after the pattern of Daniel Webster?"[33] He consequently opposed serious education for women, a doctrine that had disastrous consequences in the case of his youngest child and only daughter, Alice.

James's idealization of brotherhood was apparently also consistent, in his mind, with a belief in the natural inferiority of black people. He regarded them as "among the lowest persons intellectually, persons in whom the sensuous imagination predominates,"[34] and he declined, even as late as 1863, to join the abolitionists, on grounds that "abolitionists attack slavery as an institution rather than as a principle. . . . The practical working of the institution has been on the whole, I doubt not, favorable to the slave in a moral point of view; it is only the master who from recent developments seems to have been degraded by it."[35] When Wilky was recovering from the wounds he had suffered at Fort Wagner, Henry Senior inquired whether the black soldiers had wavered during the attack, and he remained skeptical even after Wilky insisted that they had not.[36]

James's universalism was the mandatory kind. He railed so strenuously against sectarianism ("the spirit of separatism or sect, is the identical spirit of hell,"[37] as he expressed it) that his ecumenism was sometimes indistinguishable from intolerance. He despised the Jews for believing in their chosenness and for making a fetish of the moral law—"as near to worthless as a people could well be that still wore the human form,"[38] he described them in one of his books. He considered Catholicism a superstition, and the Catholic church "a mere *scabies* upon the life of the nations."[39] He equated true spirituality with Protestantism, which he regarded as fundamentally a movement for the democratizing of religion. He regarded democracy, by the same token, as the political equivalent of Protestantism. "Democracy is not so much a new form of political life, as a dissolution or disorganization of the old forms," he explained in one of his lectures. "It is simply a resolution of government into the hands of the people, a taking down of that which has before existed, and a recommitment of it to its original sources, but it is by no means the substitution of anything else in its place."[40]

These two forces, Protestantism and democracy, working together, were, in James's view, the engines of the Swedenborgian millennium, in which all invidious distinctions among persons would be erased. It was a universal promise, but it was also the American promise. "Every church in these United States," James preached, "must disown every organization which falls short of our political proportions. . . . As our political dimensions make us a city of refuge for all the materially oppressed of the earth, so our ecclesiastical dimensions must make us a city of refuge for all the spiritually oppressed."[41] In his final work, he summed up his philosophy in an epigram: "The horse-car [in modern terms, the public bus] our true Shechinah at this day."[42]

The main pillars of Henry Senior's thought—monistic belief in the unchanging reality of an unseen world, indifference to temporal moral distinctions, and anti-individualism—are entirely alien to the views of his oldest son. They belong to the conception of a closed and predetermined universe—the "block universe"—that William James designed pragmatism specifically to subvert. William hated the idea of undifferentiated oneness; he didn't even like the fact that everyone was expected to spell the same way. He thought the universe should be renamed the "pluriverse." And his belief in the power of individual agency was so pronounced that even his philosophical allies Charles Peirce and John Dewey criticized him for it.

But William James was, like his father, a kind of super-Protestant. His own ostensibly ecumenical work, *The Varieties of Religious Experience* (1902), which assembles stories of spirituality from all over the world, acquires a supercilious tone when it discusses the legends of the Catholic saints. More significantly, James often spoke of pragmatism, the philosophy he largely created, as the equivalent of the Protestant Reformation. He intended pragmatism as an argument, in philosophy, for discarding obsolete verbal ritual and rejecting the authority of prior use. Peirce, whom James credited with the initial formulation of the pragmatist doctrine, conceived of it in the same terms, and there are echoes of this religious analogue in Dewey as well. Pragmatism belongs to a disestablishmentarian impulse in American culture—an impulse that drew strength from the writings of Emerson, who attacked institutions and conformity, and from the ascendancy, after the Civil War, of evolutionary theories, which drew attention to the contingency of all social forms. But the splintering of American Protestantism into multiple religious and quasi-religious sects over the course of the century—the protestantization, so to speak, of Protestantism—is part of the larger, more inchoate context out of which pragmatism emerged. And in that context, the writings of Henry James, Sr., do have a place.

4

Swedenborg, of course, was a mystic. His career as a religious thinker began with a hallucinatory experience in a tavern, followed by a direct communication from God; and he insisted that all his knowledge of the celestial realm was acquired from angels and other apparitions. "I enjoy," as he put it, "perfect inspiration."[43] Before he became a theologian, though, Swedenborg had been a highly accomplished man of science in eighteenth-century Denmark—he was an expert on mining engineering—and he intended his theological writings to provide a kind of unified-field theory of the cosmos, a system in which religion was congruent with modern scientific thought. When his work became fashionable in America, in the 1840s, it appealed particularly to rational and scientific minds. Swedenborgianism was a religion for liberals.

Emerson read Swedenborg with interest, even, at first, with enthusiasm, but he eventually complained that Swedenborg turned the universe into "a gigantic crystal. . . . The universe, in his poem, suffers under a magnetic sleep, and only reflects the mind of the magnetizer."[44] The magnet image is an allusion to mesmerism, and it is apt; for the Austrian physician Franz Mesmer had himself been a Swedenborgian, and when interest in hypnotism, psychic healing, and related spiritual phenomena flared up in nineteenth-century America, it found in Swedenborgianism a natural theological home. At first the Swedenborgian New Church discouraged mesmerism, but it soon found that mesmerism was a good source of converts, and in 1847, the leading Swedenborgian in America, George Bush, professor of "occult therapy" at New York University, published a book announcing the alliance, *Mesmer and Swedenborg*. For mesmerism seemed to offer scientific proof of the existence of the unseen spirit world that Swedenborg had described.[45]

So that when the Fox sisters, two girls from the Burned-over District of upstate New York who claimed to be able to communicate with spirits, burst on the scene in 1848, and spiritualism became not only a vogue but a transatlantic religious movement, Swedenborgian ministers were among the first to join up. (The earliest champion and promoter of the Fox sisters, Isaac Post, from Rochester, New York, was a Quaker.) A team of medical professors from the University of Buffalo eventually concluded that the mysterious rappings attributed to spirits were in fact the sounds of the sisters surreptitiously cracking their knee and toe joints. But it was too late. For after all, as believers in spiritualism pointed out, even if the rappings were faked, the sisters still somehow "knew" the answers to the questions audiences asked them to pose to the spirits.[46] Spiritualism was airborne, and Margaret Fox remained a minor celebrity until her death in 1893. She had prepared the way for many imitators, and for the general confusion of psychic phenomena, religious belief, and science.[47]

This was a confusion that William James, in later life, had a great deal to do with. He was fascinated by mental states that suggested the existence of an extrasensory realm. He used hypnotism regularly in his work as a psychologist; he experimented with almost every drug he could lay his hands on; he submitted himself to the ministrations of a "mind-cure" therapist (who "disentangled" his mind while he slept) when he was suffering from insomnia; and he publicly defended mind-cure practitioners, magnetic healers, Christian Scientists, and osteopaths when the Massachusetts Board of Health proposed a bill making it illegal to practice medicine without a license. He was also deeply involved with both the British and American Societies for Psychical Research. He spent a great deal of his time and energy, even in the last decade of his life, when he was suffering from heart disease and knew he had little left of either, in pur-

suit of scientific validation of what he took to be the instinctive belief
that the universe has a spiritual dimension.

His own hypothesis was that this dimension consisted of a kind of
extrapersonal consciousness with which individual minds are sublim-
inally connected. "Out of my experience" as a researcher into psychic
phenomena, he wrote near the end of his life,

> . . . one fixed conclusion dogmatically emerges, and that is this, that
> we with our lives are like islands in the sea. . . . [T]here is a contin-
> uum of cosmic consciousness against which our individuality builds
> but accidental fences, and into which our several minds plunge as
> into a mother-sea or reservoir. Our "normal" consciousness is cir-
> cumscribed for adaptation to our external earthly environment, but
> the fence is weak in spots, and fitful influences from beyond leak in,
> showing the otherwise unverifiable common connection.[48]

Psychics and mind readers, he thought, might be people with weak
spots in their mental fences, people who could penetrate the boundary that ordinarily isolates one mind from another and that sepa-
rates all individual minds from this panpsychic realm. James thought
that if the existence of such a realm could be demonstrated, it would
constitute a substantiation of the traditional religious doctrine of immortality. He never came up with the proof he was looking for, but
he never disproved his hypothesis, either. He remained, characteristically, undecided.

William felt that this turn in his professional interests toward
spiritualism, which intensified as he was finishing his first book, *The
Principles of Psychology*, published in 1890, constituted a reversion to
the thought of his father. As for life after death, he wrote to his sister
Alice when she was dying of breast cancer in London in 1891,

> there's more in it than has ever been told to so-called Science. These
> inhibitions, these split-up selves, all these new facts that are gradu-
> ally coming to light about our organization, these enlargements of
> the self in trance etc., are bringing me to turn for light in the direc-
> tion of all sorts of despised spiritualistic and unscientific ideas. Fa-
> ther would find in me to day a much more receptive listener.[49]

Actually, William might have gotten an argument. For Henry James, Sr., was not one of the Swedenborgians who developed an enthusiasm for spiritualism. When the news of the Fox sisters reached him, he warned his readers to keep away. It was not that the spirits weren't real; of course they were. It was that they were gossips and troublemakers. "They first arrest our attention by talk of those we have loved," James explained: "they gradually inflame our ascetic ambition, our ambition after spiritual distinction: and finally, having got a secure hold, who knows through what pools of voluntary filth and degradation they may drag us?"[50] His conception of the phenomenon was actually much closer to the Freudian idea of the subconscious and to the premises of psychoanalysis—which is one of the places where the therapeutic current in the spiritualist movement was ultimately directed—than his son the psychologist's was.

Still, Henry James, Sr., belonged to another era. "Unlike the cool, dry, thin-edged men who now abound," William wrote to his wife after his father's death in 1882, "he was full of the fumes of the ursprünglich [primordial] human nature; things turbid, more than he could formulate, wrought within him. . . . We must see to it that Father's remains, with a collection of extracts from all his writings are given to the world. I can't help thinking that they will soon attract a larger public eye than hitherto has known his name."[51] Two years later, William brought out that edition, *The Literary Remains of the Late Henry James*. In 1887, he wrote his brother Henry to inform him that the volume had sold, in the previous six months, one copy.[52]

5

Henry Senior's attitude toward education followed from his attitude toward religion: all institutional embodiments of it were suspect. His solution to this inconvenience was to move his children in and out of schools too quickly for any one of them to do lasting damage. By the time the family left New York City, in 1855, when William was thirteen, William and Henry had attended together at least ten different schools.[53]

As it turned out, this was a period of unusual stability. In the summer of 1855 Henry took the family to Geneva, and William and Wilky were enrolled in a nearby school (the younger Henry had come down with malaria and was too ill to attend). By October, Henry had concluded that Swiss schools were overrated, and the Jameses moved to London for the rest of the winter. In June 1856 the family left London for Paris, where William, Henry, and Wilky were assigned a private tutor. They changed residences within the city three times during the year, and in the summer of 1857 moved to Boulogne-sur-Mer. The oldest children were enrolled there in the Collège Imperial, where William was encouraged to pursue his interest in science. In the fall the family moved back to Paris, and William was enrolled in a scientific institute. In December they returned to Boulogne. At the end of the academic year William told his father that his real interest was painting, and in the summer of 1858, after three years in Europe, the family moved back across the Atlantic to Newport, so that William could study with the painter William Morris Hunt.

This was just the opening act. By the fall Henry Senior had grown unhappy with American schooling. The family returned to Geneva, where William became a student at the Geneva Academy. (Henry, for reasons not easily imagined, was sent to a polytechnic school.) In July 1860 most of the family moved to Bonn (Bob remained at school in Switzerland), with the intention of spending the year in Germany so that the children could learn German (a language Henry Senior did not speak). That plan was quickly abandoned; by September the Jameses were back in Newport and William was painting again. Henry hung around the studio. Wilky and Bob were sent off to the Concord boarding school run by Franklin Sanborn.

In the fall of 1861 William finally dropped art for science and entered the Lawrence Scientific School at Harvard to study chemistry. (In 1862 Henry joined him in Cambridge, entering, in another inexplicable miscalculation, Harvard Law School; he lasted a year.) In 1864 the Jameses all moved from Newport to Boston, and then to Cambridge, to be with William, and the family home remained there until Henry and Mary James died, in 1882.

The effect this international hopscotch had on their children varied according to the child. The one who seems to have minded it the least was Henry, who was so embarrassed about it for his father that he deliberately omitted one of the Boulogne and one of the Newport episodes from his autobiography, but whose passion for saturating himself in impressions was encouraged rather than stifled by the experience. Wilky and Bob, on the other hand, seem to have become convinced, as they trailed after their two older brothers, of their intellectual inferiority. Their ordeals in the war only set them farther apart from the rest of the family, and Bob, at least, was never able afterward to find a focus for his life. Alice, too, once wondered "whether, if I had had any education I should have been more, or less, of a fool than I am";[54] but hers was a special case, since, given Henry Senior's cosmology, her education would have been just as thoroughly neglected if the Jameses had never left New York.

For his part, William, although he was the only one of the children to enjoy anything resembling a real schooling, and although it was for his sake that most of the family's moves had been undertaken, resented the whole business. He used to say of his education that he "never had any,"[55] and he once complained that the first lecture on psychology he ever heard was the first one he gave as a professor of psychology at Harvard. He had had no education in his other main field, philosophy, either. He always felt himself at a disadvantage in arguments with people with a real training in logic (such as Peirce or Josiah Royce, his colleague, friend, and philosophical antagonist in the Harvard philosophy department). And when he retired from teaching, he complained to Henry that "as a 'professor' I always felt myself a sham, with its chief duties of being a walking encyclopedia of erudition."[56]

But William's lack of systematic education gave him one distinct advantage: it permitted him to approach intellectual problems uninhibited by received academic wisdom. The openness that characterizes both the style and the import of his writings on pragmatism seemed to some of his followers to have been specifically a consequence of his disorganized schooling. His later admirer John Dewey, for example, thought those things had "an intimate connection."[57] And the consciousness that he was not a product of a particular school or academic tradition, or even a practitioner of a particular scholarly discipline, meant that in whatever he did, James could honestly feel that he was responsible for his beliefs to no one but himself. This not only lent passion to his convictions but—something even more useful—made it easier for him to ignore those convictions when he felt them beginning to operate as prejudices. It helped him to do what his temperament inclined him to do anyway: to change his mind.

For even after he had settled on a career in science, when James arrived at Harvard in 1861, he did not settle on any particular science. And his disinclination to pledge an academic allegiance was one of the things that made it possible for him to sign up for an expedition led by the most famous of the many enemies of Charles Darwin.

Louis Agassiz at the time of his American celebrity.

FIVE

AGASSIZ

I

LOUIS AGASSIZ WAS THE MAN for whom the Lawrence Scientific School was created. He was born in Switzerland in 1807, and enjoyed a precocious European success, thanks in part to exceptional energy and ability, and in part to a gift for making himself agreeable to people in a position to promote his career. By the time he was twenty-five he had become a protégé of two of the leading scientific figures in Europe: the French paleontologist Georges Cuvier and the Prussian naturalist Alexander von Humboldt. Cuvier did Agassiz the additional, and no doubt unintended, favor of dying, in 1832, shortly after putting him in charge of a valuable collection of fish fossils, and Agassiz, through his research and publications, soon succeeded Cuvier as the leading authority in that field. His greatest early claim to fame, though, was in another area of natural science: he was one of the discoverers of the Ice Age.

But by 1845 Agassiz was overextended. He had got involved in a scientific publishing business that was losing money, and his wife, unhappy with his finances, his associates, and his obsessive work habits, had left him. Agassiz turned for help to von Humboldt, who elicited a grant from the king of Prussia for a study of the natural history of North America. To supplement this income, and to introduce himself to American audiences, Agassiz secured, with the assistance of another friend, the English geologist Charles Lyell, an appointment to deliver a series of public lectures in Boston. These were the Lowell Lectures, sponsored by John A. Lowell, the textile manufacturer, who was also a member of the corporation (the board of trustees, in effect) of Harvard College. Agassiz arrived in Boston in October 1846 and delivered the lectures that winter. Their subject was the "Plan of Creation in the Animal Kingdom," and the response was beyond anything even Agassiz, who was not a man to underestimate his own capacities, could have expected. Five thousand people turned up. Agassiz had to deliver each lecture twice to accommodate the crowds.[1]

Agassiz's zoological knowledge—in particular his knowledge of the invertebrates—was fairly prodigious, and he had a knack for conveying it in a style that nonscientists found not only accessible but intellectually thrilling. Many people found Agassiz personally thrilling as well. He was a large, handsome, self-assured man; his eyes were black, his hair was long, and his accent was French. His command of English was deliciously imperfect: when he was stumped for the correct English word during a lecture, he would draw a mollusk or some other organism on the blackboard while he searched his memory for *le mot juste*. Audiences seem to have found this irresistible. He was enormously personable, and he made friends with remarkable speed. He had the ideal personality for scholarly advancement in a city in which intellectual, financial, and social circles were still largely overlapping.

Harvard had been contemplating the establishment of a school of science since 1845, the year before Agassiz's arrival on the scene, but no funds had been raised. When it became known that Agassiz might be interested in remaining in the United States after his Prussian money ran out, John Lowell and Edward Everett, the president of Harvard (and former governor of Massachusetts), persuaded the mill-town industrialist Abbott Lawrence to donate fifty thousand dollars to found the school and to guarantee the salary for a new academic appointment intended specifically for Agassiz. The offer was made in the summer of 1847; Agassiz accepted in the fall, and he began his career as a Harvard professor in the spring of 1848. The collapse that year of the liberal revolutions in Europe, one consequence of which was the closing of the Swiss academy where Agassiz had been teaching, led to a minor exodus of European scientific talent to America, and essentially sealed Agassiz's decision to become an expatriate.

Agassiz's estranged first wife died, of tuberculosis, in Germany in 1848, and in 1850 he married Elizabeth Cabot Cary, an event that completed his conquest of Boston society. Elizabeth Cary was the daughter of a wealthy lawyer with connections to the Lowell textile industry; she had once been courted by Charles Sumner. Her sister was married to Cornelius Felton, later the president of Harvard, and Elizabeth herself was an educational pioneer: soon after the marriage, she started a school for women in her home to raise money for her husband's research, and she eventually became the first president of Radcliffe. Agassiz had three children from his first marriage, all of whom moved to the United States and married into prominent Boston families—the Shaws, the Higginsons, and the Russells. It is an indication of how commanding a presence Agassiz was in Boston in the years before the war that the Saturday Club—the literary dining and conversation society of which he was a founding member, and whose participants included Emerson, Hawthorne, Longfellow, Whittier, Lowell, Sumner, and Holmes, all at the peak of their fame—was popularly referred to as "Agassiz's Club."

Abbott Lawrence had originally intended to underwrite a school of applied science: he wanted better engineers for his mills. But with the availability of Agassiz the plan changed, and the Lawrence Scientific School was established as an institution that trained researchers. At a time when almost every American scientist received the specialized portion of his education in Europe (Dr. Holmes, for example, had spent two years in Paris as an apprentice to the pathologist Charles Louis before returning to take his medical degree from Harvard), Agassiz represented the introduction of modern scientific education to the United States. His Harvard appointment marked the beginning of the professionalization of American science.[2]

Professionalization means disciplinary autonomy. A field of study (or any line of work) is a profession when its practitioners are answerable for the content of their work only to fellow practitioners, and not to persons outside the field. One of the things that had held back scientific education in American colleges (there were no graduate schools, strictly speaking, in the United States before the Civil War) was the dominance of theology in the curriculum, which obliged scholars in every field to align their work with Christian orthodoxy. Theology was the academic trump card. Agassiz insisted on the independence of scientific inquiry from religious beliefs—and, for that matter, from political and economic beliefs as well. He did not attend church himself, but he was an outspoken deist, and that was evidence enough of religious commitment for a Unitarian institution like Harvard. It allowed Agassiz to secularize scientific research without completely alienating the ministers.

The method Agassiz preached was strict induction. "[A] physical fact," he said, "is as sacred as a moral principle."[3] Rather than derive the laws of nature from scriptural teachings or from any other set of abstractions, Agassiz's students were required to observe first and construct generalizations later. And by observation Agassiz meant hands-on contact. In one of his first American lectures, on grasshoppers, which he delivered to a group of Massachusetts schoolteachers in 1847, Agassiz supplied each teacher in the audience with a live grasshopper. If someone dropped his or her grasshopper during the lecture, Agassiz stopped speaking until the insect was recaptured.[4] The teachers in 1847 found this pedagogy bizarre; by the time of Agassiz's death in 1873, it had become legendary. Many former students later recalled how Agassiz had started them out by handing them a dead fish or some other specimen, and requiring them to produce a complete and accurate description of it before he allowed them to proceed. To meet Agassiz's standards, this sometimes took weeks, and left the students with a badly decomposed fish on their hands.[5]

Agassiz also insisted on a comparative approach. He taught that the scientist's work consists not of enumerating facts, but of making sense of facts by putting them in relation to other facts. And he was a passionate collector. His other great contribution to Harvard, besides the modernization of its science curriculum, was the creation of the Museum of Comparative Zoology, which opened in 1860. This was a prodigy of personal fund-raising: Agassiz amazed everyone by talking the Massachusetts legislature, which had no particular reason to give money to Harvard College, into putting up one hundred thousand dollars for the museum. It became known, naturally, as "Agassiz's Museum."[6]

The methods that Agassiz championed may seem the essence of modern scientific practice. The notion that the scientist is working with actual things, rather than with prior abstract conceptions about things, suggests that the world is being taken on its own terms. The scientist is not speculating about unseen or unverifiable agencies; he or she is simply assembling reliable data and generating testable hypotheses. A personal preference for one outcome over another is not being permitted to override the evidence of the senses.

But what *is* the evidence of senses? Without concepts, it is unintelligible, and without preferences, no one would bother to accumulate it. Agassiz had concepts and he had preferences. These were not modern at all, and the manner in which he used advanced scientific practices to reach reactionary conclusions is, in retrospect, the most interesting thing about him. Despite his insistence on divorcing science from politics, Agassiz provided scientific ammunition to the politicians of his own time and well beyond it. The lesson of his career is that since everything we do we do out of some interest, we had better be clear about what our interests are. This lesson was not lost on William James.

2

Soon after the news of the Confederate firing on Fort Sumter reached Cambridge, in April 1861, a student at the Lawrence Scientific School—Nathaniel Shaler, later a renowned Harvard geologist—ran into Agassiz on Divinity Avenue. He was weeping. Shaler asked him why. "They will Mexicanize the country," was Agassiz's reply.[7] The remark is cryptic, but it sums up, in its gnomic way, Agassiz's theory of the natural world. In order to understand what that theory was, and how it bore on the issues over which the Civil War was fought, we have to take a second look at the story of Agassiz's American career.

In the months between his arrival in Boston in October 1846 and his delivery of the Lowell Lectures that winter, Agassiz had made a quick tour of the Northeast for the purpose of introducing himself to the American scientific establishment. He ended up spending most of his time in Philadelphia, where he was in the frequent company of a man named Samuel George Morton. Morton was the most famous American anthropologist of his day. He had two medical degrees, one from the University of Pennsylvania, the other from the University of Edinburgh, and he had made his name by analyzing the fossils brought back by Lewis and Clark. His special passion, though, was human crania—skulls—which he began collecting around 1830. Morton's health was poor and he never went into the field himself; but he let it be known that he would be glad to receive skulls, and people all over the world began sending them in. By the time Agassiz paid his visit, the collection housed more than six hundred skulls. It was known as "The American Golgotha."

Morton had published two major works on his skulls. *Crania Americana*, which appeared in 1839, was a study of the skulls of Native Americans; *Crania Aegyptiaca*, published five years later, analyzed skulls that had been retrieved from ancient Egyptian tombs. Morton's method, like Agassiz's, was empirical and comparative: he measured the interior capacity of the skulls and then he compared the results by race. His conclusions, collated in a catalogue of the entire collection that was published in 1849 and reprinted many times, ranked the human races (as Morton classified them) by cranial capacity. In descending order of volume, these were: Caucasian, Mongolian, Malay, Native American, and Negro. Subdivisions within the five categories showed that Teutonics—Germans, English people, and Anglo-Americans—had the largest cranial capacity among all groups, and that American-born Negroes, Hottentots, and aboriginal Australians had the smallest. Morton correlated these measurements with generalizations about the attributes of the different races as he had gleaned them from anthropological and travel literature. The Caucasian race, for example, was noted to be "distinguished by the facility with which it attains the highest intellectual endowments"; the American (that is, Native American) is "averse to cultivation, and slow in acquiring knowledge; restless, revengeful, and fond of war, and wholly destitute of maritime adventure"; the Ethiopian (Negro) "is joyous, flexible, and indolent; while the many nations which compose this race present a singular diversity of intellectual character, of which the far extreme is the lowest grade of humanity."[8]

Morton's data were completely unsound. Since he possessed only the skulls and whatever information their donors chose to send along with them, he had no way of checking the reliability of his racial attributions. He failed to factor gender and overall body size—information he sometimes did not even have—into his calculations. And he dealt with skewing in his samples by making seat-of-the-pants adjustments. Some of his Caucasian skulls, for example, had belonged (as one might expect) to men who had been hanged for murder; Morton argued that the Caucasian mean should therefore be adjusted upward, on the assumption that murderers have smaller cranial capacity than law-abiding persons. He dropped Hindu skulls from his calculation of the Caucasian mean because the Hindu figure brought the overall average down, but he retained a disproportionately high number of Peruvian skulls in his calculation of the Native American mean, even though the Peruvian average was the lowest within that category.[9] And he made elementary statistical errors.[10] But his studies, published in oversized volumes with elegantly designed plates and charts, were widely circulated, and his results were cited as authoritative by scientists in the United States and Europe.

Agassiz found Morton an exceptionally congenial man; they became good friends. And he found Morton's research fascinating. Anthropology was a new field for Agassiz; his specialty, after all, was fish. His own passing remarks on the human races, back in Switzerland, had emphasized the unity of the species.[11] But Morton converted him. "After Georges Cuvier," wrote Agassiz's disciple and biographer Jules Marcou many years later, "Morton was the only zoologist who had any influence on Agassiz's mind and scientific opinions. . . . He had, at last, found a naturalist to his liking, without any reserve."[12] Agassiz became a polygenist.

Two theories of racial difference predominated in Western science in the century before Darwin; neither was egalitarian.[13] People who believed that all humans are descended from a common origin (a position known as monogenism) attributed racial inequalities to differing rates of degeneration. The entire species had declined since the creation, monogenists thought, but some groups, due (usually) to the effects of climate, had declined farther than others. Polygenists, on the other hand, believed that the races were created separately and that they had been endowed with different attributes and unequal aptitudes from the start.

Polygenists rejected the degeneration theory on the grounds that archaeological evidence indicated no change in racial types over time. Their usual proof was the statues, drawings, and remains found in ancient Egyptian tombs. This is why Morton published his second volume on human skulls, *Crania Aegyptiaca*: he wanted to show that the capacity of the crania of sub-Saharan blacks found in those tombs (Morton classified Egyptians as Caucasian) was just as small, relative to Caucasian crania, three thousand years ago. The depiction of blacks as servants in ancient Egyptian art, Morton argued, indicated that secondary racial characteristics had not changed either. (Since sub-Saharan blacks in ancient Egypt were people who had been captured in battle and made into slaves, it is not surprising that they were portrayed as such in Egyptian art. Polygenists did not consider this a point: "It is said that when the Negro has been with other races, he has always been a slave," one of them explained. "This is quite true; but why has he been a slave?")[14]

There will not seem, in the end, to be very much to choose between monogenism and polygenism. Both assume the existence of deeply ingrained racial differences, and both are hierarchical. But polygenism is the more radical theory, because it supports the con-

tention not just that black people and white people have evolved (or
devolved) at different rates, but that they belong to entirely different
species. And this is the view to which Samuel Morton converted
Louis Agassiz.

The effect on Agassiz was visceral. In December 1846 he wrote a
long letter to his mother about his American tour. The visit to Morton was the high point: "That collection alone was worth the trip to
America," he told her. It was also in Philadelphia, he continued, that
he had come into contact with actual Negroes for the first time in his
life. "All the servants at the hotel I stayed in were men of color. I
scarcely dare tell you the painful impression I received, so contrary
was the sentiment they inspired in me to our ideas of the fraternity
of humankind and the unique origin of our species. But," he says,
"truth before all":

> As much as I try to feel pity at the sight of this degraded and degen-
> erate race, as much as their fate fills me with compassion in thinking
> of them as really men, it is impossible for me to repress the feeling
> that they are not of the same blood as us. Seeing their black faces
> with their fat lips and their grimacing teeth, the wool on their heads,
> their bent knees, their elongated hands, their large curved finger-
> nails, and above all the livid color of their palms, I could not turn my
> eyes from their face in order to tell them to keep their distance, and
> when they advanced that hideous hand toward my plate to serve me,
> I wished I could leave in order to eat a piece of bread apart rather
> than dine with such service. What unhappiness for the white race to
> have tied its existence so closely to that of the negroes in certain
> countries! God protect us from such contact!

Agassiz had been in the United States just two months; his observations of black people were limited to the staff of a Northern hotel.
And it is surely almost instinctive, in most people, to find human beings of a kind one has never encountered before unpleasantly alien.
The interesting thing about Agassiz's reaction is that he grasped immediately its political implications. The abolitionists (or "the philanthropists," as he called them) and the defenders of slavery were both
in error:

The philanthropists who want to make them citizens of their community constantly forget that in according them political rights, they cannot give them either the African sun to favor their full development, nor a domestic hearth among them, for they would refuse them their daughters if they demanded them, and none of them would dream of marrying a negress. The defenders of slavery forget that for being black these men have as much right as we do to the enjoyment of their liberty, and they don't go into the question except as a question of property, a heritage which is protected by law and the loss of which would be their ruin.[15]

Agassiz delivered his inaugural Lowell lecture later that month, and in it he announced, for the first time in his career, that although Negroes and whites belonged to the same species, they had had separate origins. Ten months later he went to South Carolina and repeated the lecture to the Charleston Literary Club at a meeting attended by local scientists and theologians eager to hear Agassiz on just this point. Pressed by his audience, Agassiz now stated that Negroes were, physiologically and anatomically, a distinct species.[16] The response was gratifying to many of his listeners, and it was promptly reported back to Morton in Philadelphia. Agassiz became a regularly invited visitor to Charleston.

Morton's skulls had made an impression. But Morton's ideas about race were also appealing to Agassiz because they were entirely consistent with his own theory of natural history. For Agassiz not only believed that every species was created separately—which was, of course, the orthodox pre-evolutionist view. He also believed that all life forms had been created in the same numbers as currently inhabit the planet, and in the same geographical locations. Nothing had changed since the creation. "Time," as he put it, "does not alter organized beings."[17]

But what about the fossil record? What about the evidence of extinct species and of ancestral versions of contemporary species? This is where the Ice Age proved a useful discovery. Agassiz believed not only that God had created the world as it now exists, but that he had done so many times before. (This had also been the belief of Agassiz's mentor Cuvier.) Each previous creation had been succeeded by a catastrophe, like the Ice Age, wiping out everything, and each catastrophe had been followed by a new creation, introducing superior species to the planet. Happily, the end of this process had been reached. "I think it can be shown by anatomical evidence," Agassiz wrote in what he intended as his major work, *Contributions to the Natural History of the United States of America* (1857–62), "that man is not only the last and highest among the living beings, for the present period, but that he is the last term of a series beyond which there is no material progress possible upon the plan upon which the whole animal kingdom is constructed."[18]

A theory like Morton's, according to which the different races originated in the places where they are currently found (or where the modern European first discovered them), was therefore more congenial to Agassiz than a theory in which the progeny of an original couple multiply, migrate, and mutate over time. Agassiz didn't think that plants or animals had multiplied, migrated, and mutated over time; it was awkward to have to make an exception for human beings. But he was drawn to polygenism for another reason as well: it was an idealist, rather than a materialist, theory. It made the differences we observe in the natural world the product of intelligence rather than accident.

Monogenism, the belief that all humans have a common origin, was scarcely a pure materialism. The Bible, after all, is a monogenist text: it traces all of humanity back to an original pair. But monogenism attributes the subsequent differentiation of the races to material causes, such as the effects of climate on skin color and intelligence (tropical climates being considered the most deleterious; temperate zones, such as Northern Europe, the most salubrious). On the polygenist view, all differences are attributable to the intentions of a thoughtful Creator. The races differ because they were created different. They don't just form a hierarchy; they form an *intelligible* hierarchy. They instantiate a plan.

By the time he met Morton, Agassiz was already busy with his own exegesis of this plan as he detected it in the animal kingdom— the plan that he made the subject of those first, enormously successful Lowell Lectures. Agassiz thought that the different species could be ranked according to their degree of complexity, and that the evidence for this ranking could be found in the development of the embryo. In its earliest stage, he believed, the embryo resembles the adult version of the lowest-ranked organisms; as it develops, it passes through stages of resemblance to adult versions of higher and higher types of organisms until it attains its own level. The "higher" the organism in the scale of life forms, the greater the number of stages it passes through. "There is a period when the young bird has the structure, not only the form, but the structure, and even the fins, which characterize the Fish," Agassiz explained in a second series of Lowell Lectures, delivered in the winter of 1848–49.

> And of the young mammals the same may be said. There is a period in the structure of the young Rabbit . . . when the young Rabbit resembles so closely the Fish, that it even has gills, living in a sac full of water breathing as Fishes do. So that the resemblance is as complete as it can be, though each of these types grows to a complication of structure, by which the young Mammal, for instance, leaving behind this low organization of the lower types, rises to a complicated structure, to higher and higher degrees, and to that eminence even which characterizes mankind.[19]

The stages of embryonic development constitute, in short, "a natural scale by which we can measure and estimate the position to ascribe to any animal belonging to this family. . . . We read here the intelligent action of the Creator." And the fossil record, the remains of all those previous creations, reveals the same progression of animal types; so that "in whatever point of view we consider the animal kingdom," embryonically or geologically, "we find its natural series agree with each other."[20]

This is the theory of recapitulation, or what is sometimes called the biogenetic law: ontogeny (the development of the individual organism) recapitulates phylogeny (the evolutionary history of the entire group). In more cosmic terms: the process by which the universe becomes itself is replicated in the life history of the individual. Agassiz did not invent this theory; he had picked it up during his education, in the 1820s, in Munich, where he had been a student of both

Lorenz Oken, a cosmically minded embryologist who devised a system of classification on recapitulationist principles, and the philosopher Friedrich Schelling, who taught that all change, natural or historical, can be understood as the unfolding of an idea.[21] But Agassiz gave the theory scientific grounding by supplementing it with what his German teachers, for the most part, did not have much of: empirical data. After he left Munich, Agassiz had gone to Paris to work with Cuvier on fish fossils, and it was from Cuvier that he learned the importance of physical evidence. A man who found divine intention in the dimensions of skulls was therefore a man after his own heart.

What Agassiz took from Morton's rankings was the idea that the Negro represented the lowest stage of human being, which the Caucasian recapitulated in the course of his or her fetal development. "The brain of the Negro," Agassiz told his Charleston audience in 1847, "is that of the imperfect brain of a 7 month's infant in the womb of a White."[22] It is important to realize how deep this statement goes. For Agassiz did not mean that the brain of the Negro had evolved that way. He meant that it had been created that way. The races were immutable ("Time does not alter organized beings"): they were what Agassiz called "the living expression of a gigantic conception."[23] Nothing could alter their relations with one another. They were part of an idea.

In 1850 Agassiz returned to Charleston for a meeting of the American Association for the Advancement of Science. He delivered a paper in which he explained that although all human beings, morally speaking, enjoyed the same special relation to their Creator, "viewed zoologically, the several races of men were well marked and distinct. . . . These races did not originate from a common centre, nor from a single pair."[24] Agassiz's remarks were welcomed by the person who had delivered the previous paper at that meeting, "An Examination of the Physical History of the Jews, in Its Bearings on the Question of the Unity of Races." This was Josiah Nott.

Nott was a physician, from a Connecticut family, who practiced in Mobile, Alabama, and who had become the leading polygenist in the South. His polygenism arose from a desire to prevent interbreeding, which he believed would lead to extinction, since (he thought) hybrids—the offspring of parents of differing species—are either sterile themselves or produce sterile descendants. Nott professed to dislike slavery, but he did not profess to like black people (he expressed little concern about any form of race-mixing besides black and white), and he claimed to see no way besides slavery of preventing eugenic catastrophe. Nott's initial publications on the issue were conspicuously short on data: he relied heavily on allusions to his own experience as a physician and on ordinary prejudice.

> Look, first, upon the Caucasian female with her rose and lily skin, silky hair, Venus form, and well chiseled features—and then upon the African wench, with her black and odorous skin, woolly head and animal features—next compare their intellectual and moral qualities, and their whole anatomical structure, and say whether they do not differ as much as the swan and the goose, the horse and the ass, or the apple and pear trees,[25]

he wrote, for example, in the *American Journal of Medical Sciences* in 1843.

Morton's work gave Nott empirical ammunition. In 1844 Nott published *Two Lectures on the Natural History of the Caucasian and Negro Races* (he referred to them as his lectures on "niggerology") and embarked on a campaign to preserve the purity of the races, which he believed was threatened, even in the South, by the sentimental monogenism of Christianity. Nott regarded his work as fundamentally a crusade of science against religion, and he was delighted to welcome so renowned a scientist as Agassiz to the cause. "With Agassiz in the war," he wrote to Morton after hearing Agassiz's Charleston paper, "the battle is ours."[26]

Nott had by this time acquired a teammate, George Gliddon. Gliddon was an Englishman who, thanks to an odd confluence of circumstances, had once served as the American vice-consul in Cairo and, in that capacity, had been responsible for providing Samuel Morton with most of his Egyptian specimens. *Crania Aegyptiaca* was dedicated to him. Gliddon had come to the United States in 1837, and had toured the country giving lectures on Egyptology, including, in 1843, a series of Lowell Lectures. After Morton died, in 1851, of the heart disease that had prevented him from leaving Philadelphia, Nott and Gliddon began the project of making Morton's research the basis for an authoritative work of racial science. Through their efforts polygenism became known as the American school of anthropology.

They cultivated Agassiz assiduously. During his visit to Charleston in 1850, Agassiz had been taken to visit some local plantations. He interviewed slaves and found, he claimed, that he could identify the African tribes to which they had belonged from their physical features, "even when they attempted to deceive him." "These races," he concluded, "must have originated where they occur. . . . Men must have originated in nations, as the bees have originated in swarms."[27] In 1853 Agassiz went to Mobile, Nott's home base, to deliver a series of lectures. Nott and Gliddon attended, and one day Agassiz told them that his next lecture was "for *you*." In it he announced that "we see in the races a gradation parallel to the gradations of animals up to man. . . . The inferior races, by successive gradations, are linked to a higher humanity. How could climatic influences produce these results? How could all physical causes combined? It would be to make accident produce a logical result; in short, an absurdity."[28]

A year later, Nott and Gliddon published *Types of Mankind*, the first of two huge tomes based on Morton's researches. The leading theme of the volume was the supremacy of the white race: the servitude of Negroes and the extinction of Native Americans were explained as the natural outcomes, scientifically confirmed, of human history.[29] Agassiz sent Nott and Gliddon an essay, which they placed, with much fanfare, at the beginning of the volume. The diversity of life forms, Agassiz explained, "is a fact determined by the will of the Creator, and their geographical distribution part of the general plan which unites all organized beings into one great organic conception: whence it follows that what are called human races, down to their specialization as nations, are distinct primordial forms of the type of man."[30] God made the Greeks in Greece. It was the last refinement of polygenist doctrine.

Types of Mankind was a popular book. It had wide circulation among scientists and physicians—Dr. Holmes was a subscriber—

and it went through ten editions between 1854 and 1871. Some Northerners regarded the volume as a political defense of slavery under scientific cover, and Agassiz's participation in it as ingenuous or worse. Agassiz was unmoved. "I do not regret contributing," he replied to one Northern scientist. "Nott is a man after my heart, for whose private character I have the highest regard. . . . I know him to be a man of truth and faith. Gliddon is coarse. . . . But I would rather meet a man like him . . . than any . . . who shut their eyes against evidence."[31]

And when Nott and Gliddon brought out their second volume, *Indigenous Races of the Earth*, in 1857, Agassiz again supplied some remarks expanding on his earlier theory of the separate creation of nations. Nott and Gliddon also submitted for his approval a chart, assembled by Gliddon, on "The Geographical Distribution of Monkeys in Their Relation of That of Some Inferior Types of Men": it demonstrated that "the most superior types of Monkeys are found to be indigenous exactly where we encounter races of some of the most inferior types of Men." "Europe," Gliddon pointed out, ". . . has not contained any monkeys."[32] Agassiz approved.

3

Despite its obvious usefulness in defenses of slavery, polygenism was a controversial doctrine in the South because it contradicted the account in Genesis. And even proslavery polemicists like George Fitzhugh were uncomfortable with the implication that Negroes were effectively animals and could be treated as such. But as the political temperature rose, polygenism was cited in support of the view that slavery did not violate the spirit of the Declaration of Independence, on grounds that Jefferson's term "all men" did not, scientifically, mean blacks. "The abolition delusion is founded upon the error of using the word *man* in a generic sense, instead of restricting it to its primary specific sense," wrote Samuel Cartwright, a Louisiana physician, in *De Bow's Review*, a leading Southern journal. Cartwright popularized the work of the American school of anthropology by making polygenism compatible with Christianity. The

Bible, he explained, describes two creations, a black one (with the animals) and a white one (Adam and Eve). The Hebrew word for the serpent who tempts Eve is *Nachash*, meaning "to be or become *black*": the biblical serpent is, Cartwright was thus able to reveal, "the *negro gardner*."[33]

Agassiz himself argued that the Bible is simply silent on the question of the origin of any other race than the Caucasian: "We have no statements relating to the origin of the inhabitants now found in those parts of the world which were unknown to the ancients." And he was insistent that his views were not intended as a defense of slavery. He was a scientist, not a politician or a minister, and he was obliged to follow the evidence no matter where it led. At the same time, he was confident that "human affairs with reference to the colored races would be far more judiciously conducted, if, in our intercourse with them, we were guided by a full consciousness of the real differences existing between us and them, and to foster those dispositions that are eminently marked in them, rather than by treating them on terms of equality." Slavery seemed to him a violation of the moral status enjoyed by every human being in the eyes of the Creator, and therefore beyond the pale. The political lesson of polygenism was not that Caucasians had a right to oppress the members of other races. It was that the races had never been intended to interact at all. "For our part," he wrote in an article published a few months after the Compromise of 1850, "we have always considered it a most injudicious proceeding to attempt to force the peculiarities of our white civilization of the nineteenth century upon all nations of the world."[34]

In America, of course, the civilizations had long since intersected. Black people had been forcibly resettled in a part of the planet where God had intended only white people to live. (And, evidently, Native Americans. The presence of Native Americans in a temperate climate was an embarrassment to polygenists and monogenists alike: if God had created these people in North America, Caucasians from Europe had no business displacing them; on the other hand, if climate was a factor in the evolution of the races, the alleged disparity between Caucasian and Native American capacity was inexplicable.)

Agassiz viewed the racial confusion in the United States with grave alarm—as is already clear in the letter he sent to his mother in his first months in America. He genuinely deplored slavery—he was, after all, a Swiss republican—but he dreaded social equality among the races nearly as much.

In 1863, the year the Emancipation Proclamation went into effect, Lincoln appointed Samuel Gridley Howe to head the American Freedmen's Inquiry Commission, which was charged with formulating policies for dealing with a large freed black population. Howe wrote to Agassiz to ask whether, in his opinion as a scientist, "the African race, represented by less than two million blacks, & a little more than two million mulattoes . . . will be a *persistent* race in this country; or, will it be absorbed, diluted, & finally effaced by the white race, numbering twenty four millions."[35]

Agassiz was sufficiently stirred to write Howe four letters on the subject in less than a week. He had, it turned out, become a subscriber to the eugenic views of Josiah Nott. He believed that racial interbreeding would be a biological catastrophe, on grounds that hybrids were defective or sterile. (This had not, incidentally, been Samuel Morton's view. The supposed sterility of hybrids was a leading monogenist argument—the races manifestly do interbreed, after all—and Morton preferred to concede the point by arguing that many animal species also interbreed successfully. He thought the races simply felt a natural sexual repugnance for one another.)[36] The one policy to be avoided at all costs, therefore, was the policy of racial amalgamation.

Sexual intercourse between whites and blacks, Agassiz told Howe, was the moral and biological equivalent of incest. The government ought "to put every possible obstacle to the crossing of the races, and the increase of half-breeds."

It is immoral and destructive of social equality as it creates unnatural relations and multiplies the differences among members of the same community in a wrong direction. . . . [W]hile I believe that a wise social economy will foster the progress of every pure race according to its natural dispositions and abilities . . . I am convinced also that no efforts should be spared to check that which is abhorrent to our better nature, and inconsistent with the progress of higher civilization and a purer morality.

As Howe had explained, though, mulattoes actually outnumbered Negroes in the United States, a statistic not exactly compatible with the notion that racial interbreeding is instinctively repugnant and leads to extinction. Agassiz recognized the anomaly, and he had an argument ready to address it. Those mulattoes, he explained, were simply products of the abnormal conditions of a slave society.

> As soon as the sexual desires are awakening in the young men of the South, they find it easy to gratify them by the readiness with which they are met by colored house servants. . . . The first gratification under the pressure of so great a stimulus as the advantages accruing to the family negress, from the connection with young masters, already blunts his better instincts in that direction and leads him gradually to seek more "spicy partners," as I have heard the full blacks called by fast young men. Moreover it is not difficult physiologically to understand why mulattoes with their peculiar constitution should be particularly attractive physically, even though that intercourse should be abhorrent to a refined moral sensibility. Again whatever be the merit of this explanation, . . . [i]t is altogether a physical connection and in the lowest condition of life.[37]

It was possibly not the most scientific argument. The next day, in a new letter, Agassiz tried another tack. "Conceive for a moment the difference it would make in future ages for the prospect of republican institutions and our civilization generally, if instead of the manly population descended from cognate nations, the United States should hereafter be inhabited by the effeminate progeny of mixed races, half indian, half negro, sprinkled with white blood," he suggested. "In whatever proportion the amalgamation may take place, I shudder at the consequences." He advised Howe to contemplate the racial condition of Latin America. "Can you devise a scheme to rescue the Spaniards of Mexico from their degradation?" he asked. "Beware, therefore, of any policy which may bring our own race to their level." It was the fear he had expressed, through his tears, to Nathaniel Shaler when the war broke out: "They will Mexicanize the country." "They" were the abolitionists.

The only way to avoid the disaster of racial intermarriage, Agassiz thought, was (given the unfeasibility of mass exportation) to deny black Americans social equality. "We ought," he advised,

> . . . to beware how we give to the blacks rights by virtue of which they may endanger the progress of the whites. . . . Social equality I deem at all times impracticable. It is a natural impossibility, flowing from the very character of the negro race. . . . [T]hey are incapable of living on a footing of social equality with the whites, in one and the same community, without becoming an element of social disorder.[38]

Howe wrote back a little shaken by the tone of Agassiz's letters. He was in favor of political equality, he explained, but that did not mean he countenanced racial amalgamation, and he was a little hurt to feel that Agassiz had assumed otherwise. He was not willing to concede that black people were inferior to whites, but he agreed with Agassiz completely about mulattoes, and he assured him that he would never recommend any policy "discordant with natural instincts and cultivated tastes." "[M]ulattoism," he affirmed, "is hybridism, and . . . is unnatural and undesirable." Those who favor amalgamation "forget that we may not do the wrong that right may come of it. They forget that no amount of diffusion will exterminate whatever exists; that a pint of ink diffused in a lake is still there, and the water is only the less pure."[39]

Howe was a physician, a philanthropist, and an abolitionist. He had served in the bodyguard of Wendell Phillips; he had been a member of John Brown's Secret Six; he was married to the author of "The Battle Hymn of the Republic." Yet he accepted, as scientific, racial myths that helped sustain a hundred years of segregation.

SIX

BRAZIL

I

WILLIAM JAMES'S FIRST ENCOUNTER with Louis Agassiz took place in September 1861, five months after the outbreak of the Civil War. James was nineteen and had just arrived at Harvard to enter the Lawrence Scientific School. Agassiz was giving another series of Lowell Lectures in Boston that fall, this one on "Methods of Study in Natural History," and James attended. "He is evidently a great favorite with his audience and feels so himself," James reported to his family, back in Newport. "But he is an admirable, earnest lecturer, clear as day and his accent is most fascinating. I should like to study under him."[1]

He did. James began at Lawrence as a student of Charles William Eliot's, who would eventually become, as president of Harvard, the most important figure in the history of American higher education, but who was then a chemist of no special distinction. James's own enthusiasm for chemistry was small, and he hated laboratory work. (Though he later established the first laboratory for experimental psychology in America, the aversion was lifelong.) In his second year at

Head of Alexandrina (1865), woodcut made from a drawing by William
James, in Teffé, Brazil, at the request of Louis Agassiz.
(From Louis and Elizabeth Agassiz, *A Journey in Brazil.*)

Lawrence he switched to natural history to study with Agassiz and
the biologist Jeffries Wyman. In 1864 (conforming to his pattern of
changing career tracks regularly) he quit the Scientific School and
entered the Medical School. But he maintained an interest in zoology and anatomy, and in 1865, when Agassiz began recruiting volunteers for his trip to Brazil, James signed up.

The Brazil expedition was a classic Agassiz operation.[2] It arose out
of a series of public lectures on glaciers which he gave in the winter
of 1864–65. Agassiz, of course, took glaciers to be one of the tech-
niques God employed to wipe out existing life forms in preparation
for a new creation. This theory doesn't work, though, if the Ice Age is
restricted to the Northern Hemisphere; it has to have been a global
event. God is supposed to start each time from scratch. Agassiz
therefore remarked, in his final lecture, on the desirability of exploring Brazil for evidence of glacial action in the Southern Hemisphere.
Nathaniel Thayer, a wealthy businessman who was also the treasurer
of the board of trustees at the Museum of Comparative Zoology
("Agassiz's Museum"), was in the audience, and he took the bait. He
offered to underwrite a yearlong expedition for Agassiz, four paid assistants, and a number of students (one of whom turned out to be his
own son Stephen). Samuel Ward, the American agent for Baring
Brothers, arranged for the Pacific Mail Steamship Company, whose
financial interests he represented, to provide free passage to Rio de
Janeiro on a new ship, the *Colorado*. (Ward's son, Tom, also signed
up as a student assistant; Samuel Ward was the James family banker,
and Tom was one of William James's best friends.)

The services of the United States government were enlisted as
well. The administration was interested in counteracting Confederate influence in Brazil (a consideration that had become irrelevant by
the time the expedition arrived) and in opening the Amazon up to
trade (an event that indeed took place about a year after the expedition returned, and for which Agassiz legitimately claimed some
credit). The government notified its officers to give the expedition
any aid it required, and entrusted Agassiz with various messages for
the emperor, Dom Pedro II—who, within days of the expedition's arrival in Rio (and after a few personal visits from its leader), became

another delighted captive of Agassiz's charm. Dom Pedro, it turned out, was an amateur devotee of natural history, and he arranged for free transportation and meals, provided government steamships for river travel, appointed a major from his army to accompany the expedition, and undertook to collect certain rare fish specimens, desired by Agassiz, personally.

As was his habit, Agassiz made generosity easy by accepting everything as his due. "*Offering* your services to Agassiz," as James explained to his mother in a letter written on board the *Colorado*, "is as absurd as it wd. be for a S. Carolinian to *invite* Gen. Sherman's soldiers to partake of some refreshment when they called at his house." James had just witnessed a scene in which a passenger on the ship, a man named Frederick Billings, who was on his way to California, had offered to lend Agassiz some books. "Ag: 'May I enter your state room & take them when I shall want them, Sir?' Billings, extending his arm, said genially: 'Sir, all that I have is yours!' To which, Agassiz, far from being overcome, replied, shaking a monitory finger at the foolishly generous wight: 'Look out, Sirr, dat I take not your skin!' That," wrote James, "expresses very well the man."[3]

The Thayer expedition, as it was officially known, lasted sixteen months, from April 1865 to August 1866 (although William and his friend Tom Ward went home early, in January). Scientific drawings were made, photographs were taken, and over eighty thousand specimens—an enormous haul—were collected and shipped back to Cambridge.[4] But as many people felt afterward, there was something slightly bogus about the whole enterprise. For the expedition was designed to score predetermined points. It was a mission with a mission. Agassiz intended to gather evidence that would disprove the theories of Charles Darwin; and, knowing in advance exactly what he was looking for, he found it.

2

On the Origin of Species was published on November 24, 1859. The word "evolution" does not appear in it. Many scientists by 1859 were evolutionists—that is, they believed that species had not been cre-

ated once and for all, but had changed over time. The French naturalist Jean-Baptiste Lamarck had advanced his theory of progressive
adaptation in *Philosophie zoologique* in 1809; the English philosopher
Herbert Spencer had published his evolutionary theory of mind and
behavior, *Principles of Psychology*, in 1855. Darwin's book decisively
tipped the balance of educated opinion to evolutionism; but even after 1859, more nineteenth-century evolutionists were (whether they
identified themselves as such or not) Lamarckians or Spencerians
than Darwinians. The purpose of *On the Origin of Species* was not to
introduce the concept of evolution; it was to debunk the concept of
supernatural intelligence—the idea that the universe is the result of
an idea.

For a belief that species evolve is not incompatible with a belief
in divine creation, or with a belief in intelligent design. Progressive
adaptation might simply be the mechanism God has selected to realize his intentions. What was radical about *On the Origin of Species*
was not its evolutionism, but its materialism. Darwin wanted to establish something even his most loyal disciples were reluctant to admit, which is that the species—including human beings—were
created by, and evolve according to, processes that are entirely natural, chance-generated, and blind. In order to do this, he had to do
more than come up with a new set of scientific arguments. He had to
develop what amounted to a new way of thinking.[5]

The world is filled with unique things. In order to deal with the
world, though, we have to make generalizations. On what should we
base our generalizations? One answer, and it seems the obvious answer, is that we should base them on the characteristics things have
in common. No individual horse is completely identical to any other
horse; no poem is identical to any other poem. But all things we call
horses, and all things we call poems, share certain properties, and if
we make those properties the basis for generalizations, we have one
way of "doing things" with horses or poems—of distinguishing a
horse from a zebra, for example, or of judging whether a particular
poem is a good poem or a bad poem. These common properties
can be visible features or they can be invisible qualities; in either
case, we create an idea of a "horse" or a "poem," or of "horseness" or

"poetry," by retaining the characteristics found in all horses or poems and ignoring characteristics that make one horse or poem different from another. We even out, or bracket, the variations among individuals for the sake of constructing a general type.

Darwin's fundamental insight as a biologist was that among groups of sexually reproducing organisms, the variations are much more important than the similarities. "Natural selection," his name for the mechanism of evolutionary development that he codiscovered with Alfred Russel Wallace, is the process by which individual characteristics that are more favorable to reproductive success are "chosen," because passed on from one generation to the next, over characteristics that are less favorable. Darwin regretted that the word "selection" suggested an intention: natural selection is a blind process, because the conditions to which the organism must adapt in order to survive are never the same. In periods of drought, when seeds are hard to find, finches that happen to have long narrow beaks, good for foraging, will be favored over finches with broad powerful beaks: more of their offspring will survive and reproduce. In periods of abundance, when seeds are large and their shells are hard, the broad-beaked finches will hold the adaptive advantage. "Finchness" is a variable, not a constant.

Darwin thought that variations do not arise because organisms need them (which is essentially what Lamarck had argued). He thought that variations occur by chance, and that chance determines their adaptive utility. In all seasons it happens that some finches are born with marginally longer and narrower beaks than others, just as children of the same parents are not all exactly the same height. In certain environmental conditions, a narrower beak may have positive or negative survival value, but in other conditions—for example, when seeds are plentiful and finches are few—it may make no difference. The "selection" of favorable characteristics is therefore neither designed nor progressive. No intelligence, divine or otherwise, determines in advance the relative value of individual variations, and there is no ideal type of "finch," or essence of "finchness," toward which adaptive changes are leading.

Natural selection is a law that explains *why* changes occur in nature—because, as Darwin and Wallace both realized after reading, independently, Thomas Malthus's *Essay on the Principle of Population* (1798), if all members of a group of sexually reproducing organisms were equally well adapted, the population of the group would quickly outgrow the resources available to sustain it. Since some members of the group must die, the individuals whose slight differences give them an adaptive edge are more likely to survive. Evolution is simply the incidental by-product of material struggle, not its goal. Organisms don't struggle because they must evolve; they evolve because they must struggle. Natural selection also explains *how* changes occur in nature—by the relative reproductive success of the marginally better adapted. But natural selection does not dictate *what* those changes shall be. It is a process without mind.

A way of thinking that regards individual differences as inessential departures from a general type is therefore not well suited for dealing with the natural world. A general type is fixed, determinate, and uniform; the world Darwin described is characterized by chance, change, and difference—all the attributes general types are designed to leave out. In emphasizing the particularity of individual organisms, Darwin did not conclude that species do not exist. He only concluded that species are what they appear to be: ideas, which are provisionally useful for naming groups of interacting individuals. "I look at the term species," he wrote, "as one arbitrarily given for the sake of convenience to a set of individuals closely resembling each other. . . . [I]t does not essentially differ from the term variety, which is given to less distinct and more fluctuating forms. The term variety, again, in comparison with mere individual differences, is also applied arbitrarily, and for mere convenience sake."[6] Difference goes all the way down.

Once our attention is redirected to the individual, we need another way of making generalizations. We are no longer interested in the conformity of an individual to an ideal type; we are now interested in the relation of an individual to the other individuals with which it interacts. To generalize about groups of interacting individuals, we need to drop the language of types and essences, which is prescriptive (telling us what all finches should be), and adopt the language of statistics and probability, which is predictive (telling us what the average finch, under specified conditions, is likely to do). Relations will be more important than categories; functions, which are variable, will be more important than purposes, which are fixed in advance; transitions will be more important than boundaries; sequences will be more important than hierarchies.

Still, relational and probabilistic thinking is just another way of making generalizations. It is no less abstract than typological and prescriptive thinking. You can't see a relation any more than you can see an essence. Until well into the twentieth century, in fact, no one had ever documented a case of natural selection in action. Darwin gleaned his evidence for the inheritability of variations from domestic dog and pigeon breeding, which is intelligent selection *par excellence*. Natural selection was only a hypothesis. And since Darwin did not know the science of genetics, he was unable even to explain how characteristics get passed on. He could only claim that he had come up with a way of thinking about living things that did a better job of accounting for what we do know and what we can see than any previous scientist.

On the Origin of Species was therefore not only a challenge to Louis Agassiz's view of natural history at almost every point; it also represented a completely different method of scientific thought.[7] Agassiz had been an opponent of evolutionary theories (or transmutation theories, as he called them) long before Darwin's book appeared. His mentor Georges Cuvier had been a colleague of Lamarck's at the Muséum National d'Histoire Naturelle, in Paris, and had flavored his own attacks on Lamarck's theory of adaptation with the special contempt collegiality breeds. Agassiz's inaugural Lowell Lectures, "The Plan of Creation in the Animal Kingdom," in 1846, were explicitly a response to *Vestiges of the Natural History of Creation*, a work, published anonymously in 1844 by an English journalist named Robert Chambers, which purported to offer scientific evidence that the "higher" species had descended from "lower" ones.

Darwin himself "discovered" the law of natural selection in 1838, after reading Malthus, and he had become convinced of the mutability of species ("it is like confessing a murder," he told his friend

Joseph Hooker)[8] by 1844. He delayed formal presentation of his ideas, in part because of the critical reaction to Chambers's book, for twenty years—and even then he was only pushed into it by the news of Wallace's independent arrival at the same theory. But he was in continual correspondence with scientists all over Europe and the United States. Everyone knew what he was working on.

One of Darwin's American correspondents was Asa Gray. Gray was a botanist who knew Agassiz well: they had met in Princeton, during Agassiz's initial American tour, and traveled together to Philadelphia, where Agassiz had his productive encounter with Samuel Morton. When the Lawrence Scientific School got under way, Gray joined the faculty, and he and Agassiz became colleagues. Gray disapproved of Agassiz's association with Nott and Gliddon, partly for political reasons, but also because Gray was a religious man, and he believed that polygenism—the theory of the separate creation of the races—contradicted Christian teaching. He also distrusted what he regarded as an element of showmanship in Agassiz's scientific style. Agassiz "has a touch of the empiric about him," he wrote to Darwin's friend Hooker in 1858, when the storm over *On the Origin of Species* was already visible on the North Atlantic horizon, "in that he is always writing and talking *ad populum*—fond of addressing himself to an incompetent tribunal."[9]

The best evidence Darwin had for his theory of natural selection was the geographical distribution of species. (This was also the principal evidence adduced by Wallace, who had studied the distribution of butterflies in the Malay archipelago.) Darwin thought that the distribution of species was consistent with the theory of common descent—the theory, that is, that the members of a species, no matter where they are found, are descendants of a single pair. In 1855 Darwin wrote to Gray asking him for information about the distribution of plants in North America; Gray responded with an article on "Statistics of the Flora of the Northern United States," published in three parts in 1856–57. Statistical analysis of the distribution of plant species in eastern Asia and North America, Gray argued, showed that many species have migrated (due to changes in climate and in the relations of the continents) from a single origin. Specimens of a

North American species, for example, can be found in Nepal. Only one of two theories, he suggested, could explain such phenomena: a theory that assumes a common origin and looks for the causes of migration, or a theory that assumes that each type of organism originated in its present locale. But the second theory, Gray said, is only an act of faith: it "leaves species no objective basis in nature, and seems to make even the ground of their limitation a matter of individual opinion"[10]—that is, it allows the naturalist simply to assert that the Nepalese plant must be a different species from its North American look-alike.

This was a direct slap at Agassiz. In 1858 and 1859 Gray published more findings supporting his theory of plant distribution and showing that examples of the same species could be found in Japan and in eastern North America; and in the winter of 1859 he and Agassiz had a debate over his findings at the American Academy of Arts and Sciences in Boston. Gray was an academic specialist and Agassiz was a celebrity accustomed to spellbinding. But Gray won the debate easily, as he would win a second debate with Agassiz a year later, following the publication of *On the Origin of Species*.

For Gray understood something Agassiz did not, which was that there were new rules for scientific argument. The problem with Agassiz's theory, Gray argued in their first debate, was "[t]hat it offers no *scientific* explanation for the present distribution of species over the globe."[11] It was a scandalous thing to say to a man who regarded himself as the walking embodiment of modern science; but Agassiz had no reply. For he could not explain *how* species came to inhabit the places where they are currently found; he could only repeat his conviction that since this is where we find them, God must have put them there. "[T]he present races of animals were originally created on the earth in about the same proportionate numbers as they are found to have at the present time, and in about the same localities as those they now occupy,"[12] was his rebuttal of Gray. It was not an argument.

Gray, of course, had not actually seen species migrate, any more than Agassiz had seen God create them. He only had his data. But by subjecting them to statistical analysis he was able to show that the geographical distribution of plant species followed patterns consistent with evidence of glacial activity and movements of the earth's crust. Gray was thinking in terms of relations and probabilities. Agassiz, though, was still thinking in terms of types and ideas. He was unable to see how chance could be a cause of order, and he was unable to imagine order that was not the product of a mind. Agassiz called Darwin's theory, when he finally wrote about it, "a scientific mistake, untrue in its facts, unscientific in its method, and mischievous in its tendency."[13] This was not bluster, or it was not only bluster: Agassiz simply could not recognize Darwinian thinking as science.

It was perfectly possible to believe in Darwin and God at the same time in nineteenth-century Cambridge. Gray, for example, thought that Agassiz's theism and Darwin's naturalism could somehow be synthesized, and even claimed (a little bizarrely) that a theistic view of nature was implied in Darwin's book. Organic life evolved the way Darwin said it did, by the natural selection of variations, Gray thought; but there was no reason why God could not be supplying the variations.[14] Like many other nineteenth-century scientists (including Darwin's English champion Thomas Huxley), Gray had interpreted Darwin phenomenalistically: he took natural selection to be an explanation of phenomena, not an account of final causes. In Gray's view, science was only concerned with the things we experience; it left questions about ultimates, questions like whether God exists or life has a purpose, where it found them. The theory of natural selection, Gray announced, had done nothing to disturb his own "profound conviction that there is order in the universe; that order presupposes mind; design, will; and mind or will, personality."[15] But Darwin did not believe he had left questions about ultimates where he had found them, and he eventually wrote *The Variation of Plants and Animals under Domestication* (1868) to show why Gray was wrong: because nothing in the process by which organisms evolve can be explained by a theory of design.

Agassiz, on the other hand, had given himself no room for compromise. He *couldn't* separate the phenomenal from the transcendental: his entire system was tied to the belief that all observable order in nature is prima facie evidence of a supernatural intention.

The species, he insisted, were "categories of thought embodied in individual living forms," and natural history was ultimately "the analysis of the thoughts of the Creator of the Universe, as manifested in the animal and vegetable kingdoms."[16] This intransigence left him, after 1860, with very few scientific allies in Cambridge. He was reduced to relying on the support of people like Francis Bowen, the Harvard philosophy professor who had campaigned against Emerson and whose classes the young Wendell Holmes was busy disrupting, and his own patron, John A. Lowell, who reviewed (anonymously) *On the Origin of Species* in a Boston journal, the *Christian Examiner*. "[W]e hope to be excused," Lowell wrote of Darwin, "if we say that we deem his case as really a psychological curiosity."[17] Lowell was a businessman. ("[I]t is clear," wrote Darwin after seeing the review, that "he is not [a] naturalist.")[18]

It was a fairly stunning peripeteia. Agassiz was unaccustomed to life on the professional margins, and the experience became so disorienting that in 1864 he got into a quarrel with Gray on a train from New Haven and called him "no gentleman." Gray stopped speaking to him after that. The rumor in Cambridge was that Agassiz had challenged Gray to a duel.[19] By the winter of 1865, when he mentioned the possibility of looking for glacial activity in Brazil, it was clear to Agassiz's friends that it might indeed be a good idea for him to get out of town for a while.

And on March 29, 1865, the *Colorado*, with the Thayer expedition on board, set out from New York Harbor. Elizabeth Cary Agassiz was a member of the party: she was to serve as the expedition's official diarist. On April 2, a Sunday, as the ship steamed south, the passengers noticed a column of smoke on the western horizon. It was Richmond. Grant was about to enter Petersburg, and the Confederates had set their own capital on fire. It was the last battle of the Civil War.

3

From the start William James was much more interested in Agassiz than he was in glacial activity—or in any other aspect of natural history, for that matter. And he was perfectly aware of the extent to which the expedition was, in its grander ambitions, a charade. One of the passengers on board the *Colorado* was the Episcopal bishop of Pennsylvania, Alonzo Potter, who was traveling to California with his new wife, Frances. She was Potter's third wife; he was sixty-five. Potter had an ancient connection with the Jameses. Back in 1829, in his black-sheep days, Henry Senior had dropped out of college in Albany and run away to Boston, where he ended up staying for a while with the Potters. Henry was extremely taken with the then Mrs. Potter, Sarah—"what Eve might have been before the fall,"[20] as he described her at the time. He thought it a disgrace that a woman with her attractions had been obliged to take such a plebeian married name. (Sarah Potter's maiden name, as it happened, was Nott; her father was a cousin of Josiah Nott.) The bishop evidently had an interesting track record.

Agassiz's endorsement of polygenism in the 1850s had annoyed the churchmen, but his leadership in the fight against Darwinism brought them back; and though Potter was an outspoken antislavery figure—one of his sons was a general in the Union Army—he and Agassiz quickly bonded. The bishop offered weekly sermons on the trip south, and Agassiz delivered daily lectures to the ship's company, including the captain and crew, in which he rehearsed his own theories of intelligent creation and embryological recapitulation, and expanded on his reasons for going to Brazil. "I am often asked," he explained, "what is my chief aim in this expedition to South America? . . . [T]he conviction which draws me irresistibly, is that the combination of animals on this continent, where the faunae are so characteristic and so distinct from all others, will give me the means of showing that the transmutation theory is wholly without foundation in facts."[21]

The bishop backed him up. "He and Prof. furnish as good an illustration of the saying: 'You caw me & I'll caw you,' as I ever saw," James told his parents.

> Though I think Agassiz will be left a little in the debt of the worthy Bish. unless he makes it up to morrow. The Bish tells me he . . . has

read Substance & Shadder [Henry Senior's book *Substance and Shadow*], & tho' disagreeing with the doctrine, admires the ability displayed & the very fine style. Last Sunday he preached a sermon particularly to us "savans" as the outsiders call us, and told us we must try to imitate the simple child like devotion to truth of our great leader. We must give up our pet theories of transmutation, spontaneous generation &c, and seek in nature what God has put there rather than try to put there some system wh. our imagination has devised &c &c. (Vide Agassiz passim.) The good old Prof. was melted to tears, and wepped profusely.[22]

It was a little like the Duke and the Dauphin in *Huckleberry Finn*.

But James admired Agassiz's powers of mind and will—so focused when his own seemed so fickle—and he spent much of his time in Brazil trying to distinguish the meritorious from the meretricious in his teacher's character. It was not a simple task. "Professor is a very interesting man," William wrote to his brother Henry in May from Rio. "I don't yet understand him very well. His charlatanerie is almost as great as his solid worth; and it seems of an unconscious childish kind that you can't condemn him for as you wd most people. He wishes to be too omniscient. But his personal fascination is very remarkable." "[O]f his 11 assistants," he added, "3 are absolute idiots." He meant that three knew nothing about natural history, and that one of the three was himself.

A week later, his opinion of Agassiz had shifted. "Since seeing more of Agassiz, my desire to be with him, so as to learn from him has much diminished," he now informed Henry. "He is doubtless a man of some wonderful mental faculties, but such a politician & so self-seeking & illiberal to others that it sadly diminishes one's respect for him. Don't say anything about this outside, for heaven's sake."[23]

But Agassiz had not achieved his position in the world by failing to cultivate people who happened to drift into his orbit, and he must have sensed that with a young man like James patronizing encouragement would be the wrong tack to take. So when James, one morning, proposed an ingenious theory about some natural phenomenon, Agassiz responded by calling him "totally uneducated."[24] This hit a nerve—James had good reasons for feeling insecure about his education—and he respected Agassiz for saying it. By September, the appreciative mood had returned. "I have profited a great deal by hearing Agassiz talk," William wrote to his father,

> not so much by what he says, for never did a man utter a greater amount of humbug, but by learning the way of feeling of such a vast practical engine as he is. No one sees farther into a generalisation than his own knowledge of details extends, and you have a greater feeling of weight & solidity about the movement of agassiz's mind, owing to the continual presence of this great background of special facts, than about the mind of any other man I know. He has great personal tact too, and I see that in all his talks with me he is pitching in to my loose and . . . superficial way of thinking. I have said a great deal against him wh., if repeated to strangers, wd. generate an impression that I disliked him very much. This is not at all the case so I wish you wd. repeat none of it. Now that I am more intimate with him & can talk more freely to him, I delight to be with him. I only saw his defects at first, but now his wonderful qualities throw them quite in the background. I am convinced that he is the man to do me good.[25]

James's chief assignment in Brazil, besides the mindless one of constructing barrels for the thousands of specimens to be shipped back to the Museum of Comparative Zoology in Cambridge, was to travel up selected tributaries of the Amazon, with a Brazilian guide and a few colleagues, and collect fish. It is unclear whether he reflected much on the purpose of the exercise: it was to help Agassiz establish, by collecting specimens simultaneously from up- and downriver locations, that fish do not migrate, and that God must therefore have created the species where they are found. James's data were to be his answer to Darwin and Gray. Agassiz was also keen to collect embryos to support his theory of recapitulation—particularly alligator eggs. A study of alligator fetal development, he thought, would yield a natural classification for all the reptiles.

And of course he was searching for evidence of glaciation. When the expedition made its first trip up a Brazilian hill outside Rio, Agassiz decided that the ground under the mule path they were traveling on was "a drift hill with numerous erratic boulders." It was, he wrote to his Harvard colleague and close friend Benjamin Peirce, "one of the happiest days of my life"; for the erratic boulders suggested geological activity of some kind. He had not, Agassiz confessed to Peirce, actually seen traces of glacial action, such as scratches and furrows a glacier might have left behind. But this just suggested that he was on the verge of discovering "a new geological agency, thus far not discussed in our geological theories"—that is, another one of God's methods for inducing catastrophe. James was on that trip; he just noted that "erratic drift" made for an extremely uncomfortable ride.[26]

Agassiz had another item on his agenda, though, which he does not seem to have expanded on in his shipboard lectures, and which James apparently learned about by accident. One of the assistants on the expedition was a photographer, Walter Hunnewell, a man James grew friendly with, and in November Hunnewell and Agassiz set up a photographic studio in Manáos, their base of operations for exploring the upper Amazon. One day James dropped by. "I . . . was cautiously admitted by Hunnewell with his black hands," he wrote in his diary.

> On entering the room found Prof. engaged in cajoling 3 moças [môças: young women] whom he called pure indians but who I thought, & as afterwards appeared, had white blood. They were very nicely dressed in white muslin & jewelry with flowers in their hair & an excellent smell of pripioca. Apparently refined, at all events not sluttish, they consented to the utmost liberties being taken with them and two without much trouble were induced to strip and pose naked. While we were there Sr. Tavares Bastos [a Brazilian official who occasionally accompanied the expedition] came in and asked me mockingly if I was attached to the Bureau d'Anthropologie.[27]

The scene was embarrassing because Agassiz had a reputation for a certain libidinal gusto. "[H]e has the joy of animal vigour to a degree rare among men," as his fellow Saturday Clubber James Russell Lowell once put it, "—a true male, in all its meaning."[28] A few years after his arrival in Boston Agassiz had been involved in a scandal concerning his relations with a servant named Jane: a witness claimed he had discovered Agassiz and Jane in a room together with the front of Agassiz's trousers in disarray; Jane is supposed to have explained that she had been sewing on a button. (The accusation was part of a complaint brought against Agassiz by an embittered associate; the charges were investigated with due solemnity by a panel of Boston dignitaries—including John A. Lowell, who already had a good deal invested in Agassiz—and were dismissed.)[29]

It's plain that James was not impressed with the scientific rigor of the session he had barged in on, but whatever other interests they may have served (Mrs. Agassiz was, after all, traveling with the expedition), the photographs did have a scientific rationale. Agassiz was trying to do with pictures what Morton had done with skulls: he was attempting to document the hierarchy of racial types and the deterioration of mixed-race populations. It was indeed anthropological fieldwork—though Senhor Bastos's sarcastic remark suggests that this was one aspect of the expedition Agassiz had not cleared with the emperor.

And with good reason, for race was a contentious issue in Brazil in 1865. Brazil was by then the only independent state in the Western world that officially tolerated slavery. (Spain still permitted slavery in its Caribbean colonies; the United States, of course, had issued the Emancipation Proclamation in 1863, and ratified the Thirteenth Amendment, outlawing slavery, in 1865.) The government of Dom Pedro II had ended the slave trade in 1850, but until then three million Africans had been imported from Angola and the Congo. Brazil was under international pressure, particularly from Great Britain, to abolish slavery; but it was also fighting the so-called War of the Triple Alliance, against Paraguay, and the government was reluctant to deal with the domestic turmoil abolition would entail. For Brazil was an agricultural economy with a complex caste system based on race, religion, and country of birth. Still, manumission was contemplated, and Brazilian politicians were immersed in the details. Bastos, in fact, was a historian and statistician of the slave trade—which is why he would have had a particular interest in Agassiz's photographic operations.

After the slave trade was outlawed, there were some attempts to import Chinese into Brazil for labor, but these were resisted on grounds that Chinese blood would corrupt Brazil's racial stock. (Portuguese from the Azores were impressed instead.) The fear of racial impurity was peculiar in a country where more people were of mixed race than were either white or black. According to its first national census, in 1872, Brazil had just under 10 million inhabitants; fewer than 3.8 million of them were classified as white, about 2 million were black, and the rest—just under 4.2 million, or 42 percent of the population—were mestizos (of mixed white and Indian ancestry) or mulattoes. Mestizos, in fact, were the dominant caste socially, outnumbering the slaveowners (of Portuguese descent) and the slaves (of African descent), and they tended to determine the mores of race-mixing.[30] Their numbers and social position did not suggest declining fertility rates among "hybrids"—but that was what Agassiz was looking for. He was seeking to reinforce the polygenetic theories of the American school of anthropology, of which he was by now the leading light, and to back up, with more science, the case against racial amalgamation he had made to Samuel Gridley Howe.

The human variety on display in Brazil fascinated both the Agassizes. "Perhaps nowhere in the world can the blending of types among men be studied so fully as in the Amazons, where mamelucos, cafuzos, mulattoes, cabocos, negroes, and whites are mingled in a confusion that seems at first inextricable,"[31] Elizabeth Agassiz wrote in her diary. Perhaps the racial mixture seemed inextricable because it *was* inextricable; but the Agassizes were conditioned to look for types, and types is what they found. On April 23, a few days after the expedition arrived, Elizabeth attended a festival to watch Negroes dance. "Looking at their half-naked figures and unintelligent faces," she wrote, "the question arose, so constantly suggested when we come in contact with the race, 'What will they do with this great gift of freedom?' The only corrective for the half doubt is to consider the whites side by side with them: whatever one may think of the condition of slavery for the blacks, there can be no question as to its evil effects on their masters."[32] It was a distinctly Bostonian view of race—revulsion at the racism of others.

Elizabeth Agassiz's diary is filled with her observations of racial characteristics, including the characteristics of Brazilian whites, whom she and her husband considered triply degraded—by their southern European and Catholic origins, by their fraternization with Indians, and by their role in a slave economy. On July 30, as the expedition traveled by ship to Pará at the mouth of the Amazon, James, Hunnewell, and the Agassizes had a long moonlight conversation on deck with a Brazilian senator, a Senhor Sinimbu, about the consequences of emancipation for Brazil. "The absence of all restraint upon the free blacks, the fact that they are eligible to office, and that all professional careers are open to them, without prejudice on the ground of color, enables one to form some opinion as to their ability and capacity for development," Elizabeth Agassiz reported. "Mr. Sinimbu tells us that here the result is on the whole in their favor; he says that the free blacks compare well in intelligence. . . . But it must be remembered, in making the comparison with reference to our own country, that here they are brought into contact with a less energetic and powerful race than the Anglo-Saxon."[33] She was referring to the Portuguese.

In September, when the expedition was quartered in Teffé, Elizabeth Agassiz acquired a young housemaid, named Alexandrina, who was a cafuzo—a child of Negro and Indian parents. "She promises very well, and seems to have the intelligence of the Indian with the greater pliability of the negro,"[34] Elizabeth wrote. The Agassizes were intrigued by Alexandrina's appearance, and got James—who, after all, had once studied to be a painter—to draw her. "She consented yesterday, after a good deal of coy demur, to have her portrait taken," wrote Elizabeth.

Mr. Agassiz wanted it especially on account of her extraordinary hair, which, though it has lost its compact negro crinkle, and acquired something of the length and texture of the Indian hair, retains, nevertheless, a sort of wiry elasticity, so that, when combed out, it stands off from her head in all directions as if electrified. In the examples of negro and Indian half-breeds we have seen, the negro type seems the first to yield, as if the more facile disposition of the negro, as compared with the enduring tenacity of the Indian, showed itself in their physical as well as their mental characteristics.[35]

They found hierarchy in hair.

In his letters home James had complimentary things to say about Elizabeth Agassiz, though in his diary he calls her an "excellent but infatuated woman [who] *will* look at every thing in such an unnatural & romantic light that she don't seem to walk upon the solid earth."[36] James's own very casual observations tend to stress the ordinariness underneath the exotic appearance of the Brazilians he meets. "About sunrise," he writes, for example, in his diary about one of his upriver expeditions,

> we met a large montaria coming up close to the bank manned entirely by indian women 7 in all. The patroness a little old lady sat at the mouth of the toldo smoking her pipe. As we met we hailed her and stopped together. Altho' they spoke portuguese I could not make out whether all their men had gone to the war [against Paraguay] or whether they had stayed back for fear of being sent to the war. How can a population with such habits and aims as this care for the war or wish to enter the army? I marvelled, as I always do, at the quiet urbane polite tone of the conversation between my friends [the Indians in his boat] and the old lady. Is it race or is it circumstance that makes these people so refined and well bred? No gentleman of Europe has better manners and yet these are peasants.[37]

"Is it race or is it circumstance"? It is the beginning of relational thinking.

About the expedition as a whole James's feelings performed their usual somersaults. He was susceptible to seasickness, and he found the voyage out unpleasant and tedious. ("We have seen a few little flying fish skip," he writes his parents from the *Colorado*, "but they are not near as interesting as toads at home. . . . The Ocean is a d——d wet, disagreeable place anyhow, is my conclusion.")[38] As soon as he gets to Rio, though, he is enraptured by the tropical landscape, and his letters are filled with enthusiasm. A month later, the landscape and the climate have become unbearably monotonous, and he regrets the entire business. "My coming," he writes to his father from Rio, "was a mistake."[39] Once the group moves outside Rio, he is reenchanted. "[N]ow that the real enjoyment of the expedition is beginning & I am tasting the sweets of these lovely forests here, I find it impossible to tear myself away,"[40] he writes to his mother in August from somewhere on the Xingu River.

In the end, though, James found the experience uninspiring, including his own performance. He was (as he realized very quickly) not a dedicated collector, or even a competent one; and he hated mosquitoes. But mostly he was bored. He developed an antipathy to the repetitiveness of the work and the languidness of the environment. "I am on the whole very glad this thing is winding up," he told his mother in December, after he had made his plans to return to Cambridge,

> —not that I have not enjoyed parts of it intensely and regard it as one of the best spent portions of my life; but enough is as good as a feast; I thoroughly *hate* collecting, and long to be back to books, studies &c after this elementary existence. . . . [T]he idea of the people swarming about as they do at home, killing themselves with thinking about things that have no connexion with their merely external circumstances, studying themselves into fevers, going mad about religion, philosophy, love & sich, breathing perpetual heated gas & excitement, turning night into day, seems almost incredible and imaginary. . . . Still more remarkable seems the extraordinary variety of character that results from it all—here all is so monotonous, in life and in nature that you are rocked into a kind of sleep.[41]

He had evidently missed something he had once hoped to find—to have set out with an expectation of dangers much more interesting than mosquito bites, adventures that might call out qualities of fortitude and boldness in himself. It seems that Brazil was to be, in effect, his Civil War. In his letters he identifies Agassiz, more than once, with General Sherman, and himself with his brothers who had fought. "I have felt more sympathy with Bob and Wilk than ever from the fact of my isolated circumstances being more like theirs than the life I have led hitherto," he tells his parents on the way down. "Please send them this letter. It is written as much for them as for any one."[42] He even suffered a sort of wound. Soon after the expedition arrived, he came down with a form of smallpox, probably varioloid, and spent two and a half weeks in a *maison de santé*. The disease left his face, in the end, unscarred, but it ruined his eyes. He had to wear dark glasses for part of the trip, and he suffered from chronic eye trouble for the rest of his life.

James had set off as if to the front, but he found no opportunity, or found he could make no opportunity, for heroism. After eight months, he seems to have decided that the war was really back in Cambridge, as his last letter home suggests—"the people swarming about as they do . . . killing themselves with thinking . . . breathing perpetual heated gas & excitement." He could not know that for soldiers war is mostly boredom, too.

Almost as soon as Agassiz returned, in August 1866, he went to Washington and gave a series of lectures on "Traces of Glaciers under the Tropics" at the National Academy of Sciences, which he closed with the remark: "So here is the end of the Darwinian theory."[43] He had already had a pamphlet on "The Geology of the Amazons" printed up; Charles Lyell, the English geologist who, long before, had once secured the Lowell Lectureship for Agassiz, sent Darwin a copy. "I was very glad to read it," Darwin replied, "though chiefly as a psychological curiosity. I quite follow you in thinking Agassiz glacier-mad."[44]

And Lyell himself was not yet fully converted to Darwinism. By his inflexibility and his refusal to acknowledge the research of others (Alfred Wallace, the codiscoverer of natural selection, had been to Brazil already and had detected no signs of glaciation there), Agassiz had lost most of his scientific audience. His response was to turn his wife's diary, with considerable annotation by himself, into a book. This appeared in January 1868 as *A Journey in Brazil*. Agassiz was moving his personal battle against Darwinism onto less challenging terrain. *A Journey in Brazil*, a kind of travelogue with scientific editorials, was designed to reach over (or under) the heads of the scientists. The Agassizes sent it as a Christmas present to their Boston friends, some of whom were a little puzzled how to respond. "Please tell Mr. Agassiz there is not a word too much of science to my perception, though of course *I* do not understand it," wrote George Ticknor's wife, Anna. "What a beautiful book it is, so handsomely and accurately printed."[45]

Anna Ticknor was an intelligent person. Possibly there were things about the book she chose not to understand too quickly. What Agassiz was eager to show, of course, was that he had found nothing in Brazil either to support Darwin's theories or to contradict his own. But he also wished, even more fervently, to impress his audience with the dangers of racial amalgamation. Brazil was a warning. "Let any one who doubts the evil of this mixture of races, and is inclined, from a mistaken philanthropy, to break down all barriers between them, come to Brazil," he wrote in one of his lengthy footnotes to his wife's diary.

> At a time when the new social status of the negro is a subject of vital importance in our statesmanship, we should profit by the experience of a country where, though slavery exists, there is far more liberality toward the free negro than he has ever enjoyed in the United States. Let us learn the double lesson: open all the advantages of education to the negro, and give him every chance of success which culture gives to the man who knows how to use it; but respect the laws of nature, and let all our dealings with the black man tend to preserve, as far as possible, the distinctness of his national characteristics, and the integrity of our own.[46]

His ethnographic observations, photographically aided, had confirmed the polygenist view:

> I am satisfied that, unless it can be shown that the differences between the Indian, negro, and white races are unstable and transient, it is not in keeping with the facts to affirm a community of origin for all the varieties of the human family, nor in keeping with scientific principles to make a difference between human races and animal species in a systematic point of view. . . . The natural result of an uninterrupted contact of half-breeds with one another is a class of men in which pure type fades away as completely as do all the good qualities, physical and moral, of the primitive races, engendering a mongrel crowd as repulsive as the mongrel dogs, which are apt to be

their companions, and among which it is impossible to pick out a single specimen retaining the intelligence, the nobility, or the affectionateness of nature which makes the dog of pure type the favorite companion of civilized man.[47]

And he added an appendix on the "Permanence of Characteristics in Different Human Species," in which he summarized the results of his and Hunnewell's work. It is an imitation of the racial typology of Morton's *Crania Americana*: "while the Indian female is remarkable for her masculine build, the Negro male is equally so for his feminine aspect"; the mulatto's "features are handsome, his complexion clear, and his character confiding, but indolent"; the "Mammeluco [mestizo] . . . is pallid, effeminate, feeble, lazy, and rather obstinate"; and so on.[48] Between 1868 and 1875 *A Journey in Brazil* was reprinted nine times.

4

"He was a Darwinian for fun," wrote Henry Adams about Henry Adams in *The Education of Henry Adams*. He meant that he had, as a young man, regarded the theory of natural selection as unproved, and probably unprovable, but had accepted it anyway. Two of the most striking things about the reception of Darwin's theory are the degree to which it was regarded, even by its supporters, as highly speculative, and the speed with which it was nevertheless assimilated by younger intellectuals. "One could not stop to chase doubts as though they were rabbits," as Adams explained. "One had no time to paint the surface of Law, even though it were cracked and rotten. For the young men whose lives were cast in the generation between 1867 and 1900, Law should be Evolution."[49] Darwinism dropped into a cultural configuration already aligned to accommodate it. Its fitness was generally appreciated before its rightness was generally established.

William James, Adams's friend and contemporary, was also quick to respond to Darwin's ideas. The first two articles he ever published, written in 1865, just before he left for Brazil, were reviews, largely sympathetic, of works by Thomas Huxley and Alfred Wallace. James was clearly already an evolutionist. "[I]n the case of Darwin's original law," he wrote in the Wallace review, "what most astonishes the reader is the fact that the discovery was made so late."[50] "He was a Darwinist before the letter,"[51] is the way Adams described himself at the same point in his own life.

But James differed from Adams, and from most of the rest of his generation, in his relation to Darwin. James's thought, as a psychologist and later on as a philosopher, belongs to the tradition initiated by *On the Origin of Species*; but he refused to regard evolution as a "law," in Adams's sense, and he devoted much of his life to attacking the way Darwin's work was interpreted by people like Huxley and Herbert Spencer. James had the same attitude about Darwin that he had, toward the end of his life, about Freud: he liked the ideas but hated seeing them treated as the exclusive truth. He was Darwinian, but he was not a Darwinist. This made him truer to Darwin than most nineteenth-century evolutionists.

On James's view, two incorrect lessons were drawn from the success of *On the Origin of Species*. The first was the conclusion that science is an activity that is properly independent of our own (or our society's) interests and preferences. Darwin's book had, of course, scandalized the faithful; one way to defend it was to explain that the scientist can only stick to the facts. But for James, anti-Darwinian scientists like Agassiz were mistaken not because they ignored the facts in favor of preconceived theories, but for the opposite reason— because they collected facts without a working hypothesis to guide them. When we look at Agassiz's work we think we are seeing a confusion between science and belief. But what we are really seeing is a disjunction between those things. This is what Asa Gray had meant when he said that Agassiz had no *scientific* explanation for the phenomena he observed; for Agassiz had only his observations on one side and his theory on the other. His science wasn't theoretical and his theory wasn't scientific. His ideas are edifices perched on top of mountains of data. Darwin's ideas are devices for generating data. Darwin's theory opens possibilities for inquiry; Agassiz's closes them.

In 1868 James was in Germany, where he spent a year that turned out to be even less inspiring than his eight months in Brazil; he was trying to study physiology, but a bad back and low spirits drove him to a spa, in Bohemia, where he spent most of his time reading Goethe. But when Darwin's book on *The Variation of Animals and Plants under Domestication* came out that winter, James wrote two reviews of it, one for the *North American Review* (whose editor, Charles Eliot Norton, was a good friend of his brother Henry) and the other for the *Atlantic Monthly* (whose assistant editor, William Dean Howells, was also a good friend of his brother Henry). Darwin's book introduced nearly as many difficulties as it solved, James wrote: "the only 'law' under which the greater mass of the facts the author has brought together can be grouped seems to be that of Caprice,—caprice in inheriting, caprice in transmitting, caprice everywhere, in turn. To look for laws at all in the chaos seems absurdly presumptuous."

But James thought that this was what made the work profound. For it is in the nature of experience to offer exceptions and eccentricities, and a theory that anticipates them—that is, in fact, predicated on them—is far more useful than a theory that bulldozes them. "It is one of the fortunate points of the general theory which bears [Darwin's] name (and which is, after all, only a descriptive or historical, and not a physiological hypothesis)," James pointed out, "that the more idiosyncracies are found, the more the probabilities in its favor grow [since idiosyncrasies are evidence of chance variation]. Its adversaries are those whose interest it is to establish the rigor of these descriptive laws. . . . Hence, the great value of the hypotheses in setting naturalists to work, and sharpening their eyes for new facts and relations."[52] One of the adversaries James had in mind, of course, was Agassiz. "The more I think of Darwin's ideas," he wrote to Henry while he was working on his reviews, "the more weighty do they appear to me—tho' of course my opinion is worth very little—still I *believe* that that scoundrel Aggassiz is unworthy either intellectually or morally for him to wipe his shoes on, & I find a certain pleasure in yielding to the feeling."[53]

The other wrong lesson James thought people took from *On the Origin of Species* is, in effect, the flip side of the first. It is the belief that evolutionary science can lay a foundation for norms—that natural selection serves as a kind of "bottom-line" arbiter of merit. This is the doctrine of "the survival of the fittest," a concept that originated not with Darwin, but with Herbert Spencer, seven years before *On the Origin of Species* appeared.[54] It makes the logic of evolution the logic of human values: it suggests that we should pursue policies and honor behavior that are consistent with the survival of characteristics understood to be "adaptive," and it justifies, as "natural," certain kinds of coercion. In a society that had just been through a civil war the appeal of Darwin's theory, on this interpretation, is plain—as Adams, in his mordant way, recognized. Adams had spent the Civil War years in London, serving as secretary to his father, Charles Francis Adams, who was Lincoln's minister to the Court of St. James's; evolution, he wrote in the *Education*, was the perfect theory for a "young man who had just helped to waste five or ten thousand million dollars and a million lives, more or less, to enforce unity and uniformity on people who objected to it."[55] The war was just part of the struggle for existence, a means by which the species moved ahead.

James believed that scientific inquiry, like any other form of inquiry, is an activity inspired and informed by our tastes, values, and hopes. But this does not, in his view, confer any special authority on the conclusions it reaches. On the contrary: it obligates us to regard those conclusions as provisional and partial, since it was for provisional and partial reasons that we undertook to find them. A theory good for explaining why finches have differently sized beaks in different environments has no further necessary claim on us—and maybe we will come up with a better explanation for finch beaks someday, too. The mistake is not simply endowing science with an authority it does not merit. It is turning one belief into a trump card over alternative beliefs. It is ruling out the possibility of other ways of considering the case. That there is always more than one way of considering a case is what James meant by the term (which he introduced to English-language philosophy) "pluralism."

For when circumstances change, trumps have a tendency to change as well. Even in his brief career as a naturalist James had had a chance to see how malleable an authority science can be. For twenty years Agassiz and Nott had insisted that the races must be segregated because science had determined them to be separately created species. But in 1866, after Darwin had persuaded most scientists of the theory of common descent, Nott published a book called *The Negro Race: Its Ethnology and History* in which he coolly conceded that Darwin might perfectly well be correct, but that since the theory of natural selection required millions of years for the races to differentiate, the practical effect was the same: Caucasian superiority, Negro inferiority.[56] Two years later, in *A Journey in Brazil*, and with equal aplomb, Agassiz abandoned the theory of multiple human origins on which he had based his opinions about racial policy— though he did not abandon the opinions. "[F]or my purpose, it does not matter whether there are three, four, five, or twenty human races, and whether they originated independently from one another or not," he now explained. "The fact that they differ by constant permanent features is in itself sufficient to justify a comparison between the human races and animal species."[57] Both men were anticipated by Samuel Morton himself. Alexander von Humboldt, Agassiz's old mentor, had attacked Morton's polygenist ethnology in his major work, *Cosmos* (1849), and had maintained the unity of the human species. Morton wasn't bothered a bit. "[I]t makes little difference," he replied, "whether the mental inferiority of the Negro, the Samoyede, or the Indian, is natural or acquired; for, if they ever possessed equal intelligence with the Caucasian, they have lost it; and if they never had it, they had nothing to lose."[58] So much for the evidence of the tombs.

James was alert to this use and abuse of science. In 1868, around the same time he was reviewing *The Variation of Animals and Plants under Domestication*, he also reviewed a report on the state of anthropology in France by Armand de Quatrefages. Quatrefages (or as James called him in one of his letters home to Henry, "4fages")[59] was a prominent French monogenist. Anthropology had become a subject of great popular interest, James noted in his review, but

[m]uch of this popular interest has anything but a purely scientific source. The zeal for and against orthodoxy has always formed a by no means insignificant factor in the popularity of the question of the

original unity ("Monogenism") or diversity ("Polygenism") of our species, and we in America all know too well how often "science" has been appealed to in the least calm of public assemblies to bear evidence in favor of one view or another of the way in which we ought to treat the inferior races that live with us.[60]

The passage suggests two things: that James was comfortable with a hierarchical conception of race ("the inferior races who live with us"), and that he was doubtful that science had much to do with people's opinions about it.

And if we try to assign a role to scientific and religious beliefs in the politics of slavery, we find that nothing like a pattern emerges. Polygenism would seem the natural scientific theory for a supporter of slavery to hold, but most Southerners who had an opinion on the subject were monogenists. Some Americans felt compelled by their Christian faith to demand the abolition of slavery; some felt compelled by it to defend slavery to the death. There were atheists, like Wendell Holmes, who opposed slavery and there were atheists, like Josiah Nott, who defended it. Samuel Morton was a Philadelphia Quaker; so was Penrose Hallowell. Theodore Parker believed that people with dark skin were inferior; Wendell Phillips believed that all men were created equal. Both risked their lives to free the slaves. The Episcopal bishop of Vermont got into a heated dispute with the Episcopal bishop of Pennsylvania (Alonzo Potter, Agassiz's shipboard crony) over whether the Bible countenanced slavery (Potter thought it did not).[61] Scientific and religious beliefs are important to people; but they are (usually) neither foundational premises, backing one outcome in advance against all others, nor ex post facto rationalizations, disguising personal preferences in the language of impersonal authority. They are only tools for decision making, one of the pieces people try to bundle together with other pieces, like moral teachings and selfish interests and specific information, when they need to reach a decision.

James believed that the theory of natural selection should be regarded like any other idea—as a hypothesis, good in some situations, not so good in others, and not as a basis for values. Natural selection is, after all, a chance process. The finch with the better-adapted beak isn't smarter or nobler than the other finches; it just lucked out. A characteristic that helps an organism survive may be completely undesirable from every other point of view, and survival in one season can mean extinction in the next. The real lesson of *On the Origin of Species* for James—the lesson on which he based his own major work, *The Principles of Psychology* (1890)—was that natural selection has produced, in human beings, organisms gifted with the capacity to make choices incompatible with "the survival of the fittest." There *is* intelligence in the universe: it is ours. It was our good luck that, somewhere along the way, we acquired minds. They released us from the prison of biology.

James's understanding of the Civil War was different, therefore, from Adams's: it had another layer, so to speak. If the war is seen simply as an elemental struggle for existence between two groups, nothing about it deserves either credit or discredit—any more than the surviving finches deserve credit for the shape of their beaks. But if it is seen as the sum of many individual actions, the war was an event bristling with moral significance; for everything human beings do by intelligence rather than instinct, any course of conduct they choose when they might have chosen differently, is a moral action.

The wounds Wilky James suffered in the failed assault of the Fifty-Fourth Massachusetts on Fort Wagner, in the summer of 1863, were severe; he was unconscious when he was brought, all the way from South Carolina, into the Jameses' house in Newport, and it took him a year and a half to recover. He then rejoined his regiment and served until the end of the war. In 1866 he and his brother Bob started a farm in Florida using freed blacks as labor, but the racism of local whites and the falling price of cotton brought the enterprise to a disastrous end. Bob bailed out early; Wilky stayed on for six years, long enough to see that the emancipation for which he had fought had only brought a new kind of misery to black people in the South.

He finally moved to Milwaukee and got a job as a clerk for the railroad, but he became too crippled by kidney problems, a weak heart, rheumatism, and the lingering effects of his wounds to work.

In 1882 Henry James, Sr., died, leaving a will from which (in a bizarre reversion to the behavior of his own father fifty years earlier) he excluded Wilky, on grounds that Wilky had used up his share of the inheritance on the Florida venture. He also reduced the bequest to Bob. Wilky called it "a death stab at the only two of his children who dared fight through the war for the defense of the family."[62] A year later, he died of kidney disease. He was thirty-eight. As a boy, he had been considered the most affable and gregarious of all the James children.

In 1897 the Commonwealth of Massachusetts erected a monument on Boston Common, designed by Augustus Saint-Gaudens and dedicated to Robert Gould Shaw, the man who had led the Fifty-Fourth and had died at Fort Wagner. William James was invited to deliver the oration at the unveiling. It is the finest of his speeches. Shaw had begun the war as a private in the Seventh New York Regiment, and was then commissioned an officer in the Second Massachusetts before accepting, in the winter of 1863, the colonelcy of the Fifty-Fourth, the so-called black regiment. Veterans of all Shaw's regiments were in the audience when James spoke. Shaw was being honored for having been a valiant soldier, James told them, but that was not what made him worthy of a memorial. For the instinct to fight is bred into us through natural selection; it hardly needs monuments or speeches to be reinforced. "[T]he survivors of one successful massacre after another are the beings from whose loins we and all our contemporary races spring," James said; ". . . pugnacity is the virtue least in need of reinforcement by reflection."

What had made Shaw admirable, James explained, was not "the common and gregarious courage" of going off to fight.

It is that more lonely courage which he showed when he dropped his warm commission in the glorious Second to head your dubious fortunes, negroes of the Fifty-fourth. That lonely kind of courage (civic courage as we call it in peace-times) is the kind of valor to which the monuments of nations should most of all be reared, for the survival of the fittest has not bred it into the bone of human beings as it has bred military valor; and of five hundred of us who could storm a battery side by side with others, perhaps not one could be found who would risk his worldly fortunes all alone in resisting an enthroned abuse.

A great nation is not saved by wars, James said; it is saved "by acts without external picturesqueness; by speaking, writing, voting reasonably; by smiting corruption swiftly; by good temper between parties; by the people knowing true men when they see them, and preferring them as leaders to rabid partisans or empty quacks."[63] This is the behavior that monuments should honor.

Shaw was a war hero. He had been shot through the heart on the ramparts of a Confederate fort, about as glorious a death as any soldier's in the Union Army. Saint-Gaudens's monument was Boston's tribute to what it regarded as its own best character, to its fittest. In the minds of everyone listening to James's speech, Shaw was a paragon of breeding. He was the very type of the heroic Brahmin. It was a little perverse, in those circumstances, for James to speak of Shaw's courage as "lonely" or his actions as unpicturesque. But William James was not a Brahmin, and he was not thinking about Robert Shaw. He was thinking about Wilky.

PART THREE

Louis Agassiz and Benjamin Peirce. Peirce is indicating the global
position of Harvard College.

SEVEN

THE PEIRCES

I

"THERE IS A SON OF PROF. PEIRCE, who I suspect to be a very 'smart' fellow with a great deal of character, pretty independent & violent though,"[1] William James wrote to his family soon after he entered the Lawrence Scientific School in the fall of 1861. This was Charles Sanders Peirce. Peirce's field at Lawrence was chemistry, which was also James's field in his first year, though Peirce was in the class ahead of him. Unlike James, he was a college graduate and an all-around prodigy of science, mathematics, and philosophy, and he was not shy about displaying his erudition or his disdain for less initiated minds. It was in James's character not to be put off by a little arrogance in someone he found otherwise intriguing, and he was immediately intrigued by Charles Peirce. He began recording in his class notebook remarks of Peirce's he found provocative—for example: "He makes a test of any man's right to write upon freedom that he explain the authority of a Father over his child. Unknown as yet—no one can even say what relation of Father & child *may* be."[2]

James had personal reasons for being interested in the metaphysics of the relations between fathers and sons, but Peirce had reasons too. His father was one of the most dominant figures at Harvard, Benjamin Peirce, the "Prof. Peirce" of James's letter. And unlike James (or, for that matter, Wendell Holmes), Charles was never interested in distancing himself from his father's views. He began his career under his father's patronage, and for the rest of his life he regarded his work as an amplification and extension of what his father had done. This essentially meant adapting the worldview of science before Darwin to post-Darwinian thought—adapting, that is, a view predicated on the conviction that there is certainty in the universe to views predicated on the presumption that there is not. The task was impossible, and Peirce's philosophical difficulties, though he faced them with genius, were exacerbated by professional difficulties which, because they stemmed in part from a temperamental idiosyncrasy, he could never overcome. But he left behind many brilliant insights on his road to unsuccess. His failure was of a singular and spectacular kind.

2

The Peirces were not quite Brahmins in Dr. Holmes's definition of the term—they were not a line of scholars—but they had been in Massachusetts since the early seventeenth century (the name was English, and originally spelled "Pers"), and they had been associated with Harvard since 1826, which is the year Benjamin Peirce's father, also Benjamin, quit the family shipping business in Salem (it was about to go broke anyway) and moved to Cambridge to become the librarian of Harvard College. The younger Benjamin graduated from Harvard in 1829 in a class that included Holmes, Benjamin R. Curtis, William Henry Channing, and the Transcendentalist James Freeman Clarke. He began teaching at the Round Hill School in Northampton, an experimental secondary school established on the model of the German gymnasium by the historian George Bancroft; but in 1831 he returned to teach at Harvard, and in 1833, at the age of twenty-four, he was appointed professor of mathematics and natural philosophy. In 1842 he was made the first Perkins Professor of Astronomy and Mathematics, a chair he held until his death, in 1880, by which time he had served at Harvard longer than any other member of the faculty but one. (The record holder, as it happened, was a near-namesake, the Reverend John Pierce, the man who once called Emerson's "American Scholar" "unintelligible.")

Peirce was probably the first world-class—in the sense of internationally recognized—mathematician the United States produced. He cultivated a certain wizardliness of manner. His hair was iron-gray, and he wore it long, with, in later years, a thick beard. And his obscurity was legendary. It was said at Harvard that you never realized how truly incapable you were of understanding a scientific matter until Professor Peirce had elucidated it for you. Even his most loyal students admitted that impenetrability was a large part of the appeal. "Few men could suggest more while saying so little, or stimulate so much while communicating next to nothing that was tangible and comprehensible," is the way Franklin Sanborn, the abolitionist whose school in Concord Wilky and Bob James later attended, remembered his classes with Peirce; and almost every memoir of Peirce's pedagogy strikes the same note.[3] Peirce enjoyed the reputation, and even played up to it, because he was a confirmed intellectual elitist, a pure meritocrat with no democracy about him. "Do you follow me?" he is supposed to have asked one of his advanced classes during a lecture. No one did. "I'm not surprised," he said. "I know of only three persons who could."[4]

It was Peirce's view that mathematics was the supreme science, but a science accessible only to a few. This made him an enthusiastic proponent of the elective system at a time when most of the Harvard curriculum was still prescribed. In 1838, as chair of the math department, he persuaded the college to drop the mathematics requirement after the freshman year, with the consequence that in the following year, only eight sophomores in a class of fifty-five took a math course. Peirce undertook to improve on these results, and, over the years, he succeeded. In the class of 1851 only two students elected advanced mathematics, and both dropped it. There were complaints, and a committee of the overseers conducted an investigation, which concluded that "the Perkins professor of mathematics and astronomy is working in his deep mines for one infant prodigy and one eminent Senior." The math requirement was reinstated.[5]

But Peirce had his disciples. In the course of his career he taught three presidents of Harvard: Thomas Hill (1862–69), Charles William Eliot (1869–1909), and A. Lawrence Lowell (1909–33), who wrote a thesis on quaternions (a type of abstract number devised by the Irish mathematician William Rowan Hamilton) and who regarded Peirce as "the most massive intellect with which I have ever come into close contact, and . . . the most inspiring teacher that I ever had."[6] Lowell's predecessor as president of Harvard, Charles Eliot, was less enthusiastic. He once asked in class whether something Peirce had been saying wasn't merely theoretical. "Professor Peirce looked at me gravely," Eliot later recalled, "and remarked gently, 'Eliot, your trouble is that your mind has a skeptical turn. Be on your guard against that tendency or it will hurt your career.' That was new light to me; for I had never thought at all about my own turns of mind. The diagnosis was correct."[7] It was also a foreshadowing of friction to come.

Peirce carried this air of superiority into the public realm. For several years in the 1860s, during the presidency of Thomas Hill, he delivered public lectures at Harvard for advanced students and local residents. A woman was asked after one of his lectures what she had got out of it. "I could not understand much that he said," she explained; "but it was *splendid*. The only thing I now remember in the whole lecture is this—'Incline the mind to an angle of 45°, and periodicity becomes non-periodicity and the ideal becomes real.'"[8] Peirce once represented Harvard at a town meeting at which some college policy was being debated. One of the townspeople, in response to something Peirce had said, called him a nabob. After the meeting, Peirce was asked why he had not responded. He said he hadn't taken it as an insult: "I so enjoyed sitting up there and seeing all that crowd look up to me as a nabob that I could not say one word against the fellow."[9] He cast himself, in short, as the enemy of sentimental egalitarianism.

"Mathematics is the science which draws necessary conclusions," Peirce wrote at the start of what he regarded as his most important work, *Linear Associative Algebra*, published in 1870. "It deduces from a law all its consequences, and develops them into the suitable form for comparison with observation, and thereby measures the strength of the argument from observation in favor of a proposed law or of a proposed form of application of a law."[10] What he meant was that knowledge consists of generalizations that we make up based on our experience of the facts. We observe the orbits of various bodies in space, and then we guess that a law of gravity explains them. But before we formulated a law of gravity, we had invented different hypotheses about the movements of the planets, hypotheses we now regard as mistaken. The problem, as Peirce saw it, is not that there is no single law governing the attraction of bodies in space; the problem is that observation is imperfect. We make mistakes; and even if we didn't, we are unable to observe every case. We have to form a hypothesis based on the limited number of cases we can observe. We then infer (that is, deduce), as a logical consequence of that hypothesis, the existence of further identical cases: in the case of gravity, we assume that a hypothesis drawn from the observation of *some* bodies in space will apply to *all* bodies in space, whether we have observed them or not. If we discover that this is incorrect, if we find cases where our hypothesis breaks down, then we need to revise it. Mathematics, Peirce maintained, is the language in which hypotheses can be formulated most accurately, their logical consequences deduced most rigorously, and their limits thereby ascertained. Mathematics tells us, based on what we do know, what are entitled to infer about what we don't know. If observations continue to conform to our hypothesis, then we have a law, which we may now treat as a fact about the world. Near the end of his life, Peirce summed it up this way:

> Observation supplies fact. Induction ascends from fact to law. Deduction, applying the pure logic of mathematics, reverses the process and descends from law to fact. The facts of observation are liable to the uncertainties and inaccuracies of the human senses; and the first inductions of law are rough approximations to the truth. The law is freed from the defects of observation and converted by the speculations of the geometer into exact form. But it has ceased to be pure induction, and has become ideal hypothesis. Deductions are made from it with syllogistic precision, and consequent facts are

logically evolved without immediate reference to the actual events of Nature. If the results of computation coincide, not merely qualitatively but quantitatively, with observation, the law is established as a reality, and is restored to the domain of induction.[11]

Peirce called himself an idealist, by which he meant that he believed that the universe is knowable because our minds are designed to know it. "In every form of material manifestation," he explained, "there is a corresponding form of human thought, so that the human mind is as wide in its range of thought as the physical universe which it thinks. The two are wonderfully matched."[12] Thought and matter obey the same laws because both have a common origin in the mind of a Creator. This is why the truths of mathematical reasoning (as Peirce often reminded his students) are God's truths. "The universe is a book written for man's reading," he said, echoing a metaphor of Galileo's. "The universal plan is apparent to every mind which yields itself to logical induction."[13] There are, of course, minds that do not yield, or are not capable of yielding, to logical induction. These minds make errors. But our minds are theoretically capable of reasoning logically, and we are thus theoretically capable of knowing the truth about the nature of things. Peirce therefore believed—and this is the distinctive feature of his cosmology—that mathematics is the language not just of scientific thought, but of all thought. Mathematics "belongs to every enquiry," as he put it in *Linear Associative Algebra*, "moral as well as physical."[14]

A person with these views is a person who might be expected to find Louis Agassiz a congenial colleague, and Peirce did. He helped to lobby for the creation of the Lawrence Scientific School, which brought Agassiz to Harvard in 1848, and he became a member of the Lawrence faculty himself. Though they sometimes quarreled— neither man had an elastic ego—Peirce and Agassiz became lifelong professional allies. They were also friends. The Agassizes, after Louis's marriage to Elizabeth Cary, moved into a house across from the Peirces on Quincy Street, and Peirce was, along with Agassiz, one of the eleven founding members of the Saturday Club. Though their specialties were different, they felt they shared a scientific understanding. Peirce once concluded a lecture before the National Academy of Sciences with the remark (not uncharacteristic): "There is only one member of the Academy who can understand my work and he is in South America."[15] It was, of course, the time of the Thayer expedition. And when Agassiz, on that expedition, made his first "discovery" of glacial activity in the Southern Hemisphere, he announced it in the form of a letter to Peirce.

Peirce and Agassiz had more in common than cosmology. They were both institution builders. Before Agassiz came to Harvard, Peirce had already helped to bring about the construction of a new observatory in Cambridge; and in 1849, when Congress established a bureau for the publication of a nautical almanac (so that if the United States went to war American sailors would not be obliged to rely on foreign almanacs), Peirce was appointed consulting astronomer. (The superintendent of the almanac, Charles Henry Davis of the United States Navy, was Peirce's brother-in-law. He, too, had a house on Quincy Street.)

Peirce had also been an early champion of the career of a man named Alexander Dallas Bache, a great-grandson of Benjamin Franklin's. Bache's own scientific talent was small, but his political talent was great, and in 1843 Peirce agitated successfully to get him appointed superintendent of the United States Coast Survey, an agency of the Treasury Department. The Survey (which is now known as the Coast and Geodetic Survey) is the oldest government scientific agency in America; it was established during the administration of Thomas Jefferson and it was already, in 1843, very well funded. In ten years, Bache managed nearly to quintuple its appropriation, mainly by tying its activities to national territorial expansion. He made Peirce his chief astronomical consultant, and in 1852 put him in charge of longitude determination.

By the late 1840s Bache, Peirce, Davis, and Agassiz, along with a few friends, had maneuvered themselves into a position to control, to a great extent, the institutional shape of American science. They were a clique, and were careful to keep it that way. At first they called themselves the Florentine Academy (in honor of an oyster bar favored by Bache), but they eventually became known as the Lazzaroni—"the beggars"—for their success in soliciting government funds for science and then directing the money to work they approved. In 1848 they took over the Association of American Geologists and Naturalists, making membership more selective and changing the name to the American Association for the Advancement of Science, an organization they proceeded to dominate for the next decade. Peirce was elected president twice, in 1853 and 1854. Still, despite their reforms, the Lazzaroni came to find the Association too democratic. They envisioned a national scientific organization modeled on the French Academy—a body that would be frankly elitist, with limited membership, and whose pronouncements would carry incontrovertible authority—and in 1863 they persuaded a wartime Congress to establish the National Academy of Sciences as the official scientific advisory body of the federal government. Bache became its first president. Thus, by the time Charles Peirce was ready to begin his career, he was connected, through his father, to the most powerful figures in American science.

3

Charles was the second of Benjamin Peirce's five children. His mother was the former Sarah Hunt Mills, the daughter of a United States senator, Elijah Hunt Mills, whose seat, after he left office in 1827, had been taken by Daniel Webster. Charles was born in 1839 and named after a distant relative—his father's grandmother's sister's husband, a wealthy man who later left Harvard the money to build Sanders Theatre. Charles grew up in a house (Benjamin called it Function Grove, a reference to the calculus; his nickname for himself was The Functionary) in which Webster, Longfellow, Charles Eliot Norton, Dr. Holmes, and most of the Harvard science faculty were frequent visitors.

Benjamin Peirce was not exactly a wit, but he enjoyed a heavy kind of jocularity; he loved children; and his tastes were, in fact, quite expansive. He believed in the education of the senses. He had four sons and a daughter, and he introduced them to poetry, music, and fine food, and organized recitals and family theatricals. Benjamin indulged all of his children, but he knew that Charles was a prodigy, and he gave his training special attention. They discussed complex mathematical problems together when Charles was a boy, and sometimes stayed up late at night playing games of double dummy (bridge with two of the hands laid out) as a way of acquiring powers of concentration. Charles wrote a history of chemistry when he was eleven; he had his own laboratory when he was twelve; he introduced himself to formal logic by reading his older brother's textbook when he was thirteen. He played chess and invented card tricks. He is supposed to have been able to write with both hands simultaneously—a problem with the right hand and its solution with the left. So that when he entered Harvard, he was thoroughly bored by the level of instruction and extremely undisciplined. He got reported for being drunk in public, and when he graduated, in 1859, he ranked seventy-ninth in a class of ninety.[16]

Charles suffered from facial neuralgia, a chronic and painful neurological disorder, and used opium (then a commonly prescribed painkiller) for relief, apparently developing an addiction. Later in life he relied on ether, morphine, and cocaine as well.[17] He was also an assiduous womanizer. He seems to have seduced a Boston girl named Carrie Badger, the daughter of a shipbuilder, by persuading her to contract a secret marriage with him. When, having got what he wanted, he broke off the relationship, she accused him of trying the same hoax on her best friend.[18] His neuralgia, and the drugs he used to alleviate it, made him susceptible to violent fits of temper. In his senior year, he assembled a private class book in which he wrote thumbnail characterizations of the members of his class. Under his own name, he put: "1 Vanity 2 Snobbishness 3 Incivility 4 Recklessness 5 Lazyness 6 Ill-tempered."[19] It was, by most accounts, an accurate self-portrait.

But it omitted one item, which is that Peirce was also a person who was able to pass such judgments on himself. He *had* a better nature; but he knew, even at twenty, that his personality was his enemy, and his entire adult life was a continual cycle of self-indulgence and self-rebuke. "[My father] took great pains to teach me concentration of mind," he wrote late in life, during one of the self-rebuking phases. "But as to moral self-control, he unfortunately presumed that I would have inherited his own nobility of character, which was so far from being the case that for long years I suffered unspeakably, being an excessively emotional fellow, from ignorance of how to go to work to acquire a sovereignty over myself."[20]

The one group of Boston intellectuals not welcomed at Function Grove was the abolitionists. Benjamin Peirce had good friends in the South—before the war he had been a correspondent of Jefferson Davis—and he also believed that slavery was completely justified. It was a corollary of his cosmology: "No man of the African Race has ever shewn himself capable of any advance in the mathematical *sciences*," he explained in a letter to two Southern friends, John and Josephine Le Conte.

> If therefore we would insist upon it that the knowledge of God in the physical universe was the duty of all men and that this knowledge could only be acquired through mathematics, and that therefore any man of that race should be compelled to become a student of mathematical science—we should labour in vain. We might as well hope to wash out his colour, as we should be attempting to prevent the order of God's creation.

To require black people to civilize themselves "would be for a teacher to introduce the Principia of Newton into the infant school."[21] He opposed universal human suffrage, and he regarded abolitionism as its extreme logical consequence: it made people dissatisfied with the position for which nature had fitted them.[22]

Benjamin Peirce was not a unionist; he was, in his own mind, a secessionist. The more radicalized antislavery politics became in Boston and Cambridge, the more isolated he felt. He was careful about the language he chose to express his views, but he did not conceal them. "If the separation takes place," he wrote to the Le Contes in 1858,

> remember that I am on the other side of Mason and Dixon's line. I belong to the other pole of the Republic. I need the genial clime to warm my cold insides. Take me to your hearts, my true southern

friends. My constant text now is I have seen slavery and I believe in it. You may believe that some looks are averted—but I am persuaded that the earnestness of my sincerity gains at least many listening ears.[23]

The abolitionist Thomas Wentworth Higginson had been one of Peirce's students in an advanced mathematics class at Harvard. In 1854, when he was under indictment for the attempted rescue of the fugitive Anthony Burns, Higginson ran into his old teacher on the street. "[I] told him," Higginson remembered, "that if I were imprisoned I should have time to read Laplace's *Méchanique Céleste* [a classic nineteenth-century treatise on astronomy that Peirce had helped translate]. 'In that case,' said the professor . . . 'I sincerely wish you may be.' "[24]

Charles, all his life, shared his father's views on slavery and on the war. He liked to use the syllogism

> All men are equal in their political rights;
> Negroes are men;
> . ˙ . Negroes are equal in political rights to whites

to illustrate the unreliability of traditional forms of logic.[25] He despised Charles Sumner—"one of the absurdest figures of vanity I have ever laid eyes on,"[26] he later called him. And he dreaded the draft: "I should feel that I was ended & thrown away for nothing,"[27] as he put it in a letter to Bache. After his graduation from Harvard in 1859, his father got him attached as an aide to Coast Survey expeditions—one to Maine, led by Bache, and a second to Mississippi and Louisiana. When he returned, in the spring of 1860, he studied natural classification for six months as a private pupil of Agassiz's and then entered Lawrence. In July 1861, three months after war broke out, he was made assistant computer (a job performing mathematical calculations) in the Coast Survey, an appointment that, he was relieved to learn, exempted him from conscription. He remained an employee of the Survey for thirty years.

Once the war started, Benjamin Peirce dropped his secessionist talk and became, like Agassiz, a devoted Union partisan. He gave money to the Sanitary Commission, the leading Northern war charity (Bache was its vice-president); and his daughter remembered coming in on him one day sitting with Agassiz and discussing some bad news from the front while tears ran down their faces.[28] Still, no member of the Peirce family volunteered or enlisted. A cousin of Charles's on his mother's side, Charley Mills, did serve in the Union Army. He was killed in 1865 at Hatcher's Run, in Virginia, in one of the last battles of the war.

Charles Peirce married Harriet Melusina Fay, called Zina (or sometimes, by her husband, Zero) in 1862. She was the daughter of a Harvard classmate of Benjamin Peirce's and the granddaughter of the Episcopal bishop of Vermont, John Henry Hopkins—the man who had once engaged Alonzo Potter in debate over whether the Bible sanctioned slavery. (Bishop Hopkins believed that it did.) Zina was devout: a religious experience when she was twenty-three had convinced her that the Holy Ghost represented the feminine principle in the universe. Before the ceremony, Charles was baptized into the Episcopal church (the Peirces were Unitarians) and he remained observant all his life. Zina Peirce was also a feminist—a few years after her marriage she established the Cooperative Housekeeping Society in Cambridge, which undertook to relieve married women of domestic drudgery by demanding, among other things, that men pay their wives for housework—and a nativist. She detested Irish-Americans and was an outspoken opponent of immigration. She was, in short, a somewhat flamboyant member of a generally decorous society. "Mrs. P—— is a nice woman," William James's sister Alice reported to him after a visit, "she seems very intelligent and energetic; if only she would refrain from throwing up her head and glaring at one like a wild horse on the prairies."[29] It is a measure of the flamboyance of Charles Peirce, therefore, that in the view of his family, Zina was a moderating influence. "Zina is all the more acceptable," Benjamin wrote to Dallas Bache, "that she has been the instrument of bringing him to a serious state of mind."[30]

In 1864 Bache suffered a stroke, which largely incapacitated him, and in 1867 he died. The National Academy of Sciences, compro-

mised from the beginning by scientific infighting between the Lazzaroni and their enemies, was in disarray. But the Coast Survey was
thriving. It had established itself as the scientific authority backing
the political agenda of national expansion, an activity finally unleashed after decades of constraint imposed by the South's insistence
on coupling territorial acquisition with the spread of slavery. On February 26, 1867, Benjamin Peirce succeeded Bache as superintendent
of the Coast Survey. He held the job until 1874. Those seven years
were the period of the closest association between Charles and his
father, and they were also, in many respects, the period of the most
consistent professional attainment in Charles's life. His father's
stature gave him stature; it also insulated him from the consequences of his temper and his recklessness.

The father and the son were collaborators. A few months after he
took over as superintendent of the Coast Survey, Benjamin was engaged as an expert witness in one of the most celebrated trials of the
century, *Robinson v. Mandell*, popularly known as the Howland will
case. He employed Charles on the assignment, and they testified together. Their efforts did not affect the outcome of the trial, but it
made them notorious, and it is a nice illustration of their scientific
beliefs.

4

The Howland will case was a suit over the disposition of a fortune
made in whaling. Despite the apprehensions of the unionists, the
Civil War did not destroy the New England textile industry. But—
something no one seems to have predicted—it ruined the whaling
business. Before the war, whaling had been one of the most lucrative
growth industries in America. Between 1815 and 1859, the value of
the industry's total production rose by 1,144 percent. Harvesting
whale oil was not like harvesting cotton; it was a high-risk enterprise.
Sailors mutinied and ships sank. Between 1820 and the start of the
Civil War, eighty-eight whaling ship captains out of a single port,
New Bedford, died at sea. Three of them were killed by Pacific
islanders; ten were killed by whales. (One, John Fisher, in 1856, was

last seen holding fast, like Ahab, to the side of a whale.) But the profit from a successful voyage could be prodigious, and even after the industry had fully expanded, in the 1840s, it was returning investors an annual average of almost 15 percent.[31]

Half of all American whalers listed New Bedford as their home port. Their voyages were underwritten by local firms, known as "agencies," which raised the capital needed to mount an expedition and took about a third of the profits in return. Two characteristics distinguished the principals in these New Bedford whaling firms: they were mostly Quakers, and they tended to intermarry. The Quakerism conduced to thrift; the intermarriage conduced to accumulation; and the consequence was that by the 1850s, New Bedford was the wealthiest community, per capita, in Massachusetts, and one of the wealthiest in the United States. And the wealthiest agency in New Bedford was the firm of Isaac Howland, Jr.

Like many successful agents, Isaac Howland, Jr. (a man, history has found it important to record, who weighed less than 100 pounds), commanded a number of income streams. He underwrote whaling expeditions; he was a founder and director of the New Bedford Commercial Bank and of an insurance company associated with it; he owned a retail store; and he was a moneylender. Howland opened his own agency in 1817, and two years later he took in two partners: his son-in-law, whose name (such was the degree of intermarriage among whaling families) was Gideon Howland, and a local businessman named Thomas Mandell. In 1833 a third partner joined the firm, Edward Mott Robinson, a Quaker from Rhode Island, who entered the trade in the customary manner: he married Isaac Howland's granddaughter—Gideon Howland's daughter—Abby. Gideon Howland had another child, Sylvia Ann. She, too, eventually became a partner in the firm. In 1835 Edward and Abby Robinson had a daughter, whom they named Hetty.

Isaac Howland, Jr., died in 1834; his son-in-law, Gideon Howland, died in 1847, and Gideon's daughter Abby died in 1860. In 1861, Abby's widower, Edward Robinson, quit the whaling business and moved to New York City, where he joined a commercial shipping concern, and a year later, the two remaining partners, Thomas Mandell and Sylvia Ann Howland, closed up shop. In forty-five years the firm of Isaac Howland, Jr., and Company had sponsored 171 whaling expeditions, more than any other New Bedford agency would mount in the whole of the nineteenth century.[32]

Whether they were smart or just lucky, the Howland partners got out of the whaling business at exactly the right moment. Between 1860 and 1865, industry revenues fell by 50 percent, in part because the Confederates made Northern whaling ships a military target—they captured or sank forty-six of them during the war, mostly in the Pacific—and in part because the Union government bought forty vessels from whaling firms and sank them outside Charleston and Savannah in an unsuccessful attempt to blockade the harbors. Those eighty-six lost vessels represented a sixth of the American fleet. But the chief reason for the demise of whaling was that the war, by raising demand, spurred the development of the main commercial rivals for whale oil and sperm oil: kerosene and petroleum. When these became cheaper to produce than whale oil, investors found other businesses besides whaling—for instance, railroads—to put their money into. After 1865 the industry was kept alive only by the continually increasing demand for whalebone, a product used in the manufacture of corsets. (It is a little poignant to think of sailors risking their lives in the extremely dangerous business of killing whales in order to keep the United States in a decent supply of affordable corsets. In 1904, with the invention of cheaper flexible steel hoops, the whalebone market collapsed, too, and so did the American whaling industry.)[33]

Edward Robinson died on June 14, 1865, in New York City, leaving an estate worth almost $6 million; less than three weeks later, Sylvia Ann Howland died in New Bedford at the age of fifty-nine. Her estate was worth $2,145,029; she was said to have been, at the time of her death, the richest person in New Bedford. She had never married; she suffered from a spinal affliction, and was obliged to have herself carried around town in a litter. Her death left a single heir-at-law to the entire Howland fortune: her niece (Edward Robinson's daughter), Hetty Robinson.

Hetty Robinson was now thirty years old. She was a handsome

woman, but she had, as it turned out, only one interest in life. By her
father's will, she had received $910,000 outright and the income from
most of the remaining $5 million. Sylvia Ann Howland's will, written
in 1863, ordered that roughly half of her estate be given in bequests
to various individuals and corporations and the rest, $1,132,929, be
placed in trust, with the income to go to Hetty during her lifetime
and the principal to be distributed to the lineal descendants of Sylvia
Ann's grandfather, Gideon Howland, after Hetty's death. The will
named Thomas Mandell, the former Howland partner, as executor.

Hetty Robinson was thus left with nearly $1 million of her own
plus the income for life on some $6 million more. But she did not
feel well used, and on December 2, 1865, she sued. She filed a bill of
complaint in federal court (she was a resident of New York) against
the executor and trustees of her aunt's estate, claiming that, according to an earlier will, the entire estate, minus $100,000 in unspecified
bequests, should have gone to her outright. Hetty produced a copy of
this earlier will, which had been signed on January 11, 1862, by Sylvia
Ann Howland and three witnesses; and she produced as well two
copies of an additional page, signed only by Sylvia Ann Howland, re-
voking "all wills made by me before or after this one." "I give this will
to my niece," it said, "to shew, if absolutely necessary to have it, to
appear against another will found after my death." This piece of paper became known during the trial as "the Second page."[34]

Hetty Robinson swore that she had personally drawn up the 1862
will, including the "Second page," at her aunt's request, and had then
left the will and one signed copy of the "Second page" with her aunt
and taken the duplicate, also signed, back to New York City. She and
her aunt had concealed the "Second page" from the three witnesses
to the will proper, she explained, in order to keep a secret, which was
that the will was one-half of a "mutual will." Sylvia Ann Howland,
Hetty told the court, had become estranged from her brother-in-law,
Edward Robinson, and she wanted to make sure that none of the
Howland fortune ended up in his hands. So she made Hetty promise
to write her own will, excluding her father from any money she might
inherit; in exchange, she agreed to leave all her property, excluding
$100,000 in "presents to my friends and relations," to Hetty, with no

strings attached. The two women agreed that neither would alter her own will without notifying the other (an understanding memorialized on the "Second page"); and since Hetty Robinson had not, she claimed, been notified of her aunt's later will, dated 1863—the will in probate—that will must be invalid. Hetty was therefore asking the court to award her aunt's entire estate to herself. She would take care of the $100,000 in bequests, she said. She said she knew the beneficiaries her aunt had had in mind.[35]

The case presented a number of legal questions (should courts recognize "mutual wills"?, for example), but the trial turned into a protracted and expensive battle over a single piece of evidence. For the defense claimed that Sylvia Ann Howland's signature on the "Second page" of the 1862 will had been forged. An enormous array of legal and professional talent was enlisted to settle this question. The estate's lawyers included a former member of Congress and a retired justice of the Massachusetts Supreme Judicial Court; the lawyers for Hetty Robinson included Benjamin R. Curtis, the man who had resigned from the United States Supreme Court in the aftermath of the Dred Scott decision. The judge in the case, John H. Clifford, was a former governor of Massachusetts.[36] Testimony was taken in camera before a master in chancery; it took over a year to complete and produced a thousand pages of evidence for submission to the U.S. Circuit Court.

There were three signatures in evidence: the one on the 1862 will, which had been witnessed by three people and which both sides agreed was genuine, and the signatures on the two copies of the "Second page," which the estate charged were forgeries. Those signatures did look remarkably alike, and also remarkably like the signature on the will. They even appeared at the same place on the page—the same distance from the margins—as the witnessed signature. Had Hetty drawn up the "Second page" herself, without her aunt's knowledge, and then traced her aunt's signature?

No expense was spared (there was, after all, plenty of money available) to decide this question. Photographs of the three signatures were taken and blown up; photographs were taken of the signatures of other people and introduced into evidence for comparison. Chemists analyzed the ink and engravers evaluated the handwriting. Bankers and brokers were brought in from Boston and New York to testify based on their extensive experience with signatures. The presidents of commercial colleges offered their views. It was, after all, an era in which penmanship was still a professional skill. People made a living from handwriting.

Hetty Robinson's lawyers produced a draftsman, two engravers, a teacher of penmanship, the principal of French's Commercial and Nautical College, and the chief of the electrotype and photographic division of the United States Coast Survey, along with many other witnesses who could claim to be expert in matters of signatures and copying. All duly swore that, in their informed opinion, the signatures on the "Second page" had indeed been written by Sylvia Ann Howland. There was no evidence of forgery.

Hetty's lawyers had another, even more spectacular witness to bring forward. This was John Quincy Adams, grandson of the former president. Adams had found 110 returned checks in his grandfather's papers, which he handed over to an experienced engraver, one J. C. Crossman, who came up with twelve signatures that appeared to be virtually identical. These twelve signatures were photographed, enlarged, and printed on both opaque and oiled (that is, transparent) sheets, so that they could be superimposed on each other and their similarity demonstrated. They were submitted to show that some people do duplicate their signatures with mechanical exactitude.

The lawyers for the Howland estate scoffed at the demonstration. John Quincy Adams, they pointed out, was actually famous for the uniformity of his handwriting; the court was being asked to conclude that because a legend of precision occasionally duplicated his signature, Sylvia Ann Howland, who evidently had been too infirm to have written anything in her life *except* her signature, could have done so as well. "Are not the improbabilities of a race horse, impossibilities for the draft horse?" they inquired.[37] But Hetty's lawyers repeated the demonstration with the signatures of the president of the Suffolk National Bank, Samuel W. Swett. They had Crossman compare Swett's signatures on sixty-four checks, which yielded seventeen "covering" cases. These, too, were photographed, enlarged, and entered into evidence. The same exercise was performed with the signatures of the former treasurer of the Western Railroad, the clerk of the Massachusetts Supreme Judicial Court, a former clerk to the governor of Massachusetts, and the superintendent of the Boston Lunatic Asylum. All exhibited instances of remarkable uniformity.[38]

Hetty Robinson's star expert witnesses were Louis Agassiz and Oliver Wendell Holmes, Sr., men introduced to the court as persons skilled in the use of the microscope. Holmes testified that after inspecting the signatures in question under a microscope, he had found nothing to indicate that different inks had been used on the different documents, or that the signatures on the "Second page" had been traced. Agassiz (recently returned from Brazil) was a good deal more expansive; he treated the lawyers to a disquisition on the microscopic interactions of ink and paper fiber which all parties claimed to have found fascinating. But he came to the same conclusion as his Harvard colleague: examined under a compound microscope, the fibers of the paper revealed no evidence of lead from a pencil (which might have been used to do the tracing), and the distribution of the ink did not suggest unusual movements of the hand when the signatures were written. There was no reason, he concluded, to believe that the signatures on the "Second page" had been forged.

The lawyers for the estate dismissed the testimony of Agassiz and Holmes as academic grandstanding. They had used microscopes a good deal, it was true, but they had never used them to analyze signatures. "When the instrument is arranged over a signature, the microscopist's work is done; and now who is entitled to give opinions as to the picture of *handwriting*? The whole human race can see what is to be seen,"[39] they complained. But the estate produced, in turn, its own battery of experts. These included Albert Sands Southworth, a pioneer of American photography who had also once taught penmanship; the presidents of the Metropolitan Bank of New York, the Webster National Bank, the American Bank Note Company of New York, and the Commercial College in Boston (a man who had testified about handwriting in more than two hundred cases); the assistant paymaster of the Suffolk National Bank; the treasurer of the city of New Bedford; the state assayer of Massachusetts; and (a delightful coup) Joseph E. Paine of Brooklyn, the man who had inscribed the Emancipation Proclamation. But to offset the testimony of Holmes and Agassiz, the defendants needed their own giant of science from Harvard, and the man they selected was Benjamin Peirce. He brought Charles along with him. The Peirces testified on June 5 and 6, 1867.

Charles was deposed first. He explained that his father had given him forty-four samples of Sylvia Ann Howland's signature (not including the ones in dispute) and had identified thirty separate "positions" for him to compare. These "positions" were places in the signature where the formation of a letter required a downward stroke of the pen: there were two such places on each letter S, two on each y, one on each l, and so on. The forty-four signatures had been enlarged and printed on oiled paper, and Charles's assignment was to superimpose each signature on the other forty-three, one at a time, and to count the number of downstrokes that coincided. (A coincidence was counted when two downstrokes were started at the same point on the letter in question in both signatures.) Benjamin had already determined that the downstrokes in the disputed signature (the signature on the "Second page") coincided with the downstrokes in the genuine signature (the one on the will itself) at all thirty positions. What he was attempting to determine was the likelihood that the disputed signature was produced independently of the signature on the will proper—the likelihood that the degree of coincidence had happened by chance.

Two of the reproductions were flawed, so Charles ended up comparing forty-two signatures. That required 861 comparisons; but since thirty separate "positions" had to be compared in each case, he had to tabulate the results of a total of 25,830 comparisons. (People who did this sort of work in the nineteenth century were not called "computers" for nothing.) Charles found 5,325 cases of coincidence—5,325 out of 25,830 possible cases in which the start of a downstroke in one signature coincided with the start of the same downstroke on the same letter in another signature. In other words, one out of every five of Sylvia Ann Howland's downstroke positions overlapped. To put it technically, the relative frequency of coincidence in the position of Sylvia Ann Howland's downstrokes was one-fifth. (The Peirces had hypothesized, of course, that each downstroke was an independent event—that is, that the existence of a coincidence on the first downstrokes in two signatures does not affect the probability that the second downstrokes will also coincide, and so on.) Charles telegraphed this information to his father, who was at the Coast Survey offices in Washington.[40]

Benjamin Peirce was now supplied with two pieces of information: the total number of signature comparisons (861) and the relative frequency of coincidence of the downstrokes (one-fifth). He proceeded to calculate the number of comparisons in which—if the coincidences were occurring by chance—just one of the thirty downstrokes should overlap, the number in which two should overlap, and so on, up to the number of cases in which all thirty could be expected to overlap. He ended up with the following table:

NUMBER OF COINCIDING DOWNSTROKES (out of a possible 30)	NUMBER OF CASES OF EXPECTED COINCIDENCE (out of 861)
3	68
4	114
5	148
6	154
7	132
8	95
9	58
10	31
11	14
12	6

Number of cases of less than 3 or more than 12 expected coincidences: 41.

Up in Cambridge, Charles was making the same tabulation by actually counting the number of cases in which one downstroke, two downstrokes, three downstrokes, and so on coincided. These were his results:

NUMBER OF COINCIDING DOWNSTROKES	NUMBER OF CASES OF ACTUAL COINCIDENCE
3	97
4	131
5	147
6	143
7	99
8	88
9	55
10	34
11	17
12	15

Cases of less than 3 or more than 12 actual coincidences: 35. (Charles counted 15 cases of 2 coincidences, and 20 cases of more than 12.) In other words, Charles's results, produced by counting actual matches, approximated Benjamin's predictions, produced mathematically, remarkably closely.

When he was deposed on the day after his son, Benjamin Peirce was asked what conclusion he drew from these results. He had an impressive answer prepared. The chance that Sylvia Ann Howland could have produced two signatures in which all thirty downstrokes coincided was, he said, one in 5^{30}, "or, more exactly it is once in . . . two thousand six hundred and sixty-six millions of millions of millions of times, or 2,666,000,000,000,000,000,000." Such a number, he advised the court,

> transcends human experience. So vast an improbability is practically an impossibility. Such an evanescent shadow of probability cannot belong to actual life. They are unimaginably less than those least things which the law cares for.
> The coincidence which is presented in this case cannot there-

fore be reasonably regarded as having occurred in the ordinary course of signing a name. Under a solemn sense of the responsibility involved in the assertion, I declare that the coincidence which has here occurred must have had its origin in an intention to produce it. . . . [I]t is utterly repugnant to sound reason to attribute this coincidence to any case but design.[41]

He hadn't even bothered, he added, to factor in the likelihood of any two signatures being exactly the same distance from the margins of the paper, as was the case with all three of the signatures in question. If he had, he estimated that this would have increased the improbability of mere coincidence by at least a factor of 10, and probably by a factor of 100.

The lawyers for Hetty Robinson treated the whole demonstration as mathematical voodoo, and they had some fun during oral arguments that fall, when the testimony was presented to the Circuit Court, ridiculing Benjamin Peirce's portentousness. "[A] most extraordinary piece of evidence drawn from the shades of the academy," Hetty's lead attorney, Sidney Bartlett, told the judges. "It is a pleasure to read it, may it please your Honors, to me, illustrating as it does the fervor and breadth with which science, only grant it its postulates, can express itself. Give it its postulates, and nothing can be more beautiful to read; but it is the most baseless statement that ever came from a learned man."[42]

Many people who were not parties to the lawsuit had a similar reaction. There was, they felt, an air of the parlor trick about the Peirces' performance—the father in Washington predicting with uncanny accuracy the figures the son in Cambridge would get when he tallied up the comparisons. And Peirce's fantastically infinitesimal number, $1/5^{30}$, representing the odds that the similarities in the disputed signatures had occurred by chance, seemed a hyperbolic flourish. People didn't like the idea that something it was humanly possible to do could be declared inconceivable by statistics; it was an inverse case of the irritation people feel when they are told that their own behavior is statistically normal. It was as though some boundary had been transgressed, as though Sylvia Ann Howland had somehow been denied the faculty of free will. "It is always a person's *intention* to make the signature similar to others as nearly as possible every time," complained a letter writer in the *Nation* a few weeks after the Peirces' testimony was presented in court. "The elements of will and desire unfit it for judgment by such laws. Figures can be prostituted to prove almost anything, and were it not for Prof. Peirce's high position, one might be led to think his evidence nothing more than a special plea. And the tone of his testimony is arrogant and positive, as if he were charging the judges."[43]

But of course Benjamin Peirce did not believe that "elements of will and desire" made a thing unfit for mathematical reasoning, and the procedure he had followed with the signatures in the Howland will case was exactly the procedure he would articulate in *Linear Associative Algebra* three years later. He started with an idea: that hidden within the randomness of the collection of different Sylvia Ann Howland signatures was a certain kind of statistical order, an idea that might be tested by comparing pairs of signatures in the way he and his son devised. The empirical test of this idea yielded a hypothesis: that the relative frequency of coincidence in the downstrokes in Sylvia Ann Howland's signatures was one-fifth. Peirce's next step was to deduce the logical consequence of this hypothesis, which was that the number of coincidences would be distributed among the 861 signature comparisons in a particular way. He then compared the results he had arrived at by calculation (the distribution that *ought* to exist if one-fifth is the frequency when the coincidences occur by chance) with his son's observations (the actual distribution in the samples at hand), and the fit confirmed the hypothesis.

If Charles had already determined that the relative frequency of coincidence was one-fifth, why did he and his father have to calculate the way the coincidences were distributed? Because if the actual distribution had differed significantly from the predicted distribution, then either the coincidences were not occurring by chance or the sample of forty-two signatures was not a random sample. By establishing that the actual distribution matched the predicted one, the Peirces had verified that one-fifth was indeed the relative frequency with which coincidences appeared by chance. The final step was simply a matter of raising that fraction to the power represented by the total number of coincidences required for all thirty positions to match—each pair of downstrokes having a one in five chance of coinciding—in order to arrive at a numerical expression of the probability that the thirty-for-thirty rate of coincidence in the disputed signatures had occurred by chance, or, to put it another way, at a numerical expression of how often Sylvia Ann Howland could be expected to duplicate her signatures unintentionally but exactly: once in every 2,666,000,000,000,000,000,000 attempts.

5

In the end, all the expensive evidence about the signatures turned out to be irrelevant. In its verdict, handed down in 1868, the Circuit Court held that Hetty Robinson's testimony on her own behalf during the trial had violated a federal statute prohibiting parties to a suit over a will from giving testimony unless called by the other side or commanded to testify by the court. Since Hetty was the only witness supporting the contention that her and her aunt's wills had been mutual, "the court is of the opinion that the contract is not proved."[44] The estate won. The Howland will case was decided on a technicality.

The plaintiff had already skipped town. In 1867, while her case was still under way, Hetty Robinson had married Edward Green, a wealthy Vermont businessman. Seeing the shadow of a criminal fraud charge across her path if the signatures in dispute were proved to be forgeries, she took the precaution of moving to London, where she and her husband lived for eight years, and where they had two children. After their return, the Greens moved to New York City, and the money that had come out of the New Bedford whaling industry was put to work on Wall Street. Hetty Green became a moneylender, a phenomenally successful one—eventually, a character in the popular imagination. As one might imagine, she proved to be a ruthless businesswoman and a great miser. She became known as the Witch of Wall Street, and when she died, in 1916, at the age of eighty-two, her fortune was estimated to be between $100 and 200 million. The *New York Times*, in its obituary, called her the richest woman in the country.

Hetty Green's estate, of course, was not entirely hers to dispose of: she had had only a life interest in most of the money she had inherited back in the 1860s. That was, of course, the situation she was trying to undo in her lawsuit. After her death, the portion of her wealth that derived from Sylvia Ann Howland's estate reverted, under the terms of the will, to the lineal descendants of Gideon Howland. Many people showed up to claim the distinction. The huge sum Hetty Green had made on her own she kept, in Quaker fashion, within the family. It finally reverted to her daughter, who died, childless, in 1951. She gave away $100 million. The Howland whaling fortune was not finally disbursed until 1952.[45]

The Peirces' testimony was therefore legally moot. But the reason it remained so controversial was that it was based on a mathematical "law" that had entered scientific thinking only a few decades earlier, and that many people in 1868 found distressing, and even shocking. This was the law of errors—one of the most far-reaching inventions of the nineteenth century, and an idea central to the thought of Charles Peirce.

EIGHT

THE LAW OF ERRORS

I

THE LAW OF ERRORS AROSE OUT of two closely related bodies of thought, both of which had their origins in the seventeenth century: probability theory, which sought to understand chance events, such as throwing dice, and statistics, which sought to measure large-scale fluctuating phenomena, such as birthrates and life expectancies. These two lines of thought converged around 1800 in the field of astronomy.[1]

If a team of astronomers wishes to chart the position of a star, and its members make a series of individual observations of that star, the results they get will almost always vary. The same problem arises when a single astronomer makes multiple observations of the same star. In fact, when we measure anything repeatedly with exactitude, we generally get discrepancies in the results. In the case of astronomy, the discrepancies can have many causes: changes in atmospheric conditions, the effects of temperature or humidity on the apparatus, unequal powers of eyesight among the observers, and plain old human ineptitude. But these causes are largely un-

Charles S. Peirce in 1859, the year he graduated from
Harvard, ranked 79th in a class of 90.

detectable (otherwise we could correct for them). So when we don't know what is producing the discrepancies, how do we know which result is the usable one and which are the errors?

The solution to this problem was borrowed from probability theory—specifically, from a formula published in 1738 by a mathematician named Abraham De Moivre, a Huguenot who had emigrated to England, in the second edition of a work called *The Doctrine of Chances*.[2] When you roll two dice, you get one of thirty-six possible combinations (one and one, one and two, one and three, and so on, up to six and six). These thirty-six combinations can produce eleven possible totals (two through twelve). The total with the greatest likelihood of coming up is seven, since a seven can be produced by any of six different combinations (one and six, two and five, three and four, four and three, five and two, six and one). Only five of the thirty-six combinations will produce an eight or a six, only four will produce a nine or a five, and so on, down to the two and the twelve. If you chart on a graph the results of many rolls of the dice, with the totals (two through twelve) on the horizontal axis and the number of times each total comes up on the vertical axis, you will eventually get points that connect to form a bell-shaped curve. The highest point on this curve will be at seven on the horizontal axis (approximately one-sixth of your throws will produce some combination of numbers adding up to seven), and the curve will slope downward symmetrically on either side to two at one end and twelve at the other.

The basis of the law of errors in astronomy was the discovery that multiple observations of a star also tend to conform to a bell-shaped curve—as does any group of measurements of a fixed object. You can think of the act of measuring on the analogy of shooting arrows at a target. Some shots will be above the bull's-eye, some to the right or left, some below. But if you shoot enough arrows, always aiming at the center of the target, the misses will sort themselves out like the throws of the dice: many arrows will hit close to the bull's-eye, some will clearly miss the bull's-eye but strike the target, and a few will sail past the target altogether. And so with astronomical observations: although the differences in the results are produced by chance (since none of the errors is deliberate), they nevertheless distribute themselves more or less symmetrically around a mean, and this mean can be taken as the likeliest position of the star. The reasoning is that if there is no single hidden variable, no unknown cause responsible for the discrepancies, a measurement is just as likely to be too great as it is to be too small.

In the archery example, we know where the bull's-eye is even if none of the arrows strikes it. How do we make this determination in the star example, where it is precisely the center of the observational target we are seeking? The solution to this problem became known as "the method of least squares": the likeliest position is the one such that the sum of the squares of the differences between it and each of the aberrant observed positions is the smallest possible. This position may not correspond to any actual observation, just as no arrows may have hit the bull's-eye. The bull's-eye is "implied" by the distribution of the shots that miss it, and the position of the star is the position implied by—is the arithmetical mean of—the discrepant observations. Using the method of least squares to find the mean of a series of numbers or equations is the equivalent of finding the center of gravity in a body of matter.

When the object being observed is fixed, like a star, determining the mean is a relatively simple arithmetical calculation. When the object is moving, like a comet, the calculation is much more difficult, since each determination of a comet's orbit consists of three (or more) observations of the comet over time, from which an equation is derived that expresses the curve of the comet's path through space. The computational problems involved in taking the mean of these equations by the method of least squares was worked out by the German mathematician Carl Friedrich Gauss, who was the first person to use the method, around 1795; the French mathematician Adrien Marie Legendre, who was the first person to publish it, in 1805; and the French scientist Pierre-Simon Laplace, who ended up getting most of the credit.[3]

Laplace was a man skilled at self-positioning. The span of his career—from 1773, the year of his election to the Académie Royale des Sciences, to 1827, the year of his death—obliged him to respect the dispositions of, successively, a king, a revolutionary government, a republican government, a dictatorship, an emperor, and a king. He managed it well enough for Louis XVIII (the last in the series) to make him a marquis. But he was a formidable scientist, and in the case of the law of errors, his work deserved the attention it received.

Laplace was, in effect, his own popularizer. He produced two major scientific works: a five-volume work on astronomy, *Traité de mécanique céleste* (1798–1825), and a mathematical study of probability theory, *Théorie analytique des probabilités* (1812). But he also published nontechnical versions of both books: *Exposition du système du monde* (1796) and *Essai philosophique sur les probabilités* (1814). This enabled his ideas to reach both specialists and nonspecialists, and they enjoyed tremendous influence as a result.

Laplace's astronomical work was a completely mechanical explanation of the solar system based on Newtonian principles—thus the term, which he coined, "celestial mechanics." (Napoleon is supposed to have asked Laplace why the word "God" did not appear in his book. "Sire," Laplace replied, "je n'ai pas besoin de cette hypothèse"—"I have no need of that hypothesis.")[4] Laplace's popular version of his astronomy, the *Système du monde*, was famous for introducing what came to be known as the nebular hypothesis, the theory that the solar system was formed by the condensation, through gradual cooling, of the gaseous atmosphere (the nebulae) surrounding the sun. (Immanuel Kant had proposed a similar theory earlier, but Laplace was apparently unaware of it.) Laplace regarded this hypothesis as speculative, and the last thing he intended by it was to suggest that the solar system "develops" in an evolutionary sense. On the contrary, he was trying to explain why the solar system, having come into being, persists in a stable form; he even alluded to the work of Georges Cuvier, Agassiz's old teacher, who had maintained the permanence of species.[5] But in the years after Laplace's death, the nebular hypothesis was picked up by evolutionists—in particular, Herbert Spencer—as the astronomical corollary of geological and biological theories of development.

The impact of Laplace's writings about probability was a lot closer to what their author had in mind. This work was influential for two reasons. First, Laplace was explicit about the probabilistic nature of statistical calculations. When we try to determine the orbit of a comet or the mortality rate of a population, we are attempting a precise measurement of a phenomenon that eludes precision. Observations of the same comet differ; the annual number of deaths fluctuates. How can we know with absolute certainty which observation or which number is the correct one? Laplace's point was that we can never know with absolute certainty; we can only know with greater or lesser degrees of probability. The question we are asking ourselves when we use the method of least squares is, essentially, What are the chances that our best guess about the orbit of this comet is right? Probability theory—what De Moivre had called "the doctrine of chances"—demonstrates that just as the more times we throw the dice, the ratio of sevens to the other ten possible outcomes will get closer and closer to one-to-six, so the chances that the mean of our measurements is not the correct measurement will grow smaller and smaller the more measurements we take. When the chances of being wrong become infinitesimal, we have arrived, if not at complete certainty, at virtual certainty. This is the operation the Peirces were performing on Sylvia Ann Howland's signatures. They were asking the question, How likely is it that we would be wrong if we decided that the signatures on the will were traced? They concluded that the odds were 2,666,000,000,000,000,000,000 to 1 in their favor. Not absolute certainty, but most people would take the bet.

The genius of statistics, as Laplace defined it, was that it did not ignore errors; it quantified them. In the case of the bell-shaped curve—or the normal distribution, as it is also known—the deviations from the mean are as predictable as the mean itself (which is why Benjamin Peirce could predict the number of times the signatures would have more or less than six coinciding downstrokes). The right answer is, in a sense, a function of the mistakes. By uncoupling the idea of precision from the idea of a single absolute value, statistics and probability theory allowed scientists to achieve far greater degrees of precision than they had ever imagined possible. Statistics conquered uncertainty by embracing it. At the beginning of the nineteenth century, the English astronomer royal, Nevil Maskelyne, fired one of his assistants for coming up with observations that differed consistently from his own. By the 1820s, astronomers had developed the concept of the "personal equation," which measures the tendency of an individual observer, by virtue of whatever idiosyncrasy, to deviate from the mean. All Maskelyne had to do was discount the assistant's results by his "personal equation" and he would have had usable estimates. The law of errors quantified subjectivity.[6]

Laplace saw no reason to limit probability theory to comets and dice, and this was the second reason for the influence of his book. What the law of errors (whose curve, he showed, need not always be symmetrically shaped) suggested was that all phenomena that vary vary within ascertainable limits. They have a central limit, which represents their most probable state, and they have outer limits, which represent possible but improbable extreme states; and the dispersion of variations within these limits can be measured, giving us the likelihood of any particular state deviating from the mean. (This measurement became known as "probable error." Dispersions obviously differ: the arrows of the expert archer cluster differently from the arrows of the novice, and therefore have a different degree of probable error.) Laplace proceeded to demonstrate, in the *Essai sur les probabilités*, the ways that probability could be used to assess the reliability of legal testimony and the fairness of verdicts, to ascertain rates of mortality and marriage, to predict the ratio of male to female births, and to calculate premiums for insurance and annuities.

In short, Laplace extended the application of probability from physics to people, with the promise that events that seem random and unpredictable—such as, in his most celebrated illustration, the number of letters that end up every year in the Paris dead-letter office—can be shown to obey hidden laws. People marry and letters get misaddressed for apparently subjective and unreproducible reasons, but statistics reveals that the total number of marriages or of dead letters every year gravitates, as if by necessity, around a mean value. The consistency of that value, Laplace thought, signified the operation of a natural law. "All events, even those which, by their insignificance, seem not to follow the great laws of nature, follow them as necessarily as the revolutions of the sun," he wrote.

> In our ignorance of the ties that bind these events to the entire sys-
> tem of the universe, we have taken them to depend on final causes
> or on chance, depending on whether they occur and are repeated
> with regularity or without apparent order. But these imaginary
> causes have gradually receded with the widening scope of our
> knowledge, and they will disappear entirely before a sound philoso-
> phy, which sees in them nothing but the expression of our ignorance
> of the true causes.[7]

He had pointed the way from celestial mechanics to social mechanics.

2

Benjamin Peirce was a disciple of Laplace. Peirce's teacher when he
was a schoolboy in Salem, Nathaniel Bowditch, was the author of
the standard English translation of Laplace's *Traité de méchanique
céleste*; Peirce helped to check the proof sheets while he was a student at Harvard College. (This was the book he hoped Thomas Higginson would have time to read if he went to prison for violating the
Fugitive Slave Act.) Peirce thought that "no grander conception of
the physical universe has ever been presented to philosophical discussion"[8] than the nebular hypothesis. And a great deal of his own
renown derived, in fact, from his work as an astronomer.

He analyzed the rings of Saturn (a popular nineteenth-century astronomical problem) and concluded that they must be fluid. (This
turned out to be mistaken.)[9] And he caused a small scandal by announcing that the discovery of the planet Neptune, in 1846, had
been a "happy accident." Neptune was located by inferring its position from the perturbations of Uranus: that is, since something was
interfering with Uranus's orbit, making it deviate from a normal el-
lipse, there must be an eighth planet somewhere in the solar system
exerting gravitational pull. Peirce argued that the calculations used
by the astronomers initially credited with the discovery, Urbain-Jean-
Joseph Le Verrier and Johann Gottfried Galle, were wrong: Neptune's actual orbit, seen from Earth, just happened to coincide with
their incorrectly computed orbit in the year 1846, a coincidence that

could have occurred, according to Peirce, only once every 650 years. Neptune had been simultaneously discovered by a British mathematician, John Couch Adams, working with the astronomer John Frederick William Herschel, and negotiations over priority were delicate. The Royal Astronomical Society of London asked Peirce to suppress his paper calling the discovery accidental on grounds that its conclusions were improbable. "But it is still more improbable that there could be an error in my calculations," Peirce is supposed to have replied, and he published the paper anyway. (It was later shown to have been mistaken.)[10]

Peirce also made a contribution to the method of least squares. There had always been a question about what to do with observations (known as "outliers") that are wildly discrepant from the mean. Obviously the observer has made a huge mistake somewhere—for example, reversing the digits when transcribing a number—but the fundamental premise of the law of errors is that mistakes should never be thrown out. How are astronomers supposed to distinguish between inaccuracies and sheer blunders? The practical solution had been to use common sense. You just *know* that some results are off the wall, mathematicians like Gauss thought, and you don't need any better reason for dropping them out of your calculations. This was not scientific enough for Peirce, and in 1852 he published a paper on the "Criterion for the Rejection of Doubtful Observations." His purpose, he explained, was "to produce an exact rule for the rejection of observations, which shall be legitimately derived from the fundamental principles of the calculus of probabilities." (For the record, the rule he came up with was: *the proposed observations should be rejected when the probability of the system of errors obtained by retaining them is less than that of the system of errors obtained by their rejection multiplied by the probability of making so many, and no more, abnormal observations.*)[11] This became known as "Peirce's criterion"; it was widely adopted in the United States, though never accepted in Europe. (It, too, was eventually shown to be mistaken.)[12]

Measuring things is what, as scientists, the Peirces did. Benjamin used the method of least squares regularly in his work as an astronomer, and in his work as a geographer after Bache put him in charge of longitude determinations at the Coast Survey. Charles not only used the method on his many expeditions for the Survey and published papers on the theory of errors; he became one of the leading metrologists of the nineteenth century. (Metrology is the science of measurement.) His perfection of the pendulums used to measure the force of gravity (the method used for attempting to determine the shape of the geoid—that is, the earth at sea level) made him famous in Europe, and he established a universal standard for the meter based on the wavelength of light. It was therefore natural for the Peirces to assess the validity of the signatures in the Howland will case by constructing an error curve. The whole history of the fields in which they had been trained told them that such things are regulated by laws.

What made the law of errors so important to nineteenth-century thought, though, was not only its application to the study of nature. The realization that even "errors," even the unpredictable and accidental fluctuations that make phenomena seem to deviate from their normal "laws," are themselves bound by a statistical law thrilled scientists. But what captivated, and sometimes appalled, the popular imagination was the application of the law of errors—hinted at by Laplace in his discussion of dead letters and marriage rates—to the study of human beings. What scandalized people about the Peirces' testimony in the Howland will case was their apparent reduction of a human activity—signing one's name—to a set of numbers. For in the 1860s such reductions had a particular philosophical implication. They were understood to point toward determinism.

3

The man who seized Laplace's hint most firmly and exploited it most fully was Adolphe Quetelet.[13] Quetelet was an ambitious Belgian mathematician—he also wrote poetry, literary criticism, and an opera libretto—who, when he was still in his early twenties, helped persuade the government of Belgium to build an observatory, and then to give him a grant to go to Paris so he could learn some astronomy. He arrived in 1823. Whether he studied with Laplace himself, who

was then seventy-four years old, is unclear, but it is clear that he became infatuated with probability theory, and especially with the idea
of adapting the law of errors to social data. Paris is supposed to be a
place where people fall in love. Adolphe Quetelet fell in love with a
curve.

Quetelet did study astronomy in Paris, but he also studied statistics and probability theory with the leading French statistician,
Joseph Fourier; and when he returned to Belgium (where he was appointed astronomer royal) he began to collect demographic and meteorological data and to analyze it statistically. This was something
statisticians had been doing since the seventeenth century. The term
"statistics" is etymologically linked to "state": statisticians were sometimes called "statists," and before the adoption of the German term
Statistik, their work was referred to, in English, as "political arithmetic." A statistician was someone who monitored the state of the
state—population, mortality, marriage, disease, crime, climate, and
so on. But Quetelet did something new with his statistical data: he
analyzed it in terms of the law of errors. He published some of his results in 1835 in a two-volume work called *Sur l'homme et le deve-
loppement de ses facultés*. It was a blockbuster.

"Man is born, grows up, and dies according to certain laws which
have never been studied,"[14] Quetelet began, and he printed a table
showing that the annual number of murders reported in France from
1826 to 1831 was relatively constant. This was not, perhaps, an unexpected finding. But Quetelet's table also showed that the proportion
of murders committed with guns each year was also relatively constant, as were the proportions of murders committed using swords,
knives, canes, stones, cutting and stabbing instruments, kicks and
punches, strangulation, drowning, and fire. He concluded that although we may not know who will kill whom by what means, we do
know, with a high degree of probability, that a certain number of
murders of a certain type will happen every year in France. This
number is the mean of the annual totals; according to Quetelet's
adaptation of the astronomer's error curve, it constitutes the "true"
rate of (say) French murder-by-sword. Higher or lower totals in a particular year are, in effect, "errors," whose probable range can be pre-

dicted. There was, as Quetelet said elsewhere, "a sort of French national budget of the scaffold, whose regularity is, without doubt, more reliable than the French financial budget."[15] The table of murders categorized by technique was the first in a staggering array of data, all of which Quetelet showed to follow regular patterns, and all of which, he argued, demonstrated the existence of social laws just as determinate as the law of gravity. He called the science he had invented *physique sociale*—social physics.

Quetelet was not coy about generalization, and two of the claims he made in *Sur l'homme* attracted special attention. The first was that since (as he believed he had shown) there is a "law" governing the amount of crime in a society, moral responsibility for crime must lie with the society and not with the individual criminal. "It is society that prepares the crime and . . . the guilty person is only the instrument who executes it,"[16] is the rather dramatic way he expressed it. People who murder—like people who marry and people who commit suicide—are only fulfilling a quota that has been preset by social conditions. The rate of murder or marriage might go up or down in certain periods, but Quetelet thought that these fluctuations could be explained on the analogy of perturbations in the orbit of a planet. Variations in the murder rate do not mean that there is an element of chance in the number of murders in a given year; it means that some unidentified transient cause is pulling the curve out of alignment. In the long run, planets adhere to their normal orbits, and societies produce their normal number of murders. This was, of course, a determinist conclusion.

The second influential generalization Quetelet drew from his research was the concept of *l'homme moyen*—the average man. The average man (strictly speaking, the "mean" man) is a statistical fiction, but he became one of the leading characters in nineteenth-century thought. "*L'homme moyen* is in a nation what the center of gravity is in a planet," is the way Quetelet explained his concept: *l'homme moyen* sets the standard against which deviance in a particular society is measured. And this standard is by no means a morally neutral one. It represents the bull's-eye, so to speak, at which that society is aiming. "An individual who sums up, for a given era, all the qualities of the average man will represent everything that is grand, beautiful, and good," as Quetelet explained it in *Sur l'homme*.[17] The appeal of *l'homme moyen* was that it represented a norm that was derived not philosophically or theologically but scientifically, from the actual social data of a nation. And like all early statisticians, Quetelet believed in the distinctive character of national types: the distinctive character of specific nations was, after all, what statisticians studied. The French *homme moyen* and the Belgian *homme moyen* were different entities.

Quetelet's most famous case study concerned, in fact, the Scottish *homme moyen*. A few years after publishing *Sur l'homme*, he came across a list of the height and chest measurements of some 5,738 Scottish soldiers in an old issue of the *Edinburgh Medical and Surgical Journal*. (Presumably these had originally been made for the purpose of ordering uniforms.) Quetelet analyzed the chest measurements and found extreme limits of 33 inches (three soldiers) and 48 inches (one soldier), and a central limit between 39 inches (1,073 soldiers) and 40 inches (1,079 soldiers). (Strangely, he did not pay attention to height, which might be assumed to bear some relation to the significance of chest size.) He then calculated the probable results of drawing 999 balls, one at a time, from an urn containing an equal number of white and black balls, replacing the ball each time (a procedure equivalent to flipping a coin), and showed that the bell-shaped curve resulting from this procedure matched (more or less) the curve produced by the measurements of Scottish chests. He concluded that chest circumferences among Scotsmen are distributed according to the law of errors.[18]

This was a big conceptual leap. Quetelet was essentially claiming that the distribution arrived at by measuring 5,738 Scottish chests is analogous to the distribution you would arrive at if you measured one Scottish chest 5,738 times—since that, after all, is the procedure the law of errors was invented to regularize. What enabled Quetelet to make this leap was the astronomical basis of his notion of *l'homme moyen*. He thought that Scottish social conditions produce men of a certain-sized chest (39.83 inches was the mean of his data) in the same way that a planet's mean distance from the sun determines its orbit. Extraneous causes—perhaps an unusual diet—might produce Scotsmen with smaller or larger chests; but these were "perturbations." As long as conditions in Scotland remain relatively constant, the norm for male chest size will be 39.83 inches. Quetelet published his findings in a paper in 1844 and then in a popular work, *Lettres à S. A. R. Duc Règnant de Saxe-Coburg et Gotha sur la théorie des probabilités,* in 1846.

Quetelet was a sociologist, not a physiologist—he explained things by reference to society, rather than to biology—and this gave his categorizations of human types a different emphasis from the categorizations of a scientist like Samuel Morton. The discovery of different national *hommes moyens* implied the existence of different social conditions operating as causes on human development. Types are not providentially ordered once and for all (as they are in Morton's and Agassiz's thinking); if you change the social conditions, you will, eventually, change the type. Quetelet's was a theory superficially much closer to Darwin's. It did not require the hypothesis of a god.

Quetelet did, in fact, practice the method of least squares on racial types. (He seems to have practiced the method of least squares on almost everything: one of the "laws" he discovered was that Belgian lilacs bloom when the sum of the squares of the mean daily temperature since the last frost adds up to $[4264° \text{ C}]^2$.)[19] In 1846 twelve Indians from North America came through Brussels, and Quetelet took their measurements; in 1854, he did the same thing with a small number of Negroes. On the whole, he thought, the Indians were better physical specimens than most Belgians; but in general, statistical analysis indicated no significant variations in physique among the races. "The major features of the human species," he concluded, "appear to be pretty much the same."[20] He thought his results supported a belief in the unity of the species.

Quetelet was an obsessive and, from a scientific point of view, something of a crank, but he was also a brilliant promoter of statistical methods. He helped found statistical organizations all over Europe, and many scientists undertook to imitate the methods that had produced the "average man": one analyzed samples taken from a urinal in a train station through which Europeans of many nationalities

passed, in an effort to determine "average European urine."[21] German scientists tended to be skeptical of Quetelet's results: it was
pointed out that the "laws" announced in *Sur l'homme* were based on
only six years' worth of data (the conclusions about racial physique
were, similarly, drawn from tiny samples), and that many social phenomena in fact exhibit wide variations.[22] The French, on the other
hand, were highly receptive. It had been from the French, after all,
that Quetelet had learned his technique, and many French scientists
had already adopted statistical methods. Charles Louis, the medical
researcher under whom Oliver Wendell Holmes, Sr., once studied,
was an early practitioner of medical statistics, and Holmes's famous
paper on childbed fever was statistical in spirit: it based its conclusion that the disease is spread by germs carried by the obstetrician on
data showing that some doctors have many patients who die from it
while some have none.

Quetelet's work was especially well received in Great Britain.
When *Sur l'homme* appeared, in 1835, the *Athenaeum* gave it a three-
part review, concluding with the announcement: "We consider the
appearance of these volumes as forming an epoch in the literary history of civilization."[23] When the *Lettres* was translated, in 1849, it was
reviewed by the astronomer John Herschel, who praised the application of the law of errors to social phenomena as a major scientific advance. Quetelet's most zealous British disciple, though, was Henry
Thomas Buckle. Buckle published the first volume of his *History of
Civilization in England* in 1857, when he was thirty-six. He presented
the book as a new thing: history written from an entirely statistical
point of view—which, for Buckle, meant from the point of view of an
implacable determinism. Free will, he informed his readers, was an
unscientific concept. Statistics

> has already thrown more light on the study of human nature than all
> the sciences put together. . . . The great truth that the actions of
> men, being guided by their antecedents, are in reality never incon-
> sistent, but, however capricious they may appear, only form part of
> one vast scheme of universal order, of which we in the present state
> of knowledge can barely see the outline . . . is at once the key and
> the basis of history.[24]

This is pretty plainly an echo of Laplace's *Essai sur les probabilités*; but Buckle did not mention Laplace in his book. He mentioned Quetelet instead—Quetelet was the first authority he cited—and the particular argument of Quetelet's Buckle borrowed was the argument that it is society, and not the individual, that is responsible for vice. "This is an inference resting on broad and tangible proofs accessible to all the world," Buckle maintained, "and as such cannot be overturned, or even impeached, by any of those hypotheses with which metaphysicians and theologians have hitherto perplexed the study of past events."[25] He meant the hypothesis of free will.

Buckle believed that human behavior, and thus human history, is determined by four conditions: climate, food, soil, and what he called the "General Aspect of Nature."[26] Like Laplace with his dead letters and Quetelet with his Scottish chests, Buckle had his own special example. It concerned the rate of marriage and the price of corn. These things bear, Buckle claimed, "a fixed and definite relation"; and since that fixed relation can be proved statistically, it follows that "instead of having any connexion with personal feelings, [marriages] are simply regulated by the average earnings of the great mass of the people; so that this immense social and religious institution is not only swayed, but is completely controlled, by the price of food and by the rate of wages."[27]

Buckle's *History of Civilization in England* was written in a statistical spirit in another respect as well. It was a blatantly nationalist project. The first volume (many more were planned) is a survey of other European nations undertaken for the purpose, chiefly, of invidious comparison with England. Buckle's stance of disinterestedness, in other words, did not inhibit him from offering conclusions gratifying to the chauvinism of British readers. (The French, for example, are "an admirable people . . . [but] looking at this matter historically, it is unquestionably true that we have worked out our civilization with little aid from them, while they have worked out theirs with great aid from us.")[28]

His great point, though, was the superiority of European to non-European civilizations. This was the result of the influence of the fourth of his all-powerful causes, the "General Aspect of Nature." In nations where the beauty and power of nature are overwhelming, such as India, the rational faculty remains undeveloped; in nations, such as (he suggested) Greece, where nature is less impressive and can be readily subdued, reason flourishes. Thus "it is . . . in Europe alone, that man has really succeeded in taming the energies of nature, bending them to his own will, turning them aside from their ordinary course, and compelling them to minister to his happiness, and subserve the general purposes of human life."[29] The triumph of reason is the result of climate.

That Buckle should have regarded it as no inconsistency to offer a determinist account in praise of reason—for what is reason worth if behavior is entirely conditioned by circumstance?—is a fair indication of the cogency of his thinking. But even people who found the thesis overstated believed that Buckle had produced an important book. "One of the most remarkable philosophical works of the present generation," concluded the legal and political writer Fitzjames Stephen in the *Edinburgh Review*, "although in point of execution it must be termed unequal, heterogeneous, and paradoxical."[30] *History of Civilization in England* was read all over Europe, by novelists and by physicists; hundreds of responses to it were published. The first volume was reprinted several times in England between 1857 and 1861; it was translated into French; it went through four German editions before 1871; and there were several Russian translations. Darwin read it (and was not impressed); Alfred Russel Wallace read it (and was). Dostoevsky read it twice, and gave a line about Buckle to the Underground Man. In 1861, the year volume two appeared, Buckle died. He was forty. (The cause of death was typhus. Buckle was traveling in Damascus, and was offered the services of a local physician. He declined the offer on the grounds that the doctor was French.) Buckle's grand design was hopelessly incomplete; but he had instigated a debate over the existence of free will that obsessed North Atlantic intellectuals for more than a decade.[31]

For people who believed—as most nineteenth-century scientists did believe—that understanding something was synonymous with being able to measure it, the appeal of statistics was plain. It permitted observations of phenomena—not just orbits and molecules, but risks, genes, suicides, nose size, almost anything—to be expressed in mathematical language. It was a way of cataloguing the universe and creating models for manipulating it. The broader appeal of statistics lay in the idea of an order beneath apparent randomness. Individuals—molecules or humans—might act unpredictably, but statistics seemed to show that in the aggregate their behavior conformed to stable laws. One reason for the relatively rapid acceptance of Darwin's theory of natural selection was that it seemed another example of order underlying chance, a phenomenon already addressed, in their own rather different ways, by Laplace and Quetelet.

It was therefore tempting to conclude that the world must be set up in such a way that things regulated themselves, and this was taken to confer a kind of cosmic seal of approval on the political doctrines of individualism and laissez-faire. In fact, nearly all the nineteenth-century champions of statistics were laissez-faire liberals.[32] Herschel ended his review of Quetelet's *Letters* with an attack on government intervention in social and economic affairs; Buckle called Adam Smith's *The Wealth of Nations* "probably the most important book that has ever been written," and announced the burden of all his researches to be that "the great enemy of civilization, is the protective spirit; by which I mean the notion that society cannot prosper, unless the affairs of life are watched over and protected at nearly every turn by the state and the church."[33] (The failure of the French and the Germans to grasp this truth, he explained, was a reason for the superiority of British civilization.) Herbert Spencer titled his philosophical defense of laissez-faire, published in 1851, *Social Statics*.

Darwinism, too, seemed to justify political laissez-faire. Huxley thought that one of the lessons the theory of natural selection taught was that white people did not need the institution of slavery to maintain their superiority over black people: nature would take care of it. This was, he claimed, the best argument for abolition. "The highest places in the hierarchy of civilisation will assuredly not be within the reach of our dusky cousins, though it is by no means necessary that they should be restricted to the lowest," he wrote in 1865. "But whatever the position of stable equilibrium into which the laws of social gravitation may bring the negro, all responsibility for the result will henceforward lie between Nature and him. The white man may wash his hands of it, and the Caucasian conscience be void of reproach for evermore."[34] It was a theology for the postslavery era.

What statistics seemed to show, in short, was that the market was not, as people like Matthew Arnold complained, an invitation to anarchy. Markets operate just the way nature does: left to themselves, they can be counted on to produce the optimum outcome over the long run. The individual pursuit of self-interest conduces to aggregate efficiency. Of course, like all appeals to natural laws as a justification for human arrangements, the "discovery" of the laws reflected the arrangements to be justified. Nineteenth-century liberals believed that the market operated like nature because they had already decided that nature operated like a market.

4

Charles Peirce was an enemy of economic individualism. He was also an enemy of determinism. He did not believe that evidence of statistical regularity licensed individual self-interest, and he did not believe that the universe is a machine. He thought that life is everywhere, and that life means spontaneity. He believed that the universe is charged with indeterminacy; like his father, though, he also believed that the universe makes sense, and he devoted his life to devising a cosmology that would show how both of those things—the indeterminacy and the intelligibility—could be the case. He never abandoned his father's faith that the world is constructed to be known by the mind—that, in Benjamin Peirce's words, "the two are wonderfully matched."[35] But he worked with scientific concepts predicated on a fundamentally different conception of the universe.

The story of that difference—the difference between Benjamin Peirce's scientific generation and Charles's—is the story of two demons. The first made its public appearance in 1812 in Laplace's *Théorie analytique des probabilités.* "We must . . . imagine the present state of the universe as the effect of its prior state and as the cause of the state that will follow it," Laplace wrote.

An intelligence which, for a given instant, could know all the forces by which nature is animated, and the respective situation of the beings who compose it, if, moreover, it was sufficiently vast to submit these data to analysis, if it could embrace in the same formula the movements of the greatest bodies in the universe as well as those of the lightest atom—nothing would be uncertain for it, and the future, like the past, would be present to its eyes.[36]

This is Laplace's demon. It stands for the billiard-ball theory of matter, the belief that every event, including the actions of human beings, is the singular and inevitable consequence of a chain of antecedent events in which chance does not play a role. The demon is a figural embodiment of what was called "the doctrine of necessity"—that is, the philosophy of determinism—and Laplace's passage inspired many imitations.

The particle of dust, that is snatched into the air by some sudden gust, and then passed from one space to another, by the shifting breezes that seize successively upon it, after describing its contortions and circumvolutions, through aerial whirlpools and eddies, swifter than sight, and more interlaced and interwoven than the reason can trace or unravel, describes its peculiar and intricate orbit as obediently as the planets; and a higher reason than man's, and a keener analysis than he has yet invented, would be able to calculate and predict the point in space which the atom would pass through after years of such labyrinthine circuits, as precisely as he now tells the place of the Moon, or the time of the perihelion passage of Halley's comet, after its solitary and disturbed journey of 76 years.[37]

The date was 1842, the writer was Joseph Lovering, a Harvard science professor, and the passage is from an article in a journal called the *Cambridge Miscellany*, co-edited by Lovering and Benjamin Peirce. Many nineteenth-century scientists were infatuated with Laplace's demon. It was a promise—if scientists could only get in there among the molecules and the brainwaves—of perfect knowledge.

Laplace introduced his demon in order to explain the purpose of probability theory: it was to compensate for human incapacity. We strive for the demon's omniscience, but "it remains always infinitely remote."[38] Our problem is not that events occur only with probable predictability; they occur (as the demon knows) with perfect predictability. Our problem is that we don't know enough to be able to make the predictions. Probability—the law of errors—is a tool for quantifying our ignorance. It refers not to events themselves, but to the degree of certainty with which we have grasped them. "The doctrine of chances," Lovering explained, paraphrasing Laplace, "reduces to definiteness and shape the loose and inadequate ways in which men calculate upon future events."[39] Events themselves are not chancy.

The second demon proposed otherwise. This demon made its public appearance in 1871 in a work called *Theory of Heat*, by the Scottish physicist James Clerk Maxwell. Maxwell had been an interested reader of Herschel's review of Quetelet and of Buckle's *History of Civilization in England*, and he had made, in 1859, one of the most brilliant uses of the law of errors in nineteenth-century science. The temperature within a sealed container is determined by the velocity of the molecules inside—the faster the molecules, the more frequently they collide and the higher the temperature. But that velocity is an average, for the individual molecules are all moving at different speeds. Since it is impossible to measure the speed of each molecule, how can we represent their behavior? Maxwell's proposal was that "the velocities are distributed among the particles according to the same law as the errors are distributed among the observations in the theory of the 'method of least squares.' "[40] His demonstration (along with work by the German physicist Rudolph Clausius and the Austrian physicist Ludwig Boltzmann) was a key contribution to the kinetic theory of gases, and helped to establish the science of statistical mechanics.

In *Theory of Heat*, Maxwell invited his reader to imagine, inside such a sealed chamber, "a being whose faculties are so sharpened that he can follow every molecule in its course"—an omniscient being, in other words, exactly like Laplace's. "Now let us suppose," he went on, that such a vessel is divided into two portions, A and B, by a division in which there is a small hole, and that a being, who can see the individual molecules, opens and closes this hole, so as to allow only the swifter molecules to pass from A to B, and only the slower ones to pass from B to A. He will thus, without expenditure of work, raise the temperature of B and lower that of A, in contradiction to the second law of thermodynamics.[41]

The second law of thermodynamics is the law of the dissipation of energy. It had been dramatically invoked by the British physicist William Thomson in 1852 to explain why, since energy cannot be created without the expenditure of energy, the universe will eventually reach a state of maximum entropy (a term coined by Clausius to describe the same process) and suffer a heat death. "Within a finite period of time to come," Thomson proclaimed, "the earth must be unfit for the habitation of man."[42] Many people considered the second law of thermodynamics some sort of ultimate judgment on the meaning of human history. The second law became a deep obsession of Henry Adams's.

Maxwell's demon was invented to refute this version of the doctrine of necessity. The obvious objection to his hypothetical is that the demon is expending energy in opening and shutting the door (never mind in picking out the right molecules); but that was not the point. What Maxwell was trying to show was that the second law of thermodynamics is only probabilistic. If the molecules inside a container are all moving at different velocities, we can only say that they will maintain a uniform temperature *most of the time*. There is always the infinitesimal chance that the molecules will sort themselves out spontaneously in such a way that the faster ones will all end up on one side of the container, thus raising the temperature and producing energy spontaneously. The moral, as Maxwell put it in a letter to a friend, is that "[t]he 2nd law of thermodynamics has the same degree of truth as the statement that if you throw a tumblerful of water into the sea, you cannot get the same tumblerful of water out again."[43] Physical laws are not absolutely precise.

An analogy with Darwin's theory of natural selection is not hard to see.[44] Most finches will be born with beaks inside the normal range of beak-size distributions—around the crest of the bell-shaped curve—but every once in a while a finch with an exceptionally long (or exceptionally broad, or exceptionally short) beak will appear, and if the environment (operating like Maxwell's demon) "selects" that characteristic by making it requisite for survival, an evolutionary development will have occurred. The appearance of the lucky bird is, for all intents and purposes, a matter of chance, "spontaneous," like drawing the card you want from a shuffled deck. Darwin was not a statistician; his mathematical aptitude was, in fact, quite small ("irrational angles produce a corresponding effect on my mind,"[45] he once confessed to an American follower). And the notion that nature "selects" in the self-consciously creative manner of Maxwell's gas demon probably reflects a slightly wishful interpretation of the theory of natural selection by chance variation. But that theory was in many ways both the most profound and the most representative product of what, in 1904, John Theodore Merz, in his massive intellectual history of nineteenth-century Europe, named "the statistical century."[46]

Darwinism was a scandal to many Laplaceans. In the Laplacean worldview, randomness is only appearance; in the Darwinian, it is closer to a fact of nature—in some respects, it is *the* fact of nature. Herschel, the man who had helped introduce Quetelet to British readers, wrote in 1850 that if all the literature of Europe were to perish and only Laplace's *Système du monde* and *Essai sur les probabilités* remained, "they would suffice to convey to the latest posterity an impression of the intellectual greatness of the age which could produce them, surpassing that afforded by all the monuments antiquity has left us."[47] But when *On the Origin of Species* appeared, in 1859, he ridiculed Darwin's theory as "the law of higgledy-piggledy."[48] Which, in a sense, it is.

What does it mean to say we "know" something in a world in which things happen higgledy-piggledy? Virtually all of Charles Peirce's work—an enormous body of writing on logic, semiotics, mathematics, astronomy, metrology, physics, psychology, and philosophy, large portions of it unpublished or unfinished—was devoted to this question. His answer had many parts, and fitting them all together—in a form consistent with his belief in the existence of a personal God—became the burden of his life. But one part of his answer was that in a universe in which events are uncertain and perception is fallible, knowing cannot be a matter of an individual mind "mirroring" reality. Each mind reflects differently—even the same mind reflects differently at different moments—and in any case reality doesn't stand still long enough to be accurately mirrored. Peirce's conclusion was that knowledge must therefore be social. It was his most important contribution to American thought, and when he recalled, late in life, how he came to formulate it, he described it—fittingly—as the product of a group. This was the conversation society he formed with William James, Oliver Wendell Holmes, Jr., and a few others in Cambridge in 1872, the group known as the Metaphysical Club.

NINE

THE METAPHYSICAL CLUB

I

"IT WAS IN THE EARLIEST SEVENTIES that a knot of us young men in Old Cambridge, calling ourselves, half-ironically, half-defiantly, 'The Metaphysical Club,'—for agnosticism was then riding its high horse, and was frowning superbly upon all metaphysics,—used to meet, sometimes in my study, sometimes in that of William James," Charles Peirce wrote in 1907, in a manuscript he never published. The other members of the club, he recalled, were Oliver Wendell Holmes, Jr., Nicholas St. John Green ("a skillful lawyer and a learned one"), Joseph Bangs Warner (also a lawyer), John Fiske, Francis Ellingwood Abbot, and Chauncey Wright.[1]

None of these people besides Peirce ever mentioned a Metaphysical Club anywhere—in letters, diaries, or published or unpublished writings. Peirce's own recollections were thirty-five years old, and his memory of the participants is almost certainly faulty. But there was a group, and James and Holmes were among its members. It was formed in January 1872. Henry James, writing that month to his friend Elizabeth Boott, reported that "[m]y brother has just helped to

Chauncey Wright, the Cambridge Socrates, around 1870.

found a metaphysical club, in Cambridge, (consisting of Chauncey Wright, C. Pierce etc.) to which you may expect to be appointed corresponding member."[2] (This was a Jamesian tease. Lizzie Boott was no kind of philosopher.) A couple of weeks later, Henry sent the news to Charles Eliot Norton, who was then living in Germany: "Wendell Holmes is about to discourse out here on jurisprudence," he wrote. "He, my brother, and various other long-headed youths have combined to form a metaphysical club, where they wrangle grimly and stick to the question." Then he added, possibly for Norton's gratification (Norton and William did not especially admire one another), possibly for his own: "It gives me a headache merely to know of it."[3]

Peirce's friendship with James dated, of course, from their time together at Lawrence. James had some trouble, in the beginning, grasping Peirce's ideas. "Your 1st question is 'where have I been?,'" he wrote in a letter to his sister Alice in 1866. " 'To C. S. Peirce's Lecture [at the Lowell Institute] of wh. I cd. not understand a word but rather enjoyed the sensation of listening to for an hour. [']"[4] Three years later James was not much further enlightened. "I have just been quit by Chas. S. Peirce, with whom I have been talking about a couple of articles in the St Louis 'Journal of Speculative Philosophy' by him wh. I have just read," he wrote to a fellow medical student, Henry Bowditch. "They are exceedingly bold subtle & incomprehensible and I can't say that his vocal elucidations helped me a great deal to their understanding, but they nevertheless interest me strangely."[5]

Eventually, though, he discovered the formula. "[T]he way to treat him," he wrote in 1875 to his brother Henry, who had run into Peirce in Paris and was dining with him occasionally,

> is after the fabled "nettle" receipt: grasp firmly, contradict, push hard, make fun of him, and he is as pleasant as anyone; but be overawed by his sententious manner and his paradoxical & obscure statements, wait upon them as it were, for light to dawn, and you will never get a feeling of ease with him any more than I did for years, until I changed my course & treated him more or less chaffingly. I confess I like him very much in spite of his peculiarities, for

he is a man of genius and there's always something in that to compel one's sympathy.[6]

It was a strategy William stuck to for the rest of his life. He treated Peirce the way Emerson treated other people's books: he skimmed him, in effect, for insight and stimulation, and abandoned the effort at complete comprehension. Much of Peirce's work involving mathematics and logic was, in any case, over James's head. This style of intellectual friendship came to exasperate Peirce, who could never understand James's habit of bouncing off other people's ideas. But it suited James perfectly.

Wendell Holmes went off to war before William James arrived in Cambridge, in September 1861. But Holmes was soon back to recover from the wound he suffered at Ball's Bluff, and he was in Boston again for several months in the fall of 1862, recovering from the wound he suffered at Antietam. By this time he and James had friends in common—notably John Ropes, whose brother Henry was in Holmes's regiment and died at Gettysburg—and they almost certainly got together, because after his return to the front that December, Holmes noted in a letter home: "Wrote James in the afternoon (may not send it)."[7] And their fathers were close. In 1863 Henry Senior was voted a member of the Saturday Club, and Dr. Holmes became his favorite companion there.

After the war, William and Wendell became best friends. "The only fellow here I care anything about is Holmes, who is on the whole a first rate article, and one which improves by wear," William wrote to Tom Ward after getting back from Brazil. "He is perhaps too exclusively intellectual but sees things so easily & clearly & talks so admirably that its a treat to be with him."[8] Until James went to Germany, in 1867, he and Holmes had a date to get together every Saturday evening at 8:30 to discuss philosophy.

Holmes was a famously brilliant talker on any subject—it was a gift he inherited from his father—and James found in him a degree of clarity and wit he missed in Peirce. He found as well a degree of social accomplishment that he possibly envied a little. Holmes was a war hero, a professional, and a man confident of his appeal to women. Apart from reading, flirtation was Holmes's single hobby, and he took it extremely seriously. James was not romantically adept, and he had an unfortunate habit of picking targets already pierced by the arrows of other men. He admired Clover Hooper ("a perfect Voltaire in petticoats,"[9] as Henry once described her), but she married Henry Adams. He admired Clover's sister Ellen as well; she married Ephraim Gurney, a Harvard historian who later became the first dean of the college. He even developed a wan sort of crush on Holmes's longtime girlfriend, Fanny Bowditch Dixwell. (She was the granddaughter of Benjamin Peirce's old mathematics mentor, Nathaniel Bowditch.) "I have made the acquaintance of the eldest Miss Dixwell of Cambridge lately," William wrote to Wilky in the spring of 1866. "She is about as fine as they make 'em. That villain Wendell Holmes has been keeping her all to himself out at Cambridge for the last 8 years; but I hope I may enjoy her acquaintance now. She is *A1*, if any one ever was."[10]

James's hope that he might enjoy her acquaintance *now* sprang from the circumstance that in 1866 Holmes happened to be spending the summer in Europe. The door may have been open, but James did not get in. It was not for lack of trying. Holmes's mother was moved to send her son a warning on the subject, though in language suggesting that she did not regard William James as much of a threat to the future happiness of a Holmes. Fanny Dixwell is "living quietly in Cambridge," she wrote to Wendell (who was flirting away furiously in England), "with the exception of visits from Bill James, who appears to go there at any time from 9 o'clock in the morning—I told her to let me know how the flirtation got on—she says he is a person who likes to know his friends very well."[11] James continued to call on Fanny Dixwell for several years. She married Holmes in 1872. That was the year in which Holmes, James, Peirce, and a few friends formed their club.

2

The pivotal figure in this group was not James or Holmes or Peirce. It was Chauncey Wright, a man who, almost literally, lived for conversation. Wright was a computer. He had come to Cambridge from Northampton, where Wrights had lived since the seventeenth century, and had been a student of Benjamin Peirce's at Harvard College. After his graduation, in 1852, he went to work for the *American Ephemeris and Nautical Almanac*, the federally financed publication at which Peirce was consulting astronomer and Peirce's brother-in-law Charles Davis was superintendent. Wright composed ephemerides—tables giving the future positions of the sun, moon, planets, and principal fixed stars for use in navigation. It was a full-time job, but he squeezed the entire year's work into three months, partly by devising new methods of calculation (he was a talented mathematician) and partly by working (aided by a constant infusion of nicotine) almost around the clock. The other nine months he talked.

When he was in college Wright had developed a habit of turning up in his friends' rooms and sitting quietly, sometimes for hours, doing nothing in particular until someone asked him a question. Then he would begin to converse; and once he got going, people had a hard time stopping him. "He could talk well," said Charles Eliot Norton, in whose home Wright was at one period an almost daily habitué, "too long for average human nature."[12] Wright was a large, phlegmatic man, but he was gentle, serene to the point of indolence, and, in a bland and unassuming way, a kind of genius. He had a knack for assimilating ideas. People rarely saw him do more with a book than glance at the table of contents and read a page or two at random, but he always seemed thoroughly informed about the latest work in philosophy, mathematics, and science. And he could explain anything. He once wrote a young woman a thousand-word letter explaining why taffy turns white when you pull it.

Wright was unmarried. He lodged, after 1861, in the home of Mary Walker, a fugitive former slave from North Carolina whose children Wright helped locate and bring north during the war. His published work consisted almost entirely of book reviews for the *Nation* and the *North American Review*—dense, dry pieces that his friends thought gave a poor idea of the quality of his mind. But he had few literary or scientific aspirations; he was content to serve as the local

Socrates. He was also a depressive and an alcoholic. It seems likely that the hospitality he enjoyed was due partly to his gifts as an interlocutor (he also invented card tricks, built ingenious mechanical toys, and juggled), and partly to a general concern for his welfare. He was the kind of loner loneliness makes miserable.

Socrates was Wright's role model, but unlike Socrates, Wright had a doctrine. He was a positivist, and positivism was the view he defended in conversation against all comers. In the nineteenth century positivism was a movement associated principally with French thinkers—Saint-Simon, Auguste Comte, Charles Fourier, Joseph Proudhon—but Wright despised the French, whose culture he thought fetishized ideas, and he considered positivism a quintessentially Anglo-Saxon philosophy. His heroes were Englishmen: Francis Bacon and John Stuart Mill.

What Wright meant by positivism was, at bottom, an absolute distinction between facts and values. Fact was the province of science and value was the province of what he called, always a little deprecatingly, metaphysics. Wright thought that metaphysical speculation—ideas about the origin, end, and meaning of life—came naturally to human beings. He didn't condemn such ideas out of hand. He just thought they should never be confused with science. For what science teaches is that the phenomenal world—the world we can see and touch—is characterized, through and through, by change, and that our knowledge of it is characterized, through and through, by uncertainty.

His favorite illustration was the weather. Everyone believes that the weather is purely a product of physical cause and effect, but no one can predict it with certainty. "[U]nlike planetary perturbations, the weather makes the most reckless excursions from its averages, and obscures them by a most inconsequent and incalculable fickleness,"[13] he maintained in one of the first articles he ever published, "The Winds and the Weather," in 1858. We accept this state of affairs about the weather—that it is a perfectly lawful, rather mundane phenomenon whose complexity nevertheless vastly exceeds our ability to understand it—and yet we freely pontificate about the causes of human unhappiness and the future progress of society, things determined by factors presumably many times more complex than the weather. It would be too much to say that this inconsistency roused Chauncey Wright—he was not an excitable man—but it attracted his attention, and he spent much of his career attempting to correct it.

It is not, Wright believed, that every event is not completely determined by physical causes. It is just that precise knowledge of those causes and how they operate is inaccessible to science in its present state—and, considering the multitude of factors, each with its own probability of occurrence, involved in producing the outcome of even the simplest events, such as flipping a coin, that knowledge will probably remain inaccessible. Thus, he thought, the "scientific" claims of historians like Buckle reduce to mere superstition. Statistical explanations of history are no different from the providential explanations they purport to displace. "The interest is nearly the same, whether the lesson be on Divine Providence or on the force of an inscrutable and irresistible fate,"[14] as he wrote in a review of a book by an American disciple of Buckle.

Wright had a theory about the fickleness of the weather. He thought that it was the reason organic change occurred. Plants and the lower orders of animals have no power to develop by themselves, he argued; they need the stimulation of external forces that act on them destructively. The inconstancy of the weather, he thought, might perform this function.

> Changes of growth are effected by those apparent hardships to which life is subject; and progression in new directions is effected by retrogression in previous modes of growth. The old leaves and branches must fall, the wood must be frost-bitten or dried, the substance of seeds must wither and then decay, the action of leaves must every night be reversed, vines and branches must be shaken by the winds, that the energies and the materials of new forms of life may be rendered active and available.

And it may be that the changes we observe in plants and other simple organisms due to the weather also explain the evolution, long ago, of all life forms. For

[t]he classification of organic forms presents to the naturalist, not the structure of a regular though incomplete development, but the broken and fragmentary form of a ruin. We may suppose . . . that the creation of those organic forms which constitute this fragmentary system was effected in the midst of an elemental storm, a regulated confusion, uniting all the external conditions which the highest capacities and the greatest varieties of organized life require for their fullest development; and that as the storm subsided into a simpler, but less genial diversity,—into the weather,—whole orders and genera and species sank with it from the ranks of possible organic forms. The weather, fallen from its high estate, no longer able to develope, much less to create new forms, can only sustain those that are left to its care.[15]

The vision is very close to Darwin's; and so it is not surprising that when *On the Origin of Species* appeared, a year later, Wright was enchanted. It is one of the few books he was observed to have read all the way through, and he read it more than once. Darwin became his hero. Wright had been teaching in the Agassizes' school for girls when the *Origin* came out, and he witnessed Agassiz's reaction to it. He resigned at the end of the year and afterward regarded Agassiz with what was, for him, an uncharacteristically energetic distaste. Agassiz's "theory of creation," Wright wrote to a friend, simply "covers ignorance with a word pretending knowledge and feigning reverence. To admit a miracle when one isn't necessary seems to be one of those works of supererogation which have survived the Protestant Reformation."[16] In 1866 Wright heard Agassiz lecture on the findings of the Brazil expedition: Agassiz just "repeated . . . what he has said at every scientific meeting at which I have heard him speak," he complained to Norton; "and he said it with as much animation as if the world were not weary of it. . . . [I]t is a chronic case of public speaking,—a brilliant idea which occurred to him once upon a time, and has been a standing marvel of inspiration ever since."[17]

Wright did not consider himself an evolutionist. To him the term denoted a belief that the world was getting, on some definition, "better." His loyalty was only to the theory of natural selection, which he thought corresponded perfectly to his notion of life as weather.

"[T]he principle of the theory of Natural Selection is taught in the discourse of Jesus with Nicodemus the Pharisee,"[18] he explained in a letter to Charles Norton's sister Grace. The allusion may be a little gnomic today. The discourse with Nicodemus is in the Gospel of John, and the words of Jesus Wright was referring to are these: "The wind bloweth where it listeth, and thou hearest the sound thereof, but canst not tell whence it cometh, and whither it goeth: so is every one that is born of the Spirit." Wright was, in short, one of the few nineteenth-century Darwinians who thought like Darwin—one of the few evolutionists who did not associate evolutionary change with progress. "Never use the word[s] higher & lower,"[19] Darwin scribbled in the margins of his copy of the *Vestiges of the Natural History of Creation* in 1847. The advice proved almost impossible to follow to the letter, even for Darwin, but if anyone respected its spirit, it was Chauncey Wright.

Wright's particular bête noire was the evolutionist Herbert Spencer, whose work seemed to him a flagrant violation of the separation of science and metaphysics. "Mr. Spencer," as he declared, "is not a positivist."[20] Spencer's mistake was to treat the concepts of science, which are merely tools of inquiry, as though they were realities of nature. The theory of natural selection, for example, posits continuity in the sequence of natural phenomena (evolution does not proceed by leaps). But "continuity" is simply a verbal handle we attach to a bundle of empirical observations. It is not something that actually exists in nature. Spencer failed to understand this, and he therefore imputed cosmic reality to what are just conceptual inferences— just words. He did with the word "evolution" what Agassiz did with the word "creation": he erected an idol.

"Mr. Spencer's philosophy contemplates the universe in its totality as having an intelligible order, a relation of beginning and end—a development,"[21] Wright said. But the universe is only weather.

> Everything out of the mind is a product, the result of some process. Nothing is exempt from change. Worlds are formed and dissipated. Races of organic beings grow up like their constituent individual members, and disappear like these. Nothing shows a trace of an

original, immutable nature, except the unchangeable laws of change. These point to no beginning and to no end in time, nor to any bounds in space. All indications to the contrary in the results of physical research are clearly traceable to imperfections in our present knowledge of all the laws of change, and to that disposition to cosmological speculations which still prevails even in science.[22]

"No *real* fate or necessity is indeed manifested anywhere in the universe," he wrote to a friend, "—only a phenomenal regularity."[23]

Wright especially objected to Spencer's adoption of Laplace's nebular hypothesis, which Wright regarded as a classic example of evolutionism in the bad sense: it described a development from lower to higher, from chaos to system. Possibly the solar system had evolved out of the sun's nebulae, Wright argued; if so, what was to prevent it from devolving right back into gas again? "[T]he constitution of the solar system is not archetypal, as the ancients supposed, but the same corrupt mix of law and apparent accident that the phenomena of the earth's surface exhibit," he argued. And since all natural movements produce, eventually, countermovements—since the sun eventually drives out the rain—there is no reason to think that the present solar system constitutes the final state of anything. Judging from what we observe in the rest of nature, in fact, there is every reason to assume that the solar system will some day swing back in the direction of relative chaos (or homogeneity), from which it will again evolve into a different kind of relative order (or heterogeneity). In explaining how this process might work, Wright introduced his signature phrase:

> Of what we may call cosmical weather, in the inter-stellar spaces, little is known. Of the general cosmical effects of the opposing actions of heat and gravitation, the great dispersive and concentrative principles of the universe, we can at present only form vague conjectures; but that these two principles are the agents of vast countermovements in the formation and destruction of systems of worlds, always operative in never-ending cycles and in infinite time, seems to us to be by far the most rational supposition which we can form concerning the matter.[24]

For Wright's friends, "cosmical weather" became the term that summed up his thought.

Since he considered metaphysical speculation groundless, how did Wright propose people should approach moral and religious questions? In public matters he was content with the standard utilitarian formula—the good is equal to the greatest happiness of the greatest number—but in personal matters his indifference was settled: "about what we really know nothing we ought not to affirm or deny any thing,"[25] he wrote to his friend the philosopher Francis Ellingwood Abbot. Still, though he professed neutrality on the question of the existence of a god ("Atheism is speculatively as unfounded as theism, and practically can only spring from bad motives,"[26] he told Abbot), he was hostile to organized religion, which he considered oppression through the fetishization of words. "Religion" and "religious," he wrote to Norton, are "*good* words through which one of the subtlest forms of tyranny is exercised over freedom of thought."[27] In the modern world, Wright believed, concepts were at last being properly understood as the means, and not the ends, of inquiry. " 'Fixed ideas,' once controlling elements, are now subservient instruments of great purposes or characters," he informed Norton (who was traveling in Italy, a perilous recreation that moved Wright to send him a number of reminders about the baleful history of superstition). "They are still needed for discipline, but are not worshipped as masters."[28]

Wright thought that religious faith was beyond argument. If faith satisfied an emotional need, there was nothing more to be said about it, except that no one had the right to impose his or her religion on anyone else. Morality was another matter. Religion is personal and unconditional, but morality is social and conventional. Morals do not require philosophical grounding, and they can be imposed on other people, since they simply represent the rules a given society has found reason to enforce. Yet philosophers persist in devising abstract moral systems. Since, on Wright's view, all such systems are speculative, sheer metaphysical word worship, how are we supposed to justify our moral choices?

Wright believed that this was not a problem, and he laid out his views in a letter to Abbot. "I have always believed that the really *essential* positions of morals and religion could be sustained on the 'lower' ground of common-sense,—on what men generally understand and believe independently of their philosophical theories," he explained. Philosophers like to deduce dire practical consequences from the theories of their opponents; but in daily life people's philosophical beliefs don't have very much to do with the way they actually behave.

> Men conclude in matters affecting their own welfare so much better than they can justify rationally,—they are led by their instincts of reverence so surely to the safest known authority, that theory becomes in such matters an insignificant affair. . . . To stake any serious human concern on the truth of this or that philosophical theory seems to me, therefore, in the highest degree arrogant and absurd, as coming from a confused begging of some philosophical question,—from taking for granted that something is important practically which is in theory problematical; from taking for granted, for example, that our duties would be different, or be more or less binding on us according as our faith in a future life should be well or ill founded.[29]

Wright wrote those words in 1867, two years after one of his brothers died from wounds suffered at Cold Harbor. If the war taught anything, it was that beliefs have consequences; in this sense, Wright's whole position was a form of denial. Where, after all, is the bright line that divides common sense from philosophy, or the practical from the theoretical, or what we call facts from what we call values? The effect of belief on conduct may be impossible to predict in an individual case (this, too, was a lesson of the war), but what is imponderable is not therefore irrelevant—as any student of the weather ought to know. "Where we cannot be certain, we must affirm nothing" was the motto to which Wright's positivism reduced.

What Wright might have said in his letter to Abbot is that people are better off relying on their instincts of sympathy and common sense than they are trying to obey the dictates of a system of abstractions. But that would have sounded like constructing a morality from first principles, and Wright had ruled this out as an empty exercise. He had, with impressive scientific authority, driven himself into a moral dead end. For some young intellectuals in the years after the war, Wright's thought represented a mature debunking of the philosophical and scientific certitudes that had failed to prevent—in some cases had even incited—four years of mutual destruction. Their challenge, as they perceived it, was to devise a theory of conduct that made sense in a universe of uncertainty, a universe like the one Wright described. But for Wright himself no such theory was imaginable. His nihilism was fairly complete.

3

Before it was published, in the *Atlantic Monthly*, Wright had read his paper on "The Winds and the Weather" to a small group of male friends who called themselves the Septem. The group had come together in 1856, and its seven members included two old friends of Wright's from Northampton who had also been his classmates at Harvard—James Bradley Thayer, later a professor of law at Harvard, and Ephraim Gurney, the historian and future Harvard dean—along with a Boston lawyer named George Shattuck. The group met usually in Wright's rooms, and its transactions were not exclusively philosophical. Thayer, who served as secretary, recorded in the minutes after one meeting that the only thing he could remember was that someone had made a motion to change the name of the group to the Whiskey Punch Club.

In 1859, after Shattuck and then Thayer got married, the group broke up. In 1863 Wright fell into a depression and began drinking heavily. He had somehow injured his foot and healing was slow: the more he drank, the longer it took. Gurney and Charles Eliot Norton undertook to resuscitate him by doing duty as conversationalists; Norton began soliciting pieces regularly from him for the *North American Review*, which he took over as editor in 1864; and in 1865 the Septem (with some new members) was revived by Gurney, and Wright had his school back.

The impulse to form schools was in Wright's nature. They were his surrogate for family. Sometimes his school was someone else's actual family, as was the case with the Nortons. Sometimes it took the form of a tutorial, as was the case with the philosopher Francis Abbot, to whom Wright sent long letters gently correcting his philosophical errors. (Abbot lived in New Hampshire, where he worked as a Unitarian minister until he was fired by his congregation for preaching that the authority of Jesus was no greater than the authority of his own reason, a doctrine too unsupernatural even for Unitarians.) And sometimes the school was an actual club, usually composed of younger, unmarried men.

In 1868 Gurney married Ellen Hooper, the Nortons went abroad, where they remained for four years, and Wright suffered another alcoholic breakdown. This one lasted nearly two years and forced him to abandon his work for the *Almanac*. Once again he was helped out by the intercession of friends and by the formation of a new club, consisting entirely of himself and two epigones: Eldridge Cutler, a young Harvard professor, and Charles Salter, another former Unitarian minister who had resigned because of theological doubts and had turned to the law. (It was a short-lived club: Cutler and Salter both died, unexpectedly, in 1870.) Wright never fully recovered from this second collapse, but he was back in business.

Wright's habit of convening private philosophical societies was idiosyncratic only in the sense that it gave him relief from the solitude he seems to have felt otherwise condemned to endure. For private philosophical and literary societies were one of the venues in which intellectual work got done in the United States in the years before the emergence of the university. Some of these societies were more social than others. The Saturday Club was a dinner club: it met in a restaurant, and no formal presentations seem to have been expected of its members. But it plainly served as a medium for intellectual exchange in a world in which the disciplines, in the modern academic sense, did not exist. The Saturday Club was where Emerson and Hawthorne talked to Agassiz and Benjamin Peirce.

In 1868 a kind of junior edition of the Saturday Club—known simply as The Club—was founded in Boston. It met for dinner on the second Tuesday of every month, and its members included the lawyers Wendell Holmes, John Ropes, John Gray, Moorfield Story, and Arthur Sedgwick; the *littérateurs* William Dean Howells, Thomas Sergeant Perry, and Henry James; the freelance Spencerian philosopher John Fiske; the banker and musicologist Henry Lee Higginson; the historian Henry Adams; and the vocationally challenged William James. Like its senior model, the setting was social but the conversation was intellectual. "[I]t used to be great fun," Higginson later recalled, "to hear William James and Wendell Holmes . . . spar, or at any rate excite each other to all sorts of ideas and expressions."[30] The Metaphysical Club memorialized by Peirce was therefore one of many places where Cambridge intellectuals got together. Its members all knew each other from other gatherings. And they all knew Chauncey Wright.

Holmes was probably not a frequent participant in Metaphysical Club discussions. He had a busy 1872. He was in practice in Boston (he had started out in a firm whose partners included Wright's old Septem comrades James Thayer and George Shattuck, but had left it to go into practice with his brother, Ned); he was lecturing at Harvard; and his spare time was consumed by his first major piece of legal scholarship, a new edition of Kent's *Commentaries on American Law*, a standard legal reference work. It was an assignment Holmes became obsessed with. He used to carry the manuscript around with him in a green bag. He made his family practice fire drills in which the bag, placed each night outside his bedroom door, was evacuated first, and when he visited the Jameses for dinner he amused them by taking the bag with him when he went to wash his hands. In June Holmes was appointed sole editor of the *American Law Review*, a journal founded by his friends John Ropes and John Gray in 1866. (He had been co-editor with Arthur Sedgwick, a fellow veteran of the Massachusetts Twentieth and a law school classmate, since 1870.) The same month, he married Fanny Dixwell, who almost immediately came down with rheumatic fever, a dangerous disease. She remained an invalid for several months; she was still unable to come downstairs (the Holmeses lived with Wendell's parents) in October.

Holmes was never keen to acknowledge the influence of other people on his views, but he never had trouble acknowledging

Wright's. He identified with Wright's positivism: it suited perfectly his own disillusionment. He took satisfaction in the notion that values are epiphenomenal—that beneath all the talk of principles and ideals, what people do is just a fancy version of what amoebas do. And he therefore agreed with Wright that philosophy and logic don't have much to do with the practical choices people make. He certainly thought this was true in the law. "It is the merit of the common law that it decides the case first and determines the principle afterwards,"[31] is the first sentence of the first law review article he ever wrote, in 1870, two years before the Metaphysical Club came into existence; and he spent much of his career as a philosopher of jurisprudence explaining how the fact that judges conclude before they reason does not mean that legal decision making is arbitrary.

Holmes eventually lost sympathy with the views of his friend William James, which he thought too hopeful and anthropocentric. He never had much interest in Peirce; he thought Peirce's genius "overrated."[32] But he continued to admire Wright, and years later cited him as the inspiration for what he liked to call his philosophy of "bettabilitarianism." "Chauncey Wright[,] a nearly forgotten philosopher of real merit, taught me when young that I must not say *necessary* about the universe, that we don't know whether anything is necessary or not," he wrote to Frederick Pollock in 1929, when he was in his eighties. "So that I describe myself as a *bet*tabilitarian. I believe that we can *bet* on the behavior of the universe in its contract with us. We bet we can know what it will be. That leaves a loophole for free will—in the miraculous sense—the creation of a new atom of force, although I don't in the least believe in it."[33]

In his own way, and despite Holmes's distaste, William James was a bettabilitarian, too. But he did believe in free will—what would it mean to bet, after all, if we were not free to choose the stakes? He was repelled by Wright's reduction of the world to pure phenomena—he thought Wright made the universe into a "Nulliverse"[34]—and he regarded the abyss Wright insisted on placing between facts and values as a fiction. James thought that Wright's decision to separate science from metaphysics was itself a metaphysical choice—that Wright's disapproval of talk about values was just an expression of Wright's own values. Wright was a positivist because positivism suited his character: moral neutrality was his way of dealing with the world—and that, in James's view, is what all beliefs are anyway, "scientific" or otherwise.

Wright was a regular visitor to the James family home in Cambridge long before 1872, and in any case William James did not need the Metaphysical Club to reach his conclusion about the nature of beliefs. He had already arrived there by experimentation on what was always his favorite human subject, himself. When he was living in Germany in the late 1860s, he had got caught up in the speculative frenzy about free will and determinism inspired by Buckle's book. As usual, he found merits on both sides. "I'm swamped in an empirical philosophy," he wrote to Tom Ward shortly after getting back to Cambridge in 1869; "—I feel that we are Nature through and through, that we are *wholly* conditioned, that not a wiggle of our will happens save as the result of physical laws, and yet notwithstanding we are en rapport with reason. . . . It is not that we are all nature *but* some point which is reason, but that all is Nature *and* all is reason too."[35]

After he took his M.D. from Harvard, in June 1869, James collapsed. He descended into a deep depression, exacerbated by back pains, eye trouble, and various other complaints. His diary for the winter of 1869–70 is a record of misery and self-loathing. Then in the spring, after reading the second installment, published in 1859, of a three-part work called the *Essais de critique générale* by the French philosopher Charles Renouvier, he had a breakthrough.

Renouvier was a French Protestant from a family active in liberal politics, but he had quit political life after the rise of the Second Empire, in 1848, to devote himself to the construction of a philosophical defense of freedom. Renouvier's argument was that "the doctrine of necessity" is incoherent, since if all beliefs are determined, we have no way of knowing whether the belief that all beliefs are determined is correct, and no way of explaining why one person believes in determinism while another person does not. The only noncontradictory position, Renouvier held, is to believe that we freely believe, and therefore to believe in free will. Even so, we cannot be absolutely certain of the truth of this belief, or of anything else. "Certainty is not and cannot be absolute," he wrote in the second *Essai*. "It is . . . a condition and an action of human beings. . . . Properly speaking, there is no certainty; there are only people who are certain."[36]

This was, in effect, Wright without the nihilism, and it was entirely appealing to James. "I think that yesterday was a crisis in my life," he wrote in his diary on April 30, 1870.

> I finished the first part of Renouvier's 2nd Essays and see no reason why his definition of free will—the sustaining of a thought *because I choose to* when I might have other thoughts—need be the definition of an illusion. At any rate I will assume for the present—until next year—that it is no illusion. My first act of free will shall be to believe in free will. . . . Hitherto, when I have felt like taking a free initiative, like daring to act originally, without carefully waiting for contemplation of the external world to determine all for me, suicide seemed the most manly form to put my daring into; now, I will go a step further with my will, not only act with it, but believe as well; believe in my individual reality and creative power.[37]

As bold as this resolution sounds, it did not release James from his depression. He seems to have been incapacitated by psychosomatic disorders—in particular, an inability to use his eyes for reading or writing—for another eighteen months, and he suffered chronically from depression, eyestrain, and insomnia all his life. Henry's mention of the formation of the Metaphysical Club in January 1872 is one of the first signs, after the diary entry about Renouvier, written a year and a half earlier, that William was socially active again.[38]

Still, James believed that Renouvier had cured him, and he sent him thanks. "I must not lose this opportunity of telling you of the admiration and gratitude which have been excited in me by the reading of your *Essais*," he wrote to Renouvier in the fall of 1872. "Thanks to you I possess for the first time an intelligible and reasonable conception of freedom. . . . I can say that through that philosophy I am beginning to experience a rebirth of the moral life; and I assure you, sir, that this is no small thing."[39] Renouvier had taught James two things: first, that philosophy is not a path to certainty, only a method of coping, and second, that what makes beliefs true is not logic but results. To James, this meant that human beings are active agents—that they get a vote—in the evolving constitution of the universe: when we choose a belief and act on it, we change the way things are.

In 1875 James published a review of a book called *The Unseen Universe*, by two Scottish physicists, Peter Guthrie Tait (a close friend of James Clerk Maxwell's) and Balfour Stewart, which undertook to refute William Thomson's interpretation of the second law of thermodynamics—the conclusion that the universe is fated to run down and die through the loss of heat. Tait and Stewart suggested that the energy being expended in the material world is not lost, but gets absorbed into the "unseen" world of what nineteenth-century scientists called the "ether"—the invisible medium in which molecules, the elemental units of matter, were imagined to circulate. When the material universe is depleted, Tait and Stewart suggested, this "invisible" universe will remain, charged with spiritual life. Contrary to Clausius's and Thomson's theory, the entropy of the universe remains constant. It was a thermodynamic argument for heaven. James regarded the theory as fanciful and probably unprovable, but—this was his main point—that didn't make it illegitimate. "[A]ny one *to whom [such an argument] makes a practical difference* (whether of motive to action or of mental peace) is in duty bound to make it," he wrote. "If 'scientific' scruples withhold him from making it, this proves his intellect to have been simply sicklied o'er and paralyzed by scientific pursuits."[40]

Wright interpreted this as a personal attack, and he was uncharacteristically annoyed. He called the review "boyish" and James's behavior (in effect) Oedipal. "One remains a boy longer in philosophy than in any other direction," he wrote to Grace Norton. "[James] has been for some time . . . in a rebellious mood towards the views I argue for; and he has written many private essays or notes on the subject; and very unwisely committed himself to expressions of his animosity in published writings."[41] He hurried over to the James home, caught "Dr. James" (as he mockingly called him; William was then a Harvard instructor) just returned, and delivered a critique of James's doctrine of "the duty of belief." Two days later, Wright re-

turned to Quincy Street for another session. He got James to concede that Wright was indeed the person he had had in mind when he
wrote his attack on " 'scientific' scruples," and he got him to retract
the word "duty." But he did not succeed in disabusing James of his
idea. James later referred to "the duty of belief" as "the subjective
method"; much later he called it "the will to believe," and, when that
phrase was criticized, "the right to believe." The name he finally
chose for it was "pragmatism."

Charles Peirce met Wright in 1857, when Peirce was eighteen and
Wright was twenty-seven, at another private scholarly gathering—a
Shakespeare Club, presided over by the wife of Charles Russell Lowell (father of the Civil War hero). They soon began getting together,
almost daily, to debate philosophy. "We must have fought out nearly a
thousand close disputations, regular set-tos concerning the philosophy of Mill, perfectly dispassionate of course, before the Metaphysical Club had been started,"[42] Peirce later recalled.

Peirce and Wright had a lot in common besides their interest in
mathematics, astronomy, and argument. They both invented card
tricks, for example, which they traded with one another; and, of
course, Wright made his living working for Charles's father. When
the Peirces were attacked in the *Nation* after their testimony in the
Howland will case, Wright defended them in print. (At least, he defended their math: "If he appears arrogant," Wright explained of
Benjamin Peirce, "it is probably from a desire to make up in the
earnestness of his statements the lack of convincing clearness—to
supply his audience with a lively faith in default of a clear understanding. He is a little too much given to impute a certainty to the
processes and not to the data of the computation."[43] The article was
signed with a pseudonym.) Unlike James—unlike most people in
Cambridge—Wright was up to Peirce's speed in mathematics and
logic, and Peirce regarded him as a kind of mental trainer, a philosophical workout specialist. Wright was "our boxing-master," as he
later wrote, "whom we,—I, particularly,—used to face to be severely
pummelled."[44]

Their bouts concerned the nature of the universe. (People do not
seem to have been shy about cosmological speculation in mid-

nineteenth-century Cambridge.) Wright was a Laplacean, though without the Laplacean hubris. He did not think that things happen by chance; he just thought that causation is generally too complex for our minds to grasp, and that the future course of the universe, like the future course of the weather, is largely unchartable. When he used the word "uncertainty," he meant *our* uncertainty—just as when Laplace used the word "probability," he was referring not to events themselves, but to our imperfect knowledge of them.

Peirce was a Maxwellian. He thought that physical laws are not absolutely precise, and his experience as a scientist seemed to confirm this. Scientific laws rely on the assumption that like causes always produce like effects, but as Maxwell himself once put it, this assumption is a "metaphysical doctrine. . . . [I]t is not of much use in a world like this, in which the same antecedents never again concur, and nothing ever happens twice."[45] As all efforts to measure phenomena repeatedly with exactitude reveal, things never cease varying. The facts are always susceptible to (as Peirce later put it) "a certain swerving"[46] from the paths their laws dictate, and Peirce interpreted this to open the door to the possibility of pure chance.

Darwin, Peirce thought, had done with organisms what Maxwell had done with gases: he "proposed to apply the statistical method to biology."[47] When *On the Origin of Species* came out, in late 1859, Peirce was in the Louisiana wilderness, working for the Coast Survey, but he exchanged letters with Wright about the book, and when he got back to Cambridge that summer and found Wright a convert to Darwinism, he told him that if the theory of natural selection by chance variation was correct, there was more spontaneity in the universe than Wright's mechanistic views allowed. The remark, according to Peirce, "impressed him enough to perplex him."[48]

If scientific laws are not absolutely precise, then scientific terminology has to be understood in a new way. Words like "cause" and "effect," "certainty" and "chance," even "hard" and "soft" cannot be understood as naming fixed and discrete entities or properties; they have to be understood as naming points on a curve of possibilities, as guesses or predictions rather than conclusions. Otherwise, scientists are in danger of reifying their concepts—of imputing an unvarying essence to phenomena that are in a continual state of flux. Peirce was the first scientist to perceive all the implications of this problem, and his mature philosophy—his theory of signs and his elaboration of what he called "the logic of relations"—is obsessed with it. The problem boils down to this question: What does it mean to say that a statement is "true" in a world always susceptible to "a certain swerving"? Peirce got a hint of how this question might be answered from another member of the Metaphysical Club, Nicholas St. John Green.

Green was one of Wright's Northampton connections. He had studied with Wright in preparation for Harvard, and remained one of his closest friends. He came from a political family. His father, the Reverend James D. Green, was four times mayor of Cambridge; his mother was the daughter of a New Hampshire Congressman. Green himself was a lawyer. Before the Civil War, he had been a junior partner in the law office of Benjamin Butler, the notorious Union general (and later governor of Massachusetts), and he served under Butler during the war. Afterward, he became a law professor at Harvard. Green wrote frequently for the *American Law Review*, articles much admired by his friend and editor Wendell Holmes, and also by Charles Peirce. His favorite target was legal formalism—the belief that legal concepts refer to something immutable and determinate. His criticism of legal formalism was Wright's criticism of Spencer's evolutionary philosophy: he thought it treated what were merely tools of analysis as though they named actual entities.

Judges and lawyers, for example, use the phrase "chain of causation," which is the concept behind the legal distinction between "proximate cause" (the cause immediately preceding an event, and therefore, if that event constitutes a crime or a private wrong, a point of exposure to legal liability) and "remote cause" (a cause farther back in the chain, and therefore a point generally exempt from liability). But "the chain of causation," Green argued, is only a metaphor. In reality, every event has a multiplicity of interdependent causes. The "proximate cause" is just the antecedent event people choose to pick out in order to serve whatever interest they happen to have in the case at hand. Similarly, labeling a cause "remote" is just a way of announcing a decision not to attach liability to it. Independent of someone's interests, one cause is not more "proximate" or "remote" than any number of other causes.

"In as many different ways as we view an effect," Green wrote,

> so many different causes . . . can we find for it. The true, the entire, cause is none of these separate causes taken singly, but all of them taken together. There is no chain of causation consisting of determinate links ranged in order of proximity to the effect. They are rather mutually interwoven with themselves and the effect, as the meshes of a net are interwoven. As the existence of each adjoining mesh of the net is necessary for the existence of any particular mesh, so the presence of each and every surrounding circumstance, which, taken by itself we may call a cause, is necessary for the production of the effect. . . . The same cause and effect which would be considered proximate in one class of [legal] actions, the attendant circumstances being unchanged, would be considered remote in others. The meaning of the terms, proximate and remote, is contracted or enlarged, according to what is the subject-matter of the inquiry.[49]

This was entirely compatible with Peirce's understanding of causation in nature, and Peirce found the method of analysis thrilling. He praised, in one of his recollections of the Metaphysical Club, Green's "extraordinary power of disrobing warm and breathing truth of the draperies of long worn formulas."[50]

In criticizing the notion that "proximate cause" means anything more than "the place we choose to attach liability in this particular fact situation," Green was not suggesting that the term is empty of truth value. He was arguing that its truth value is a function of its usefulness in sorting out the facts in the case at hand, very much as Darwin had argued that the term "species" doesn't refer to anything definitive in nature, but is nevertheless a useful way of lumping organisms together. Legal cases, like natural phenomena, are classifiable into groups (negligence cases, breach of promise cases, libel cases, and so on), but the resemblance is only rough, since no two cases are completely identical, any more than two stars or two frogs or two chambers of gas molecules are completely identical. Things are unique before they are alike. Legal terms, therefore, should be understood as naming not a single discrete entity, but a set of limits within which a thing can plausibly be counted as (for instance) "negligence" or "libel" or a "proximate cause." These limits do not exist independently of our interest; but that does not mean they have no reality. They have precisely the reality that legal liability attaches to whatever is commonly understood to fall within them.

Green thought that all beliefs have this purposive character—that knowledge is not a passive mirroring of the world, but an active means of making the world into the kind of world we want it to be— and this was a point he insisted on in meetings of the Metaphysical Club. "He often urged the importance of applying Bain's definition of belief as 'that upon which a man is prepared to act,' "[51] as Peirce explained it. Bain was Alexander Bain, a Scotsman who was a close friend of John Stuart Mill's and who established the New Psychology—that is, physiological psychology—in Britain. In *The Emotions and the Will*, published in 1859 and in use as a standard psychology textbook for the rest of the century, Bain had proposed such a definition of belief; but (contrary to Peirce's attribution) that was probably not where Green picked it up. He probably got it from a work well known to him and to his friend Holmes, James Fitzjames Stephen's *A General View of the Criminal Law in England*, published in 1863. (Holmes read it immediately after returning from Europe, where he had met Stephen, in 1866.)

"The desire to act and the desire to act successfully are ultimate facts in human nature," Stephen wrote;

> but we are so constituted that all actions involve belief, and the world is so arranged that all actions involve belief, and all successful actions involve true belief. Hence, the ultimate reason for believing is, that without belief men cannot act. And the reason for believing what is true is, that without true belief they cannot act successfully; thus the advantage derived from true as distinguished from false belief, and not the bare fact that the thing is true, is the reason for believing what is true. . . . If all the affairs of life, moral and intellectual education included, could be conducted as well by a person who believed that twice two make six, as by one who believed that twice

two make four, there would be no reason for believing the one proposition rather than the other. Hence, belief is not mere impression which the mind receives passively from the contemplation of facts external to it, but an active habit involving an exertion of will.[52]

"[W]hat a man really believes is what he would be ready to act upon, and to risk much upon," is the way Peirce described Green's rendition of the theory. Peirce was struck by it, and he "endeavoured," he said, "to weave that truth in with others which he had made out for himself, so as to make a consistent doctrine of cognition."[53] The result was a paper which Peirce read at the last meeting of the Metaphysical Club.

The Metaphysical Club had started to pull apart toward the summer of 1872. In April Benjamin Peirce appointed Charles acting assistant in charge of the Washington office of the Coast Survey, and Charles began spending much of his time there. In June Holmes got married, and in July Wright went to Europe for four months. (He found it overrated. "C.W. seems in Paris just as he did in Cambridge," Henry James reported home, "—serenely purpurine [purple-complexioned]. . . . I frequently see him trundling on tip-toes along the Boulevard, as he did at home along the Main Street";[54] he "seems to do nothing but loaf and absorb knowledge apparently from the asphalte of the Boulevards."[55]) Wright returned in October; as soon as he got off the boat in New York City, he fell into a severe depression.

In December Charles Peirce was made assistant in charge of gravimetric experiments at the Coast Survey (part of its project to determine the shape of the earth), and he and his wife moved to Washington soon after. The club's last meeting was evidently arranged to coincide with their departure. "Wendell H. spent an eve[g] here this week," William wrote to Henry on November 24.

> He grows more & more concentrated upon his law. His mind resembles a stiff spring, which has to be abducted violently from it, and which every instant it is left to itself flies tight back. He works less since his marriage and feels the better for it. His wife is getting well and he seems now quite cheerful about her. Chas. Peirce & wife are going to washington again for the winter and perhaps for good. He

says he is appreciated there, & only tolerated here and wd. be a fool not to go there. He read us an admirable introductory chapter to his book on logic the other day.[56]

Exactly what Peirce read is uncertain. He had been working since the spring on a book about logic (producing such a book was a life-long and unfulfilled aspiration), but the surviving drafts are fragmentary. He may have patched together his paper for the Metaphysical Club from bits and pieces. Its argument, though, is not hard to reconstruct. Peirce proposed, first, to give Green's theory about beliefs a name: he called it "pragmatism." The term was borrowed from a passage in Kant's *Kritik der reinen Vernunft* (the *Critique of Pure Reason*), a book Peirce had studied closely when he was younger. "Once an end is accepted, the conditions of its attainment are hypothetically necessary," Kant wrote.

> The physician must do something for a patient in danger, but he does not know the nature of his illness. He observes the symptoms, and if he can find no more likely alternative, judges it to be a case of phthisis. Now even in his own estimation his belief is contingent only; another observer might perhaps come to a sounder conclusion. Such contingent belief, which yet forms the ground for the actual employment of means to certain actions, I entitle *pragmatic belief*.
>
> The usual touchstone, whether that which someone asserts is merely his persuasion—or at least his subjective conviction, that is, his firm belief—is *betting*. . . . Thus pragmatic belief always exists in some specific degree, which, according to differences in the interests at stake, may be large or may be small.[57]

Kant thought of "pragmatic belief" as one of several kinds of belief; Peirce thought it was the only kind of belief. In a world that never repeats itself with exactitude, *all* believing is betting. Our beliefs and concepts are, in the end, only guesses about how things will behave most of the time. As Peirce expressed it six years later, in a series of articles he said were based on his Metaphysical Club paper: "Consider what effects, which might conceivably have practical bearings, we conceive the object of our conception to have. Then, our conception of these effects is the whole of our conception of the object."[58]

So far, Peirce was only coining a philosophical term—pragmatism—for an idea already shared by Wright, Green, Holmes, and James (and, for that matter, by James Stephen and Alexander Bain). The idea implied a doctrine, though, which Peirce was concerned to refute. This was nominalism—the belief that since concepts are generalizations about things that, taken individually, are singular and unreproducible, they do not refer to anything real. Nominalism is the doctrine that reality is just one unique thing after another, and that general truths about those things are simply conventions of language, simply names. Peirce balked at this conclusion. He believed what his father had taught him to believe: that the world is made to be known by the mind—that (in Benjamin Peirce's words) "the two are wonderfully matched." We think in generalizations; that is what inferences are—general truths drawn from the observation of particular events. Therefore, there must be things in the universe to which our generalizations correspond.

The nominalist's mistake, Peirce argued, is the definition of belief as *individual* belief. Of course the beliefs of individuals are flawed; no individual mind is capable of an accurate and objective knowledge of reality. But the aggregate beliefs of many individual minds is another matter; and here Peirce invoked the astronomer's law of errors. "No two observers can make the same observation," he wrote in one of the drafts of his book on logic. "The observations which I made yesterday are not the same which I make today. Nor are simultaneous observations at different observatories the same, however close together the observatories are placed. Every man's senses are his observatory." But just as a star exists independently of the observations made by individual astronomers, "reality is independent of the individual accidental element of thought." The real star is the object around which repeated observations ineluctably converge. The purpose of all scientific investigation is therefore to push our collective opinions about the world closer and closer to agreement with each other, and thus closer and closer to the limit represented by reality itself.

Theoretically, *complete* certainty about, say, the position of a star requires an infinite number of observations. But Peirce was not in a hurry. "The personal prejudices or other peculiarities of generations of men may postpone indefinitely an agreement in this opinion," he wrote; "but no human will or limitation can make the final result of an investigation to be anything else than that which it is destined to be. The reality, then, must be identified with what is thought in the ultimate true opinion."[59] In the end, he put it this way: "The opinion which is fated to be ultimately agreed to by all who investigate, is what we mean by the truth, and the object represented in this opinion is the real."[60]

For Peirce, there was much more at stake than a theory about knowledge. Nominalism, he believed, was a philosophy in aid of selfishness. This was not simply because nominalism denies knowledge its social character; it was because by acknowledging the reality only of individuals, nominalism denies the social altogether. "The question whether the *genus homo* has any existence except as individuals," Peirce wrote in an essay in the *North American Review* in 1871,

> is the question whether there is anything of any more dignity, worth, and importance than individual happiness, individual aspirations, individual life. Whether men really have anything in common, so that the *community* is to be considered as an end in itself . . . is the most fundamental practical question in regard to every public institution the constitution of which we have it in our power to influence.[61]

This was the conviction at the bottom of all of Peirce's thought. It was that knowledge cannot depend on the inferences of single individuals. For individuals die: "the number of probable inferences, which a man draws in his whole life, is a finite one, and he cannot be absolutely *certain* that the mean result will accord with the probabilities at all," Peirce wrote in the series that grew out of his Metaphysical Club paper. Reasoning "inexorably requires that our interests shall *not* be limited. They must not stop at our own fate, but must embrace the whole community. . . . He who would not sacrifice his own soul to save the whole world, is, as it seems to me, illogical in all his inferences, collectively. Logic is rooted in the social principle."[62]

4

In the end, the Metaphysical Club unraveled because Harvard University was reformed. In 1869 Charles William Eliot had been named president of Harvard. Eliot's academic field was chemistry, and he had once been on the faculty of the Lawrence Scientific School. He was not a very accomplished chemist, though, and he had quit Harvard in 1863 after being passed over for a new chair in chemistry. The position, the Rumford Professorship, went to Wolcott Gibbs (who *was* an accomplished chemist). When Harvard called him back to the presidency, Eliot was on the faculty of the Massachusetts Institute of Technology, which had recently been founded in Boston as a school to prepare students for the scientific professions. His appointment constituted a recognition that American higher education was changing—that science, not theology, was the educational core of the future—and that Harvard was in danger of losing its prestige. Harvard picked Eliot because it wanted to be reformed. Eliot did not disappoint it. He became the greatest professionalizer in the history of American higher education.

William James had been Eliot's student at Lawrence when he was starting out there in 1861. "A very interesting and agreeable pupil, but . . . not wholly devoted to the study of Chemistry,"[63] is the way Eliot remembered him. (James's assignment seems to have been to investigate the effects of a particular brand of baking powder on the kidneys—in other words, self-urinalysis. After three weeks, he asked Eliot to assign the experiment to someone else. It was the beginning of a lifelong aversion to laboratory work.) James soon switched fields, but Eliot was impressed by his talents, and in 1872 began the difficult business of coaxing him to join the faculty. By 1874, after a few false starts, he had succeeded.

In his first year as president Eliot inaugurated a series of lecture courses designed for graduates and local residents. Wendell Holmes gave one course; Chauncey Wright was invited to offer another.

Wright's topic was "Expositions of the Principles of Psychology, from the text of Bain," and his lectures were a disaster. He never had more than twelve students in attendance, and he turned out to have no flair for classroom instruction. "The lectures were delivered in a monotonous way, without emphasis, and they failed to arouse interest," Joseph Warner recalled with some pain. "The picture which is vividly before me is of his face rather a blank, his eyes fastened on the desk below him and therefore appearing shut, his frame almost motionless, and his voice even, to a monotonous degree."[64]

Wright's friends persisted, and in 1874–75 he was given a class in mathematical physics. This, too, was a failure, and in July 1875 Eliot wrote him to say the course would not be repeated. "I am very sorry to find that only one person has elected physics 1," he explained. "We cannot give the elective for less than four students, and I very reluctantly give you notice therefore that the elective will be discontinued."[65] On September 12, Wright's landlady found him slumped over at his desk; he had suffered a stroke during the night. That day he had a second stroke, and he died without recovering consciousness. St. John Green and the younger Henry James were at his bedside. William was out of town. "He had been drinking moderately for a few days, but not harmfully," Henry Senior wrote him. "[H]e was in here a few days ago to read to you a proof of his article on Darwinism in this last week's Nation. He sat with me *two hours & over* and we had a charming conversation. . . . I said to the family when he left, that Chauncey was in his very best bloom."[66] Wright was forty-five.

Green had quit Harvard Law School in 1873. He was disgusted by the legal formalism that came to dominate the curriculum after Eliot's appointment, in 1870, of his old college roommate Christopher Columbus Langdell (then an obscure New York attorney) to the deanship. Green moved to Boston University Law School, at a lower salary, where he became acting dean. On September 8, 1876, almost exactly a year after his old friend's death, he took an overdose of laudanum. Green was forty-six. He had been ill for some time; there is some evidence that he, too, had been an alcoholic.[67]

Benjamin Peirce had not ingratiated himself with Eliot. Peirce had been one of the promoters of Gibbs for the Rumford Professorship in chemistry, and he and Agassiz had opposed reforms Eliot planned for the Scientific School. (Eliot instituted them anyway; indifference to established interests was his greatest gift as an administrator.) Chemistry had been Charles Peirce's subject at Lawrence, but he had worked with Josiah Cooke, not with Eliot, and Eliot had broken with Cooke in a religious dispute. (Cooke was a defender of natural theology.) Through his father, Charles had gotten a position as assistant to the director of the Harvard College Observatory, Joseph Winlock; but Eliot found Charles's conduct obnoxious—he made his ambitions too plain—and when Winlock died, in 1875, he declined to consider Charles for the position. Eliot's presidency was the principal reason Charles left for the Coast Survey in Washington: Benjamin was no longer able to serve as his son's promoter and protector in Cambridge. Charles's older brother, James Mills Peirce, a professor of mathematics, became director of graduate studies under Eliot, but he was never able to get Charles a Harvard appointment. Eliot had him banned from the campus. When, almost twenty-five years later, James arranged for Peirce to come to Cambridge to speak on pragmatism, the lectures had to be held in a private house.

PART FOUR

Daniel Webster in 1819, in a portrait by Gilbert Stuart,
commissioned by the trustees of Dartmouth College
after Webster argued their case before the
United States Supreme Court.

TEN

BURLINGTON

I

O N January 18, 1859, in Burlington, Vermont, a little boy named John Dewey fell into a pail of scalding water. His parents applied oil to his burns and wrapped him in cotton batting, but there was another accident and the batting caught fire. The next day the child died. He was two and a half. It is a sad and terrible story, but the parents found a means of consolation, and nine months later almost to the day, on October 20, 1859, they had another baby. He was named after his dead brother.

This John Dewey lived to be ninety-three and became one of the most celebrated public intellectuals of his time. He published books on psychology, ethics, education, logic, religion, politics, philosophy, and art; he wrote for scholarly journals and for journals of opinion; and he lectured before almost every kind of audience. He helped to create, and sometimes to lead, many prominent political and educational organizations: the American Civil Liberties Union, the National Association for the Advancement of Colored People, the

League for Industrial Democracy, the New York Teachers Union, the American Association of University Professors, and the New School for Social Research. "It is scarcely an exaggeration to say that for a generation no major issue was clarified until Dewey had spoken,"[1] Henry Steele Commager wrote in 1950, when Dewey was ninety-one and still active. And there were few public issues on which Dewey did not speak.

The organizations Dewey's name is associated with make it natural to think of him as a representative American liberal. In the very broad sense that liberalism stands for an opposition to the reproduction of hierarchies—political, social, cultural, and even conceptual— Dewey was probably as liberal a thinker as the United States has produced. He seems never to have come across a distinction he did not find inherently invidious and wish to break down. But in almost every other respect the identification is misleading. In the nineteenth century liberalism meant a commitment to free markets; in the twentieth century it meant a commitment to individual liberties. Those were not commitments Dewey shared—at least not in the terms in which they are usually framed. Usually, Americans think of freedom as a condition of personal autonomy, independence from the will of others. This way of thinking reflects just the kind of distinction— between oneself and the rest of the group of which one is a part— that Dewey considered false.

In the beginning, Dewey's reasons for rejecting a hard distinction between the individual and society, between autonomy and heteronomy, were philosophical. But he reached maturity as a thinker at exactly the moment American social and economic life was tipping over into modern forms of organization, forms whose characteristics reflect the effects of size: impersonal authority, bureaucratic procedure, mass markets. The persistence of older notions of individualism in this new dispensation was a cause of confusion, disruption, and conflict, some of it violent. Dewey's success as a public intellectual derived from the acuity with which he saw how his philosophical beliefs might be relevant to these new conditions, and from the speed with which he shed the metaphysical husks of those beliefs in order to attempt to make philosophy (as he hopefully put it) "a method . . . for dealing with the problems of men."[2]

Dewey was more radical than most American liberals because he rated solidarity higher than independence. Though he was never a socialist, his political views were closer to socialism than they were to even New Deal welfare liberalism: he voted for Norman Thomas, and against Franklin Roosevelt, three times. But Dewey was also more conservative than many American liberals because he refused to regard the perpetuation of modern forms of social and economic organization as necessarily evil, or as displacing ways of life people should be sorry to give up. He believed that people could achieve satisfaction—"self-realization," to use his term—within the world in which they found themselves. This meant (and this is where the philosophy came in) understanding the world and its connection to the self in a new way. Dewey rethought the relation between liberty and conformity. Unlike almost every other serious thinker of his time, he was at home in modernity.

Dewey was one of the world's most mild-mannered people, but his career was that of a man who never looked back. He kept what he wanted from what he had learned and he left the rest behind without regret. Nostalgia was not an element of his temperament. His father, Archibald Dewey, was a storekeeper, a witty man who recited Milton around the shop but whose greatest hope for his sons was that one of them might grow up to be a mechanic. Dewey's mother, Lucina, was an evangelical woman who demanded regular avowals of piety from her children. ("Are you right with Jesus?" she used to ask them.)[3] Dewey does not seem to have quarreled with his parents, but he was glad to leave Burlington. Many years later he used to say to his colleagues on the faculty at Columbia University that he didn't see why they had summer places in Vermont. "I got out as soon as I could," he told them.[4]

The way out was through the local college in Burlington, which happened to be the University of Vermont. When Dewey graduated, in 1879, there were eighteen students in his class; one was his brother Davis, and another was a cousin who had been raised in their family. Dewey went off briefly to teach high school in a place called South Oil City, in Pennsylvania, but he returned to Burlington to study philosophy privately with one of his former professors. So that by the time he entered graduate school at Johns Hopkins, in 1882, Dewey had already been trained as a certain kind of philosopher. He was sent into the world as the last of the Vermont Transcendentalists.

2

The first of the Vermont Transcendentalists was James Marsh. Marsh was born in Hartford, Vermont, in 1794, and he attended Dartmouth College at what turned out to be the most famous moment in its history. It was a defining moment for Marsh as well.

Dartmouth was the creation of a Connecticut minister named Eleazar Wheelock, who had raised money in England from a group led by the Earl of Dartmouth for a charity school for Native Americans. In 1769 Wheelock obtained a land grant from the crown colony of New Hampshire to establish his college up the Connecticut River in Hanover. The colonial government issued the college a charter of incorporation, which stipulated that it would be governed by a board of twelve trustees, with power to remove the president, and that Wheelock would be the first president of the college and would have the right to name his successor. It was characteristic of Wheelock's method of doing business that this charter conflicted with the understanding he had had with his British backers, since, by creating a new board of trustees, it deprived them of control over educational policy, and the school for Native Americans was subsequently separated from the college. Dartmouth became, like Harvard and Princeton (then known as the College of New Jersey), primarily a finishing school for Anglo-American men.

In 1779 Eleazar Wheelock died. As was his prerogative under the charter, he had named his son John to succeed him. John Wheelock was twenty-five years old. He had been serving as a colonel in the Revolutionary Army when his father died, and he regarded Dartmouth as more or less the personal property of the Wheelock family.

He ran it in that spirit. He was an autocrat. By the time James Marsh was a student there, John Wheelock was engaged in a full-blown feud with the board of trustees.

The politics of the dispute were strictly academic—that is, the issues were myriad, they were interrelated in arcane ways, and they were fantastically petty. The principals were fighting over things like which pew Dartmouth students should sit in when they attended the village church. In 1815 Wheelock, finding himself blocked by the trustees on virtually every front, asked the New Hampshire legislature to investigate. The trustees responded by firing Wheelock. Wheelock then composed and distributed a pamphlet abusing the trustees, and the affair became a topic of public debate throughout New England.

The key element in these events was the timing of Wheelock's appeal to the legislature. In the 1810s New Hampshire politics was consumed by an all-out war between the Federalists and the Republicans. The Federalists were the party of the Founders, but by the end of the War of 1812 (which they had opposed) they were a dying political faction. Their principal constituents were wealthy merchants, major property owners, and religious conservatives. The Republicans were the party of Jefferson. They believed in freedom of conscience and grassroots democracy, and they were hostile to the large commercial interests.

New England had been the last bastion of Federalist hegemony, but in 1816 the Republicans regained control of the state government in New Hampshire. The new governor, William Plumer, had started his career as a Federalist, but he was now a Republican, and with a convert's zeal. He announced his intention to intervene in the feud at Dartmouth in his inaugural address to the state legislature, a speech praised by Jefferson himself, who called it "replete with sound principles and truly Republican," and who endorsed Plumer's decision to set Dartmouth trustees straight. "The idea that institutions, established for the use of the nation, cannot be touched or modified, even to make them answer this end, because of rights gratuitously supposed in those employed to manage them in trust to the public, may, perhaps, be a salutory provision against the abuses of a monarch, but it is most absurd against the nation itself," Jefferson wrote to Plumer. The notion that the terms in the original charter were forever immune to change, Jefferson said, was equivalent to the notion "that the earth belongs to the dead, and not to the living."[5]

Plumer wasted little time getting the New Hampshire legislature to rewrite the college's charter. The trustees were replaced (by expanding the board to twenty-one and then having the old members voted off), the school was renamed Dartmouth University, complete religious freedom was mandated, Wheelock was reappointed president, and a board of overseers was established to represent the public interest. In short, Plumer engineered a state takeover.

Wheelock's alliance with Plumer was entirely opportunistic. For Wheelock himself was a Federalist and an orthodox Calvinist; the trustee who had been giving him the hardest time, a man named Nathaniel Niles, happened to be a prominent Republican. The troubles in Hanover were largely ego effects. But Plumer's intervention changed the terms of the dispute and turned Dartmouth into a site of ideological confrontation. The new board of trustees dismissed the faculty (there were only five) and removed them from the college buildings. The fired professors responded by setting themselves up in private houses in town and reconstituting their college under the direction of the old board of trustees. Most of the students went with them.

By 1817, therefore, there were two Dartmouths in Hanover: Dartmouth University, a public institution operated on Jeffersonian principles, and Dartmouth College, a private institution run by people who despised the Republicans as radical democrats and who regarded themselves as the defenders of true religion and private property. In 1817 the board of the college sued its former treasurer, William Woodward, who had defected to the university, to recover the original charter and other corporate property. This was the action that gave birth to the *Trustees of Dartmouth College v. Woodward*— the Dartmouth College case.

The case was first argued before the New Hampshire Superior Court, all three of whose members were Plumer appointees. The original charter of incorporation, the trustees of the college argued, constituted a contract between Dartmouth and the state; in unilaterally rewriting it, the legislature was in violation of the Contract Clause of the United States Constitution—the clause which provides that no state may pass any law "impairing the Obligation of Contracts."[6] To meet this argument, the New Hampshire court proceeded to draw a distinction between private corporations and public corporations. If a corporation is established to benefit individuals, the court said, it is private, and the Contract Clause protects it from government intervention. But if a corporation is established to benefit the public, that corporation is ipso facto a public company, and is therefore subject to public control. It doesn't matter where the money comes from, the court said: the state can fund a private corporation, and private money can endow a public one. It is solely a question of who benefits.

On this definition, the court concluded, Dartmouth College was plainly a public corporation. "The *College*," the court pointed out,

> was founded for the purpose of "spreading the knowledge of the Great Redeemer," among the savages and of furnishing "the best means of education" to the province of *New-Hampshire*. These great purposes are surely, if any thing can be, matters of public concern. . . . The trustees themselves have no greater interest in the spreading of christian knowledge among the indians, and in providing the best means of education, than any other individuals in the community. Nor have they any private interest in the property of this institution. . . . If all the property of the institution were destroyed, the loss would be exclusively public, and no private loss to them. . . . The office of trustee of *Dartmouth College* is, in fact, a public trust, as much so as the office of governor, or of a judge of this court.[7]

If the people of New Hampshire, through their elected representatives, wished to intervene in matters of college governance, the Contract Clause therefore did not stand in their way. "These trustees are the servants of the public," the court held, "and the servant is not to resist the will of his master, in a matter that concerns that master alone."[8] This was Republican reasoning. It undertook to limit the immunity of private corporations from the exercise of the democratic will.

The college appealed to the United States Supreme Court, before which it was represented by its favorite son, Daniel Webster, Dartmouth class of 1801. Webster was a champion of nation and of industry: those were the views that underlay the position he would stake out, more than thirty years later, in the Seventh of March speech, which was essentially an argument to preserve the union for the benefit of commerce. From 1813 to 1817 he had represented New Hampshire in Congress as a Federalist and a defender of the New England shipping interests. Webster's argument to the Supreme Court was that the New Hampshire judges had erred in designating Dartmouth a public corporation. Dartmouth was "an *eleemosynary* corporation," he explained. "It is a *private charity*, originally founded and endowed by an individual, with a charter obtained for it at *his request*, for the better administration of *his charity*."[9] Wheelock's whole reason for seeking incorporation was to prevent the money he had raised from being administered in ways he had not intended. A private charity, Webster said, is no less private than a business. "Who ever appointed a legislature to administer his charity?"[10] he asked.

Webster's peroration in the case became legendary, though it is impossible to know precisely what he said since no one recorded his words at the time. "It is . . . a small College," he is supposed to have told the court at the end of his oral argument. "And yet, *there are those who love it*"—and he went on to describe, in full sonority, his filial attachment to Dartmouth, winding up with an allusion to the assassination of Julius Caesar. Some people in the audience (quite sparse, actually: mostly lawyers waiting for their own cases to come up) are reported to have swooned. The chief justice, John Marshall, wept.[11]

Webster's histrionics were probably supererogatory. Federalism was nearly a religion with Marshall. He hated Jefferson and all things Jeffersonian; and he had already issued two opinions, in *Fletcher v. Peck* (1810) and *State of New Jersey v. Wilson* (1812), ruling that contracts to which the state is a party are covered by the Contract

Clause. Apart from building a majority among his brethren, he had
no trouble finding the actions of the New Hampshire legislature "repugnant to the constitution of the United States."[12] In his concurring
opinion, Associate Justice Joseph Story explicitly repudiated the
New Hampshire court's definition of "public" and "private." "[P]ublic
corporations are such only as are founded by the government for
public purposes, where the whole interests belong also to the government," Story held. "If, therefore, the foundation be private,
though under the charter of the government, the corporation is private, however extensive the uses may be to which it is devoted. . . .
[T]he uses may, in a certain sense, be called public, but the corporations are private; as much so, indeed, as if the franchises were vested
in a single person."[13] The Court's opinion, handed down in 1819, effectively returned control of the college to the old board of trustees
under the terms of the original charter. Dartmouth University was
abolished. The case made Webster famous. The trustees paid him a
fee of one thousand dollars and commissioned Gilbert Stuart to
paint his portrait.

The Dartmouth College case is cited as a landmark in the history
of academic freedom, because it made private educational institutions safe from government interference. But Marshall deliberately
cast his reasoning in broad language, and his opinion became the basis for claims by any corporation having business with the public that
the Contract Clause protected it from state regulation. People who
wished to subject such corporations to some measure of public ac-
countability were obliged to carve out exceptions from the ruling in
Dartmouth College. As Webster and Marshall intended, the decision
expanded the privileges of private property against the claims of
the public interest, and it helped to unleash capitalist enterprise in
nineteenth-century America.

3

James Marsh was a Dartmouth College loyalist. His uncle Charles, a
prominent Vermont lawyer, was one of the leaders of the trustees
who fired Wheelock, and James was a student at the college-in-exile,

from which he graduated in 1817. He and his college friends looked upon the actions of the New Hampshire legislature as mob tyranny; they considered the university a bastion of radicals, deists, and infidels; and they believed that the poison at the root of the outrage was the philosophy of John Locke.[14]

In Marsh's time the name of Locke stood for two theories. The first theory was based on the belief that the mind is a blank slate, written on by experience. We possess, according to this view, no innate ideas, no mental contents that just automatically come with having minds. All our ideas derive from the world outside ourselves, to which we have no unmediated access, but which we experience through the senses in the form of images and impressions. This is empiricism. The second theory associated with Locke was based on the belief that societies are composed of autonomous individuals who establish governments in order to protect their natural rights, which include the right to rebel against tyrannous regimes. This is liberal individualism, the philosophical foundation of the Declaration of Independence, a document drafted, of course, by Jefferson. In Lockean thinking, human beings are essentially rights-bearing ciphers.

Like Newtonian physics, Lockean philosophy is atomistic: it imagines everything as a concatenation of independent entities. In the Lockean theory of knowledge, mental contents are aggregations of discrete items of sense data linked by chains of association; in the Lockean theory of politics, social groups are aggregations of autonomous individuals linked by voluntary and revokable contractual bonds. These are theories that contemplate no whole greater than its parts. Also like Newtonian physics, Lockean empiricism explains everything as a matter of cause and effect. Apart from the possibility of a start-up god, a divinity who winds the universe's clock, it seems to leave no room for the supernatural (that which we cannot know through the senses) or for the miraculous (the uncaused cause).

James Marsh's distaste for atomistic thinking had two dimensions. One was political. He rejected the idea that societies are associations of already fully realized individuals. He believed, on the contrary, that selves can be realized only in and through communities, and he thought the distinction implicit in Lockean political theory between "the individual" and "the state" was therefore insupportable. What individuates individuals, what enables them to realize themselves *as* individuals, is their role within a group. Outside of the group, they have no identity.

Marsh's second objection was religious. Marsh was an evangelical Christian. He had taken Jesus as his savior during a religious revival in Hanover when he was a Dartmouth student, and he refused to accept the divorce empiricism seemed to mandate between matters of philosophy and matters of faith. It was common in the nineteenth century to make modern science and philosophy compatible with Christian belief by pronouncing questions of faith to be, by their nature, unprovable. The argument was that although the truth of religious beliefs cannot be established empirically (by scientific observation) or rationally (by philosophical argument), it does not follow that faith is untenable. It simply means that science and philosophy have to do only with the world we can see and touch, the world of phenomena; about things of the spirit, they can properly have nothing to say. Marsh refused to adhere to this decorum, and it became the quest of his short life to find a philosophy on all fours with evangelical Christianity.

He found it (or he thought he found it) in the work of Samuel Taylor Coleridge. Coleridge, when Marsh took him up, was regarded in the United States as a distinguished poet with an unfortunate taste for German metaphysics. He was not esteemed as a thinker. But in 1829 Marsh published an edition of Coleridge's *Aids to Reflection*, to which he contributed a long introduction announcing that Coleridge had proved that Christianity is indeed consistent with philosophy—that (in Marsh's words) "so far from being irrational, CHRISTIAN FAITH IS THE PERFECTION OF HUMAN REASON."[15] It makes no sense, Marsh argued, to have two systems of belief—a philosophical system for natural things and a theological system for spiritual things. "We cannot, as rational beings, believe a proposition on the grounds of reason, and deny it on the authority of revelation," he insisted. "We cannot believe a proposition in philosophy, and deny the same proposition in theology."[16] We need a single system, and

Coleridge had produced one. He had rescued evangelicism from superstition. He had provided rational grounds for believing in the supernatural agency of Jesus Christ.

Coleridge had accomplished this by the trick of looking inward instead of outward. Looking outward onto the phenomenal world, which is where the empiricist looks, we find no justification for faith because faith does not justify itself by the evidence of the senses; all the evidence of the senses tells us (as Locke's successor David Hume had seemed to show) is that the universe is just one phenomenal event after another. Faith justifies itself instead by the evidence of introspection—the evidence we gather by looking into our own minds and reflecting on the laws of our being. For we do have innate ideas, mental contents that automatically come with being human; and we find in those ideas a consistency and a harmony missing from the fallen world we know through the senses—and thus discover a rational basis for faith.

This is an echo of Plato's distinction between an inconstant world of appearance, apprehended by the senses, and an eternal world of ideal forms, apprehended by the intellect. Coleridge had read Plato and the Neoplatonic British writers of the seventeenth century (as had Marsh) with enthusiasm; but he had another source as well. This was the philosophy of Immanuel Kant, whom he understood (somewhat erroneously) to have made a distinction between "understanding," defined as the mental faculty that perceives empirical particulars, and "reason," the mental faculty that perceives universals. When Coleridge and Marsh said that Christianity is "rational," this is what they meant: that its doctrines are consistent with the universal laws of being as these are known by the faculty of reason. As Marsh put it: "though we may believe what 'passeth all *understanding*' [that is, what we cannot perceive through our senses: the miraculous], we *cannot* believe what is *absurd*, or contradictory to *reason*."[17]

Coleridge learned his Kant through the mediation of later German philosophers, notably Friedrich Schelling, the man who had furnished Louis Agassiz's mind with the teachings of *Naturphilosophie* at the University of Berlin, and large chunks of whose prose Coleridge had a habit of incorporating into his own writings without the trouble of quotation marks. It was from Schelling that Coleridge took the key concept of his own thought, which is the organic unity, the ultimate indivisibility, of part and whole, matter and spirit, mind and nature. This transcendent and metaphysical unity—transcendent because it is "greater" than the parts that compose it, metaphysical because it is "beyond" the world that we know through the senses—is what "reason" perceives. "Christianity," Coleridge wrote, in a passage noted by Marsh, "is not a *Theory*, or a *Speculation*; but a *Life*. Not a *Philosophy* of Life, but a Life and a living process."[18] This is the essence of the Romantic reaction, the great renunciation of mechanism in post-Enlightenment European culture. In Blake's lines:

> The Atoms of Democritus
> And Newton's Particles of Light
> Are sands upon the Red sea shore,
> Where Israel's tents do shine so bright.[19]

In the final pages of his introduction to the *Aids to Reflection*, Marsh made his polemical point. It was that Lockean empiricism and the philosophical tradition descended from it were now prevalent in American theological and philosophical circles, and were "of an injurious and dangerous tendency."[20] They were sensuous philosophies: they turned human beings into brutes, mere reactors to external stimuli, the toys of matter. By making everything inside us determined by something outside us, these philosophies denied the possibility of human agency, and thus removed the foundation for morality.

Marsh's edition of Coleridge is one of the originary texts of American Transcendentalism. Emerson read it the year it appeared and wrote to his aunt of his new enthusiasm for Coleridge (though it took him a while to feel he understood what Coleridge was saying), and that enthusiasm led him to Kant, Fichte, and Schelling, and to the other major English-language conduit of German philosophy, Thomas Carlyle. Frederick Henry Hedge's review of Marsh's edition of the *Aids to Reflection* in 1833 was the first place in which the term "transcendental philosophy" was used in the sense Emerson and his associates would use it: as the name for a philosophy based on the superiority of what Hedge called "a free intuition."[21] And the first meeting of what became the Transcendentalist Club, in the Boston parsonage of George Ripley in 1836, was convened by a group of young clergymen who were unhappy with (in Hedge's words) "the reigning sensuous philosophy, dating from Locke,"[22] and who had been inspired by reading Marsh's edition of Coleridge. Marsh provided Emerson and his friends with an alternative to the Unitarianism and empiricism they were trying to find a way to renounce. He helped bring Romanticism to America.

By the time he wrote his introduction, when he was thirty-five, Marsh had been president of the University of Vermont for three years, and he had already begun to reform the university on Coleridgean principles. This meant integrating the curriculum so that (in the words of the university's published rationale) "all that is taught in the institution, forms but one ample course, the several parts of which may be acquired in any number and to any extent that the purposes of the individual may require."[23] Marsh instituted an elective system (the first in the country), admitted part-time students, allowed students to graduate in as few or as many terms as they needed to master the material, discouraged formal examinations, and capped the curriculum with a senior-year philosophy course designed to introduce students to the unity of all knowledge. As the program was summed up twenty-five years later by a member of the faculty, it sought

> to give a coherence to the various studies, in each department, so that its several parts shall present, more or less, the unity, not of an aggregation, nor of a juxtaposition, nor of a merely logical arrangement, but of a natural development, and a growth; and therefore the study of it, rightly pursued, would be a growing and enlarging process, to the mind of the student.[24]

It was educational organicism.

And it was a big success. The university had been struggling when Marsh arrived; by the time he stepped down as president, in

1833, to take a chair in philosophy, it was one of the most respected institutions of advanced learning in New England. Marsh took care to assure an orderly succession. After he returned to teaching, he was succeeded as president by an old Dartmouth College friend, John Wheeler; after Marsh's death from tuberculosis, in 1842, his chair in philosophy was taken by another Dartmouth friend, Joseph Torrey, who later became president of the university as well. These were people who shared Marsh's Dartmouth background and Marsh's philosophical and pedagogical views, and they ensured that for more than forty years students at the University of Vermont were trained in what was known as "the Burlington philosophy."

The Burlington philosophy was Transcendentalist, but it was not Emersonian. When Marsh spoke of "intuition," he didn't mean "feeling." He meant almost the opposite of feeling: he meant rigorous introspection and analysis. The whole basis for his interest in Coleridge was his belief that Coleridge had created (with assistance from Kant) a complete and logically sound philosophical system. But Emerson, Marsh thought (and he was not wrong), used the concept of intuition as an excuse for abandoning systematic thinking altogether. In the winter of 1837–38 Emerson delivered a series of lectures on "Human Culture" at the Masonic Temple in Boston. When accounts of the talks reached Marsh in Burlington, he was disgusted. "[T]hey . . . contain with scarcely a decent disguise nothing less than an Epicurean Atheism dressed up in a style seducing and to many perhaps deceptive,"[25] he wrote to Richard Henry Dana. "The whole of Boston transcendentalism," he complained to another correspondent a few years later, "I take to be rather a superficial affair. . . . They pretend to no system of unity, but each utters, it seems, the inspiration of the moment, assuming that it all comes from the universal heart, while ten to one it comes only from the stomach of the individual."[26] It was the sensuous philosophy all over again, and without the philosophy.

True to its origins in the Dartmouth College crisis and in the writings of its hero, Coleridge, Vermont Transcendentalism was fundamentally conservative. It was about preserving institutions, not (like the Concord edition) about ignoring, debunking, or reinventing them. Its communitarianism was the communitarianism of the Christian communion, not the communitarianism of Brook Farm. Marsh had taught at a college in Virginia before coming to Vermont, and he disliked slavery; but he thought the proper means for reform lay in the hearts of Southern whites. His successor as president, John Wheeler, opposed the Civil War: he believed the slave system might become more benevolent, but he did not think it needed to be abolished. These were the views of people who clung to the very Calvinist dogma the Boston Transcendentalists so scandalously repudiated: the belief that the moral depravity of human beings can never be eradicated in this world.

4

The political views of the Vermont Transcendentalists were not the political views of most Vermonters. Vermont was possibly the most abolitionist state in the country. It had outlawed slavery in 1777, the first colony to do so, and of 37,000 Vermont men liable for military duty during the Civil War, almost 34,000 volunteered. More men from Vermont died in the course of the war than from any other Northern state.[27]

Though he was nearly fifty when Lincoln issued his first call for volunteers in the summer of 1861, Archibald Dewey sold his shop and signed up as a quartermaster in the First Vermont Cavalry. He was mustered out in 1862, reenlisted, and was promoted to captain. The First Vermont Cavalry took part in seventy-five engagements; more than a third of its original number died, and it fought to the very end of the Civil War. It was in the middle of executing the order for the last cavalry charge in the history of the Army of the Potomac, at Appomattox Court House, when Lee surrendered.[28] Archibald Dewey stayed in the army for the entire war. In 1864, when John was five, Lucina Dewey sold the family's house and moved to Virginia to be with her husband. The Deweys did not return to Burlington until 1867.

John Dewey was raised in a family with a culture of social commitment. Archibald remained a die-hard Republican all his life. In the contested presidential election of 1876, when it appeared that the Democrat Samuel Tilden had defeated Rutherford B. Hayes, John Dewey brought the news to his father. "Then we fought the war in vain," Archibald Dewey said.[29] (Hayes was later declared the winner, by one vote, in the electoral college. He was the third of four Union generals elected president between 1868 and 1892.) Lucina Dewey was an orthodox Congregationalist and a believer in original sin, but she was a social activist as well. She worked in the Adam's Mission House, a local charitable institution, and she was known in Burlington as a reformer and a person who looked after the interests of the poor.

Lucina Dewey's best friend was Sarah Paine Torrey, the daughter of Joseph Torrey, the man who had been Marsh's successor first as professor of philosophy and then as president of the University of Vermont. Sarah Torrey was also the wife of Joseph Torrey's nephew (in other words, her own cousin), Henry Augustus Pearson Torrey. Henry Torrey had been born in Massachusetts, but had moved to Burlington when he was young and was raised in his uncle's house (where he presumably had plenty of opportunity to win the favor of his future wife). He graduated from the University of Vermont in 1858, and after Joseph Torrey died, in 1867, he took over the chair of philosophy. He had had no special training as a philosopher—he was working as a pastor elsewhere in Vermont when the appointment was made—and he spent his first three years on the job working his way through Kant in German to get himself up to speed with the Burlington philosophy. Henry Torrey was, academically speaking, the direct descendant of James Marsh. He used *The Remains of the Rev. James Marsh*, a volume edited by his uncle, as a textbook. He was John Dewey's teacher.

Dewey was an exceptionally shy and self-effacing young man. He resented his mother's intrusive evangelicalism, but he seems to have had a hard time resisting it, possibly because he disliked contentiousness, possibly because the idea of unworthiness resonated with his own sense of ineffectuality. He was not completely tame as a student, but he took to books as a refuge from social stress. The rousing of his philosophical ambitions happened in biology class. He had been assigned a physiology textbook by Thomas Huxley, and he found Huxley's description of the human body as an interdependent and interrelated organism an inspiring image of life. The book provided "a kind of type or model of a view of things to which material in any field ought to conform," Dewey wrote many years later. "Subconsciously, at least, I was led to desire a world and a life that would have the same properties as had the human organism in the picture of it derived from study of Huxley's treatment."[30]

This was the way James Marsh himself had conceived of knowledge, as an interfused and interrelated whole; so that when Dewey became Henry Torrey's student, he was primed to receive the Burlington philosophy. Torrey's class was known as "the Mansfield course," after the Vermont mountain the classroom looked out on. It began with a consideration of Mount Mansfield as a material fact, and then moved on to a discussion of Mount Mansfield as a mental concept—in other words, first the mountain as perceived by the understanding, and then the mountain as perceived by reason. Dewey read Marsh's edition of the *Aids to Reflection* in the class and he embraced its synthesis of philosophy and faith enthusiastically. It had on him its intended effect of making Christian piety seem compatible with modern thought—with, for example, Darwinian biology. Marsh's edition, he said many years later, was "my first Bible."[31]

In its day, Marsh's Kantianism had been iconoclastic, but by the time Dewey was a student in Burlington, in the late 1870s, the edge had long since worn off. Henry Torrey was deeply devout. He took little interest in social issues, or in anything else outside his study and his church. Dewey remembered him as a strong thinker but a timid man. Still, when Dewey returned to Burlington from his two-year teaching stint in Pennsylvania, he hooked up with Torrey again for a private tutorial. Torrey taught Dewey how to read German, and they took walks together in the woods and talked about Kant. In this setting Dewey found Torrey a little less inhibited, but only a little. His later impression was of a man shackled to doctrine. "Undoubtedly pantheism is the most satisfactory form of metaphysics intellectually," Dewey remembered Torrey saying to him during one of their walks, "but it goes counter to religious faith."[32] The comment is a pretty clear indication that the Burlington tank was on empty. Marsh had invented his philosophy, after all, to ensure that *no* belief worth holding would be philosophically satisfactory and religiously unacceptable at the same time. Torrey's confession that he could not square what he thought logical with what he thought orthodox was a confession that Kant and Coleridge had not cured the split Marsh claimed they had.

But Torrey seems to have given Dewey confidence in his philosophical abilities. While they were working together, Dewey wrote two short articles—"The Metaphysical Assumptions of Materialism" and "The Pantheism of Spinoza," both defenses of Burlington theories—and sent them off to the *Journal of Speculative Philosophy* (the place where, thirteen years earlier, the young Charles Peirce had published the articles on cognition that had intrigued and baffled William James). The articles were accepted, and in 1882, Dewey applied to graduate school at the Johns Hopkins University in Baltimore. Torrey wrote him two letters of recommendation, one for admission and a second, a year later, for a fellowship. They were positive about Dewey's abilities, and promised that Dewey's "natural reserve . . . diminishes considerably on more intimate acquaintance."[33] The president of the University of Vermont, Matthew Buckham, sent a letter, too. "He is sound and sweet all through," he wrote of Dewey—though, he added, rather reticent. Buckham wondered whether Dewey had "the amount of dogmatism that a teacher ought to have."[34]

Dewey was accepted as a student at Hopkins, but he was turned down for a fellowship for his first year. When he wrote personally to the president of the university asking for a scholarship, he was turned down again. It is a sign of his impatience to get out of Vermont that he borrowed five hundred dollars from an aunt and went anyway.

Juliette Peirce in 1883, the year she married Charles Peirce.

ELEVEN

BALTIMORE

I

THE JOHNS HOPKINS UNIVERSITY did not really have a philosophy department in 1882. It was not for lack of resources. The university was then only six years old, but it was very well endowed, and it had gotten off to a spectacular start. It had been created from half of what was at the time the largest private bequest ever made in America, $7 million, mostly in the form of Baltimore and Ohio Railroad Company stock, left by a Baltimore financier. (The other half of the $7 million was dedicated to founding a hospital. By contrast, the largest private gift to an educational institution up to the time of the Civil War was the $50,000 Abbott Lawrence had given to Harvard in aid of its Agassiz retention program.) Though Johns Hopkins left no special instructions about the nature of the university he wished to be founded in his name, the trustees of his estate decided to build a school dedicated primarily to research and doctoral education. Hopkins did offer undergraduate instruction, but the university was designed to be known as a center of advanced learning, the first of its kind in the country.

The person the trustees chose to oversee the job was Daniel Coit Gilman. Gilman had been recommended by Charles William Eliot. The two men had had similar careers. Gilman had gone to Yale; in the 1850s he traveled to Europe, where he served as an attaché to the American legation in St. Petersburg, examined the school systems, and studied for a year at the University of Berlin (his field was geography). He returned in 1856 to help Yale build up its scientific school, the Sheffield School, just as Eliot had set about to raise standards at the Lawrence Scientific School at Harvard. Gilman was serving as president of the University of California when he was called, at the age of forty-three, to Baltimore.

More than nine thousand Americans studied in Germany in the nineteenth century. Like many of them, Gilman was impressed by the German university—in particular, by two features conspicuous to someone coming from an American setting. The first was a well-established principle of academic freedom (at least at the universities most Americans attended, Göttingen and Berlin); the second was a commitment to *Wissenschaft*, "pure learning"—the idea of knowledge for its own sake. In Germany, academic freedom and "pure learning" had specific connotations: they were associated with a spirit of nationalism and with the concept of personal mental development, *Bildung*. For most Americans who saw the German university as an adaptable institutional model, though, they tended to reduce to a single term: science.[1]

At Harvard, Eliot modernized the curriculum in the name of "freedom"—a value he invoked continually—by instituting an elective system for undergraduates. (By 1900 he had eliminated virtually all requirements at Harvard, with the unintended result that over half the students who graduated had taken nothing but introductory courses for four years.) And he modernized the professional schools—medicine, law, and science—by making a college degree a prerequisite for admission. (In 1869–70, Eliot's first year as president, half the students at Harvard Law School and nearly three-quarters of the students at Harvard Medical School did not have B.A.s—which is how it was that Henry James, who had never spent a day in college, enrolled at Harvard Law School in 1862. His brother William took his M.D. without any prior degree, though he had spent a few desultory years at Lawrence.)

Eliot was too much of a utilitarian to be comfortable with the notion of pursuing knowledge for its own sake, however. He thought research ought to yield practical benefits—he once addressed a convention of philologists by commending them for their contributions to industrial civilization—and though he established a kind of adult education program for college graduates (the program Chauncey Wright taught in), he was slow to create a real graduate school.[2] Harvard's delay gave Gilman his opportunity.

Gilman set out to buy up the world's top researchers for Hopkins, and he had few compunctions about raiding the school of the man who had helped to get him the job. He tried to recruit Benjamin Peirce; he tried to recruit the Rumford Professor of Chemistry, Wolcott Gibbs (who would have been prudent to accept: Eliot never forgave him for winning the chair he had coveted). These efforts failed, but Gilman was successful elsewhere, and by 1880, four years after it opened, Johns Hopkins had more than a hundred graduate students (to Harvard's forty-one), and its faculty had published almost as much research as had been published during the previous twenty years by the faculties of all other American universities combined. By the time Dewey graduated, in 1884, almost every one of Hopkins's fifty-three professors had studied in Germany, and thirteen of them held the Ph.D., a degree not even granted in the United States until 1861. Hopkins was known as the Göttingen of Baltimore.

But Gilman had trouble finding a philosopher.[3] There were two difficulties. The first was a public relations problem that had to do with the connotations understood to attach to the term "science" in the late nineteenth century. The reason many Americans attended German universities was to do laboratory work, and the notion of science they brought back with them when they returned to the United States was empirical and positivist—that is, hostile to explanations that invoked unobservable entities. "Pure science" meant an unsentimental effort to reduce the explanation of phenomena to the physical laws of cause and effect, to restrict the scope of knowledge to things that can be measured. It meant doing without the hypothesis of a god—not only in the case of stars and rocks and fishes, but, since Darwin, in the case of human beings as well. Squaring this enterprise with moral principles understood by most Americans to derive from divine revelation and to depend on the existence of a faculty of free will in human beings was a tricky business.

Just how tricky Gilman had brought home to him on almost the day his new university opened, in September 1876. The inaugural address was delivered by Thomas Huxley, who, besides being more intimately associated with Darwinism than anyone in the world besides Darwin himself, also happened to be the person who had invented the term "agnostic." His presence sent a message. And as the newspapers noted, so did the absence of prayers, benedictions, or references to religion of any kind during the ceremonies. Gilman, who was a religious man, found himself dealing with the public impression that Hopkins was a godless institution. He needed to demonstrate a commitment to Christian values within a university dedicated to a positivist scientific agenda.

It was exactly the problem James Marsh had faced fifty years before: the problem of reconciling reason and faith. Gilman could finesse the conflict, but only so far. He could rely on the decorum that granted the scientist and the theologian autonomy within their separate realms in every area of academic inquiry except one, and that was philosophy. It would be counterproductive, at a research institution, to hire a philosopher who was antagonistic to science; it would be fatal to hire one who was antagonistic to revelation. Marsh's dream became Gilman's dream: to find a philosopher whose research project was the synthesis of scientific and religious worldviews, someone who could reconcile mechanics with miracles. Gilman's task was harder, of course, because unlike Marsh, he really believed in the mechanics.

The task was additionally vexed by a problem within the discipline of philosophy itself.[4] In Marsh's day, to talk about the "laws of the human mind" was to talk philosophically. This is why Marsh and Coleridge were able to "refute" Locke and Hume's entirely speculative account of how the mind works by replacing it with their own entirely speculative account. The question whether what these writers were doing was "philosophy" or "psychology" would not have made sense to them. Psychology was just what philosophers did when they talked about minds. It was part of the same field, "mental science."

In Gilman's day, this field was splitting in two. When William James went to Germany, in 1867, he did so to study what was then the hottest area in science: physiological psychology, sometimes called psychophysics. Physiological psychology was founded on a distinction between the mind (consciousness) and the brain (an organ of the body), and its premise was that all mind processes are correlated with brain processes, that every conscious event has a physical basis. "Mental science" therefore meant experimentation rather than introspection. It meant measuring the reactions of the nervous system in a laboratory rather than speculating on the universal laws of reason in a library.

In its most uncompromising form, physiological psychology treated feelings and thoughts as, in effect, brain secretions, the by-products of purely organic changes. Matter (the body) ran along the track laid down for it by physical laws, and mind was the shadow that accompanied it. Huxley's steam-whistle analogy became famous. "The consciousness of brutes," he wrote in 1874,

> would appear to be related to the mechanism of their body simply as a collateral product of its working, and to be as completely without any power of modifying that working, as the steam-whistle which accompanies the work of a locomotive engine is without influence upon its machinery. . . . [T]he argumentation which applies to brutes holds equally good of men; . . . all states of consciousness in us, as in them, are immediately caused by molecular changes of the brain-substance. . . . [T]here is no proof that any state of consciousness is the cause of change in the motion of matter of the organism. . . . We are conscious automata.[5]

Huxley didn't think that this left no place for philosophy. He just thought that nothing philosophers said about minds could count as science. Philosophy was "metaphysics," the study of what is without spatial or temporal dimension and therefore cannot be measured.

This was what he had meant by "agnosticism": that whatever is not susceptible to measurement must remain unknown and unknowable. Huxley rejected the hypothesis that mental processes cause physical changes—that the *mind* is the engine and the body is the whistle—because it was scientifically untestable.

Physiological psychology put the study of the mind on an experimental basis—it made epistemology into a laboratory science—and the field that emerged was known as the New Psychology. The consequence was that what we now call psychology established itself as an academic discipline in the modern sense—that is, as a field with a distinctive program of research—well before what we now call philosophy did.[6] If the mind could be studied scientifically, and if what could not be studied scientifically was not knowledge, what exactly was the research program of philosophy? The institutional bias toward hard data gave psychology the advantage in its claim to be the real mental science. Philosophy had to redefine itself or run the risk of going the way of theology. So that when Gilman set out to hire a philosophy professor for his new university, he was searching in a field whose future was up for grabs. He had no way of knowing which horse to back in a race none of them might finish.

One of the Harvard professors Gilman tried to steal away was William James. The courtship was typically Jamesian: between 1875 and 1881 James changed his mind about whether he would be receptive to an offer from Hopkins four times. James's academic field in those years was physiology. He created the first psychology laboratory in the United States at Harvard in 1875 (he set it up in what had once been Louis Agassiz's private office in the Museum of Comparative Zoology), and in 1878 he signed a contract with the publisher Henry Holt to produce a textbook he proposed to call "Psychology, as a Natural Science"[7]—a phrase borrowed from the leading German experimental psychologist of the time, Wilhelm Wundt. So James was naturally drawn to Hopkins as a place that promised to be uninhibited by old ways of thinking about thinking. "I have more sympathy in many respects with your university than with this," he wrote to Gilman in 1879.

But James had also gotten married in 1878, an event that drove

his sister Alice into a permanent condition of psychosomatic inva-
lidism, and his parents were old and infirm. These family responsi-
bilities, James explained to Gilman, obliged him to remain in
Cambridge (though they did not prevent him two years later from
writing to Gilman again to announce his availability for a Hopkins
appointment). Meanwhile, he had some suggestions about the philosophy department. "If you want original work done by your first-
appointed professor I hardly know who to recommend," he told
Gilman.

> If you want a philosophic scholar and expert who would guide stu-
> dents through the history of the subject, I suppose Morris would be
> an excellent man. . . . In the psychological line proper the only work-
> ers I know of are Peirce and Hall. Peirce's drawbacks you know.
> Hall, although a thoroughly original and able worker is perhaps defi-
> cient in the practical and organizing qualities which the J. H. U. es-
> pecially needs *now* in its professors.[8]

Not the most glowing recommendations ever written, but Gilman
hired all three. He hedged his bets, though, by making all of the ap-
pointments part-time lectureships. He wanted to see which horse
showed the best legs before making any arrangement permanent.

2

It is a mark of Gilman's skepticism about the academic future of philosophy that when John Dewey arrived at Hopkins in the fall of 1882,
Gilman tried to persuade him to switch to science. But Dewey preferred to study with a philosopher. He had the three mentioned in
James's letter to pick from: George Sylvester Morris and G. Stanley
Hall, who taught in alternate semesters, and Charles Peirce, who
taught all year but half-time, splitting his appointment with his job at
the Coast Survey. Dewey chose Morris. For a Vermont Transcendentalist, it was the logical move.

The most interesting thing about the Burlington philosophy was
how long it managed to survive. For the whole system was based on
a rather glaring misunderstanding. Contrary to what Coleridge,

Marsh, and Marsh's heirs at the University of Vermont all taught, Kant had never claimed that we can establish religious truths by looking into our own minds, or by any other means. Kant accepted empiricism's distinction between the things we can know through the senses and the things we cannot hope to know because they are supersensible—for example, God. Kant's ambition was not to debunk empiricism; he hoped, in fact, to develop a philosophy consistent with Newtonian science. He only wanted to improve on empiricism by explaining how it is that human beings do "know" certain things that they can't have apprehended through the senses.

One of these things—a concept indispensable to Newtonian science—is causality. We cannot see causation. What we see is just one phenomenon followed by another phenomenon. David Hume had famously argued that the belief in causality is only a mental habit acquired from the repeated experience of seeing event x followed by event y. Hume thought that this experience gives us no grounds for believing that x "causes" y, or even for believing that the next time we perceive an x we will necessarily perceive a y immediately following. Empirically speaking, belief in causality is a superstition. Space and time, too, cannot be explained as impressions received through the senses. The retinal image is two-dimensional. How do we "know" there is a third dimension in the physical world when we look at it? Yet we not only believe in the reality of space, time, and causality; we cannot *not* believe in these things. Knowing them is a precondition for knowing anything else about the world we experience. It is knowledge that is both universal and necessary. If it isn't acquired through the senses, where does it come from?

The question Kant was trying to answer was, essentially: How does the world hang together? Our senses don't apprehend the world as a unified totality. What they pick up is an apparently endless procession of discrete phenomena, one unique event after another. But all minds, after only a little bit of experience, take for granted a world that is organized spatially, temporally, and causally—a world that hangs together. This can't be merely a subjective projection of order onto a random flux, since all minds order experience in roughly the same way (that is, causally, temporally, and spatially), and they never encounter a sensible phenomenon that fails to conform to that order. If there are uncaused or timeless entities out there, we are unable to perceive them with our senses.

Kant's conclusion was that the mind must not be a totally blank slate. It must come accessorized with certain "categories," like causality, that organize experience for us. And the raw phenomena of the external world must themselves be knowable only insofar as they conform to this way of being organized. The mind's structuring categories are not imposed on phenomena, in other words; they are constitutive of phenomena. The knowable is limited to whatever can be experienced in the context of these categories; whatever is omnipresent, eternal, or without antecedent cause—God, free will, immortality—is therefore unknowable. Kant had theories for why people believe in these supersensible entities, but he did not think that the mind was equipped to "know" them. The gap between the sensible and the spiritual that Marsh had declared closed was not closed by Kant.

Marsh's mistake arose because Coleridge had acquired his understanding of Kant through the work of two disciples of Kant's whose desire to get beyond empiricism was far more thoroughgoing: Fichte and Schelling. When Marsh stepped down from the presidency of the University of Vermont, it was in order to devote all his time to the creation of a systematic theory of all knowledge; but once he got started, he realized that Coleridge had misled him, and that Kant's philosophy was an inadequate foundation for the project he had in mind. Marsh died before he could complete his system, but before his death he turned from Kant to Hegel.[9]

Hegel certainly did have a systematic theory of all knowledge. He completed the revision of Kant that Fichte and Schelling had begun, and ended up devising one of the most grandly architectonic answers to the question, How does the world hang together? ever formulated. He got there not by rejecting Kant's theory but (he believed) by "completing" it.[10] Though we assume that the world is unified, we cannot grasp this unity ourselves. Our minds are temporally and spatially conditioned—we can only perceive whatever is present to us now—and our knowledge is consequently partial and relational. But although human minds cannot know all of reality all at once, there must be *some* mind that can—because as Kant had established, things don't hang together by themselves. They require a mind to make their existence intelligible. Such a mind—a mind capable of perceiving the world in its completeness—must be unconditioned by time, place, or antecedent cause. Hegel's name for this ineffable entity was the Absolute. From the perspective of the Absolute Mind, entities that Kant's philosophy treated as independent and opposed, like "mind" and "phenomena," are revealed to be simply two aspects of an organic whole, partial ways of understanding an indivisible unity.

Hegel believed that the Absolute reveals itself not only in nature (which is what Schelling believed, and had taught, for example, to Louis Agassiz), but also in history. Reality is an Idea in the mind of the Absolute, and history is that Idea's gradual coming into consciousness itself. (It is easy to see the analogy with Agassiz's notion that embryological development recapitulates the timeless "idea" of a Creator.) The Idea is always present, but it can realize itself concretely only in the collective consciousness of human beings, and only through time—like (Hegel said) "the circle which presupposes its end as its purpose, and has its end for its beginning; it becomes concrete and actual only by being carried out, and by the end it involves." True knowledge of this "inner being of the world"[11] Hegel called "science" (*Wissenschaft*); the education required to achieve it is what the Germans meant by *Bildung*. In the German conception, therefore, scientific education wasn't about amassing data; it wasn't even about individual enlightenment. It was about communal growth, and its end was spiritual completeness.

George Sylvester Morris, the man Dewey chose to work with at Hopkins, was a Hegelian. Like Dewey, Morris was a Vermonter and the son of an abolitionist. He was born in Norwich, in 1840, and went to Dartmouth. After serving in the Sixteenth Vermont Regiment during the Civil War (he was assistant postmaster), he enrolled at Union Theological Seminary in New York City, where he made the mistake of reading the work of David Hume and underwent a serious crisis of faith as a result. In 1866 Morris went to Berlin, where he spent two somewhat despondent years (partly coinciding with William James's similarly melancholy visit to the same city) studying with the philosopher Friedrich Adolph Trendelenburg, an opponent of Hegelianism. When Morris got back to the United States, his fiancée refused to see him, on grounds that "he had grown so learned and had changed so much in his religious opinions, that she was afraid of him."[12]

The same apprehension—that his religious commitment was shaky—made it impossible for Morris to find a job teaching philosophy. He ended up tutoring the children of a New York banker named Jesse Seligman until, in 1870, he got a position as a professor of modern languages and literature at the University of Michigan. In 1877 he started teaching part-time at Hopkins, but he remained on the Michigan faculty. His philosophical views, meanwhile, had been evolving steadily away from empiricism. In 1880 he began reading the British Hegelian Thomas Hill Green, and by the time Dewey showed up at Hopkins, Morris was a full-fledged Hegelian.

Morris used Hegel exactly as Marsh, had he lived long enough, would have used him: to reconcile reason with faith. For the attributes of the Absolute that Hegel arrived at working philosophically coincided perfectly (it was no accident) with the attributes of the God of Christian revelation. Morris thought that people like Huxley were wrong to claim that scientific thought and religious belief had separate ends and belonged to separate realms. "Religion," Morris argued, "as presupposing and requiring knowledge of the Absolute, and philosophy, as the pure, unbiased search for and demonstration of it, occupy like ground. . . . '[H]uman reason' is not confounded by the content of the Christian consciousness, but is strengthened, illuminated, satisfied, nay, completed by it."[13] It was an almost exact echo, more than half a century later, of Marsh's assertion in his introduction to Coleridge: "CHRISTIAN FAITH IS THE PERFECTION OF HUMAN REASON." Morris's organic conception of education was an echo of Marsh's as well. No subject, Morris insisted, can be pursued "unless such pursuit be accompanied by an appropriate knowledge of the whole, of which, rightly conceived, it is an organic, living member."[14]

Morris was a serious person—"his sparse and tense frame seemed but an organ for the realization of thought,"[15] Dewey later said of him—which is perhaps why his fiancée became so alarmed at the thought of life with him as a dedicated atheist. But he was not (unlike, for example, Henry Torrey) a contemplative. His Hegelianism made his Christianity a religion of engagement—since in Hegel the Absolute is realized not in thought, but in the unfolding of history. "The Christian victory," Marsh taught, "is not won through an attempted withdrawal from the world, but by overcoming it;—by remaining in the world and conquering it. The 'universal self' of man is not an abstraction, but, like all true universals, a power to realize itself in and through the materials of particular circumstances and opportunity, in the midst of which the individual may be placed."[16] Self-realization is a social process.

Morris and Dewey were quick to appreciate one another. Morris's antipathy to British empiricism—he seems to have held Hume responsible for damaging his life—resonated with the philosophical prejudices Dewey had already been exposed to in Vermont. Morris thought that the British philosophical frame of mind, with its atomizing sensationalism, showed "all the quality of a disease,"[17] and he used to tell his classes that John Stuart Mill's greatest misfortune was to have been born the son of the arch-utilitarian James Mill rather than of Johann Gottlieb Fichte. But Dewey was a serious person, too. He wasn't interested in philosophy as a form of mental exercise. He was interested in it as a guide to living, and Hegel turned out to be just what he was looking for. Hegel's philosophy made a much closer corollary to Huxley's picture of the body as an integrated organism than Torrey's attenuated Kantianism had. It answered, Dewey recalled many years later,

a demand for unification that was doubtless an intense emotional craving, and yet was a hunger that only an intellectualized subject-matter could satisfy. . . . [T]he sense of divisions and separations that were, I suppose, borne in upon me as a consequence of a heritage of New England culture, divisions by way of isolation of self from the world, of soul from body, of nature from God, brought a painful oppression—or, rather, they were an inward laceration. . . . Hegel's synthesis of subject and object, matter and spirit, the divine and the human, was . . . no mere intellectual formula; it operated as an immense release, a liberation. Hegel's treatment of human culture, of institutions and the arts, involved the same dissolution of hard-and-fast dividing walls, and had a special attraction for me.[18]

In his two years at Hopkins, Dewey took every graduate course Morris offered. There were five: on "the science of knowledge" in Greek philosophy, on Spinoza, on British philosophy, on German philosophy ("with special references to the movement from Kant to Hegel"),[19] and on Hegel's philosophy of history. By the end of his first semester, Dewey had become Morris's prize student. He was singled out for special mention in Morris's reports to Gilman on his classes ("Mr. Dewey's paper on Empedocles embodied an ingenious attempt to find, in the fragments of doctrine attributed to the philosopher, justification for a spiritualistic interpretation of his maxim, 'Like is known by like' ")[20] and he was inquired after in Morris's letters to Gilman from Michigan during the off-semesters. At the end of his first year, Dewey got his fellowship. By his fourth semester, he was teaching Hopkins undergraduates.

3

Morris alternated semesters at Hopkins with a man for whom he had once served as a professional role model, Granville Stanley Hall. Hall, too, was the son of an abolitionist. He was from Ashfield, in western Massachusetts (not Vermont, but less than twenty miles away). His father secured an exemption from military service for him, though, so he could attend Williams College, and after graduating in 1867 he went to Union Theological Seminary, where he met Morris on his return from Germany and was so impressed that he decided to become a philosopher, too. Hall proceeded to trace Morris's footsteps with impressive exactitude: he went to Berlin in 1869, studied with Trendelenburg, returned to New York City, was unable to find a job teaching philosophy, succeeded Morris as tutor to the

Seligman family, and ended up, in 1872, as professor of rhetoric and English literature at a Midwestern college—in his case, Antioch.

Hall loved Germany, in part because not all the freedoms he encountered there were academic. He met some young German women and (as he described it many years after, when it was professionally safe to do so),

> with two of these *Mädchen*, one after the other, I first realized what love really meant and could do. . . . I realized that I was a man in the full normal sense of that word. . . . Not only did these companions facilitate my use of German but, what was vastly more important, they awoke capacities hitherto unusually dormant and repressed and thus made life seem richer and more meaningful.[21]

Despite whatever countervailing influence Trendelenburg may have exerted, Hall also took up Hegel; among his first publications were translations of essays by German Hegelians for the *Journal of Speculative Philosophy*. But Hall was an intent reader of academic signals: he was not a man who regarded his intellectual interests and his professional prospects as necessarily exclusive concerns. While he was at Antioch, he soured on Hegel, and after reading Wilhelm Wundt's *Grundzüge des physiologischen Psychologie* ("Principles of Physiological Psychology"), he decided to go into business all over again as a New Psychologist. So in 1876 he moved to Cambridge and became a student of the man who was virtually the only professional physiological psychologist in the country, William James.

"I was immensely impressed and fascinated by his personality," Hall later said of James, "and looked up to him, who was several years my senior, somewhat as I had done before to George Morris."[22] In fact, James was only two years Hall's senior—he was still living with his parents in 1876—and later on, when Hall was no longer dependent on James's patronage, the competitiveness in their relationship ceased to be latent. In the 1870s, though, Hall and James quickly bonded. Part of the reason was that they both understood (James a little in advance of Hall) that the true ambition of German experimental psychology was not to reduce mental phenomena to physical laws, but to solve traditional philosophical problems—and validate traditional philosophical conclusions—using laboratory methods.

Wundt, for example, had started out, around 1860, by working on the "personal equation" in astronomy—the measurement of differences between individual observers in their determinations of the position of a star. He found that one of the factors that surfaced in analyzing these differences was whether the astronomer had the practice of looking first at the star and then at the instrument that indicated its position, or first at the instrument and then at the star. What this told Wundt was that minds are capable of attending to only one thing at a time—that consciousness is unitary—and also that they are not just passive receivers of stimuli, not just blank slates. There is something "in there," some faculty of attention, that chooses its object. Minds select. Isn't that just what German philosophy since Kant had insisted? And now this faculty of attention (Kant had called it "apperception") could be analyzed by empirical means. It could be measured: its study was a science. The New Psychology was born.

In his two-volume *Grundzüge*—the textbook, published in 1873–74, that had inspired Hall out in Ohio—Wundt thus felt entitled to conclude his positivistic account with five pages of what a British scientist like Huxley would have called pure metaphysics. "Human consciousness," Wundt wrote, "constitutes a decisive point in nature's course, a point at which the world becomes aware of itself."

> Our consciousness encompasses only an infinitesimal point of the world in its inner being. We cannot assume that the world outside ourselves lacks this inner being. But if we wish to imagine what it is like, we cannot possibly do so otherwise than in the form of our own self-perception and of our apprehension of mankind as a whole, . . . that is, as a unified complex that is articulated into independent units of different orders, each developing in accordance with inner ends. Thus, psychological experience is compatible only with a monistic world view that acknowledges the worth of the individual without dissolving it into the contentless form of a simple monad

that can attain complexity only through the miracle of supernatural aids. It is not as a simple entity but as an ordered unit of many elements that the mind is what Leibniz called it: *a mirror of the world*.[23]

As the mind unifies the impressions of the nervous system, so the "inner being" of the world unifies phenomena. The passage is shot through with Kantian and Hegelian thinking.

In 1878, with a thesis published under the title "The Muscular Perception of Space" (that is: a Kantian "category" physiologically explained), Hall received the first Ph.D. ever granted by the Harvard philosophy department. It was also the first Ph.D. in psychology awarded in the United States. He immediately returned to Germany (the trip was paid for by a gift from his old employer Jesse Seligman) and made the scientific rounds. He met, attended classes by, or worked with nearly every German celebrity in the field: the founder of psychophysics, Gustav Fechner; the physicist and physiologist Hermann von Helmholtz; the neurologist Emil Du Bois-Reymond; the cardiovascular pioneer Carl Ludwig; and, in Leipzig, Wilhelm Wundt himself, who was just setting up his Institut für Experimentelle Psychologie, the first psychology laboratory in Europe. Hall worked in Ludwig's lab and attended Wundt's lectures; he was Wundt's first American student. James, even though he had lived almost two years in Germany, had met none of these people; he had spent most of his time at the spa in Teplitz, reading Goethe and trying to get over his bad back and depression. Hall returned to Cambridge as the most thoroughly credentialed psychologist in America.

Thinking that a demonstration of the New Psychology's practical applications might make it less threatening to traditionalists, Hall delivered a series of lectures on education in Boston (arranged by Charles Eliot). The lectures drew on the work of a man named Francis Parker, who had become famous as the superintendent of schools in Quincy, Massachusetts, and the founder of a theory of pedagogy known as "the Quincy system." Parker had served as a colonel in the Union Army (he retained the title ever after); after the war, he had spent several years in Europe, returning with a philosophy of education derived from Kantian and Fichtean ideas of mental growth, and emphasizing the importance of experience in acquiring knowledge. Hall expressed the germ of the theory in recapitulationist language: "The pupil should, and in fact naturally does, repeat the course of the development of the race, and education is simply the expediting and shortening of this course."[24] The lectures, attended mostly by teachers, were hugely successful. Hall still couldn't get a job. He started to think about going to medical school.

Hall had been bombarding Gilman with unsolicited letters of recommendation for himself since 1875, when he was still a philosopher manqué at Antioch and Hopkins had not even opened, and he kept it up. James warned him about Gilman's coyness (a character trait on which James should have been expert), but it took Hall a while to figure out which buttons he needed to push. In the beginning he advertised himself as a hard scientist: "My line of work has been entirely physiological for the last three years, with daily laboratory work, latterly with Wundt & Helmholtz,—thus entirely in the same line as James,"[25] he wrote to Gilman in 1879. (He knew, of course, that Gilman had been trying to lure James to Baltimore.) But eventually he figured out that this was not the note Gilman was hoping to hear, and in 1880, he wrote again to explain that

> I am as far as *possible* from materialism in every form. My physiological studies of the nervous system bring me recurrently before the question of thought & matter, & I can only say that my deepest private feeling, like that of most investigators in Germany whose intimacy it has been my privilege to share, is that materialism is simply want of education.
>
> As to my religious sentiments, I am a graduate in divinity, & without agreeing entirely with all I hear, am in the habit of churchgoing, & indeed am still a nominal church member I believe. I do not think it is possible for any one to become deeply interested in philosophy without a devout respect for religion growing more profound at every step.[26]

Meanwhile, he arranged for more testimonials: from James (again), from Charles Eliot Norton (who had gotten to know Hall in Ashfield, where they both spent their summers), and even from Ludwig and Wundt. Gilman at last acceded, and in the spring of 1883 Hall taught his first graduate course at Hopkins. It was an advanced psychology class, with a lab requirement, and the recommended texts were Wundt's *Grundzüge des physiologischen Psychologie* and an English translation of Kant. Dewey took it. The next year, Dewey took two more courses with Hall: one on physiological psychology, the other on psychological and ethical theories. Hall was by this time on a different track from his former idol, George Morris, but for Dewey their approaches must not have seemed incompatible. Dewey's interest in philosophy had begun, after all, with a physiology textbook. The New Psychology represented the potential transcendence of Huxley's division: it promised to map the convergence of physics and metaphysics. In 1884, the year he took his degree, Dewey was able to defend the New Psychology as "making possible for the first time an adequate psychology of man's religious nature and experience":

> As it goes into the depths of man's nature it finds, as stone of its foundation, blood of its life, the instinctive tendencies of devotion, sacrifice, faith, and idealism which are the eternal substructure of all the struggles of the nations upon the altar stairs which slope up to God. . . . [I]t can discover in its investigations no reason which is not based upon faith, and no faith which is not rational in its origin and tendency.[27]

The school of Burlington still survived.

4

In 1882–83, Dewey's first year at Hopkins, Charles Peirce taught a yearlong course on logic. The syllabus began with two articles Peirce had written based on his 1872 Metaphysical Club paper, "The Fixation of Belief" and "How to Make Our Ideas Clear," and it included units on the theory of probabilities, the method of least squares, inductive reasoning, the kinetic theory of gases, and the effect of probability-based reasoning on philosophy. Dewey did not take the class. Peirce announced in his introductory lecture that "no brilliant talent for mathematics is at all necessary,"[28] but Dewey sensed that Peirce's idea of what would count as even average mathematical talent did not encompass him, and he did not take a class with Peirce until his third semester at Hopkins. But he saw a good deal of him anyway.

Peirce had been recommended to Gilman back in 1875, first by his father, who suggested Charles be appointed to teach physics, and then by James, who told Gilman that "I don't think it extravagant praise to say that of late years there has been no intellect in Cambridge of such a general power & originality as his, unless one should except the late Chauncey Wright [who had died only two months before], and *effectively*, Peirce will always rank higher than Wright."[29] (Peirce returned the favor two years later by writing to Gilman to recommend James as the only person in the country qualified to teach the New Psychology.)

In his letter to Gilman four years later, James was less enthusiastic ("Peirce's drawbacks you know"). This may have been in part because Peirce had by then written Gilman several rather pompous letters on his own behalf ("I believe that my system of logic . . . must stand, or else the whole spirit of the physical sciences must be revolutionized," he explained in one of them. "I have measured my powers against those of other men; I know what they are").[30] But there was a personal issue as well.

Zina Fay Peirce was both a feminist and a religious person, and she believed that the punishment for adultery should be life imprisonment or death. This was not a view conducive to a happy marriage with Charles Peirce, and in 1875, in the middle of a European trip on Coast Survey business, Zina abandoned her husband and returned to America. Charles, alone in Paris, suffered a severe breakdown. He and Zina were reunited and briefly reconciled; but when, back in the United States in 1876, Charles moved to New York City, she remained in Cambridge, and they were never together again.

Zina may have walked out on Peirce simply because it had finally dawned on her that the man she had married was a disaster waiting to happen. During the European trip, Peirce had squandered the money advanced to him by the Survey, made a hash of his accounts, caused some expensive scientific instruments to be broken, and, by neglecting to provide the Survey with his address in any of the frantic letters he wrote to Washington requesting additional funds, was unable to get the money he needed to pay his bills. In the middle of this debacle (and this is the *echt* Peircean touch) he hired an expensive French *sommelier* to give him instruction in the wines of Médoc.

But Zina had already complained before the trip to Europe—not only to her parents, but to Peirce's as well—of her husband's infidelity, and it is hard not to imagine (since she remained solicitous about Peirce's health and financial condition) that it was some sort of sexual escapade in Paris that broke the marriage apart. In any case, the Fays were outraged by what Zina reported; the story of Peirce's philandering was spread; and Peirce, whose quarrel with Eliot over the directorship of the observatory had already made him persona non grata at Harvard, became a pariah in Cambridge.

That there was some sexual offense at the root of the separation is suggested by a letter Peirce wrote to Gilman in 1878 discussing the possibility of a Hopkins appointment. One potential obstacle, Peirce explained, was his Survey job, which he was unwilling to give up.

> The second is a very painful personal matter upon which I dislike to speak at all, & of which I will say the least possible. It is that I have been for a number of years in disagreement with my wife, not having lived with her for a long time, & not having even seen her for over a year; and the reasons for this on the one side and on the other will, I hope, never be known. It is however certain that we shall never live together again. This is a fact to which you will naturally give a weight, should you seriously consider inviting me to Baltimore.[31]

Considering his public relations problem, Gilman could not have received this as good news, but he must have been impressed by Peirce's frankness, because eighteen months later, he gave him a job. He was sorry.

One of the first things Peirce did after he arrived at Hopkins in the fall of 1879 was to start a Metaphysical Club. It was open to faculty and graduate students from any department, and it met once a month to discuss papers presented, usually, by the members themselves. Peirce was the club's first president, and though later on Morris and Hall held that office as well, Peirce generally went to the meetings when he was in Baltimore. (One was devoted to a talk by Morris on the life and work of Henry James, Sr. It was held in January 1883, less than a month after the subject's death, and Peirce, who had been a close friend of Henry Senior—he shared James's interest in Swedenborg—and a great admirer of *Substance and Shadow*, was there to comment. What was said is not recorded.)

When he got to Hopkins, Dewey became an active member of the club. (He was present for the discussion of Henry James, Sr., and delivered a paper of his own at the same meeting, on T. H. Green.) At one meeting, presided over by Morris, Dewey heard Peirce read a paper called "Design and Chance," and joined in the discussion afterward. The paper is the germ of Peirce's later cosmology, and it sums up in a few pages what was probably the substance of the year-long class Dewey had chosen not to take. Peirce's subject was the laws of nature—the laws that Newtonian physicists believed explained the behavior of matter and that physiological psychologists believed explained the behavior of minds—and he began with a simple question: Does the principle that everything can be explained have an explanation? Or, as he also put it: Does the law of causality (which is another name for the principle that everything can be explained) have a cause?

Though he disparaged his own literary abilities, in his nontechnical work Peirce was a vivid writer. His weakness (apart from a chronic inability to finish things) is a little unexpected in a person so committed to logic and the art of clear thinking: a lack of proportion. Every relevant idea seemed equally important to him, and while he was composing he rarely glimpsed a path down which he was not tempted to wander (a tendency he shared with Coleridge, a person Peirce resembled in other ways as well). This accounts for a lot of the incompleteness: almost every time he wrote a fresh draft (and he customarily wrote many), Peirce sooner or later found himself on an unanticipated detour with no clear route back to his main point. His drafts tend to start in the same place and wind up in widely divergent cul-de-sacs. His impulse to nail all the little points frequently kept him from ever getting to the big one. He was not skilled at subordination.

But it was also very much a part of Peirce's picture of the world that all paths *do* ultimately converge, and in his completed essays ("Design and Chance," unpublished in his lifetime, is not one of them), there is a shape, if not exactly an order, a clump of ideas rather than a row of arguments. Peirce was a system builder—by virtue of the range of his expertise, possibly the most ambitious (and possibly the most frustrated) system builder of late-nineteenth-century North Atlantic culture. And it was a culture that took system building extremely seriously.

Summarizing Peirce's Metaphysical Club paper on "Design and Chance" is therefore not quite the same thing as paraphrasing it. The argument begins with the point James Clerk Maxwell had made with his imaginary demon: that a scientific law is only a prediction of what will happen most of the time. Even "the axioms of geometry," said Peirce, "are mere empirical laws whose perfect exactitude we have no reason whatever to feel confident of."[32] The decision to treat a particular law as absolute is a pragmatic one: sometimes we feel that questioning it will only lead to confusion, and sometimes we feel that questioning it is necessary in order to try out a new hypothesis. A law, in Peirce's pragmatic view (derived, of course, from Wright), is essentially a path of inquiry. It helps us find things out—as the law of gravitation, for example, helped us discover Neptune—and Peirce's first rule as a philosopher of science was that the path of inquiry should never be blocked, not even by a hypothesis that has worked for us in the past.

Maxwell's view was that laws are fundamentally uncertain because there is always a chance that the next time around things will behave in an improbable (though not an impossible) way—a chance that all the fast molecules will congregate on one side of the container. Peirce's point was that a chance occurrence like this can change the conditions of the universe. His illustration was drawn from classic probability theory: in a game with fair dice, a player's wins and losses will balance out in the long run; but if one die is shaped so that there is an infinitesimally greater chance that after a winning throw the next throw will be a losing throw, in the long run the player will be ruined. A minute variation in what seemed a stable and predictable system can have cosmic consequences. In the natural world, Peirce said, such minute variations are happening all the time. Their occurrence is always a matter of chance—"chance is the one essential agency upon which the whole process depends"—and, according to probability theory, "everything that can happen by chance, sometime or other will happen by chance. Chance will sometime bring about a change in every condition."[33] Peirce thought that even the terrible second law of thermodynamics—the law of the dissipation of energy—was subject to reversal by such means.

As Peirce acknowledged, this was a Darwinian argument: "my opinion is only Darwinism analyzed, generalized, and brought into the realm of Ontology,"[34] he said. What he meant was that since nature evolves by chance variation, then the laws of nature must evolve by chance variation as well. Variations that are compatible with survival are reproduced; variations that are incompatible are weeded out. A tiny deviation from the norm in the outcome of a physical process can, over the long run, produce a new physical law. Laws are adaptive.

Pragmatically defined, variations are habits. They constitute a behavioral tendency—for if they had no behavioral consequences, they would have no evolutionary significance. Bigness in beak size is whatever big beaks do for you (if you are a finch), just as (to use an example from "How to Make Our Ideas Clear") "hardness" is just the sum total of what all hard things do. What Peirce proposed in "Design and Chance" was that natural laws are also habits. This was not a new thought for him. There is a story, attributed to William James, about a meeting of the original Metaphysical Club in Cambridge, in which the members waited patiently for Peirce to arrive and deliver a promised paper.

> They assembled. Peirce did not come; they waited and waited; finally a two-horse carriage came along and Peirce got out with a dark cloak over him; he came in and began to read his paper. What was it about? He set forth . . . how the different moments of time got in the habit of coming one after another.[35]

It sounds like a joke, but the story is probably true. Peirce's paper must have been an extrapolation from the nebular hypothesis—the theory that the universe evolves from a condition of relative homogeneity, in which virtually no order exists, not even temporal order, to a condition of relative heterogeneity, in which, among other things, time has become linear. How did time get straightened out in this way? By developing good habits. In "Design and Chance," Peirce put it this way:

> Systems or compounds which have bad habits are quickly destroyed, those which have no habits follow the same course; only those which have good habits tend to survive.
>   Why . . . do the heavenly bodies tend to attract one another? Because in the long run bodies that repel or do not attract will get thrown out of the region of space leaving only the mutually attracting bodies.[36]

If you are a heavenly body, in other words, gravitational attraction is a good habit to have, in the same way that if you are a proto-giraffe, a long neck is a good attribute to have. It keeps you in the system. When gravitational attraction becomes the habit of *all* heavenly bodies, then we can speak of "the law of gravity," just as when all surviving proto-giraffes have long necks, we can speak of a giraffe species, and (presumably) when all moments of time have the habit of following one another, we can speak of past, present, and future. But the law of gravity did not preexist the formation of the universe, any more than the idea of a giraffe did. It evolved into its present state while the universe was evolving into *its* present state. Gravity was a chance variation that got selected. Objects that didn't have the gravitational habit didn't survive.

So far, Peirce was following a line of thought already laid down by other writers. The idea that nature is subject to a continuous "change of type" was advanced by (besides Darwin) the English logician John Venn in a book called *The Logic of Chance*, which Peirce had reviewed back in 1866 and called "a book which should be read by every thinking man."[37] Venn was attacking people who used statistics—specifically, Quetelet—to define national types. There are no fixed types (forget about fixed *national* types) in nature, Venn argued, because organisms are continually evolving. The notion that the laws derived from hypothetical dice games and target practice could be applied to living beings was absurd: "It is as if the point on the target at which we aim, instead of being fixed, were slowly changing its position as we continue to fire at it; changing almost certainly to some extent and temporarily, and not improbably to a considerable extent and permanently."[38]

That natural laws themselves evolve was the argument of a well-known book by the French philosopher Émile Boutroux, *De la contingence des lois de la nature* ("The Contingency of the Laws of Nature"), published in 1874—a defense of free will written very much in the spirit of William James's own French inspiration, Charles Renouvier. "Scientific laws are the bed over which passes the torrent of facts," Boutroux wrote; "they shape it even as they follow it. . . . They do not precede things, they derive from them, and they can vary, if the things themselves happen to vary." The tendencies of living beings to follow predictable paths, he said, although they "can look, viewed from outside, like necessary laws,"[39] are only habits. Without variation, everything would be dead matter.

Still, none of these arguments answered the question Peirce had started out with, which was whether the law of causation has a cause. To say that causality "evolved" is not an answer, because it uses another law—the law of evolution by chance variation—as an explanation, and leaves us with the question, Did the law of evolution evolve? The search for a primal cause seems to suck us into an infinite regression. Darwin and Maxwell's conception of chance can't help us, because that conception simply expresses the statistical notion of causality—the notion that outcomes are distributed along a curve of probabilities on which extremes are always possible. Darwin did not think that variations were spontaneous in the sense of being uncaused, only in the sense of being unpredictable, and he was willing to leave it at that. *On the Origin of Species* is actually silent on the question of the origin.

But the origin was the problem that interested Peirce. His conclusion was that there must be something he called "absolute chance" in the universe. This was another way of saying that the answer to the question, Does the law of causation have a cause? is, no. Causation came about not as a consequence of the operation of some other law, but by pure chance, out of the blue. Peirce spelled this idea out more clearly a few years later in an essay—one of his most ambitiously speculative, also unfinished and unpublished— called "A Guess at the Riddle." "We are brought, then, to this," he says toward the end of it:

> conformity to law exists only within a limited range of events and even there is not perfect, for an element of pure spontaneity or lawless originality mingles, or at least, must be supposed to mingle, with law everywhere. Moreover, conformity with law is a fact requiring to be explained; and since Law in general cannot be explained by any law in particular, the explanation must consist in showing how law is developed out of pure chance, irregularity, and indeterminacy. . . . According to this, three elements are active in the world, first, chance; second, law; and third, habit-taking.
> Such is our guess of the secret of the sphynx.[40]

Peirce's faith in the existence of absolute chance seems a vote for freedom and originality and against statistics and systems; but that is not how Peirce thought of it. Chance, in his theory, changes the system, but it does not make it any less systematic. On the contrary. As he put it in the paper on "Design and Chance": "Chance is indeterminacy, is freedom. But the action of freedom issues in the strictest law."[41] Unlike Renouvier and Boutroux, Peirce did not think that he had come up with a scientific justification for liberty and a belief in free will. He thought that he had found the Holy Grail of post-Kantian system builders. He thought he had located the uncaused cause.

5

Peirce read his paper on "Design and Chance" to the Hopkins Metaphysical Club on January 17, 1884. Nine days later, he was fired. The Zina problem had finally surfaced in Baltimore.

Peirce had not been oblivious of the rumors surrounding his separation from his first wife, but he had not exactly been daunted by them, either. Soon after the split, he took up with a woman who called herself Juliette Annette Froissy Pourtalai. On Peirce's later account, they were introduced in 1876 in New York City, at a ball at the Brevoort, on Fifth Avenue, where (since it was a luxury hotel) Peirce liked to stay when he was in town, and where they probably began their affair. Juliette's origins are a mystery, and she and Peirce, all their lives, were careful to keep them that way. (In this endeavor, anyway, they seem to have had a lasting success.) She was apparently French—though in one version of her story she was a Hapsburg princess—and Pourtalai is supposed to have been the name of a deceased husband, despite the likelihood that she was still a teenager when she met Peirce (he was thirty-seven). In any event, she was childlike, frail, a bit of an actress, and intensely possessive. Charles's family thought she was a "vampire."[42]

Peirce probably abused Juliette physically—he could be a violent man—but he was devoted to her, and after they met she began traveling with him on his trips for the Coast Survey. Outside Baltimore they apparently did not feel it necessary to keep their relationship a secret. On April 26, 1883, two days after Charles's divorce from Zina became final, they married, and they set up house in Baltimore when school started again in the fall. That was when the rumors caught up with them. One of Benjamin Peirce's successors as superintendent of the Coast Survey, a man named Julius Hilgard, told a Hopkins astronomy professor, Simon Newcomb, the stories about Charles and Juliette cohabiting on Survey expeditions, and when Newcomb ran into a Hopkins trustee on the train one day, he repeated the news— that (in his unforgettable Victorian ellipsis) the Peirces' marriage had "made no change in the relations of the parties."[43] Gilman's worst fears were about to be realized.

Gilman was quick to control the damage. As soon as he had confirmed Newcomb's report, he engineered a resolution by the executive committee of the trustees terminating all the part-time positions in philosophy at the end of the academic year, ostensibly for lack of funds. Shortly afterward, Morris and Hall were reinstated. Peirce got the message, and he spent the winter and spring writing increasingly frantic and aggrieved letters to Gilman and to the trustees trying to discover the grounds for his severance. He never did.

Peirce had been behaving erratically ever since he had come to Hopkins, possibly because he had started relying on cocaine to alleviate the pain from his neuralgia and to keep up his energy. For almost two months in the middle of his first year he stayed in New York and missed his classes, sending Gilman letters claiming various maladies as his excuse. In 1881 he suddenly resigned from Hopkins, announcing his intention to give up philosophy forever and offering to sell his personal library to the university. He was evidently only trying to pressure Gilman into giving him a permanent appointment; instead, he got a raise and agreed to withdraw his resignation. But the books had already been purchased by the Hopkins library, and though Peirce immediately set about trying to get them back—or at least arrange for special borrowing privileges—he was unsuccessful. Years after he left Hopkins, Peirce was still trying to retrieve his books: he could not afford to buy them, and Hopkins was unwilling to give them up. Peirce also got into a protracted dispute with another Hopkins professor, the mathematician J. J. Sylvester, over who should get credit for an algebraic theory. Peirce's general state of nerves by the winter of 1884 is suggested by an item in a Baltimore newspaper the month after he learned of his termination:

> Margaret Hill, an old lady, was charged with assaulting her employer, Dr. Pierce [sic] of Calvert street, with a brick. Harris J. Chilton, her counsel, pleaded strongly that a doubt existed in her favor.
> Judge Duffy—It is only on that doubt that I act. I strongly suspect that the woman struck the man with the brick, but I give her the benefit of the doubt. Not guilty.[44]

Peirce was plainly a high-maintenance employee. Gilman was undoubtedly glad to be rid of him.

Peirce did not depart quietly—he was still assailing the trustees with letters maligning Gilman in the fall of 1884, though he was by then no longer on the faculty—but he had no options. He never held another academic position. A few years later, Gilman left a house where he was visiting two former Hopkins students after learning that Peirce was there: he told his hosts he "would not stay under the same roof with so immoral a man."[45]

In April, three months after dismissing Peirce, Gilman finally decided which of his part-time lecturers he was ready to offer a full-time appointment. G. Stanley Hall was made professor of psychology and pedagogy. Morris, feeling slighted (he *had* been slighted: his mildness of manner did not appeal to Gilman), returned to the University of Michigan and took Dewey with him. Dewey became a member of the Michigan philosophy department; when Morris died, unexpectedly, in 1889, he succeeded him as chair.

Triumphant at last after fifteen years in the academic wilderness, Hall bought a big house and began riding to hounds in full regalia.[46] He took over as president of the Metaphysical Club on what he announced as a new plan; within three months, the club had folded. In the fall of 1884, he delivered his inaugural lecture as the permanent professor of psychology. "The new psychology," he said,

> . . . is I believe Christian to its root and centre. . . . The Bible is being slowly re-revealed as man's great text-book in psychology,—dealing with him as a whole, his body, mind, and will, in all the larger relations to nature and society,—which has been so misappreciated simply because it is so deeply divine. That something may be done here to aid this development is my strongest hope and belief.[47]

The following winter, in a speech celebrating the university's connections to Baltimore, Daniel Gilman quoted these sentences as proof that philosophy and religion were indeed on the same wavelength. "[A]s I believe that one truth is never in conflict with another truth," Gilman said, "so I believe that the ethics of the New Testament will be accepted by the scientific as well as the religious faculties of man; to the former, as Law; to the latter, as Gospel."[48] Huxley's split had been cured at Hopkins.

Hopkins still did not have a philosophy professor, though, and

Hall was diligent about making sure Gilman did not find one. In 1885 Gilman considered trying Morris again for a chair in ethical philosophy. Hall wrote him to express his admiration for Morris's learning, but he added that "I sincerely hope there is something better than a light that is so *dry* & am very sure there is."[49] Morris was not invited. Then, in 1888, still with no philosophy professor on the faculty, Hall left Gilman in the lurch. He resigned to become the president of the newly founded Clark University, in Worcester, Massachusetts. Johns Hopkins did not get a full-time professor of philosophy until Arthur O. Lovejoy joined the faculty in 1910.

TWELVE

CHICAGO

I

$\mathbf{I}$N 1894, WHEN HE WAS THIRTY-FIVE, John Dewey became chairman of the philosophy department at the University of Chicago. He was by no means the first choice for the job. The
University of Chicago had been founded in 1857 under the auspices
of Senator Stephen A. Douglas, but had had to shut its doors in 1886
when its mortgage was foreclosed. A group called the Baptist Education Society decided to resuscitate the university, and persuaded
John D. Rockefeller, who had never been to college himself but who
was a devout Baptist, to act as its principal patron.[1]

The person chosen to be the new university's first president was
William Rainey Harper, a prodigy from Ohio who had received his
Ph.D. in philology at Yale when he was nineteen with a dissertation
comparing the use of prepositions in Latin, Greek, Sanskrit, and
Gothic. Harper was a Baptist (he needed to be: the Baptist Education Society stipulated that the president and two-thirds of the
trustees must be Baptists), but he was a liberal Baptist, and he was
determined to make Chicago a great university, which, in his view,

Jane Addams, the founder of Hull-House, in Chicago, 1896.

meant a nonsectarian university. Harper's approach to the knowledge business was imperialist. Chicago grew quickly and in many directions, its ability to attract exciting scholars and launch innovative programs enhanced by its chief donor's willingness to pump vast sums into the institution (by the time of his death, in 1937, Rockefeller had given more than $80 million) and to stay out of policy matters, and the university became known as Harper's Bazaar.

Harper began searching for faculty in 1889, and like Gilman fifteen years earlier (what else could they have done?), he raided other people's schools. As it happened, the victim of his most successful raid was G. Stanley Hall. Jonas Clark, the founder of Clark University, had made his fortune selling goods to California gold miners, and he did not share Rockefeller's noninterventionist posture toward the institution he was underwriting. He began compromising his support for his university soon after Hall arrived to be its first president. Under financial pressure, Hall did not deal as straightforwardly with his faculty as they considered their due, and by the spring of 1892, the professors were in revolt. That's when Harper came to town. By the end of the academic year, two-thirds of Clark's faculty and 70 percent of the student body had left; half of these, including five professors of biology, went directly to Chicago. When the new university opened that fall, fifteen of the 120 members of the faculty were Clark refugees.

Harper was still looking for a star to head his philosophy department, however. William James (a professor of psychology in 1892) suggested Charles Peirce, but the recommendation was killed by a member of the Harvard philosophy department, George Herbert Palmer, who told Harper: "I am astonished at James's recommendation of Peirce; . . . from so many sources I have heard of his broken and dissolute character that I should advise you to make most careful inquiries before engaging him. I am sure it is suspicions of this sort which have prevented his appointment here, and I suppose the same causes procured his dismissal from Johns Hopkins."[2] Harper did not need to hear more. He tried to recruit Palmer himself, but that effort failed, though he did persuade Palmer's wife, Alice, who was the president of Wellesley, to become dean of women at

Chicago. Attempts to hire the philosophers Jacob Gould Schurman (who declined in order to become president of Cornell) and E. Benjamin Andrews (who declined in order to remain president of Brown) were unsuccessful as well. Harper got Dewey's name from James Tufts, a member of the Chicago faculty who had once studied Hebrew with Harper at Yale and later worked as an instructor under Dewey in the Michigan philosophy department. "As a man," Tufts wrote to Harper about Dewey, "he is *simple*, modest, utterly devoid of any affectation or self-consciousness, and makes many friends and no enemies. He is a man of religious nature."[3] Harper offered Dewey the chairmanship.

The reference to Dewey's lack of affectation echoes so many earlier and later accounts that it is easy to miss what should be obvious, which is that people were trying to explain a quality that was rather mysterious to them. When people remarked on Dewey's simplicity, they were not referring to naïveté. They were referring to equanimity, a kind of poise—a quality that did not translate into charisma, exactly (Dewey was never a galvanic presence in the classroom), but that gave Dewey an unusual sort of personal authority. To older men like Stanley Hall or George Palmer, whose personal authority was of the more mundane variety, Dewey's manner seemed merely unthreatening and bland. "[He] conveys in his appearance little sign of being a man of consequence,"[4] Palmer observed privately. But younger people had a very different impression. "Mr Dewey is a tall, dark, thin young man, with long black hair, and a soft, penetrating eye, and looks like a cross between a Nihilist and a poet," wrote one of his Michigan students. "He is, I believe, thirty-five, but seems much younger. I gazed on him with much awe."[5] He "left a lasting mark, but rather by his personality . . . than by his lectures," remembered another Michigan student, the future sociologist Charles Cooley. "[H]is character was deeply admired, for its singularity. . . . We believed that there was something highly original and significant in his philosophy, but had no definite idea as to what it was."[6]

By 1894 Dewey was beginning to find Ann Arbor a little insular. Most of his work at Michigan had been along the lines indicated by his Hopkins training—an effort to integrate the New Psychology, evolutionary theory, Hegelianism, and Christianity. But he had gotten married there to one of his students, Alice Chipman, a person with a strong interest in social reform, and he had started getting involved in public affairs himself—serving, for example, on a university committee charged with evaluating standards at state high schools. After negotiating his salary up to $5,000 (the Deweys had three children), he took the job at Chicago.

Harper could pay only $4,000 for the first year, though, so Dewey made a deal under which he would start work July 1, 1894, teach through the fall semester, and then take the following spring off. He planned to spend the leave with his family in Europe. In May 1894 he sent Alice and the two older children, Frederick and Evelyn, on to Europe ahead of him. He kept the youngest with him—a little boy called Morris, after his father's mentor. On July 1, 1894, Dewey left Morris with the child's grandparents in Fenton, near Ann Arbor, and took a train to Chicago. He arrived at a critical moment in American social history. It was the middle of the Pullman strike.

2

George Pullman was an engineering entrepreneur. He had made his reputation when Chicago was young by raising large downtown buildings out of the Lake Michigan mud in which they were starting to sink. He spent nine years on the design of his famous sleeping car, scoring a tremendous promotional coup by arranging to have the prototype car, called the *Pioneer*, attached to Lincoln's funeral train as it made its way from Chicago to Springfield in 1865. (Whether the *Pioneer* actually made it onto the train is unclear; if it didn't, the fact did not prevent Pullman from publicizing the connection.)[7] In 1867 he established the Pullman Palace Car Company and went into the railroad car–making business.[8]

The Pullman sleeping car was a luxury vehicle. It cost $20,000 to manufacture, four times as much as the standard sleeping car. What made it pay was that Pullman didn't sell his sleepers to the railroads. He essentially leased them: he provided their crews, including a conductor and a porter; he maintained the interiors (the railroads had to agree to keep the outsides washed); and he took fifty cents from every fare. The sleeping cars were in demand among people who wanted to travel in comfort and style and who could afford the upgrade; railroads all over the country contracted to attach them to their passenger trains; and Pullman got rich. The Pullman Palace Car Company also built and leased dining and buffet cars; it built and sold passenger cars, freight cars, refrigerator cars, and streetcars. But the sleeping car was the franchise product. From its very first year in operation, the company paid shareholders an annual dividend of 8 percent. Pullman stock was famous for its reliability.

Pullman's first factory was in Palmyra, New York, but he wanted a shop near Chicago, which was where he lived and which had become a railroad hub: twenty-four railroads had terminals there. So in 1880 he bought a large plot of vacant land twelve miles south of the city and built a car works. He also built, from scratch, an entire town to go with it: Pullman, Illinois. Pullman was a model town, the first of its kind of the United States. (Pullman apparently got the idea from the Krupp family's model town near their steel plant in Prussia.)[9] The town had 1,400 housing units and a population of 8,000, all employees, or family members of employees, of the Pullman Company. It contained a mall (an indoor arcade that housed all the shops), a five-room library stocked with 5,000 volumes donated by Pullman himself, a school with a playground (a rarity in 1880), a park with a miniature lake, a thousand-seat theater, a hotel, a bank, and a church. The streets were all paved and the houses had lawns manicured by the company.

Pullman's idea was to provide his workers with a morally salubrious environment. The sale of liquor was prohibited (except at the hotel bar, too expensive for most residents); so was prostitution. Adult education classes were available; there was an athletic club; an eighty-piece military band gave free weekly concerts during the summer. The children were vaccinated for smallpox, and schooling from kindergarten through the eighth grade was free. The theater booked only entertainments suitable for family audiences.

But Pullman also wanted his town to turn a profit. Everything in Pullman was owned by the Pullman Company, even the bank, and each facility, from the apartment houses to the church, was expected to yield a 6 percent return on its cost. (This requirement made the church so expensive that no denomination could afford to rent it, and the library had to charge an annual membership fee. It did not have many members.) Rents in Pullman were significantly higher than rents for comparable living space in Chicago, though it was widely agreed that the amenities were exceptional. Garbage and sewage were regularly disposed of, for example, something not exactly the norm in the working-class districts of Chicago. (The sewage was piped to a company farm outside the town, where it was put to an appropriate use.) Home ownership was prohibited, and the leases provided that any tenant could be evicted on ten days' notice. Until the Illinois legislature outlawed the practice, in 1891, rent was deducted automatically from the residents' paychecks. And as he did on his sleeping cars, Pullman employed "spotters"—informers—to report derelictions. Residents who complained about the company risked eviction. By 1893, the population had reached 12,600. Seventy-two percent were immigrants.

On June 27, 1893, the New York stock market crashed, triggering a major depression. The American economy after the Civil War was driven by the expansion of the railroads.[10] The Northern wartime Congress had enacted a land grant program that made 158 million acres available to companies wanting to build new railroads. The program was one more piece of that Congress's nationalizing agenda, for the railroads helped to bring a national economic system into being. Railroad construction attracted European capital; it stimulated the growth of the iron and steel industries; it was a magnet for immigrants looking for work. One purpose of the land grants was to facilitate the completion of a transcontinental railroad (a goal accomplished in 1869), and by making it possible for goods and materials to be shipped rapidly from one end of the continent to the other, the railroads laid the foundation for the mass-market economy.

In keeping with the laissez-faire business philosophy of the Republican Party, the growth of the railroad industry was largely unregulated. The system that emerged after the war was characterized by private ownership (the capital required to build tracks and buy cars was too great for state governments to raise) and by short-distance lines—which, until the mid-1880s, often had differing track gauges, making it necessary for passengers and freight to change trains frequently during long trips. The system was also characterized by redundancy. Twenty-four independent lines running into Chicago, for example, was a virtual guarantee of excess capacity and ruinously competitive pricing practices. When the economy grew, the railroads prospered—they carried the goods—but when the economy stalled, cars became idle and workers were laid off. And when track and car construction stopped, the iron and steel industries, over half of whose product went into railroad building and maintenance, suffered slowdowns; weaker companies and the banks that lent to them went under; capital fled. Since the railroad economy was a national economy, these effects spread quickly. The Gilded Age business cycle ran about ten years; before 1893, there had been depressions in 1884 and in 1873.

Chicago's experience in the depression of 1893 was atypical. The panic struck in the middle of the World Columbian Exposition, a kind of world's fair being held in Chicago to commemorate the 400th (plus one) anniversary of Columbus's voyage. The Exposition was one of the greatest tourist attractions of the nineteenth century: between May and October 30, 1893, 27 million people—a number equal to nearly half the population of the United States—came to Chicago to see the show. The crowds kept the local economy flush. But the Exposition employed a lot of people, and when it closed, those people, many of whom had moved to Chicago for the jobs, were thrown out of work. There was nowhere for them to go, and Chicago became a city roamed by armies of unemployed men. (It also underwent a smallpox epidemic, and, two days before the Exposition ended, its mayor was assassinated.)

Businesses like Pullman thus faced a drastically reduced demand for their products (by the end of the summer of 1893, seventy-four railroads had gone bankrupt) and an oversupply of labor. So Pullman did what he thought was the prudent thing: in December he cut wages by an average of 25 percent and laid off a fifth of the workforce at the shops in Pullman, Illinois. He did not, however, reduce the rents. Profit from the town had dropped below 4 percent in 1892 and 1893; Pullman expected 6 percent, and he did not see what wages, which were governed by market conditions, had to do with rents, which were governed by leases freely entered into by the town's residents. The residents did not see it in quite the same way, and by the spring of 1894, Pullman had a very unhappy model town on his hands.

Even some Republicans found Pullman's position a little rigid. Mark Hanna, the Ohio tycoon and future Republican kingmaker, is supposed to have said of Pullman that "a man who won't meet his men half-way is a God-damn fool."[11] But with a large labor pool on one side and a nervous investment community on the other, which group did it make more sense to keep satisfied? Pullman stockholders did not suffer from the downturn in the car business: in 1893 the company paid $7,223,719 in wages and $2,520,000 in dividends; in 1894 it paid $4,471,701 in wages and $2,880,000 in dividends, and had an undistributed surplus of $2,320,000.[12] So on May 11, 90 percent of the workforce in Pullman failed to show up for work. The company fired the rest and closed down the shops.

There had been work stoppages in Pullman before. What made the situation in 1894 different was the existence of a new labor organization, the American Railway Union. The ARU was the personal creation of Eugene Victor Debs. Debs's parents were Alsatian immigrants who had settled in Terre Haute in 1851 and had raised their son on the literature of European Romanticism. Debs was named after Eugène Sue and Victor Hugo, novelists and social reformers. His favorite book was *Les Misérables*. His hero was John Brown. He began working on the railroads as a fireman when he was sixteen, and he soon became active in the Brotherhood of Locomotive Firemen.

The Brotherhood was a trade union: that is, it represented the interests of firemen. To the extent that what was good for firemen was not good for switchmen, brakemen, conductors, repairmen, telegraphers, or engineers—all of whom had their own brotherhoods—the Brotherhood of Locomotive Firemen might find itself at odds not only with management but with the unions of other railroad workers. And all railroad workers often found themselves at odds with another group, farmers, who had an interest in keeping shipping costs low and food prices high. Business owners' ability to pit different groups of workers against each other was one reason labor was so politically feeble in the nineteenth century. The American Federation of Labor, formed by Samuel Gompers in 1886, was just an association of trade unions. Debs's American Railway Union was something different: it was an industrial union. It represented everyone who worked for a railroad, including unskilled laborers—workers who didn't have a trade and therefore weren't in the AF of L. If the ARU called a strike, it could shut down the system.

The ARU was formed in June 1893. Less than a year later, it struck James Hill's Great Northern Railroad and in eighteen days forced an arbitration in which the workers won virtually all of their demands. It was the first successful strike against a major railroad in American history, and by June 1894, a year after its founding, the ARU had 150,000 members. Workers in the Pullman factories were eligible to join because the company operated a short stretch of track running between the shops and downtown Chicago, which technically made it a railroad. In June, Pullman workers approached the ARU and requested a boycott of all railroads running Pullman sleepers.

Debs was not thrilled. He seems to have sensed that the stakes this time were much higher than they had been in the Great Northern strike. But a series of approaches to company management were rebuffed. (Pullman himself, after establishing the policy that pay and rents were nonnegotiable, had taken the precaution of leaving town; he spent most of the strike in isolation at his vacation house on the New Jersey shore.) And on June 26, the ARU ordered all switchmen to refuse to switch Pullman sleeping cars onto trains. If the switchmen were disciplined or discharged as a result, all ARU members on that line would strike. It was exactly the kind of coordinated job action the brotherhoods had been incapable of pulling off.

Debs's premonition was correct. This time the railroads were ready for him. The twenty-four lines running into Chicago had formed their own organization—the General Managers' Association of Railroads—in contemplation of just such a turn of events, and they announced that all lines holding contracts with the Pullman

Company would refuse to operate trains unless Pullman sleeping cars were attached. By June 29, twenty lines had stopped running, 125,000 ARU members had quit work, and the entire rail transport system west of Chicago was effectively shut down.

John Dewey therefore had some trouble getting into Chicago on July 1. He was finally able to find a seat on the Michigan Central line, which used sleeping cars manufactured by a Pullman competitor, the Wagner Company. During the trip he got into a brief conversation with one of the strike organizers. It was a kind of relevation. "I only talked with him 10 or 15 minutes," he wrote to Alice,

> but when I got through my nerves were more thrilled than they had been for years; I felt as if I had better resign my job teaching & follow him round till I got into life. One lost all sense of the right or wrong of things in admiration of his absolute almost fanatic sincerity & earnestness, & in admiration of the magnificent combination that was going on. Simply as an aesthetic matter, I don't believe the world has seen but few times such a spectacle of magnificent, widespread union of men about a common interest as this strike evinces. . . . The gov't is evidently going to take a hand in & the men will be beaten almost to a certainty—but it's a great thing & the beginning of greater.

He was also amused to listen to the other passengers.

> Two or three well dressed men were voluble on the outrage & tyranny which Labor was exercising. One man was greatly troubled because they had now "forfeited all public sympathy"—because he couldn't get home to dinner. Debbs . . . ought to be tried for treason; another man was great on Debbs being a "Jesuit." This was explained in the morning paper when I found this same man was a lecturer for the Am. Patriotic Ass'n—an Anti Cath. organization.[13]

Dewey was right about the government. The next day, July 2, the attorney general of the United States, Richard B. Olney, obtained a court order enjoining Debs and the rest of the ARU leadership from any actions, including speeches, intended to encourage the boycott.

Debs ignored the injunction. Olney then prevailed on the president, Grover Cleveland (a Democrat who had been elected in 1892 with the support of labor), to call out the army for the purpose of protecting interstate commerce and the delivery of the mails. There was no reason, of course, for mail trains to carry sleeping cars, and the ARU had instructed its members not to do anything that might interfere with mail delivery. But official concern for the mails was just a pretext for getting the federal government into the act. On the morning of July 4, Debs looked out the window of his hotel room in downtown Chicago and saw federal soldiers encamped along the lakefront. The entire command of Fort Sheridan had been put on active duty. In all, 2,000 troops and 5,000 federal marshals were mobilized to break the strike.

That afternoon Dewey was a guest at the mansion of Adolphus C. Bartlett. Bartlett was a leading civic figure in Chicago who had made his fortune in the wholesale hardware business. (His second wife, Abby, was a Michigan alumna, which is how Dewey got the invitation.) One of the Bartletts' other guests was John Barrows, the pastor of the First Presbyterian Church in Chicago and a lecturer on religion at the university. "It was interesting," Dewey reported to Alice the next day,

> to see how much more violent the minister was on the Strike than the business man; Bartlett wants to see the strikers downed for business reasons naturally. Barrows surrounds their suppression with a halo of good order, maintaining law, teaching lessons & piety in general. . . . I think professional people are probably worse than the capitalists themselves. Von Holst [chair of the history department at Chicago] talks about "crisis in history of republic; Debbs tyranny worse than that of Czar of Russia" &c, all of which Barrows quotes with great glibness, & fears lest the strike be settled before some of the men be shot & thus learn a lesson—which is fair for a minister of the gospel of Christ. The Univ. is evidently in very bad repute with "Labor."[14]

On July 6 Debs offered to call off the boycott on condition that everyone be allowed to go back to work, but the railroads now had the upper hand, and they turned him down. The confrontation became violent. Twelve people, strikers and onlookers, were killed; hundreds of thousands of dollars of railroad property was destroyed; and on July 10, Debs and other ARU officials were indicted for conspiracy to disrupt the mails and to obstruct the flow of interstate commerce. Debs was arrested. He posted bail, but the end was plainly at hand.

"As you will have found out by the papers," Dewey wrote to Alice on the 14th,

> the strike is lost, & "Labor" is rather depressed. But if I am a prophet, it really won. The business made a tremendous impression; & while there has been a good deal of violent talk—particularly it seems to me by the "upper classes" yet the exhibition of what the unions might accomplish, if organized and working together, has not only sobered them, but given the public mind an object lesson that it won't soon forget. I think the few thousand freight cars burned up a pretty cheap price to pay—it was the stimulus necessary to direct attention, & it might easily have taken more to get the social organism thinking.

He had also, he added, been learning more about Harper and his new colleagues at the university. The place seemed rather conservative and status-conscious. "[M]y main impression," he said, "is that I am a good deal of an anarchist."[15]

On July 17 Debs was arrested again, for violating the July 2 injunction. This time he declined to post bail: he knew the battle was lost, and he was prepared, like John Brown, to assume the martyr's role. The next day, the boycott ended. The railroad brotherhoods had refused to join it; so had the American Federation of Labor. One thousand of the original striking workers in Pullman were left destitute, and everyone who went back to work for the company was required to sign a pledge never to join a union.

Throughout the boycott Debs had been reviled in the press as a dictator. *Harper's Weekly* ran some anti-Debs articles, under the headlines "Suppress the Rebellion" and "Monopoly," during the week of Debs's arrest. When Dewey read them he was disgusted. "I don't know when I have seen anything that seemed so hopeless & discouraging," he wrote to Alice.

> [T]he only wonder is that when the "higher classes"—damn them—take such views there aren't more downright socialists. . . . [T]hat a representative journal of the upper classes—damn them again—can take the attitude of that Harper's weekly & in common with all other journals, think Debs is a simple lunatic or else doing all this to show his criminal control over the criminal "lower classes"—well, it shows what it is to become a higher class. And I fear Chicago Univ. is a capitalistic institution—that is, it too belongs to the higher classes.[16]

Three days later, Dewey was more hopeful. "The Debs crowd still claim that the roads are badly crippled," he reported,

> but so far as the outside is concerned the strike & boycott, *per se, qua strike* &c, &c, have failed dismally. The arrest of Debs is a mighty good thing; the courts have got to face the problem & either say that strikes & boycotts presuppose a leader who can issue orders, & thus discharge Debs, or else hold him criminally responsible (interfering with mail, interference with commerce by conspiracy &c) simply for running the thing. . . . It seems to me a decision either way is a victory for "Labor." . . . Slavery can't have gone so far yet that the kick of such a decision won't be more effective than the thing itself.[17]

In the end the conspiracy case against the ARU collapsed (the ARU officials were defended by Clarence Darrow), but Debs and the others were held in contempt for violating the July 2 injunction. Debs's lawyers filed a petition for a writ of habeas corpus to the United States Supreme Court, but the petition was denied and Debs served six months in the McHenry County Jail in Woodstock, Illinois. Some local farmers threatened to break into the prison facility and lynch him.[18] When he got out, in November 1895, he tried to revive the ARU, but no one wanted anything to do with it. On January 1, 1897, he announced that he had become a socialist.

3

Dewey's view of the Pullman strike was consistent: he thought that whatever the outcome, it was a way (as he put it in one of his letters to Alice) "to get the social organism thinking." The social organism had a lot to think about. For the strike showed what a tangle of contradictions and anachronisms lay in the accumulated mixture of Christian piety, laissez-faire economics, natural law doctrine, scientific determinism, and popular Darwinism that characterized many people's attitudes toward social and economic life in the decades after the Civil War.

It was not the violence that made the Pullman affair such a telling moment. The suppression of the Homestead strike at Andrew Carnegie's Pennsylvania steel plant two years earlier had been at least as brutal. What made Pullman a kind of national alarm bell was its scale. We think of the strike as a conflict between two groups, business and labor. Most people in 1894 thought of it as a conflict between two individuals, George Pullman and Eugene Debs. And what was shocking was that their quarrel could paralyze half the country. This is why Debs was caricatured as Dictator Debs. To nineteenth-century eyes, the boycott seemed an extension of his personal will. In fact, Debs had resisted the calls for a boycott, he had continually attempted to negotiate a settlement, and he had tried to prevent the acts of violence and sabotage that (despite the presence of *agents provocateurs*) were almost certainly perpetrated by ARU members.[19] But in creating the ARU, he had given birth to a tiger. He could sit on its back; he could not control it. Pullman, too, seems to have been stunned by the magnitude of the turmoil his obstinacy had provoked.

One of the things the Pullman strike exposed, therefore, was the extent to which the principles of classical economic theory—that is, the principles of laissez-faire—were based on an individualistic psychology. From the point of view of classical economics, the town of Pullman was the personal property of an individual, George Pullman, which he was entitled to do with as he pleased, on the assumption that his pleasure would be most gratified by maximizing the town's financial potential. This was the argument Webster had used to win the Dartmouth College case: that Dartmouth was the private charity of Eleazer Wheelock, which it was his right, ratified by charter, to administer as he saw fit. Justice Story's dictum that a private corporation has the same rights as a person was the legal corollary.

Classical economic theory regarded the Pullman worker in the same light. The worker was the sole proprietor of his own labor, which he was free to sell to Pullman, to sell to an employer offering greater compensation, or to withhold in the hope of seeing its price bid up (or because he gave a higher value to leisure than to wages). The assumption, again, was that his pleasure would best be served by maximizing the return on his "property." For Pullman and for the worker alike, economic behavior was understood to be dictated by this "hedonistic calculus." What neither Pullman nor the worker was entitled to do, however, was to conspire to prevent other individuals from pursuing their own economic interests. Such a conspiracy was signified by the term of opprobrium "combination."

Thus the indictment of Debs for conspiracy to obstruct interstate commerce was brought under the Sherman Anti-Trust Act of 1890— a measure originally designed to curtail the anticompetitive practices of a *business* combination, the Standard Oil Trust, set up in 1881 by the man who would become the chief benefactor of the University of Chicago, John D. Rockefeller. The American Railway Union was unlawful, Circuit Court Judge William Howard Taft declared in sentencing an ARU official to jail for helping to organize the boycott in Cincinnati, because although Pullman's own employees had a right to strike, the involvement of workers with no "natural relation" (as Taft called it) to Pullman constituted a combination in restraint of trade. "The gigantic character of the conspiracy of the American Railway Union staggers the imagination," he wrote. "[T]he starvation of a nation cannot be a lawful purpose of a combination."[20] This is why the railroad brotherhoods had been organized by craft: all firemen were presumed to have a "natural relation" to developments affecting the interests of firemen. If those developments did not affect the interests of, say, engineers, engineers stayed out of it. And it is why when *Harper's Weekly* called one of its antistrike editorials "Monopoly," it was referring not to the town of Pullman, but to the ARU.

The General Managers' Association of Railroads, the group that coordinated the industry's response to the strike, was a combination, too, of course, and it played its part in ratcheting up the level of damage caused by the boycott.[21] It was obvious that the federal government's intervention was an intervention on behalf of the railroad companies; but it was just as obvious that without that intervention the antagonists really might have starved the nation, or part of it, in their efforts to squeeze each other into submission. The size of the entities involved in the Pullman affair was much too great to allow them to test the economic merits of their positions in the open market.

And what was, legally speaking, the state's interest in their dispute? It was the interest that had inspired Governor Plumer, seventy-eight years earlier, to intervene in the Dartmouth College affair: the public welfare. "If it takes the entire army and navy of the United States to deliver a postal card in Chicago, that card will be delivered,"[22] Cleveland is supposed to have said, and the Supreme Court backed him up. "The entire strength of the nation may be used to enforce in any part of the land the full and free exercise of all national powers and the security of all rights entrusted by the Constitution to its care," the Court held in denying Debs a writ of habeas corpus. "The strong arm of the government may be put forth to brush away all obstructions to the freedom of interstate commerce or the transportation of the mails."[23] The target of these sentences was organized labor, but for big business the writing was on the wall.

It is natural to assume that the belief system behind the antilabor sentiments exhibited during the Pullman strike—and as Dewey had occasion to observe, those sentiments were widespread among the professional classes—was Social Darwinism. Social Darwinism was an extrapolation from evolutionary theory (the idea that life is a struggle for survival) and statistical thinking (the idea that the results of that struggle are always optimal and are determined by natural laws). It was a rather unsubtle justification for existing hierarchies of wealth and power, and obviously a philosophy entirely compatible with classical economics. Its attitude toward reform is summed up in the title of an article published by its leading American theorist, William Graham Sumner, just two months before the Pullman strike began: "The Absurd Effort to Make the World Over." But Social Darwinism probably had only a little to do with the responses people had to the strike. And in any case, it was a fading ideology in 1894.

Pullman himself, for instance, though in many respects a prime specimen of the Gilded Age tycoon, was plainly not a Social Darwinist. His model town was predicated on the reformist idea that character is a function of things like good housing and regular garbage collection rather than genes, and his intransigence about the rents almost certainly had as much to do with moral values (and *amour propre*) as it did with economic theory. What looks like Social Darwinism in the businessmen of Pullman's generation was generally just a Protestant belief in the virtues of the work ethic combined with a Lockean belief in the sanctity of private property. It had nothing to do with evolution.[24]

And even though Sumner was a professor at Yale, American social science essentially created itself as a discipline by reacting against the laissez-faire views associated with Sumner and Sumner's philosophical master, Herbert Spencer. After all, which assumption offers a more promising basis for a field of inquiry: the assumption that societies develop according to underlying laws whose efficiency cannot be improved by public policies, or the assumption that societies are multivariable organisms whose progress can be guided by scientific intelligence? Professions come into existence because there is a demand for expertise. The expertise required to repeat, in every situation, "Let the market decide" (or as Sumner liked to say, "Root, hog, or die")[25] is not great.

The academic world Dewey inhabited exposed him continually to ideas antagonistic to laissez-faire individualism, some far more radical than the Burlington philosophy or George Morris's Christian Hegelianism. While he was still a student at Hopkins, in 1884, he heard Sumner's most vigorous opponent, Lester Ward, read a paper before the Metaphysical Club on "Mind as a Social Factor." The year before, Ward (a practicing scientist: he was a government paleontologist) had published the first American sociology textbook, *Dynamic Sociology*, which emphasized the role of intelligence in human evolution, and he repeated its argument in his talk. "The *laissez faire* doctrine is a gospel of inaction, the scientific creed is struck with sterility, the policy of resigning all into the hands of Nature is a surrender," he told the club. "The survival of the fittest is simply the survival of the strong, which . . . might as well be called, the destruction of the weak. And if nature progresses through the destruction of the weak, man progresses through the *protection* of the weak."[26]

The same year, an assistant professor at Hopkins, Richard Ely, published a widely read attack on classical economics, "The Past and Present of Political Economy," in the Hopkins journal *Studies in Historical and Political Science*. Soon after, Ely was commissioned by *Harper's Magazine* to visit the town of Pullman and write a report; his piece appeared in the winter of 1885. (Ely had just gotten married; since *Harper's* was paying expenses, he economized by taking his honeymoon in Pullman.) Ely recognized immediately that the town represented an abandonment of the principles of laissez-faire. "The pretty dream of a perfect, natural order of things brought about by the free play of unrestrained social forces has vanished," he wrote. "The conviction has become general that the divine order never contemplated a social and economic world left to itself." Still, he found it almost impossible to get the residents of Pullman to talk frankly: they suspected that he was a "spotter." He started tearing the buttons off his wife's boots and taking them to different shoemakers to be repaired, on the theory that "no one could avoid a free discussion with a man who came on so harmless an errand." For all its architectural and sanitary excellence, he concluded, "the idea of Pullman is un-American. . . . It is benevolent, well-wishing feudalism."[27] (That fall, Ely founded the American Economic Association—in order, he wrote privately, "to combat the influence of the Sumner crowd.")[28]

Laissez-faire liberalism was under attack at Michigan, too. One of Dewey's favorite colleagues there was the economist Henry Carter Adams, who argued that private property should be subject to state regulation when the public welfare was affected, and who had lost his position at Cornell in 1886 for speaking in support of a railroad strike. Dewey's best friend at Michigan, whom he later brought to Chicago, was George Herbert Mead, a former student of William James's and one of the founders of social psychology, a field premised on the idea that selfhood is a function of one's relations with others. And Charles Cooley, the student who had found Dewey inspiring without understanding exactly what he was saying, began teaching sociology at Michigan in 1892 (his Ph.D. was in economics), and developed a theory based on the notion, similar to Mead's, of "the looking-glass self"—the notion that people acquire their sense of themselves as individuals from their reflection in the social mirror.

Dewey himself, while he was at Michigan, had been working on a theory of democracy that dispensed with Lockean assumptions. "The Ethics of Democracy," published in the *University of Michigan Philosophical Papers* in 1888, is one of his most luminous pieces of writing. (In later years Dewey deliberately adopted an antirhetorical style, in the belief that readers should be persuaded by the cogency of the thought rather than the felicities of the prose. He was uncommonly successful in getting rid of the felicities.) "The Ethics of Democracy" was a reply to a critique of democracy called *Popular Government*, by the British legal historian Henry Maine. Maine was an enemy of majoritarianism—he considered popular prejudice an obstacle to progress—and he was a particular admirer of the Supreme Court's opinion in the Dartmouth College case, which he called "the basis of the credit of many of the great American Railway Incorporations. . . . [I]t has secured full play to the economical forces by which the achievement of cultivating the soil of the North American Continent has been performed; it is the bulwark of American individualism against democratic impatience and Socialistic fantasy."[29]

Dewey argued that in thinking of majority decisions as the sum of so many independent selfish preferences, Maine had committed the empiricist's error of assuming that what we can see is more real than what we can't see—that individuals exist but "the popular will" is a fiction. This, Dewey thought, was exactly backward. "Society in its unified and structural character is the fact of the case," he wrote; "the non-social individual is an abstraction arrived at by imagining what man would be if all his human qualities were taken away. Society, as a real whole, is the normal order, and the mass as an aggregate of isolated units is the fiction."[30] Democracies are not just the sum of their constituent atoms because atoms are not independent of their molecules. They are always functioning as parts of a greater whole. Participation changes everything.

And (despite Dewey's first impressions) the University of Chicago was already on its way to becoming a center of post-laissez-faire thought when he arrived there. Harper had created the first sociology department in the country, and its chair, Albion Small, was a Hopkins graduate and a disciple of Lester Ward. ("I would rather have written *Dynamic Sociology* than any other book that has ever appeared in America,"[31] he once claimed.) Small was not a radical reformer (neither, for that matter, was Ward), but he believed that sociology should be an engaged discipline. "The most impressive lesson which I have learned in the vast sociological laboratory which the city of Chicago constitutes," he wrote in 1896 in one of the first issues of the *American Journal of Sociology*, which he founded, along with George Herbert Mead and another Chicago sociologist and Christian reformer, Charles Henderson, "is that action, not speculation, is the supreme teacher."[32]

And there was a genuine iconoclast at Chicago. Thorstein Veblen, too, had been a graduate student at Hopkins, entering in the same year as Dewey: he had taken the yearlong logic course taught by Peirce that Dewey decided was too intimidating. Veblen was turned down for a fellowship, though, and he had to drop out. He reentered graduate school at Cornell in 1891, and came to Chicago a year later as a teaching fellow. Veblen's view of property—set out in 1899 in *The Theory of the Leisure Class*, a debunking of classical economic assumptions so caustic that some readers mistook it for a satire—was that property originates in theft, and that its acquisition beyond necessity has nothing to do with survival and nearly everything to do with status.

Veblen's view of the hedonistic calculus was that it was founded on "a faulty conception of human nature," picturing a person as "a homogeneous globule of desire of happiness"[33] played upon by external forces. Like most academic opponents of Social Darwinism, Veblen did not reject the Darwinism; he only thought that by reading Darwin in the light of classical economic theory, Spencer and his American epigones had missed the point. Real evolutionary economics, Veblen thought, required a picture of human beings not as passive reactors to stimuli, but as actors for ends. And not all our ends can be expressed in the language of profit and loss. "In the organic complex of habits of thought which make up the substance of an individual's conscious life," as he put it in *The Theory of the Leisure Class*, "the economic interest does not lie isolated and distinct."[34]

By the time Dewey arrived in Chicago, in short, the opposition to laissez-faire thinking was well established intellectually, even though (and this was what Dewey was trying to take the measure of in his first weeks at the university) it was still embattled politically and institutionally. Criticism of capitalism made Harper nervous—understandably, since his career was dependent on the largesse of a man who was virtually the symbol of capitalist success in America. But since he dreamed of making a great university, Harper could not afford to be inhospitable to faculty on the leading edges of their disciplines. Professors were subject to administrative pressure for their political opinions in the 1890s, and some were fired, even at Chicago. (Veblen's problems were a little different: the record of his sexual escapades puts Charles Peirce's in the shade. He had the custom of sleeping with his colleagues' wives, who are reported to have found him irresistible.) But many of those who got into trouble for their political views before 1900 became stars of the profession afterward.

The interpretation of the Pullman strike Dewey found most penetrating, though, was not written by an academic social scientist. It was written by a practicing social scientist.

4

Jane Addams was a sociologist, and Hull-House, the neighborhood center she founded in Chicago with her friend Ellen Gates Starr, was a sociology laboratory. Neither started out that way.[35]

Addams was born in a small Illinois town, Cedarville, in 1860. Her father, John, was a successful businessman and a friend of Lincoln's. He participated in the founding of the Republican Party, and during the Civil War he helped to raise and equip a regiment subsequently known as "the Addams Guard." He also served for sixteen years in the Illinois state senate, where his rectitude was proverbial: he became famous as a man who not only had never taken a bribe, but had never been offered one. Jane Addams had a tubercular spine, which made her stoop-shouldered and pigeon-toed, and she was coddled as a child and depressive as a young woman. But she had her father's qualities: righteousness, formality (in college she annoyed her friends by asking them to address her as Miss Addams), and ambition. She was also, particularly to women, fantastically charismatic. People thought she was a saint. To some extent this was a nineteenth-century way of explaining the aura of authority and integrity surrounding a person who happened to be female. Still, she had the aura.

Addams and Starr became friends in college, at an Illinois school for women called Rockford Seminary. (Addams had wanted to go to Smith but her father thought it was too far away.) They got the idea for Hull-House during a trip to England in 1888, when they visited a place called Toynbee Hall. Toynbee Hall had been created in 1884; it was the original social settlement—that is, a building in an impoverished urban area where college men (the "settlers") lived and worked for social reform. Toynbee Hall had a theory. Its founder and warden was a clergyman, Samuel A. Barnett—he had been the vicar of St. Jude's, in the poor London parish of Whitechapel—and his theory was a combination of Christian Samaritanism and the social gospel of Victorian critics of industrialism like Arnold, Carlyle, and Ruskin. The theory had two implications for the practice. The first (stemming from the Christianity) was that Toynbee Hall's greatest benefit, since it was the spiritual benefit, was understood to be the one conferred on the settlers: brotherly contact with the poor was improving to the soul. The second (stemming from the social criticism) was the belief that a crucial element of social reform was exposure to literature and art—that the cultural impoverishment of working-class Londoners was at least as significant as their material deprivation.

Starr was a religious woman; Addams was a devotee of the most transcendental of the American Transcendentalists. (She is supposed to have competed for the privilege of scraping the mud off Bronson Alcott's boots when he visited Rockford.[36] Alcott was someone who thought the use of fire in cooking was wicked.) Starr and Addams therefore had no difficulty picking up the Toynbee philosophy, and soon after they got back to the United States, they raised the money, some of it from Chicago ministers, to start Hull-House. It opened in 1889 in one of the worst urban areas in the United States, on a block of Halsted Street in Chicago's Nineteenth Ward—a district whose directory listed nine churches and 250 saloons.[37] Apart from a small number of African-Americans, most of the people in the neighborhood were immigrants. (In fact, in 1889 60 percent of all Chicagoans were foreign-born.) Addams and Starr and their colleagues later counted eighteen different national groups in the vicinity of Hull-House.[38]

Hull-House was not a welfare agency in the twentieth-century meaning of the term. It did have relief funds for people who were out of work or faced other sorts of financial emergencies, and the "settlers" were, of course, engaged in providing assistance to people who lived nearby. But Hull-House was primarily, and in the broadest sense, an educational institution. It sponsored classes, lectures, dietetic instruction, athletics, and boys', girls', men's, and women's clubs. It had a kindergarten, a playground, a nursery, and a day-care center, a drama group and a choral group, a Shakespeare Club and a Plato Club. It was furnished attractively and decorated with reproductions of famous paintings. The idea was to provide people with an escape from the conditions in which their poverty, and the city's inability to provide decent public services, obliged them to live. It was also to inculcate them with American civic and cultural norms in a setting where their particular national heritages were acknowledged and respected. (The last part was not always easy for Addams. She had trouble, for example, getting used to the notion that alcohol could serve as a medium of hospitality.)

In the beginning, Addams and Starr followed, in effect, the Toynbee manual. "One of its chief aims," explained a women's magazine article, called "A Chicago Toynbee Hall," publicizing Hull-House a few months before it opened,

> will be to make it . . . a retreat for other young women, who need rest and change, or who desire a safe refuge from the inordinate demands of society, and in whom it is believed that a glimpse of the reverse side of life, of the poverty and struggles of half of the people, will beget a broader philanthropy and a tenderer sympathy, and leave less time and inclination for introspection, for selfish ambition, or for real or fancied invalidism.[39]

It sounds like social work as therapy, and in a sense it was. But it was also a response to the forced inanition of middle- and upper-class women—a kind of feminism. The initial activities at Hull-House were inspired, similarly, by Ruskinian theories of cultural uplift. One of the first events, for local Italian immigrants, was a series of evening readings from George Eliot's *Romola*, accompanied by a viewing of photographs of Florence.[40]

The tone soon changed. One of the reasons was the arrival, in 1891, of Florence Kelley. Kelley was a far more worldly character than either Addams or Starr. She had graduated from Cornell, attended the University of Zurich, translated Friedrich Engels's *The Condition of the Working Class in England in 1844*, married and then separated (her married name was Wischnewetzky), and published a pamphlet on child labor. Unlike Starr, she was an atheist; unlike both Starr and Addams, she was a socialist. She was not in it for the spiritual rewards. Her presence helped transform Hull-House into a center of reform advocacy. Her investigation of Chicago sweatshops, for example, was so effective that she was appointed chief factory inspector for Illinois by the progressive governor, John Peter Altgeld. Kelley helped make Hull-House a center of sociological investigation as well. She was one of the forces behind *Hull-House Maps and Papers*, a study of the area around Hull-House clearly inspired by Engels's book on Manchester. It was published in 1895, one of the first serious examinations of an American working-class urban neighborhood.

(Jacob Riis's sensational *How the Other Half Lives*, on the slums of New York City, had appeared in 1890.)

The educational programs at Hull-House continued, including talks by distinguished visitors; and one of these was John Dewey. In January 1892, while he was still on the Michigan faculty, Dewey lectured at Hull-House on "Psychology and History." "I cannot tell you how much good I got from my stay," he wrote to Addams when he got back to Ann Arbor.

> My indebtedness to you for giving me an insight into matters there is great. . . . Every day I stayed there only added to my conviction that you had taken the right way. I am confident that 25 years from now the forces now turned in upon themselves in various church &c agencies will be finding outlet very largely through just such channels as you have opened.[41]

It was the start of a long association.

Hull-House was not the first social settlement in the United States. A man named Stanton Coit, who had spent two months as a resident of Toynbee Hall, had opened one on the Lower East Side of New York City in 1886. But Hull-House quickly became the most famous. By the time of the Pullman strike, it was a place distinguished figures from Europe made it a point to visit, and Addams was a leading citizen of the city. She was a member of a group called the Civic Federation of Chicago (so was Adolphus Bartlett, the hardware king at whose mansion Dewey was a guest during the strike); and in that capacity, she approached the Pullman Company when the strike began to propose that an impartial committee investigate the grievances of the workers. Addams knew George Pullman; she had served with Pullman's daughter Florence on the board of the Chicago Visiting Nurses' Association; Pullman himself had made a contribution to Hull-House (oddly, given his views about the rents, to the relief fund). But she was informed that the problems in Pullman were none of her business.

Hull-House sympathies, as one would expect, were generally pro-boycott. On July 5, the day after the troops were called out, Dewey stopped in on his way back from the Bartletts. "The atmosphere is somewhat different you may imagine," he wrote to Alice. Addams was away; but "Miss Starr warmed with enthusiasm for the magnificence of men all over the country throwing away their bread & butter in order that their fellows hundreds of miles away might get their rights—she is the only person I have seen who feels that side of things."[42] Florence Kelley was active in the union's behalf. She helped raise bail for Debs after the July 10 indictment, and she covered for him with the press while he went out on a drinking binge afterward.[43] (Debs was a terrible drinker, the kind who is knocked out by the second round, but he did a lot of it: barhopping was apparently his way of bonding with his constituents.)

Addams took a different line. She deplored the boycott. The reason she was out when Dewey came by was because she was visiting her sister, Mary Linn, who was dying of cancer at a hospital in Kenosha, Wisconsin. Jane was able to get to Kenosha by private train, but Mary's husband, John, and their four children had trouble. John Linn eventually signed a statement releasing the railroad from responsibility if their train was attacked en route, and the family rode sitting on the floor for fear of being hit by rocks. They got to Kenosha, but too late. Addams always insisted that her sister forgave the strikers on her deathbed,[44] but the experience seems to have left her with a sick sense of the destructive effects of industrial warfare.

She had philosophical objections as well. Florence Kelley was one reason for Addams's abandonment of the Toynbee philosophy, but another had to do with her own encounters with her neighbors on Halsted Street. She found that the people she was trying to help had better ideas about how their lives might be improved than she and her colleagues did. She came to believe that any method of philanthropy or reform premised on top-down assumptions—the assumption, for instance, that the reformer's tastes or values are superior to the reformee's, or, more simply, that philanthropy is a unilateral act of giving by the person who has to the person who has not—is ineffectual and inherently false. She decided that for the settlement movement to be successful, it needed to correct for the antidemocratic animus that ran through the social criticism of Arnold, Carlyle, and Ruskin (as Dewey had set out to correct a similar animus in the political writings of Henry Maine). The obliteration of invidious group and class distinctions became her obsession. Anything that made division sharper—such as a strike—she deprecated. Anything that promoted the cooperative idea—such as arbitration—she encouraged.

"We must learn," as she put it in her contribution to *Hull-House Maps and Papers*, "to trust our democracy, giant-like and threatening as it may appear in its uncouth strength and untried applications."[45] And her idea of democratic participation was universal. "We have learned to say," she wrote a few years later, "that the good must be extended to all of society before it can be held secure by any one person or any one class; but we have not yet learned to add to that statement, that unless all men and all classes contribute to a good, we cannot even be sure that it is worth having."[46] The moment Addams had this insight into the nature of her own work was the moment she ceased being a do-gooder, or even a reformer, and became a social scientist. She became the sociologist of her own profession: she was the first sociologist of social work.

In the fall of 1894, a few months after the demise of the Pullman boycott, the University of Chicago began making arrangements to establish its own settlement house. (Harper had made a bid to take over Hull-House, but Addams refused the offer.) The university's effort was led by Alice Palmer, the wife of the Harvard philosopher who had turned down the chairmanship that went to Dewey, and Dewey attended some of the planning meetings, including one, in October, at which Addams was invited to speak. Dewey reported her remarks to his wife. "There was no special aim," he said Addams told the meeting, "because [a settlement] wasn't a thing but a way of living—hence had the same aims as life itself. . . . Miss Addams hoped [the university's] settlement wasn't being started . . . from the desire to do good. Philanthropy had been identified with helping instead of with interpretation."[47] Alice Palmer evidently did not get the message: she made a pitch for money by suggesting that each student should donate two dollars and each faculty member five dollars in a spirit of philanthropic self-sacrifice. Addams was disgusted. She told Dewey she thought Palmer "a dangerous nuisance"—which, Dewey added, "I fear is true."[48]

The next day, though, Addams and Dewey got into an argument. It was an argument about argument. Addams said she believed that antagonism was always unnecessary. It never arose from real, objective differences, she told Dewey, "but from a person's mixing in his own personal reactions—the extra emphasis he gave the truth, the enjoyment he took in doing a thing because it was unpalatable to others, or the feeling that one must show his own colors." If Christ drove the money changers out of the temple, she said, so much the worse for Christianity. The Civil War, too, showed the futility of antagonism: "we freed the slaves by war & and had now to free them all over again individually, & pay the costs of the war & reckon with the added bitterness of the Southerner beside."

Dewey was baffled. He asked Addams whether there weren't antagonisms between certain institutions—for example, capital and labor, or the church and democracy—which it made sense to take seriously. She said there never were: "The antagonism of institutions was always unreal; it was simply due to the injection of the personal attitude & reaction; & then instead of adding to the recognition of meaning, it delayed & distorted it." It was, Dewey confessed to Alice, "the most magnificent exhibition of intellectual & moral faith I ever saw. She converted me internally, but not really, I fear. . . . [W]hen you think that Miss Addams does not think this as a philosophy, but believes it in all her senses & muscles—Great God."

By morning he had changed his mind. Addams, he decided, was right. "I can see that I have always been interpreting the [he wrote "Hegelian," but crossed it out] dialectic wrong end up," he wrote to Alice, "—the unity as the reconciliation of opposites, instead of the opposites as the unity in its growth, and thus translated the physical tension into a moral thing." He saw, in other words, that the resistance the world puts up to our actions and desires is not the same as a genuine opposition of interests. "I don't know as I give the reality of this at all," he concluded, "—it seems so natural & commonplace now, but I never had anything take hold of me so."

I don't know whether I told you some time about Miss Starr's account of what they went thro' with at the outset—the hootings, the
throwing of stones in at the window & all the other outbreaks, &
how Miss A. said she would give the whole thing [up] before she
would ask for a policeman; one day a negro spat straight in her face
in the street, & she simply wiped it off, & went on talking without
noticing it.[49]

It was a degree of equanimity awesome even to Dewey. The next day
he sent Addams a letter. "I wish to take back what I said the other
night," he told her. "Not only is actual antagonizing bad, but the assumption that there is or may be antagonism is bad. . . . I'm glad I
found this out before I began to talk on social psychology. . . . This is
rather a suspiciously sudden conversion," he added, "but then it's
only a beginning."[50]

The little debate between Addams and Dewey sounds fairly abstract, but the subtext was concrete enough: they were arguing over
the proper response to the Pullman affair. For at the same time that
Addams was explaining her views on antagonism to Dewey and her
views on philanthropy to Palmer and the other university dignitaries,
she was composing her own interpretation of the strike, which she
delivered that month as a talk before the Chicago Woman's Club.
She called it "A Modern Lear." Her idea was that the conflict between
Pullman and his workers was analogous to the conflict between King
Lear and his daughter Cordelia in Shakespeare's play: an old set of
values, predicated on individualism and paternalism, had run up
against a new set of values, predicated on mutuality and self-
determination. She saw, in other words, and even more clearly than
Dewey, that the Pullman affair—she called it "an industrial tragedy"—represented a rupture in the cultural system.

A rupture in the cultural system is not a tragedy; even a revolution is not a tragedy. What made the Pullman strike tragic, Addams
thought, was the belief of both parties that their interests were genuinely opposed—that a gain for one must mean a loss for the other.
But antagonism (as she had tried to explain to Dewey) was only misunderstanding, a tension in the progress toward a common outcome.

Cordelia, after all, does love her father. Lear doesn't oppose her; he only misinterprets her. Pullman was the same. "The man who persistently paced the seashore, while the interior of his country was racked with a strife which he alone might have arbitrated, lived out within himself the tragedy of King Lear," Addams said. "He, too, lost the faculty of affectionate interpretation, and demanded a sign." Interests, if they are worth securing, are mutual. "Affectionate interpretation" is the means by which we understand how.

Pullman had wished to be a great man and to do good, but he didn't understand the meaning of greatness or the method of goodness. "It is easy for the good and powerful to think that they can rise by following the dictates of conscience by pursuing their own ideals, leaving those ideals unconnected with the consent of their fellowmen,"[51] Addams said. She was echoing a point Richard Ely had made after his visit to Pullman ten years earlier—that "[t]he loss of authority and distrust of the people is the fatal weakness of many systems of reform and well-intentioned projects of benevolence."[52] True greatness, Addams said, consists of identification with the widest possible interest: "Popular opinion calls him the greatest of Americans who gathered to himself the largest amount of American experience." She was referring to Lincoln, her father's hero.

The workers, too, Addams told the Woman's Club, needed to understand that their interests and the businessmen's were the same; otherwise they risked reproducing the divisions they hoped to overcome. ("In reading the tragedy of King Lear, Cordelia does not escape our censure," she said.) For "[t]he new claim on the part of the toiling multitude, the new sense of responsibility on the part of the well-to-do, arise in reality from the same source. They are in fact the same 'social compunction,' and, in spite of their widely varying manifestations, logically converge into the same movement."[53] The right outcome is always the outcome democratically reached. Otherwise we cannot know if it is right. "It is easy for the good and powerful to think that they can rise by pursuing their own ideals": Addams might have been thinking of Alice Palmer. She was certainly thinking of herself. Addams understood Pullman because she had been like him once, too.

Addams sent "A Modern Lear" to the *Forum* (known as a muck-raking journal), the *North American Review*, and the *Atlantic Monthly*. All three turned it down on grounds that it was an ad hominem attack on George Pullman. ("A Modern Lear" wasn't published until 1912.) Addams showed the essay to Dewey as well. He called it "one of the greatest things I ever read."[54] Three years later, on October 19, 1897, George Pullman died of a heart attack. His estate was valued at $8 million. He left his two sons only $3,000 a month, because he thought they were dissolute and unworthy; but he left $1.25 million to his model town, to be spent on a manual training school for the inhabitants. Pullman was buried in a special grave of his own design: it was ten feet deep and filled with concrete. He was afraid workers might dig up his body and desecrate it. He was Lear to the end.

Exactly a year after Pullman's death, the Illinois Supreme Court ordered the Pullman Palace Car Company to divest itself of the model town. The court said it could find no mention of a town in the corporation's charter. Company towns, the judges observed, were opposed to good public policy. The Pullman Company was then being run by Robert Todd Lincoln, a close counselor to Pullman during the strike and the son of the American president.

5.

It was in Chicago that Dewey did the work that made him famous around the world and among people who are not philosophers. This was his work on the school. What Dewey accomplished helped to change the way children are taught, and it gave him a reputation as a great educator. But Dewey did not get into the field as a reformer, and he did not regard himself as an educator.

Dewey became interested in education, he once remarked, "mainly on account of the children."[55] He meant his own children, whose development he followed with close attention and, in the case of Morris particularly, documented in detail. Morris Dewey was an exceptional little boy. He was only twenty months old when the

John Dewey at the University of Chicago in 1902, when he was chair
of the Department of Philosophy, director of the School of Education,
and head of the Laboratory School, internationally known as
"the Dewey School." (Photograph by Eva Watson Schutze.)

family left Michigan, but he was verbally precocious and, to Dewey's continual amazement, uncannily serene in his relations with the world. "Morris is so good, so sweet and tractable, that it doesnt seem possible that he should have spirit & force, but he doesn't show lack of them," Dewey he wrote to the rest of the family a few weeks before he left Morris with the grandparents and set off for Chicago in the summer of 1894. "It is almost incredible that there should be such a combination of goodness & sense as he is."[56] And two months later: "He is the most perfect work of art in his attitude toward the world I have ever seen."[57] In August Morris and his father were reunited and Dewey became a student of his son's growth, mailing anecdotes regularly to Alice and the other children. "I hope I shall never forget the lessons I have learned from Morris," he wrote in October; ". . . he is social intelligence incorporate."[58]

At the end of the fall semester, Dewey took Morris to Europe, where they rejoined the rest of the family in Paris. While the Deweys were traveling through Germany, Morris contracted diphtheria, probably in Freiburg, and he died in Milan on March 12, 1895. He was not quite two and a half. It was, Dewey's daughter Jane wrote many years later, "a blow from which neither of his parents ever fully recovered."[59] (A little more than a year after Morris's death, the Deweys had another son, Gordon. He, too, was a gifted child, and he, too, died, when he was eight, during a family trip to Europe. Jane Addams held a memorial service for him at Hull-House. Jane Dewey—she was named after Jane Addams—said that her mother never got over this second loss.) Dewey was not given to self-reflection (in print, anyway), and it is hard to know what Morris's death meant to him. But it is possible to feel, reading his letters after March 1895, that a light has gone out.

Morris was one reason Dewey became interested in education. Chicago was another. Dewey was ambivalent about the university, but he loved the city. "Chicago is the place to make you appreciate at every turn the absolute opportunity which chaos affords," he wrote to Alice less than two weeks after arriving; "—it is sheer Matter with no Standards at all."[60] Six weeks later, he expanded on his impression:

Every conceivable thing solicits you; the town seems filled with problems holding out their hands & asking somebody to please solve them—or else dump them in the Lake. I had no conception that things could be so much more phenomenal & objective than they are in a country village, & simply stick themselves at you, instead of leaving you to think about them. . . . [Y]ou can't really get rid feeling here that there is a "method" & if you could only get hold of it, things could be so tremendously strengthened out; it's such a loose jointed quantitative chaos after all,—and not an Ann Arbor parterre. Think of all hell turned loose, & yet not hell any longer, but simply material for a new creation.[61]

It is like Albion Small's notion of the city as a laboratory. Chicago seems to have struck the social-scientific mind at the end of the nineteenth century as an animated simulacrum of social life, a sort of living textbook. Max Weber, passing through the city in 1904, compared it to a man whose skin has been peeled off so that you can see the intestines working.

A third ingredient was regular exposure to Hull-House; and by November of 1894, Dewey had his vision. He wrote it down in a letter to Alice that expresses (in language several degrees more excited than he used again) all the essential elements in his philosophy of the school. "I think I'm in a fair way to become an educational crank," he wrote;

I sometimes think I will drop teaching phil—directly, & teach it via *pedagogy*. When you think of the thousands & thousands of young 'uns who are practically being ruined negatively if not positively in the Chicago schools every year, it is enough to make you go out & howl on the street corners like the Salvation Army. There is an image of a school growing up in my mind all the time; a school where some actual & literal constructive activity shall be the centre & source of the whole thing, & from which the work should be always growing out in two directions—one the social bearings of that constructive industry, the other the contact with nature which supplies it with its materials. I can see, theoretically, how the carpentry etc involved in building a model house should be the centre of a social training on one side, & a scientific on the other, all held within the grasp of a

positive concrete physical habit of eye & hand. . . . The school is the
one form of social life which is abstracted & under control—which
is directly experimental, and if philosophy is ever to be an experimental science, the construction of a school is its starting point—
This general theorizing is very edifying when our own children can't
get even a poor school to go to; but it's largely that that has started
me off—with the pleasure of being with an absolute normal intelligence like Morris's.[62]

A little more than a year later, in January 1896, Dewey opened the
University Elementary School of the University of Chicago. The
school had sixteen children, all under twelve, and two teachers. It
was a local sensation. That fall, it reopened in a new space with
three teachers and thirty-two students. By 1902, there were 140 students, twenty-three teachers, and ten graduate students working as
assistants; it had become an international sensation; and it was
known as the Dewey School.

The official name the school eventually acquired was the Laboratory School. The name actually came from the school's supervisor of
instruction, Ella Flagg Young (who later became superintendent of
the Chicago school system), but it expressed Dewey's intention exactly. The Dewey School was a philosophy laboratory, in the same
way that Hull-House was a sociology laboratory. It was a place, as
Dewey later put it, "to work out in the concrete, instead of merely in
the head or on paper, a theory of the unity of knowledge."[63]

Morris Dewey, Jane Addams, and the city of Chicago represented
a set of influences unique to Dewey. From a professional point of
view, though, the move into education was a perfectly natural career
development. As Stanley Hall, with his customary shrewdness, had
realized back in the early 1880s, the theory and practice of education
was a sensible application for a discipline, like the New Psychology,
in search of legitimacy. Hall's own work was principally in pedagogy
and developmental psychology. (He became identified with the recapitulationist theory—derived, of course, from German sources—
which he first advanced in his Harvard lectures: that the child's intellectual development repeats the development of the species. Hall

called this "the general psychonomic law.") And William James, two years after the appearance in 1890 of his *Principles of Psychology*, gave a series of lectures on education that were published in 1899 as *Talks to Teachers on Psychology* and became one of James's most popular books. Two of the leading American figures in the field of educational research after the turn of the century, James McKeen Cattell, of Columbia University, and his student Edward L. Thorndike, of Teachers College, were trained as experimental psychologists. Cattell took his Ph.D. under Wundt in Leipzig; Thorndike, before transferring to Columbia, had begun his dissertation (on learning curves in chickens) with James at Harvard. (When Thorndike was refused space for his chickens in the Agassiz Museum, James housed them in his cellar.) As an academic psychologist, Dewey was applying his expertise in the approved way.

The condition of American elementary education was also a leading public issue in 1896, and for a philosopher to be engaged with it was hardly eccentric. The United States Commissioner of Education was William Torrey Harris, who also happened to be the leading American Hegelian and founder and editor of the *Journal of Speculative Philosophy*, where Dewey had published his first essays. In 1892 and 1893 a series of investigative articles on American schools by a New York pediatrician named Joseph Mayer Rice, published in the *Forum* (one of the magazines that would reject "A Modern Lear" three years later), had drawn national attention. Before touring the United States and examining its schools, Rice had spent two years studying pedagogy in Germany, in Jena and Leipzig. He was, not surprisingly, appalled by the lack of psychological sophistication in the rote approach to learning that dominated American elementary education. (He was appalled by many other things as well, including the political corruption in many school districts.)

One of the few schools Rice found it possible to praise was near Chicago. This was the Cook County Normal School, in Englewood, whose principal was the same Colonel Francis Parker whose work in the Quincy schools Hall had talked about in his Harvard lectures. Parker, too, had learned his pedagogy in Germany, and his "Quincy System" was distinguished by the hands-on approach: the use of manipulatives (like blocks) to teach arithmetic, for example, or field trips to teach geography. Parker created a teacher training program at the Cook County Normal School based on his system, and in his first semester at Chicago Dewey gave a university extension course there on psychology. He was impressed by what he saw—he had just returned from giving one of those lectures, in fact, when he wrote his wife the letter of November 1894 announcing his inspiration.

Dewey didn't conceive of his school as a teacher training institute, though, and he didn't conceive of it as a psychology laboratory, either. He conceived of it as a *philosophy* laboratory. Dewey wasn't conducting curricular experiments or collecting data on mental development. He was trying out a theory. It was a theory, as he said, of "the unity of knowledge."

The phrase "unity of knowledge" echoes James Marsh and George Morris, and the passion for holism that inspired their philosophies of education—their idea that every subject should be taught as an aspect of a greater whole—was certainly inherited by Dewey. But in Marsh and Morris that idea was metaphysical in Huxley's sense: it rested on a belief that the ultimate whole was an extrasensory entity—the divine will, or the Absolute. It belonged to the German idea of *Bildung*, education as growth toward the apprehension of a spiritual oneness. This part of his inheritance Dewey now rejected.

By "unity of knowledge" Dewey did not mean that all knowledge is one. He meant that knowledge is inseparably united with doing. Education at the Dewey School was based on the idea that knowledge is a by-product of activity: people do things in the world, and the doing results in learning something that, if deemed useful, gets carried along into the next activity. In the traditional method of education, in which the things considered worth knowing are handed down from teacher to pupil as disembodied information, knowledge is cut off from the activity in which it has its meaning, and becomes a false abstraction. One of the consequences (besides boredom) is that an invidious distinction between knowing and doing—a distinction Dewey thought socially pernicious as well as philosophically erroneous—gets reinforced.

At the Laboratory School, therefore, children were involved in workshop-type projects in which learning was accomplished in a manner that simulated the way Dewey thought it was accomplished in real life: through group activity. Since the project was being carried out in the present, and since it was supposed to proceed in accordance with the natural instincts of the children ("I think . . . that the development of the children's interests will follow very closely a truly scientific development of the subject,"[64] Dewey stated in one of his planning letters), what was learned was precisely what was useful. Relevance was built into the system.

One of Dewey's curricular obsessions, for instance, was cooking. (Like all courses at the school, including carpentry and sewing, cooking was coeducational.) The children cooked and served lunch once a week. The philosophical rationale is obvious enough: preparing a meal (as opposed to, say, memorizing the multiplication table) is a goal-directed activity, it is a social activity, and it is an activity continuous with life outside school. But Dewey incorporated into the practical business of making lunch: arithmetic (weighing and measuring ingredients, with instruments the children made themselves), chemistry and physics (observing the process of combustion), biology (diet and digestion), geography (exploring the natural environments of the plants and animals), and so on. Cooking became the basis for most of the science taught in the school. It turned out to have so much curricular potential that making cereal became a three-year continuous course of study for all children between the ages of six and eight—with (on the testimony of two teachers) "no sense of monotony on the part of either pupils or teacher."[65] And as cooking established a continuity with the sphere of the home, other activities established continuities with the spheres of industry and business. There was much work, for example, with iron. The children built their own tiny smelters.

The pedagogical challenge, crucial to the theory, was to make the chemistry indivisible from the lunch, the learning indivisible from the doing. "Absolutely no separation is made between the 'social' side of the work, its concern with people's activities and their mutual dependencies, and the 'science,' regard for physical facts and forces,"[66]

Dewey wrote in 1899 in his best-selling book about the school, *The School and Society* (a work that has never been out of print). This is one of the things Addams had meant when she told Alice Palmer that a social settlement "wasn't a thing but a way of living—hence had the same aims as life itself." And it is one of the things Dewey meant by "the unity of knowledge."

But "unity" had another connotation: it was the fighting term of functionalism. Most work in experimental psychology in the nineteenth century was predicated on the theories of two people who had never seen the inside of a laboratory, Locke and Kant. Kant had a more generous view of the mind than Locke, but he did not think of himself as superseding Locke's theory, only as correcting for a few inadequacies. A Kantian like Wundt therefore assumed that every mental state, no matter how complicated, can be broken down into simple bits of sense data that have been combined by the operation of various mental processes—perception, attention, cognition, discrimination, comparison, association, and so on. Wundt thought that the purpose of physiological psychology was to study these processes; and to study something meant for him (as it would for almost any nineteenth-century scientist) to measure it. When people came to work in Wundt's laboratory in Leipzig, that was what they did.

How exactly do you measure "attention"? The answer was: you time it. You place a subject in front of a screen and instruct him or her to press a key when a light appears, and then you record the time between the appearance of the light and the pressing of the key. The technical term for what you are measuring is the "reflex arc"—the sequence of sensory stimulus (the light), idea ("the light is the signal for me to press the key"), and motor response (pushing down on the key). Like many other nineteenth-century psychologists, Wundt believed that the reflex arc—sensation, idea, action—was the basic structure of all mental activity. It was, after all, perfectly Newtonian, a straightforward causal model—the billiard-ball picture of the mind.

When you measure the total time between a stimulus and a response, you are measuring more than an act of attention, of course. The total time also includes, for example, the time it takes for the brain's command to press the key to be transmitted through the nerves to the hand. So which portion of the time between the shining of the light and the pressing of the key is taken up specifically by attention (Wundt preferred the Kantian term "apperception")—that is, by picking up the stimulus and recognizing it as a signal to press the key?

The problem was addressed in 1888 by a psychologist working in Wundt's laboratory named Ludwig Lange. Lange instructed half his subjects to concentrate on seeing the light and half to concentrate on pressing the key. He found that the people who concentrated on what their hands were doing reacted about a tenth of a second faster than the people who concentrated on what they were seeing. He concluded that the extra tenth of a second was the time required to pick the light out from all the objects in the field of vision and interpret it as the signal to press the key—the time required for attention. (The experiment was virtually a reproduction of the study that was one of the origins of the New Psychology, Wundt's discovery of the difference between astronomical observers who look at the star first and observers who look at the instrument first.) It is an indication of the glamour surrounding experimental psychology that Lange's finding was treated as a major scientific advance. It generated almost as much excitement as Gustav Fechner's earlier discovery that the intensity of a sensation (of brightness, say, or of weight) increases as the logarithm of the intensity of the stimulus—a principle Fechner believed comparable in significance to the law of gravity. Measuring reaction times became an academic industry.

One person unimpressed by whole business was William James. Though he had once hoped to study with Wundt, by the time he came to write *The Principles of Psychology* James had lost all sympathy with the Leipzig approach—"brass instrument psychology," as it was known to its detractors. He thought Wundt "a Napoleon without genius,"[67] and he considered reaction time studies largely pointless. "It is a sort of work which appeals particularly to patient and exact minds," he noted drily in the *Principles*, "and they have not failed to profit by the opportunity."[68] (Patience and exactitude were not, of course, James's most notable qualities.) James's assessment of Fechner's great discovery was more blunt: "in the humble opinion of the present writer," he says in the *Principles*, "the proper psychological outcome is just *nothing*."[69]

What irritated James most about Lange's study was that in order to get uniform results showing the tenth of a second difference, the subjects were required to repeat the experiment many times. For in the beginning, as one would expect, reaction times were wildly inconsistent. Some people were good at it right away and some people had to repeat the sequence over and over in order to get their times down. James's point was that after a large number of trials, Lange was no longer measuring attention, because the whole act had become a muscular reflex: see light, press key. What is genuinely an act of attention, James suggested, was what happens the *first* time the subjects pick out the light and press the key, before they become habituated to it. That's when they really have to be paying attention. And first-time reactions are various because individuals are various. No general "law of attention" is possible.

Lange's procedures were defended by the leading Wundtian in America, Edward B. Titchener, an Englishman who had written his thesis in Leipzig on reaction times and, in 1892, became professor of psychology at Cornell. Titchener thought getting individual differences out of the way was the obvious starting point for any scientific investigation. If you are looking for the underlying elements of psychic life, the basic structure of the mind, then you want to get past the accidental in order to reach the constant. In putting forward this position, Titchener became embroiled in a dispute with a Princeton psychologist, James Mark Baldwin, who claimed to have gotten reaction times that contradicted the Leipzig results, and who called himself a functionalist. A functionalist, according to Baldwin, is interested in what people do, not what is going on in their brains while they're doing it. You cannot break an act up, as Wundt and Titchener believed you could, into so many distinct elementary processes. Behavior is a matter of the relation between the whole organism and the whole situation. (Thorndike would soon after make the same point with his chickens.)

The debate between Titchener and Baldwin became intense— the issue seems trivial, but they were arguing, in a sense, over the

future of their discipline—and in 1895, James Rowland Angell undertook to mediate it. James Rowland Angell was the son of James Burrill Angell, who had been president of the University of Vermont
when Dewey was growing up and president of the University of
Michigan when Dewey was teaching there. James R. was a Michigan
undergraduate, and in 1891, his senior year, he read *The Principles of
Psychology* in Dewey's class and became inspired. On Dewey's advice, he went to Harvard to work with James, whom he came to consider "my spiritual father."[70] At Harvard, Angell decided he needed a
German Ph.D. (though his father pointed out to him that "Dewey is
proof that one can succeed without going abroad");[71] when he arrived in Leipzig, however, he found there was no room in Wundt's
classes. He went to Berlin instead, but accepted a position at the
University of Minnesota, in 1893, before getting his degree. In 1894
Dewey brought him to Chicago. (The lack of a doctorate did not prevent Angell from becoming, many years later, the president of Yale.)

Along with a teaching fellow in the Chicago department named
Addison Moore, Angell conducted a version of Lange's experiment.
The results partially confirmed both the "Leipzig" and the "Princeton" claims: individual times varied according to skill and experience,
but after sufficient practice concentration on the physical response
rather than the sensory stimulus generally yielded the faster times.
They showed their results to Dewey and George Herbert Mead, and,
after consultation (all of them were familiar, of course, with James's
criticisms of Lange's original experiment), Angell and Moore composed an interpretation.

They said the obvious thing, which is that subjects concentrating
on their response are "attending" just as much as subjects concentrating on the stimulus are. What, after all, is "attention"? It is what
happens when we are performing an act that is not, or is no longer,
habitual. For example, we don't pay attention to the way we walk until we encounter an obstacle that makes walking in the normal, un-
selfconscious way a problem. Attention, Angell and Moore said, is
just "the process of mediating the tension between habit and new
conditions," and it therefore comes into play wherever "this tension
is strongest, *i.e.*, where habit is least able to cope with the situa-

tion."[72] For most of the subjects in the experiment, picking up a stimulus becomes habitual more readily than producing a physical response, which is the real explanation for the tendency of the people focusing on their hands to get faster times: they're directing attention where it's most needed. Attention is functional. It is not a process measurable from the outside; it is something that falls "inside" the complete act. And the complete act is not composed of discrete units; the act *is* the unit.

Equipped with Angell and Moore's results, Dewey proceeded to write "The Reflex Arc Concept in Psychology," a very short, very technical paper, which he published in 1896 and never reprinted, and which is the key to his thought. To put it anachronistically but accurately: Dewey deconstructed the reflex arc. In the reflex arc's billiard-ball picture, a sensory stimulus (Dewey used the standard textbook illustration of a child seeing a candle flame) triggers an idea (for example: "This light might be amusing to play with"), which triggers a physical response (reaching out to touch the flame). There follows another sensation (of burning), another idea ("Get away from this light!"), and another response (withdrawal of hand and concomitant symptoms of distress). But this account commits the empiricist's fallacy: it assumes that the parts are prior to the whole, when in fact it is the whole that makes the parts what they are. "[I]n its failure to see that the arc of which it talks is virtually a circuit, a continual reconstitution," Dewey said, the reflex arc theory "breaks continuity and leaves us nothing but a series of jerks, the origin of each jerk to be sought outside the process of experience itself."[73]

In other words, the reflex arc pretends to be a description when it is really just an ex post facto interpretation. "A set of considerations which hold good only because of a completed process," Dewey complained, "is read into the content of the process which conditions this completed result. A state of things characterizing an outcome is regarded as a true description of the events which led up to this outcome."[74] Analytically speaking, the response actually *precedes* the stimulus—that is, we label the seeing a "stimulus" because we have already labeled another part of the act, the reaching, a "response." As

Dewey provocatively put it: "The burn is the original seeing."[75] For actions have goals built into them. The child wasn't seeing and then, as a separate act, touching; the child was seeing-in-order-to-touch. The correct way to picture an act is therefore not as a series of concatenating billiard balls, or as an arc, but as an organic circuit. It has to be indivisible before it can be divided.

The language of Dewey's paper is secular and Darwinian: it dissolves mental states into the unified biological activity of adapting to the environment. And his attack on the scientist's tendency to treat terms of inquiry as though they are real things derives from what James, in a passage in *The Principles of Psychology*, termed "the psychologist's fallacy."[76] ("Let me say that I think the discovery & express formulation of this *alone* would have marked the book as 'epoch-making,' "[77] Dewey said of this passage in his first fan letter to James.) And James's passage derives in turn from the thought of Charles Peirce and Chauncey Wright and St. John Green. But Dewey's idea of the priority of the complete act to any of its aspects is not found in James or Peirce, or even in Baldwin and the other functionalists. It has a very different source: it is an echo of Hegel's description of the realization of the Idea in history—"the circle which presupposes its end as its purpose, and has its end for its beginning, [becoming] concrete and actual only by being carried out, and by the end it involves." The only thing missing is the Absolute. The "organic circuit" is biologized Hegel.

In fact, Dewey had used the metaphor of the organic circuit before he wrote the paper on "The Reflex Arc Concept," and even before he knew the results of Angell and Moore's experiment. It appears everywhere in his writings on the school. "There is a circuit in any material," he explained to one of his future teachers in 1895. "The beginning and the end is the individual activity."[78] Knowledge is not the result of experience, any more than a response is the result of a stimulus; knowledge is experience itself in one of its manifestations. "[T]he facts and truths that enter into the child's present experience, and those contained in the subject-matter of studies, are the initial and final terms of one reality," as Dewey put it in 1902. "To oppose one to the other is . . . to set the moving tendency and the final result of the same process over against each other; it is to hold that the nature and the destiny of the child war with each other."[79]

The "Reflex Arc" paper is the essential expression of Dewey's particular mode of intelligence. It is the strategy he followed in approaching every problem: expose a tacit hierarchy in the terms in which people conventionally think about it. We think that a response follows a stimulus; Dewey taught that there is a stimulus only because there is already a response. We think that first there are individuals and then there is society; Dewey taught that there is no such thing as an individual without society. We think we know in order to do; Dewey taught that doing is why there is knowing.

Dewey was not reversing the priority of the terms he identified in these analyses. Invidiousness was precisely what he wished always to avoid. In condemning (as he did) the elevation of thinking over doing as a reflection of class bias (Veblen would have said that philosophical speculation is a form of conspicuous consumption: it shows we can afford not to work with our hands), Dewey was not proposing to elevate doing over thinking instead. He was only applying the idea Addams was trying to explain to him when she said that antagonism is unreal: he was showing that "doing" and "thinking," like "stimulus" and "response," are just practical distinctions we make when tensions arise in the process of adjustment between the organism and its world. Later in his career, Dewey would criticize, in the same manner, the distinctions between mind and reality, means and ends, nature and culture. As Henry Steele Commager testified, a generation (or part of a generation, anyway) seems to have found Dewey's manner of calmly and often rather colorlessly chewing through received ideas irresistible and indispensable. Dewey thought chewing through ideas was just his job, the philosopher's way of helping people adjust to the conditions in which they find themselves. "Sorry," he would say when people praised him as an educator, "I'm just a philosopher. I'm just trying to think. That's all I'm doing."[80]

6

Though Rockefeller was generally benignly neglectful of policy matters at the University of Chicago, he was diligent in his supervision
of budgetary matters, and Harper, whose instincts were expansive
and expensive, had a difficult time keeping the deficits within limits
acceptable to his principal patron. He therefore preferred to have the
Laboratory School support itself by tuition and donations, despite
Dewey's contention that it should be funded on a par with any other
laboratory in the university. Nevertheless, Harper insisted on reviewing the school's budget. A great deal of Dewey's energy was therefore spent justifying his school's expenses to an administration that
did not contribute significantly to its income. This did not enhance
collegiality.

In 1901, in a characteristically acquisitory move, Harper announced that Colonel Parker's elementary school and teacher training institute were being incorporated into the university. Parker was
almost a cult figure in educational circles, and he arrived at the university with a patron, Anita McCormick Blaine, of the McCormick
reaper fortune, who had endowed his schools with a million-dollar
gift. How Parker would occupy the same institutional and financial
space as Dewey was a delicate question; but the difficulty disappeared when Parker died unexpectedly in 1902.

His schools, however, had already been joined to the university,
and Harper was anxious to keep Anita Blaine happy by retaining and
sustaining them. On Dewey's suggestion, it was decided to combine
Parker's elementary school with Dewey's Laboratory School, with
Dewey in charge of the school and of every other aspect of the university's educational programs, which included a School of Education, a Department of Pedagogy, a high school, and a manual training
school. Dewey had made his wife principal of the Laboratory School,
and he chose to have her continue as the principal of the newly combined school.

Alice Dewey does not seem to have possessed strong personnel
skills. Her new authority over the teachers in the combined school

(many of whom felt a personal devotion to Parker), with her husband to back her, was contemplated with apprehension. Anxieties were communicated to Harper; Anita Blaine was drawn into the matter; and Harper made the mistake of assuring Blaine and the trustees, but without informing either Dewey, that Alice Dewey would step down after a year as principal. When the time came and Alice was informed that her resignation was expected, the Deweys promptly resigned, she as principal of the elementary school and he as director of the School of Education. Five days later, on April 11, 1904, John Dewey resigned as chair and professor in the Department of Philosophy, effectively terminating his relations with the university. He had four children and no other source of income.

Harper realized he was losing his star, and he set about trying frantically to walk the cat backward into the house. He consulted with Mead and Angell, who urged him to apologize and conciliate; he consulted with Albion Small, who was less sympathetic to the Deweys. On April 18, Harper wrote Dewey requesting a meeting, pleading that there had been a misunderstanding. But Dewey had already written, six days earlier, to McKeen Cattell, at Columbia, informing him that "I have finally taken a step which has been in my mind for two or three years—I have resigned from the Univ. of Chicago. . . . I have nothing in view and shall have to rely on my friends to let me know of things that might appropriately come within my scope."[81] Cattell knew how to take a hint, and he did not waste time. Nicholas Murray Butler, the president of Columbia, was a former member of the philosophy department and a former president of the institution that had become Teachers College. By April 23, he had offered Dewey a position as professor of philosophy, with a course at Teachers College to increase his salary. Dewey accepted, and the appointment was announced on May 2, 1904.

Harper had managed to have several interviews with the Deweys in the interim, but they only served to widen the breach. Dewey's final letter to Harper is dated May 10. He wishes to make it clear, he says, that contrary to Harper's representations, the firing of Alice Dewey was by no means the reason for his departure. "Your willingness to embarrass and hamper my work as Director by making use of the fact that Mrs. Dewey was Principal," he explained, "is but one incident in the history of years."[82] If Dewey had regrets about leaving Chicago, he does not seem to have expressed them. In 1936 he supervised closely the composition of a history of the Laboratory School, by two former teachers; Harper's name does not appear in its pages. Dewey went off to Cattell and Thorndike, to Teachers College, and to New York City, where he lived, ultimately on Fifth Avenue, for the rest of his life—forty-eight years. He never accepted another administrative post at a university, and he never looked back.

PART FIVE

William James in the 1890s, when he was turning from
psychology to philosophy.
(Photograph by Mrs. Montgomery Sears.)

THIRTEEN

PRAGMATISMS

I

THE FRIENDSHIP BETWEEN Oliver Wendell Holmes and William James began to unravel in the 1870s, not long after the Metaphysical Club ended its brief life. In part the unraveling was just the ordinary weakening of the bonds of young male attraction in the presence of a different kind of attraction. Holmes married Fanny Dixwell in 1872; James married Alice Gibbens in 1878. But in part it was the consequence of a decision by each of the friends that what seemed a stimulating difference of opinion was also a personal difference deep enough to make for incompatibility. In the dispute between James and Chauncey Wright—the dispute over whether our wishes and desires have any effect on the business of the universe—Holmes sided, unequivocally, with Wright. He came to think James incurably soft-hearted, and James, in response, came to think Holmes repellently hard-headed. "I spent three very pleasant days with the Holmes' at Mattappoissett," William wrote to his brother Henry in 1876. (The Holmeses had bought a farm, which they used as a summer house, in Mattapoisett, on Buzzards Bay.) "I fell quite in love with she; & he exemplified in the most ridiculous way Michelet's 'marriage de l'homme et de la terre.' . . . He is a powerful battery, formed like a planing machine to gouge a deep self-beneficial groove through life."[1] James and Holmes maintained a cordial relationship all their lives. Each sent his published works to the other, and the other always responded with polite admiration. But they felt themselves to be on different frequencies.

William James was not the only person to consider Wendell Holmes self-centered and ambitious. Like his father (and unlike James), Holmes was socially adept, and he cultivated the skill; but he was privately dismissive of people whose views he found sentimental or pious—and that took in, for him, a lot of views. He was also, indisputably, ambitious. He believed that no one was worth anything who had not produced a major achievement before the age of forty, and he determined to beat the deadline. He just made it. The achievement he produced was *The Common Law*.

The Common Law originated as a series of Lowell Lectures, in 1880. Holmes was still working as a lawyer in 1880; he was recommended as a speaker by A. Lawrence Lowell, future president of Harvard (and former star pupil of Benjamin Peirce's), then a student at Harvard Law School. Holmes was an exceptionally disciplined worker (a characteristic not only William but all the Jameses found strange and bemusing), and he spent almost a year composing the lectures. He delivered all twelve to a packed hall, without notes. They bristle with pedantic details of legal antiquarianism and with technical analyses, and they propose a complicated and somewhat tendentious argument about the evolution of legal doctrine. But at bottom they are an attempt to explain the remark Holmes had made in his very first law review article, back in 1870: "It is the merit of the common law that it decides the case first and determines the principle afterwards."[2] For that sentence leaves us with the question: If principles don't decide cases, what does? Holmes's answer formed the basis of all his later jurisprudence.

2

Jurisprudential theories, like theories of literary criticism or historical methodologies, are generally categorized according to the element of their subjects they take to be essential. A legal theory that stresses the logical consistency of judicial opinions is called formalist; a theory that emphasizes their social consequences is called utilitarian; a theory that regards them as reflections of the circumstances in which they were written is called historicist. The problem with all such theories is that they single out one aspect of the law as the essential aspect. It was Holmes's genius as a philosopher to see that the law has no essential aspect.

A case comes to court as a unique fact situation. It immediately enters a kind of vortex of discursive imperatives. There is the imperative to find the just result in this particular case. There is the imperative to find the result that will be consistent with the results reached in analogous cases in the past. There is the imperative to find the result that, generalized across many similar cases, will be most beneficial to society as a whole—the result that will send the most useful behavioral message. There are also, though less explicitly acknowledged, the desire to secure the outcome most congenial to the judge's own politics; the desire to use the case to bend legal doctrine so that it will conform better with changes in social standards and conditions; and the desire to punish the wicked and excuse the good, and to redistribute costs from parties who can't afford them (like accident victims) to parties who can (like manufacturers and insurance companies).

Hovering over this whole unpredictable weather pattern—all of which is already in motion, as it were, before the particular case at hand ever arises—is a single meta-imperative. This is the imperative not to let it appear as though any one of these lesser imperatives has decided the case at the blatant expense of the others. A result that seems just intuitively but is admittedly incompatible with legal precedent is taboo; so is a result that is formally consistent with precedent but appears unjust on its face. The court does not want to seem to excuse reckless behavior (like operating a railroad too close to a heavily populated area), but it does not want to raise too high a liability barrier to activities society wants to encourage (like building railroads). It wants the law to run in a politically desirable direction, but it does not want to be caught appearing to bend an anachronistic legal doctrine in order to compel a politically correct result.

There is also (to put the final spin on the system), within each of these competing imperatives, the problem of deciding what counts as relevant within that particular discourse and what does not. This series of problems begins with the question of what the legally relevant "facts" in the case really are; it runs through the questions of what counts as an analogous case, what counts as an applicable general legal principle, what counts as a benefit to society, and so on; and it ends with the question of what counts as a "just result." Holmes thought that there were no hard-and-fast distinctions in any of these areas; he believed that the answer always boils down to a matter of degree. But he thought more: he thought that even if we were to select one imperative to trump all the others, we would still find that the consequences for any particular case were indeterminate. Principles are manipulable. Many years later, when he was on the Supreme Court, Holmes used to invite his fellow justices, in conference, to name any legal principle they liked, and he would use it to decide the case under consideration either way. "Cost-benefit analysis" is as malleable as "rights talk." When there are no bones, anybody can carve a goose.

Yet there must be bones of some sort. For cases get decided and verdicts get returned and opinions get written, and by a process that does not seem arbitrary or subjective to the people who do the deciding, returning, and explaining. If the various discourses of fairness, policy, precedent, and so forth are simply being manipulated rather than applied, they are being manipulated to justify an outcome which has been reached in obedience to some standard. When Holmes said that common law judges decided the result first and figured out a plausible account of how they got there afterward, the implication was not that the result was chosen randomly, but that it was dictated by something other than the formal legal rationale later adduced to support it. Holmes announced what this "something" was in the famous fourth sentence of the opening lecture of *The Common Law*: "The life of the law has not been logic; it has been experience."[3]

The sentence was taken by many people at the time as a challenge to the dean of the Harvard Law School, Christopher Columbus Langdell. Langdell was the man Charles William Eliot had appointed during his campaign to clean up Harvard's professional schools, and who had introduced the case method to legal education. Under the case method, students read appellate decisions and attempt to extract legal doctrine from them; the assumption is that the law is a structure of logically related principles, and that judges apply the relevant principles to the particular cases before them in order to reach the correct results. Langdell thought that this was a way of treating law as a science, but his idea of science was plainly pre-Darwinian. He thought that behind the variety of actual judicial opinions there was an ideal order, just as Agassiz had taught that there was an ideal order behind the variety of actual living organisms.

But Holmes had, in fact, praised Langdell's casebooks in his law review articles, and he had used the case method himself when he had taught a course at Harvard. For there plainly are formalist elements in the law. Doctrinal continuity is highly valued by judges; it is, at a minimum, the best hedge against reversal. At the same time, Holmes believed that the law was susceptible to a utilitarian analysis, since the law is also an instrument of social policy; a moral analysis, since the law is a record of the conduct a society sees fit to penalize; and a historical analysis, since the law has historical roots and evolves in response to changing social conditions. "The life of the law has not been logic; it has been experience," does not say that there is no logic in the law. It only says that logic is not responsible for what is living in the law. The active ingredient in the compound, what puts the bones in the goose, is the thing called "experience." It's a word with a number of associations, but Holmes was using it in a particular sense. He meant it as the name for everything that arises out of the interaction of the human organism with its environment: beliefs, sentiments, customs, values, policies, prejudices—what he called "the felt necessities of the time."[4] Another word for it is "culture."

Understanding Holmes's conception of "experience" is the key to understanding almost everything that is distinctive about his view of the law. Three features are especially significant. The first is that experience is not, in Holmes's view, reducible to propositions, even though human beings spend a lot of time so reducing it. "All the pleasure of life is in general ideas," Holmes wrote to a correspondent in 1899. "But all the use of life is in specific solutions—which cannot be reached through generalities any more than a picture can be painted by knowing some rules of method. They are reached by insight, tact and specific knowledge."[5] Even people who think their thinking is guided by general principles, in other words, even people who think thought is deductive, actually think the way everyone else does—by the seat of their pants. First they decide, then they deduce.

This is the idea that stands behind the assertion, which appears in many places in Holmes's writing, most prominently in his dissent in the Supreme Court case of *Lochner v. New York* (1905), that "[g]eneral propositions do not decide concrete cases."[6] Logical reasoning from a priori truths is just not the way people make practical choices most of the time. Holmes thought that learning the abstract legal doctrines on which judicial decisions are expressly based— what used to be called "black letter law"—was therefore poor training for a lawyer. Judges do invoke these doctrines when they are explaining their decision, but (as Holmes was pointing out when he volunteered to use the same principle to decide a given case either way) the doctrines are never sufficient to account for the result reached. The hole always has a different shape from the arrow sticking out of it. So that anything that might operate as a motive for a judge's decision—a moral conviction, a political preference, even (as Holmes once put it) "the blandishments of the emperor's wife"[7]— might be legally material if it helps lawyers guess the result correctly.

This is the essence of the so-called prediction theory of the law, which Holmes presented in 1897 in the essay that is the most succinct expression of his judicial philosophy, "The Path of the Law."

"The prophecies of what the courts will do in fact, and nothing more pretentious, are what I mean by the law,"[8] he said there. Like the idea that judicial decisions precede legal reasons, the prediction theory was something Holmes had articulated very early in his career as a judicial philosopher. It appears in an essay he published in the *American Law Review* in 1872, where he argued that it is not the law that determines the outcome in a particular case; it is what judges *say* is the law. For "a precedent may not be followed; a statute may be emptied of its contents by construction. . . . The only question for the lawyer is, how will the judges act?"[9] From the very beginning, Holmes's view of the law was premised on the assumption that law is simply and empirically judicial behavior. A rule may be written down, it may express the will of the sovereign, it may be justified by logic or approved by custom; but if courts will not enforce it, it is not the law, and lawyers who bet their cases on it will lose.

A second distinctive feature of Holmes's conception of experience is that it is not individual and internal but collective and consensual; it is social, not psychological. This is the feature responsible for his most important contribution to the civil law, which is the invention of the reasonable man. The reasonable man is the fictional protagonist of modern liability theory. If you are injured as a result of an act of mine, what triggers civil liability? There are, traditionally, three ways to answer this question. The first is to say that it is enough merely to prove causation: I act at my peril, and I am therefore liable for any costs my actions incur, whether I could have foreseen them or not. The legal term for this is "strict liability." The second way of answering it is to say that I am liable for your injury if I wickedly intended it, but cannot fairly be held liable for injuries I never contemplated. This is the theory of *mens rea*—"the guilty mind." And the third is to say that even if I neither wished for nor anticipated the possibility of your injury, I am liable to you anyway if my act was careless or imprudent. When I act recklessly, then I do act at my peril. This is the theory of negligence.[10]

It is often hard to distinguish, in Holmes's writing, between the descriptive and the prescriptive—between what Holmes believed the law was in practice and what he thought the law ought to be.

Holmes didn't do a lot to help his readers make this distinction, but the reason is that his favorite method of argument was to show that what the law ought to be is what it pretty much already is, only under a wrong description. In the case of tort law (the common law governing civil liability for an injury not arising out of a contract), for example, Holmes argued for answer three—liability ought to be triggered by a finding of negligence—but he did so by attempting to demonstrate that negligence was already, and more or less always had been, the rough basis for tort liability. He argued, in other words, that if in our analysis of tort cases we dropped terms like "guilt" and "fault" and replaced them with terms like "carelessness" and "recklessness," we would find that we generally got the same results. The advantage of replacing the moral language of sin with the economic language of risk was not to punish a different class of wrongdoers or a different category of wrongs. It was simply to make explicit what moral language tends to disguise, which is that (in the words of *The Common Law*): "The substance of the law at any given time pretty nearly corresponds, so far as it goes, with what is then understood to be convenient"[11]—a sentence in which, as the context makes clear, we are meant to understand "convenient" in the widest possible sense.

The problem for Holmes wasn't, therefore, what the basis for tort liability ought to be. The problem was what the basis for deciding that a particular act was negligent ought to be. Assuming we want to make persons who act recklessly or carelessly pay the cost of cleaning up their tortious messes, how do we determine what sort of behavior counts as reckless or careless? How do we distinguish a tort from an accident, or from the permissible by-product of a socially desirable activity? One way of doing this would be to devise a series of general rules for conduct, violation of which would ipso facto constitute negligence; but this solution was obviously ruled out for Holmes by his contempt for the malleability of general rules. His alternative proposal was that we should do judicially what we all do anyway when we are confronted with a judgment call, which is to evaluate the conduct at issue by the lessons of experience. "Experience is the test," as he put it in *The Common Law*, "by which it is decided whether the degree of danger attending given conduct under certain known circumstances is sufficient to throw the risk upon the party pursuing it."[12]

Whose experience? The experience, Holmes said, of "an intelligent and prudent member of the community."[13] He didn't mean by this a *particularly* prudent and intelligent person—a judge, for instance. He meant, precisely, a person who is neither particularly prudent nor particularly imprudent, an "average member of the community"—in other words, a jury. "When men live in society," he explained, "a certain average of conduct, a sacrifice of individual peculiarities going beyond a certain point, is necessary to the general welfare. If . . . a man is born hasty and awkward, is always having accidents and hurting himself or his neighbors . . . his slips are no less troublesome to his neighbors than if they spring from guilty neglect. His neighbors accordingly require him, at his proper peril, to come up to their standard, and the courts which they establish decline to take his personal equation into account."[14] Putting it this way made blameworthiness, Holmes thought, into what he approvingly called "an external standard," a standard before which the defendant's state of mind (a legal imponderable anyway) becomes irrelevant. "A man may have as bad a heart as he chooses," as he wrote elsewhere, "if his conduct is within the rules."[15]

"The reasonable man" is the phrase commonly associated with this theory of liability. Holmes didn't coin it—it began appearing in American and English opinions around 1850—but, along with his English friend Frederick Pollock, he probably did as much as anyone to define and establish it. What makes the concept work (on Holmes's theory) is that it represents a composite. It is a collective noun, a statistical fiction, an averaging out across the whole population. It is the legal cousin of Adolphe Quetelet's *homme moyen*, though its basis is behavioral, not racial. The "reasonable man" knows, because "experience" tells him, that a given behavior in a given circumstance—say, taking target practice in a populated area— carries the risk of injuring another person. Of course, any action in any circumstance carries some risk, however remote, of injuring another person; and reasonable people know this. But this knowledge is not what reasonableness consists in. What reasonableness consists in is the knowledge of the greater or lesser *probability* of an injury being caused by such and such an action in such and such circumstances. "[E]ven in the domain of knowledge," as Holmes put it, "the law applies its principle of averages."[16]

Putting negligence at the center of tort liability made it easier for industry to escape liability for injuries, to workers or customers, incidental to its enterprise, injuries for which it would have had to pay under a theory of strict liability. There is little doubt that the "reasonable man" standard for tort liability was a boon to industrial development—that it is a modern legal standard because it is compatible with the economic imperatives of modern societies. Still, Holmes did accept a principle of strict liability for what he called "extrahazardous" activity. Under this principle, a company that uses dynamite in the normal course of its business, for example, can be held accountable for any injuries it causes, even if it has taken reasonable precautions to avoid them. Holmes didn't regard strict liability as inconsistent with the concept of reasonableness, though, or even with the concept of negligence; for the activities society labels extrahazardous are just activities experience has led the reasonable man to believe to be risky per se. "Negligence" is infected a little by the kind of moral coloration Holmes deprecated in legal language: it suggests a personal failing on the part of the defendant. But all Holmes meant by it was acting in the face of foreseeable risk. We may have perfectly honorable reasons for doing so, but we also have to be willing to take our legal chances.

When Holmes remarked, therefore, in "The Path of the Law," that although "[f]or the rational study of the law the black-letter man may be the man of the present . . . the man of the future is the man of statistics and the master of economics,"[17] he meant that the more it became obvious that legal liability can be thought of as a function of the probability of injury, and that courts will weigh the cost of such injuries against the social benefit of the activity in question, the more irrelevant a knowledge of formal legal doctrine would be to the ability to predict what courts will do. In his theory of torts, Holmes did what Darwin did in his theory of evolution by chance variation and Maxwell did in his kinetic theory of gases: he applied to his own special field the great nineteenth-century discovery that the indeterminacy of individual behavior can be regularized by considering people statistically at the level of the mass.

As it happened, Christopher Columbus Langdell was in the audience for Holmes's Lowell Lectures, and he was sufficiently impressed (and unoffended) to offer Holmes a job soon afterward. Holmes became a professor at Harvard Law School in 1882. He had not even finished his first term of teaching there, though, when he was offered a seat on the Massachusetts Supreme Judicial Court. He accepted immediately. His colleagues, who had gone to some trouble to raise the money for his professorship, were annoyed. One of these was James Bradley Thayer, Chauncey Wright's old Northampton friend and the former secretary of the Septem, Wright's original discussion group, back in the 1850s. Thayer had known Holmes for many years, and had helped him get the assignment that led to his first work of legal scholarship, the edition of Kent's *Commentaries on American Law*. Holmes had not given Thayer credit in the published volume, and his hasty departure from the Law School brought the memory back. "[H]e is," Thayer wrote in his diary, "with all his attractive qualities and his solid merits, wanting sadly in the noblest region of human character—selfish, vain, thoughtless of others."[18] Holmes ended up sitting on the Supreme Judicial Court for twenty years, the last three as chief justice. It was while he was on that court that he wrote "The Path of the Law," the essay that sums up his judicial philosophy—his belief that law is nothing more or less than what judges do. That was in 1897. The following year, William James introduced the philosophy known as pragmatism to the world.

3

William James invented pragmatism as a favor to Charles Peirce. Peirce needed one. In 1887, three years after his dismissal from Hopkins, he and Juliette had moved to Milford, Pennsylvania, a Delaware River resort town, two hours by train from New York City, where they bought a house and two thousand acres of land. They named their property Arisbe and embarked on an ambitious program of improvements. Then, in 1891, Peirce lost his job at the Coast Survey.

The superintendent of the Survey, Thomas Mendenhall, was a protégé of Simon Newcomb's, the man who had spilled the news to the Hopkins trustees about the Peirces' premarital sleeping arrangements. Peirce already had a reputation in Washington for procrastination and prodigality, and Mendenhall seems to have been persuaded by Newcomb that it would be prudent to let him go. Peirce was terminated on December 31, 1891.[19] He had been an employee of the federal government for thirty years, but there was no pension system. His father was dead. Peirce knew his lifeline had been cut. On January 1, 1892, he began a diary. "I have a hard year, a year of effort before me," he wrote. "I think I shall very soon be completely ruined, it seems inevitable. What I have to do is to peg away and try to do my duty, and starve if necessary. One thing I must make up my mind to clearly. I must earn some money every day."[20] It was an accurate assessment in every respect.

Peirce did not lack initiative. His difficulty finishing things never seemed to depress his enthusiasm for starting them, and he plunged into a series of schemes—among them the construction of a hydro-electric power station in upstate New York, the marketing of a patented bleaching process, and the establishment of a correspondence school in logic—guaranteed to make him rich. He appears sometimes to have been swindled; at other times, he must merely have thrown his or his investors' money away. Meanwhile, serenely ignorant of the nature of the opinion arrayed against him, he pursued another academic appointment. In 1890, he asked Stanley Hall for a job at Clark. In 1891, he asked Newcomb to recommend him for a position at Stanford. In 1893, after Harper had dropped him from consideration for the job at Chicago that went to John Dewey, Peirce's brother James, a Harvard dean, wrote to Gilman begging him to give Charles a lectureship to save him from penury. No one would touch him. When the depression of 1893 arrived, Peirce's sole source of regular income was the Nation, whose editor, Wendell Phillips Garrison (son of one famous abolitionist and namesake of another), paid him a small stipend in return for unsigned book reviews.

He couldn't get a job. He could still, however, get arrested. In 1894, he was sued by workers he had hired to fix up his estate despite having no money to pay them. James Peirce bailed him out by arranging a mortgage on the property. But various creditors continued to sue, and in 1895, Peirce was charged with aggravated assault and battery by one of his servants, and a warrant was issued for his arrest. He spent most of the next two years on the lam in New York City, cadging food from the Century Club, of which he was still a member, and sometimes sleeping on the street. When he visited Milford to check up on his property, he wore a disguise.

In 1897 James published a collection of essays called *The Will to Believe* and dedicated the book to Peirce. Peirce was pleased by the attention. "I have learned a great deal about philosophy in the last few years," he wrote to James from New York after getting his copy, "because they have been very miserable and unsuccessful years,— terrible beyond anything that the man of ordinary experience can possibly understand or conceive. . . . [A] new world of which I knew nothing, and of which I cannot find that anybody who has written has really known much, has been disclosed to me, the world of misery."[21] He had gone without food, he said, for three days.

James swung into action. He arranged for Peirce to give a series of lectures in Cambridge and raised a thousand dollars for the honorarium. (Peirce's spending habits were well known; in order to persuade people to contribute, James agreed to have half the money sent directly to Juliette Peirce in small weekly installments.) James's idea was that the lectures might lead to a book, a means for Peirce to restore his academic credibility, and he urged Peirce to make them as accessible as possible. "You are teeming with ideas," he told Peirce, "—and the lectures need not by any means form a continuous whole. Separate topics of a vitally important character would do perfectly well."[22] It was a misfire typical of their relationship. "My philosophy," Peirce responded with some stiffness, ". . . is not an 'idea' with which I 'brim over'; it is a serious research."[23]

He could not afford to walk away from the offer, though, and in the winter of 1898 he delivered the lectures in a private house on Brattle Street. James thought them a success; Josiah Royce, James's colleague in the Harvard philosophy department (to which James now belonged), thought them an inspiration. James tried to get Paul Carus, the editor of the *Monist*, to which earlier in the decade Peirce had contributed a series of articles derived from his Hopkins Metaphysical Club talk on "Design and Chance," to print them. Nothing came of the suggestion.

Still, in May, with the income from the lectures and other financial support (the Century Club had finally kicked him out), the Peirces were able to return to Arisbe. And in August, in a talk at the University of California in Berkeley, James introduced the term "pragmatism" to the world. Its source, he told his audience, was

> a philosopher whose published works . . . are no fit expression of his powers. I refer to Mr. Charles S. Peirce, with whose very existence as a philosopher I dare say many of you are unacquainted. He is one of the most original of contemporary thinkers; and the principle of practicalism—or pragmatism, as he called it, when I first heard him enunciate it in Cambridge in the early '70s—is the clue or compass by following which I find myself more and more confirmed in believing we may find our feet upon the proper trail.[24]

People in 1898 may not have known who Charles Peirce was, but they knew who William James was, and although the attribution did not restore Peirce's fortunes—nothing in his lifetime ever would—James's lecture made pragmatism a subject of international discussion and debate for twenty years. It is a minor peculiarity of that debate that none of the principal figures who became identified with pragmatism much liked the name. James used it only because it was the term he remembered Peirce coining back in their Metaphysical Club days; he would have preferred "humanism," which was the term used by James's chief British ally, Ferdinand Canning Scott Schiller, at Oxford. John Dewey, who quickly became James's chief American ally, called his own philosophy "instrumentalism." ("I object root and branch to the term 'pragmatism,' "[25] he once confessed privately.) Peirce himself, who had never used the word in print until James's lecture, saw the chance he had been given to repackage his views with a label publicized by a celebrity; but he soon realized that the resemblance between his own thought and what James and Dewey were doing was not deep, and he began calling his philosophy "pragmaticism" (a word he said he thought too ugly to be kidnapped) in order to distinguish what he meant from what everyone else meant. But by then—around 1905—what Peirce meant had ceased, for most people, to matter.

4

Pragmatism is an account of the way people think—the way they come up with ideas, form beliefs, and reach decisions. What makes us decide to do one thing when we might do another thing instead? The question seems unanswerable, since life presents us with many types of choices, and no single explanation can be expected to cover every case. Deciding whether to order the lobster or the steak is not the same sort of thing as deciding whether the defendant is guilty beyond a reasonable doubt. In the first case (assuming price is not an object) we consult our taste; in the second we consult our judgment, and try to keep our taste out of it. But knowing more or less what category a particular decision belongs to—knowing whether it is a matter of personal preference or a matter of impersonal judgment—doesn't make that decision any easier to make. "Order what you feel like eating," says your impatient dinner companion. But the problem is that you don't *know* what you feel like eating. What you feel like eating is precisely what you are trying to figure out.

"Order what you feel like eating" is just a piece of advice about the criteria you should be using to guide your deliberations. It is not a solution to your menu problem—just as "Do the right thing" and "Tell the truth" are only suggestions about criteria, not answers to actual dilemmas. The actual dilemma is what, in the particular case staring you in the face, the right thing to do or the honest thing to say really is. And making those kinds of decisions—about what is right or what is truthful—*is* like deciding what to order in a restaurant, in the sense that getting a handle on tastiness is no harder or easier (even though it is generally less important) than getting a handle on justice or truth.

People reach decisions, most of the time, by thinking. This is a pretty banal statement, but the process it names is inscrutable. An acquaintance gives you a piece of information in strict confidence; later on, a close friend, lacking that information, is about to make a bad mistake. Do you betray the confidence? "Do the right thing"— but what is the right thing? Keeping your word, or helping someone you care about avoid injury or embarrassment? Even in this two-sentence hypothetical case, the choice between principles is complicated—as it always is in life—by circumstances. If it had been the close friend who gave you the information and the acquaintance who was about to make the mistake, you would almost certainly think about your choice differently—as you would if you thought that the acquaintance was a nasty person, or that the friend was a lucky person, or that the statute of limitations on the secret had probably run out, or that you had acquired a terrible habit of betraying confidences and really ought to break it. In the end, you will do what you believe is "right," but "rightness" will be, in effect, the compliment you give to the outcome of your deliberations. Though it is always in view while you are thinking, "what is right" is something that appears in its complete form at the end, not the beginning, of your deliberation.

When we think, in other words, we do not simply consult principles, or reasons, or sentiments, or tastes; for prior to thinking, all those things are indeterminate. Thinking is what makes them real. Deciding to order the lobster helps us determine that we have a taste for lobster; deciding that the defendant is guilty helps us establish the standard of justice that applies in this case; choosing to keep a confidence helps make honesty a principle and choosing to betray it helps to confirm the value we put on friendship.

Does this mean that our choices are arbitrary or self-serving— that standards and principles are just whatever it is in our interest to say they are, pretexts for satisfying selfish ends or gratifying hidden impulses? There is no way to answer this question, except to say that it rarely *feels* as though this is the case. We usually don't end up deciding to do what seems pleasant or convenient at the moment; experience teaches us that this is rarely a wise basis for making a choice. ("If merely 'feeling good' could decide, drunkenness would be the supremely valid human experience," as James once put it.)[26] When we are happy with a decision, it doesn't feel arbitrary; it feels like the decision we *had* to reach. And this is because its inevitability is a function of its "fit" with the whole inchoate set of assumptions of our self-understanding and of the social world we inhabit, the assumptions that give the moral weight—much greater moral weight than logic or taste could ever give—to every judgment we make. This is why, so often, we know we're right before we know *why* we're right. First we decide, then we deduce.

It does not follow that it is meaningless to talk of beliefs being true or untrue. It only means that there is no noncircular set of criteria for knowing whether a particular belief is true, no appeal to some standard outside the process of coming to the belief itself. For thinking just *is* a circular process, in which some end, some imagined outcome, is already present at the start of any train of thought. "Truth *happens* to an idea," James said in the lectures he published in 1907 as *Pragmatism*. "It *becomes* true, is *made* true by events. Its verity *is* in fact an event, a process: the process namely of its verifying itself."[27] And, elsewhere in the same lectures: " 'the true' is only the expedient in the way of our thinking, just as 'the right' is only the expedient in the way of our behaving."[28] Thinking is a free-form and boundless activity that nevertheless leads us to outcomes we feel justified in calling true, or just, or moral.

James invented pragmatism—that is, he named his own philosophical views after a principle Peirce had published twenty years earlier in an article, based on his Cambridge Metaphysical Club paper, called "How to Make Our Ideas Clear"—in order to defend religious belief in what he regarded as an excessively scientistic and materialistic age. That had not been part of Peirce's intention (though Peirce certainly believed that his principle was compatible with religious faith), but there was nothing eccentric about what James was doing. Defending religious belief was a task almost every nineteenth-century scientist felt obliged to take on. Some did it by rejecting modern science (as Agassiz did); some did it by drawing a bright line between science and faith (as Huxley did); some did it by claiming that science and Scripture were on the same page (as Hall did). James thought all these methods of defending religious belief were based on a mistaken understanding of the nature of belief; and he proposed to show that what science—specifically, what the New Psychology—had to say about how minds work applies to the way people think about God as much as it does to the way they think about whether the world is round or what to have for dinner.

This is how, in Berkeley in 1898, James summarized what he called "the principle of Peirce, the principle of pragmatism":

> the soul and meaning of thought . . . can never be made to direct itself towards anything but the production of belief. . . . When our thought about an object has found its rest in belief, then our action on the subject can firmly and safely begin. Beliefs, in short, are really rules for action; and the whole function of thinking is but one step in the production of habits of action. If there were any part of a thought that made no difference in the thought's practical consequences, then that part would be no proper element of the thought's significance.[29]

Peirce, of course, had adapted his "principle" (via St. John Green) from Alexander Bain, one of the founders of the New Psychology in Britain, who, in *The Emotions and the Will*, had defined belief as that upon which a person is prepared to act. James knew Bain's book well; it was one of the sources for his chapter on "Habit" in *The Principles of Psychology*. "The whole plasticity of the brain," James said there, "sums itself up in two words when we call it an organ in which currents pouring in from the sense-organs make with extreme facility paths which do not easily disappear."[30] These neural paths, once established, constitute habits: they ensure that our reaction to stimulus will—on average, for habit is a statistical concept—be predictable, repeatable, habitual.

A simple illustration of what James is talking about is the acquisition of some physical skill—say, shooting free throws in basketball— by practice. That the organism is neurologically equipped to learn to shoot free throws is proved by the fact that the more we do it, the better we get. Success and failure are not randomly distributed over the total number of attempts. Each time a coordinated sequence of movements meets with success—each time the ball goes through the hoop—we attempt to duplicate the sequence. We're wiring ourselves, in effect, to become a machine for making free throws—so that someday, with the score tied and no time left on the clock, while the arena howls, we can calmly sink the winning basket.

This was exactly the lesson James's student Edward Thorndike had drawn from his work with chickens. Thorndike had put chickens (and other tame animals, like cats) in boxes with doors on them, and measured how long it took the chickens to learn how to open the doors (by pressing a lever, for example) and get at the food pellets outside. He observed that although at first many actions were tried, apparently unsystematically, only successful actions performed by chickens who were hungry—only actions that opened the door to the food they wanted to get at—were learned. He concluded that success caused those movements to be imprinted in the brains of the chickens. His results were published two months before James's Berkeley talk.[31]

Shooting free throws if you are a basketball player, or learning how to get out of a box if you are a chicken, are simple examples of what James was talking about. A difficult example is belief in God. James thought that belief in God "works" in the same way that learning to shoot free throws—or to tie your shoes, honor your father and mother, or get out of the box—works: each time it issues in a successful action, it gets reinforced as an organic habit. What "imprints" the belief is the action. James did not need Peirce's principle to arrive at this belief about beliefs; it dates from his decision, in 1870, to act as though there were such a thing as free will. If behaving as though we had free will or God exists gets us results we want, we will not only come to believe those things; they will be, pragmatically, true. In James's formulation: "the true is the name of whatever proves itself to be good in the way of belief."[32] In his final lecture in *Pragmatism*, James suggested that "if the hypothesis of God works satisfactorily in the widest sense of the word, it is true."[33] If we have the will to act on our belief, James thought, the universe should meet us halfway. We will stand a better chance of getting the pellets. If we stop getting them, we may not drop the belief—we may keep going to church, for example—but we will cease using it as a rule for action. Our belief in God will no longer have cash value.

This verification by experience is how, in Peirce's terms, beliefs become "fixed."[34] Beliefs that make no difference therefore have no significance. ("Consider what effects, which might conceivably have practical bearings, we conceive the object of our conception to have," Peirce had said, in the passage James cited repeatedly. "Then, our conception of these effects is the *whole* of our conception of the object.")[35] A great deal of philosophical language, on a pragmatist view, is incantation. The chicken that makes a special cluck every time it pushes the lever and opens the door may "believe" the cluck is an indispensable element in the sequence of actions producing the desired outcome, but to the human observer the cluck is meaningless and belief in its efficacy is a superstition. Peirce and James wanted to put philosophy to the same test. This is how, to use, again, Peirce's term, they proposed to make ideas "clear." This is the pragmatist razor: it is designed to strip problems of metaphysical irrelevancies.

Pragmatists think that the mistake most people make about beliefs is to think that a belief is true, or justified, only if it mirrors "the way things really are"—that (to use one of James's most frequent targets, Huxley's argument for agnosticism) we are justified in believing in God only if we are able to prove that God exists apart from our personal belief in him. No belief, James thought, is justified by its correspondence with reality, because mirroring reality is not the purpose of having minds. His position on this matter was his earliest announced position as a professional psychologist. It appears in the first article he ever published, "Remarks on Spencer's Definition of Mind as Correspondence," which appeared in the *Journal of Speculative Philosophy* in the same month that "How to Make Our Ideas Clear" was appearing in the *Popular Science Monthly*—January 1878. "I, for my part," James wrote, cannot escape the consideration . . . that the knower is not simply a mirror floating with no foot-hold anywhere, and passively reflecting an order that he comes upon and finds simply existing. The knower is an actor, and co-efficient of the truth. . . . Mental interests, hypotheses, postulates, so far as they are bases for human action—action which to a great extent transforms the world—help to *make* the truth which they declare. In other words, there belongs to mind, from its birth upward, a spontaneity, a vote. It is in the game.[36]

James returned to the argument in the last chapter—the chapter of which he was proudest—of *The Principles of Psychology*, where he proposed to answer scientifically the question that Locke and Kant had tried to answer philosophically: How do we acquire our ideas about the world outside ourselves? Locke, of course, had attributed all our ideas to sensory experience; Kant had pointed out that some ideas, such as the idea of causation, cannot be explained by sensory experience, since we do not "see" causation, we only infer it, and he had concluded that such ideas must be innate, wired in from birth.

James agreed with Kant that many of the ideas we more or less instinctively have about the world do not derive from what we experience through the senses, but he thought there was a Darwinian explanation: "innate" ideas are fortuitous variations that have been naturally selected. Minds that possessed them were preferred over minds that did not. But why? It doesn't make sense to say, Because those minds mirrored reality more accurately. From a Darwinian point of view, "mirroring accurately" is a gratuitous compliment, an ex post facto rationalization—like saying that long necks have been selected in giraffes because long necks look better on a giraffe. Traits are selected because they help the organism adapt. There are no other criteria.

The reason human beings came to possess the idea of causation, James concluded, is not because causation really exists and would exist whether we were around to believe in it or not. We have no way of knowing whether this is so, and no reason to care. "The word 'cause,'" as he remarked in *The Principles of Psychology*, "is . . . an altar to an unknown god."[37] The reason we believe in causation is because experience shows that it pays to believe in causation. Causation is a cashable belief. It gets us pellets. "The whole notion of truth, which naturally and without reflexion we assume to mean the simple duplication by the mind of a ready-made and given reality, proves hard to understand clearly," James declared seventeen years later in the lectures on *Pragmatism*. "[A]ll our thoughts are *instrumental*, and mental modes of *adaptation* to reality, rather than revelations or gnostic answers to some divinely instituted world-enigma."[38]

5

After his Berkeley lecture, James did not do much with pragmatism. The following summer he damaged his heart while hiking in the Adirondacks. He had agreed to give the Gifford Lectures at the University of Edinburgh in 1900, but was forced to postpone them. He fell into a depression almost as prolonged and incapacitating as the nervous collapse he had suffered after getting his medical degree in 1869. As usual, he experimented with a variety of therapies. The one that seemed to work best involved twice-daily injections of a substance called Robert-Hawley Lymph Compound—extracts from the lymph glands, brains, and testicles of a goat.[39] With (or conceivably in spite of) this assistance, he was able to deliver the Gifford Lectures, finishing in June 1902. These became *The Varieties of Religious Experience*, published later that year. Then, James rediscovered Dewey.

James had read Dewey's psychology textbook, written while Dewey was still at Michigan and in his Hegelian phase, while he was working on *The Principles of Psychology*, and had been disappointed. There was no philosopher (Schopenhauer was a possible exception) for whom James felt a deeper loathing than Hegel. (Herbert Spencer he regarded as a writer for people who did not have a philosopher.) James had not actually read very much Hegel, but he took the view that the sort of philosopher one is drawn to is a reflection of one's own personality; his colleague George Herbert Palmer (the man who had killed Peirce's chances at Chicago) was a Hegelian, and James considered Palmer an insufferable prig. But in 1891 James sent

Dewey a nice letter about an essay Dewey had written on Leibniz. Dewey had just read *The Principles of Psychology*, and he wrote back to tell James of his admiration for the book—also to suggest that parts of it were perhaps more Hegelian than James might wish to admit.

James weathered the blow, and the correspondence continued in a collegial vein. Then, in 1903, after *The Varieties of Religious Experience* had come out, James wrote to ask Dewey to recommend a speaker for an educational convention to be held in Cambridge; his advice had been solicited, he explained, by the philanthropist sponsoring the affair, Mrs. Quincy Adams Shaw—the former Pauline Agassiz, daughter of the scientist. He added that he had just read, "with almost absurd pleasure," a book by Addison Moore on "existence, meaning and reality. I am years behindhand in my reading," he told Dewey, "and don't know how close *you* may have come to anything like that since 1898. I see an entirely new 'school of thought' forming."[40] In fact, James had been tipped off that something was happening at Chicago by James Angell, soon after James's Berkeley lecture, who had written him that Dewey was "driving at"[41] something very like Peirce's pragmatism. And in 1902 Schiller had informed James that Dewey "seems to be teaching a sort of pragmatism at Chicago."[42] But James had been focused on his Edinburgh lectures and on his health. Now he was ready to get back to pragmatism.

Dewey was thrilled to receive James's "school of thought" letter. Addison Moore was the person who, while a graduate student, had co-authored the reaction time study with Angell that was the empirical basis for Dewey's essay on "The Reflex Arc Concept in Psychology"; he was now a professor in the Chicago philosophy department. A "school" was just what Dewey had been trying to build at Chicago, made up mostly of people who had been inspired by James's *Principles of Psychology*. "[I walked] on air for a long time after getting such a letter from you," Dewey told James. He sent along his "Reflex Arc" paper, along with an advance copy of a volume of essays by Moore, Angell, George Herbert Mead, himself, and other members of the Chicago faculty, called *Studies in Logical Theory*. "I wish you would glance them over," he said, ". . . to see whether you could stand for a dedication to yourself."[43]

James found that he could stand for it. "You can count on my zealous cooperation,"[44] he told Dewey, and he reviewed the book, in 1904, in the *Psychological Bulletin*, where he announced that "Chicago has a School of Thought!"[45] Dewey responded that he and his colleagues "have simply been rendering back in logical vocabulary what was already your own."[46] That was in January. In February, James paid a visit to Chicago and spoke to the graduate students on what he was now calling "the 'New Thought.' "[47] He was struck, like many people, by Dewey's unworldliness of manner. "[S]trange that that long-necked and abstracted dreamer should really put his stamp on a genuine new school of philosophic thought,"[48] he wrote to a friend. By May, Dewey had left for Columbia, and Chicago had lost, though not quite its school, its leader. But pragmatism had become a movement.

Dewey's pragmatism was a consequence of the success of the Laboratory School. The school established for him the validity of his hypothesis that thinking and acting are just two names for a single process—the process of making our way as best we can in a universe shot through with contingency. It also showed him what was wrong with philosophy, and Dewey's career after Chicago can be divided into two parts: from his arrival at Columbia until the United States entered the war in 1917, he defended pragmatism against the arguments of other philosophers (frequently in the pages of the *Journal of Philosophy*, founded in 1904 by two members of the Columbia faculty: the psychologist J. McKeen Cattell and the chairman of the philosophy department, Frederick J. E. Woodbridge).[49] From the war until the end of his life, he addressed the issues of his time in a pragmatist spirit.

Philosophers, Dewey argued, had mistakenly insisted on making a problem of the relation between the mind and the world, an obsession that had given rise to what he called "the alleged discipline of epistemology"[50]—the attempt to answer the question, How do we know? The pragmatist response to this question is to point out that nobody has ever made a problem about the relation between, for example, the *hand* and the world. The function of the hand is to help the organism cope with the environment; in situations in which a hand doesn't work, we try something else, such as a foot, or a fish-hook, or an editorial. Nobody worries in these situations about a lack of some preordained "fit"—about whether the physical world was or was not made to be manipulated by hands. They just use a hand where a hand will do.

Dewey thought that ideas and beliefs are the same as hands: instruments for coping. An idea has no greater metaphysical stature than, say, a fork. When your fork proves inadequate to the task of eating soup, it makes little sense to argue about whether there is something inherent in the nature of forks or something inherent in the nature of soup that accounts for the failure. You just reach for a spoon. But philosophers have worried about whether the mind is such that the world can be known by it, and they have produced all sorts of accounts of how the "fit" is supposed to work—how the mental represents the real. Dewey's point was that "mind" and "reality," like "stimulus" and "response," name nonexistent entities: they are abstractions from a single, indivisible process. It therefore makes as little sense to talk about a "split" that needs to be overcome between the mind and the world as it does to talk about a "split" between the hand and the environment, or the fork and the soup. "Things," he wrote, ". . . are what they are experienced as."[51] Knowledge is not a copy of something that exists independently of its being known, *"it is an instrument or organ of successful action."*[52] "The chief service of pragmatism, as regards epistemology," he wrote to a friend in 1905, "will be . . . to give the *coup de grace* to *representationalism."*[53]

Dewey regarded the tendency to ascribe a special status to the mind and its ideas as a reflection of class bias. The Greek philosophers belonged to a leisure class, and this made it natural for them to exalt reflection and speculation at the expense of making and doing—to talk about "reasoning" as something that transcends the circumstances of the being who reasons. Philosophy since the Greeks, Dewey thought, amounted to a history of efforts to establish, in the interests of similar class preferences, the superiority of one element over the other in a series of false dichotomies: stability over change, certainty over contingency, the fine arts over the useful arts, what minds do over what hands do.

The penalty was anachronism. While philosophy pondered its artificial puzzles, science, taking a purely instrumental and experimental approach, had transformed the world. Dewey believed that it was time for philosophy to catch up; like James, he thought that pragmatism's insistence that ideas and beliefs are always in the service of interests—that "the trail of the human serpent is . . . over everything,"[54] as James put it—was the beginning of a philosophical revolution. "The moment the complicity of the personal factor in our valuations is recognized, is recognized fully, frankly, and generally," Dewey wrote a year after James's *Pragmatism* appeared, "that moment a new era in philosophy will begin."[55]

When the British writer G. K. Chesterton complained, soon after, that "[p]ragmatism is a matter of human needs, and one of the first of human needs is to be something more than a pragmatist,"[56] Dewey was delighted. The remark "spilled the personal milk in the absolutist's cocoanut,"[57] he said. For the objection that pragmatism's account of belief doesn't satisfy all our needs confirms pragmatism's most basic claim, which is that what people choose to believe is just what they think it is good to believe. Every philosophical account of the way people think is a support for those human goods the person making the account believes to be important. Dewey thought that recognizing this could help philosophers make a difference in the world. "Philosophy recovers itself," he wrote in 1917 in a famous sentence in his essay "The Need for a Recovery of Philosophy," "when it ceases to be a device for dealing with the problems of philosophers and becomes a method, cultivated by philosophers, for dealing with the problems of men."[58]

6

Peirce had been touched by James's dedication of *The Will to Believe* to him, but he was not entirely pleased by the book. "Will" seemed to him exactly the wrong word to use about something—belief—which he thought meaningless if not instinctive. James came to regret the title, too; he later said he wished he had used the phrase "the right to believe"[59]—though that would scarcely have been more palatable to Peirce. But that is because individualism and voluntarism were values fundamental to James's thought, and they were values despised by Peirce.

Peirce could not afford to buy *Studies in Logical Theory* when it came out in 1904, but he got a copy through the *Nation*. He was sympathetic to the spirit, but appalled by what he regarded as a lack of rigor. He wrote a letter to Dewey accusing him of "intellectual licentiousness,"[60] but did not send it. He did, however, review the book anonymously in the *Nation*, where he was a little less damning, but only a little. "[T]hey make *truth*, which is a matter of fact, to be a matter of a way of thinking or even of linguistic expression," he complained. "The Chicago school or group are manifestly in radical opposition to the exact logicians, and are not making any studies which anybody in his senses can expect, directly or indirectly, in any considerable degree, to influence twentieth-century science."[61]

Peirce's account of the way people think was the same as James's and Dewey's. He, too, regarded a belief as a kind of bet in a probabilistic universe, and successful beliefs—winning bets—as habits. And he, too, rejected the theory that the mind is the mirror of an external reality. There was no way to hook up ideas with things, Peirce thought, because ideas—mental representations—do not refer to things; they refer to other mental representations. When we hear the word "tree," we do not perceive an actual tree; we perceive the conception of a tree that already exists in our minds. Peirce called this mediating representation an "interpretant"[62] (a term he introduced in 1866, in a lecture in Boston attended by James and Wendell Holmes). "The meaning of a representation," he wrote in a later, undated manuscript,

> can be nothing but a representation. In fact, it is nothing but the representation itself conceived as stripped of irrelevant clothing. But this clothing can never be completely stripped off; it is only changed for something more diaphanous. So there is an infinite regression here. Finally, the interpretant is nothing but another representation

to which the torch of truth is handed along; and as representation, it has its interpretant again. Lo, another infinite series.[63]

Peirce thought that our representations can be classified, filled out, and elaborated in all sorts of ways, that they can even become "better," in the sense of "more useful," as we peel off their metaphysical husks. But we can never (as individuals) say that they are identical with their objects. This is not just because our knowledge always "swims," as Peirce put it, "in a continuum of uncertainty and of indeterminacy";[64] it is also because—and this is the distinctive feature of Peirce's theory of signs—there are no prerepresentational objects out there. Things are themselves signs: their being signs is a condition of their being things at all. You can call this notion counterintuitive, because that is exactly what it is: it is part of Peirce's attack on the idea that we can know some things intuitively—that is, without the mediation of representations. For Peirce, knowing was inseparable from what he called semiosis, the making of signs, and of the making of signs there is no end. If you look up a word in the dictionary, you find it defined by a string of other words, the meanings of which can be discovered by looking them up in a dictionary, leading to more words to be looked up in turn. There is no exit from the dictionary. Peirce didn't simply think that language is like that. He thought that the universe is like that.

So what did he mean when he accused the Chicago school of treating truth as a matter of linguistic expression rather than a matter of fact? He meant that Dewey had no teleology. The evolutionary concept of teleology is confusing. Darwin's theory is teleological in that it conceives of everything about an organism as designed for a purpose—ultimately, the purpose of survival. That was one of the most revolutionary aspects of Darwin's thinking, and the source of James and Dewey's functionalism—their idea that beliefs are instruments for action. We don't act because we have ideas; we have ideas because we must act, and we act to achieve ends. But Darwin's theory is antiteleological in that it does not conceive of the universe itself as designed for an end. Change is continual but not directional.

Evolutionary development is not guided by anything prior to or outside of itself.

Peirce joined with James and Dewey on the first kind of teleology;
he broke with them, and with Darwin, on the second. He did not
think chance variation could explain evolution adequately—he
thought God's love must play a more important role, a theory he
called "agapism,"[65] and derived in part from the Swedenborgian writings of Henry James, Sr.—and he could not imagine a universe
devoid of ultimate meaning. He was quite explicit on this point:
"physical evolution works towards ends in the same way that mental
action works towards ends," he wrote in 1902 in an entry for a dictionary of philosophy and psychology edited by the functionalist James
Mark Baldwin. (Baldwin would one day come to share a distinction
with Peirce: he was dismissed from the Hopkins faculty, in 1909, after he was discovered by the Baltimore police during a raid on a
black brothel. He ended his career in Mexico.)[66] For Peirce, habits
are therefore not provisional adaptive responses to fluctuating environmental conditions; they are steps on the universal road from
indeterminacy to law, a road traveled by objects as well as by organisms. For matter, Peirce thought, was simply "mind whose habits
have become fixed so as to lose the powers of forming them and losing them."[67]

Habit, in Peirce's theory, is what makes all things, from molecules
to philosophers, what they are. It is what enables them to persist in
their condition of sameness—as we are (to other people) the set of
repeated behaviors observable in us. If our behavior was perfectly arbitrary—that is, not habitual—we would have no identity; the price
of having an identity is an inability fundamentally to transform it.
Habit-taking is a "plastic" faculty, in the sense that every organism
has the potential to produce a variety of responses to a given stimulus: the peculiar characteristic of habit, as Peirce explained, is "not
acting with exactitude."[68] But those responses cannot be random,
since if they were, law would not be possible. They cluster around a
norm. This definition of a thing as the sum of its possible behaviors
is what Peirce had meant by his "principle of pragmatism."

But Peirce also believed, as his father had, in a version of the nebular hypothesis: he thought that the universe is evolving from a condition of chaos, in which things happen entirely by chance, toward a condition of absolute law, or complete determinism, in which chance will disappear and all habits will be perfectly fixed. In the long run, as he had argued in his Hopkins Metaphysical Club paper on "Design and Chance," the evolutionary process weeds out bad habits and encourages the reproduction of good ones, and the consequence is a continual reduction of indeterminacy.

Among the habits subject to selection are our beliefs. As the universe becomes more predictable, our beliefs about it become truer, less individual, more "fixed." "[J]ust as conduct controlled by ethical reason tends toward fixing certain habits of conduct, the nature of which . . . does not depend upon any accidental circumstances, and *in that sense*, may be said to be *destined*," Peirce wrote, in 1905, in the essay that was his answer to James and Dewey; "so, thought, controlled by rational experimental logic, tends to the fixation of certain opinions, equally destined, the nature of which will be the same in the end, however the perversity of thought of whole generations may cause the postponement of the ultimate fixation."[69] For Peirce, the whole purpose of thinking philosophically was "to grind off," as he put it, "the arbitrary and the individualistic character of thought," and to recover our instincts, which he called "racial ideas."[70]

Peirce had a number of examples he liked to use to support his contention that instincts are unconscious decision-making powers that have been bred into us. One involved a lost watch. In 1879, Peirce's watch was apparently stolen during a trip to New York on a steamship called the *Bristol*. Peirce made all the African-American waiters on the boat come on deck, and talked briefly with each. Finding no clue to indicate which was the thief (or indeed that any African-American or any waiter was the thief), Peirce decided to guess. He approached one of the men and confidently accused him of the crime. "[A]ll shadow of doubt had vanished. There was no self-criticism,"[71] as he later described his feeling. The waiter denied the charge. Peirce hired a Pinkerton detective and ultimately, he claimed, recovered the watch from the very person he had accused on no evidence. Peirce concluded that he must have received clues subconsciously during his conversation with the waiter that led him to reach the correct conclusion—an accomplishment he compared, in the essay he wrote about it, with Kepler's discovery of the laws of planetary motion. Kepler, too, did not have enough evidence to *know* that his laws were correct; he must have guessed. This kind of guessing Peirce called "abduction"; he thought that it was a method integral to scientific progress, and that it pointed to an underlying affinity between the mind and the universe.

A few years after the *Bristol* incident, while he was teaching at Hopkins, Peirce and his prize student, Joseph Jastrow, performed a version of what had been the pioneering experiment in physiological psychology, Gustav Fechner's study of the amount a weight needs to be increased for a person to become aware of the change. Fechner was trying to determine the liminal threshold for a sensation; Peirce and Jastrow decided to investigate subliminal sensations. They increased or decreased a stimulus by a degree too small to be registered consciously, and then asked their subjects to guess which way it had changed. They found that 60 percent guessed correctly—a result, they argued, that "gives new reason for believing that we gather what is passing in one another's minds in large measure from sensations so faint that we are not fully aware of having them, and can reach no account of how we reached our conclusions about such matters." (They suggested that this might explain, among other things, "[t]he insight of females.")[72] It was another confirmation, for Peirce, of the notion that we are evolving, as a species, toward a complete epistemological rapport with reality. Peirce called this final condition, in which the universe is perfectly lawlike and beliefs are perfectly true, "concrete reasonableness." And "concrete" is unquestionably *le mot juste*.

This is the vision behind Peirce's argument, in "How to Make Our Ideas Clear," that "[t]he opinion which is fated to be ultimately agreed to by all who investigate, is what we mean by the truth, and the object represented in this opinion is the real."[73] James may have taken this to mean that our opinions become true insofar as they continue to cash out for us in experience; but that is not what Peirce

Juliette and Charles Peirce at their estate, Arisbe, in 1907. Earlier that year
Peirce had been found malnourished and near death in a Cambridge rooming house
by a student of William James's.

meant, and he almost certainly had James in mind when he warned, in a footnote added when he was recasting the essay with an eye to making it part of a book (a project never completed), that his theory should not be taken "in too individualistic a sense."[74] For Peirce, inquiry is always communal—it is the median of many observations that gives the position of the star—and the last analysis really is the last. In Peirce's cosmology, everyone's beliefs *have* to be the same in the end, because all opinion must converge. Doubt will disappear, and beliefs will be perfectly instinctive, the genetic legacy of the species. Individuality and choice are obviously not features of such a universe. Neither, for that matter, is mind. Peirce's pragmatism has the Midas touch.

7

Why, on a pragmatist account of ideas, did the idea of pragmatism arise? According to Peirce's version, pragmatism has to be explained as a necessary rung on the ladder to concrete reasonableness. For James and Dewey, though, no idea is necessary in that sense: a new idea is not the inexorable next link in a chain of prior ideas; it is a chance outgrowth, a lucky variant that catches on because it hooks people up with their circumstances in ways they find useful.

As James saw right away, he and Dewey came to pragmatism from nearly opposite philosophical directions. James took his inspiration from (besides Charles Renouvier, a philosopher Dewey does not seem to have taken an interest in) the British empiricists—John Locke, David Hume, and George Berkeley—writers James thought had reduced philosophical terms like "matter" and "identity" to their cash value. James dedicated *Pragmatism* to John Stuart Mill, "whom my fancy likes to picture as our leader were he alive today."[75] Mill and the British empiricists were, of course, the bane of the tradition in which Dewey had been trained—just as Hegel, whose work Dewey said "left a permanent deposit in my thinking,"[76] was the particular bête noire of William James.

James and Dewey were both affected by the New Psychology, it's true, but James was contemptuous of most of the prevailing assumptions in that field, even when he was composing his landmark summation of its findings, and the compliment was returned. "James's influence both in philosophy & psychology appears to me to be getting positively unwholesome," the Wundtian Edward Titchener complained to McKeen Cattell a few months after James introduced pragmatism in the Berkeley lecture: "his credulity and his appeals to emotion are surely the reverse of scientific."[77] Pragmatism was in many respects a reaction *against* experimental psychology. It rejected not only the static, structural model of Wundtian psychology, the model Dewey demolished in the "Reflex Arc" paper, but the behaviorism implicit in the early-twentieth-century version of the functionalist model as well.

The bigger intellectual picture is similarly equivocal. Pragmatism seems a reflection of the late-nineteenth-century faith in scientific inquiry—yet James introduced it in order to attack the pretensions of late-nineteenth-century science. Pragmatism seems Darwinian—yet it was openly hostile to the two most prominent Darwinists of the time, Herbert Spencer and Thomas Huxley; it was designed, in James's version, to get God back into a picture many people felt Darwin had written him out of; and it had nothing in common with the thought of people like William Graham Sumner, or with the eugenics movement, which was based on the work of Darwin's cousin, the statistician Francis Galton. Pragmatism seems to derive from statistical thinking—but many nineteenth-century statisticians were committed to principles of laissez-faire James and Dewey did not endorse, and many turn-of-the-century statisticians (Galton was one of the most renowned) were committed to ideas of race-building and social engineering that are alien to everything James and Dewey wrote. Pragmatism shares Emerson's distrust of institutions and systems, and his manner of appropriating ideas while discarding their philosophical foundations—but it does not share his conception of the individual conscience as a transcendental authority.

In short, pragmatism was a variant of many strands in nineteenth-century thought but by no means their destined point of convergence. It fit in with the stock of existing ideas in ways that made it seem recognizable and plausible: James subtitled *Pragmatism* "A

New Name for Old Ways of Thinking." But pragmatism was the product of a group of individuals, and it took its shape from the way they bounced off one another, their circumstances, and the mysteries of their unreproducible personalities.

A pragmatic account of pragmatism's emergence would, in any case, look not to its origins but to its consequences. What changes in American life made pragmatism seem to some people the right philosophical utensil for a few decades after 1898? Though the immediate outcome of the Pullman boycott was disastrous for labor, Dewey and Jane Addams had been right when they predicted that the episode would eventually be seen to mark the obsolescence of nineteenth-century economic arrangements. The year James introduced pragmatism was also the year the American economy began to move away from an individualist ideal of unrestrained competition and toward a bureaucratic ideal of management and regulation.[78]

Starting with the Erdman Act, passed by Congress in 1898, which recognized the right of workers to organize and provided for the mediation of labor disputes by a government board, the state began assuming a role in economic affairs. And as epitomized by the creation of United States Steel, in 1901, which merged 158 companies into one organization, American business began exchanging an entrepreneurial model, in which an individual like George Pullman could run his company largely according to his own wishes (and straight into the ground, if he liked), for a corporate model, in which a board of directors, dominated usually by bankers, oversaw company policy in the interest of investors—the system of finance capitalism. The period of pragmatism's efflorescence, from 1898 to 1917, was a period when the values of corporate management, public oversight, and political reform were in ascendance. The intellectual elite was finished with the Gilded Age, and so, for its own reasons, was the business elite.

Pragmatism's appeal in these circumstances is not hard to understand. Everything James and Dewey wrote as pragmatists boils down to a single claim: people are the agents of their own destinies. They dispelled the fatalism that haunts almost every nineteenth-century system of thought—the mechanical or materialist determinism of writers like Laplace, Malthus, Darwin, Spencer, Huxley, and Marx, and the providential or absolutist determinism of writers like Hegel, Agassiz, Morris, and the Peirces. James and Dewey described a universe still in progress, a place where no conclusion is foregone and every problem is amenable to the exercise of what Dewey called "intelligent action." They spoke to a generation of academics, journalists, jurists, and policy makers eager to find scientific solutions to social problems, and happy to be given good reasons to ignore the claims of finished cosmologies.

For James, this was not entirely the reception he had intended. The period from 1898 to 1917 in the United States was a period of adjustment to life under industrial capitalism, and James was temperamentally averse to many of the conditions such a life entailed. The Spanish-American War, in 1898, in which the United States acquired the Philippines in what seemed an almost reflexive gesture of imperialism, exposed, he thought, the soul of modern America: its mindless drive toward expansion, conglomeration, massification. "As for me, my bed is made," he wrote to a friend in 1899:

> I am against bigness and greatness in all their forms, and with the invisible molecular moral forces that work from individual to individual, stealing in through the crannies of the world like so many soft rootlets, or like the capillary oozing of water. . . . The bigger the unit you deal with, the hollower, the more brutal, the more mendacious is the life displayed. So I am against all big organizations as such, national ones first and foremost; against all big successes and big results; and in favor of the eternal forces of truth which always work in the individual and immediately unsuccessful way, underdogs always, till history comes, after they are long dead, and puts them on the top.[79]

James's pragmatism was not a philosophy for policy makers, muckrakers, and social scientists. It was a philosophy for misfits, mystics, and geniuses—people who believed in mental telepathy, or immortality, or God. James was never able to believe unreservedly in any of those things himself; but to the end of his life, he tried.

Dewey and Jane Addams did believe in adjustment. They were reformers, and reform is about improving the quality of life under a given regime, not about overthrowing the established order. Dewey was no friend of industrial capitalism, but he was not under the illusion that it was about to go away. His strategy was to promote, in every area of life, including industrial life, democracy, which he interpreted as the practice of "associated living"—cooperation with others on a basis of tolerance and equality. He hoped that in the long run this would lead to a more just order. The hope had its philosophical justifications, which Dewey spent his career trying to spell out. But it was also the expression of a singularly irenic personality. He had taken Addams's teaching to heart: that antagonism is unnecessary, that it is based on a misunderstanding of one's best interests, and that it leads to violence.

And the fear of violence is possibly at the bottom of the whole matter of pragmatism's "fit." At the beginning of the Pullman affair, Eugene Debs addressed the strikers in the Illinois shops. "Pullman's pretended philanthropy," he told them, "makes this a question of emancipation. His specious interest in the welfare of the 'poor workingman' is in no way different from that of the slaveowner of fifty years ago. . . . You are striking to avert inevitable slavery and degradation."[80] And soon after, when the Cleveland administration was poised to intervene in order to end the boycott, Debs warned that if the army were called out, it would instigate a new civil war.[81] Debs was not a militant, but he had taken his inspiration from John Brown, and he was happy, once the battle was engaged, to become a martyr. His behavior is likely to look to us like the behavior of a person firmly committed to principle. To many people in 1894 it looked like the behavior of a fanatic, and precisely because it was the behavior of a person firmly committed to principle. Those people thought they had seen commitment to principle of that type before: abolitionism.

For many white Americans after 1865, the abolitionists were the century's villains—not only because they were thought to have been responsible for the war, but because they and their heirs were thought to have been responsible for the humiliation of the South during Reconstruction. They had driven a wedge into white America, and they did it because they had become infatuated with an idea. They marched the nation to the brink of self-destruction in the name of an abstraction. The United States in the 1890s was a society fractured along many lines: the South against the North, the West against the East, labor against capital, agriculture against industry, borrowers against lenders, people who called themselves natives against the new immigrants. In a time when the chance of another civil war did not seem remote, a philosophy that warned against the idolatry of ideas was possibly the only philosophy on which a progressive politics could have been successfully mounted.

It is possible to go a little farther, and to say that the price of reform in the United States between 1898 and 1917 was the removal of the issue of race from the table. When the Populist Party was founded in 1892 with a platform that included demands for an income tax, government ownership of the railroads, and laws to protect unions, its leaders set out to recruit black voters. By 1906 the Populists had become the party of white supremacy. In *Plessy v. Ferguson*, in 1896, the Supreme Court sanctioned apartheid; in *Williams v. Mississippi*, in 1898, it sanctioned the disenfranchisement of Southern blacks. In 1896, there had been 130,334 African-Americans registered to vote in Louisiana; by 1904, there were only 1,342.[82] White Americans were free to appropriate the rhetoric of abolition and emancipation, but they were not free to apply it to the situation of black Americans. This was a fact of life Debs knew perfectly well; for although all Pullman sleeping car porters were African-American, none of them participated in the boycott, because the American Railway Union, Debs's own organization, did not admit blacks.

In its day pragmatism attracted relentless criticism from other philosophers, which James and Dewey spent a great deal of their time responding to. James and Dewey did not consider pragmatism an attack on philosophy as such, only a tool to help philosophy become more practical and effective. But philosophers, not surprisingly, saw it differently, and they were not always nuanced in imagining the dangers of doing without metaphysics. If pragmatism had its way, Bertrand Russell wrote in 1909, then "ironclads and Maxim guns must be the ultimate arbiters of metaphysical truth."[83]

(Russell's attacks on pragmatism were so intemperate that he earned the distinction of being one of the few people known to have provoked Dewey to express irritation. "You know, he gets me sore," Dewey said.)[84]

But leaving aside its merits as philosophy—leaving aside, for example, the question of whether its theory of truth is logically supportable—turn-of-the-century pragmatism does have two larger deficiencies as a school of thought. One is that it takes interests for granted; it doesn't provide for a way of judging whether they are worth pursuing apart from the consequences of acting on them. We form beliefs to get what we want, but where do we get our wants? This is a question asked by writers like Veblen and Weber and Freud, but it is not a question that figures centrally in the thought of James and Dewey. The second deficiency is related to the first. It is that wants and beliefs can lead people to act in ways that are distinctly unpragmatic. Sometimes the results are destructive, but sometimes they are not. There is a sense in which history is lit by the deeds of men and women for whom ideas were things other than instruments of adjustment. Pragmatism explains everything about ideas except why a person would be willing to die for one.

Alain Locke at Hertford College, University of Oxford, in 1908, at the
end of his year as the first African-American Rhodes Scholar.

FOURTEEN

PLURALISMS

I

PLURALISM IS AN ATTEMPT to make a good out of the circumstance that goods are often incommensurable. People come at life from different places, they understand the world in different ways, they strive for different ends. This is a fact that has proved amazingly hard to live with, and the reason is that as associated beings, we naturally seek to find our tastes, values, and hopes reflected in other people. It would be one thing, in other words, if each individual simply had his or her own spin and there were no way to get groups of individuals spinning in the same direction. But individuals do belong to groups, they take their identities from groups, and it tends to be as members of groups that they pursue the goods they desire. To the extent that one group perceives its goods to be incompatible with the goods of another group, there are collisions.

Philosophically, pluralism is the view that the world consists of independent things. Each thing relates to other things, but the relations depend on where you start. The universe is plural: it hangs together, but in more ways than one. Reality, as William James liked to say, is distributive, by which he meant that things are connected loosely, provisionally, and every which way, and not, as in a monistic philosophy like Hegel's, logically, ineluctably, and in one ultimate and absolute way. "Everything is many directional, many dimensional, in its external relations," James wrote in a notebook;

> and after pursuing one line of direction from it, you have to go back, and start in a new dimension if you wish to bring in other objects related to it, different from those which lay in the original direction. No one point of view or attitude commands everything at once in a synthetic scheme. . , .
>
> [A] sensible "experience" of mine, say this book written on by this pen, leads in one dimension into the world of matter, paper-mills, etc., in the other into that psychologic life of mine of which it is an affection. Both sets of associates are contiguous with it, yet one set must be dropped out of sight if the other is to be followed. They decline to make one universe in the absolute sense of something that can be embraced by one individual stroke of apprehension.[1]

The notebook was used to record ideas for the Hibbert Lectures, which James delivered at Manchester College, Oxford, in May 1908, and published a year later under the title *A Pluralistic Universe*. "Things are 'with' one another in many ways," James put it there,

> but nothing includes everything, or dominates over everything. The word "and" trails along after every sentence. Something always escapes. . . . The pluralistic world is . . . more like a federal republic than like an empire or a kingdom. However much may be collected, however much may report itself as present at any effective centre of consciousness or action, something else is self-governed and absent and unreduced to unity.[2]

Though the lectures attracted overflow crowds, there was little response from Oxford philosophers.[3] James was disappointed, but not entirely surprised. For one of the things he was suggesting was that in a pluralistic universe, there is no one vocabulary, no one discourse, that covers every case, and the idea that it might be the discourse that covers every case is one of the oldest dreams of philosophy. It was a dream philosophers were not willing to give up.

Politics had not been a prominent interest of James's before 1898, but the suppression of the Philippine independence movement in the aftermath of the Spanish-American War and, a little later on, newspaper reports of lynchings in the South moved him to become active in public affairs. He may have come to think of his pragmatism and his pluralism as philosophical expressions of his anti-imperialism and antiracism,[4] but his announced adherence to the former ideas predated the Spanish-American War (his pluralism predated even his pragmatism: he identified his point of view as pluralist in the preface to *The Will to Believe* in 1897), and he did not present them in political terms. The remark in the Hibbert Lectures that the universe is "more like a federal republic than like an empire or a kingdom" was probably just a figure of speech, an American (in fact, an Irish-American) tweaking his British listeners. It was taken to heart, though, by two members of his audience, and it became one of the inspirations for the idea of cultural pluralism.

2

Cultural pluralism is an analogue of political pluralism, and the American idea of political pluralism was also inspired by James, though less directly. Its first major expression appeared in the same year that James delivered the Hibbert Lectures, 1908, in the form of a book called *The Process of Government*. *The Process of Government* was for many years a relatively obscure text, and part of the reason was that its author was a person without an academic affiliation. Arthur Bentley was born in Illinois in 1870.[5] He dropped out of several colleges, eventually graduating, in 1892, from Johns Hopkins, where he was a student of Richard Ely's. He studied in Germany under the sociologist Georg Simmel and the philosopher Wilhelm Dilthey, and returned to Hopkins for his Ph.D., which he received in 1895. He then went to the University of Chicago, where he served as an instructor in sociology for one year.

Bentley was a learned man but a reclusive person, and students found his assignments absurdly demanding. His class was disbanded by mutual agreement, and apart from a visiting professorship at Columbia almost fifty years later, in 1941–42, he never held another academic appointment. But during his year at Chicago, he sat in on John Dewey's course on logic[6] (apparently without informing Dewey), and when he left in 1896, to begin a career as a reporter and editorial writer for Chicago newspapers, he began writing *The Process of Government*. He finished the book twelve years later; it was published by the University of Chicago Press, and its one-sentence preface indicates plainly enough the influence of Dewey's pragmatism: "This Book Is an Attempt to Fashion a Tool."

Bentley's theory of government was pure Chicago-school functionalism. It derived from Dewey and Mead, and through Dewey and Mead from James's *Principles of Psychology*; it was also influenced by Dilthey's theory of interpretation in the social sciences, according to which understanding is achieved by a continuous movement from parts to wholes and back again; and it clearly reflected its author's inveterate distaste for simple explanations. Bentley's undergraduate thesis at Hopkins had been a study of the economic condition of the Nebraska farmer that stressed the complexity of the reasons for the agricultural depression; his doctoral thesis was an attack on mechanistic causal explanations of social phenomena. Bentley's argument in *The Process of Government* was directed at the fiction (as he regarded it) of sovereignty. Political scientists talk about "the state" and its institutions as though those things existed independently of the people who exercise political power. The state, Bentley pragmatically argued, just *is* the people who exercise political power, and these people organize themselves into groups, for the Deweyan reason that individuals are products of their social circumstances and always define and express themselves socially.

Bentley referred to these groups, whose struggle with one another constitutes "government," as "interest groups," but he cautioned that "interest" was just a name for one aspect of group activity, the label for a particular good arising at a particular moment out of the ongoing process of associated living. What was radical about Bentley's

theory wasn't his definition of the state in terms of competing interests: James Madison (a writer to whom Bentley strangely did not refer) had famously defined constitutional democracy in these terms in
the *Federalist* papers. What was radical was his insistence that simply
identifying interest groups did not allow us to construct an explanatory model, since interests are never fixed. We can describe the
process, but the constituent elements of the process at any given
moment are always unique. This is because groups are continually
defining and redefining themselves in relation to other groups, and
all groups, no matter how marginal or disenfranchised they seem, are
in the game. "No interest group has meaning except with reference
to other interest groups," Bentley wrote; "and those other interest
groups are pressures; they count in the government process. The
lowest of despised castes, deprived of rights to the protection of
property and even life, will still be found to be a factor in the government. . . . No slaves, not the worst abused of all, but help to form the
government. They are an interest group within it."[7]

The year his book came out, Bentley fell into a long depression,
and in 1911 he moved to rural Indiana, where he devoted himself, for
the rest of his life, to writing. Many years later, he renewed contact
with Dewey and they became correspondents and eventually collaborators, producing, in 1949, when Dewey was ninety and Bentley was
nearly eighty, a book on logic called *Knowing and the Known*. But although *The Process of Government* did not get a lot of attention when
it appeared, it was in every other respect well timed. For 1908 was
also the year of Israel Zangwill's popular play *The Melting Pot*. Bentley's book offered a way of understanding a situation Americans
had become obsessed with—the growing presence of immigrant
groups.

Between 1901 and 1910, 8,795,386 immigrants were admitted to
the United States; 70 percent were from Southern and Eastern Europe, principally Catholics and Jews. Between 1911 and 1920, another
5,735,811 people were admitted from abroad, 59 percent of whom
came from Southern and Eastern Europe.[8] By 1910, 40 percent of the
population of New York City was foreign-born. (Not all these immigrants remained in the United States permanently, of course.) At a

time when nationality was defined racially, and when race was conceived hierarchically, the anxiety that Louis Agassiz had expressed at the time of the Civil War reasserted itself: would the presence of large numbers of non-Anglo-Saxon peoples lead to national degeneration?

The question was given an ugly edge by what was actually an advance in evolutionary theory.[9] A number of prominent American natural scientists in the late nineteenth century had been students of Agassiz. They retained their teacher's faith in the rational intelligibility of the natural world, but they dropped his antagonism to evolution. These scientists' evolutionism was not Darwinian, however; it was Lamarckian. They believed in the inheritability of acquired characteristics—the theory that species can progress by the cultivation of good habits transmitted genetically from one generation to the next. It was a theory considered compatible with Social Darwinism, and it was sometimes used to explain the alleged superiority of the Anglo-Saxon; but it held out the promise at least that "lesser" races might also improve themselves (generally with Anglo-Saxon guidance, as in the case of the Philippines) over time.

Then, in 1889, the German biologist August Weismann disproved the Lamarckian theory by showing that mice whose tails had been cut off never produced short-tailed offspring—a finding reached just in time to be discussed by James in the closing pages of *The Principles of Psychology*. (The scientist whose experimental results Weismann specifically set out to refute, Charles Brown-Séquard, had been one of James's teachers at the Harvard Medical School.) Weismann's conclusions were furiously contested, by Herbert Spencer especially, but they could not, of course, be disproved, and one of the results was that racial difference suddenly seemed, once again, immutable. Americans who regarded Southern and Eastern Europeans, not to mention Asians and African-Americans, as biologically inferior now envisioned racial catastrophe. They believed—because they did not know any scientific reason not to believe it—that the presence of what they assumed were inferior human types would lower the standard of American civilization.

Many of these people considered themselves progressives. The sociologist Edward A. Ross, for instance, who taught first at Stanford and then at the University of Wisconsin, was a student of Richard Ely and a disciple and associate of Lester Ward. (He was married, in fact, to Ward's niece.) Ross was one of the best-known public intellectuals of his day; his books sold more than 300,000 copies.[10] He had a strong interest in socialism, and sometimes jeopardized his academic career by championing the labor movement. But he was also a eugenicist and an opponent of immigration, on grounds that racial inequality is a fact of nature. "The theory that races are virtually equal in capacity," he wrote in the *American Journal of Sociology* in 1907, "leads to such monumental follies as lining the valleys of the South with the bones of half a million picked whites in order to improve the condition of four million unpicked blacks."[11] (How it is that the surviving group is the one that qualifies as "unpicked" Ross did not explain.) But just as eugenicism was on the verge of becoming the enlightened political view and biological determinism seemed back for good, the whole applecart was upset by a completely unexpected discovery.

The person who made the discovery was Franz Boas.[12] Boas was from Germany, but his career oddly shadowed Dewey's. He was born in 1858, a year before Dewey, and received a Ph.D. from the University of Kiel in 1881, but he sought to leave Germany because of anti-Semitism. (Boas was Jewish, and he had lifelong scars on his face that were rumored to have been the results of a duel he insisted on fighting with a student who had made an anti-Semitic remark—a report people who knew him later in America found completely consistent with his personality. Boas was not known for his willingness to suffer fools.) He applied for a fellowship to study at Johns Hopkins in 1882, the year Dewey entered, but was refused. So instead he went to Baffin Island to study the Eskimos.

Boas began as a psychophysicist and a disciple of Gustav Fechner. His dissertation was entitled *Beiträge zur Erkenntniss der Farbe des Wassers*—"Contribution to the Understanding of the Color of Water." It was a topic that entailed an inquiry into the classic Fechnerian problem of sensory thresholds: How much does light have to increase or decrease in brightness before we perceive a change in the color of water? Boas's consideration of this problem led him to the conclusion that contrary to the founding assumption of psychophysics, there can be no general law of sensory thresholds, because perception is always situational. Different observers have different responses depending on expectations and experience, and these differences are not innate; they are, consciously and unconsciously, learned. It was a tiny crack in the foundations of physical anthropology, but it eventually led to the establishment of a new explanatory concept in the human sciences: culture.

After his work with the Eskimos, Boas returned to Germany. He came back to North America in 1886 to do fieldwork on the Bella Coola Indians of the Pacific Northwest, and ended up taking a job as a writer for *Science* magazine in New York City. His ethnographic work had confirmed for him "the fact," as he put it in 1887, "that civilization is not something absolute, but that it is relative, and that our ideas and conceptions are true only so far as our civilization goes. . . . The physiological and psychological state of an organism at a certain moment is a function of its whole history."[13] And he began using the term "culture" in this relational sense. He was the first social scientist to refer to "cultures," in the plural.[14]

In 1888, on a train to Cleveland to attend a scientific meeting, Boas got into a conversation with the man in the seat next to him, who, at the end of the trip, offered him a job. The friendly passenger was G. Stanley Hall, recruiting for the newly opened Clark University. Boas taught at Clark for four years. Like most of the rest of the faculty, he eventually became exasperated with what he and his colleagues regarded as Hall's duplicity, and he departed in the general exodus of 1892. He went to Chicago, but not to the university. William Rainey Harper was reluctant to hire him—he was concerned that Boas was not a person who could "take direction"[15]—and Boas went to work at the World Columbian Exposition, collecting anthropological data. (Joseph Jastrow, Charles Peirce's Hopkins protégé, did similar work at the Exposition.) In 1896 Boas moved to New York again and became assistant curator of the American Museum of Natural History. J. McKeen Cattell got him an appointment as a lecturer at Columbia, he was tenured in 1899, and in 1904 Dewey finally caught up with him. They found themselves on the same intellectual page.

In 1908, after persistence on Boas's part, the Dillingham Commission of the United States Senate agreed to fund a study of the bodily form of the descendants of immigrants as part of its general charge to look into the problem of immigration and assimilation. Over two years, Boas and his team examined 17,000 people, and the results astonished even him. For he discovered that children born in the United States of immigrant parents had different physical features from children born in Europe of the same parents.

Boas's principal statistic was the cephalic index—the ratio of the width of the head to the length, expressed as a percentage. Boas had always considered head shape one of the most stable characteristics of racial types, and he was amazed to find that it could change not only within a single generation, but among the offspring of the same biological parents. Children born in Sicily had relatively long heads, and Jewish children born in Eastern Europe had relatively wide heads; but American children of Sicilian parents had wider heads than their Sicilian-born siblings, and American children of Eastern European Jewish parents had longer heads. The more time the parents had spent in the United States before conception, the more pronounced the difference. The American descendants of Sicilians and Eastern European Jews seemed to be converging on a similar cranial shape, and genes plainly had nothing to do with it—since, as Weismann had shown, inherited characteristics are impervious to environmental influence. (Weismann hypothesized that they were transmitted through something he called the "gene plasm"; genetics and evolutionary theory had not yet been synthesized.) Boas tested for illegitimacy, differences in infant mortality rates, swaddling practices, and many other possible explanations, and he ruled them all out. He did not even offer a theory to explain his results; he thought they spoke for themselves. "[W]e are compelled to conclude," he announced in the report he submitted in 1910, "that when these features of the body change, the whole bodily and mental make-up of the immigrant may change. . . . [A]ll the evidence now is of a great plasticity of human types."[16]

In fact, the change Boas had detected was, though statistically significant, fairly small: the Sicilian-descended cephalic index went from 78 percent to a little over 80 percent, the Jewish-descended cephalic index from 83 percent to 81 percent. And it was a leap to conclude that if head shape changed, everything else about a person must be susceptible to change as well. Boas was not a leaper; he was a rigorous scientist. But he was already disposed to believe in what he called the "plasticity of human types"—the capacity of racial groups to change their characteristics over time. He had long admired a book published in 1858 by Theodor Waitz, a professor at the University of Marburg, called *Ueber die Einheit des Menschengeschlechtes und den Naturzustand des Menschen* ("On the Unity of the Human Species and the Natural Condition of Man"), which was an attack on polygenism and the American school of anthropology—the school founded on the craniological researches of Samuel Morton and represented in Waitz's time by Josiah Nott, with the endorsement and encouragement of Agassiz. In 1894, long before his work on the head shapes of immigrant children, Boas had delivered an address to the American Association for the Advancement of Science (the organization before which Agassiz had once announced his conversion to polygenism), in which he dismissed as utterly unreliable virtually all nineteenth-century research on racial difference. That research had been undertaken, Boas pointed out, as though colonialism and racial oppression had never happened. It was absurd to attribute the absence of a developed civilization to racial inferiority when no possibility of developing a civilization had been permitted to exist: "The rapid dissemination of Europeans over the whole world cut short all promising beginnings," Boas said. "[N]o race except that of eastern Asia was given a chance to develop a civilization." He specifically ridiculed the scientific pretensions of Nott and Gliddon, writers whose "generalizations," he said, ". . . either do not sufficiently take into account the social conditions of race, and thus confound cause and effect, or were dictated by scientific or humanitarian bias or by the desire to justify the institution of slavery."[17] The talk was incorporated almost without change into Boas's most influential book, *The Mind of Primitive Man*, published in 1911, the year his final report on the descendants of immigrants appeared. Boas's heads undid the work of Morton's skulls.

They did not end the hysteria over immigration, though. The Dillingham Commission issued a forty-two-volume report that, in spite of Boas's contribution, concluded that immigration must be restricted, and although the outbreak of war in Europe in 1914 cut the flow of immigrants to the United States, the war years were the years of possibly the most intense racial xenophobia in American history. D. W. Griffith's *The Birth of a Nation*, released on January 1, 1915, was an immediate box-office sensation. President Wilson saw it at a special White House screening and is supposed to have supplied a blurb—"It is history written by lightning,"[18] he said—and the movie was shown to the members of the United States Supreme Court as well. The chief justice, Edward Douglass White, who did not think much of movies, was persuaded to see it after being told it was about the Ku Klux Klan: it turned out that White had been a member of the Klan in Louisiana after the Civil War. Jane Addams attended a screening in New York City and called for the movie to be banned.[19] Griffith did change some scenes in response to her criticisms, but his movie was almost as popular in the North as it was in the South, and it is very likely that one of the reasons was that many Northerners read into a story about the unassimilability of black people an analogue to their belief in the unassimilability of European immigrants.

The Birth of a Nation also inspired a revival, by William J. Simmons of Georgia, of the Ku Klux Klan, which added anti-Catholicism, anti-Semitism, and nativism to its principles. In the same year, 1915, a new English abridgment of Arthur Gobineau's *The Inequality of the Human Races*, a work translated fifty-nine years earlier by Josiah Nott, was published. By 1915 thirteen states had laws permitting the involuntary sterilization of persons judged defective. (The first, Indiana's, had been passed in 1907.) In 1916 the summa of American anti-immigrant works was published, Madison Grant's *The Passing of the Great Race*—by which Grant meant the Nordic race, which he called "the white man par excellence."[20] And in 1918, the last year of the war, a little book called *New York: A Symphonic Study* appeared. It called for the creation of a new political party of "Hereditary Americans" whose platform would include immigration restriction, mandatory domestic labor for unmarried immigrant women, and a complete ban on the admission of Asians—

> the sole and all-sufficient and imperative reason being their attitude toward and treatment of their womankind as an inferior caste, and their unblushing polygamy, profligacy, and sodomy. . . . Better our lands lie fallow, better our mines go unworked, than expose ourselves to the contamination of pagans settling among us and disseminating the loathsome practices which have reduced themselves to the moral lepers and intellectual echoes and effetes that they so often are. Besides, what with Hawaiian, Philippine, and Negro licentiousness, have we not already more paganism growing up with our Christian ideals and institutions than we are eliminating?[21]

The author was Melusina Fay Peirce, the feminist and former wife of Charles Peirce.

This was the context in which two listeners at James's Oxford lectures, seven years earlier, undertook to articulate the concept of cultural pluralism.[22]

3

Both were Americans. Horace Kallen and Alain Locke had met at Harvard, where Kallen was a graduate teaching assistant in a course on Greek philosophy taught by George Santayana. Locke was a student in the class, and he and Kallen became friends. In 1907 Kallen received a Sheldon traveling fellowship to study at Oxford; Locke graduated in the same year and also went to Oxford, as a Rhodes Scholar—which is how both of them happened to be in the audience for James's lectures in 1908.

Though philosophy was his field, Locke had never taken a class with James. Kallen had; he considered himself, in fact, James's disciple and philosophical heir. Kallen was born in Silesia, then part of Germany, and had come to the United States in 1887, when he was five. His family were Orthodox Jews—his father was a Boston rabbi—but by the time he entered Harvard, Kallen had lost his reli-

gion. He did not wish to be identified as a Jew; he wished to be identified as an American.[23]

His mind was changed by a Harvard English professor named
Barrett Wendell. Wendell had been a student of James's back when
James was teaching physiology and anatomy, and they had a close
friendship based on the pleasure they took in being considered flamboyant by their colleagues. (As a student, Wendell had especially
admired James's attire: James was known in Cambridge for his European style of dress, more casually elegant than the usual academic
outfits.)[24] Wendell did not share James's taste for human variety,
though; he was a socially conservative Brahmin and a strict nativist.
He had an interest in the Old Testament influence on the Puritans—
he was a biographer of Cotton Mather, and had a theory that the Puritans had Hebrew blood—and he persuaded Kallen that being a Jew
was consistent with being an American, or, at least, with being a
Yankee. Kallen found this suggestion extremely appealing, and he
revised his assimilationist plans accordingly. In 1903 he became a
Zionist, and in 1906, as a graduate student, he helped to found the
Harvard Menorah Society, an organization intended to encourage
Jewish students to take pride in their religious and cultural heritage—to learn how to base their Americanness on their Jewishness.
When Alain Locke turned up in his class, Kallen believed he had
found another candidate for conversion to his theory of dual identity.

Locke's situation was not exactly parallel to Kallen's. Locke's situation was not exactly parallel to anyone's.[25] He had heart trouble and
an unusually slight physique (he was five feet tall and weighed
ninety-nine pounds); he was homosexual; and he was black. He had
come to Harvard from Philadelphia, where his parents were schoolteachers, and where he had been a brilliant student in mostly white
schools. His undergraduate career at Harvard was similarly distinguished. But he maintained—Kallen was correct—a complicated relation to the matter of identity. He was born on September 13, 1885,
but always gave his birthday as September 13, 1886; his parents
named him Arthur, but he changed it to Alain LeRoy; and he was
careful not to associate too much with other black students at Harvard, not because he aspired to acceptance by white people, but be-

cause he was a follower of George Santayana and a philosophical aesthete. He regarded his life as an experiment in blocking out physical accidents like race. He was the first African-American to win a Rhodes Scholarship, and the fact received considerable attention, but it was not how he wished to be known. "I am not a race problem," he wrote to his mother after winning the Rhodes. "I am Alain LeRoy Locke."[26]

When Locke arrived at Oxford, his race did become a problem. Five Oxford colleges denied him admission, and the Southern Rhodes Scholars in his class, who had formally appealed to the Rhodes trustees to overturn Locke's award before they left the United States, shunned him and made his presence an issue with other Americans there. Locke found himself the personal focus of racial politics; he was taken up by nonwhite colonial students from India, Egypt, and Ceylon—many of them members of a group that called itself the Oxford Cosmopolitan Club. By the time James arrived to give the Hibbert Lectures at the end of the academic year, Locke had a much richer appreciation of the social salience of race. The whole experience was traumatic. Locke left Oxford without taking a degree—he felt himself, for the first time in his life, an academic failure—and he spent the next two years studying Kant at the University of Berlin and traveling in Eastern Europe. He returned to the United States in 1911 and (with the help of Booker T. Washington) secured a teaching position at Howard University; by then he had abandoned the notion that racial difference was a fact of life one could ignore.

Many years later, after Locke's death, Kallen claimed that the phrase "cultural pluralism" was first formulated in conversations between him and Locke during Locke's senior year at Harvard.[27] The history seems a little more complicated.[28] Kallen was outraged by the treatment Locke was subjected to at Oxford, and he made a public point of showing solidarity with him: Locke was not invited to the traditional Thanksgiving Day dinner at the American Club at Oxford, so Kallen refused to attend. What got Kallen particularly upset, however, was the insult to Harvard. He sent a letter about the situation to Barrett Wendell, asking him to intervene with the Americans he knew at Oxford. "As you know," Kallen said of Locke in his letter, "I have neither respect nor liking for his race—but individually they have to be taken, each on his own merits and value, and if ever a negro was worthy, this boy is."[29]

Wendell wrote back that he was unable to enter completely into Kallen's view of the matter. He had always refused, he said, to meet black people at table, even Booker T. Washington, whom he otherwise respected, and he agreed with the Southerners that the award to Locke was inappropriate. He advised Kallen to let the business about the Thanksgiving dinner drop, and to invite Locke to tea to meet some of Kallen's Oxford acquaintances, if that would soothe his feelings. Kallen was quick to respond. He had taken the advice, he wrote back to Wendell; he had had Locke to tea, and was planning to do so again—"tho' it is personally repugnant to me to eat with him. . . . [B]ut then, Locke is a Harvard man and as such he has a definite claim on me."[30] It is possible that Kallen was playing to prejudices he knew his old teacher to have; but it is difficult to see how he could have come to an agreement on a theory of tolerance based on ethnicity—which is what the theory of cultural pluralism essentially is—with someone for whose ethnicity he had no respect. For his part, Locke never seems to have credited his own version of pluralism to any conversations he had had as a college student. The influences he named were the British colonials he had met at the Oxford Cosmopolitan Club and his subsequent travels through Europe—all postgraduate experiences.[31]

Whatever the degree of reciprocity in their thinking, Kallen and Locke articulated their ideas of pluralism at virtually the same moment. Kallen's appeared in an essay called "Democracy Versus the Melting-Pot," which he first delivered as a talk to the American Philosophical Association in December 1914 and then published in the *Nation* the following February. By then Kallen was teaching at the University of Wisconsin, which happened to be the home institution of Edward Ross, and his article was explicitly a response to Ross's *The Old World in the New*, a volume of his anti-immigration pieces published in 1914. Kallen began by taking issue with an unnamed "eminent lawyer" who had referred to the Declaration of Independence as a collection of "glittering generalities." The remark was unfair, Kallen said; the Declaration was an instrument of its time, and its assertion of natural rights was the appropriate response to the rival assertion of the divine right of kings. Still, times had changed, and the Declaration needed to be rewritten. "To conserve the inalienable rights of the colonists in 1776," Kallen explained, "it was necessary to declare all men equal; to conserve the inalienable rights of their descendants in 1914, it becomes necessary to declare all men unequal."[32] This was not merely a dramatic opening move (though it was dramatic enough); it was the essential first step in the version of pluralism Kallen went on to formulate.

The key to Kallen's thinking was his belief—inspired by his recovery of his own Jewishness—that fulfillment in life is a function of cultural identity, that cultural identity is a function of ethnicity (which he also called "race" or "nationality"), and that ethnicity is immutable. "Men may change their clothes, their politics, their wives, their religions, their philosophies, to a greater or lesser extent," he wrote in a passage that became famous; "they cannot change their grandfathers."[33] Or as he put it elsewhere a few years later: "an Irishman is always an Irishman, a Jew always a Jew. . . . Irishman and Jew are facts in nature; citizen and church-member artefacts in civilization."[34] Racial ancestry is the one unalterable constituent of selfhood, and the happiness people pursue in their lives "has its form implied in ancestral endowment."[35] Your hopes and fears are in your genes.

Kallen's view was not, in short, Boasian. Its scientific assumptions were the scientific assumptions of the anti-immigrationists, the Wendells and the Rosses. Kallen shared their belief that race is a determining element of character; he implicitly shared their fear of interbreeding, though he thought interbreeding was not a danger because (he argued) people prefer their own kind, and ethnic types appear to be permanent. What he wished was simply to acknowledge ethnic difference as a fact of twentieth-century American life, and to recognize it as a virtue. He thought that becoming an American should be understood not as a melting down of difference, but as a result of the assertion of difference. "Democracy means self-realization through self-control, through self-government," he wrote (echoing Dewey), "and . . . the one is impossible without the other."[36]

"Democracy Versus the Melting-Pot" does not descend frequently to particulars. Kallen offered the essay primarily as a vision, not a blueprint, and he issued two warnings about the alternatives. The first had to do with the consequences of allowing assimilationist tendencies to take their natural course. The children of immigrants who lose their parents' culture, Kallen explained, replace it not with a genuine Anglo-Saxon culture, but with a manufactured culture purveyed for a deracinated audience—the culture of motion pictures, baseball, and the "yellow press."[37] The preservation and protection of national cultural traditions was therefore a bulwark against the debilitating effects of mass culture. The other warning was a reference to the war in Europe: Germany and Russia, continually trying to absorb the nations of Central Europe, showed the violent consequences of cultural imperialism, an impulse that had led the whole continent to war. The proper system, Kallen said, borrowing James's figure, was "that of a Federated republic, its substance a democracy of nationalities, cooperating voluntarily and autonomously in the enterprise of self-realisation through the perfection of men according to their kind." Thus

> "American civilization" may come to mean the perfection of "European civilization," the waste, the squalor, and the distress of Europe being eliminated—a multiplicity in a unity, an orchestration of mankind. As in an orchestra, every type of instrument has its specific tonality, founded in its substance and form; as every type has its appropriate theme and melody in the whole symphony, so in society each ethnic group is the natural instrument, its spirit and culture are its theme and melody, and the harmony and dissonances and discords of them all make the symphony of civilization, with this difference: a musical symphony is written before it is played; in the symphony of civilization the playing is the writing.[38]

Why does this kind of society—a society imagined on the orchestra metaphor—require a revision of the Declaration of Independence? If Kallen was proposing that all ethnic traditions be treated equally, why did he begin his essay by arguing for the principle that all men are unequal? Because he did not think of pluralism as a means to facilitate social mobility; he thought of it as a means to eliminate the lure of social mobility. The great evil of popular culture, he believed, was that it encouraged workers to aspire to the lifestyle of the rich. But immigration meant that the United States was becoming more stratified, not less, since each immigrant group naturally gravitated to the social and economic position appropriate to it. Dissatisfaction with that position, fed by the movies and the commercial press, was a threat to personal fulfillment and the civic order. Kallen wanted each ethnic group to keep its proper place; he only wanted it to be honored for doing so—for adhering to the idea of "the perfection of men according to their kind." Kallen's pluralism was a formula for a kind of noninvidious segregation.

The ethnic groups in Kallen's pluralist vision were all European. He did not address the situation of African-Americans in his essay, and it is just as well, since a theory that celebrates socioeconomic stratification does not hold an obvious appeal for the group already consigned to the bottom rung. For an African-American, the notion of dual identity had a rather different significance than it did for an American Zionist like Kallen, and the significance was summed up in a term introduced by another student of William James's—the term "double-consciousness." Its author, W. E. Burghardt Du Bois, entered Harvard in 1888 as a junior (he already had a B.A. from Fisk University in Nashville), and James became his favorite teacher— "my friend and guide to clear thinking,"[39] he later described him. Though generally supportive, James advised Du Bois not to pursue a career in philosophy. So Du Bois pursued a career in history instead, and in 1895, following two years of study in Germany, he became the first black person to receive a Harvard Ph.D., with a dissertation published in 1896 as *The Suppression of the African Slave-Trade to the United States of America, 1638–1870*. (The Harvard Glee Club, however, had refused to admit him.)

Unlike Locke, Du Bois was engaged with the issue of race from the start. At his high school graduation in the predominately white town of Great Barrington, in western Massachusetts, he delivered an

oration on Wendell Phillips; at his Harvard commencement, he delivered an oration on Jefferson Davis. Du Bois was political, but he
was also an intellectual; he found the concept of race exceedingly
slippery, and he spent much of his life working through its difficulties. In 1895 Booker T. Washington delivered the address, at the Cotton States Exposition, in Atlanta, in which he endorsed social
segregation as a basis for racial cooperation. "In all things that are
purely social we can be as separate as the fingers, yet one as the
hand in all things essential to progress,"[40] was the metaphor he used.
Du Bois, then teaching at Wilberforce University, in Ohio, wrote
Washington a congratulatory note on the speech: "a word fitly spoken,"[41] he called it. Two years later, Du Bois gave a talk to the American Negro Academy, a scholarly organization he had helped to
found, called "The Conservation of Races," in which he, too, argued
that each race has its own traditions and "spirit," and is destined to
make its peculiar contribution to civilization. It was a vision not too
distant from the one Kallen would announce eighteen years later. In
the same year, though, Du Bois published an article in the *Atlantic
Monthly*, "Strivings of the Negro People," in which he used the term
"double-consciousness," and the article reappeared six years later as
part of the first chapter of Du Bois's most famous book, his study of
the situation of black Americans at the turn of the century, *The Souls
of Black Folk*.

Du Bois thought that African-Americans were torn by what he
called "two warring ideals," an apparently unrealizable desire to be
black and American at the same time. But "double-consciousness"
does not refer to this tension between identities. It refers to a lack of
identity. "[T]he Negro is a sort of seventh son," Du Bois wrote,

> born with a veil, and gifted with second-sight in this American
> world,—a world which yields him no true self-consciousness, but
> only lets him see himself through the revelation of the other world.
> It is a peculiar sensation, this double-consciousness, this sense of al-
> ways looking at one's self through the eyes of others, of measuring
> one's soul by the tape of a world that looks on in amused contempt
> and pity.[42]

It is the key insight of the book—that self-conception is a function of how others see you. Identity is not biological and static; it is social and relational.

Du Bois prefixed each chapter in *The Souls of Black Folk* with two epigraphs—in most cases, lines from a poem about freedom by a white American or European followed by several measures, in musical notation, of a Negro spiritual, what Du Bois called a "sorrow song." The intention seems to be to reveal a commonality in the two cultural traditions, one literary and Euro-American, the other oral and African-American. But the juxtaposition suggests something else as well, which is that the white-American sentiment of liberty would not be the same without the black-American sentiment of oppression to set beside it. By the time he came to write *The Souls of Black Folk*, Du Bois understood group identity not as something essentially fixed, as Washington saw it and as Kallen would see it, but as something essentially plastic, as Boas and Bentley would see it. And (as Bentley would argue in *The Process of Government*) if groups define themselves by their difference from other groups, a change in the status of one group affects every group that defines itself in relation to it. To the degree that black identity becomes more like white identity, in other words, it is not only blackness that changes. Whiteness changes as well. *The Souls of Black Folk* was in part a book about the stake white Americans had in racial division.

Did this mean that black Americans were stuck with an identity defined for them by other groups? This was the problem Alain Locke addressed in a series of lectures he delivered at Howard University in the spring of 1915, shortly after Kallen's article appeared in the *Nation*. Locke had hoped to offer a course on the subject, but the white ministers who ran Howard opposed him. Howard was a school to educate black professionals; they did not want it associated with controversial subjects like race. But Locke was able, with help from the Howard chapter of the National Association for the Advancement of Colored People, to give his course in the form of a series of public lectures called "Race Contacts and Interracial Relations."

Locke knew Boas's work well, and he began by asserting Boas's distinction between racial difference and racial inequality. The first is

biological, the second is social; but they are constantly being confused. As Boas had said back in 1894, it is illogical to prevent a group
from developing a civilization and then to attribute its failure to develop a civilization to biological inferiority; but that is what Europeans had done. They had created a history of racial invidiousness
and then they had called it natural. And whether they choose it or
not (and Locke had once tried not to), individuals are the bearers of
that history. "Really, when the modern man talks about race," Locke
said, "he is not talking about the anthropological or biological idea at
all. He is really talking about the historical record of success or failure of an ethnic group. . . . [T]hese groups, from the point of view of
anthropology, are ethnic fictions."[43]

They are fictions whose effects are real enough, however. Locke
had learned that lesson at Oxford. What he now proposed was a way
to make the fiction useful for minority ethnic groups. He did not
think those groups could improve their situation by maintaining
separateness, as Washington had advised in the case of African-
Americans and as Kallen had advised in the case of European
immigrants. For—and this was Locke's special insight—modern civilization does not tolerate separateness. "Modern systems are systems
that require or seem to require social assimilation," he said. People
may eat their own ethnic food, but in the things that matter, they are
obliged to adhere to the dominant standard. Modern societies

> are not necessarily so arbitrary about their social culture as . . . ear-
> lier societies were, but they are at least arbitrary to this extent: that
> in the interests of what they call a common standard of living, com-
> mon institutions, and a common heritage, they exact that a man who
> elects . . . to live in a modern society must adopt, more or less
> wholesale, the fundamental or cardinal principles of that social
> culture.

This is the real meaning of the melting pot, he argued: "America,
. . . for all its boasted absorption of types, absorbs them only to re-
make them or re-cast them into a national mold. . . . [T]o enjoy the
privileges of such a society means to conform to that type."[44] The

price of cultural separatism is social subordination. Locke had given Kallen's pluralist vision the equivalent of a cold shower.

Yet as Du Bois had suggested, the fiction of "the Anglo-Saxon," as the name for an ethnic type that defined itself against other types, had proved crucial to the self-conception of white Americans. For people do identify themselves with ethnic or national groups, and many accomplishments are stimulated by group pride. Civilizations are among them: they are created and defended as group projects—whether there is any biological content in the distinction or not. As Locke put it: "that the group needs to consider itself an ethnic unit is very different from the view that the group *is* an ethnic unit."[45]

So that if it is a mistake to cling to ethnic identity, it is also a mistake to abandon it. The trick is to use it in order to overcome it. "The group needs . . . to get a right conception of itself," Locke said,

> and it can only do that through the stimulation of pride in itself. Pride in itself is race pride, and race pride seems a rather different loyalty from the larger loyalty to the joint or common civilization type. Yet . . . through a doctrine of racial solidarity and culture, you really accelerate and stimulate the alien group to rather more rapid assimilation of the . . . general social culture, than would otherwise be possible.[46]

Although racial identity has no basis in biology, in other words, and although racial pride is, in itself, socially divisive, the only way to overcome social divisiveness is to stimulate racial pride—to encourage minority ethnic groups to take satisfaction in their particular practices and achievements. The desire to be accepted as like everyone else—the desire to meet the "common standard"—flows from the desire to be recognized as different from everyone else. You want to prove that your group is as good as every other group. The elegance of Locke's formulation is that neither human sameness nor human difference is treated as real and essential. They are defined functionally. Universality and diversity are both effects of social practice. They are not given in nature; they are outcomes of what people do. Locke did not publish his lectures, but the argument he worked out in them led him, ten years later, to edit and introduce *The New Negro*, the most important anthology of the literary and artistic movement known as the Harlem Renaissance.

Scientifically and philosophically Locke's pluralism is plainly distinct from Kallen's, but the crucial difference lies in his attitude toward modernity. Modernity is the condition a society reaches when life is no longer conceived as cyclical. In a premodern society, where the purpose of life is understood to be the reproduction of the customs and practices of the group, and where people are expected to follow the life path their parents followed, the ends of life are given at the beginning of life. People know what their life's task is, and they know when it has been completed. In modern societies, the reproduction of custom is no longer understood to be one of the chief purposes of existence, and the ends of life are not thought to be given; they are thought to be discovered or created. Individuals are not expected to follow the life path of their parents, and the future of the society is not thought to be dictated entirely by its past. Modern societies do not simply repeat and extend themselves; they change in unforeseeable directions, and the individual's contribution to these changes is unspecifiable in advance. To devote oneself to the business of preserving and reproducing the culture of one's group is to risk one of the most terrible fates in modern societies, obsolescence. It was not a question, for Locke, of approving or disapproving of modernity. It was a question of coping with it.

4

By 1915, when his *Nation* article appeared, Kallen had become a figure in pragmatist circles. James had died in 1910, of the heart condition he had been suffering from, sometimes agonizingly, since 1899. He had asked Kallen to prepare for publication material he had been hoping to turn into a book on metaphysics; this was published, in 1911, as *Some Problems in Philosophy*. Kallen then began assembling what would become one of the most important pragmatist anthologies of the period, *Creative Intelligence*, published in 1917—the volume in which Dewey published his essay on "The Need for a

Recovery of Philosophy." So that when Dewey read "Democracy Versus the Melting-Pot" in the *Nation*, he and Kallen were already in correspondence.

Dewey wrote Kallen to say he had been interested in his article, but had a few reservations. "Chiefly I am inclined to ask whether you do underestimate the reminiscent and literary quality of these culture revivals," he explained. He was partly English and partly Flemish himself, he said, but had never had much interest in his ethnic background. "I want to see this country American and that means the english tradition reduced to a strain along with others," he told Kallen.

> I quite agree with your orchestra idea, but upon condition we really get a symphony and not a lot of different instruments playing simultaneously. I never did care for the melting pot metaphor, but genuine assimilation *to one another*—not to Anglo-Saxondom—seems to be essential to an America. That each cultural section should maintain its distinctive literary and artistic traditions seems to me most desirable, but in order that it might have the more to contribute to others. I am not sure you mean more than this, but there seems to be an implication of segregation geographical and otherwise. That we should recognize the segregation that undoubtedly exists is requisite, but in order that it may not be fastened upon us.[47]

When Dewey came to comment on ethnic identity himself, in an essay published in 1916, he underscored the criticism by borrowing Kallen's metaphor and bending it to his own assimilationist point. "Neither Englandism nor New-Englandism, neither Puritan nor Cavalier any more than Teuton or Slav, can do anything but furnish one note in a vast symphony," he wrote.

> The way to deal with hyphenism [German-American, Jewish-American, and so on] . . . is to welcome it, but to welcome it in the sense of extracting from each people its special good, so that it shall surrender into a common fund of wisdom and experience what it especially has to contribute. All of these surrenders and contributions taken together create the national spirit of America. The dangerous

thing is for each factor to isolate itself, to try to live off its past, and then to attempt to impose itself upon other elements, or, at least, to keep itself intact and thus refuse to accept what other cultures have to offer, so as thereby to be transmuted into authentic Americanism.[48]

Locke was an Americanist and a modernist by necessity: he felt that those were conditions African-Americans had no choice but to accept. Dewey was an Americanist and a modernist by desire. To Dewey, Americanism meant democracy, and modernity meant a life in which possibilities are unforeclosed. It is therefore appropriate that the most militantly modernist version of pluralism should have come from one of Dewey's own renegade disciples.

This was Randolph Bourne. Bourne was from New Jersey. His family was Presbyterian and not undistinguished—his great-grandfather had been an abolitionist and an acquaintance of Emerson's—but business failures had reduced its circumstances, and though Bourne was a precocious student, he could not afford to attend college until he was twenty-three, when, in 1909, he entered Columbia on a full academic scholarship. Bourne was—he wrote an essay about it—severely disabled. A forceps delivery had badly mangled his features at birth, and when he was four, he had come down with tuberculosis of the spine, the disease that had stricken Jane Addams. In Bourne's case the effects were more serious: his growth was stunted and he developed a hunchback. He was always self-conscious about his condition: he thought his appearance made people underestimate his capacities, and he compensated for it with a brilliance that could be exceptionally caustic. "[M]y fate," he wrote to a friend while he was still in college, "seems to lie in poking holes in what other people are saying."[49]

Bourne was introduced to the writings of William James in a philosophy class taught by Frederick Woodbridge. He was, as he put it, "hypnotized."[50] "James' books," he explained to a friend in 1913, are "the most inspiring modern outlook on life and reality."[51] He became a student of Dewey's, and contracted what he called "the virus of the Bergson-James-Schiller-instrumental-pragmatism."[52] He was also an admirer of Boas's *The Mind of Primitive Man*, which he reviewed in the *Columbia Monthly*; he knew the work in social psychology of J. McKeen Cattell and E. L. Thorndike; and he developed a socialist politics in part through his classes with the historian Charles Beard. The effect of all this education, enhanced by a year spent traveling through Europe after graduation, was distinctive: it turned Bourne into a new sort of American radical, a cultural radical.[53] He believed that American society must be transformed, and that the site of that transformation must be the culture. And he thought pragmatism supplied the method. Dewey's "philosophy of 'instrumentalism,'" he wrote in the *New Republic* in 1915, "has an edge on it that would slash up the habits of thought, the customs and institutions in which our society has been living for centuries."[54] It is not a claim Dewey or James would ever have made, but it was how Bourne interpreted their legacy. He had contempt for what he called "the blind recalcitrancy of progressives and feminists of the Jane Addams type."[55] He was not a reformer. He wanted a movement.

He thought he found one in the ethnic transformation of American society by immigration. Bourne knew Kallen personally, and found his *Nation* essay extremely stimulating. He had already discussed the issue of assimilation with his Columbia friends, and one of them—probably Alexander Sachs, a graduate student of Dewey's who later became an economic adviser to Franklin Roosevelt—suggested "trans-nationalism" as a description of a pluralist America. Bourne adopted the term for the title of what would become his best-known essay, "Trans-National America." It was published in the *Atlantic Monthly* in July 1916.

Bourne's essay is a kind of synthesis of pluralist ideas. Bourne evoked Boas's conception of racial plasticity: "Let us speak, not of inferior races, but of inferior civilizations. . . . It is not what we are now that concerns us, but what this plastic next generation may become in the light of a new cosmopolitan ideal." He repeated Dewey's critique of liberal individualism:

> If freedom means the right to do pretty much as one pleases . . . the immigrant has found freedom, and the ruling element has been singularly liberal in its treatment of the invading hordes. But if freedom

means democratic cooperation in determining the ideals and purposes and industrial and social institutions of a country, then the immigrant has not been free, and the Anglo-Saxon element is guilty of
just what every dominant race is guilty of in every European country:
the imposition of its own culture upon the minority peoples.

He echoed Kallen's warning about the effects of mass culture:

Already we have far too much of this insipidity—masses of people
who are cultural half-breeds, neither assimilated Anglo-Saxons nor
nationals of another culture. . . . [L]etting slip whatever native culture they had, they have substituted for it only the most rudimentary
American—the American culture of the cheap newspaper, the
"movies," popular song, the ubiquitous automobile.

He adopted James's figure of the federation: "there is no distinctively
American culture. It is apparently our lot rather to be a federation of
cultures." He embraced the concept of dual identity: "dual citizen-
ship seems to us profound and right. For it recognizes that, although
the Frenchman may accept the formal institutional framework of his
new country and indeed become intensely loyal to it, yet his Frenchness he will never lose."[56]

Most importantly, though—and like Locke, but in a different
spirit—he praised cultural identity in order to transcend it. Bourne's
ideal was not Americanism; it was an international cosmopolitanism
which America might lead by example. He aspired not to preserve
cultural traditions, but to create new cultural possibilities. He was a
true modernist.

His fear, therefore, was that official recognition of the integrity
and autonomy of ethnic subcultures would lead to the persistence in
the United States of customs and folkways that were already disap-
pearing in Europe. The last thing he wanted was to preserve the premodern culture of the peasant village or the *shtetl*. His image of
cosmopolitanism was an enlightened ethnicity, a kind of postethnic
ethnic identification. Specifically, it was Zionism. He made the point
explicit three months after "Trans-National America" appeared, in an
address to the Harvard Menorah Society, the group Kallen had

helped to found. Trans-nationalism, Bourne told the members, "is a Jewish idea."[57] The accommodation that diaspora Jews had had to make to the dominant culture was the model for the accommodation every ethnic group must make. Zionism was the ideal because "a genuine trans-nationalism would be modern," and "[t]he Zionist's outlook is intensely modern. . . . The Jew in America is proving every day the possibility of this dual life."[58]

Dewey's reaction to his student's version of the pluralist idea is unknown, because in 1917, they broke over the issue of American entry into the war in Europe. The war split American intellectuals. Dewey supported intervention, and he was not equivocal about his position. "I have been a thorough and complete sympathizer with the part played by this country in this war and I have wished to see the resources of this country used for its successful prosecution,"[59] he declared in 1917, in an address printed in the *New York Post*. He dismissed as squeamish objections to the use of force, and he argued that the military means were justified by the likely outcome, which was the chance for the United States to take a formative role in the establishment of democracy in Europe. He echoed, in short, the position of the Wilson administration, and this put him at odds not only with his friend Jane Addams, who announced herself to be a pacifist, but with Bourne as well.

In 1917, in the *Seven Arts*, Bourne published an essay called "Twilight of Idols," in which he denounced pragmatism, and Deweyan instrumentalism in particular, for being "against concern for the quality of life as above machinery of life." Pragmatism provided no stable criteria for how values are to be judged, Bourne now complained. Dewey "always meant his philosophy, when taken as a philosophy of life, to start with values. But there was always that unhappy ambiguity in his doctrine as to just how values were created, and it became easier and easier to assume that just any growth was justified and almost any activity valuable so long as it achieved ends." This had led to an inability to see that "war always undermines values." "A philosophy of adjustment," Bourne concluded, "will not even make for adjustment."[60] It was not a criticism; it was a renunciation.

Dewey could not have taken kindly to Bourne's defection or to the tone of his attack. Bourne had written his master's thesis under Dewey; he had championed Dewey's philosophy in many magazines; he had been a close friend of the family. He had carried on a mildly flirtatious correspondence with Dewey's daughter Evelyn (they were about the same age) when the Deweys were traveling in Europe in 1913. But the final rupture came about in a bizarre way. In 1918, Bourne reviewed a book called *Man's Supreme Inheritance*, by a man named F. Matthias Alexander, for the *New Republic*. Alexander was a theorist of posture: he believed that evolution had led to a disjunction between the mind and the body, which had produced all sorts of muscular infirmities, such as backaches; and he advanced a system of exercise designed to put the mind in touch with bodily processes. Dewey was prone to backaches of just the sort Alexander proposed to cure, and he contributed an introduction to the book. In his rather supercilious review, Bourne took the occasion to criticize Alexander's theory as another instance of instrumentalism run amok.

Dewey was, uncharacteristically, incensed. The *New Republic* was, in effect, his magazine; he was one of its star contributors. He wrote Bourne a long letter accusing him of deliberately misreading Alexander's book, and then he published a reply to Bourne's review in the magazine. Bourne published a reply to Dewey's reply, but Dewey was not appeased. When he was invited soon after to become a member of the editorial board of the *Dial*, he made his acceptance conditional on Bourne's removal from the board. The editors complied.

The *Dial* had been one of the last places left in which Bourne could get published. The *Atlantic Monthly* had printed "Trans-National America" despite the fact that its editor, the Boston Brahmin Ellery Sedgwick, found its argument an objectionable attack on Anglo-Americans (and said so to Bourne); Bourne's criticisms of American war policy had made him an undesirable at the *New Republic*, a magazine closely identified with the Wilson administration; the *Seven Arts* folded because its patron, Annette Rankin, could not tolerate its antiwar articles, among which Bourne's were notable. "The magazines I write for die violent deaths, and all my thoughts seem unprintable,"[61] Bourne wrote to a friend in November 1917.

Thirteen months later he was dead, a victim of an influenza epidemic introduced into New York City by American troops returning from victory in Europe.

Dewey never referred publicly to Bourne or his criticisms again, but after seeing Wilson's vision for a democratic Europe dissolve in the Treaty of Versailles, he became a pacifist, too. His momentary advocacy of violent means during the First World War is a peculiar episode in his career, but his reaction to the Alexander review is even more peculiar. For it is hard to understand how Dewey could not see that a book advocating the conquest of physical infirmity by the training and exercise of the mind was not a book that could be expected to appeal to Randolph Bourne.

5

The term "cultural pluralism" did not appear in print until 1924, when Kallen introduced it in his book *Culture and Democracy in the United States*—a work dedicated to the memory of Barrett Wendell.[62] Three years earlier, the United States had established a quota system designed specifically to restrict immigration from Southern and Eastern Europe. That proved unsatisfactory to the people who had supported it, and in 1924, the year of Kallen's book, an even more restrictive immigration law went into effect. The phenomenon that had inspired Kallen and Bourne to create their visions of a pluralist society ceased to be a pressing public issue. The phenomenon that had inspired Du Bois and Locke to create theirs still had not become a pressing public issue.

Cultural pluralism was a brave idea at a time when Woodrow Wilson himself was on record as opposed to even the notion of groups. "America does not consist of groups," he announced in 1915, the year Kallen's essay appeared. "A man who thinks of himself as belonging to a particular national group in America has not yet become an American; and the man who goes among you to trade upon your nationality is no worthy son to live under the Stars and Stripes."[63] But cultural pluralism makes a problematic politics, and the reason is that identifying people by culture has the same effect as identifying people by race: it prejudges their possibilities. In Kallen's theory, this tendency is fairly plain, but even in Bourne's and Locke's more dynamic conceptions of pluralism, there is an assumption that people carry their cultures in the same way that they carry their genes ("his Frenchness he will never lose," said Bourne). Only in Dewey's conception does the specter of race completely disappear, and Dewey did not consider himself a cultural pluralist. Like Addams, he insisted that divisions are just temporary alignments within a common whole. And he preferred to stress the whole.

There is also the problem that "culture" names a rather amorphous entity. Human beings produce culture in the same sense that they produce carbon dioxide: they can't help it, but the stuff has absolutely no value in itself. It's just there. It is one thing to attribute a group's characteristics to its culture, as Boas did; it is another thing to elevate that culture into a discrete set of traditions and practices in which the members of the group can take pride simply because they are, willy-nilly, theirs. Culture is only a response to the conditions of life; when those conditions change—and in modern societies they change continuously—cultures change as well. "Frenchness" is as variable as "finchness," and no more worthy of respect as a thing in itself. It's all a question of what people make of it.

And finally, cultural pluralism seems to violate the premise of its philosophical parent concept. The whole purpose of the philosophical term, as Dewey wrote in his entry on "Pluralism" for James Mark Baldwin's *Dictionary of Philosophy and Psychology* in 1902, was to lay the foundations for "the possibility of real change, . . . the possibility of real variety, . . . [and] the possibility of freedom"[64]—all because pluralism considers individual things, and therefore individual human beings, not as partial aspects of greater metaphysical wholes, but as complete in themselves, free to enter into relations as they choose or as life unfolds. Culture is not an individual acquirement; it is the name for a set of products, practices, and perspectives of which individuals can avail themselves. In modern societies, which are the kind of societies Locke and Bourne and Dewey contemplated, culture is a Rubik's Cube of possibilities. Bentley's argument about political interest groups applies to culture as well: every combination produces a new relation among the elements. The only thing prescriptive one can say about culture as a political matter is that the more access individuals have to whatever other human beings have produced, the greater the number of new combinations that are possible. Since there is no way out of the Cube, the most useful thing is to secure a degree of freedom within it.

FIFTEEN

FREEDOMS

I

COERCION IS NATURAL; freedom is artificial. Freedoms are socially engineered spaces where parties engaged in specified pursuits enjoy protection from parties who would otherwise naturally seek to interfere in those pursuits. One person's freedom is therefore always another person's restriction: we would not have even the concept of freedom if the reality of coercion were not already present. We think of a freedom as a right, and therefore the opposite of a rule, but a right *is* a rule. It is a prohibition against sanctions on certain types of behavior. We also think of rights as privileges retained by individuals against the rest of society, but rights are created not for the good of individuals, but for the good of society. Individual freedoms are manufactured to achieve group ends.

This way of thinking about freedoms helps to explain why the two people most closely associated with the establishment of the modern principles of freedoms of thought and expression in the United States were indifferent to the notion of individual rights. John Dewey and Oliver Wendell Holmes had no particular interest in providing a

Eugene Debs in Canton, Ohio, June 16, 1918, delivering the speech for which he was arrested under the Espionage and Sedition Act.

benefit to persons at the expense of the group. Dewey took a benign pleasure and Holmes took a cynical pleasure in the spectacle of personal wishes being subordinated to community will. But they both saw the social usefulness of creating a zone of protection for individual thought and expression, and the freedoms they helped to establish are responsible for much of what is distinctive about American life in the twentieth century and after.

2

Americans owe the establishment of the principle of academic freedom in part to the racism of the man whose work later provided the occasion for Horace Kallen's "Democracy Versus the Melting-Pot," Edward A. Ross.[1] After receiving his Ph.D. in economics from Johns Hopkins in 1891, Ross took a job at Indiana State University and a year later moved to Stanford. The university had been founded by a founder and president of the Central Pacific Railroad and former governor of California, Leland Stanford, and his wife, Jane Lathrop Stanford, in memory of their son, who had died at the age of fifteen during a trip to Europe. (The institution's legal name is still Leland Stanford Junior University.) The Stanfords regarded the university as their personal operation, to such an extent that they declined to accept money from other donors. After Leland Senior died in 1893, his widow became the university's sole trustee. Edward Ross was a free-spirited young man and not shy of controversy, and he seems to have set out to get a rise out of Mrs. Stanford.

On May 7, 1900, after several earlier efforts had fallen short, he succeeded. He delivered a speech to a group of San Francisco labor leaders in which he condemned Asian immigration on eugenicist grounds. Labor unions opposed immigration, of course, because it was a source of cheap labor; railroad owners supported it for the same reason. The Central Pacific had been built with coolie labor, and the Stanfords are supposed to have developed a paternalistic affection for their Asian workers. Ross had already caught the attention of Jane Stanford with earlier political pronouncements; now he roused her to action. "I must confess I am weary of Professor Ross," she wrote to the school's president, David Starr Jordan, on May 9, "and I think he ought not to be retained at Stanford University. . . . I trust that before the close of this semester Professor Ross will have received notice that he will not be re-engaged for the new year."[2] Jordan dragged his feet for six months, but Jane Stanford's irritation did not fade, and in November Ross was forced to resign.

There had been plenty of incidents before the Ross case in which professors had been warned, sanctioned, or fired for giving offense to presidents or trustees. Charles William Eliot had once told Barrett Wendell that too pronounced a display of eccentricity would delay his promotion. Richard Ely had had to submit to a "trial" at the University of Wisconsin in 1894 after making remarks about the right to strike that offended a regent. And in a famous case at the University of Chicago in 1895, shortly after Dewey arrived, William Rainey Harper forced the resignation of a young economics professor named Edward Bemis for speaking out in favor of the Pullman boycott and against monopolies, an awkward subject at a university patronized by John D. Rockefeller. (Bemis ended up superintendent of the water department in Cleveland.)

But Ross was not blindsided by the firing, and he was careful to engineer maximum publicity for his cause. Seven Stanford professors resigned in protest (their places were quickly filled by Harvard Ph.D.s), and the American Economic Association, the group founded by Ross's old dissertation director, Richard Ely, took up the matter. It was the first professorial investigation of an abuse of academic freedom in the United States.[3] Jordan stiff-armed the inquiry, and no remedial action came out of it, but the abridgment of academic freedom had finally been recognized as a systemic problem in higher education. Ross went on first to Nebraska, then to Wisconsin and celebrity; fifteen years later, the American Association of University Professors came into being.

The desire to protect academic freedom was not, as it happened, the chief motivation for the formation of the AAUP. Its principal organizers were John Dewey and the Hopkins philosopher Arthur O. Lovejoy. Lovejoy was no friend of pragmatism. He had received an M.A. from Harvard, in 1897, but he was a philosophical realist, and the author of an article, "The Thirteen Pragmatisms," published in the *Journal of Philosophy* in 1908, frequently cited by critics of James and Dewey. But Lovejoy had been one of the seven professors who had resigned from Stanford in the wake of Ross's dismissal; he had taught at Columbia for a year before going to Hopkins, and he respected Dewey. Along with a number of other prominent academics, including J. McKeen Cattell, the psychologist who had helped bring Dewey and Franz Boas to Columbia, they met in Baltimore in 1913 and began planning their organization.

What Dewey envisioned—as he put it in a letter to Boas soliciting his participation—was "an association representing the interests of American university teachers, comparable to the American Bar or Medical Associations."[4] He did not imagine a trade union. When Dewey invited Barrett Wendell to join, Wendell wrote back to say he didn't much like the idea of a professional guild. Dewey replied that he didn't either; it was not at all what he had in mind. "If I thought an organization could or would lessen the freedom of individual scholars," he told Wendell, "I should be heartily opposed to it. . . . And if I thot there was any danger of an organization attempting to 'run' institutions instead of allowing the constituted authorities to 'run' them, I should be at least suspicious of the organization."[5] As Dewey saw it, the role of the AAUP was to make the case for scholarship to the American public. One of the chief questions he and the other founders debated had to do with the criteria for admission: it was felt that the membership should be restricted to prominent scholars, since they would represent the profession at its finest; and, for the first few years, it was.

In 1915 the AAUP came into formal existence and Dewey was made its first president. In his address at the first meeting, he dismissed the notion that the organization would be required to devote much of its time to investigating violations of academic freedom. At the end of the year, he was obliged to report that he had been too optimistic.[6] Thirty-one academic freedom cases came before the AAUP in its first two years, and they didn't stop coming. It seemed that the right of university teachers to express their views was not as secure as Dewey had imagined. In the end, most membership restrictions were lifted and the AAUP became just what Dewey hoped it would not have to become: a union for professors and the national academic freedom watchdog.

The creation of the AAUP was the capstone event in the process of the professionalization of the university that got under way after the Civil War, and in which Charles William Eliot, Daniel Coit Gilman, and William Rainey Harper played leading roles. And as it turned out, the concept of academic freedom was the key to the whole development. For professions, unlike other types of occupations, are self-regulating. No professional, no doctor or lawyer or architect, wants to have the terms of his or her practice dictated by someone other than his or her peers, people who have the interests of the profession, rather than the interests of some group outside the profession, at heart. Doctors don't want insurance companies to decide what constitutes good medical practice; architects don't want developers to determine who is qualified to practice architecture; lawyers don't want politicians to define legal ethics. (This is one of the reasons education in those fields is confined almost exclusively to professional schools, which get to pick the students they want to initiate.)

American universities became modern when they finally arrived, around the time the AAUP came into existence, at an institutional structure designed to make academic work self-regulating. This meant making the Ph.D. the normal requirement for employment at a university—since people with Ph.D.s have been credentialed by established experts in their fields. It meant requiring publication in peer-reviewed journals for professional advancement—since, again, peer review is a way of maintaining professorial control over the kind of scholarship that gets produced and rewarded. It meant establishing the department as the basic administrative unit of the university—since departments hire, promote, tenure, and fire their own members and set their own curricula.

All these mechanisms are ways of ensuring that only specialists get to judge the work of other specialists, and of insulating the content of academic work from the political, financial, and personal interests of administrators, trustees, legislators, alumni, and amateurs.

Academic freedom is a freedom specifically for academics: it can be enjoyed only by people already admitted to the club. Professions are democratic in the sense that they are open to anyone with talent, but they are guilds in the sense that they protect their members from market forces with which all nonprofessionals have to cope. The tenured professor not only has access to resources—libraries, students, scholarly networks—almost entirely off-limits to the independent scholar; he or she has a lifetime guaranteed income as well. Professionalization is a system of market control.

Academic freedom for a professor is therefore, actually or potentially, a restriction on everyone who is not a professor. But what is the social good? Why should society prefer that Edward Ross, an employee of a private institution, be permitted to say whatever he chooses, but that Jane Stanford, who pays his salary, be prevented from trying to shape the intellectual content of her own university? She (with her husband) had created Stanford; she was free to close it down whenever she liked. But she could not fire Edward Ross.

The AAUP's answer to this question appeared in a document called the "Report on Academic Freedom and Tenure," drawn up by Committee A of the Association—the committee charged with investigating violations of academic freedom—and printed in the first volume of the Association's *Bulletin*, in December 1915. The reason administrators and trustees should have no power to sanction professors for their views, the statement said, was because professors did not work for the trustees. They worked for the public.

> The responsibility of the university teacher is primarily to the public itself, and to the judgment of his own profession; and while, with respect to certain external conditions of his vocation, he accepts a responsibility to the authorities of the institution in which he serves, in the essentials of his professional activity his duty is to the wider public to which the institution itself is morally amenable. . . . University teachers should be understood to be, with respect to the conclusions reached and expressed by them, no more subject to the control of the trustees, than are judges subject to the control of the President, with respect to their decisions.[7]

Whether Dewey wrote these sentences is not known, but they plainly express his own rationale for academic freedom. During Dewey's year as president of the AAUP, the trustees of the University of Pennsylvania refused to renew the contract of the economist Scott Nearing, who was on the faculty of the Wharton School of Finance and Commerce, because of his reformist views. (Despite its name, the University of Pennsylvania was essentially a private institution, but it received some state support, and it was the threat of reduced state funding that provoked the trustees to dismiss Nearing.) The incident got a lot of attention, and the *New York Times* published an editorial, under the headline "The Philadelphia Martyr," maintaining that the trustees had the right to dismiss anyone they saw fit, and no obligation to provide their reasons for doing so.

Dewey's letter to the editor in reply was unusually pointed. "It is doubtless fitting and natural that the *New York Times* should find university professors 'chartered libertines of speech,' given to 'too much foolish babbling,' whenever the results of the investigations of university scholars lead them to question any features of the existing economic order," he began. The *Times* was perfectly entitled, in other words, to express opinions flattering to its constituency. But it misunderstood the nature of academic work. "You apparently take the ground that a modern university is a personally conducted institution like a factory," Dewey explained,

> and that if for any reason the utterances of any teacher, within or without the university walls, are objectionable to the Trustees, there is nothing more to be said. This view virtually makes the Trustees owners of a private undertaking. . . . [But] the modern university is in every respect, save its legal management, a public institution with public responsibilities. [Professors] have been trained to think of the pursuit and expression of truth as a public function to be exercised on behalf of the interests of their moral employer—society as a whole. . . . They ask for no social immunities or privileges for themselves. They will be content, for their own protection, with any system which protects the relation of the modern university to the public as a whole.[8]

The Dartmouth College case is often cited as the foundation for academic freedom in the United States; but the argument the Supreme Court rejected in that case in 1819 is precisely the argument Dewey and the AAUP advanced, almost a century later, as academic freedom's rationale. The Court took Dartmouth College away from a state legislature and returned it to its "owners" on the grounds that it was a private corporation immune from public control. In rescuing private colleges from the politicians, the Court effectively turned them over to the trustees. It did not turn them over to the professors. What Dewey and the AAUP accomplished was therefore a rather remarkable end run around *Dartmouth College*: they created a nongovernmental organization, the AAUP, that claimed to represent the public interest against the university's own benefactors, and they defined that interest as a need for disinterested scholarship. The deal they offered was that in return for exemption from ordinary market conditions, professors would commit themselves to the unselfish and disinterested pursuit of truth. Implicit in the argument they made was that the public—though supposedly the real "owners" of universities—would abstain from interference in university affairs out of its own self-interest. Edward Ross's freedom from Jane Stanford would have been worth nothing, after all, if the voters of California could have fired him instead. And the most remarkable thing about this deal was that American society—with, to be sure, many reservations and regrets along the way—bought it.

3

They did not buy it right away. The Harvard philosophy department, for example, spent several years trying to get permission to fill the position left vacant by the retirement of William James. When the line was finally made available, the department unanimously recommended Lovejoy. He was rejected by A. Lawrence Lowell, Charles Eliot's successor (and former protégé of Benjamin Peirce), because Lovejoy had been involved in the creation of the AAUP. When Josiah Royce died, in 1916, the department proposed Bertrand Russell (who had taught at Harvard as a visitor) as his replacement; Lowell re-

fused because Russell was a pacifist. Two years later, Dewey was proposed; Lowell thought he was too old. (Dewey was fifty-nine; he
would teach for another twelve years and publish for another thirty-
four.)[9] On most campuses, the presidents still ruled.

Of course, university presidents do have a say in faculty appoint-
ments and promotions. A university president is an academic officer,
and exercises power as such. But university presidents, unlike professors, are answerable to trustees and other parties, like legislators
and alumni, whose happiness matters to the health of the institution;
that is their job, and in the 1910s they were still accustomed to exercising peremptory authority over faculty opinion when they saw fit. It
was a combustible arrangement, and it was ignited by the event that
also drove a wedge between intellectuals like Dewey and Randolph
Bourne: the American entry, in April 1917, into the war in Europe.

Anti-German sentiment in the United States had been incited by
the sinking of the *Lusitania* back in 1915, but the commitment of
American troops provoked a display of nationalism peculiar in a conflict in which national borders were never threatened. Of the many
acts of patriotic symbolism inspired by the war, the decision by the
city of Pittsburgh to ban the music of Beethoven was possibly the
most imaginative. Americans who opposed intervention had different
reasons for doing so. In Jane Addams's case, it was simply an opposition to violence. In many other cases, though, it was a fear on the
part of socialists that the United States had a covert reason for sending its army into Europe: to engineer the overthrow of the Bolshevik
regime in Russia. Bourne, for instance, never offered this as a reason
for his disagreement with Dewey on the war; but Bourne was, after
all, some kind of a socialist, and Dewey was not.

In June 1917, two months after the declaration of war, Nicholas
Murray Butler announced at the Columbia University commencement that although opposition to American intervention had been
tolerable when the country was still at peace, he was now imposing a
ban on the expression of disloyal views on campus. "This is the university's last and only warning to any among us, if such there be, who
are not with whole heart and mind and strength committed to fight
with us to make the world safe for democracy," he explained.[10] In Au-

gust, McKeen Cattell sent a petition to three congressmen requesting them to support a bill that would prohibit the use of draftees in
battle. The congressmen complained to Butler, Butler informed the
trustees, and the trustees fired Cattell.

Butler had been eager to rid the university of McKeen Cattell for
many years. Cattell was a person obnoxious even to many of his colleagues, and he was especially obnoxious to Butler, whose autocratic
pretensions he criticized publicly and often. (It is probably not irrelevant that Butler and Cattell had once been members of the same
department.) This latest movement to force Cattell out had really
been precipitated not by his petition to Congress but by his behavior
during a dispute over the much more parochial question of whether
the Columbia Faculty Club should be torn down. But the flouting of
Butler's ban on antiwar expressions put the final dismissal procedures into motion, and Dewey was naturally drawn into the affair.

In Dewey's conception, the principle of academic freedom was
far from absolute. "We may insist that a man needs tact as well as
scholarship," he wrote, about the idea of academic freedom, in 1902,
in the aftermath of the Ross case;

> or, let us say, sympathy with human interests—since "tact" suggests
> perhaps too much a kind of juggling diplomacy with the questions at
> issue. . . . Lack of reverence for the things that mean much to hu-
> manity, joined with a craving for public notoriety, may induce a man
> to pose as a martyr to truth when in reality he is a victim of his own
> lack of mental and moral poise.[11]

Dewey felt that Cattell had behaved less than tactfully—he had
his own unpleasant run-in with Cattell during the affair—and he was
not sorry to see him suffer the consequences of his obstreperous-
ness. But he thought that in writing to the congressmen, Cattell had
"merely exercised the right of every American citizen, to give his
opinion on matters pending before the legislative branch of government,"[12] and that in giving disloyalty as the reason for his removal,
the trustees had acted improperly.

In October, on the heels of the dismissal of Cattell, and, on similar grounds, of a junior professor in the English department named Henry Wadsworth Longfellow Dana, Charles Beard resigned. He had been warned by the trustees against expressing views they considered unpatriotic; he found the warning ridiculous, and he quit. Dewey issued a statement to the press. After the firing of Cattell, he announced, he was not surprised by Beard's action. "To my mind this college is nothing but a factory, and a badly run factory at that," he said. "It is factory tactics that enable a professor to be expelled from a university on the recommendation of men who know nothing about his work and who are not his associates"[13]—and that was what had happened to Cattell. The criticism was blunt but the wording was circumspect. Dewey was not saying that Cattell should not have been dismissed, only that his dismissal was the business of his professional peers, not of the president or the trustees. Academic freedom is a privilege enjoyed at the pleasure of a community; fights over academic freedom are, at bottom, fights over how that community should be defined. It is all a question of who gets to decide.

Two more Columbia professors followed Beard and resigned in protest. Dewey was not one of them. Butler went on to win the Nobel Peace Prize, in 1931, for his work on behalf of disarmament and international peace. He shared the award with Jane Addams.

4

The reason the Columbia trustees were so agitated by the activities of professors like Cattell, Dana, and Beard was not entirely because they were possessed by an exaggerated conception of loyalty. There was a real legal issue at stake. On June 15, 1917, two months after the declaration of war, Congress passed the Espionage Act, which made it a crime to utter false statements calculated to interfere with the success of the armed forces, to foster insubordination among the troops, or to obstruct the draft. A little less than a year later, on May 7, 1918, the act was amended to make it also a crime to speak or publish any views, false or not, disloyal to the United States or intended to interfere with the war effort. The 1918 act, known as the Espionage and Sedition Act, was the trigger for one of the most celebrated opinions in Supreme Court history, Oliver Wendell Holmes's dissent in the case of *Abrams v. United States*. That dissent was also one of the unlikeliest opinions in Supreme Court history. It was not an opinion most people who knew Holmes's views on the law would have been likely to predict.

In 1919, when the Abrams case was decided, Holmes was seventy-eight and had been sitting on the Supreme Court for seventeen years. He had by then become, to his pleasure (for he enjoyed being lionized) but also to his bemusement, a hero to progressives. The reason was not because he shared their political hopes; it was because he shared their philosophy of judicial restraint. In the view of progressives, the part played by the courts in the movement for social and economic reform since the 1890s had been principally the negative one of declaring laws regulating business to be in violation of the Fourteenth Amendment's prohibition against depriving citizens of "life, liberty, or property, without due process of law." The Fourteenth Amendment was one of the Civil War amendments; it had been intended to protect black citizens after emancipation. But in 1873, in the *Slaughter-House Cases*, the Supreme Court had ruled that the amendment was not binding on state governments, thus laying the constitutional groundwork for the regime of Jim Crow, and by the 1890s the "due process" clause had become a protection for private enterprise rather than a guarantee of racial equality. This was why turn-of-the-century progressives opposed an active judiciary: they wanted judges to stop using the Fourteenth Amendment to kill reform legislation.

Holmes had declared his contempt for the economic interpretation of the Fourteenth Amendment in 1905 in the case of *Lochner v. New York*—also known as the Sugar Baker's case. The state of New York had passed a law limiting the number of hours people could work in a bakery to ten per day; in its majority opinion, the Court declared the law an unconstitutional infringement on bakery owners' "right to property" as embodied in the Fourteenth Amendment. Holmes's dissent was brief, and its point can be reduced (as it was many times afterward) to one sentence: "The Fourteenth Amendment does not enact Mr. Herbert Spencer's Social Statics."[14]

Social Statics was published in 1851, two years after John Her-schel's review of Adolphe Quetelet's *Letters on the Theory of Probabil-ity*. It was Spencer's first important work, and, as the title suggests, it was an attempt to derive a principle from the social "laws" that sta-tistics was supposed to have revealed. The principle Spencer an-nounced was: "Every man has freedom to do all that he wills, provided he infringes not the equal freedom of any other man"[15]— the classic doctrine of laissez-faire. (Herschel had reached a similar conclusion in his review.) Holmes's point was that there was nothing "natural" about laissez-faire; it was just an economic theory, and "a constitution," he said,

> is not intended to embody a particular economic theory. . . . It is made for people of fundamentally differing views, and the accident of our finding certain opinions natural and familiar or novel and even shocking ought not to conclude our judgment upon the question whether statutes embodying them conflict with the Constitution of the United States. General principles do not decide concrete cases. . . . But I think that the proposition just stated . . . will carry us far toward the end.[16]

Holmes was not saying that he thought regulation of business was good social policy; he probably thought it was not. He was saying that what he thought was irrelevant. It was the judicial credo of pro-gressivism.

Holmes's view of rights was not a secret in 1919. The year before, he had published a short article in the *Harvard Law Review* on "Nat-ural Law." "[A] right," he said there, "is only the hypostasis of a prophecy—the imagination of a substance supporting the fact that the public force will be brought to bear upon those who do things to contravene it—just as we talk of the force of gravitation accounting for the conduct of bodies in space."[17] It was an analysis derived from the teachings, almost fifty years earlier, of Chauncey Wright and St. John Green: the term "right" names the fact that there are some activities that courts will, with a high degree of predictability, prevent other parties from interfering with, just as "gravity" names a highly predictable behavior observed of bodies in space. "Right" is a term of convenience; it is not a thing in nature, or something that inheres in us simply by virtue of being human.

When the first group of Espionage Act cases came before the Supreme Court, in January 1919, the conservative chief justice, Edward Douglass White, therefore did not feel he was taking a risk in assigning the opinions to Holmes. Three cases were decided in the same session. The defendants in them were a man from Kansas City named Jacob Frohwerk, who had published articles in a German-language newspaper, the Missouri *Staats Zeitung*, advocating resistance to the draft; Charles T. Schenck, general secretary of the Socialist Party in Philadelphia, who had distributed leaflets opposing recruitment to draftees; and Eugene Debs.[18]

In 1919, Debs was sixty-four and the most famous socialist in America. He had run for president four times; in 1912, in a race against Woodrow Wilson, William Howard Taft, and Theodore Roosevelt, he had taken 6 percent of the vote. The Socialist Party, which Debs had helped to create in 1898 in the aftermath of the Pullman affair, opposed American intervention in the war and supported the Bolshevik government in Russia. On June 16, 1918, Debs addressed a large rally in Canton, Ohio, where the state Socialist Party convention was being held.[19] Eight percent of Ohio ballots had been cast for Debs in the 1912 election, the largest proportion of any state; when he arrived to speak there, three local Socialist Party leaders were already in jail for obstructing the draft. It was a politically loaded occasion.

Debs suspected that he was under surveillance, and he was correct. The United States attorney for northern Ohio, a man named E. S. Wertz, had placed stenographers in the crowd to transcribe his speech. It was mostly an appeal to join ranks with the Socialist Party and a blessing on the Bolshevik revolution, but Debs also held up his jailed comrades as examples to which true socialists might aspire. Wertz construed this as speech intended to obstruct recruitment, and therefore a violation of the Espionage and Sedition Act, passed a month earlier; and he informed the Justice Department in Washington that he had a case. The Justice Department found the evidence a little oblique, and declined to prosecute; but Wertz obtained an indictment from a federal grand jury in Cleveland. In September Debs was found guilty in a jury trial. He was sentenced to ten years in prison.

Holmes wrote separate opinions in the three cases; in all of them, he stressed the crucial relevance of context. "It may be that all this might be said or written even in time of war in circumstances that would not make it a crime," he wrote of the writings being prosecuted in *Frohwerk*. "But . . . it is impossible to say that it might not have been found that the circulation of the paper was in quarters where a little breath would be enough to kindle a flame."[20] In the case of Debs, Holmes said, it did not matter if the suggestion that the war was wrong was just an incidental remark in a plea for socialism. If "the opposition was so expressed that its natural and intended effect would be to obstruct recruiting," he argued, ". . . if, in all the circumstances, that would be its probable effect, it would not be protected by reason of its being part of a general program and expressions of a general and conscientious belief."[21] And in *Schenck*, Holmes announced his contextual test: "The question in every case," he wrote, "is whether the words used are used in such circumstances and are of such a nature as to create a clear and present danger that they will bring about the substantive evils that Congress has a right to prevent. It is a question of proximity and degree."[22] Holmes did not have much trouble seeing the government's point of view in every case, and he affirmed all the convictions. The war had been over for four months. Debs was sent to a federal penitentiary in Moundsville, West Virginia, to serve his ten-year sentence. He brought with him his most prized possession: the candlestick holder John Brown had used at Harpers Ferry.

A little to Holmes's surprise, his opinions were a source of distress to his progressive admirers. One of these was Learned Hand. Like most progressives, Hand had no particular enthusiasm for the idea of individual rights, which he associated with what he regarded as constitutionally bogus concepts such as "the right to property" and "liberty of contract." In 1919, Hand had been a United States district judge for the Southern District of New York for ten years. He had graduated in 1893 from Harvard College, where he had studied psychology under William James and philosophy under Josiah Royce. He considered a career in philosophy, but Royce was not enthusiastic when Hand approached him for advice about it, and he went to Harvard Law School instead, where he became a student of James Thayer's. Thayer had just published what would be his most famous work, "The Origin and Scope of the American Doctrine of Constitutional Law," an argument for judicial restraint. "[T]he constitution," Thayer explained, "often admits of different interpretations. . . . [It] does not impose upon the legislature any one specific opinion, but leaves open this range of choice. . . . The judicial function is merely that of fixing the outside border of reasonable legislative action."[23] It was Holmes's *Lochner* dissent twelve years before *Lochner*.

Hand took Thayer's class on constitutional law and found it, as he later put it, "subversive." For Thayer taught that (in Hand's words)

> most of constitutional law had been constructed out of circular propositions, which justified the predetermined attitudes of the judges, who—being, more often than not, primarily men of action— were unaware of the verbal traps that lay about them and into which they often unwittingly fell. . . . [T]he result was to imbue us with a skepticism about the wisdom of setting up courts as the final arbiters of social conflicts.[24]

Thayer was, of course, just repeating Chauncey Wright's warning about the idolatry of concepts. Thayer taught Hand the danger of principle. As a young lawyer in New York City, Hand became involved in progressive circles, and in 1908, just before his appointment to the bench (where he foreswore all political activity), he published a *Harvard Law Review* article called "Due Process of Law and the Eight-Hour Day"—an attack on the majority opinion in *Lochner*.

Holmes was therefore Hand's judicial ideal; he modeled his opinions on Holmes's all his life. Many years later, in the case of *United States v. Carroll Towing* (1947), he announced a formula that used the probability of injury to determine whether a defendant had exercised due care—the statistical instantiation of Holmes's reasonable man standard. But Hand was unhappy with Holmes's Espionage Act decisions, and especially with *Debs*. He had reason to be sensitive to those decisions, because he had been badly burned himself on the same constitutional terrain. The Espionage Act of 1917 had empowered the postmaster to suppress materials judged to violate the provisions of the act, and on July 3, 1917, eighteen days after the act was passed, the postmaster of New York City, Thomas G. Patten, following the directive of the postmaster general, refused to mail the August issue of the *Masses*. The magazine petitioned the federal district court for an injunction, and on July 24, Hand issued his opinion.

The *Masses* was a small radical magazine with an impressive list of contributors: John Reed, Louis Untermeyer, Carl Sandburg, Floyd Dell, John Sloan, George Bellows, Stuart Davis. It was edited by Max Eastman, a graduate student of Dewey's at Columbia. Hand knew Eastman a little, and though his own politics were closer to the *New Republic*'s—he supported American intervention in the war without hesitation—he was disposed to be sympathetic.[25] The August *Masses* contained a good deal of material critical of the war, including a cartoon of dead women and children captioned "Conscription," but it did not explicitly counsel interference with the war effort or resistance to the draft, and this became Hand's loophole. He crafted what he must have imagined an extremely diplomatic opinion.

There was "no question," Hand said, that Congress had the authority, under the war powers, to suppress speech it considered a threat to national safety. But Congress could not possibly have intended to suppress mere criticisms of government policy, because in democratic countries, "the free expression of opinion [is] the ultimate source of authority." Criticism of government policy was by no means the same thing as counsel to violate the law; and "to assimilate agitation, legitimate as such, with direct incitement to violent resistance, is to disregard the tolerance of all methods of political agitation, which in normal times is a safeguard of free government." Since he was unable to find any "direct advocacy of resistance" to the draft in the August *Masses*, Hand concluded that the expressions suppressed by the postmaster did not rise to the level of culpability contemplated by Congress.[26] He granted the injunction.

Four months later, he was reversed by a unanimous Circuit Court of Appeals. "[I]t is not necessary that an incitement to crime must be direct," the court said. "That one may willfully obstruct the enlistment service, without advising in direct language against enlistments, . . . seems to us too plain for controversy."[27] Hand was a brilliant jurist, but he was also a sensitive and insecure person; he did not like to see his logic rejected so summarily. What was more, there had been an opening on the Second Circuit Court of Appeals to which he had aspired and which he had had reason to assume was within his grasp. It now went to another judge.

Hand summered in New Hampshire; Holmes summered in Massachusetts. The following June, they ran into each other on the train to Boston, and they discussed Hand's *Masses* opinion (which Holmes had not yet read) and the law of free speech. Hand was naturally eager to have his argument confirmed by his hero, and he pressed on Holmes the virtue of his "direct incitement" test—the theory that the state cannot suppress speech unless it explicitly advocates the commission of a crime. Holmes enjoyed the conversation, but he was not convinced about Hand's test, and it is easy to see why. For Holmes's whole approach to the law was reflected in the argument of the Circuit Court's reversal of Hand: it isn't the words themselves that determine liability. It's the context.

Still, having opened the topic for discussion, Hand felt entitled to write to Holmes after reading his opinion in the *Debs* case nine months later. "I haven't a doubt that Debs was guilty under any rule conceivably applicable," Hand began. (He was being disingenuous: he almost certainly thought Debs had been wrongly convicted.)[28] But he wanted to suggest again that responsibility for speech only begins "when the words [are] directly an incitement."[29] Holmes wrote back to say that he had been "so busy propagating new sophistries &c. that I haven't had time to defend the old ones," but that "I am afraid that I don't quite get your point. . . . I don't know what the matter is, or how we differ."[30] And he quoted his "clear and present danger" test from *Schenck*. The next fall, though, Holmes wrote an opinion Hand was happier with. This was the *Abrams* dissent.

Jacob Abrams was a Russian Jewish immigrant who lived in Manhattan and belonged to an anarchist group. On September 12, 1918, he and six associates—Mollie Steimer, Samuel Lipman, Hyman Lachowsky, Jacob Schwartz, Gabriel Prober, and Hyman Rosansky—were indicted by a federal grand jury for interfering with the war effort by printing two leaflets (one in English and the other in Yiddish) protesting American policy toward Russia, and throwing them from the roof of a building on Second Avenue. The indictments were handed up in Hand's jurisdiction, and, as the senior judge, Hand would likely have presided over the trial; but because of his court's caseload, he had invited several federal judges to come to New York to help out, and the case went to one of them. This was Henry De-Lamar Clayton, Jr., of Alabama, the son of a major general in the Confederate Army. On October 24, Abrams, Steimer, Lipman, Lachowsky, and Rosansky were convicted by a New York jury (Prober was acquitted; Schwartz had died during the trial). Clayton fined Rosansky; he sentenced Steimer to ten years in prison; and he gave Abram, Lipman, and Lachowsky twenty years.[31]

The case was argued before the Supreme Court on October 21, 1919—the fifty-eighth anniversary, as it happened, of the battle of Ball's Bluff. Holmes had not been hearing only from Hand about his opinions in the Espionage Act cases of the previous spring; he had been bombarded with articles and letters by many progressive intellectuals with whom he was on friendly terms, including three Harvard professors, Zechariah Chafee, Ernst Freund, and Harold Laski. Laski was himself in trouble on a speech issue. Laski was a precocious British political scientist, known for a book on political pluralism, *Studies in the Problem of Sovereignty*, which he had published in 1917, when he was twenty-four; he had been teaching at Harvard and corresponding regularly with Holmes since 1916. Holmes was exceptionally fond of him. In September 1919 the Boston police had gone out on strike, and Laski had spoken out publicly in their support.

The strike was suppressed by the governor, Calvin Coolidge, who called out the state militia, and Laski's position made him unpopular at Harvard. He was the subject of anti-Semitic caricatures in the *Lampoon*, and Lowell eventually forced his resignation. Holmes had many motives, in short, for recasting his view of First Amendment challenges to the Espionage and Sedition Act. And when, on November 10, 1919, the Court affirmed the convictions of Abrams and the other defendants, rejecting their First Amendment claim by citing Holmes's own opinion in *Schenck*, Holmes filed a dissent.

As always, he was reluctant to trump a legislative act with the assertion of a right. "I do not doubt for a moment," he wrote, "that by the same reasoning that would justify punishing persuasion to murder, the United States constitutionally may punish speech that produces or is intended to produce a clear and imminent danger that it will bring about forthwith certain substantive evils that the United States constitutionally may seek to prevent." But he could not find, in the facts before him, such a danger. "[N]obody can suppose," he said, "that the surreptitious publishing of a silly leaflet by an unknown man, without more, would present any immediate danger that its opinions would hinder the success of the government arms or have any appreciable tendency to do so."[32] And he declined to affirm the judgment against them.

Despite Hand's appeals, Holmes had not abandoned his contextual test. He had simply interpreted the facts to place the case against Abrams and the others too far out on the curve to come within the purview of the statute. Hand's test was more speech-protective than Holmes's, but Holmes's was more language-sensitive. From a civil libertarian point of view, a contextual interpretation seems to invite juries to read their own prejudices into the evidence. But Holmes thought that juries would do that no matter what—that dominant opinion would have its way in the end, anyway. The only reasonable attitude was to assume that if a jury understood the standard, it would apply it correctly. It was not that Holmes had a deep faith in the judgment of the average person. He just thought that was the way the system worked.

Holmes always insisted that his dissent in *Abrams* was perfectly consistent with his opinion for the court in *Schenck*, and he was correct. What made *Abrams* different was Holmes's recognition that in order to justify his reading of the facts, he needed a theory. In upholding an individual right of free speech, he needed to explain why it was in the majority's interest to grant such a right. He supplied his theory in his final paragraph. "Persecution for the expression of opinions seems to me perfectly logical," he wrote.

> If you have no doubt of your premises or your power and want a certain result with all your heart you naturally express your wishes in law and sweep away all opposition. . . . But when men have realized that time has upset many fighting faiths, they may come to believe even more than they believe the very foundations of their own conduct that the ultimate good desired is better reached by free trade in ideas—that the best test of truth is the power of that thought to get itself accepted in the competition of the market, and that truth is the only ground upon which their wishes safely can be carried out. That at any rate is the theory of our Constitution. It is an experiment, as all life is an experiment. Every year if not every day we have to wager our salvation upon some prophecy based upon imperfect knowledge. While that experiment is part of our system I think that we should be eternally vigilant against attempts to check the expression of opinions that we loathe and believe to be fraught with death.
> . . . Only the emergency that makes it immediately dangerous to leave the correction of evil counsels to time warrants making any exception to the sweeping command, "Congress shall make no law . . . abridging the freedom of speech." . . . I regret that I cannot put into more impressive words my belief that in their conviction upon this indictment the defendants were deprived of their rights under the Constitution of the United States.[33]

It was not until 1925 that the United States Supreme Court recognized free speech as one of the liberties protected by the Fourteenth Amendment's due process clause, and not until 1927, in an opinion by Louis Brandeis, that it adopted Holmes's argument for protecting political speech from state sanctions.[34] After the Second World War, the positions Hand and Holmes had put forward in 1917 and 1919 became judicial touchstones, and the basis for a broad expansion of First Amendment freedoms.

The constitutional law of free speech is the most important benefit to come out of the way of thinking that emerged in Cambridge and elsewhere in the decades after the Civil War. It makes the value of an idea not its correspondence to a preexisting reality or a metaphysical truth, but simply the difference it makes in the life of the group. Holmes's conceit of a "marketplace of ideas" suffers from the defect of all market theories: exogenous elements are always in play to keep marketplaces from being truly competitive. Some ideas just never make it to the public. But it is the metaphor of probabilistic thinking: the more arrows you shoot at the target, the better sense you will have of the bull's-eye. The more individual variations, the greater the chances that the group will survive. We do not (on Holmes's reasoning) permit the free expression of ideas because some individual may have the right one. No individual alone can have the right one. We permit free expression because we need the resources of the whole group to get us the ideas we need. Thinking is a social activity. I tolerate your thought because it is part of my thought—even when my thought defines itself in opposition to yours.

5

Academic freedom and the freedom of speech are quintessentially modern principles. Since the defining characteristic of modern life is social change—not onward or upward, but forward, and toward a future always in the making—the problem of legitimacy continually arises. In a premodern society, legitimacy rests with hereditary authority and tradition; in a modernizing society, the kind of society in which Louis Agassiz and Oliver Wendell Holmes, Sr., and Benjamin Peirce lived and wrote, legitimacy tends to be transferred from leaders and customs to nature. Agassiz and the senior Holmes and Benjamin Peirce all assumed that social arrangements are justified if they correspond with the design of the natural world—and so did Adolphe Quetelet, Henry Thomas Buckle, Thomas Huxley, and William Graham Sumner. But in societies bent on transforming the past, and on treating nature itself as a process of ceaseless transformation, how do we trust the claim that a particular state of affairs is legitimate?

The solution has been to shift the totem of legitimacy from premises to procedures. We know an outcome is right not because it was derived from immutable principles, but because it was reached by following the correct procedures. Science became modern when it was conceived not as an empirical confirmation of truths derived from an independent source, divine revelation, but as simply whatever followed from the pursuit of scientific methods of inquiry. If those methods were scientific, the result must be science. The modern conception of law is similar: if the legal process was adhered to, the outcome is just. Justice does not preexist the case at hand; justice is whatever result just procedures have led to. Even art adopted the same standards in the modern period: it became defined as the realization of the aesthetic potential of the artistic medium. Poetry was talked about as an exploration of the resources of language, painting as a manipulation of canvas and paint, figure and ground. The argument of Hand and Holmes—which was also the argument of Jane Addams and John Dewey—about democracy had the same logic. It is that a decision can be called democratic only if everyone has been permitted to participate in reaching it.

The marketplace is not the only metaphor in Holmes's opinion, though. The image of the Civil War is everywhere in its language— "sweep away all opposition," "fighting faiths," "fraught with death." Like Hand, Holmes believed that political opinion should be protected because that is the only way for democratic governments to maintain legitimacy. Like Dewey, he believed that the freedom of speech is not an individual good, but a social good—that we have an interest in allowing individuals to express themselves because we need the ideas. What is distinctive in Holmes's view is the insistence that ideas are also dangerous. He defended free speech in the language of risk. Holmes would never have called himself a pragmatist; he associated the term with a desire to smuggle religion back into modern thought under a pseudo-scientific cover. But his belief that life is an experiment, and that since we can never be certain we must tolerate dissent, is consistent with everything James, Peirce, and Dewey wrote. What Holmes did not share with those thinkers was their optimism. He did not believe that the experimental spirit will necessarily lead us, ultimately, down the right path. Democracy is an experiment, and it is in the nature of experiments sometimes to fail. He had seen it fail once.

Oliver Wendell Holmes in Washington, D.C., in December 1934, three months before his death. (Photograph by Clara Sipprell.)

EPILOGUE

IN 1907, ONE OF WILLIAM JAMES's students discovered Charles Peirce ill, and near death from malnourishment, in a Cambridge rooming house. James realized that Peirce's hopes for professional resurrection were finished, and he organized a fund to support him. It yielded about a thousand dollars a year, and Peirce, in gratitude, added a middle name, Santiago—St. James. Three years later, James died of the heart condition from which he had been suffering for more than a decade. His brother Henry had come from England to be with him, and William, just before he died, asked him to remain in Cambridge for six weeks after his death: he would try to communicate with him from beyond the grave. If William sent any posthumous messages, his brother did not receive them.

After James's death, Peirce continued to write, but he was already taking morphine daily for the pain from cancer, and he knew that he had been cut off for too long from the work of other thinkers—he could not afford to buy their books—to make a contribution. "I came within an ace of teaching men something to their profit," he wrote in 1911 to one of the few correspondents he had left. "But certain misfortunes have prevented my keeping up with the times."[1] Even when he was dying, he would ask Juliette to give him paper and something to write with: he said it was the only way he knew to relieve the pain. He lived until 1914. His book was finished, he told Juliette just before he died; it would revolutionize science, and they would be able to travel. After his death, his sister, Helen, wrote a brief memorial. "He loved to recall in our rare meetings of late when we would reminisce his association with his friends in the sixties," she said. "That time was the one he would like to dwell upon with me."[2]

Juliette stayed on at Arisbe, a recluse. In 1932 Peirce's old Hopkins student Joseph Jastrow went to see her and found the house in decay; the outdoor pump was the only source of water. But Juliette was glad to see him. "She recited the details of Mr. Peirce's Lowell lectures in Boston," Jastrow later wrote, "which must have taken place soon after her marriage. Most of all she wanted to meet William and Alice James. A seat was reserved for her in the brilliant audience that had assembled to hear her husband. She was delighted to find that her neighbor was Mrs. James."[3] Juliette died in 1934. She had survived her husband by twenty years.

Wendell Holmes attended James's funeral, but privately he made a point of his lack of sympathy with James's views. He thought that James had made scientific uncertainty an excuse for believing in the existence of an unseen world. "His wishes made him turn down the lights so as to give miracle a chance,"[4] as Holmes complained in a letter to Frederick Pollock. But he had not forgotten what their friendship had meant. In 1912, James's son Henry began preparing an edition of his father's letters, and wrote to Holmes asking for any he might have. Holmes had saved his letters from James, and he read them over. They "revive a lifelong pain," he wrote when he sent them to Henry, "—the partial drawing asunder of two who loved each other."[5]

The last years of Holmes's life, as he often said, were the happiest. In the 1920s, when the memory of the political hostilities of the progressive period had begun to fade in the public mind, he became a kind of popular icon of American liberalism. He did not bother to disabuse his public of their view of him; he liked the attention too well. In 1925, John Dewey published his most wide-ranging philosophical book, *Experience and Nature*. Dewey used the term "experience" in that book exactly as Holmes had used it forty years earlier in the famous opening paragraph of *The Common Law*—as a name for culture. (Dewey later said that he wished he had called the book *Culture and Nature*.) And in the final chapter, he praised Holmes as "one of our greatest American philosophers,"[6] and went on to quote a long passage from Holmes's essay on "Natural Law." Holmes read the book several times, with growing pleasure. He thought he had found in Dewey a philosopher whose conception of existence seemed to match his own. "[A]lthough Dewey's book is incredibly ill written," he told Pollock, "it seemed to me . . . to have a feeling of intimacy with the universe that I found unequaled. So methought God would have spoken had He been inarticulate but keenly desirous to tell you how it was."[7]

Holmes sat on the Supreme Court for thirty years. He was finally persuaded to retire in 1932, and he died, in Washington, D.C., in 1935, two days before his ninety-fourth birthday. After his death, two Civil War uniforms were found hanging in his closet with a note pinned to them. It read: "These uniforms were worn by me in the Civil War and the stains upon them are my blood."[8]

Dewey was sixty-six when he wrote *Experience and Nature*, and he was by no means finished. He retired from Columbia in 1930, but he continued to write and lecture; and in 1937, when he was seventy-eight, he traveled to Mexico to head a committee to investigate Joseph Stalin's charges against Leon Trotsky. Dewey admired Trotsky's courage and the dialectical sophistication of his mind; but, as he told one of the Americans traveling with him, he thought him "tragic. To see such brilliant native intelligence locked up in absolutes,"[9] he said. Alice Dewey died in 1927, and in 1946, Dewey, now eighty-seven, married Roberta Lowitz Grant, who was forty-two. They adopted two Belgian war orphans, and Dewey enjoyed having them around while he did his work. In late 1951, while he was playing with them, he fell and broke a hip, and he never fully recovered. The following spring, he contracted pneumonia, and he died on June 1, 1952.

Five months later, the United States exploded a hydrogen bomb over the Pacific island of Elugelab, and to many Americans (also to many people who were not Americans) the world looked like a very different place. For the next forty years, Holmes, James, and Dewey, figures who had dominated American intellectual life for half a century, seemed to go into almost total eclipse. A movement of thought that had grown out of the experience of the Civil War appeared to reach an end with the Cold War. Why did this happen?

A full answer is difficult because the Cold War changed almost everything about American intellectual life; the fading of interest in Holmes, James, and Dewey was just part of a much larger shift in values and priorities. The simple explanation for the change in their status is the common explanation for changes of this kind, which is that Holmes, James, and Dewey became identified with the work of disciples whose stature was a lot less intimidating and whose claims struck many people as a lot more controversial. The criticism of legal formalism Holmes had pressed in *The Common Law* and "The Path of the Law" was taken up in the 1920s and 1930s by the school of jurisprudence known as Legal Realism, whose representatives made assertions about the political bias in legal principles (while dropping entirely Holmes's opposition to judicial activism) that went beyond anything in Holmes. In a similar way Dewey's emphasis, in his writings on education, on the importance of the child's own interests became the basis for a greatly expanded conception of child-centeredness in the progressive education movement, which was criticized, especially during the Cold War years, for a lack of discipline and rigor. Efforts within American universities to make the pragmatism of James and Peirce into a research program for philosophy professors were sidelined by work in philosophical traditions more obviously suited to academic modes in inquiry. And the therapeutic side of James's thought—the conviction, born out of his struggles with indecision and depression, that philosophy can be motivational—did not survive a transplant from a culture in which emotional restraint was counted a virtue to one in which emotional release was considered a panacea.

Holmes, James, Peirce, and Dewey were modernists; the eventual obsolescence of their work would hardly have shocked them. Even Peirce, who did not share with the others a belief in the pure provisionality of ideas, thought that the opinions of one generation were destined to be superseded by the opinions of the next. And Holmes liked to say (though it wasn't true of his own habits as a reader) that there was no point in reading anything more than twenty years old. Styles of thought do run into the ground; ideas lose their cogency. Holmes, James, and Dewey had once helped to run a style of thought into the ground themselves—the one represented by their parents and teachers, by Dr. Holmes and Benjamin Peirce and Henry James, Sr., by James Marsh and Louis Agassiz and George Sylvester Morris. In doing so they helped to put an end to the idea that the universe is an idea, that beyond the mundane business of making our way as best we can in a world shot through with contingency, there exists some order, invisible to us, whose logic we transgress at our peril.

Still, the reputations of Holmes, James, and Dewey during the Cold War years were not just the reputations of thinkers whose style had come to seem antique. They were also the reputations of thinkers whose style had come to seem naïve, and even a little dangerous. The reason has to do with the difference between the intellectual climate after the Civil War and the intellectual climate of the Cold War. The value at the bottom of the thought of Holmes, James, Peirce, and Dewey is tolerance. The United States was created in part by Europeans who emigrated in the name of religious tolerance (more precisely, in the name of opposition to religious intolerance). The various offshoots of the pragmatist way of thinking—the educational philosophy, the pluralist conception of culture, the argument for expanded freedoms of expression—were, in a sense, translations of this individualist, Protestant ethic into social and secular terms. But the modern idea of tolerance is analogous not so much to the

Protestant belief in the freedom of each person to worship according to the dictates of his or her own conscience as it is to the idea of tolerance in engineering—the tolerance, say, of a piece of steel. The pragmatists wanted a social organism that permitted a greater (though by no means unrestricted) margin for difference, but not just for the sake of difference, and not even because they thought principles of love and fairness required it. They wanted to create more social room for error because they thought this would give good outcomes a better chance to emerge. They didn't just want to keep the conversation going; they wanted to get to a better place.

This does not sound like an attitude inconsistent with the self-conception of the United States during the Cold War, and many of the social reforms set in motion in the 1900s and 1910s were vastly accelerated in the 1950s and 1960s. Holmes, James, and Dewey—along with, it is important to remember, many people who did not share their philosophical views—helped to make tolerance an official virtue in modern America. But the intellectual grounds for that virtue changed after 1945. Beliefs, Holmes, James, Peirce, and Dewey had said repeatedly, are just bets on the future. Though we may believe unreservedly in a certain set of truths, there is always the possibility that some other set of truths might be the case. In the end, we have to act on what we believe; we cannot wait for confirmation from the rest of the universe. But the moral justification for our actions comes from the tolerance we have shown to other ways of being in the world, other ways of considering the case. The alternative is force. Pragmatism was designed to make it harder for people to be driven to violence by their beliefs.

This sounds unexceptionable, and in many ways it is. But it is important to see that the idea is a compromise. Holmes, James, Peirce, and Dewey wished to bring ideas and principles and beliefs down to a human level because they wished to avoid the violence they saw hidden in abstractions. This was one of the lessons the Civil War had taught them. The political system their philosophy was designed to support was democracy. And democracy, as they understood it, isn't just about letting the right people have their say; it's also about letting the wrong people have their say. It is about giving space to minority and dissenting views so that, at the end of the day, the interests of the majority may prevail. Democracy means that everyone is equally in the game, but it also means that no one can opt out. Modern American thought, the thought associated with Holmes, James, Peirce, and Dewey, represents the intellectual triumph of unionism.

The Cold War was a war over principles. In many parts of the world—Korea, Vietnam, Nicaragua—it was, of course, a hot war, but in the United States it was a war fought mostly with images and ideas. A style of thought that elevated compromise over confrontation therefore did not hold much appeal. Even the opponents of the Cold War mounted their opposition on principle. The notion that the values of the free society for which the Cold War was waged were contingent, relative, fallible constructions, good for some purposes and not so good for others, was not a notion compatible with the moral imperatives of the age. The great movement to secure civil liberties in the United States during the Cold War arose out of a religious community, black Southern Baptists, and it was founded on the belief that every individual has an inalienable right to those freedoms by virtue of being human—precisely the individualism that Holmes and Dewey felt they needed to discredit. Martin Luther King, Jr., was not a pragmatist, a relativist, or a pluralist, and it is a question whether the movement he led could have accomplished what it did if its inspirations had come from Dewey and Holmes rather than Reinhold Niebuhr and Mahatma Gandhi. Americans did not reject the values of tolerance and liberty during the Cold War—on the contrary—but they replanted those values in distinctly non-pragmatic soil.

And once the Cold War ended, the ideas of Holmes, James, Peirce, and Dewey reemerged as suddenly has they had been eclipsed. Those writers began to be studied and debated with a seriousness and intensity, both in the United States and in other countries, that they had not attracted for forty years. For in the post–Cold War world, where there are many competing belief systems, not just two, skepticism about the finality of any particular set of beliefs has begun to seem to some people an important value again. And so has the political theory this skepticism helps to underwrite: the theory

that democracy is the value that validates all other values. Democratic participation isn't the means to an end, in this way of thinking;
it is the end. The purpose of the experiment is to keep the experiment going. This is the point of Holmes's *Abrams* dissent, of James's
insistence on the "right to believe," of Peirce's insistence on keeping
the path of inquiry open, of Jane Addams's and John Dewey's insistence on understanding antagonism as a temporary stage in the
movement toward a common goal. Whether this nineteenth-century
way of thinking really does have twenty-first-century uses is not yet
clear.

For we are a long way from 1872, when the members of the mysterious Metaphysical Club got together in Cambridge to talk about
the place of ideas in *their* postwar world. It is true that those people,
and the way they thought, can seem familiar to us today in rather uncanny ways. But it is worth trying to see how almost unimaginably
strange they and their world were, too. The relevance and the
strangeness are forever bound together in their thought.

ACKNOWLEDGMENTS

I HAD NO IDEA, when I started out, how huge a mountain this would be to climb. I also had no idea how many amazing characters I would be seduced by along the way—Pen Hallowell, trying to coax one last idealistic exertion out of his reluctant friend Wendell Holmes; Hetty Green, tracing the signature of her invalid aunt and dreaming of millions; the sober-sided Henry Torrey, pacing through the Vermont woods discussing Kant with the young John Dewey; the ambitious G. Stanley Hall; the sensitive but unsentimental Alain Locke; the obnoxious McKeen Cattell. And the fantastic demons of Maxwell and Laplace. There was no part of the trek I did not find almost fatally fascinating, and (this is something I never thought I would say about writing a book) I am sorry it is over.

I could not have even begun without the great fortune of being granted fellowships by the National Endowment for the Humanities and the John Simon Guggenheim Foundation. The Guggenheim not only supported me for a year with money; they sustained me for many more years with expressions of interest and encouragement. I am grateful to my friends at the Foundation Peter Kardon, Tom Tanselle, and Joel Connaroe. My research was also assisted by a grant from the Professional Staff Congress of the City University of New York.

At the beginning of my work I was lucky to be given space in the offices of the New York Institute for the Humanities at New York University. I am very grateful to its director in those years, A. Richard Turner, and to its irrepressible associate director, Jocelyn Carlson, for the space and the companionship. I am also grateful to all my colleagues at the Graduate Center of the City University of New York, who have been unfailingly supportive, and especially to John Brenkman, John Patrick Diggins, and Joan Richardson, with whom I have taught some of the material in this book. At the end, Cathleen Schine kindly lent me the perfect place in which to write the final pages.

Sections from the work were given as talks at the Center on Violence and Human Survival at the John Jay College of Criminal Justice, Rutgers University, the University of Nebraska at Lincoln, Brown University, Pomona College, and the Center for Ideas and Society at the University of California at Riverside. I am grateful to the sponsors of these events and to members of the audience for their reactions.

Several friends read sections of the book as it was being written, and so did several people whose expertise far exceeds mine, and their reactions were thoughtful, thorough beyond the obligations of friendship or the call of duty, and extremely valuable. I thank Paul Berman, William Kelly, David Layzer, Nancy K. Miller, Richard Rorty, and Kenneth Sacks. I also profited from advice and information anxiously solicited from and generously provided by Edward Abrahams, Bruce Kuklick, and Beverly Palmer. Jonathan Galassi and Joan Richardson made many helpful suggestions about the entire manuscript. Catherine S. Menand did heroic (and thankless) archival work in Boston, both at the beginning and the end of the project—but she's my mother. Emily Abrahams talked me through many stretches, she commented wisely on the entire manuscript, and the pleasure she took in the book I was able to produce is what mattered to me the most—but she's my wife.

Henry Finder read the whole manuscript, apparently overnight, and produced a scrupulous and learned set of suggestions, most of which I took up, and the rest of which I wished I had the competence to take up. For many years, on many occasions, I have relied on the astonishing editorial intelligence of my friend Ann Hulbert. She was the first reader of the first section, the chapters on Holmes, and without her reaction the rest of the mountain would have remained unclimbed. At the end she gave me advice on many points in the manuscript and was the biggest help in the business of putting a frame around what I had done.

I learned a tremendous amount about America by writing this book, and the greatest kindness all the people I have thanked did me was not to say what I know to be true: that I have not begun to do justice to the people and the events I have tried to bring to life in these pages.

Louis Menand

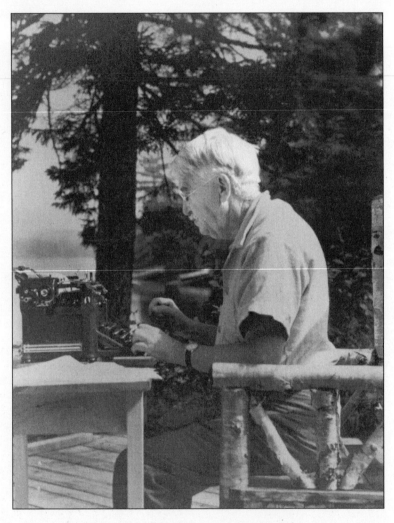

John Dewey at "Hubbard's," in Nova Scotia, in the 1940s.
(Photograph by Robert Norwood.)

NOTES

PREFACE

1. I have used primary material whenever feasible, but I have also relied on a large body of work by other writers for historical and biographical information, general guidance, and many insights and references. The following were works indispensable throughout:

On Holmes: Mark DeWolfe Howe, *Justice Oliver Wendell Holmes: The Shaping Years, 1841–1870* (Cambridge, Mass.: Harvard University Press, 1957) and *Justice Oliver Wendell Holmes: The Proving Years, 1870–1882* (Cambridge, Mass.: Harvard University Press, 1963); Sheldon M. Novick, *Honorable Justice: The Life of Oliver Wendell Holmes* (Boston: Little, Brown, 1989); Liva Baker, *The Justice from Beacon Hill: The Life and Times of Oliver Wendell Holmes* (New York: Harper-Collins, 1991); and G. Edward White, *Justice Oliver Wendell Holmes: Law and the Inner Self* (New York: Oxford University Press, 1993).

On James: Ralph Barton Perry, *The Thought and Character of William James*, 2 vols. (Boston: Little, Brown, 1935); F. O. Matthiessen, *The James Family* (New York: Knopf, 1947); Gay Wilson Allen, *William James: A Biography* (New York: Viking, 1967); Leon Edel, *Henry James*, 5 vols. (Philadelphia: Lippincott, 1953–72); Jean Strouse, *Alice James: A Biography* (Boston: Houghton Mifflin, 1980); Howard M. Feinstein, *Becoming William James* (Ithaca, N.Y.: Cornell University Press, 1984); Gerald E. Myers, *William James: His Life and Thought* (New Haven: Yale University Press, 1986); Jane Maher, *Biography of Broken Fortunes: Wilkie and Bob, Brothers of William, Henry, and Alice James* (Hamden, Conn.: Archon Books, 1986); R. W. B. Lewis, *The Jameses: A Family Narrative* (New York: Farrar, Straus and Giroux, 1991);

Alfred Habegger, *The Father: A Life of Henry James Senior* (New York: Farrar, Straus and Giroux, 1994); and Linda Simon, *Genuine Reality: A Life of William James* (New York: Harcourt Brace, 1998).

On Peirce: Max H. Fisch, *Peirce, Semeiotic, and Pragmatism: Essays*, ed. Kenneth Laine Ketner and Christian J. W. Kloesel (Bloomington: Indiana University Press, 1986); Joseph Brent, *Charles Sanders Peirce: A Life* (Bloomington: Indiana University Press, 1993); Kenneth Laine Ketner, *His Glassy Essence: An Autobiography of Charles Sanders Peirce* (Nashville: Vanderbilt University Press, 1998); and the introductions by Max H. Fisch and Nathan Houser in *Writings of Charles S. Peirce: A Chronological Edition*, Peirce Edition Project, 30 vols. (Bloomington: Indiana University Press, 1982–).

On Dewey: George Dykhuizen, *The Life and Mind of John Dewey*, ed. Jo Ann Boydston (Carbondale: Southern Illinois University Press, 1973); Neil Coughlan, *Young John Dewey: An Essay in American Intellectual History* (Chicago: University of Chicago Press, 1975); Steven C. Rockefeller, *John Dewey: Religious Faith and Democratic Humanism* (New York: Columbia University Press, 1991); Robert B. Westbrook, *John Dewey and American Democracy* (Ithaca, N.Y.: Cornell University Press, 1991); and Alan Ryan, *John Dewey and the High Tide of American Liberalism* (New York: Norton, 1995).

Two works of intellectual history were especially germane: Philip P. Wiener, *Evolution and the Founders of Pragmatism* (Cambridge, Mass.: Harvard University Press, 1949); and Bruce Kuklick, *The Rise of American Philosophy: Cambridge, Massachusetts, 1860–1930* (New Haven: Yale University Press, 1977).

CHAPTER ONE: THE POLITICS OF SLAVERY

1. Oliver Wendell Holmes, *Elsie Venner* (1861), *The Works of Oliver Wendell Holmes* (Boston: Houghton Mifflin, 1892), vol. 5, 4.

2. Oliver Wendell Holmes, *The Professor at the Breakfast-Table* (1860), *The Works of Oliver Wendell Holmes*, vol. 2, 83.

3. Oliver Wendell Holmes, *The Autocrat of the Breakfast-Table* (1858), *The Works of Oliver Wendell Holmes*, vol. 1, 125.

4. [Oliver Wendell Holmes], "The Autocrat of the Breakfast Table, No. II," *New England Magazine*, 2 (1832): 137.

5. Petitions dated December 10 and 11, 1850, and Oliver Wendell Holmes, Sr., to Abraham R. Thompson, n.d., Harvard Medical School Dean's Office Files c. 1839–1900, box 3 [Archives AA 1.20], Harvard Medical Library in the Francis A. Countway Library of Medicine.

6. See Werner Sollors, Caldwell Titcomb, and Thomas A. Underwood, eds., *Blacks at Harvard: A Documentary History of African-American Experience at Harvard and Radcliffe* (New York: New York University Press, 1993), 18–31; Victor Ullman, *Martin R. Delany: The Beginnings of Black Nationalism* (Boston: Beacon Press, 1971), 113–21; Dorothy Sterling, *The Making of an Afro-American: Martin Robison Delany 1812–1885* (Garden City, N.Y.: Doubleday, 1971), 122–35; and Edwin P. Hoyt, *Improper Bostonian: Dr. Oliver Wendell Holmes* (New York: Morrow, 1979), 146–51.

7. See James M. McPherson, *Battle Cry of Freedom: The Civil War Era* (New York: Oxford University Press, 1988), 81–3; Lawrence Lader, *The Bold Brahmins: New England's War Against Slavery: 1831–1863* (New York: Dutton, 1961), 161; Jane H. Pease and William H. Pease, *They Who Would Be Free: Blacks' Search for Freedom, 1830–1861* (New York: Atheneum, 1974), 206–32; and Albert J. von Frank, *The Trials of Anthony Burns: Freedom and Slavery in Emerson's Boston* (Cambridge, Mass.: Harvard University Press, 1998).

8. McPherson, *Battle Cry of Freedom*, 95.

9. Ulysses S. Grant, *Personal Memoirs of U. S. Grant* (1885–86), *Memoirs and Selected Letters* (New York: Library of America, 1990), 773.

10. Edward L. Pierce, *Memoir and Letters of Charles Sumner* (Boston: Roberts, 1894), vol. 3, 295.

11. See *The Journals of Richard Henry Dana, Jr.*, ed. Robert F. Lucid (Cambridge, Mass.: Harvard University Press, 1968), vol. 4, xxv; and E. Digby Baltzell, *Puritan Boston and Quaker Philadelphia: Two Protestant Ethics and the Spirit of Class Authority and Leadership* (New York: Free Press, 1979), 41–3.

12. See Daniel Walker Howe, *The Unitarian Conscience: Harvard Moral Philosophy, 1805–1861* (Cambridge, Mass.: Harvard University Press, 1970), 271–3, 287.

13. See Howe, *The Unitarian Conscience*, 311.

14. See Edward Waldo Emerson, *The Early Years of the Saturday Club: 1855–1870* (Boston: Houghton Mifflin, 1918), 162; and Pierce, *Memoir and Letters of Charles Sumner*, vol. 3, 219–20.

15. See Mark DeWolfe Howe, *Justice Oliver Wendell Holmes: The Shaping Years, 1841–1870* (Cambridge, Mass.: Harvard University Press, 1957), 72n.

16. See Richard Hofstadter, *The American Political Tradition and the Men Who Made It* (New York: Knopf, 1951), 146; and, generally, Stanley M. Elkins, *Slavery: A Problem in American Institutional and Intellectual History*, 2nd. ed. (Chicago: University of Chicago Press, 1968).

17. William Lloyd Garrison, "No Compromise with Slavery," *Selections from the Writings and Speeches of William Lloyd Garrison* (Boston: R. F. Wallcut, 1852), 139.

18. James G. Birney, *A Letter on the Political Obligations of Abolitionists, with a Reply by William Lloyd Garrison* (Boston: Dow and Jackson, 1839), 32.

19. W[illia]m Lloyd Garrison, "Address," *Liberator*, 9 (July 19, 1839): 114.

20. [William Lloyd Garrison], "Prospectus of the Liberator," *Liberator*, 8 (December 28, 1838): 207.

21. Wendell Phillips, "Philosophy of the Abolition Movement" (1853), *Speeches, Lectures, and Letters* (Boston: Lee and Shepard, 1884), 113.

22. See Hofstadter, *The American Political Tradition*, 139.

23. See C. Vann Woodward, *American Counterpoint: Slavery and Racism in the North-South Dialogue* (Boston: Little, Brown, 1971), 144.

24. Wendell Phillips, "Idols" (1859), *Speeches, Lectures, and Letters*, 243.

25. Wendell Phillips, "Public Opinion" (1852), *Speeches, Lectures, and Letters*, 53–4.

26. See Oliver Wendell Holmes, *The Poet at the Breakfast-Table* (1872), *The Works of Oliver Wendell Holmes*, vol. 3, 26; Holmes was referring to *The New-York Conspiracy, or A History of the Negro Plot, with the Journal of the Proceedings Against the Conspirators, at New-York in the Year 1741–2* (New York: Southwick & Pelsue, 1801).

27. Oliver Wendell Holmes, "Oration, Semi-centennial Celebration of the New England Society in the City of New York" (1855), *The Autocrat's Miscellanies*, ed. Albert Mordell (New York: Twayne, 1959), 77, 80.

28. See Eleanor M. Tilton, *Amiable Autocrat: A Biography of Dr. Oliver Wendell Holmes* (New York: Henry Schuman, 1947), 224; Hoyt, *Improper Bostonian*, 159–61; and Len Gougeon, *Virtue's Hero: Emerson, Anti-Slavery, and Reform* (Athens: University of Georgia Press, 1990), 219.

29. Quoted in Tilton, *Amiable Autocrat*, 320.

30. See Tilton, *Amiable Autocrat*, 344.

31. [James Russell Lowell], "Thoreau's Letters," *North American Review*, 101 (1865): 600.

32. Quoted in Samuel Eliot Morison, *Three Centuries of Harvard, 1636–1936* (Cambridge, Mass.: Harvard University Press, 1936), 248–9.

33. Ralph Waldo Emerson, "Self-Reliance" (1841), *Essays and Lectures* (New York: Library of America, 1983), 272.

34. See Morison, *Three Centuries of Harvard*, 244.

35. Ralph Waldo Emerson, Sermon CLVII, *The Complete Sermons of Ralph Waldo Emerson*, ed. Albert J. von Frank (Columbia: University of Missouri Press, 1989–92), vol. 4, 157.

36. Ralph Waldo Emerson to Oliver Wendell Holmes, March 1856 (draft), *The Letters of Ralph Waldo Emerson*, ed. Ralph L. Rusk and Eleanor M. Tilton (New York: Columbia University Press, 1939–95), vol. 5, 17–18.

37. Ralph Waldo Emerson, "The American Scholar" (1837), *Essays and Lectures*, 71.

38. William Ellery Channing, "Remarks on Associations" (1829), *Works of William Ellery Channing, D.D.* (Boston: J. Munroe, 1841–43), vol. 1, 290.

39. Ralph Waldo Emerson, journal, April 26, 1838, *The Journals and Miscellaneous Notebooks of Ralph Waldo Emerson*, ed. William H. Gilman et al. (Cambridge, Mass.: Harvard University Press, 1960–82), vol. 5, 479.

40. Ralph Waldo Emerson, "The Transcendentalist" (1842), *Essays and Lectures*, 203.

41. Ralph Waldo Emerson, Journal HO, 1853–54(?), *The Journals and Miscellaneous Notebooks*, vol. 13, 281–2.

42. Ralph Waldo Emerson, Journal BO, 1851, *The Journals and Miscellaneous Notebooks*, vol. 11, 346.

43. Ralph Waldo Emerson, "Address to the Citizens of Concord" (1851), *Emerson's Antislavery Writings*, ed. Len Gougeon and Joel Myerson (New Haven: Yale University Press, 1995), 65.

44. Emerson, "Address to the Citizens of Concord," *Emerson's Antislavery Writings*, 53.

45. Oliver Wendell Holmes, *Ralph Waldo Emerson* (Boston: Houghton Mifflin, 1884), 211.

46. See Gougeon, *Virtue's Hero*, 7–12.

47. Ralph Waldo Emerson to Oliver Wendell Holmes, March 1856, *The Letters of Ralph Waldo Emerson*, vol. 5, 17.

48. Emerson, "The American Scholar," *Essays and Lectures*, 64.

49. Oliver Wendell Holmes to Ralph Waldo Emerson, March 26, 1856, quoted in Tilton, *Amiable Autocrat*, 227.

50. See Tilton, *Amiable Autocrat*, 227.

CHAPTER TWO: THE ABOLITIONIST

1. Oliver Wendell Holmes to Morris Cohen, February 5, 1919, "The Holmes-Cohen Correspondence," ed. Felix S. Cohen, *Journal of the History of Ideas*, 9 (1948): 15.

2. Oliver Wendell Holmes, "Books" (1858), *The Collected Works of Justice Holmes: Complete Public Writings and Selected Judicial Opinions of Oliver Wendell Holmes*, ed. Sheldon M. Novick (Chicago: University of Chicago Press, 1995–), vol. 1, 141.

3. Ellen Tucker Emerson to Edith Forbes, January 29, 1859, *The Letters of Ellen Tucker Emerson*, ed. Edith E. W. Gregg (Kent, Ohio: Kent State University Press, 1982), vol. 1, 166.

4. Oliver Wendell Holmes to Patrick Augustine Sheehan, October 27, 1912, *Holmes-Sheehan Correspondence: Letters of Justice Oliver Wendell Holmes, Jr., and Canon Patrick Augustine Sheehan*, ed. David H. Burton, rev. ed. (New York: Fordham University Press, 1993), 71.

5. Oliver Wendell Holmes to Elizabeth Shipley Sargeant, December 7, 1926, Oliver Wendell Holmes Papers, Harvard Law School Library.

6. Holmes, "Books," *The Collected Works of Justice Holmes*, vol. 1, 140–1.

7. Oliver Wendell Holmes, "Notes on Albert Dürer" (1860), *The Collected Works of Justice Holmes*, vol. 1, 154–5.

8. See Liva Baker, *The Justice from Beacon Hill: The Life and Times of Oliver Wendell Holmes* (New York: HarperCollins, 1991), 88.

9. See Oliver Wendell Holmes to Harold J. Laski, November 5, 1926, *Holmes-Laski Letters: The Correspondence of Mr. Justice Holmes and Harold J. Laski*, ed. Mark DeWolfe Howe (Cambridge, Mass.: Harvard University Press, 1953), 2: 893; and Holmes to Arthur Garfield Hays, April 20, 1928, quoted in Mark DeWolfe Howe, *Justice Oliver Wendell Holmes: The Shaping Years, 1841–1870* (Cambridge, Mass.: Harvard University Press, 1957), 49.

10. Oliver Wendell Holmes, "Class Book 1861—Entry," *The Collected Works of Justice Holmes*, vol. 1, 170.

11. Amos A. Lawrence to Giles Richards, June 1, 1854, quoted in James M. McPherson, *Battle Cry of Freedom: The Civil War Era* (New York: Oxford University Press, 1988), 120.

12. *Dred Scott v. Sandford*, 60 U.S. 393 (1857), 404–5.

13. Herman Melville, "The Portent" (1859), *American Poetry: The Nineteenth Century*, ed. John Hollander (New York: Library of America, 1993), vol. 2, 2.

14. Theodore Parker to Francis Jackson, November 24, 1859, in John Weiss, *Life and Correspondence of Theodore Parker: Minister of the Twenty-Eighth Congregational Society* (New York: D. Appleton, 1864), vol. 2, 178.

15. James Elliot Cabot, *A Memoir of Ralph Waldo Emerson* (Boston: Houghton Mifflin, 1888), vol. 2, 597.

16. Ralph Waldo Emerson, "Speech at a Meeting to Aid John Brown's Family" (1859), *Emerson's Antislavery Writings*, ed. Len Gougeon and Joel Myerson (New Haven: Yale University Press, 1995), 119.

17. See C. Vann Woodward, "John Brown's Private War," *The Burden of Southern History* (Baton Rouge: Louisiana State University Press, 1960), 53–61; and McPherson, *Battle Cry of Freedom*, 208–13.

18. See Lawrence Lader, *The Bold Brahmins: New England's War Against Slavery, 1831–1863* (New York: Dutton, 1961), 257.

19. See Irving H. Bartlett, *Wendell Phillips: Brahmin Radical* (Boston: Beacon Press, 1961), 227–9.

20. Samuel Gridley Howe to Charles Sumner, January 20, 1861, Charles Sumner Papers, Houghton Library, Harvard University, 074/394.

21. Richard Price Hallowell to Oliver Wendell Holmes, January 23, 1861, Oliver Wendell Holmes Papers.

22. Ralph Waldo Emerson, "Attempted Speech" (1861), *Emerson's Antislavery Writings*, 127.

23. George Ticknor to Edmund Head, April 21, 1861, in George S. Hillard, *Life, Letters, and Journals of George Ticknor* (Boston: Osgood, 1876), vol. 2, 433–4.

24. Cabot, *A Memoir of Ralph Waldo Emerson*, 2: 601.

25. Cornelius Conway Felton to Oliver Wendell Holmes, Sr., June 11, 1861, Harvard University Archives, UAI.15.890.3 (170–171).

26. Oliver Wendell Holmes to Cornelius Conway Felton, July 24, 1861, quoted in Mark DeWolfe Howe, *Holmes of the Breakfast-Table* (London: Oxford University Press, 1939), 102–4.

27. George McClellan to Ellen Marcy McClellan, November 2(?), 1861, quoted in McPherson, *Battle Cry of Freedom*, 364.

28. See Allan Nevins, *The War for the Union, Volume One: The Improvised War, 1861–1862* (New York: Scribner, 1959), 298–9; and McPherson, *Battle Cry of Freedom*, 362.

29. Louis-Philippe-Albert d'Orléans, Comte de Paris, *History of the Civil War in America*, trans. Louis F. Tasistro (Philadelphia: Coates, 1875–88), vol. 1, 413.

30. See George A. Bruce, *The Twentieth Regiment of Massachusetts Volunteer Infantry, 1861–1865* (Boston: Houghton Mifflin, 1906), 52–5.

31. See Oliver Wendell Holmes, *Touched with Fire: Civil War Letters and Diary of Oliver Wendell Holmes, Jr., 1861–1864*, ed. Mark DeWolfe Howe (Cambridge, Mass.: Harvard University Press, 1946), 23–33.

32. See Richard B. Irwin, "Ball's Bluff and the Arrest of General Stone," in Robert Underwood Johnson and Clarence Clough Buel, eds., *Battles and Leaders of the Civil War* (Rpt. New York: Thomas Yoseloff, 1956), vol. 2, 123–34.

33. See William F. Fox, *Regimental Losses in the American Civil War, 1861–1865* (Albany: Albany Publishing, 1889), 164.

34. Holmes, *Touched with Fire*, 30; and see Irwin, "Ball's Bluff and the Arrest of General Stone," in *Battles and Leaders of the Civil War*, vol. 2, 123–34.

35. Holmes, *Touched with Fire*, 32.

36. Holmes, *Touched with Fire*, 27–8.

37. Holmes, *Touched with Fire*, 32.

38. See Saul Touster, "In Search of Holmes from Within," *Vanderbilt Law Review*, 18 (1965): 439 n. 3.

39. Holmes, *Touched with Fire*, 57 n. 1.

40. Norwood Penrose Hallowell to Richard Price Hallowell, November 24, 1861 (copy by R. P. Hallowell), Wendell Phillips Papers, Houghton Library, Harvard University, bMS Am 1953 (650).

41. Norwood Penrose Hallowell to Wendell Phillips, October 31, 1861, Wendell Phillips Papers (649).

42. Richard Price Hallowell to Wendell Phillips, December 6, 1861, Wendell Phillips Papers (650).

43. See Lewis Einstein, Introduction to *The Holmes-Einstein Letters: The Correspondence of Mr. Justice Holmes and Lewis Einstein, 1903–1935*, ed. James Bishop Peabody (New York: St. Martin's, 1964), xvii.

44. Henry Livermore Abbott to Elizabeth Livermore, January 10, 1863, *Fallen Leaves; The Civil War Letters of Major Henry Livermore Abbott*, ed. Robert Garth Scott (Kent, Ohio: Kent State University Press, 1991), 161.

45. Henry Livermore Abbott to Josiah Abbott, August 17, 1863, *Fallen Leaves*, 201.

46. Henry Livermore Abbott to Josiah Abbott, September 18, 1863, *Fallen Leaves*, 215.

47. Oliver Wendell Holmes, Civil War scrapbook, Oliver Wendell Holmes Papers.

48. See Oliver Wendell Holmes, "My Hunt after 'The Captain,'" *Atlantic Monthly*, 10 (1862): 738–64.

49. See Howe, *Justice Oliver Wendell Holmes: The Shaping Years*, 135.

50. Oliver Wendell Holmes to his parents, November 16(?), 1862, *Touched with Fire*, 69–70.

51. Oliver Wendell Holmes to Amelia Holmes, November 16(?)–19, 1862, *Touched with Fire*, 73.

52. See McPherson, *Battle Cry of Freedom*, 544.

53. Quoted in McPherson, *Battle Cry of Freedom*, 572, 574.

54. See Paul E. Steiner, *Disease in the Civil War: Natural Biological Warfare in 1861–1865* (Springfield, Ill.: Charles C. Thomas, 1968), 10.

55. Oliver Wendell Holmes, "Memorial Day" (1884), *The Collected Works of Justice Holmes*, vol. 3, 465.

56. See Fox, *Regimental Losses in the American Civil War*, 164.

57. See Oliver Wendell Holmes to his parents, December 12, 1862, *Touched with Fire*, 74.

58. See Henry Livermore Abbott to Josiah Abbott, November 7, 1861, *Fallen Leaves*, 74.

59. Henry Livermore Abbott to Caroline Livermore Abbott, May 17, 1863, *Fallen Leaves*, 182.

60. Henry Livermore Abbott to Caroline Livermore Abbott, December 21, 1862, *Fallen Leaves*, 155.

61. Oliver Wendell Holmes to Oliver Wendell Holmes, Sr., December 20, 1862, *Touched with Fire*, 79–80.

62. Ralph Waldo Emerson to Edith Emerson, January 8, 1863, *The Letters of Ralph Waldo Emerson*, ed. Ralph L. Rusk and Eleanor M. Tilton (New York: Columbia University Press, 1939–95), vol. 5, 305.

63. See Norwood Penrose Hallowell to Oliver Wendell Holmes, February 7, 1863, Oliver Wendell Holmes Papers; and Howe, *Justice Oliver Wendell Holmes: The Shaping Years*, 157–8.

64. Benjamin F. Butler, *Autobiography and Personal Reminiscences of Major-General Benjamin F. Butler: Butler's Book* (Boston: Thayer, 1892), 566.

65. Oliver Wendell Holmes to Oliver Wendell Holmes, Sr., March 29, 1863, *Touched with Fire*, 86, 90–1.

66. Oliver Wendell Holmes, Sr., to John Lothrop Motley, November 29, 1863, *The Correspondence of John Lothrop Motley*, ed. George William Curtis (New York: Harper, 1889), vol. 2, 44.

67. John Codman Ropes to Oliver Wendell Holmes, July 7, 1863, Oliver Wendell Holmes Papers.

68. Norwood Penrose Hallowell to Oliver Wendell Holmes, August 4, 1863, Oliver Wendell Holmes Papers.

69. Henry Livermore Abbott to Oliver Wendell Holmes, September 5, 1863, *Fallen Leaves*, 211.

70. Henry Livermore Abbott to Oliver Wendell Holmes, October 18, 1863, Abbott Brothers—Civil War letters, Houghton Library, Harvard University, MS Am 800.26. (The editor of Abbott's published correspondence excises the final phrase without ellipsis.)

CHAPTER THREE: THE WILDERNESS AND AFTER

1. See James M. McPherson, *Battle Cry of Freedom: The Civil War Era* (New York: Oxford University Press, 1988), 472–7.

2. See William F. Fox, *Regimental Losses in the American Civil War, 1861–1865* (Albany: Albany Publishing, 1889), 3.

3. See George M. Fredrickson, *The Inner Civil War: Northern Intellectuals and the Crisis of the Union* (New York: Harper & Row, 1965), 69–70, 80; and James Turner, *The Liberal Education of Charles Eliot Norton* (Baltimore: Johns Hopkins University Press, 1999), 180–1.

4. [Charles Eliot Norton], "The Advantages of Defeat," *Atlantic Monthly*, 8 (1861): 363, 365.

5. Charles Eliot Norton to Aubrey de Vere, October 2, 1861, Charles Eliot Norton Papers, Houghton Library, Harvard University, bMS Am 1088.2, Box 3.

6. Oliver Wendell Holmes to Charles Eliot Norton, April 17, 1864, Charles Eliot Norton Papers (3532).

7. Oliver Wendell Holmes to Ralph Waldo Emerson, February [?] 1864, *The Journals and Miscellaneous Notebooks of Ralph Waldo Emerson*, ed. William H. Gilman et al. (Cambridge, Mass.: Harvard University Press, 1960–82), vol. 15, 200.

8. Oliver Wendell Holmes to his parents, May 3, 1864, *Touched with Fire: Civil War Letters and Diary of Oliver Wendell Holmes, Jr., 1861–1864*, ed. Mark DeWolfe Howe (Cambridge, Mass.: Harvard University Press, 1947), 102–3.

9. Ulysses S. Grant, *Personal Memoirs of U. S. Grant* (1885–86), *Memoirs and Selected Letters* (New York: Library of America, 1990), 534.

10. Holmes, *Touched with Fire*, 104–5.

11. Oliver Wendell Holmes to his parents, May 6, 1864, *Touched with Fire*, 105.

12. See George A. Bruce, *The Twentieth Regiment of Massachusetts Volunteer Infantry, 1861–1865* (Boston: Houghton Mifflin, 1906), 353–4, 357.

13. Oliver Wendell Holmes to Amelia Lee Jackson Holmes, May 11, 1864, *Touched with Fire*, 114.

14. Holmes, *Touched with Fire*, 116.

15. See McPherson, *Battle Cry of Freedom*, 730.

16. See McPherson, *Battle Cry of Freedom*, 730; and Grant, *Personal Memoirs, Memoirs and Selected Letters*, 554.

17. Holmes, *Touched with Fire*, 116–17.

18. Oliver Wendell Holmes to his parents, May 16, 1864, *Touched with Fire*, 121–3.

19. Oliver Wendell Holmes to his parents, May 30, 1864, *Touched with Fire*, 135.

20. Holmes, *Touched with Fire*, 137 n. 4.

21. Oliver Wendell Holmes to Amelia Lee Jackson Holmes, June 7, 1864, *Touched with Fire*, 142–3.

22. Oliver Wendell Holmes to his parents, June 24, 1864, *Touched with Fire*, 149–50.

23. Oliver Wendell Holmes to Amelia Lee Jackson Holmes, July 8, 1864, *Touched with Fire*, 152.

24. See Francis Biddle, *Mr. Justice Holmes* (New York: Scribner, 1942), 35–6.

25. [Oliver Wendell Holmes], "The Autocrat of the Breakfast Table, No. II," *New-England Magazine*, 2 (1832): 134.

26. See Edward Waldo Emerson, *The Early Years of the Saturday Club: 1855–1870* (Boston: Houghton Mifflin, 1918), 145.

27. Quoted in M. A. DeWolfe Howe, *Holmes of the Breakfast-Table* (London: Oxford University Press, 1939), 53.

28. Oliver Wendell Holmes, "Some of My Early Teachers" (1882), *Medical Essays, 1842–1882, The Works of Oliver Wendell Holmes* (Boston: Houghton Mifflin, 1892), vol. 9, 434.

29. Ralph Waldo Emerson, "Self-Reliance" (1841), *Essays and Lectures* (New York: Library of America, 1983), 259.

30. See Fredrickson, *The Inner Civil War*, 175–6.

31. Oliver Wendell Holmes to Ralph Waldo Emerson, April 16, 1876, Ralph Waldo Emerson Papers, Houghton Library, Harvard University, bMS Am 1280 (1535).

32. Oliver Wendell Holmes to Lewis Einstein, July 17, 1909, *The Holmes-Einstein Letters: The Correspondence of Mr. Justice Holmes and Lewis Einstein, 1903–1935*, ed. James Bishop Peabody (New York: St. Martin's, 1964), 48.

33. Oliver Wendell Holmes, "The Profession of the Law" (1886), *Collected Works of Justice Holmes: Complete Public Writings and Selected Judicial Opinions of Oliver Wendell Holmes*, ed. Sheldon M. Novick (Chicago: University of Chicago Press, 1995–), vol. 3, 472.

34. Ralph Waldo Emerson, "The American Scholar" (1837), *Essays and Lectures*, 69.

35. Holmes, "The Profession of the Law," *The Collected Works of Justice Holmes*, vol. 3, 472–3.

36. Oliver Wendell Holmes, "H. L. A.: Twentieth Massachusetts Volunteers" (1864), *The Collected Works of Justice Holmes*, vol. 1, 172.

37. Oliver Wendell Holmes to Harold J. Laski, October 24, 1930, *Holmes-Laski Letters: The Correspondence of Mr. Justice Holmes and Harold J. Laski, 1916–1935*, ed. Mark DeWolfe Howe (Cambridge, Mass.: Harvard University Press, 1953), 2: 1291.

38. Oliver Wendell Holmes to Harold J. Laski, May 12, 1927, *Holmes-Laski Letters*, 2: 942.

39. Oliver Wendell Holmes to Frederick Pollock, August 30, 1929, *Holmes-Pollock Letters: The Correspondence of Mr. Justice Holmes and Sir Frederick Pollock, 1874–1932*, ed. Mark DeWolfe Howe (Cambridge, Mass.: Harvard University Press, 1941), vol. 2, 252–3.

40. See Oliver Wendell Holmes to Morris Cohen, February 5, 1919, "The Holmes-Cohen Correspondence," ed. Felix Cohen, *Journal of the History of Ideas*, 9 (1948): 14–15.

41. Oliver Wendell Holmes to Harold J. Laski, June 1, 1927, *Holmes-Laski Letters*, 2: 948.

42. Oliver Wendell Holmes, "Natural Law" (1918), *The Collected Works of Justice Holmes*, vol. 3, 446.

43. Oliver Wendell Holmes to Lewis Einstein, November 9, 1913, *Holmes-Einstein Letters*, 82; see also Oliver Wendell Holmes to Harold J. Laski, April 13, 1929, *Holmes-Laski Letters*, 2: 1146.

44. Oliver Wendell Holmes to Alice Stopford Green, October 1, 1901, Oliver Wendell Holmes Papers.

45. Oliver Wendell Holmes, "The Gas-Stokers' Strike" (1873), *The Collected Works of Justice Holmes*, vol. 1, 325.

46. Oliver Wendell Holmes, *The Common Law* (1881), *The Collected Works of Justice Holmes*, vol. 3, 137.

47. See *The Collected Works of Justice Holmes*, vol. 3, 154 n. 5.

48. Oliver Wendell Holmes to Lewis Einstein, October 28, 1912, *Holmes-Einstein Letters*, 74; and Oliver Wendell Holmes to Harold J. Laski, May 24, 1919, *Holmes-Laski Letters*, 1: 207.

49. Oliver Wendell Holmes to Lewis Einstein, October 28, 1912, *Holmes-Einstein Letters*, 74.

50. Oliver Wendell Holmes to Frederick Pollock, February 1, 1920, *Holmes-Pollock Letters*, vol. 2, 36; see also Oliver Wendell Holmes to Harold J. Laski, December 9, 1921, *Holmes-Laski Letters*, 1: 385.

51. See Holmes's opinions in *Giles v. Harris*, 189 U.S. 475 (1903); *Bailey v. Alabama*, 219 U.S. 219 (1911); and *United States v. Reynolds*, 235 U.S. 133 (1914).

52. *Buck v. Bell*, 274 U.S. 200, 207 (1927).

53. Oliver Wendell Holmes to John T. Morse, November 28, 1926, Oliver Wendell Holmes Papers.

54. See Lewis Einstein, Introduction to *Holmes-Einstein Letters*, xix.

55. Oliver Wendell Holmes, Sr., to John Lothrop Motley, February 16, 1861, quoted in John T. Morse, Jr., *Life and Letters of Oliver Wendell Holmes* (Boston, Houghton Mifflin, 1896), vol. 2, 157.

56. See Mark DeWolfe Howe, *Justice Oliver Wendell Holmes: The Proving Years, 1870–1882* (Cambridge, Mass.: Harvard University Press, 1963), 8.

57. Vernon Louis Parrington, *Main Currents in American Thought: An Interpretation of American Literature from the Beginnings to 1920* (New York: Harcourt, Brace, 1927–30), vol. 2, 459.

58. Oliver Wendell Holmes to Harold J. Laski, June 28, 1928, *Holmes-Laski Letters*, 2: 1069–70.

59. Oliver Wendell Holmes, "Memorial Day" (1884), *The Collected Works of Justice Holmes*, vol. 3, 467.

60. Oliver Wendell Holmes to Lewis Einstein, April 7, 1914, *Holmes-Einstein Letters*, 90.

61. Oliver Wendell Holmes to Frederick Pollock, May 20, 1930, *Holmes-Pollock Letters*, vol. 2, 264.

62. See *Holmes and Frankfurter: Their Correspondence, 1912–1934*, ed. Robert M. Mennel and Christine L. Compston (Hanover: University Press of New England, 1996), xxix.

63. Einstein, Introduction to *Holmes-Einstein Letters*, xvi.

CHAPTER FOUR: THE MAN OF TWO MINDS

1. William James to Carlotta Lowell, 1905, quoted in Ferris Greenslet, *The Lowells and Their Seven Worlds* (Boston: Houghton Mifflin, 1946), 289. See also Caroline Tappan to Henry Lee Higginson, May 7, 1863, in Bliss Perry, *Life and Letters of Henry Lee Higginson* (Boston: Houghton Mifflin, 1921), 192:

   > Mrs. Tweedie [*sic*] has just been in and says Willie James saw the colored regiment reviewed,—Bob Shaw's,—and that they were a very fine set of men, finer looking than any white regiment he had seen. Charles Lowell and Effie Shaw sat on their great war horses looking on, and looked so like a king and queen that he did not venture to speak to them. Charles appears perfectly happy, as well he may be, for Effie is a very fine girl, true and full of character.

2. Quoted in Ralph Barton Perry, *The Thought and Character of William James* (Boston: Little, Brown, 1935), vol. 1, 441.

3. William James to Alice Howe Gibbens, April 23, April 24, and April 30, 1877, *The Correspondence of William James*, ed. Ignas K. Skrupskelis and Elizabeth M. Berkeley (Charlottesville: University Press of Virginia, 1992–), vol. 4, 558, 559, 560.

4. Alice James, Diary, November 18, 1889, *The Diary of Alice James*, ed. Leon Edel (London: Rupert Hart-Davis, 1965), 57.

5. George Santayana, *Persons and Places: Fragments of Autobiography* (1944), *The Works of George Santayana*, ed. William G. Holzberger and Herman J. Saatkamp, Jr. (Cambridge, Mass.: MIT Press, 1986–), vol. 1, 402.

6. See Bernard Berenson, *Sunset and Twilight: From the Diaries of 1947–1958*, ed. Nicky Mariano (London: Hamish Hamilton, 1964), 67.

7. Oliver Wendell Holmes to Frederick Pollock, April 25, 1920, *Holmes-Pollock Letters: The Correspondence of Mr. Justice Holmes and Sir Frederick Pollock, 1874–1932*, ed. Mark DeWolfe Howe (Cambridge, Mass.: Harvard University Press, 1941), vol. 2, 41.

8. Edward Waldo Emerson, *The Early Years of the Saturday Club: 1855–1870* (Boston: Houghton Mifflin, 1918), 328.

9. Quoted in Alfred Habegger, *The Father: A Life of Henry James, Sr.* (New York: Farrar, Straus and Giroux, 1994), 107.

10. See Habegger, *The Father*, 114–19.

11. Alexis de Tocqueville, *Democracy in America* (1835), trans. Henry Reeve, ed. Phillips Bradley (New York: Knopf, 1945), vol. 1, 303.

12. See Nathan O. Hatch, *The Democratization of American Christianity* (New Haven: Yale University Press, 1989), 3–4.

13. See Jon Butler, *Awash in a Sea of Faith: Christianizing the American People* (Cambridge, Mass.: Harvard University Press, 1990), 225–56; Sydney E. Ahlstrom, *A Religious History of the American People* (New Haven: Yale University Press, 1972), 472–90; and Hatch, *The Democratization of American Christianity*, 49–66.

14. See R. W. B. Lewis, *The Jameses: A Family Narrative* (New York: Farrar, Straus and Giroux, 1991), 39–40; and Habegger, *The Father*, 157–71.

15. Henry James, *Society the Redeemed Form of Man, and the Earnest of God's Omnipotence in Human Nature* (Boston: Houghton, Osgood, 1879), 44–5.

16. Henry James, *Notes of a Son and Brother* (New York: Scribner, 1914), 205.

17. Henry James, Sr., to Ralph Waldo Emerson, October 3, 1843, William James Papers, Houghton Library, Harvard University, bMS Am 1092.9 (4099).

18. Henry James, Sr., "Emerson A" (1872), William James Papers (4587).

19. Ellery Channing to Henry David Thoreau, March 5, 1845, *The Correspondence of Henry David Thoreau*, ed. Walter Harding and Carl Bode (New York: New York University Press, 1958), 161.

20. Henry David Thoreau to H. G. O. Blake, January 1, 1859, *The Correspondence of Henry David Thoreau*, 537.

21. Mrs. James T. Fields, Diary, July 28, 1864, quoted in Mark A. DeWolfe Howe, *Memories of a Hostess: A Chronicle of Eminent Friendships* (Boston: Atlantic Monthly Press, 1922), 76.

22. Quoted in James, *Notes of a Son and Brother*, 235.

23. William James to Henry James, Sr., December 14, 1882, *The Correspondence of William James*, vol. 5, 327.

24. Charles Eliot Norton to Eliot Norton, June 11, 1907, *The Letters of Charles Eliot Norton*, ed. Sara Norton and M. A. DeWolfe Howe (Boston: Houghton Mifflin, 1913), vol. 2, 379 ("I was speaking to him of Dr. James's new book [i.e., *Pragmatism*], and said that it was brilliant but not clear. 'Like his father,' said Mr. Howells, 'who wrote the Secret of Swedenborg and kept it' ").

25. William James to Henry James, October 2, 1869, *The Correspondence of William James*, vol. 1, 102.

26. Henry James, *Substance and Shadow: Or, Morality and Religion in Their Relation to Life: An Essay upon the Physics of Creation* (Boston: Ticknor and Fields, 1863), 6.

27. Henry James, *Society the Redeemed Form of Man*, 47.

28. Henry James, "Property as a Symbol," *Lectures and Miscellanies* (New York: Redfield, 1852), 76.

29. Henry James, *A Small Boy and Others* (New York: Scribner, 1913), 216.

30. Y. S. [Henry James, Sr.], "Postscript to Y. S.'s Reply to A. E. F.," *Harbinger*, 8 (December 30, 1848): 68.

31. Y. S. [Henry James, Sr.], "Remarks," *Harbinger*, 8 (December 2, 1848): 37.

32. H[enry] J[ames], "Marriage Question," *New York Tribune*, September 18, 1852, p. 6. See, generally, Habegger, *The Father*, 277–98, 329–42.

33. Henry James, "Woman and the 'Woman's Movement,' " *Putnam's Monthly*, 1 (1853): 285; "Marriage Question," 6; "Woman and the 'Woman's Movement,' " 287.

34. James, "Property as a Symbol," *Lectures and Miscellanies*, 69.

35. James, *Substance and Shadow*, 536.

36. See Habegger, *The Father*, 442–3.

37. Henry James, *The Secret of Swedenborg: Being an Elucidation of His Doctrine of the Divine Natural Humanity* (Boston: Fields, Osgood, 1869), 210.

38. James, *Society the Redeemed Form of Man*, 84.

39. Henry James, *The Church of Christ Not an Ecclesiasticism: Letter to a Sectarian* (New York: Redfield, 1854), 65.

40. Henry James, "Democracy and Its Issues," *Lectures and Miscellanies*, 4.

41. James, *The Church of Christ Not an Ecclesiasticism*, 67.

42. James, *Society the Redeemed Form of Man*, 90–1.

43. Quoted in Ahlstrom, *A Religious History of the American People*, 484.

44. Ralph Waldo Emerson, "Swedenborg; Or, The Mystic" (1850), *Essays and Lectures* (New York: Library of America, 1983), 682.

45. See Whitney R. Cross, *The Burned-over District: The Social and Intellectual History of Enthusiastic Religion in Western New York, 1800–1850* (Ithaca, N.Y.: Cornell University Press, 1950), 341–5; and Ahlstrom, *A Religious History of the American People*, 486–8.

46. See, for example, Frank Podmore, *Modern Spiritualism: A History and a Criticism* (New York: Scribner, 1902), vol. 1, 189–91.

47. See Henri F. Ellenberger, *The Discovery of the Unconscious: The History and Evolution of Dynamic Psychiatry* (New York: Basic Books, 1970), 83–5; Cross, *The Burned-over District*, 345–8; Ahlstrom, *A Religious History of the American People*, 488–90; and Podmore, *Modern Spiritualism*, vol. 1, 179–201.

48. William James, "The Confidences of a 'Psychical Researcher'" (1909), *Essays in Psychical Research, The Works of William James*, ed. Frederick H. Burkhardt (Cambridge, Mass.: Harvard University Press, 1975–88), 374.

49. William James to Alice James, July 6, 1891, *The Correspondence of William James*, vol. 7, 177–8.

50. Henry James, "'Spiritual Rappings,'" *Lectures and Miscellanies*, 417.

51. William James to Alice Howe Gibbens James, December 20, 1882, *The Correspondence of William James*, vol. 5, 342.

52. See William James to Henry James, September 1, 1887, *The Correspondence of William James*, vol. 2, 68.

53. See Lewis, *The Jameses*, 72.

54. Alice James, Diary, December 12, 1889, *The Diary of Alice James*, 66.

55. *The Letters of William James*, ed. Henry James (Boston: Atlantic Monthly Press, 1920), vol. 1, 20.

56. William James to Henry James, May 4, 1907, *The Correspondence of William James*, vol. 3, 339.

57. John Dewey, "William James as Empiricist" (1942), *The Later Works, 1925–1953*, ed. Jo Ann Boydston (Carbondale: Southern Illinois University Press, 1981–90), vol. 15, 9.

CHAPTER FIVE: AGASSIZ

1. See Edward Lurie, *Louis Agassiz: A Life in Science* (Chicago: University of Chicago Press, 1960), 122–7.

2. See Robert V. Bruce, *The Launching of Modern American Science, 1846–1876* (New York: Knopf, 1987), 7–74; and Dirk J. Struik, *Yankee Science in the Making*, rev. ed. (New York: Collier, 1962), 433–4.

3. Louis Agassiz, "Evolution and Permanence of Type," *Atlantic Monthly*, 33 (1874): 95.

4. See Lane Cooper, *Louis Agassiz as a Teacher: Illustrative Extracts on His Method of Instruction*, rev. ed. (Ithaca, N.Y.: Comstock, 1945), 82.

5. See William James, "Louis Agassiz" (1896), *Essays, Comments, and Reviews, The Works of William James*, ed. Frederick H. Burkhardt (Cambridge, Mass.: Harvard University Press, 1975–88), 49; Nathaniel Southgate Shaler, *The Autobiography of Nathaniel Southgate Shaler, with a Supplementary Memoir by His Wife* (Boston:

Houghton Mifflin, 1909), 98–9; Edward Waldo Emerson, *The Early Years of the Saturday Club: 1855–1870* (Boston: Houghton Mifflin, 1918), 34; and Cooper, *Louis Agassiz as a Teacher*, 26–7, 32–3, 55–61. See also Ezra Pound, *ABC of Reading* (New Haven: Yale University Press, 1934), 3–4.

6. See Samuel Eliot Morison, *Three Centuries of Harvard, 1636–1936* (Cambridge, Mass.: Harvard University Press, 1936), 297; Emerson, *The Early Years of the Saturday Club*, 35; Struik, *Yankee Science in the Making*, 359; and Bruce, *The Launching of Modern American Science*, 233.

7. Shaler, *The Autobiography of Nathaniel Southgate Shaler*, 170.

8. Samuel George Morton, *Crania Americana; or, A Comparative View of the Skulls of Various Aboriginal Nations of North and South America* (Philadelphia: J. Dobson, 1839), 5–7.

9. See Morton, *Crania Americana*, 261; and J. Aitken Meigs, *Catalogue of Human Crania in the Collection of the Academy of Natural Sciences of Philadelphia* (Philadelphia: Lippincott, 1857), 4 (the third edition of Morton's 1849 catalogue).

10. See Stephen Jay Gould, "Morton's Ranking of Races by Cranial Capacity," *Science*, 200 (1978): 503–9; and, generally, William Stanton, *The Leopard's Spots: Scientific Attitudes toward Race in America, 1815–1859* (Chicago: University of Chicago Press, 1960), 24–44; Thomas F. Gossett, *Race: The History of an Idea in America* (Dallas: Southern Methodist University Press, 1963), 54–83; John S. Haller, Jr., *Outcasts from Evolution: Scientific Attitudes of Racial Inferiority, 1859–1900* (Urbana: University of Illinois Press, 1971); George M. Fredrickson, *The Black Image in the White Mind: The Debate on Afro-American Character and Destiny, 1817–1914* (New York: Harper & Row, 1971), 71–96; and Stephen Jay Gould, *The Mismeasure of Man* (New York: Norton, 1981), 30–72.

11. See Louis Agassiz, "Notice sur la géographie des animaux," *Revue Suisse* (April 1845): "L'homme, malgré la diversité de ses races, constitue une seule et même espèce sur toute la surface du globe." Quoted in Jules Marcou, *Life, Letters, and Works of Louis Agassiz* (New York: Macmillan, 1896), vol. 1, 293.

12. Marcou, *Life, Letters, and Works of Louis Agassiz*, vol. 2, 29.

13. See Richard H. Popkin, "The Philosophical Bases of Modern Racism," in Craig Walton and John P. Anton, eds., *Philosophy and the Civilizing Arts* (Athens: Ohio University Press, 1974), 126–65.

14. James Hunt, "On the Negro's Place in Nature," *Memoirs Read before the Anthropological Society of London*, 1 (1865): 27 n. 14.

15. Louis Agassiz to Rose Agassiz, December 2, 1846, Louis Agassiz Papers, Houghton Library, Harvard University bMS Am 1419 (66).

> Cette collection à elle seule vaut un voyage en Amérique. . . . [T]ous les domestiques de l'hôtel que j'habitais étaient des hommes de couleur. J'ose à peine vous dire l'impression pénible que j'en ai reçu, tant le sentiment qu'ils m'ont inspiré est contraire à toutes nos idées de confraternité du genre humain & d'origine unique de notre espèce. Mais la vérité avant

tout. Autant j'éprouvais de pitié à la vue de cette race dégradée et dé-
générée, autant leur sort m'inspire de compassion en pensant que ce sont
réellement des hommes; autant il m'est impossible de réprimer le sentiment qu'ils ne sont pas du même sang que nous. En voyant leur faces
noires avec leurs grosse lèvres et leurs dents grimaçantes, leur laine sur la
tête, leurs genous fléchis, leur main alongée, leurs grands ongles cruchus
et surtout la tainte livide de la paume de la main, je ne pouvais détourner
les yeux de dessus leur figure, comme pour leur dire de rester à distance
et quand ils avançoient cette hideuse main sur mon assiette pour me
servir, j'aurais voulu pouvoir m'éloigner pour manger un morceau de pain
à l'écart plutôt que de diner avec un pareil service. Quel malheur pour la
race blanche d'avoir lié si étroitement son existence avec celle des nègres,
dans certaines contrées! Dieu nous préserve d'un pareil contact! . . . Les
philantropes qui veulent en faire des citoyens de leur communauté
oublient constamment qu'en leur accordait les droits politiques, ils ne
peuvent leur donner ni le soleil d'Afrique pour favoriser leur plein
développement, ni un foyer domestique parmi eux, car ils leur re-
fuseraient leurs filles s'ils les demandaient, et personne d'entr'eux ne
songerait à épouser une négresse. Les défendeurs de l'esclavage oublient
que pour être noir ces hommes ont autant le droit que nous à la jouis-
sance de leur liberté et ils ne vaient dans cette question qu'une question
de propriété, l'héritage garanti par la loi et dont la perte seroit leur ruine.

16. See Edward Lurie, "Louis Agassiz and the Races of Man," *Isis*, 45 (1954): 235.

17. Louis Agassiz, "The Diversity of Origin of the Human Races," *Christian Examiner*, 49 (1850): 116.

18. Louis Agassiz, *Contributions to the Natural History of the United States of America* (Boston: Little, Brown, 1857–62), vol. 1, 25.

19. Louis Agassiz, *Twelve Lectures on Comparative Embryology* (New York: Dewitt and Davenport, 1849), 96–7, 11.

20. Agassiz, *Twelve Lectures on Comparative Embryology*, 11, 26.

21. See Lurie, *Louis Agassiz*, 27–8, 50–2; and Stephen Jay Gould, *Ontogeny and Phylogeny* (Cambridge, Mass.: Harvard University Press, 1977), 33–68.

22. George R. Gliddon to Samuel George Morton, January 9, 1848, Samuel Morton Papers, Historical Society of Pennsylvania; quoted in Stanton, *The Leopard's Spots*, 100.

23. Agassiz, *Contributions to the Natural History of the United States*, vol. 1, 177.

24. Quoted in Lurie, *Louis Agassiz*, 260.

25. J. C. Nott, "The Mulatto a Hybrid—probable extermination of the two races if the White and Black are allowed to intermarry," *American Journal of the Medical Sciences*, n.s. 11 (1843): 253.

26. Josiah Nott to Samuel George Morton, May 26, 1850, Morton Papers; quoted in Lurie, "Louis Agassiz and the Races of Man," 237.

27. Agassiz, "The Diversity of Origin of the Human Races," 125, 128.

28. J. C. Nott and George R. Gliddon, *Indigenous Races of the Earth; or, New Chapters of Ethnological Inquiry* (Philadelphia: Lippincott, 1857), 639.

29. See J. C. Nott and George R. Gliddon, *Types of Mankind; or, Ethnological Researches* (Philadelphia: Lippincott, Grambo, 1854), xxxii–xxxiii, 79.

30. Louis Agassiz, "Sketch of the Natural Provinces of the Animal World and Their Relation to the Different Types of Man," in Nott and Gliddon, *Types of Mankind*, lxxvi.

31. Louis Agassiz to James Dwight Dana, July 18, 1856, quoted in Lurie, "Louis Agassiz and the Races of Man," 239 n. 60. Manuscript Collection, Rare Book Room, Yale University.

32. Nott and Gliddon, *Indigenous Races of the Earth*, 650.

33. Samuel A. Cartwright, "Unity of the Human Races Disproved by the Hebrew Bible," *De Bow's Review*, 29 (1860): 131, 130.

34. Agassiz, "The Diversity of Origin of the Human Races," 111, 144–5.

35. Samuel Gridley Howe to Louis Agassiz, August 3, 1863, autograph copy, Agassiz Papers (415).

36. See Samuel George Morton, "Hybridity in Animals, Considered in Reference to the Question of the Unity of the Human Species," *American Journal of Science and Art*, 2nd series 3 (1847): 39–50, 203–11.

37. Louis Agassiz to Samuel Gridley Howe, August 9, 1863, autograph copy, Agassiz Papers (150).

38. Louis Agassiz to Samuel Gridley Howe, August 10, 1863, autograph copy, Agassiz Papers (152).

39. Samuel Gridley Howe to Louis Agassiz, August 18, 1863, Agassiz Papers (416).

CHAPTER SIX: BRAZIL

1. William James to his family, September 16, 1861, *The Correspondence of William James*, ed. Ignas K. Skrupskelis and Elizabeth M. Berkeley (Charlottesville: University Press of Virginia, 1992–), vol. 4, 43.

2. See Edward Lurie, *Louis Agassiz: A Life in Science* (Chicago: University of Chicago Press, 1960), 344–50, and Christoph Irmscher, *The Poetics of Natural History: From John Bartram to William James* (New Brunswick: Rutgers University Press, 1999), 236–81. My pages on the Brazil expedition were written before Irmscher's superb account appeared.

3. William James to Mary James, March 31, 1865, *The Correspondence of William James*, vol. 4, 99.

4. See Lurie, *Louis Agassiz*, 345–6.

5. See, generally, Ernst Mayr, "Typological versus Population Thinking" (1959), *Evo-*

lution and the Diversity of Life: Selected Essays (Cambridge, Mass.: Harvard University Press, 1976), 26–9; Michael T. Ghiselin, *The Triumph of the Darwinian Method* (1969; new ed., Chicago: University of Chicago Press, 1984); Robert J. Richards, *Darwin and the Emergence of Evolutionary Theories of Mind and Behavior* (Chicago: University of Chicago Press, 1987); Ernst Mayr, *One Long Argument: Charles Darwin and the Genesis of Modern Evolutionary Thought* (Cambridge, Mass.: Harvard University Press, 1991); Jonathan Weiner, *The Beak of the Finch: A Story of Evolution in Real Time* (New York: Knopf, 1994); and Edward S. Reed, *From Soul to Mind: The Emergence of Psychology from Erasmus Darwin to William James* (New Haven: Yale University Press, 1997), esp. 168–83.

6. Charles Darwin, *On the Origin of Species* (1859), *The Works of Charles Darwin*, ed. Paul H. Barrett and R. B. Freeman (Cambridge, England: Cambridge University Press, 1988–), vol. 15, 39.

7. See, generally, Ernst Mayr, "Agassiz, Darwin, and Evolution" (1959), *Evolution and the Diversity of Life*, 251–76.

8. Charles Darwin to Joseph Dalton Hooker, January 11, 1844, *The Correspondence of Charles Darwin*, ed. Frederick H. Burkhardt and Sydney Smith (Cambridge, England: Cambridge University Press, 1985–), vol. 3, 2.

9. Asa Gray to Joseph Dalton Hooker, July 13, 1858, quoted in A. Hunter Dupree, *Asa Gray, 1810–1888* (Cambridge, Mass.: Harvard University Press, 1959), 229.

10. Asa Gray, "Statistics of the Flora of the Northern United States," *American Journal of Science and Arts*, 2nd series 23 (1857): 389.

11. Meeting of January 11, 1859, *Proceedings of the American Academy of Arts and Sciences*, 4 (1857–60): 132.

12. Meeting of February 22, 1859, *Proceedings of the American Academy of Arts and Sciences*, 4 (1857–60): 179.

13. Louis Agassiz, "Prof. Agassiz on the Origin of Species," *American Journal of Science and Arts*, 2nd series 30 (1860): 154.

14. See Asa Gray, "The Origin of Species by Means of Natural Selection" (1860) and "Natural Selection Not Inconsistent with Natural Theology" (1860), *Darwiniana: Essays and Reviews Pertaining to Darwinism* (New York: D. Appleton, 1876), 9–61, 87–177.

15. Gray, "The Origin of Species by Means of Natural Selection," 58.

16. Louis Agassiz, *Contributions to the Natural History of the United States of America* (Boston: Little, Brown, 1857–62), vol. 3, 88; vol. 1, 135.

17. [John Amory Lowell], "Darwin's Origin of Species," *Christian Examiner*, 68 (1860): 458.

18. Charles Darwin to Charles Lyell, June 14, 1860, *The Correspondence of Charles Darwin*, vol. 8, 253.

19. See Dupree, *Asa Gray*, 323.

20. Henry James, Sr., to Isaac W. Jackson, January 13, 1830, William James Papers, Houghton Library, Harvard University, bMS Am 1092.9 (4153).

21. Louis Agassiz and Elizabeth Agassiz, *A Journey in Brazil* (Boston: Ticknor and Fields, 1868), 33.

22. William James to his parents, April 21, 1865, *The Correspondence of William James*, vol. 4, 101.

23. William James to Henry James, May 3–10, 1865, *The Correspondence of William James*, vol. 1, 6–7, 8.

24. William James to Mary James, August 23, 1865, *The Correspondence of William James*, vol. 4, 111. See also William James, "Louis Agassiz" (1896), *Essays, Comments, and Reviews, The Works of William James*, ed. Frederick H. Burkhardt (Cambridge, Mass.: Harvard University Press, 1975–88), 50 ("'Mr. Blank, you are *totally* uneducated!' I heard him once say to a student who propounded to him some glittering theoretic generality").

25. William James to Henry James, Sr., September 12–17, 1865, *The Correspondence of William James*, vol. 4, 122.

26. Louis Agassiz to Benjamin Peirce, May 27, 1865, quoted in Agassiz and Agassiz, *A Journey in Brazil*, 86, 89; William James to Henry James, July 15, 1865, *The Correspondence of William James*, vol. 1, 10.

27. Notebook Z, [p. 8], William James Papers (4498).

28. Quoted in Jules Marcou, *Life, Letters, and Works of Louis Agassiz* (New York: Macmillan, 1896), vol. 2, 132.

29. See Lurie, *Louis Agassiz*, 158–9.

30. See José Honório Rodrigues, *Brazil and Africa*, trans. Richard A. Mazzara and Sam Hileman (Berkeley and Los Angeles: University of California Press, 1965), 52–73, 86, 158–60; and Lilia Moritz Schwarcz, *The Spectacle of the Races: Scientists, Institutions, and the Race Question in Brazil, 1870–1930*, trans. Leland Guyer (New York: Hill and Wang, 1999), 6–11.

31. Agassiz and Agassiz, *A Journey in Brazil*, 296.

32. Agassiz and Agassiz, *A Journey in Brazil*, 49.

33. Agassiz and Agassiz, *A Journey in Brazil*, 128–9.

34. Agassiz and Agassiz, *A Journey in Brazil*, 224.

35. Agassiz and Agassiz, *A Journey in Brazil*, 246.

36. Notebook Z, [p. 7], William James Papers.

37. Notebook Z, [pp. 12–13], William James Papers.

38. William James to his parents, April 21, 1865, *The Correspondence of William James*, vol. 4, 101.

39. William James to Henry James, Sr., June 3–7, 1865, *The Correspondence of William James*, vol. 4, 106.

40. William James to Mary James, August 23–27, 1865, *The Correspondence of William James*, vol. 4, 110–11.

41. William James to Mary James, December 9, 1865, *The Correspondence of William James*, vol. 4, 131–2.

42. William James to his parents, April 21–23, 1865, *The Correspondence of William James*, vol. 4, 103.

43. Charles Darwin to Charles Lyell, September 8, 1866, *More Letters of Charles Darwin: A Record of His Work in a Series of Hitherto Unpublished Letters*, ed. Francis Darwin and A. C. Seward (New York: D. Appleton, 1903), vol. 2, 160:

    I have just received a letter from Asa Gray with the following passage, so that, according to this, I am the chief cause of Agassiz's absurd views:— "Agassiz is back (I have not seen him), and he went at once down to the National Academy of Sciences, from which I sedulously keep away, and, I hear, proved to them that the Glacial period covered the whole continent of America with unbroken ice, and closed with a significant gesture and the remark: 'So here is the end of the Darwinian theory.'"

44. Charles Darwin to Charles Lyell, *More Letters of Charles Darwin*, vol. 2, 159.

45. Anna Eliot Ticknor to Elizabeth Agassiz, January 3, 1868, Louis Agassiz Papers, Houghton Library, Harvard University, bMS Am 1419 (636).

46. Agassiz and Agassiz, *A Journey in Brazil*, 293n.

47. Agassiz and Agassiz, *A Journey in Brazil*, 297–9.

48. Agassiz and Agassiz, *A Journey in Brazil*, 530, 532.

49. Henry Adams, *The Education of Henry Adams* (1907), *Novels, Mont Saint Michel, The Education* (New York: Library of America, 1983), 932.

50. William James, "Review of *The Origin of Human Races*, by Alfred R. Wallace" (1865), *Essays, Comments, and Reviews*, 208.

51. Adams, *The Education of Henry Adams*, 925.

52. William James, "Two Reviews of *The Variation of Animals and Plants under Domestication*, by Charles Darwin" (1868), *Essays, Comments, and Reviews*, 234–5.

53. William James to Henry James, March 9, 1868, *The Correspondence of William James*, vol. 1, 39.

54. See [Herbert Spencer], "A Theory of Population, Deduced from the General Law of Animal Fertility," *Westminster and Foreign Quarterly Review*, 57 (1852): 457–501.

55. Adams, *The Education of Henry Adams*, 926.

56. Josiah C. Nott, *The Negro Race: Its Ethnology and History* (Mobile, 1866); see also Nott, "Climates of the South in Their Relation to White Labor," *De Bow's Review*, 34 (1866): 166–73, and "The Problem of the Black Races," *De Bow's Review*, 34 (1866): 266–83.

57. Agassiz and Agassiz, *A Journey in Brazil*, 296.

58. Quoted in Josiah C. Nott and George R. Gliddon, *Types of Mankind: or, Ethnological Researches* (Philadelphia: Lippincott, Grambo, 1854), li–lii.

59. William James to Henry James, [January 1868], *The Correspondence of William James*, vol. 1, 29.

60. William James, "Review of *Rapport sur le progrès de l'anthropologie en France*, by Armand de Quatrefages" (1868), *Essays, Comments, and Reviews*, 217.

61. See John Henry Hopkins, *A Scriptural, Ecclesiastical, and Historical View of Slavery, from the Days of the Patriarch Abraham, to the Nineteenth Century, Addressed to the Right Rev. Alonzo Potter, D.D.* (New York: W. I. Pooley, 1864).

62. Garth Wilkinson James to Robertson James, December 26, 1882, quoted in Jane Maher, *Biography of Broken Fortunes: Wilkie and Bob, Brothers of William, Henry, and Alice James* (Hamden, Conn.: Archon Books, 1986), 150.

63. William James, "Robert Gould Shaw" (1897), *Essays in Religion and Morality, The Works of William James*, 72–3.

CHAPTER SEVEN: THE PEIRCES

1. William James to his family, September 16, 1861, *The Correspondence of William James*, ed. Ignas K. Skrupskelis and Elizabeth M. Berkeley (Charlottesville: University Press of Virginia, 1992–), vol. 4, 43.

2. William James, Notebook V (1862), William James Papers, Houghton Library, Harvard University, bMS Am 1092.9 (4496).

3. Edward Waldo Emerson, *The Early Years of the Saturday Club: 1855–1870* (Boston: Houghton Mifflin, 1918), 97. See also Edward Everett Hale, "My College Days," *Atlantic Monthly*, 71 (1893): 355–63; Sven R. Peterson, "Benjamin Peirce: Mathematician and Philosopher," *Journal of the History of Ideas*, 16 (1955): 93–4; and V. F. Lenzen, *Benjamin Peirce and the U.S. Coast Survey* (San Francisco: San Francisco Press, 1968), 43–4.

4. Emerson, *The Early Years of the Saturday Club*, 97–8.

5. See Florian Cajori, *The Teaching and History of Mathematics in the United States* (Washington, D.C.: Government Printing Office, 1890), 136–42; and Robert V. Bruce, *The Launching of Modern American Science, 1846–1876* (New York: Knopf, 1987), 40–1.

6. A. Lawrence Lowell, "Reminiscences," *American Mathematical Monthly*, 32 (1925): 4.

7. Charles William Eliot, "Reminiscences of Peirce," *American Mathematical Monthly*, 32 (1925): 2.

8. Eliot, "Reminiscences of Peirce," 3.

9. See Simon Newcomb, *The Reminiscences of an Astronomer* (Boston: Houghton Mifflin, 1903), 78.

10. Benjamin Peirce, *Linear Associative Algebra* (1870), ed. C. S. Peirce (New York: Van Nostrand, 1882), 1.

11. Benjamin Peirce, *Ideality in the Physical Sciences* (Boston: Little, Brown, 1881), 163–4.

12. Peirce, *Linear Associative Algebra*, 2.

13. Peirce, *Ideality in the Physical Sciences*, 54, 56.

14. Peirce, *Linear Associative Algebra*, 1.

15. R. C. Archibald, "Biographical Sketch," *American Mathematical Monthly*, 32 (1925): 11 n. 1.

16. See Charles S. Peirce, "Studies in Meaning" (1909), MS 619, Charles S. Peirce Papers, Houghton Library, Harvard University; Helen Peirce Ellis, draft of newspaper article (1914), MS 1644, Charles S. Peirce Papers; P[aul] W[eiss], "Charles Sanders Peirce," *Dictionary of American Biography* (New York: Scribner, 1928–60), vol. 7, 402; and Joseph Brent, *Charles Sanders Peirce: A Life* (Bloomington: Indiana University Press, 1993), 53–4.

17. See Brent, *Charles Sanders Peirce*, 40.

18. See Kenneth Laine Ketner, *His Glassy Essence: An Autobiography of Charles Sanders Peirce* (Nashville: Vanderbilt University Press, 1998), 213–22.

19. Charles S. Peirce, "The Class of 1859 of Harvard," MS 1635, Charles S. Peirce Papers.

20. Peirce, "Studies in Meaning," Charles S. Peirce Papers.

21. Benjamin Peirce to Josephine Le Conte, January 21, 1860, Le Conte Family Papers, Banc MSs C-B 1014, Box 1, 1852–58, Manuscripts Collection, Bancroft Library, University of California at Berkeley.

22. See, for example, Benjamin Peirce, "The National Importance of Social Science in the United States," *Journal of Social Science*, 12 (December 1880), xii–xxi.

23. Benjamin Peirce to John and Josephine Le Conte, March 3, 1858, Le Conte Family Papers, Box 1, 1859–75.

24. Thomas Wentworth Higginson, "How I Was Educated," *Forum*, 1 (1866): 176.

25. See Charles S. Peirce, "The Logic of Science; Or, Induction and Hypothesis" (1866), *Writings of Charles S. Peirce: A Chronological Edition*, Peirce Edition Project (Bloomington: Indiana University Press, 1982–), vol. 1, 444.

26. Charles S. Peirce to Victoria Welby, March 14, 1909, *Charles S. Peirce's Letters to Lady Welby*, ed. Irwin C. Lieb (New Haven: Whitlock, 1953), 37.

27. Charles S. Peirce to Alexander Dallas Bache, August 11, 1862, National Archives, Washington, D.C., Coast and Geodetic Survey, Civil Assistants.

28. See Emerson, *The Early Years of the Saturday Club*, 104, 102.

29. Alice James to William James, August 6, 1867, *The Correspondence of William James*, vol. 4, 191.

30. Benjamin Peirce to Alexander Dallas Bache, March 13, 1862, quoted in Brent, *Charles Sanders Peirce*, 62.

31. See Lance E. Davis, Robert E. Gallman, and Karin Gleiter, *In Pursuit of Leviathan: Technology, Institutions, Productivity, and Profits in American Whaling, 1816–1906* (Chicago: University of Chicago Press, 1997), 38, 416–17, 444.

32. See Davis, Gallman, and Gleiter, *In Pursuit of Leviathan*, 405–6, 418–19, 422; "The Howland Will Case," *American Law Review*, 4 (1870): 625–7; George F. Tucker, "New Bedford," *New England Magazine*, 21 (1896): 100–101; and William E. Emery, *The Howland Heirs: Being the Story of a Family and a Fortune and the Inheritance of a Trust Established for Mrs. Hetty H. R. Green* (New Bedford: E. Anthony, 1919), 46–57.

33. See Davis, Gallman, and Gleiter, *In Pursuit of Leviathan*, 41, 362–3; Walter S. Tower, *A History of the American Whale Fishery* (Philadelphia: Publications of the University of Pennsylvania, 1907), 67, 76–9; and Margaret S. Creighton, *Rites and Passages: The Experience of American Whaling, 1830–1870* (Cambridge, England: Cambridge University Press, 1995), 37–9.

34. See Thomas Dawes Eliot, *Hetty H. Robinson, in equity, vs. Thomas Mandell et al., U.S. District Court, Massachusetts District: Arguments, in 3 Parts*, reported by J. M. W. Yerrinton (Boston: Alfred Mudge, 1867), part one, 73; "The Howland Will Case," 630–1.

35. See "The Howland Will Case," 629–30; and Eliot, *Hetty H. Robinson vs. Thomas Mandell*, part one, 1–3.

36. See Eliot, *Hetty H. Robinson vs. Thomas Mandell*, part one, 3, 5; "The Howland Will Case," 626–30; Emery, *The Howland Heirs*, 60–7; Boyden Sparkes and Samuel Taylor Moore, *Hetty Green: A Woman Who Loved Money* (Garden City, N.Y.: Doubleday, Doran, 1930), 35, 100, 102–3.

37. Eliot, *Hetty H. Robinson vs. Thomas Mandell*, part two, 118.

38. See "The Howland Will Case," 650.

39. Eliot, *Hetty H. Robinson vs. Thomas Mandell*, part two, 175.

40. See Deposition of Charles Saunders [*sic*] Peirce, Supreme Court of the United States, No. 389, *Edward H. Green and Hetty H., His Wife, Appellants, vs. Thomas Mandell et al.: Appeal from the Circuit Court of the United States for the District of Massachusetts*, December 17, 1868, 761–5.

41. Deposition of Benjamin Peirce, Supreme Court of the United States, *Edward H. Green vs. Thomas Mandell*, 768.

42. Eliot, *Hetty H. Robinson vs. Thomas Mandell*, part one, 120.

43. V.X., "Mathematics in Court," *Nation*, 5 (September 19, 1867): 238.

44. *Robinson v. Mandell et al.*, Circuit Court for the District of Massachusetts, 20 Fed. Cas. 1027, 1033 (1868).

45. See Emery, *The Howland Heirs*, 358–68.

CHAPTER EIGHT: THE LAW OF ERRORS

1. See Stephen M. Stigler, *The History of Statistics: The Measurement of Uncertainty before 1900* (Cambridge, Mass.: Harvard University Press, 1986), 158; and, generally, Gerd Gigerenzer, Zeno Swijtink, Theodore Porter, Lorraine Daston, John

Beatty, and Lorenz Krüger, *The Empire of Chance: How Probability Changed Science and Everyday Life* (Cambridge, England: Cambridge University Press, 1989); Ian Hacking, *The Emergence of Probability: A Philosophical Study of Early Ideas about Probability, Induction and Statistical Inference* (Cambridge, England: Cambridge University Press, 1975), and *The Taming of Chance* (Cambridge, England: Cambridge University Press, 1990); Theodore M. Porter, *The Rise of Statistical Thinking, 1820–1900* (Princeton: Princeton University Press, 1986); and M. Norton Wise, ed., *The Values of Precision* (Princeton: Princeton University Press, 1995).

2. The first edition of De Moivre's *The Doctrine of Chances; or, A Method of Calculating the Probability of Events in Play* appeared in 1718; his theory of the bell-shaped curve, technically known as the normal approximation to the binomial distribution, was first published as a paper, in Latin, in 1733. See Stigler, *The History of Statistics*, 71.

3. See, generally, Charles Coulston Gillispie, *Pierre-Simon Laplace, 1749–1827: A Life in Exact Science* (Princeton: Princeton University Press, 1997), 13–28, 216–42; Porter, *The Rise of Statistical Thinking*, 93–109; and Stigler, *The History of Statistics*, 143–58.

4. See John Theodore Merz, *A History of European Thought in the Nineteenth Century* (Edinburgh and London: William Blackwood, 1904–12), vol. 1, 125.

5. See Gillispie, *Pierre-Simon Laplace*, 172–5.

6. See Merz, *A History of European Thought in the Nineteenth Century*, vol. 1, 325 n. 1; and Zeno G. Swijtink, "The Objectification of Observation: Measurement and Statistical Methods in the Nineteenth Century," in *The Probabilistic Revolution*, ed. Lorenz Krüger, Lorraine J. Daston, and Michael Heidelberger (Cambridge, Mass.: MIT Press, 1987), vol. 1, 261–85.

7. Pierre-Simon Laplace, *Théorie analytique des probabilités*, 3rd ed. (1820), *Oeuvres complètes de Laplace* (Paris: Gauthier-Villars, 1878–1912), vol. 7, vi (the *Essai* was originally published as the introduction to the *Théorie*):

> Tous les événements, ceux même qui par leur petitesse semblent ne pas tenir aux grandes lois de la nature, en sont une suite aussi nécessaire que les révolutions du Soleil. Dans l'ignorance des lien qui les unissent au système entier de l'univers, on les a fait dépendre des causes finales ou du hasard, suivant qu'ils arrivaient et se succédaient avec régularité ou sans ordre apparent; mais ces causes imaginaires ont été successivement reculées avec les bornes de nos connaissances, et disparaissent entièrement devant la saine philosophie, qui ne voit en elles que l'expression de l'ignorance où nous sommes des véritables causes.

8. Benjamin Peirce, *Ideality in the Physical Sciences* (Boston: Little, Brown, 1881), 52.

9. See V. F. Lenzen, *Benjamin Peirce and the U.S. Coast Survey* (San Francisco: San Francisco Press, 1968), 7.

10. See Florian Cajori, *The Teaching and History of Mathematics in the United States* (Washington, D.C.: Government Printing Office, 1890), 145; Edward Waldo Emerson, *The Early Years of the Saturday Club: 1855–1870* (Boston: Houghton Mifflin,

1918), 100; Lenzen, *Benjamin Peirce and the U.S. Coast Survey*, 8–25; "Benjamin Peirce," *Proceedings of the American Academy of Arts and Sciences*, 16 (1880–81), 446–7; and Peirce, *Ideality in the Physical Sciences*, 172–4.

11. Benjamin Peirce, "Criterion for the Rejection of Doubtful Observations," *Astronomical Journal*, 2 (1852): 161.

12. See Gigerenzer et al., *The Empire of Chance*, 83; and Lenzen, *Benjamin Peirce and the U.S. Coast Survey*, 6.

13. See, generally, C. C. Gillispie, "Intellectual Factors in the Background of Analysis by Probabilities," in *Scientific Change: Historical Studies in the Intellectual, Social, and Technical Conditions for Scientific Discovery and Technical Invention, from Antiquity to the Present*, ed. A. C. Crombie (New York: Basic Books, 1963), 431–53; Hacking, *The Taming of Chance*, 105–24; Porter, *The Rise of Statistical Thinking*, 41–55, 100–9; and Stigler, *The History of Statistics*, 161–220.

14. A. Quetelet, *Sur l'homme et le développement de ses facultés, ou Essai de physique sociale* (Paris: Bachelier, 1835), vol. 1, 1: "L'homme naît, se développe, et meurt d'après certaines lois qui n'ont jamais été étudiées."

15. Quoted in Ian Hacking, "Nineteenth-Century Cracks in the Concept of Determinism," *Journal of the History of Ideas*, 44 (1983): 469.

16. Quetelet, *Sur l'homme*, vol. 2, 324: "[C]'est la société qui prépare le crime et . . . le coupable n'est que l'instrument qui l'exécute."

17. Quetelet, *Sur l'homme*, vol. 2, 251, 276: "L'homme moyen, en effet, est dans une nation ce que le centre de gravité est dans un corps"; "un individu qui résumerait en lui-même, à une époque donnée, toutes les qualités de l'homme moyen, représenterait à la fois tout ce qu'il y a de grand, de beau et de bien." In the English translation, "l'homme moyen" appeared as "the average man" (*A Treatise on Man and the Development of His Faculties*, trans. R. Knox [Edinburgh: Chambers, 1842], 96).

18. See Hacking, *The Taming of Chance*, 109–14; and Stigler, *The History of Statistics*, 203–14. Quetelet made some mistakes with the data; for example, there were actually 5,732 soldiers.

19. See Hacking, *The Taming of Chance*, 62.

20. M. A. Quetelet, "Sur les proportions de la race noire," *Bulletin de l'académie royale des sciences, des lettres, et des beaux-arts de belgique*, 31, part 1 (1854): 100: "Les grandes linéaments de l'espèce humaine paraissent à peu près les mêmes pour les différents pays, et pour les différents races." See also Quetelet, "Sur les indiens O-Jib-Be-Wa's et les proportions de leur corps," *Bulletin de l'académie royale des sciences, des lettres, et des beaux-arts de belgique*, 15, part 1 (1846): 70–6.

21. See Gigerenzer et al., *The Empire of Chance*, 129.

22. See Gigerenzer et al., *The Empire of Chance*, 49–53; Hacking, "Nineteenth-Century Cracks in the Concept of Determinism," 473; and Merz, *A History of European Thought*, vol. 1, 587n.

23. Review of *On Man, and the Development of His Faculties, Athenaeum*, no. 409 (August 29, 1835): 661.

24. Henry Thomas Buckle, *History of Civilization in England*, vol. 1 (London: John W. Parker, 1857), 31, 30. (I have changed the order of the sentences.)

25. Buckle, *History of Civilization in England*, 27.

26. Buckle, *History of Civilization in England*, 36.

27. Buckle, *History of Civilization in England*, 29–30.

28. Buckle, *History of Civilization in England*, 216.

29. Buckle, *History of Civilization in England*, 140.

30. [James Fitzjames Stephen], "Buckle's *History of Civilization in England*," *Edinburgh Review*, 107 (1858): 471.

31. See Hacking, "Nineteenth-Century Cracks in the Concept of Determinism," 471–5, and *The Taming of Chance*, 125–32; and Silvan S. Schweber, "Demons, Angels, and Probability: Some Aspects of British Science in the Nineteenth Century," in *Physics as Natural Philosophy*, ed. Abner Shimony and Herman Feshbach (Cambridge, Mass.: MIT Press, 1982), 341–63.

32. See Schweber, "Demons, Angels, and Probability," 346–8; and Theodore M. Porter, "A Statistical Survey of Gases: Maxwell's Social Physics," *Historical Studies in the Physical Sciences*, 12 (1981): 82–3.

33. Buckle, *History of Civilization in England*, 194, 1.

34. Thomas H. Huxley, "Emancipation—Black and White" (1865), *Science and Education: Essays* (New York: D. Appleton, 1895), 67.

35. Benjamin Peirce, *Linear Associative Algebra* (1870), ed. C. S. Peirce (New York: Van Nostrand, 1882), 2.

36. Laplace, *Théorie analytique des probabilités*, vi–vii:

> Nous devons donc envisager l'état présent de l'univers comme l'effet de son état antérieur et comme la cause de celui qui va suivre. Une intelligence qui, pour un instant donné, connaîtrait toutes les forces dont la nature est animée et la situation respective des êtres qui la composent, si d'ailleurs elle était assez vaste pour soumettre ces données à l'Analyse, embrasserait dans la même formule les mouvements des plus grands corps de l'univers et ceux du plus léger atome: rien ne serait incertain pour elle, et l'avenir, comme le passé, serait présent à ses yeux.

The demon made an appearance in Laplace's lectures as early as 1795; see Hacking, *The Taming of Chance*, 11.

37. [Joseph] Lovering, "On the Application of Mathematical Analysis to Researches in the Physical Sciences," *Cambridge Miscellany of Mathematics, Physics, and Astronomy*, 1 (1842): 79.

38. Laplace, *Théorie analytique des probabilités*, vii: "il restera toujours infiniment éloigné."

39. Lovering, "On the Application of Mathematical Analysis," 122.

40. James Clerk Maxwell, "Illustrations of the Dynamical Theory of Gases" (1860), *The Scientific Papers of James Clerk Maxwell*, ed. W. D. Niven (Cambridge, England: Cambridge University Press, 1890), vol. 1, 377. The paper was read at a meeting of the British Association on September 21, 1859, and published in the *Philosophical Magazine*, January and July 1860.

41. James Clerk Maxwell, *Theory of Heat* (London: Longmans, 1871), 308–9. Maxwell first mentioned the demon in a letter to Peter Guthrie Tait, December 11, 1867; see *Maxwell on Heat and Statistical Mechanics: On "Avoiding All Personal Enquiries" of Molecules*, ed. Elizabeth Garber, Stephen G. Brush, and C. W. F. Everitt (Bethlehem, Pa.: Lehigh University Press, 1995), 177–8.

42. William Thomson, Baron Kelvin, "On a Universal Tendency in Nature to the Dissipation of Mechanical Energy," *Mathematical and Physical Papers* (Cambridge, England: Cambridge University Press, 1882–1911), vol. 1, 514.

43. James Clerk Maxwell to John William Strutt, December 6, 1870, in *Maxwell on Heat and Statistical Mechanics*, 205.

44. See Silvan S. Schweber, "The Origin of the *Origin* Revisited," *Journal of the History of Biology*, 10 (1977): 229–311, and "Demons, Angels, and Probability," 319–63.

45. Charles Darwin to Chauncey Wright, April 6, 1872, in James Bradley Thayer, *Letters of Chauncey Wright, with Some Account of His Life* (Cambridge, Mass.: privately printed by John Wilson, 1878), 236.

46. Merz, *A History of European Thought*, vol. 2, 567.

47. [John Herschel], "Quetelet on Probabilities," *Edinburgh Review*, 92 (1850): 11.

48. Charles Darwin to Charles Lyell, December 10, 1859, *The Correspondence of Charles Darwin*, ed. Frederick H. Burkhardt and Sydney Smith (Cambridge, England: Cambridge University Press, 1985–), vol. 7, 423 ("I have heard by round about channel that Herschel says my Book 'is the law of higgledy-pigglety' ").

CHAPTER NINE: THE METAPHYSICAL CLUB

1. Charles Sanders Peirce, "Pragmatism" (1907), MS 318, Charles S. Peirce Papers, Houghton Library, Harvard University; reprinted in part in *Collected Papers of Charles Sanders Peirce*, ed. Charles Hartshorne, Paul Weiss, and Arthur Burks (Cambridge, Mass.: Harvard University Press, 1931–66), vol. 5, sec. 12.

2. Henry James to Elizabeth Boott, January 24, 1872, *Letters*, ed. Leon Edel (Cambridge, Mass.: Harvard University Press, 1974–84), vol. 1, 269.

3. Henry James to Charles Eliot Norton, February 4, 1872, *Letters*, vol. 1, 273.

4. William James to Alice James, November 14, 1866, *The Correspondence of William James*, ed. Ignas K. Skrupskelis and Elizabeth M. Berkeley (Charlottesville: University Press of Virginia, 1992–), vol. 4, 144.

5. William James to Henry Pickering Bowditch, January 24, 1869, *The Correspondence of William James*, vol. 4, 361.

6. William James to Henry James, December 12, 1875, *The Correspondence of William James*, vol. 1, 246.

7. Oliver Wendell Holmes to Amelia Lee Jackson Holmes, December 12, 1866, *Touched with Fire: Civil War Letters and Diary of Oliver Wendell Holmes, Jr., 1861–1864*, ed. Mark DeWolfe Howe (Cambridge, Mass.: Harvard University Press, 1946), 75.

8. William James to Thomas Wren Ward, March 27, 1866, *The Correspondence of William James*, vol. 4, 137–8.

9. Henry James to Grace Norton, September 20, 1880, *Letters*, vol. 2, 307.

10. William James to Garth Wilkinson James, March 21, 1866, *The Correspondence of William James*, vol. 4, 135.

11. Amelia Lee Jackson Holmes to Oliver Wendell Holmes, July 3, 1866, Oliver Wendell Holmes Papers, Harvard Law School Library.

12. Charles Eliot Norton to James Bradley Thayer, in Thayer, *Letters of Chauncey Wright, with Some Account of His Life* (Cambridge, Mass.: privately printed by John Wilson, 1878), 90.

13. [Chauncey Wright], "The Winds and the Weather," *Atlantic Monthly*, 1 (1858): 273.

14. [Chauncey Wright], "John W. Draper's Thoughts on the Future Civil Policy of America," *North American Review*, 101 (1865): 597.

15. Wright, "The Winds and the Weather," 278–9.

16. Chauncey Wright to Susan Lesley, February 12, 1860, *Letters of Chauncey Wright*, 43.

17. Chauncey Wright to Charles Eliot Norton, August 10, 1866, Charles Eliot Norton Papers, Houghton Library, Harvard University, bMS Am 1088 (8280). (Agassiz's name is excised in *Letters of Chauncey Wright*.)

18. Chauncey Wright to Grace Norton, June 6, 1871, *Letters of Chauncey Wright*, 226.

19. *Charles Darwin's Marginalia*, ed. Mario A. di Gregorio (New York: Garland, 1990–), vol. 1, 164.

20. [Chauncey Wright], "The Philosophy of Herbert Spencer," *North American Review*, 100 (1865): 436.

21. [Chauncey Wright], "Spencer's Biology," *Nation*, 2 (1866): 725.

22. Wright, "The Philosophy of Herbert Spencer," 454–5.

23. Chauncey Wright to Francis Ellingwood Abbot, August 13, 1867, *Letters of Chauncey Wright*, 111.

24. [Chauncey Wright], "A Physical Theory of the Universe," *North American Review*, 99 (1864): 8–9, 10.

25. Chauncey Wright to Francis Ellingwood Abbot, August 13, 1867, *Letters of Chauncey Wright*, 109.

26. Chauncey Wright to Francis Ellingwood Abbot, October 28, 1867, *Letters of Chauncey Wright*, 133.

27. Chauncey Wright to Charles Eliot Norton, August 18, 1867, *Letters of Chauncey Wright*, 118.

28. Chauncey Wright to Charles Eliot Norton, March 21, 1870, *Letters of Chauncey Wright*, 170.

29. Chauncey Wright to Francis Ellingwood Abbot, July 9, 1867, *Letters of Chauncey Wright*, 100, 101–2.

30. Bliss Perry, *Life and Letters of Henry Lee Higginson* (Boston: Houghton Mifflin, 1920), 402.

31. Oliver Wendell Holmes, "Codes, and the Arrangement of the Law" (1870), *The Collected Works of Justice Holmes: Complete Public Writings and Selected Judicial Opinions of Oliver Wendell Holmes*, ed. Sheldon M. Novick (Chicago: University of Chicago Press, 1995–), vol. 1, 212.

32. Oliver Wendell Holmes to Harold J. Laski, November 29, 1923, *Holmes-Laski Letters: The Correspondence of Mr. Justice Holmes and Harold J. Laski, 1916–1935*, ed. Mark DeWolfe Howe (Cambridge, Mass.: Harvard University Press, 1953), 1: 565.

33. Oliver Wendell Holmes to Frederick Pollock, August 30, 1929, *Holmes-Pollock Letters: The Correspondence of Mr. Justice Holmes and Sir Frederick Pollock, 1874–1932*, ed. Mark DeWolfe Howe (Cambridge, Mass.: Harvard University Press, 1941), vol. 2, 252.

34. William James, "Against Nihilism" (1873–75), *Manuscript Essays and Notes, The Works of William James*, ed. Frederick H. Burkhardt (Cambridge, Mass.: Harvard University Press, 1975–88), 150.

35. William James to Thomas Wren Ward, March 1869, *The Correspondence of William James*, vol. 4, 370–1.

36. Charles Renouvier, *Essais de critique générale: deuxième essai: l'homme* (Paris: Ladrange, 1859), 390: "La certitude n'est donc pas et ne peut pas être un absolu. Elle est . . . un état et un acte de l'homme. . . . A proprement parler, il n'y a pas de certitude; il y a seulement des hommes certains."

37. William James, Diary, April 30, 1870, William James Papers, Houghton Library, Harvard University, bMS Am 1092.9 (4550).

38. See my "William James and the Case of the Epileptic Patient," *New York Review of Books*, 45 (December 17, 1998), 81–93; also James William Anderson, " 'The Worst Kind of Melancholy': William James in 1869," *Harvard Library Bulletin*, 30 (1982): 369–86; and Howard M. Feinstein, *Becoming William James* (Ithaca, N.Y.: Cornell University Press, 1984), esp. 298–315.

39. William James to Charles Renouvier, November 2, 1872, *The Correspondence of William James*, vol. 4, 430: "Je ne peux pas laisser échapper cette occasion de vous

dire toute l'admiration et la reconnaissance que m'ont inspirées la lecture de vos Essais. . . . Grace à vous je possède pour la première fois une conception intelligible et raisonnable de la Liberté. [J]e puis dire que par elle je commence à renaître à la vie morale, et croyez monsieur, que ce n'est pas une petite chose."

40. William James, "The Unseen Universe, by Peter Guthrie Tait and Balfour Stewart" (1875), Essays, Comments, and Reviews, The Works of William James, 293–4.

41. Chauncey Wright to Grace Norton, July 18, 1875, quoted in Ralph Barton Perry, The Thought and Character of William James (Boston: Little, Brown, 1935), vol. 1, 530.

42. Charles S. Peirce, "Essays Toward the Interpretation of Our Thoughts" (1909), MS 620, Charles S. Peirce Papers.

43. [Chauncey Wright], "Mathematics in Court," Nation, 5 (September 19, 1867): 238.

44. Peirce, "Pragmatism," Charles S. Peirce Papers; reprinted in part in Collected Papers of Charles Sanders Peirce, vol. 5, sec. 12.

45. James Clerk Maxwell, "Does the progress of Physical Science tend to give any advantage to the opinion of Necessity (or Determinism) over that of the Contingency of Events and the Freedom of the Will?" (1873), in Lewis Campbell and William Garnett, The Life of James Clerk Maxwell, rev. ed. (London: Macmillan, 1884), 363–4.

46. Charles S. Peirce, "The Architecture of Theories," Monist, 1 (1891): 165.

47. Charles S. Peirce, "The Fixation of Belief" (1877), Writings of Charles S. Peirce: A Chronological Edition, Peirce Edition Project (Bloomington: Indiana University Press, 1982–), vol. 3, 244.

48. Charles Sanders Peirce, Pragmatism as a Principle and Method of Right Thinking: The 1903 Harvard Lectures on Pragmatism, ed. Patricia Ann Turrisi (Albany: State University of New York Press, 1997), 164; reprinted in part in Collected Papers of Charles Sanders Peirce, vol. 5, sec. 64.

49. Nicholas St. John Green, "Proximate and Remote Cause" (1870), Essays and Notes on the Law of Tort and Crime (Menasha, Wis. George Banta, 1933), 13, 15.

50. Peirce, "Pragmatism," Charles S. Peirce Papers.

51. Peirce, "Pragmatism," Charles S. Peirce Papers.

52. James Fitzjames Stephen, A General View of the Criminal Law in England (London: Macmillan, 1863), 242.

53. Charles S. Peirce, "Pragmatism Made Easy" (n.d.), MS 325, Charles S. Peirce Papers.

54. Henry James to William James, September 22, 1872, The Correspondence of William James, vol. 1, 169.

55. Henry James to his parents, September 29, 1872, Letters, vol. 1, 303.

56. William James to Henry James, November 24, 1872, Correspondence of William James, vol. 1, 177.

57. Immanuel Kant, *Kritik der reinen Vernunft* (Riga: Johann Friedrich Hartnoch, 1781), 823–5: "Wenn einmal ein Zweck vorgesetzt ist, so sind die Bedingungen der Erreichung desselben hypothetisch notwendig. . . . Der Arzt muß bei einem Kranken, der in Gefahr ist, etwas tun, kennt aber die Krankheit nicht. Er sieht auf die Erscheinungen, und urteilt, weil er nichts Besseres weiß, es sei die Schwindsucht. Sein Glaube ist selbst in seinem eignen Urteile bloß zufällig, ein anderer möchte es vielleicht besser treffen. Ich nenne dergleichen zufälligen Glauben, der aber dem wirklichen Gebrauche der Mittel zu gewissen Handlungen zum Grunde liegt, den *pragmatischen Glauben*. Der gewöhnliche Probierstein: ob etwas bloße Überredung, oder wenigstens subjektive Überzeugung, d. i. festes Glauben sei, was jemand behauptet, ist das *Wetten*. . . . So hat der pragmatische Glaube nur einen Grad, der nach Verschiedenheit des Interesses, das dabei im Spiele ist, groß oder auch klein sein kann." (See *Immanuel Kant's Critique of Pure Reason*, trans. Norman Kemp Smith [London: Macmillan, 1956], 647–8.)

58. Charles S. Peirce, "How to Make Our Ideas Clear" (1878), *Writings of Charles S. Peirce*, vol. 3, 266.

59. Charles S. Peirce, "Of Reality" (1872), *Writings of Charles S. Peirce*, vol. 3, 55–9.

60. Peirce, "How to Make Our Ideas Clear," *Writings of Charles S. Peirce*, vol. 3, 273.

61. Charles S. Peirce, "Fraser's *The Works of George Berkeley*" (1871), *Writings of Charles S. Peirce*, vol. 2, 487.

62. Charles S. Peirce, "The Doctrine of Chances" (1878), *Writings of Charles S. Peirce*, vol. 3, 282, 284.

63. Charles William Eliot, memorandum, in *The Letters of William James*, ed. Henry James (Boston: Atlantic Monthly Press, 1920), vol. 1, 31–2.

64. Joseph Bangs Warner, memorandum, in *Letters of Chauncey Wright*, 213–14.

65. Charles William Eliot to Chauncey Wright, July 6, 1875, B W933, Chauncey Wright Papers, American Philosophical Society Library, Philadelphia.

66. Henry James, Sr., to William James, September 12, 1875, *The Correspondence of William James*, vol. 4, 519.

67. See file for Nicholas St. John Green, Harvard University Archives, HUG 300.

CHAPTER TEN: BURLINGTON

1. Henry Steele Commager, *The American Mind: An Interpretation of American Thought and Character Since the 1880s* (New Haven: Yale University Press, 1950), 100.

2. John Dewey, "The Need for a Recovery of Philosophy" (1917), *The Middle Works, 1899–1924*, ed. Jo Ann Boydston (Carbondale: Southern Illinois University Press, 1976–83), vol. 10, 46.

3. See Sidney Hook, *Pragmatism and the Tragic Sense of Life* (New York: Basic Books, 1974), 102.

4. See Corliss Lamont, ed., *Dialogue on John Dewey* (New York: Horizon Press, 1959), 89.

5. Thomas Jefferson to William Plumer, July 21, 1816, quoted in William Plumer, Jr., *Life of William Plumer* (Boston: Phillips, Sampson, 1856), 440–1.

6. United States Constitution, Article I, section 10 (1).

7. *The Trustees of Dartmouth College v. William H. Woodward*, 1 N.H. 111, 118–19 (1817).

8. *Dartmouth College v. Woodward*, 1 N.H. 121.

9. *The Trustees of Dartmouth College v. Woodward*, 17 U.S. 518, 562 (1819).

10. *Dartmouth College v. Woodward*, 17 U.S. 574.

11. See Albert J. Beveridge, *The Life of John Marshall* (Boston: Houghton Mifflin, 1916–19), vol. 4, 220–81; also Maurice G. Baxter, *Daniel Webster and the Supreme Court* (Amherst: University of Massachusetts Press, 1966), 65–109.

12. *Dartmouth College v. Woodward*, 17 U.S. 654.

13. *Dartmouth College v. Woodward*, 17 U.S. 668–9.

14. See, generally, Marjorie H. Nicolson, "James Marsh and the Vermont Transcendentalists," *Philosophical Review*, 34 (1925): 28–50; Lewis Feuer, "James Marsh and the Conservative Transcendentalist Philosophy: A Political Interpretation," *New England Quarterly*, 31 (1958): 3–31; and John J. Duffy, Introduction to *Coleridge's American Disciples: The Selected Correspondence of James Marsh*, ed. Duffy (Amherst: University of Massachusetts Press, 1973), 1–34.

15. James Marsh, "Preliminary Essay," in S[amuel] T[aylor] Coleridge, *Aids to Reflection, in the Formation of a Manly Character, on the Several Grounds of Prudence, Morality, and Religion* (Burlington, Vt.: Chauncey Goodrich, 1829), xiv.

16. Marsh, "Preliminary Essay," in Coleridge, *Aids to Reflection*, xviii.

17. Marsh, "Preliminary Essay," in Coleridge, *Aids to Reflection*, xv.

18. Quoted in Marsh, "Preliminary Essay," in Coleridge, *Aids to Reflection*, xxiv.

19. William Blake, "Mock on, Mock on, Voltaire, Rousseau," *Complete Writings of William Blake*, new ed., ed. Geoffrey Keynes (London: Oxford University Press, 1966), 418.

20. Marsh, "Preliminary Essay," in Coleridge, *Aids to Reflection*, xviii.

21. [Frederick Henry Hedge], "Coleridge's Literary Character," *Christian Examiner and General Review*, 14 (1833): 118, 119.

22. Frederick Henry Hedge, quoted in James Elliot Cabot, *A Memoir of Ralph Waldo Emerson* (Boston: Houghton Mifflin, 1888), 1: 244.

23. G. W. Benedict, *An Exposition of the System of Instruction and Discipline Pursued in the University of Vermont*, 2nd ed. (Burlington, Vt.: Chauncey Goodrich, 1831), 16.

24. John Wheeler, *A Historical Discourse by Rev. John Wheeler, D.D., . . . Delivered on*

the Occasion of the Semi-Centennial Anniversary of the University of Vermont (Burlington, Vt.: Free Press, 1854), 38.

25. James Marsh to Richard Henry Dana, March 8, 1838, *Coleridge's American Disciples*, 218.

26. James Marsh to Henry J. Raymond, March 21, 1841, *Coleridge's American Disciples*, 256.

27. See G. G. Benedict, *Vermont in the Civil War: A History of the Part Taken by the Vermont Soldiers and Sailors in the War for the Union, 1861–5* (Burlington, Vt.: Free Press, 1886–88), vol. 1, 1–2.

28. See Benedict, *Vermont in the Civil War*, vol. 2, 685, 692–4.

29. See Lewis Feuer, "H. A. P. Torrey and John Dewey: Teacher and Pupil," *American Quarterly*, 10 (1958): 52.

30. John Dewey, "From Absolutism to Experimentalism" (1930), *The Later Works, 1925–1953*, ed. Jo Ann Boydston (Carbondale: Southern Illinois University Press, 1981–90), vol. 5, 147–8. See also Jane M. Dewey, ed., "Biography of John Dewey," in *The Philosophy of John Dewey*, ed. Paul Arthur Schilpp and Lewis Edwin Hahn, 3rd ed. (La Salle, Ill.: Open Court, 1989), 10.

31. Lamont, ed., *Dialogue on John Dewey*, 15.

32. Dewey, "From Absolutism to Experimentalism," 148.

33. H. A. P. Torrey to Daniel Coit Gilman, April 5, 1883, Daniel Coit Gilman Papers, Ms. 1, Milton S. Eisenhower Library, Johns Hopkins University.

34. Matthew H. Buckham to Daniel Coit Gilman, April 3, 1883, Gilman Papers.

CHAPTER ELEVEN: BALTIMORE

1. See, generally, Richard Hofstadter and Walter P. Metzger, *The Development of Academic Freedom in the United States* (New York: Columbia University Press, 1955), 367–407; Hugh Hawkins, *Pioneer: A History of the Johns Hopkins University, 1874–1889* (Ithaca, N.Y.: Cornell University Press, 1960); and Laurence R. Veysey, *The Emergence of the American University* (Chicago: University of Chicago Press, 1965), 121–79.

2. See, generally, Henry James, *Charles W. Eliot, President of Harvard University, 1869–1909*, 2 vols. (Boston: Houghton Mifflin, 1930); Samuel Eliot Morison, *Three Centuries of Harvard, 1636–1936* (Cambridge, Mass.: Harvard University Press, 1936), 323–438; Veysey, *The Emergence of the American University*, 57–120; Hugh Hawkins, *Between Harvard and America: The Educational Leadership of Charles W. Eliot* (New York: Oxford University Press, 1971); and Burton J. Bledstein, *The Culture of Professionalism: The Middle Class and the Development of Higher Education in America* (New York: Norton, 1976), 129–202, 248–331.

3. See Max H. Fisch [and Jackson I. Cope], "Peirce at the Johns Hopkins University," in Fisch, *Peirce, Semeiotic, and Pragmatism: Essays*, ed. Kenneth Laine Ketner and Christian J. W. Kloesel (Bloomington: Indiana University Press, 1986), 38–45;

Julie A. Reuben, *The Making of the Modern University: Intellectual Transformation and the Marginalization of Morality* (Chicago: University of Chicago Press, 1996), 88–95; and Jon H. Roberts and James Turner, *The Sacred and the Secular University* (Princeton: Princeton University Press, 2000), 43–71.

4. See, generally, John Theodore Merz, *A History of European Thought in the Nineteenth Century*, (Edinburgh and London: William Blackwood, 1904–12), vol. 2, 465–547; Robert M. Young, *Mind, Brain, and Adaptation in the Nineteenth Century: Cerebral Localization and Its Biological Context from Gall to Ferrier* (Oxford: Clarendon Press, 1970); John M. O'Donnell, *The Origins of Behaviorism: American Psychology, 1870–1920* (New York: New York University Press, 1985); Kurt Danziger, *Constructing the Subject: Historical Origins of Psychological Research* (Cambridge, England: Cambridge University Press, 1990), 1–48; Roger Smith, *The Norton History of the Human Sciences* (New York: Norton, 1997), 492–529; and Edward S. Reed, *From Soul to Mind: The Emergence of Psychology from Erasmus Darwin to William James* (New Haven: Yale University Press, 1997).

5. T[homas] H. Huxley, "On the Hypothesis that Animals Are Automata, and Its History," *Fortnightly Review*, n.s. 16 (1874): 575, 577.

6. See Reed, *From Soul to Mind*, 185–7.

7. William James to Henry Holt, November 22, 1878, *The Correspondence of William James*, ed. Ignas K. Skrupskelis and Elizabeth M. Berkeley (Charlottesville: University Press of Virginia, 1992–), vol. 5, 24.

8. William James to Daniel Coit Gilman, January 18, 1879, *The Correspondence of William James*, vol. 5, 35–6.

9. See John J. Duffy, Introduction to *Coleridge's American Disciples: The Selected Correspondence of James Marsh*, ed. Duffy (Amherst: University of Massachusetts Press, 1973), 25–6.

10. Georg Wilhelm Friedrich Hegel to Friedrich Schelling, April 16, 1795: "From the Kantian system and its highest completion I expect a revolution in Germany" (*Hegel: The Letters*, trans. Clark Butler and Christiane Seiler [Bloomington: Indiana University Press, 1984], 35).

11. G. W. F. Hegel, *Phänomenologie des Geistes, Gesammelte Werke*, (Hamburg: Felix Meiner Verlag, 1968–), vol. 9, 18, 33: "Es ist das Werden seiner selbst, der Kreis, der sein Ende als seinen Zweck voraussetzt und zum Anfange hat, und nur durch die Ausführung und sein Ende Wirklich ist"; "Das Geistige allein ist das Wirkliche; es ist das Wesen oder an sich seyende." See *The Phenomenology of Mind*, trans. J. M. Baillie, 2nd ed. (London: Macmillan, 1931), 81, 86.

12. R. M. Wenley, *The Life and Work of George Sylvester Morris: A Chapter in the History of American Thought in the Nineteenth Century* (New York: Macmillan, 1917), 118. The passage is in quotation marks, but the source is unclear; it may be a paraphrase of a letter from Morris to his sister.

13. George Sylvester Morris, *Philosophy and Christianity: Syllabus of a Course of Eight Lectures* (New York: Robert Carter, 1883), 19, 273.

14. George Sylvester Morris, "The University and Philosophy," *Johns Hopkins University Circulars*, 2 (1883): 54.

15. John Dewey to R. M. Wenley, December 1915, quoted in Wenley, *The Life and Work of George Sylvester Morris*, 313.

16. Morris, *Philosophy and Christianity*, 250.

17. Morris, *Philosophy and Christianity*, 285.

18. John Dewey, "From Absolutism to Experimentalism" (1930), *The Later Works, 1925–1953*, ed. Jo Ann Boydston (Carbondale: Southern Illinois University Press, 1981–90), vol. 5, 153.

19. George Sylvester Morris, memorandum to Daniel Coit Gilman, 1884, Daniel Coit Gilman Papers, Ms. 1, Milton S. Eisenhower Library, Johns Hopkins University.

20. George Sylvester Morris, "Memorandum respecting the work of the Philosophical Seminary, September–December, 1882," March 12, 1883, Gilman Papers.

21. G. Stanley Hall, *Life and Confessions of a Psychologist* (New York: D. Appleton, 1923), 221–2.

22. Hall, *Life and Confessions of a Psychologist*, 218–19.

23. Wilhelm Wundt, *Grundzüge der physiologischen Psychologie* (Leipzig, 1873–74), vol. 2, 862–3; see R. W. Rieber, ed., *Wilhelm Wundt and the Making of a Scientific Psychology* (New York: Plenum, 1980), 176–7.

24. G. Stanley Hall, "The Moral and Religious Training of Children," *Princeton Review*, n.s. 9 (1882): 32.

25. Granville Stanley Hall to Daniel Coit Gilman, June 22, 1879, Gilman Papers.

26. Granville Stanley Hall to Daniel Coit Gilman, January 5, 1880, Gilman Papers.

27. John Dewey, "The New Psychology" (1884), *The Early Works, 1882–1898*, ed. Jo Ann Boydston (Carbondale: Southern Illinois University Press, 1967–72), vol. 1, 60.

28. Charles S. Peirce, "Introductory Lecture on the Study of Logic" (1882), *Writings of Charles S. Peirce: A Chronological Edition*, Peirce Edition Project (Bloomington: Indiana University Press, 1982–), vol. 5, 381.

29. William James to Daniel Coit Gilman, November 25, 1875, *The Correspondence of William James*, vol. 4, 525.

30. Charles S. Peirce to Daniel Coit Gilman, January 13, 1878, Gilman Papers.

31. Charles S. Peirce to Daniel Coit Gilman, January 13, 1878, Gilman Papers.

32. Charles S. Peirce, "Design and Chance" (1884), *Writings of Charles S. Peirce*, vol. 4, 544–5.

33. Peirce, "Design and Chance," 548, 549.

34. Peirce, "Design and Chance," 552.

35. See Max H. Fisch, "Was There a Metaphysical Club in Cambridge?" in *Studies in*

the Philosophy of Charles Sanders Peirce, Second Series, ed. Edward C. Moore and Richard S. Robin (Amherst: University of Massachusetts Press, 1964), 11. The words are attributed to Dickinson Miller.

36. Peirce, "Design and Chance," 553.

37. Charles S. Peirce, "Venn's Logic of Chance" (1867), Writings of Charles S. Peirce, vol. 2, 98.

38. John Venn, The Logic of Chance: An Essay on the Foundations and Province of the Theory of Probability, with Especial Reference to Its Application to Moral and Social Science (London: Macmillan, 1866), 37, 48.

39. Émile Boutroux, De la contingence des lois de la nature, 2nd ed. (Paris: Ancienne Librairie German Baillière, 1895), 39, 167: "Les lois sont le lit où passe le torrent des faits: ils l'ont creusé, bien qu'ils le suivent. . . . En réalité, les rapports logiques objectifs ne précèdent pas les choses: ils en dérivent; et ils pourraient varier, si les choses elles-mêmes venaient à varier"; "Elles apparaissent, vues du dehors, comme des lois nécessaires."

40. Charles S. Peirce, "A Guess at the Riddle" (1887–88), The Essential Peirce: Selected Philosophical Writings, ed. Nathan Houser, Christian Kloesel, and the Peirce Edition Project (Bloomington: Indiana University Press, 1992–98), vol. 1, 276. (A much longer draft of the essay appears in Writings of Charles Peirce, vol. 6, 166–210.)

41. Peirce, "Design and Chance," 552.

42. Herbert Henry Davis Peirce to Helen Huntington Peirce Ellis, April 23, 1914, L 680, Charles S. Peirce Papers, Houghton Library, Harvard University.

43. Simon Newcomb to Mary Hassler Newcomb, December 30, 1883, quoted in Nathan Houser, "Introduction," Writings of Charles S. Peirce, vol. 4, lxv.

44. Clipped to a letter from Charles S. Peirce to Daniel Coit Gilman, February 21, 1884, Gilman Papers.

45. Edwin Bidwell Wilson to Paul Weiss, November 22, 1946, quoted in Joseph Brent, Charles Sanders Peirce: A Life (Bloomington: Indiana University Press, 1993), 164.

46. See Dorothy Ross, G. Stanley Hall: The Psychologist as Prophet (Chicago: University of Chicago Press, 1972), 136.

47. G. Stanley Hall, "The New Psychology," Andover Review, 3 (1885): 247–8.

48. Daniel C. Gilman, "The Benefits Which Society Derives from Universities," Johns Hopkins University Circulars, 4 (1885): 49.

49. Granville Stanley Hall to Daniel Coit Gilman, August 28, 1885, Gilman Papers.

CHAPTER TWELVE: CHICAGO

1. See, generally, Laurence R. Veysey, The Emergence of the American University (Chicago: University of Chicago Press, 1965), 367–80; and Richard J. Storr, Harper's University: The Beginnings (Chicago: University of Chicago Press, 1966).

2. George Herbert Palmer to William Rainey Harper, June 4, 1892, William Rainey Harper Papers, Special Collections, University of Chicago.

3. James H. Tufts to William Rainey Harper, December 1893, William Rainey Harper Papers.

4. George Herbert Palmer to James B. Angell, May 22, 1895, typescript, Joseph Ratner/John Dewey Papers, Special Collections, Morris Library, Southern Illinois University.

5. Henry Northrup Castle to Samuel Northrup and Mary Ann Tenney Castle, June 10, 1893, *Henry Northrup Castle Letters* (London: privately printed, 1902), 729.

6. Charles Horton Cooley, *Sociological Theory and Social Research* (New York: Henry Holt, 1930), 6.

7. See David Ray Papke, *The Pullman Case: The Clash of Labor and Capital in Industrial America* (Lawrence: University Press of Kansas, 1999), 5.

8. See, generally, Ray Ginger, *Altgeld's America: The Lincoln Ideal Versus Changing Realities* (New York: Funk & Wagnalls, 1958), 143–93; Stanley Buder, *Pullman: An Experiment in Industrial Order and Community Planning, 1880–1930* (New York: Oxford University Press, 1967); Papke, *The Pullman Case*; and Victoria Brown, "Advocate for Democracy: Jane Addams and the Pullman Strike," Melvyn Dubofsky, "The Federal Judiciary, Free Labor, and Equal Rights," and David Montgomery, "Epilogue: The Pullman Boycott and the Making of Modern America," in Richard Schneirov, Shelton Stromquist, and Nick Salvatore, eds., *The Pullman Strike and the Crisis of the 1890s: Essays on Labor and Politics* (Urbana: University of Illinois Press, 1999), 130–58, 159–78, 233–49.

9. See W. T. Stead, *Chicago To-Day: The Labour War in America* (London: Review of Reviews, 1894), 116.

10. See, generally, Harold U. Faulkner, *The Decline of Laissez Faire, 1897–1917* (New York: Rhinehart, 1951), 191–8; and Samuel P. Hays, *The Response to Industrialism, 1885–1914* (Chicago: University of Chicago Press, 1957), 9–18.

11. See Almont Lindsey, *The Pullman Strike: The Story of a Unique Experiment and of a Great Labor Upheaval* (Chicago: University of Chicago Press, 1942), 318–19.

12. See Ginger, *Altgeld's America*, 150.

13. John Dewey to Alice Chipman Dewey, July 2, 1894, John Dewey Papers, Special Collections, Morris Library, Southern Illinois University. An electronic edition of Dewey's correspondence has been compiled by the Center for Dewey Studies at Southern Illinois University, Carbondale: *The Correspondence of John Dewey, Volume 1: 1871–1918*, ed. Larry A. Hickman, available on CD-ROM from the InteLex Corporation, Charlottesville, Virginia.

14. John Dewey to Alice Chipman Dewey and children, July 4–5, 1894, John Dewey Papers.

15. John Dewey to Alice Chipman Dewey and children, July 14, 1894, John Dewey Papers.

16. John Dewey to Alice Chipman Dewey and children, July 20, 1894, John Dewey Papers.

17. John Dewey to Alice Chipman Dewey and children, July 23, 1894, John Dewey Papers.

18. See Ray Ginger, *The Bending Cross: A Biography of Eugene Victor Debs* (New Brunswick: Rutgers University Press, 1949), 168.

19. See Susan E. Hirsch, "The Search for Unity among Railroad Workers: The Pullman Strike in Perspective," in Schneirov, Stromquist, and Salvatore, eds., *The Pullman Strike and the Crisis of the 1890s*, 50.

20. *Thomas v. Cincinnati, New Orleans, and Texas Pacific Railway Company*, 62 Federal Reporter 803, 820–1 (1894).

21. See Nick Salvatore, *Eugene V. Debs: Citizen and Socialist* (Urbana: University of Illinois Press, 1982), 130–1.

22. See Allan Nevins, *Grover Cleveland: A Study in Courage* (New York: Dodd, Mead, 1932), 628.

23. *In re Debs*, 158 U.S. 564, 582 (1895).

24. See Robert C. Bannister, *Social Darwinism: Science and Myth in Anglo-American Social Thought* (Philadelphia: Temple University Press, 1979), and T. J. Jackson Lears, *No Place of Grace: Antimodernism and the Transformation of American Culture, 1880–1920* (Chicago: University of Chicago Press, 1981), 19–26.

25. William Lyon Phelps, "When Yale Was Given to Sumnerology," *Literary Digest International Book Review*, 3 (1925): 661; see Richard Hofstadter, *Social Darwinism in American Thought*, rev. ed. (Boston: Beacon Press, 1955), 54.

26. Lester F. Ward, "Mind as a Social Factor" (1884), *Glimpses of the Cosmos* (New York: Putnam, 1913–18), vol. 3, 366, 371.

27. Richard T. Ely, "Pullman: A Social Study," *Harper's New Monthly Magazine*, 70 (1884–85): 452, 464, 465.

28. Richard T. Ely to E. R. A. Seligman, June 9, 1885, E. R. A. Seligman Papers, Rare Book and Manuscript Library, Columbia University.

29. Henry Sumner Maine, *Popular Government: Four Essays* (London: John Murray, 1885), 248.

30. John Dewey, "The Ethics of Democracy" (1888), *The Early Works, 1882–1898*, ed. Jo Ann Boydston (Carbondale: Southern Illinois University Press, 1967–72), vol. 1, 232.

31. Albion Small, "Lester Frank Ward," *American Journal of Sociology*, 19 (1913–14): 77.

32. Albion Small, "Scholarship and Social Agitation," *American Journal of Sociology*, 1 (1895–96): 581–2.

33. Thorstein Veblen, "Why Is Economics Not an Evolutionary Science?" *Quarterly Journal of Economics*, 12 (1898): 389.

34. Thorstein Veblen, *The Theory of the Leisure Class: An Economic Study in the Evolution of Institutions* (New York: Macmillan, 1899), 116.

35. See, generally, John C. Farrell, *Beloved Lady: A History of Jane Addams' Ideas on Reform and Peace* (Baltimore: Johns Hopkins University Press, 1967); Allen F. Davis, *Spearheads for Reform: The Social Settlements and the Progressive Movement, 1890–1914* (New York: Oxford University Press, 1967), and *American Heroine: The Life and Legend of Jane Addams* (New York: Oxford University Press, 1973); and Gioia Diliberto, *A Useful Woman: The Early Life of Jane Addams* (New York: Scribner, 1999).

36. See Diliberto, *A Useful Woman*, 72.

37. See Ginger, *Altgeld's America*, 126–7.

38. See Residents of Hull-House, *Hull-House Maps and Papers: A Presentation of Nationalities and Wages in a Congested District of Chicago* (New York: Thomas Y. Crowell, 1895), 17.

39. Leila G. Bedell, "A Chicago Toynbee Hall," *Woman's Journal*, 20 (1889): 162.

40. See Jane Addams, *Twenty Years at Hull-House, with Autobiographical Notes* (New York: Macmillan, 1910), 101.

41. John Dewey to Jane Addams, January 27, 1892, Jane Addams Papers, Rockford College Archives, Howard Colman Library, Rockford College.

42. John Dewey to Alice Chipman Dewey and children, July 4–5, 1894, John Dewey Papers.

43. See Davis, *American Heroine*, 113.

44. See Addams, *Twenty Years at Hull-House*, 216–17.

45. Jane Addams, "The Settlement as a Factor in the Labor Movement," in *Hull-House Maps and Papers*, 198.

46. Jane Addams, *Democracy and Social Ethics* (New York: Macmillan, 1913), 219–20.

47. John Dewey to Alice Chipman Dewey, October 9, 1894, John Dewey Papers.

48. John Dewey to Alice Chipman Dewey, October 10, 1894, John Dewey Papers.

49. John Dewey to Alice Chipman Dewey, October 10–11, 1894, John Dewey Papers.

50. John Dewey to Jane Addams, October 12, 1894, Jane Addams Papers, Swarthmore College Peace Collection, Swarthmore College.

51. Jane Addams, "A Modern Lear" (1894), *Survey*, 29 (1912): 135, 134, 137.

52. Ely, "Pullman: A Social Study," 465.

53. Jane Addams, "A Modern Lear," 136–7.

54. John Dewey to Jane Addams, January 19, 1896, Jane Addams Papers, Swarthmore College Peace Collection.

55. Katherine Camp Mayhew and Anna Camp Edwards, *The Dewey School: The Laboratory School of the University of Chicago, 1896–1903* (New York: D. Appleton-Century, 1936), 446. ("On one occasion when asked how it came about that he had turned his attention to educational philosophy, Mr. Dewey replied, 'It was mainly on account of the children.'")

56. John Dewey to Alice Chipman Dewey, May 24, 1894, John Dewey Papers.

57. John Dewey to Alice Chipman Dewey, July 9, 1894, John Dewey Papers.

58. John Dewey to Alice Chipman Dewey, October 16, 1894, John Dewey Papers.

59. Jane Dewey, ed., "Biography of John Dewey," in *The Philosophy of John Dewey*, ed. Paul Arthur Schilpp and Lewis Edwin Hahn, 3rd ed. (La Salle, Ill.: Open Court, 1989), 24.

60. John Dewey to Alice Chipman Dewey, July 12, 1894, John Dewey Papers.

61. John Dewey to Alice Chipman Dewey and children, August 25–26, 1894, John Dewey Papers.

62. John Dewey to Alice Chipman Dewey and children, November 1, 1894, John Dewey Papers.

63. John Dewey, "The Theory of the Chicago Experiment" (1936), *The Later Works, 1925–1953*, ed. Jo Ann Boydston (Carbondale: Southern Illinois University Press, 1981–90), vol. 11, 204.

64. John Dewey to Clara I. Mitchell, November 29, 1895, John Dewey Papers.

65. Mayhew and Edwards, *The Dewey School*, 297.

66. John Dewey, *The School and Society* (1899), *The Middle Works, 1899–1924*, ed. Jo Ann Boydston (Carbondale: Southern Illinois University Press, 1976–83), vol. 1, 98.

67. William James to Carl Stumpf, February 6, 1887, *The Correspondence of William James*, ed. Ignas K. Skrupskelis and Elizabeth M. Berkeley (Charlottesville: University Press of Virginia, 1992–), vol. 6, 202.

68. William James, *The Principles of Psychology* (1890), *The Works of William James*, ed. Frederick H. Burkhardt (Cambridge, Mass.: Harvard University Press, 1975–88), 1: 103.

69. James, *The Principles of Psychology*, 1: 504.

70. James Rowland Angell to William James, January 13, 1893, James Family Papers, Houghton Library, Harvard University, bMS Am 1092 (16).

71. James Burrill Angell to James Rowland Angell, March 10, 1892, James Rowland Angell Personal Papers, Manuscripts and Archives, Yale University.

72. James Rowland Angell and Addison W. Moore, "Reaction-Time: A Study in Attention and Habit," *Psychological Review*, 3 (1896): 254.

73. John Dewey, "The Reflex Arc Concept in Psychology," *The Early Works*, vol. 5, 99.

74. Dewey, "The Reflex Arc Concept," 105–6.

75. Dewey, "The Reflex Arc Concept," 98.

76. James, *The Principles of Psychology*, 1: 195–6.

77. John Dewey to William James, May 6, 1891, *The Correspondence of William James*, vol. 7, 160.

78. John Dewey to Clara I. Mitchell, November 29, 1895, John Dewey Papers.

79. John Dewey, *The Child and the Curriculum* (1902), *Middle Works*, vol. 2, 278.

80. See Corliss Lamont, ed., *Dialogue on John Dewey* (New York: Horizon Press, 1959), 126.

81. John Dewey to James McKeen Cattell, April 12, 1904, James McKeen Cattell Papers, Manuscript Division, Library of Congress.

82. John Dewey to William Rainey Harper, May 10, 1904, President's Papers, Department of Special Collections, University of Chicago Library.

CHAPTER THIRTEEN: PRAGMATISMS

1. William James to Henry James, July 5, 1876, *The Correspondence of William James*, ed. Ignas Skrupskelis and Elizabeth M. Berkeley (Charlottesville: University Press of Virginia, 1992–), vol. 1, 269.

2. Oliver Wendell Holmes, "Codes, and the Arrangement of the Law" (1870), *The Collected Works of Justice Holmes: Complete Public Writings and Selected Judicial Opinions of Oliver Wendell Holmes*, ed. Sheldon M. Novick (Chicago: University of Chicago Press, 1995–), vol. 1, 212.

3. Oliver Wendell Holmes, *The Common Law* (1881), *The Collected Works of Justice Holmes*, vol. 3, 115.

4. Holmes, *The Common Law*, *The Collected Works of Justice Holmes*, vol. 3, 115.

5. Oliver Wendell Holmes to Elmer Gertz, March 1, 1899, Gertz Papers, Library of Congress; quoted in Liva Baker, *The Justice from Beacon Hill: The Life and Times of Oliver Wendell Holmes* (New York: HarperCollins, 1991), 172–3.

6. *Lochner v. New York*, 198 U.S., 45, 76 (1905).

7. Oliver Wendell Holmes, Rev. of *The Law Magazine and Review* (1872), *The Collected Works of Justice Holmes*, vol. 1, 295.

8. Oliver Wendell Holmes, "The Path of the Law," (1897), *The Collected Works of Justice Holmes*, vol. 3, 393.

9. Holmes, Rev. of *The Law Magazine and Review*, *The Collected Works of Justice Holmes*, vol. 1, 295.

10. See, generally, "Origins of the Modern Standard of Due Care in Negligence," *Washington University Law Quarterly*, 54 (1976): 447–79, and G. Edward White, *Tort Law in America: An Intellectual History* (New York: Oxford University Press, 1980).

11. Holmes, *The Common Law*, *The Collected Works of Justice Holmes*, vol. 3, 115.

12. Holmes, *The Common Law*, *The Collected Works of Justice Holmes*, vol. 3, 191.

13. Holmes, *The Common Law*, *The Collected Works of Justice Holmes*, vol. 3, 191.

14. Holmes, *The Common Law*, *The Collected Works of Justice Holmes*, vol. 3, 191.

15. Oliver Wendell Holmes, "Trespass and Negligence" (1880), *The Collected Works of Justice Holmes*, vol. 3, 91.

16. Holmes, *The Common Law, The Collected Works of Justice Holmes*, vol. 3, 194.

17. Holmes, "The Path of the Law," *The Collected Works of Justice Holmes*, vol. 3, 399.

18. James Bradley Thayer, Memoranda book D, James Bradley Thayer Papers, Harvard Law School Library, L MS 2148, vol. 3, 144.

19. See Joseph Brent, *Charles Sanders Peirce: A Life* (Bloomington: Indiana University Press, 1993), 189–202.

20. Charles S. Peirce, [Autobiographical fragment] (1892), MS 1607, Charles S. Peirce Papers, Houghton Library, Harvard University.

21. Charles S. Peirce to William James, March 13, 1897, James Family Papers, Houghton Library, Harvard University, bMS Am 1092 (672).

22. William James to Charles Sanders Peirce, December 22, 1897, James Family Papers (3384).

23. Charles Sanders Peirce to William James, December 26, 1897, James Family Papers (678).

24. William James, "Philosophical Conceptions and Practical Results" (1898), *Pragmatism, The Works of William James*, ed. Frederick H. Burkhardt (Cambridge, Mass.: Harvard University Press, 1975–88), 258.

25. John Dewey to Addison W. Moore, January 2, 1905, Joseph Ratner/John Dewey Papers, Special Collections, Morris Library, Southern Illinois University.

26. William James, *The Varieties of Religious Experience* (1902), *The Works of William James*, 22.

27. James, *Pragmatism* (1907), *The Works of William James*, 97.

28. James, *Pragmatism, The Works of William James*, 106 (the original is in italics).

29. William James, "Philosophical Conceptions and Practical Results," *Pragmatism, The Works of William James*, 259.

30. James, *The Principles of Psychology* (1890), *The Works of William James*, 1:112.

31. See Edward L. Thorndike, *Animal Intelligence: An Experimental Study of the Associative Processes in Animals* (New York: Macmillan, 1898). The monograph was part of a series published as supplements to the *Psychological Review* (vol. 2, no. 4 [June 1898]).

32. James, *Pragmatism, The Works of William James*, 42 (the original is in italics).

33. James, *Pragmatism, The Works of William James*, 143.

34. See Charles S. Peirce, "The Fixation of Belief" (1877), *Writings of Charles S. Peirce: A Chronological Edition*, Peirce Edition Project (Bloomington: Indiana University Press, 1982–), vol. 3, 242–57.

35. Charles S. Peirce, "How to Make Our Ideas Clear" (1878), *Writings of Charles S. Peirce*, vol. 3, 266 (emphasis added).

36. William James, "Remarks on Spencer's Definition of Mind as Correspondence" (1878), *Essays in Philosophy, The Works of William James*, 21.

37. James, *The Principles of Psychology, The Works of William James*, 2: 1264.

38. James, *Pragmatism, The Works of William James*, 93–4.

39. See Linda Simon, *Genuine Reality: A Life of William James* (New York: Harcourt Brace, 1998), 295.

40. William James to John Dewey, March 11, 1903, William James Papers, Houghton Library, Harvard University, bMS Am 1092.9 (886).

41. James Rowland Angell to William James, November 13, 1898, James Family Papers (18).

42. Ferdinand Canning Scott Schiller to William James, December 8, 1902, James Family Papers (866).

43. John Dewey to William James, [March 1903?], James Family Papers (133a).

44. William James to John Dewey, December 3, 1903, General Manuscript Collection, Rare Book and Manuscript Library, Columbia University.

45. William James, "The Chicago School" (1904), *Essays in Philosophy, The Works of William James*, 102.

46. John Dewey to William James, January 20, 1904, William James Papers (135).

47. William James to John Dewey, February 2, 1904, William James Papers (889).

48. William James to Pauline Goldmark, February 23, 1904, William James Papers, bMS Am 1092.1.

49. See Sidney Morgenbesser, ed., *Dewey and His Critics: Essays from "The Journal of Philosophy"* (New York: Journal of Philosophy, 1977).

50. John Dewey, "Brief Studies in Realism" (1922), *The Middle Works, 1899–1924*, ed. Jo Ann Boydston (Carbondale: Southern Illinois University Press, 1976–83), vol. 6, 111.

51. John Dewey, "The Postulate of Immediate Empiricism" (1905), *Middle Works*, vol. 3, 158.

52. John Dewey, "The Bearing of Pragmatism Upon Education" (1908–09), *Middle Works*, vol. 4, 180.

53. John Dewey to Charles Augustus Strong, April 28, 1905, Charles Augustus Strong Papers, Rockefeller Archive Center, Rockefeller University.

54. James, *Pragmatism, The Works of William James*, 37.

55. John Dewey, "What Pragmatism Means by Practical" (1908), *Middle Works*, vol. 4, 113.

56. G. K. Chesterton, *Orthodoxy* (New York: John Lane, 1908), 62.

57. John Dewey, "A Short Catechism Concerning Truth" (1909), *Middle Works*, vol. 6, 11.

58. John Dewey, "The Need for a Recovery of Philosophy" (1917), *Middle Works*, vol. 10, 46.

59. William James to Leonard Trelawney Hobhouse, August 12, 1904, *The Letters of*

William James, ed. Henry James (Boston: Atlantic Monthly Press, 1920), vol. 2, 207 ("the 'Will to Believe' essay [which should have been called by the less unlucky title the *Right* to Believe]").

60. Charles S. Peirce to John Dewey, June 9, 1904, L 123, Charles S. Peirce Papers, Houghton Library, Harvard University.

61. [Charles S. Peirce], "Logical Lights," *Nation*, 79 (1904): 220.

62. Charles S. Peirce, "The Lowell Lectures: The Logic of Science; or, Induction and Hypothesis" (1866), *Writings of Charles S. Peirce*, vol. 1, 466.

63. Charles S. Peirce, ["Representation and Generality"] (n.d.), *Collected Papers of Charles Sanders Peirce*, ed. Charles Hartshorne, Paul Weiss, and Arthur Burks (Cambridge, Mass.: Harvard University Press, 1931–66), vol. 1, sec. 339.

64. Charles S. Peirce, ["Fallibilism, Continuity, and Evolution"] (c. 1897), *Collected Papers*, vol. 1, sec. 171.

65. Charles S. Peirce, "Evolutionary Love," *Monist*, 3 (1892–93): 188.

66. See Robert J. Richards, *Darwin and the Emergence of Evolutionary Theories of Mind and Behavior* (Chicago: University of Chicago Press, 1987), 496–501.

67. Charles S. Peirce, "Uniformity," in *The Dictionary of Philosophy and Psychology*, ed. James Mark Baldwin (New York: Macmillan, 1901–05), vol. 2, 727–31.

68. Charles S. Peirce, "Man's Glassy Essence," *Monist*, 3 (1892–93): 15.

69. Charles S. Peirce, "What Pragmatism Is," *Monist*, 15 (1905): 177.

70. Charles S. Peirce, ["Proem: The Architectonic Character of Philosophy"] (1896?), *Collected Papers of Charles Sanders Peirce*, vol. 1, sec. 178.

71. Charles S. Peirce, "Guessing" (1907), *Hound and Horn*, 2 (1929): 271.

72. C. S. Peirce and J. Jastrow, "On Small Differences of Sensation" (1884), *Writings of Charles S. Peirce*, vol. 5, 135; see also Joseph Jastrow, "Joseph Jastrow," in *A History of Psychology in Autobiography*, vol. 1, ed. Carl Murchison (Worcester: Clark University Press, 1930), 136.

73. Peirce, "How to Make Our Ideas Clear," *Writings of Charles S. Peirce*, vol. 2, 73.

74. Charles S. Peirce, ["The Pragmatic Maxim"] (1893), *Collected Papers*, vol. 5, sec. 402, P2.

75. James, *Pragmatism, The Works of William James*, [3].

76. John Dewey, "From Absolutism to Experimentalism" (1930), *The Later Works, 1925–1953*, ed. Jo Ann Boydston (Carbondale: Southern Illinois University Press, 1981–90), vol. 5, 154.

77. Edward Bradford Titchener to James McKeen Cattell, November 20, 1898, James McKeen Cattell Papers, Manuscripts Division, Library of Congress; see Eugene Taylor, *William James on Consciousness beyond the Margin* (Princeton: Princeton University Press, 1996), 173 n. 47.

78. See, generally, Harold U. Faulkner, *The Decline of Laissez Faire, 1897–1917* (New

York: Rhinehart, 1951); Samuel P. Hays, *The Response to Industrialism, 1885–1914* (Chicago: University of Chicago Press, 1957); and Robert H. Wiebe, *The Search for Order, 1877–1920* (New York: Hill and Wang, 1967).

79. William James to Sarah Wyman Whitman, June 7, 1899, *The Letters of William James*, vol. 2, 90.

80. Quoted in W. T. Stead, *Chicago To-Day: The Labour War in America* (London: Review of Reviews, 1894), 177. The first part of the quotation is from a speech of May 14, the second from a speech of May 16, 1894.

81. See Ray Ginger, *The Bending Cross: A Biography of Eugene Victor Debs* (New Brunswick: Rutgers University Press, 1949), 138.

82. See C. Vann Woodward, *The Strange Career of Jim Crow*, 3rd rev. ed. (New York: Oxford University Press, 1974), 85.

83. Bertrand Russell, "Pragmatism" (1909), *Philosophical Essays* (London: Longmans, Green, 1910), 109.

84. Corliss Lamont, ed., *Dialogue on John Dewey* (New York: Horizon Press, 1959), 335.

CHAPTER FOURTEEN: PLURALISMS

1. William James, Notebook J, William James Papers, Houghton Library, Harvard University, bMS Am 1092.9 (4509).

2. William James, *A Pluralistic Universe* (1909), *The Works of William James*, ed. Frederick H. Burkhardt (Cambridge, Mass.: Harvard University Press, 1975–88), 145.

3. See Linda Simon, *Genuine Reality: A Life of William James* (New York: Harcourt Brace, 1998), 357–8.

4. See Frank Lentricchia, *Ariel and the Police: Michel Foucault, William James, Wallace Stevens* (Madison: University of Wisconsin Press, 1988), 104–33; and George Cotkin, *William James, Public Philosopher* (Baltimore: Johns Hopkins University Press, 1990), esp. 123–76.

5. See Peter H. Odegard, Introduction to Arthur F. Bentley, *The Process of Government* (Cambridge, Mass.: Harvard University Press, 1967), vii–xlii; T. Z. Lavine, Introduction to *The Later Works of John Dewey, 1925–1953*, ed. Jo Ann Boydston (Carbondale: Southern Illinois University Press, 1981–90), vol. 16, xii–xvii; and Richard Hofstadter, *The Age of Reform: From Bryan to FDR* (New York: Knopf, 1955), 55–6.

6. Probably "The Logic of Ethics" (fall 1895) and "Political Ethics" (spring 1896); see John Dewey, *Principles of Instrumental Logic: John Dewey's Lectures in Ethics and Political Ethics, 1895–1896*, ed. Donald F. Koch (Carbondale: Southern Illinois University Press, 1998).

7. Arthur F. Bentley, *The Process of Government: A Study of Social Pressures* (Chicago: University of Chicago Press, 1908), 271.

8. See Samuel Eliot Morison, Henry Steele Commager, and William E. Leuchtenburg, *The Growth of the American Republic*, 7th ed. (New York: Oxford University Press, 1980), vol. 2, 108 n. 3.

9. See Peter J. Bowler, *The Eclipse of Darwinism: Anti-Darwinian Evolutionary Theories in the Decades around 1900* (Baltimore: Johns Hopkins University Press, 1983), 58–106, 118–40; and Carl N. Degler, *In Search of Human Nature: The Decline and Revival of Darwinism in American Social Thought* (New York: Oxford University Press, 1991), 3–55.

10. See Thomas F. Gossett, *Race: The History of an Idea in America* (Dallas: Southern Methodist University Press, 1963), 168–72; and, generally, Julius Weinberg, *Edward Alsworth Ross and the Sociology of Progressivism* (Madison: State Historical Society of Wisconsin, 1972), 149–76.

11. E. A. Ross, comment on D. Collin Wells, "Social Darwinism," *American Journal of Sociology*, 12 (1906–07): 715.

12. See George W. Stocking, *Race, Culture, and Evolution: Essays in the History of Anthropology*, 2nd ed. (Chicago: University of Chicago Press, 1981), 195–233; and Melville J. Herskovits, *Franz Boas: The Science of Man in the Making* (New York: Scribner, 1953), 1–24.

13. Franz Boas, "Museums of Ethnology and Their Classification," *Science*, 9 (1887): 589 (the sentences have been reversed).

14. See George W. Stocking, "Franz Boas and the Culture Concept in Historical Perspective," *American Anthropologist*, 68 (1966): 867–82, and *Race, Culture, and Evolution*, 203.

15. See George W. Stocking, ed., *The Shaping of American Anthropology, 1883–1911: A Franz Boas Reader* (New York: Basic Books, 1974), 219.

16. The Immigration Commission, *Abstract of the Report on Changes in Bodily Form of Descendants of Immigrants* (Washington, D.C.: Government Printing Office, 1911), 8. See also Franz Boas, "Instability of Human Types," *Papers on Inter-racial Problems, Communicated to the First Universal Races Congress Held at the University of London, July 26–29, 1911*, ed. Gustav Spiller (Boston: Ginn, 1912), 99–103, and "Changes in the Bodily Form of Descendants of Immigrants," *American Anthropologist*, n.s. 14 (1912): 530–62.

17. Franz Boas, "Human Faculty as Determined by Race," *Proceedings of the American Association for the Advancement of Science*, 43 (1894): 301–27.

18. See Richard Schickel, *D. W. Griffith: An American Life* (New York: Simon and Schuster, 1984), 270 ("It is like writing history with lightning").

19. See "Jane Addams Condemns Race Prejudice Film," *New York Evening Post*, March 13, 1915, 4.

20. Madison Grant, *The Passing of the Great Race, or The Racial Basis of European History* (New York: Scribner, 1916), 150.

21. Melusina Fay Peirce, *New York: A Symphonic Study* (New York: Neale, 1918), 131.

22. See, generally, Philip Gleason, "American Identity and Americanization," in Stephan Thernstrom, Ann Orlov, and Oscar Handlin, eds., *Harvard Encyclopedia of American Ethnic Groups* (Cambridge, Mass.: Harvard University Press, 1980), 38–47; John Higham, *Send These to Me: Immigrants in Urban America*, rev. ed. (Baltimore: Johns Hopkins University Press, 1984), 198–232; Werner Sollors, "A Critique of Pure Pluralism," in Sacvan Bercovitch, ed., *Reconstructing American Literary History* (Cambridge, Mass.: Harvard University Press, 1986), 250–79; and Walter Benn Michaels, *Our America: Nativism, Modernism, and Pluralism* (Durham: Duke University Press, 1995).

23. See Horace M. Kallen, *Individualism: An American Way of Life* (New York: Liveright, 1933), 5–8.

24. See Barrett Wendell to William James, November 26, 1900, in M. A. DeWolfe Howe, "A Packet of Wendell-James Letters," *Scribner's Magazine*, 84 (1928): 678.

25. See Jeffrey C. Stewart, Introduction to Alain LeRoy Locke, *Race Contacts and Interracial Relations: Lectures on the Theory and Practice of Race*, ed. Stewart (Washington, D.C.: Howard University Press, 1992), xxxvi–xlviii; and Stewart, "A Black Aesthete at Oxford," *Massachusetts Review*, 34 (1993): 411–28.

26. Alain Locke to Mary Locke, March 23, 1907, Alain Locke Papers, Manuscript Division, Moorland-Spingarn Research Center, Howard University.

27. See H. M. Kallen, "Alain Locke and Cultural Pluralism," *Journal of Philosophy*, 54 (1957): 119; and Sarah Schmidt, "A Conversation with Horace M. Kallen: The Zionist Chapter of His Life," *Reconstructionist*, 41 (November 1975): 29.

28. See Sollors, "A Critique of Pure Pluralism," esp. 269–72; and Stewart, "A Black Aesthete at Oxford," esp. 422–3.

29. Horace Kallen to Barrett Wendell, October 22, 1907, Barrett Wendell Papers, Houghton Library, Harvard University, bMS Am 1907.1 (733).

30. Horace Kallen to Barrett Wendell, November 12, 1907, Barrett Wendell Papers (733).

31. See Alain Locke, "Values and Imperatives," in Sidney Hook and Horace M. Kallen, eds., *American Philosophy Today and Tomorrow* (New York: Furman, 1935), 312.

32. Horace M. Kallen, "Democracy Versus the Melting-Pot," *Nation*, 100 (1915): 190–1.

33. Kallen, "Democracy Versus the Melting-Pot," 220.

34. Horace Kallen, *The Structure of Lasting Peace: An Inquiry into the Motives of War and Peace* (Boston: Marshall Jones, 1918), 31.

35. Kallen, "Democracy Versus the Melting-Pot," 220.

36. Kallen, "Democracy Versus the Melting-Pot," 219.

37. See Kallen, "Democracy Versus the Melting-Pot," 217, 194.

38. Kallen, "Democracy Versus the Melting-Pot," 220.

39. W. E. B. Du Bois, *Dusk of Dawn: An Essay Toward an Autobiography of a Race Concept* (1940), *Writings* (New York: Library of America, 1986), 581.

40. Booker T. Washington, "The Atlanta Exposition Address" (1895), *The Booker T. Washington Papers*, ed. Louis R. Harlan (Urbana: University of Illinois Press, 1972–89), vol. 3, 585.

41. W. E. B. Du Bois to Booker T. Washington, September 24, 1895, *The Booker T. Washington Papers*, vol. 4, 26.

42. W. E. B. Du Bois, *The Souls of Black Folk* (1903), *Writings*, 364.

43. Locke, *Race Contacts and Interracial Relations*, 12. The text is an edited version of a stenographic transcript made when the lectures were repeated in 1916.

44. Locke, *Race Contacts and Interracial Relations*, 91.

45. Locke, *Race Contacts and Interracial Relations*, 12 (emphasis added).

46. Locke, *Race Contacts and Interracial Relations*, 96–7.

47. John Dewey to Horace M. Kallen, March 31, 1915, Horace M. Kallen Collection, American Jewish Archives, Hebrew Union College, Cincinnati.

48. John Dewey, "Nationalizing Education" (1916), *The Middle Works, 1899–1924*, ed. Jo Ann Boydston (Carbondale: Southern Illinois University Press, 1976–83), vol. 10, 205.

49. Randolph Bourne to Prudence Winterrowd, April 10, 1913, *The Letters of Randolph Bourne: A Comprehensive Edition*, ed. Eric J. Sandeen (Troy, N.Y.: Whitson, 1981), 78.

50. Randolph Bourne to Prudence Winterrowd, May 18, 1913, *The Letters of Randolph Bourne*, 86.

51. Randolph Bourne to Prudence Winterrowd, January 16, 1913, *The Letters of Randolph Bourne*, 7.

52. Randolph Bourne to Prudence Winterrowd, April 10, 1913, *The Letters of Randolph Bourne*, 78.

53. See Christopher Lasch, *The New Radicalism in America, 1889–1963: The Intellectual as a Social Type* (New York: Knopf, 1965), 69–103; and Edward Abrahams, *The Lyrical Left: Randolph Bourne, Alfred Stieglitz, and the Origins of Cultural Radicalism in America* (Charlottesville: University Press of Virginia, 1986), 23–91.

54. Randolph S. Bourne, "John Dewey's Philosophy," *New Republic*, 2 (1915): 154.

55. Randolph Bourne to Alyse Gregory, March 13, 1914, *The Letters of Randolph Bourne*, 22.

56. Randolph Bourne, "Trans-National America," *Atlantic Monthly*, 108 (1916): 86–97.

57. Randolph S. Bourne, "The Jew and Trans-National America," *Menorah Journal*, 2 (1916): 280.

58. Bourne, "The Jew and Trans-National America," 283.

59. John Dewey, "Democracy and Loyalty in the Schools," *Middle Works*, vol. 10, 158.

60. Randolph Bourne, "Twilight of Idols," *Seven Arts*, 2 (1917): 695, 697–9.

61. Randolph Bourne to Everett Benjamin, November 26, 1917, *The Letters of Randolph Bourne*, 404.

62. Horace M. Kallen, *Culture and Democracy in the United States* (New York: Boni and Liveright, 1924), 3.

63. Woodrow Wilson, "An Address in Philadelphia to Newly Naturalized Citizens" (May 10, 1915), *The Papers of Woodrow Wilson*, ed. Arthur S. Link (Princeton: Princeton University Press, 1966–94), vol. 23, 148.

64. John Dewey, "Contributions to *Dictionary of Philosophy and Psychology*" (1902), *Middle Works*, vol. 2, 204.

CHAPTER FIFTEEN: FREEDOMS

1. See Orrin L. Elliott, *Stanford University: The First Twenty-Five Years* (London: Stanford University Press, 1937), 326–78; Richard Hofstadter and Walter P. Metzger, *The Development of Academic Freedom in the United States* (New York: Columbia University Press, 1955), 436–45; Laurence R. Veysey, *The Emergence of the American University* (Chicago: University of Chicago Press, 1965), 400–407; Thomas L. Haskell, "Justifying the Rights of Academic Freedom in the Era of Power/Knowledge," in Louis Menand, ed., *The Future of Academic Freedom* (Chicago: University of Chicago Press, 1996), 48–53.

2. Jane Lathrop Stanford to David Starr Jordan, May 9, 1900, quoted in Elliott, *Stanford University*, 341.

3. See Hofstadter and Metzger, *The Development of Academic Freedom*, 442.

4. John Dewey to Franz Boas, October 31, 1913, Franz Boas Papers, American Philosophical Library, Philadelphia.

5. John Dewey to Barrett Wendell, December 7, 1914, Barrett Wendell Papers, Houghton Library, Harvard University, bMS Am 1907.1 (360).

6. See John Dewey, "Introductory Address to the American Association of University Professors" (January 1, 1915) and "Annual Address of the President to the American Association of University Professors" (December 31, 1915), *The Middle Works, 1899–1924*, ed. Jo Ann Boydston (Carbondale: Southern Illinois University Press, 1976–83), vol. 8, 98–108.

7. "General Report of the Committee on Academic Freedom and Academic Tenure," *Bulletin of the American Association of University Professors*, 1 (1915): 26.

8. John Dewey, "Professorial Freedom" (October 22, 1915), *Middle Works*, vol. 8, 407–8.

9. See Bruce Kuklick, *The Rise of American Philosophy: Cambridge, Massachusetts, 1860–1930* (New Haven: Yale University Press, 1977), 409–11.

10. Commencement Day Address, June 6, 1917, Columbia University Archives; see Hofstadter and Metzger, *The Development of Academic Freedom in the United States*, 499.

11. John Dewey, "Academic Freedom" (1902), *Middle Works*, vol. 2, 60.

12. Robert Mark Wenley, "Report of my conversation with Dewey on the Cattell

Case," December 28, 1917, Wenley Papers, Bentley Historical Library, University of Michigan.

13. "Press reports of statements by Professor Dewey" (1917), Columbia University Archives.

14. *Lochner v. New York*, 198 U.S. 45, 75 (1905).

15. Herbert Spencer, *Social Statics: or, The Conditions Essential to Human Happiness Specified, and the First of Them Developed* (London: John Chapman, 1851), 103 (original in italics).

16. *Lochner v. New York*, 76.

17. Oliver Wendell Holmes, "Natural Law," *Collected Works of Justice Holmes: Complete Public Writings and Selected Judicial Opinions of Oliver Wendell Holmes*, ed. Sheldon M. Novick (Chicago: University of Chicago Press, 1995–), vol. 3, 447.

18. See, generally, David M. Rabban, *Free Speech in Its Forgotten Years* (Cambridge, England: Cambridge University Press, 1997), 249–380.

19. See Nick Salvatore, *Eugene V. Debs: Citizen and Socialist* (Urbana: University of Illinois Press, 1982), 291–4.

20. *Frohwerk v. United States*, 249 U.S. 204, 209 (1919).

21. *Debs v. United States*, 249 U.S. 211, 215 (1919).

22. *Schenck v. United States*, 249 U.S. 47, 52 (1919).

23. James Bradley Thayer, "The Origin and Scope of the American Doctrine of Constitutional Law," *Harvard Law Review*, 7 (1893): 144–5.

24. Learned Hand, "Three Letters from Alumni," *Harvard Law School Bulletin*, 1 (January 1949): 7.

25. See Gerald Gunther, *Learned Hand: The Man and the Judge* (New York: Knopf, 1994), 153–5.

26. *Masses Publishing Co. v. Patten*, 244 Federal Reporter 535, 543, 539, 540, 541 (S.D.N.Y. 1917).

27. *Masses Publishing Co. v. Patten*, 246 Federal Reporter 24, 38 (2d Cir. 1917).

28. See Gerald Gunther, "Learned Hand and the Origins of Modern First Amendment Doctrine: Some Fragments of History," *Stanford Law Review*, 27 (1975): 739–40.

29. Learned Hand to Oliver Wendell Holmes, [March] 1919, Learned Hand Papers, Harvard Law Library, Box 103, Folder 24.

30. Oliver Wendell Holmes to Learned Hand, April 3, 1919, Hand Papers, Box 103, Folder 24.

31. See Richard Polenberg, *Fighting Faiths: The Abrams Case, the Supreme Court, and Free Speech* (New York: Viking, 1987), 43–147.

32. *Abrams v. United States*, 250 U.S. 616, 627–8 (1919).

33. *Abrams v. United States*, 630–31.

34. *Gitlow v. New York*, 268 U.S. 652 (1925); *Whitney v. California*, 274 U.S. 357 (1927).

EPILOGUE

1. Charles S. Peirce to Victoria Welby, May 25, 1911, in *Charles Peirce's Letters to Lady Welby*, ed. Irwin C. Loeb (New Haven: Whitlock, 1953), 46.

2. Helen Peirce Ellis, memorial, MS 1644, Charles S. Peirce Papers, Houghton Library, Harvard University.

3. Joseph Jastrow, "Obituary: The Widow of Charles S. Peirce," *Science*, 80 (1934): 441.

4. Oliver Wendell Holmes to Frederick Pollock, September 1, 1910, *Holmes-Pollock Letters: The Correspondence of Mr. Justice Holmes and Sir Frederick Pollock 1874–1932*, ed. Mark DeWolfe Howe (Cambridge, Mass.: Harvard University Press, 1941), vol. 1, 167.

5. Oliver Wendell Holmes to Henry James, February 29, 1912, James Family Papers, Houghton Library, Harvard University, bMS Am 1092.

6. John Dewey, *Experience and Nature* (1925), *The Later Works, 1925–53*, ed. Jo Ann Boydston (Carbondale: Southern Illinois University Press, 1981–90), vol. 3, 312.

7. Oliver Wendell Holmes to Frederick Pollock, May 15, 1931, *Holmes-Pollock Letters*, vol. 2, 287.

8. John Flannery to Mark D. Howe, May 13, 1942, Oliver Wendell Holmes Papers, Harvard Law School; see G. Edward White, *Justice Oliver Wendell Holmes: Law and the Inner Self* (New York: Oxford University Press, 1993), 488.

9. James T. Farrell, "Dewey in Mexico," in *John Dewey: Philosopher of Science and Freedom*, ed. Sidney Hook (New York: Dial, 1950), 374.

WORKS CITED

Abbott, Henry L. *Fallen Leaves: The Civil War Letters of Major Henry Livermore Abbott*. Ed. Robert Garth Scott. Kent, Ohio: Kent State University Press, 1991.

Abrahams, Edward. *The Lyrical Left: Randolph Bourne, Alfred Stieglitz, and the Origins of Cultural Radicalism in America*. Charlottesville: University Press of Virginia, 1986.

Adams, Henry. *Novels, Mont Saint Michel, The Education*. New York: Library of America, 1983.

Addams, Jane. "A Modern Lear." *Survey*, 29 (November 2, 1912): 131–7.

———. *Democracy and Social Ethics*. New York: Macmillan, 1913.

———. "The Settlement as a Factor in the Labor Movement." In Residents of Hull-House, *Hull-House Maps and Papers: A Presentation of Nationalities and Wages in a Congested District of Chicago*. New York: Thomas Y. Crowell, 1895.

———. *Twenty Years at Hull-House, with Autobiographical Notes*. New York: Macmillan, 1910.

Agassiz, Louis. *Contributions to the Natural History of the United States of America*. 4 vols. Boston: Little, Brown, 1857–62.

———. "The Diversity of Origin of the Human Races." *Christian Examiner*, 49 (1850): 110–45.

———. "Evolution and Permanence of Type." *Atlantic Monthly*, 33 (1874): 92–101.

————. "Prof. Agassiz on the Origin of Species." *American Journal of Science and Arts,* 2nd series 30 (1860): 142–54.

————. "Sketch of the Natural Provinces of the Animal World and Their Relation to the Different Types of Man." In Josiah C. Nott and George R. Gliddon, eds., *Types of Mankind; or, Ethnological Researches.* Philadelphia: Lippincott, Grambo, 1857.

————. *Twelve Lectures on Comparative Embryology.* New York: Dewitt and Davenport, 1849.

Agassiz, Louis, and Elizabeth Agassiz. *A Journey in Brazil.* Boston: Ticknor and Fields, 1868.

Ahlstrom, Sydney E. *A Religious History of the American People.* New Haven: Yale University Press, 1972.

Allen, Gay Wilson. *William James: A Biography.* New York: Viking, 1967.

Anderson, James William, " 'The Worst Kind of Melancholy': William James in 1869." *Harvard Library Bulletin,* 30 (1982): 369–86.

Angell, James Rowland, and Addison W. Moore. "Reaction-Time: A Study in Attention and Habit." *Psychological Review,* 3 (1896): 245–58.

Archibald, R. C. "Biographical Sketch." *American Mathematical Monthly,* 32 (1925): 8–19.

Baker, Liva. *The Justice from Beacon Hill: The Life and Times of Oliver Wendell Holmes.* New York: HarperCollins, 1991.

Baltzell, E. Digby. *Puritan Boston and Quaker Philadelphia: Two Protestant Ethics and the Spirit of Class Authority and Leadership.* New York: Free Press, 1979.

Bannister, Robert C. *Social Darwinism: Science and Myth in Anglo-American Social Thought.* Philadelphia: Temple University Press, 1979.

Bartlett, Irving H. *Wendell Phillips, Brahmin Radical.* Boston: Beacon Press, 1961.

Baxter, Maurice G. *Daniel Webster and the Supreme Court.* Amherst: University of Massachusetts Press, 1966.

Bedell, Leila G. "A Chicago Toynbee Hall." *Woman's Journal,* 20 (May 25, 1889): 162.

Benedict, G. G. *Vermont in the Civil War: A History of the Part Taken by the Vermont Soldiers and Sailors in the War for the Union, 1861–5.* 2 vols. Burlington, Vt.: Free Press Association, 1886–88.

Benedict, G. W. *An Exposition of the System of Instruction and Discipline Pursued in the University of Vermont.* 2nd ed. Burlington, Vt.: Chauncey Goodrich, 1831.

"Benjamin Peirce." *Proceedings of the American Academy of Arts and Sciences,* 16 (1880–81): 446–7.

Bentley, Arthur F. *The Process of Government: A Study of Social Pressures.* Chicago: University of Chicago Press, 1908.

Berenson, Bernard. *Sunset and Twilight: From the Diaries of 1947–1958.* Ed. Nicky Mariano. London: Hamish Hamilton, 1964.

Beveridge, Albert J. *The Life of John Marshall*. 4 vols. Boston: Houghton Mifflin, 1916–19.

Biddle, Francis. *Mr. Justice Holmes*. New York: Scribner, 1942.

Birney, James G. *A Letter on the Political Obligations of Abolitionists, with a Reply by William Lloyd Garrison*. Boston: Dow and Jackson, 1839.

Blake, William. *Complete Writings of William Blake*. New ed. Ed. Geoffrey Keynes. London: Oxford University Press, 1966.

Bledstein, Burton J. *The Culture of Professionalism: The Middle Class and the Development of Higher Education in America*. New York: Norton, 1976.

Boas, Franz. "Changes in the Bodily Form of Descendants of Immigrants." *American Anrthopologist*, n.s. 14 (1912): 530–62.

———. "Human Faculty as Determined by Race." *Proceedings of the American Association for the Advancement of Science*, 43 (1894): 301–27.

———. "Instability of Human Types." In Gustav Spiller, ed., *Papers on Inter-racial Problems, Communicated to the First Universal Races Congress Held at the University of London, July 26–29, 1911*. Boston: Ginn, 1912.

———. "Museums of Ethnology and Their Classification." *Science*, 9 (1887): 589.

Bourne, Randolph. "The Jew and Trans-National America." *Menorah Journal*, 2 (1916): 277–84.

———. "John Dewey's Philosophy." *New Republic*, 2 (1915): 154–6.

———. *The Letters of Randolph Bourne: A Comprehensive Edition*. Ed. Eric J. Sandeen. Troy, N.Y.: Whitston, 1981.

———. "Trans-National America." *Atlantic Monthly*, 108 (1916): 86–97.

———. "Twilight of Idols." *Seven Arts*, 2 (1917): 688–702.

Boutroux, Émile. *De la contingence des lois de la nature*. 2nd ed. Paris: Ancienne Librairie German Baillière, 1895.

Bowler, Peter J. *The Eclipse of Darwinism: Anti-Darwinian Evolutionary Theories in the Decades around 1900*. Baltimore: Johns Hopkins University Press, 1983.

Brent, Joseph. *Charles Sanders Peirce: A Life*. Bloomington: Indiana University Press, 1993.

Brown, Victoria. "Advocate for Democracy: Jane Addams and the Pullman Strike." In Richard Schneirov, Shelton Stromquist, and Nick Salvatore, eds., *The Pullman Strike and the Crisis of the 1890s: Essays on Labor and Politics*. Urbana: University of Illinois Press, 1999.

Bruce, George A. *The Twentieth Regiment of Massachusetts Volunteer Infantry, 1861–1865*. Boston: Houghton Mifflin, 1906.

Bruce, Robert V. *The Launching of Modern American Science, 1846–1876*. New York: Knopf, 1987.

Buckle, Henry Thomas. *History of Civilization in England*. Vol. 1, London: John W. Parker, 1857. Vol. 2, London: Parker, Son, and Bourn, 1861.

Buder, Stanley. *Pullman: An Experiment in Industrial Order and Community Planning, 1880–1930*. New York: Oxford University Press, 1967.

Butler, Benjamin F. *Autobiography and Personal Reminiscences of Major-General Benjamin F. Butler: Butler's Book*. Boston: Thayer, 1892.

Butler, Jon. *Awash in a Sea of Faith: Christianizing the American People*. Cambridge, Mass.: Harvard University Press, 1990.

Cabot, James Elliot. *A Memoir of Ralph Waldo Emerson*. 2 vols. Boston: Houghton Mifflin, 1888.

Cajori, Florian. *The Teaching and History of Mathematics in the United States*. Washington, D.C.: Government Printing Office, 1890.

Campbell, Lewis, and William Garnett. *The Life of James Clerk Maxwell*. Rev. ed. London: Macmillan, 1884.

Cartwright, Samuel A. "Unity of the Human Race Disproved by the Hebrew Bible." *De Bow's Review*, 29 (1860): 129–36.

Castle, Henry Northrup. *Henry Northrup Castle Letters*. London: privately printed, 1902.

Channing, William Ellery. *Works of William Ellery Channing, D.D.* 6 vols. Boston: J. Munroe, 1841–43.

Chesterton, Gilbert Keith. *Orthodoxy*. New York: John Lane, 1908.

Coleridge, Samuel Taylor. *Aids to Reflection, in the Formation of a Manly Character, on the Several Grounds of Prudence, Morality, and Religion*. Burlington, Vt.: Chauncey Goodrich, 1829.

Commager, Henry Steele. *The American Mind: An Interpretation of American Thought and Character Since the 1880s*. New Haven: Yale University Press, 1950.

Cooley, Charles Horton. *Sociological Theory and Social Research*. New York: Henry Holt, 1930.

Cooper, Lane. *Louis Agassiz as a Teacher: Illustrative Extracts on His Method of Instruction*. Rev. ed. Ithaca, N.Y.: Comstock, 1945.

Cotkin, George. *William James, Public Philosopher*. Baltimore: Johns Hopkins University Press, 1990.

Coughlan, Neil. *Young John Dewey: An Essay in American Intellectual History*. Chicago: University of Chicago Press, 1975.

Creighton, Margaret S. *Rites and Passages: The Experience of American Whaling, 1830–1870*. Cambridge, England: Cambridge University Press, 1995.

Cross, Whitney R. *The Burned-over District: The Social and Intellectual History of Enthusiastic Religion in Western New York, 1800–1850*. Ithaca, N.Y.: Cornell University Press, 1950.

Dana, Richard Henry, Jr. *The Journals*. Ed. Robert F. Lucid. 3 vols. Cambridge, Mass.: Harvard University Press, 1968.

Danziger, Kurt. *Constructing the Subject: Historical Origins of Psychological Research.* Cambridge, England: Cambridge University Press, 1990.

Darwin, Charles. *Charles Darwin's Marginalia.* Ed. Mario A. di Gregorio. New York: Garland, 1990–.

———. *The Correspondence of Charles Darwin.* Ed. Frederick H. Burkhardt and Sydney Smith. Cambridge, England: Cambridge University Press, 1985–.

———. *More Letters of Charles Darwin: A Record of His Work in a Series of Hitherto Unpublished Letters.* Ed. Francis Darwin and A. C. Seward. 2 vols. New York: D. Appleton, 1903.

———. *The Works of Charles Darwin.* Ed. Paul H. Barrett and R. B. Freeman. Cambridge, England: Cambridge University Press, 1988–.

Davis, Allen F. *American Heroine: The Life and Legend of Jane Addams.* New York: Oxford University Press, 1973.

———. *Spearheads for Reform: The Social Settlements and the Progressive Movement, 1890–1914.* New York: Oxford University Press, 1967.

Davis, Lance E., Robert E. Gallman, and Karin Gleiter. *In Pursuit of Leviathan: Technology, Institutions, Productivity, and Profits in American Whaling, 1816–1906.* Chicago: University of Chicago Press, 1997.

Degler, Carl N. *In Search of Human Nature: The Decline and Revival of Darwinism in American Social Thought.* New York: Oxford University Press, 1991.

Dewey, John. *Correspondence of John Dewey, Volume I: 1871–1918.* Ed. Larry A. Hickman. Electronic edition. Center for Dewey Studies, Southern Illinois University at Carbondale, 1999.

———. *The Early Works, 1882–1898.* Ed. Jo Ann Boydston. 5 vols. Carbondale: Southern Illinois University Press, 1967–72.

———. *The Later Works, 1925–1953.* Ed. Jo Ann Boydston. 17 vols. Carbondale: Southern Illinois University Press, 1981–90.

———. *The Middle Works, 1899–1924.* Ed. Jo Ann Boydston. 15 vols. Carbondale: Southern Illinois University Press, 1976–83.

———. *Principles of Instrumental Logic: John Dewey's Lectures in Ethics and Political Ethics, 1895–1896.* Ed. Donald F. Koch. Carbondale: Southern Illinois University Press, 1998.

Diliberto, Gioia. *A Useful Woman: The Early Life of Jane Addams.* New York: Scribner, 1999.

Dubofsky, Melvyn. "The Federal Judiciary, Free Labor, and Equal Rights." In Richard Schneirov, Shelton Stromquist, and Nick Salvatore, eds., *The Pullman Strike and the Crisis of the 1890s: Essays on Labor and Politics.* Urbana: University of Illinois Press, 1999.

Du Bois, W. E. B. *Writings.* New York: Library of America, 1986.

Duffy, John J. Introduction to *Coleridge's American Disciples: The Selected Correspondence of James Marsh.* Amherst: University of Massachusetts Press, 1973.

Dupree, A. Hunter. *Asa Gray, 1810–1888*. Cambridge, Mass.: Harvard University Press, 1959.

Dykhuizen, George. *The Life and Mind of John Dewey*. Ed. Jo Ann Boydston. Carbondale: Southern Illinois University Press, 1973.

Edel, Leon. *Henry James*. 5 vols. Philadelphia: Lippincott, 1953–72.

Eliot, Charles William. "Reminiscences of Peirce." *American Mathematical Monthly*, 32 (1925): 1–4.

Eliot, Thomas Dawes. *Hetty H. Robinson, in equity, vs. Thomas Mandell, et al., U.S. District Court, Massachusetts District: Arguments, in 3 Parts*. Reported by J. M. W. Yerrinton. Boston: Alfred Mudge, 1867.

Elkins, Stanley M. *Slavery: A Problem in American Institutional and Intellectual Life*. 2nd. ed. Chicago: University of Chicago Press, 1968.

Ellenberger, Henri F. *The Discovery of the Unconscious: The History and Evolution of Dynamic Psychiatry*. New York: Basic Books, 1970.

Elliott, Orrin L. *Stanford University: The First Twenty-Five Years*. London: Stanford University Press, 1937.

Ely, Richard T. "Pullman: A Social Study." *Harper's New Monthly Magazine*, 70 (1884–85): 452–66.

Emerson, Edward Waldo. *The Early Years of the Saturday Club: 1855–1870*. Boston: Houghton Mifflin, 1918.

Emerson, Ellen Tucker. *The Letters of Ellen Tucker Emerson*. Ed. Edith E. W. Gregg. 2 vols. Kent, Ohio: Kent State University Press, 1982.

Emerson, Ralph Waldo. *The Complete Sermons of Ralph Waldo Emerson*. Ed. Albert J. von Frank. 4 vols. Columbia: University of Missouri Press, 1989–92.

———. *Emerson's Antislavery Writings*. Ed. Len Gougeon and Joel Myerson. New Haven: Yale University Press, 1995.

———. *Essays and Lectures*. New York: Library of America, 1983.

———. *The Journals and Miscellaneous Notebooks of Ralph Waldo Emerson*. Ed. William H. Gilman et al. 16 vols. Cambridge, Mass.: Harvard University Press, 1960–82.

———. *The Letters of Ralph Waldo Emerson*. Ed. Ralph L. Rusk and Eleanor M. Tilton. 10 vols. New York: Columbia University Press, 1939–95.

Emery, William M. *The Howland Heirs: Being the Story of a Family and a Fortune and the Inheritance of a Trust Established for Mrs. Hetty H. R. Green*. New Bedford: E. Anthony, 1919.

Farrell, James T. "Dewey in Mexico." In Sidney Hook, ed., *John Dewey: Philosopher of Science and Freedom*. New York: Dial, 1950.

Farrell, John C. *Beloved Lady: A History of Jane Addams' Ideas on Reform and Peace*. Baltimore: Johns Hopkins University Press, 1967.

Faulkner, Harold U. *The Decline of Laissez Faire, 1897–1917*. New York: Rhinehart, 1951.

Feinstein, Howard M. *Becoming William James*. Ithaca, N.Y.: Cornell University Press, 1984.

Feuer, Lewis. "H. A. P. Torrey and John Dewey: Teacher and Pupil." *American Quarterly*, 10 (1958): 34–54.

———. "James Marsh and the Conservative Transcendentalist Philosophy: A Political Interpretation." *New England Quarterly*, 31 (1958): 3–31.

Fisch, Max H. *Peirce, Semeiotic, and Pragmatism: Essays*. Ed. Kenneth Laine Ketner and Christian J. W. Kloesel. Bloomington: Indiana University Press, 1986.

———. "Was There a Metaphysical Club in Cambridge?" In Edward C. Moore and Richard S. Robin, eds., *Studies in the Philosophy of Charles Sanders Peirce, Second Series*. Amherst: University of Massachusetts Press, 1964.

Fox, William F. *Regimental Losses in the American Civil War, 1861–1865*. Albany: Albany Publishing, 1889.

Fredrickson, George M. *The Black Image in the White Mind: The Debate on Afro-American Character and Destiny, 1817–1914*. New York: Harper & Row, 1971.

———. *The Inner Civil War: Northern Intellectuals and the Crisis of the Union*. New York: Harper & Row, 1965.

Garrison, Wendell Phillips, and Francis Jackson Garrison. *William Lloyd Garrison, 1805–1879: The Story of His Life, Told by His Children*. 4 vols. New York: Century, 1885–89.

Garrison, W[illia]m Lloyd. "Address." *Liberator*, 9 (July 19, 1839): 114.

———. "Prospectus of the Liberator," *Liberator*, 8 (December 28, 1838): 207.

———. *Selections from the Writings and Speeches of William Lloyd Garrison*. Boston: R. F. Wallcut, 1852.

"General Report of the Committee on Academic Freedom and Academic Tenure." *Bulletin of the American Association of University Professors*, 1 (1915): 15–43.

Ghiselin, Michael T. *The Triumph of the Darwinian Method*. Chicago: University of Chicago Press, 1984.

Gigerenzer, Gerd, Zeno Swijtink, Theodore Porter, Lorraine Daston, John Beatty, and Lorenz Krüger. *The Empire of Chance: How Probability Changed Science and Everyday Life*. Cambridge, England: Cambridge University Press, 1989.

Gillispie, Charles Coulston. "Intellectual Factors in the Background of Analysis by Probabilities." In A. C. Crombie, ed., *Scientific Change: Historical Studies in the Intellectual, Social, and Technical Conditions for Scientific Discovery and Technical Invention, from Antiquity to the Present*. New York: Basic Books, 1963.

———. *Pierre-Simon Laplace, 1749–1827: A Life in Exact Science*. Princeton: Princeton University Press, 1997.

Gilman, Daniel C. "The Benefits Which Society Derives from Universities." *Johns Hopkins University Circulars*, 4 (1885): 43–54.

Ginger, Ray. *Altgeld's America: The Lincoln Ideal Versus Changing Realities*. New York: Funk & Wagnalls, 1958.

―――. *The Bending Cross: A Biography of Eugene Victor Debs*. New Brunswick: Rutgers University Press, 1949.

Gleason, Philip. "American Identity and Americanization." In Stephan Thernstrom, Ann Orlov, and Oscar Handlin, eds., *Harvard Encyclopedia of American Ethnic Groups*. Cambridge, Mass.: Harvard University Press, 1980.

Gossett, Thomas F. *Race: The History of an Idea in America*. Dallas: Southern Methodist University Press, 1963.

Gougeon, Len. *Virtue's Hero: Emerson, Anti-Slavery, and Reform*. Athens: University of Georgia Press, 1990.

Gould, Stephen Jay. *The Mismeasure of Man*. New York: Norton, 1981.

―――. "Morton's Ranking of Races by Cranial Capacity." *Science*, 200 (1978): 503–9.

―――. *Ontogeny and Phylogeny*. Cambridge, Mass.: Harvard University Press, 1977.

Grant, Madison. *The Passing of the Great Race, or The Racial Basis of European History*. New York: Scribner, 1916.

Grant, Ulysses S. *Memoirs and Selected Letters*. New York: Library of America, 1990.

Gray, Asa. *Darwiniana: Essays and Reviews Pertaining to Darwinism*. New York: D. Appleton, 1876.

―――. "Statistics of the Flora of the Northern United States." *American Journal of Science and Arts*, 2nd series 22 (1857): 204–52; 23 (1857): 62–84, 369–403.

Green, Nicholas St. John. *Essays and Notes on the Law of Tort and Crime*. Menasha, Wis.: George Banta, 1933.

Greenslet, Ferris. *The Lowells and Their Seven Worlds*. Boston: Houghton Mifflin, 1946.

Gunther, Gerald. "Learned Hand and the Origins of Modern First Amendment Doctrine: Some Fragments of History." *Stanford Law Review*, 27 (1975): 719–73.

―――. *Learned Hand: The Man and the Judge*. New York: Knopf, 1994.

Habegger, Alfred. *The Father: A Life of Henry James, Sr.* New York: Farrar, Straus and Giroux, 1994.

Hacking, Ian. *The Emergence of Probability: A Philosophical Study of Early Ideas about Probability, Induction and Statistical Inference*. Cambridge, England: Cambridge University Press, 1975.

―――. "Nineteenth-Century Cracks in the Concept of Determinism." *Journal of the History of Ideas*, 44 (1983): 455–75.

―――. *The Taming of Chance*. Cambridge, England: Cambridge University Press, 1990.

Hale, Edward Everett, "My College Days." *Atlantic Monthly*, 71 (1893): 355–63.

Hall, Granville Stanley. *Life and Confessions of a Psychologist*. New York: D. Appleton, 1923.

————. "The Moral and Religious Training of Children." *Princeton Review*, n.s. 9 (1882): 26–48.

————. "The New Psychology." *Andover Review*, 3 (1885): 120–35, 239–48.

Haller, John S., Jr. *Outcasts from Evolution: Scientific Attitudes of Racial Inferiority, 1859–1900*. Urbana: University of Illinois Press, 1971.

Hand, Learned. "Three Letters from Alumni." *Harvard Law School Bulletin*, 1 (January 1949): 7–8.

Haskell, Thomas L. "Justifying the Rights of Academic Freedom in the Era of Power/Knowledge." In Louis Menand, ed., *The Future of Academic Freedom*. Chicago: University of Chicago Press, 1996.

Hatch, Nathan O. *The Democratization of American Christianity*. New Haven: Yale University Press, 1989.

Hawkins, Hugh. *Between Harvard and America: The Educational Leadership of Charles W. Eliot*. New York: Oxford University Press, 1972.

————. *Pioneer: A History of the Johns Hopkins University, 1874–1889*. Ithaca, N.Y.: Cornell University Press, 1960.

Hays, Samuel P. *The Response to Industrialism, 1885–1914*. Chicago: University of Chicago Press, 1957.

Hedge, Frederick Henry. "Coleridge's Literary Character." *Christian Examiner and General Review*, 14 (1833): 109–29.

Hegel, Georg Wilhelm Friedrich. *Gesammelte Werke*. Hamburg: Felix Meiner Verlag, 1968–.

————. *Hegel: The Letters*. Trans. Clark Butler and Christiane Seiler. Bloomington: Indiana University Press, 1984.

————. *The Phenomenology of Mind*. Trans. J. B. Baillie. 2nd ed. London: Macmillan, 1931.

Herschel, John Frederick William. "Quetelet on Probabilities." *Edinburgh Review*, 92 (1850): 1–57.

Herskovits, Melville J. *Franz Boas: The Science of Man in the Making*. New York: Scribner, 1953.

Higginson, Thomas Wentworth. "How I Was Educated." *Forum*, 1 (1886): 172–82.

Higham, John. *Send These to Me: Immigrants in Urban America*. Rev. ed. Baltimore: Johns Hopkins University Press, 1984.

Hillard, George S. *Life, Letters, and Journals of George Ticknor*. 2 vols. Boston: James R. Osgood, 1876.

Hirsch, Susan E. "The Search for Unity among Railroad Workers: The Pullman Strike in Perspective." In Richard Schneirov, Shelton Stromquist, and Nick Salvatore, eds., *The Pullman Strike and the Crisis of the 1890s: Essays on Labor and Politics*. Urbana: University of Illinois Press, 1999.

Hofstadter, Richard. *The Age of Reform: From Bryan to FDR*. New York: Knopf, 1955.

———. *The American Political Tradition and the Men Who Made It*. New York: Knopf, 1951.

———. *Social Darwinism in American Thought*. Rev. ed. Boston: Beacon Press, 1955.

Hofstadter, Richard, and Walter P. Metzger. *The Development of Academic Freedom in the United States*. New York: Columbia University Press, 1955.

Hollander, John. *American Poetry: The Nineteenth Century*. 2 vols. New York: Library of America, 1993.

Holmes, Oliver Wendell, Jr. *The Collected Works of Justice Holmes: Complete Public Writings and Selected Judicial Opinions of Oliver Wendell Holmes*. Ed. Sheldon M. Novick. 5 vols. Chicago: University of Chicago Press, 1995–.

———. *Holmes and Frankfurter: Their Correspondence, 1912–1934*. Ed. Robert M. Mennel and Christine L. Compston. Hanover: University Press of New England, 1996.

———. "The Holmes-Cohen Correspondence," ed. Felix Cohen. *Journal of the History of Ideas*, 9 (1948): 3–52.

———. *The Holmes-Einstein Letters: Correspondence of Mr. Justice Holmes and Lewis Einstein 1903–1935*. Ed. James Bishop Peabody. New York: St. Martin's, 1964.

———. *Holmes-Laski Letters: The Correspondence of Mr. Justice Holmes and Harold J. Laski, 1916–1935*. Ed. Mark DeWolfe Howe. 2 vols. Cambridge, Mass.: Harvard University Press, 1953.

———. *Holmes-Pollock Letters: The Correspondence of Mr. Justice Holmes and Sir Frederick Pollock, 1874–1932*. Ed. Mark DeWolfe Howe. 2 vols. Cambridge, Mass.: Harvard University Press, 1941.

———. *Holmes-Sheehan Correspondence: Letters of Justice Oliver Wendell Holmes, Jr., and Canon Patrick Augustine Sheehan*. Ed. David H. Burton. Rev. ed. New York: Fordham University Press, 1993.

———. *Touched with Fire: Civil War Letters and Diary of Oliver Wendell Holmes, Jr., 1861–1864*. Ed. Mark DeWolfe Howe. Cambridge, Mass.: Harvard University Press, 1946.

Holmes, Oliver Wendell, Sr. "The Autocrat of the Breakfast Table, No II." *New-England Magazine*, 2 (1832): 134–8.

———. *The Autocrat's Miscellanies*. Ed. Albert Mordell. New York: Twayne, 1959.

———. "My Hunt after 'The Captain.' " *Atlantic Monthly*, 10 (1862): 738–64.

———. *Ralph Waldo Emerson*. Boston: Houghton Mifflin, 1884.

———. *The Works of Oliver Wendell Holmes*. 13 vols. Boston: Houghton Mifflin, 1892.

Hook, Sidney. *Pragmatism and the Tragic Sense of Life*. New York: Basic Books, 1974.

Hopkins, John Henry. *A Scriptural, Ecclesiastical, and Historical View of Slavery, from the Days of the Patriarch Abraham, to the Nineteenth Century, Addressed to the Right Rev. Alonzo Potter, D.D.* New York: W. I. Pooley, 1864.

Howe, Daniel Walker. *The Unitarian Conscience: Harvard Moral Philosophy, 1805–1861.* Cambridge, Mass.: Harvard University Press, 1970.

Howe, Mark DeWolfe. *Justice Oliver Wendell Holmes: The Proving Years, 1870–1882.* Cambridge, Mass.: Harvard University Press, 1963.

————. *Justice Oliver Wendell Holmes: The Shaping Years, 1841–1870.* Cambridge, Mass.: Harvard University Press, 1957.

Howe, Mark A. DeWolfe. *Holmes of the Breakfast-Table.* London: Oxford University Press, 1939.

————. *Memories of a Hostess: A Chronicle of Eminent Friendships, Drawn Chiefly from the Diaries of Mrs. James T. Fields.* Boston: Atlantic Monthly Press, 1922.

————. "A Packet of Wendell-James Letters." *Scribner's Magazine,* 84 (1928): 675–87.

"The Howland Will Case." *American Law Review,* 4 (1870): 625–63.

Hoyt, Edwin P. *Improper Bostonian: Dr. Oliver Wendell Holmes.* New York: Morrow, 1979.

Hunt, James. "On the Negro's Place in Nature." *Memoirs Read before the Anthropological Society of London,* 1 (1865): 1–64.

Huxley, Thomas H. "On the Hypothesis that Animals Are Automata, and Its History." *Fortnightly Review,* n.s. 16 (1874): 555–80.

————. *Science and Education: Essays.* New York: D. Appleton, 1896.

Immigration Commission. *Abstract of the Report on Changes in Bodily Form of Descendants of Immigrants.* Washington, D.C.: Government Printing Office, 1911.

Irmscher, Christophe. *The Poetics of Natural History: From John Bartram to William James.* New Brunswick: Rutgers University Press, 1999.

Irwin, Richard B. "Ball's Bluff and the Arrest of General Stone." In Robert Underwood Johnson and Clarence Clough Buel, eds., *Battles and Leaders of the Civil War.* 4 vols. Rpt. New York: Thomas Yoseloff, 1956.

James, Alice. *The Diary of Alice James.* Ed. Leon Edel. London: Rupert Hart-Davis, 1965.

James, Henry. *Letters.* Ed. Leon Edel. 4 vols. Cambridge, Mass.: Harvard University Press, 1974–84.

————. *Notes of a Son and Brother.* New York: Scribner, 1914.

————. *A Small Boy and Others.* New York: Scribner, 1913.

James, Henry. *Charles W. Eliot, President of Harvard University, 1869–1909.* 2 vols. Boston: Houghton Mifflin, 1930.

James, Henry, Sr. *The Church of Christ Not an Ecclesiasticism: Letter to a Sectarian.* New York: Redfield, 1854.

————. *Lectures and Miscellanies.* New York: Redfield, 1852.

————. "Marriage Question." *New York Tribune,* September 18, 1852, 6.

————. "Postcript to Y.S.'s Reply to A.E.F." *Harbinger*, 8 (December 30, 1848): 68.

————. "Remarks." *Harbinger*, 8 (December 2, 1848): 37.

————. *The Secret of Swedenborg: Being an Elucidation of His Doctrine of the Divine Natural Humanity*. Boston: Fields, Osgood, 1869.

————. *Society the Redeemed Form of Man, and the Earnest of God's Omnipotence in Human Nature*. Boston: Houghton, Osgood, 1879.

————. *Substance and Shadow: Or, Morality and Religion in Their Relation to Life: An Essay upon the Physics of Creation*. Boston: Ticknor and Fields, 1863.

————. "Woman and the 'Woman's Movement.'" *Putnam's Monthly*, 1 (1853): 279–88.

James, William. *The Correspondence of William James*. Ed. Ignas K. Skrupskelis and Elizabeth M. Berkeley. 12 vols. Charlottesville: University Press of Virginia, 1992–.

————. *The Letters of William James*. Ed. Henry James. 2 vols. Boston: Atlantic Monthly Press, 1920.

————. *The Works of William James*. Ed. Frederick H. Burkhardt. 19 vols. Cambridge, Mass.: Harvard University Press, 1975–88.

Jastrow, Joseph. "Joseph Jastrow." In Carl Murchison, ed., *A History of Psychology in Autobiography*. Vol. 1. Worcester: Clark University Press, 1930.

————. "Obituary: The Widow of Charles S. Peirce." *Science*, 80 (1934): 440–41.

Johnson, Robert Underwood, and Clarence Clough Buel, eds. *Battles and Leaders of the Civil War*. 4 vols. Rpt. New York: Thomas Yoseloff, 1956.

Kallen, Horace M. "Alain Locke and Cultural Pluralism." *Journal of Philosophy*, 54 (1957): 119–27.

————. *Culture and Democracy in the United States*. New York: Boni and Liveright, 1924.

————. "Democracy Versus the Melting-Pot." *Nation*, 100 (1915): 190–94, 217–20.

————. *Individualism: An American Way of Life*. New York: Liveright, 1933.

————. *The Structure of Lasting Peace: An Inquiry into the Motives of War and Peace*. Boston: Marshall Jones, 1918.

Kant, Immanuel. *Immanuel Kant's Critique of Pure Reason*. Trans. Norman Kemp Smith. London: Macmillan, 1929.

————. *Kritik der reinen Vernunft*. Riga: Johan Friedrich Hartnoch, 1781.

Kelvin, William Thomson, Baron. *Mathematical and Physical Papers*. 6 vols. Cambridge, England: Cambridge University Press, 1882–1911.

Ketner, Kenneth Laine. *His Glassy Essence: An Autobiography of Charles Sanders Peirce*. Nashville: Vanderbilt University Press, 1998.

Kuklick, Bruce. *The Rise of American Philosophy: Cambridge, Massachusetts, 1860–1930*. New Haven: Yale University Press, 1977.

Lader, Lawrence. *The Bold Brahmins: New England's War Against Slavery, 1831–1863*. New York: Dutton, 1961.

Lamont, Corliss, ed. *Dialogue on John Dewey*. New York: Horizon Press, 1959.

Laplace, Pierre-Simon. *Oeuvres complètes de Laplace*. 14 vols. Paris: Gauthier-Villars, 1878–1912.

Lasch, Christopher. *The New Radicalism in America, 1889–1963: The Intellectual as a Social Type*. New York: Knopf, 1965.

Lears, T. J. Jackson. *No Place of Grace: Antimodernism and the Transformation of American Culture, 1880–1920*. New York: Pantheon, 1981.

Lentricchia, Frank. *Ariel and the Police: Michel Foucault, William James, Wallace Stevens*. Madison: University of Wisconsin Press, 1988.

Lenzen, Victor F. *Benjamin Peirce and the U.S. Coast Survey*. San Francisco: San Francisco Press, 1968.

Lewis, R. W. B. *The Jameses: A Family Narrative*. New York: Farrar, Straus and Giroux, 1991.

Lindsey, Almont. *The Pullman Strike: The Story of a Unique Experiment and of a Great Labor Upheaval*. Chicago: University of Chicago Press, 1942.

Locke, Alain LeRoy. *Race Contacts and Interracial Relations: Lectures on the Theory and Practice of Race*. Ed. Jeffrey C. Stewart. Washington, D.C.: Howard University Press, 1992.

———. "Values and Imperatives." In Sidney Hook and Horace M. Kallen, eds., *American Philosophy Today and Tomorrow*. New York: Furman, 1935.

Lovering, Joseph. "On the Application of Mathematical Analysis to Researches in the Physical Sciences." *Cambridge Miscellany of Mathematics, Physics, and Astronomy*, 1 (1842): 73–81, 121–30.

Lowell, Abbott Lawrence. "Reminiscences." *American Mathematical Monthly*, 32 (1925): 4–5.

Lowell, James Russell. "Thoreau's Letters." *North American Review*, 101 (1865): 597–608.

Lowell, John Amory. "Darwin's Origin of Species." *Christian Examiner*, 68 (1860): 449–64.

Lurie, Edward. *Louis Agassiz: A Life in Science*. Chicago: University of Chicago Press, 1960.

———. "Louis Agassiz and the Races of Man." *Isis*, 45 (1954): 227–42.

McPherson, James M. *Battle Cry of Freedom: The Civil War Era*. New York: Oxford University Press, 1988.

Maher, Jane. *Biography of Broken Fortunes: Wilkie and Bob, Brothers of William, Henry, and Alice James*. Hamden, Conn.: Archon Books, 1986.

Maine, Henry Sumner. *Popular Government: Four Essays*. London: John Murray, 1885.

Marcou, Jules. *Life, Letters, and Works of Louis Agassiz*. 2 vols. New York: Macmillan, 1896.

Marsh, James. *Coleridge's American Disciples: The Selected Correspondence of James Marsh*. Ed. John J. Duffy. Amherst: University of Massachusetts Press, 1973.

———. "Preliminary Essay." In Samuel Taylor Coleridge, *Aids to Reflection, in the Formation of a Manly Character, on the Several Grounds of Prudence, Morality, and Religion*. Burlington, Vt.: Chauncey Goodrich, 1829.

Matthiessen, F. O. *The James Family*. New York: Knopf, 1947.

Maxwell, James Clerk. *Maxwell on Heat and Statistical Mechanics: On "Avoiding All Personal Enquiries" of Molecules*. Ed. Elizabeth Garber, Stephen G. Brush, and C. W. F. Everitt. Bethlehem, Pa.: Lehigh University Press, 1995.

———. *The Scientific Papers of James Clerk Maxwell*. Ed. W. D. Niven. 2 vols. Cambridge, England: Cambridge University Press, 1890.

———. *Theory of Heat*. London: Longmans, 1871.

Mayhew, Katherine Camp, and Anna Camp Edwards. *The Dewey School: The Laboratory School of the University of Chicago, 1896–1903*. New York: D. Appleton-Century, 1936.

Mayr, Ernst. *Evolution and the Diversity of Life: Selected Essays*. Cambridge, Mass.: Harvard University Press, 1976.

———. *One Long Argument: Charles Darwin and the Genesis of Modern Evolutionary Thought*. Cambridge, Mass.: Harvard University Press, 1991.

Meigs, J. Aitken. *Catalogue of Human Crania in the Collection of the Academy of Natural Sciences of Philadelphia*. Philadelphia: Lippincott, 1857.

Menand, Louis. "William James and the Case of the Epileptic Patient." *New York Review of Books*, 45 (December 17, 1998), 81–93.

Merz, John Theodore. *A History of European Thought in the Nineteenth Century*. 4 vols. Edinburgh and London: William Blackwood, 1904–1912.

Michaels, Walter Benn. *Our America: Nativism, Modernism, and Pluralism*. Durham: Duke University Press, 1995.

Montgomery, David. "Epilogue: The Pullman Boycott and the Making of Modern America." In Richard Schneirov, Shelton Stromquist, and Nick Salvatore, eds., *The Pullman Strike and the Crisis of the 1890s: Essays on Labor and Politics*. Urbana: University of Illinois Press, 1999.

Morgenbesser, Sidney, ed. *Dewey and His Critics: Essays from "The Journal of Philosophy."* New York: Journal of Philosophy, 1977.

Morison, Samuel Eliot. *Three Centuries of Harvard, 1636–1936*. Cambridge, Mass.: Harvard University Press, 1936.

Morison, Samuel Eliot, Henry Steele Commager, and William E. Leuchtenburg. *The Growth of the American Republic*. 2 vols. 7th ed. New York: Oxford University Press, 1980.

Morris, George Sylvester. *Philosophy and Christianity: Syllabus of a Course of Eight Lectures*. New York: Robert Carter, 1883.

——. "The University and Philosophy." *Johns Hopkins University Circulars*, 2 (1883): 54.

Morse, John T., Jr. *Life and Letters of Oliver Wendell Holmes*. 2 vols. Boston: Houghton Mifflin, 1896.

Morton, Samuel George. *Catalogue of Skulls of Man and the Inferior Animals*. Philadelphia: Lippincott, 1849.

——. *Crania Americana; or, A Comparative View of the Skulls of Various Aboriginal Nations of North and South America*. Philadelphia: J. Dobson, 1839.

——. "Hybridity in Animals, Considered in Reference to the Question of the Unity of the Human Species." *American Journal of Science and Art*, 2nd series 3 (1847): 39–50, 203–11.

Motley, John Lothrop. *The Correspondence of John Lothrop Motley*. Ed. George William Curtis. 2 vols. New York: Harper, 1889.

Myers, Gerald E. *William James: His Life and Thought*. New Haven: Yale University Press, 1986.

Nevins, Allan. *Grover Cleveland: A Study in Courage*. New York: Dodd, Mead, 1932.

——. *The War for the Union*. 4 vols. New York: Scribner, 1959–71.

Newcomb, Simon. *The Reminiscences of an Astronomer*. Boston: Houghton Mifflin, 1903.

The New-York Conspiracy, or A History of the Negro Plot, with the Journal of the Proceedings Against the Conspirators, at New-York in the Year 1741–2. New York: Southwick & Pelsue, 1801.

Nicolson, Marjorie H. "James Marsh and the Vermont Transcendentalists." *Philosophical Review*, 34 (1925): 28–50.

Norton, Charles Eliot. "The Advantages of Defeat." *Atlantic Monthly*, 8 (1861): 360–65.

——. *The Letters of Charles Eliot Norton*. Ed. Sara Norton and M. A. DeWolfe Howe. 2 vols. Boston: Houghton Mifflin, 1913.

Nott, Josiah C. "Climates of the South in Their Relation to White Labor." *De Bow's Review*, 34 (1866): 166–73.

——. "The Mulatto a Hybrid—probable extermination of the two races if the White and Black are allowed to intermarry." *American Journal of the Medical Sciences*, n.s. 11 (1843): 252–6.

——. *The Negro Race: Its Ethnology and History*. Mobile, 1866.

——. "The Problem of the Black Races." *De Bow's Review*, 34 (1866): 266–83.

Nott, Josiah C., and George R. Gliddon. *Indigenous Races of the Earth; or, New Chapters of Ethnological Inquiry*. Philadelphia: Lippincott, 1857.

——. *Types of Mankind: or, Ethnological Researches*. Philadelphia: Lippincott, Grambo, 1854.

Novick, Sheldon M. *Honorable Justice: The Life of Oliver Wendell Holmes*. Boston: Little, Brown, 1989.

Odegard, Peter H. Introduction to Arthur F. Bentley, *The Process of Government* (1908). Cambridge, Mass.: Harvard University Press, 1967.

O'Donnell, John M. *The Origins of Behaviorism: American Psychology, 1870–1920*. New York: New York University Press, 1985.

"Origins of the Modern Standard of Due Care in Negligence." *Washington University Law Quarterly*, 54 (1976): 447–79.

Papke, David Ray. *The Pullman Case: The Clash of Labor and Capital in Industrial America*. Lawrence: University Press of Kansas, 1999.

Paris, Louis-Philippe-Albert D'Orleans, comte de. *History of the Civil War in America*. 4 vols. Trans. L. F. Tasistro. Philadelphia: Porter & Coates, 1875–88.

Parrington, Vernon Louis. *Main Currents in American Thought: An Interpretation of American Literature from the Beginnings to 1920*. 3 vols. New York: Harcourt, Brace, 1927–30.

Pease, Jane H., and William H. Pease. *The Fugitive Slave Law and Anthony Burns: A Problem in Law Enforcement*. Lippincott: Philadelphia, 1975.

———. *They Who Would Be Free: Blacks' Search for Freedom, 1830–1861*. New York: Atheneum, 1974.

Peirce, Benjamin. "Criterion for the Rejection of Doubtful Observations." *Astronomical Journal*, 2 (1852): 161–3.

———. *Ideality in the Physical Sciences*. Boston: Little, Brown, 1881.

———. *Linear Associative Algebra* (1870). Ed. C. S. Peirce. New York: Van Nostrand, 1882.

———. "The National Importance of Social Science in the United States." *Journal of Social Science*, 12 (December 1880), xii–xxi.

Peirce, Charles Sanders. "The Architecture of Theories." *Monist*, 1 (1891): 161–76.

———. *Charles Peirce's Letters to Lady Welby*. Ed. Irwin C. Lieb. New Haven: Whitlock, 1953.

———. *Collected Papers of Charles Sanders Peirce*. Ed. Charles Hartshorne, Paul Weiss, and Arthur Burks. 8 vols. Cambridge, Mass.: Harvard University Press, 1931–66.

———. *The Essential Peirce: Selected Philosophical Writings*. Ed. Nathan Houser, Christian Kloesel, and the Peirce Edition Project. 2 vols. Bloomington: Indiana University Press, 1992–99.

———. "Evolutionary Love," *Monist*, 3 (1892–93): 176–200.

———. "Guessing." *Hound and Horn*, 2 (1929): 267–85.

———. "Logical Lights." *Nation*, 79 (1904): 219–20.

———. "Man's Glassy Essence." *Monist*, 3 (1892–93): 1–22.

———. *Pragmatism as a Principle and Method of Right Thinking: The 1903 Harvard Lectures on Pragmatism*. Ed. Patricia Ann Turrisi. Albany: State University of New York Press, 1997.

———. "Uniformity." In James Mark Baldwin, ed., *The Dictionary of Philosophy and Psychology.* 3 vols. New York: Macmillan, 1901–05.

———. "What Pragmatism Is." *Monist,* 15 (1905): 161–81.

———. *Writings of Charles S. Peirce: A Chronological Edition.* Peirce Edition Project. 30 vols. Bloomington: Indiana University Press, 1982–.

Peirce, Melusina Fay. *New York: A Symphonic Study, in Three Parts.* New York: Neale, 1918.

Perry, Bliss. *Life and Letters of Henry Lee Higginson.* Boston: Houghton Mifflin, 1921.

Perry, Ralph Barton. *The Thought and Character of William James.* 2 vols. Boston: Little, Brown, 1935.

Peterson, Sven R. "Benjamin Peirce: Mathematician and Philosopher." *Journal of the History of Ideas,* 16 (1955): 89–112.

Phelps, William Lyon. "When Yale Was Given to Sumnerology." *Literary Digest International Book Review,* 3 (1925): 661–3.

Phillips, Wendell. *Speeches, Lectures, and Letters.* Boston: Lee and Shepard, 1884.

Pierce, Edward L. *Memoir and Letters of Charles Sumner.* 4 vols. Boston: Roberts, 1877–93.

Plumer, William, Jr. *Life of William Plumer.* Boston: Phillips, Sampson, 1856.

Podmore, Frank. *Modern Spiritualism: A History and a Criticism.* 2 vols. New York: Scribner, 1902.

Polenberg, Richard. *Fighting Faiths: The Abrams Case, the Supreme Court, and Free Speech.* New York: Viking, 1987.

Popkin, Richard H. "The Philosophical Bases of Modern Racism." In Craig Walton and John P. Anton, eds., *Philosophy and the Civilizing Arts.* Athens: Ohio University Press, 1974.

Porter, Theodore M. *The Rise of Statistical Thinking, 1820–1900.* Princeton: Princeton University Press, 1986.

———. "A Statistical Survey of Gases: Maxwell's Social Physics." *Historical Studies in the Physical Sciences,* 12 (1981): 77–116.

Pound, Ezra. *ABC of Reading.* New Haven: Yale University Press, 1934.

Quetelet, Adolphe. *A Treatise on Man and the Development of His Faculties.* Trans. R. Knox. Edinburgh: Chambers, 1842.

———. "Sur les indiens O-Jib-Be-Wa's et les proportions de leur corps." *Bulletin de l'académie royale des sciences, des lettres, et des beaux-arts de belgique,* 15, part 1 (1846): 70–76.

———. "Sur les proportions de la race noire." *Bulletin de l'académie royale des sciences, des lettres, et des beaux-arts de belgique,* 31, part 1 (1854): 96–100.

———. *Sur l'homme et le développement de ses facultés, ou Essai de physique sociale.* 2 vols. Paris: Bachelier, 1835.

Rabban, David M. *Free Speech in Its Forgotten Years*. Cambridge, England: Cambridge University Press, 1997.

Reed, Edward S. *From Soul to Mind: The Emergence of Psychology, from Erasmus Darwin to William James*. New Haven: Yale University Press, 1997.

Renouvier, Charles. *Essais de critique générale: deuxième essai: l'homme*. Paris: Ladrange, 1859.

Residents of Hull-House. *Hull-House Maps and Papers: A Presentation of Nationalities and Wages in a Congested District of Chicago*. New York: Thomas Y. Crowell, 1895.

Reuben, Julie A. *The Making of the Modern University: Intellectual Transformation and the Marginalization of Morality*. Chicago: University of Chicago Press, 1996.

"Review of *On Man, and the Development of His Faculties*." *Athenaeum* (1835): 593–4, 611–13, 658–61.

Richards, Robert J. *Darwin and the Emergence of Evolutionary Theories of Mind and Behavior*. Chicago: University of Chicago Press, 1987.

Rieber, R. W., ed. *Wilhelm Wundt and the Making of a Scientific Psychology*. New York: Plenum, 1980.

Roberts, Jon H., and James Turner. *The Sacred and the Secular University*. Princeton: Princeton University Press, 2000.

Rockefeller, Steven C. *John Dewey: Religious Faith and Democratic Humanism*. New York: Columbia University Press, 1991.

Rodrigues, José Honório. *Brazil and Africa*. Trans. Richard A. Mazzara and Sam Hileman. Berkeley and Los Angeles: University of California Press, 1965.

Ross, Dorothy. *G. Stanley Hall: The Psychologist as Prophet*. Chicago: University of Chicago Press, 1972.

Ross, Edward A. Comment on D. Collin Wells, "Social Darwinism." *American Journal of Sociology*, 12 (1906–07): 715–16.

Russell, Bertrand. *Philosophical Essays*. London: Longmans, Green, 1910.

Ryan, Alan. *John Dewey and the High Tide of American Liberalism*. New York: Norton, 1995.

Salvatore, Nick. *Eugene V. Debs: Citizen and Socialist*. Urbana: University of Illinois Press, 1982.

Santayana, George. *The Works of George Santayana*. Ed. William G. Holzberger and Herman J. Saatkamp, Jr. Cambridge, Mass.: MIT Press, 1986–.

Schickel, Richard. *D. W. Griffith: An American Life*. New York: Simon and Schuster, 1983.

Schilpp, Paul Arthur, and Lewis Edwin Hahn, eds. *The Philosophy of John Dewey*. 3rd ed. La Salle, Ill.: Open Court, 1989.

Schmidt, Sarah. "A Conversation with Horace M. Kallen: The Zionist Chapter of His Life." *Reconstructionist*, 41 (November 1975): 28–33.

Schneirov, Richard, Shelton Stromquist, and Nick Salvatore, eds. *The Pullman Strike and the Crisis of the 1890s: Essays on Labor and Politics*. Urbana: University of Illinois Press, 1999.

Schwarcz, Lilia Moritz. *The Spectacle of the Races: Scientists, Institutions, and the Race Question in Brazil, 1870–1930*. Trans. Leland Guyer. New York: Hill and Wang, 1999.

Schweber, Silvan S. "Demons, Angels, and Probability: Some Aspects of British Science in the Nineteenth Century." In Abner Shimony and Herman Feshbach, eds., *Physics as Natural Philosophy*. Cambridge, Mass.: MIT Press, 1982.

———. "The Origin of the *Origin* Revisited." *Journal of the History of Biology*, 10 (1977): 229–311.

Shaler, Nathaniel Southgate. *The Autobiography of Nathaniel Southgate Shaler, with a Supplementary Memoir by His Wife*. Boston: Houghton Mifflin, 1909.

Simon, Linda. *Genuine Reality: A Life of William James*. New York: Harcourt Brace, 1998.

Small, Albion. "Lester Frank Ward." *American Journal of Sociology*, 19 (1913–14): 75–8.

———. "Scholarship and Social Agitation." *American Journal of Sociology*, 1 (1895–96): 564–82.

Smith, Roger. *The Norton History of the Human Sciences*. New York: Norton, 1997.

Sollors, Werner. "A Critique of Pure Pluralism." In Sacvan Bercovitch, ed., *Reconstructing American Literary History*. Cambridge, Mass.: Harvard University Press, 1986.

Sollors, Werner, Caldwell Titcomb, and Thomas A. Underwood, eds. *Blacks at Harvard: A Documentary History of African-American Experience at Harvard and Radcliffe*. New York: New York University Press, 1993.

Sparkes, Boyden, and Samuel Taylor Moore. *Hetty Green: A Woman Who Loved Money*. Garden City, N.Y.: Doubleday, Doran, 1930.

Spencer, Herbert. *Social Statics; or, The Conditions Essential to Human Happiness Specified, and the First of Them Developed*. London: John Chapman, 1851.

———. "A Theory of Population, Deduced from the General Law of Animal Fertility." *Westminster and Foreign Quarterly Review*, 57 (1852): 457–501.

Stanton, William. *The Leopard's Spots: Scientific Attitudes toward Race in America, 1815–1859*. Chicago: University of Chicago Press, 1960.

Stead, W. T. *Chicago To-Day: The Labour War in America*. London: Review of Reviews, 1894.

Steiner, Paul E. *Disease in the Civil War: Natural Biological Warfare in 1861–1865*. Springfield, Ill.: Charles C. Thomas, 1968.

Stephen, James Fitzjames. "Buckle's *History of Civilization in England*." *Edinburgh Review*, 107 (1858): 465–512.

———. *A General View of the Criminal Law in England*. London: Macmillan, 1863.

Sterling, Dorothy. *The Making of an Afro-American: Martin Robison Delany, 1812–1885*. Garden City, N.Y.: Doubleday, 1971.

Stewart, Jeffrey C. "A Black Aesthete at Oxford." *Massachusetts Review*, 34 (1993): 411–28.

Stigler, Stephen M. *The History of Statistics: The Measurement of Uncertainty before 1900*. Cambridge, Mass.: Harvard University Press, 1986.

Stocking, George W. "Franz Boas and the Culture Concept in Historical Perspective." *American Anthropologist*, 68 (1966): 867–82.

———. *Race, Culture, and Evolution: Essays in the History of Anthropology*. 2nd ed. Chicago: University of Chicago Press, 1982.

———, ed. *The Shaping of American Anthropology, 1883–1911: A Franz Boas Reader*. New York: Basic Books, 1974.

Storr, Richard J. *Harper's University: The Beginnings*. Chicago: University of Chicago Press, 1966.

Strouse, Jean. *Alice James: A Biography*. Boston: Houghton Mifflin, 1980.

Struik, Dirk J. *Yankee Science in the Making*. Rev. ed. New York: Collier, 1962.

Swijtink, Zeno G. "The Objectification of Observation: Measurement and Statistical Methods in the Nineteenth Century." In Lorenz Krüger, Lorraine J. Daston, and Michael Heidelberger, eds., *The Probabilistic Revolution*. Vol. 1. Cambridge, Mass.: MIT Press, 1987.

Taylor, Eugene. *William James on Consciousness beyond the Margin*. Princeton: Princeton University Press, 1996.

Thayer, James Bradley. *Letters of Chauncey Wright, with Some Account of His Life*. Cambridge, Mass.: privately printed by John Wilson, 1878.

———. "The Origin and Scope of the American Doctrine of Constitutional Law." *Harvard Law Review*, 7 (1893): 129–56.

Thoreau, Henry David. *Correspondence*. Ed. Walter Harding and Carl Bode. New York: New York University Press, 1958.

Thorndike, Edward L. *Animal Intelligence: An Experimental Study of the Associative Processes in Animals*. New York: Macmillan, 1898.

Tilton, Eleanor M. *Amiable Autocrat: A Biography of Dr. Oliver Wendell Holmes*. New York: Schuman, 1947.

Tocqueville, Alexis de. *Democracy in America*. Trans. Henry Reeve. Ed. Phillips Bradley. 2 vols. New York: Knopf, 1945.

Touster, Saul. "In Search of Holmes from Within." *Vanderbilt Law Review*, 18 (1965): 437–72.

Tower, Walter S. *A History of the American Whale Fishery*. Philadelphia: Publications of the University of Pennsylvania, 1907.

Tucker, George F. "New Bedford." *New England Magazine*, 21 (1896): 97–117.

Turner, James. *The Liberal Education of Charles Eliot Norton*. Baltimore: Johns Hopkins University Press, 1999.

Ullman, Victor. *Martin R. Delany: The Beginnings of Black Nationalism*. Boston: Beacon Press, 1971.

Veblen, Thorstein. *The Theory of the Leisure Class: An Economic Study in the Evolution of Institutions*. New York: Macmillan, 1899.

———. "Why Is Economics Not an Evolutionary Science?" *Quarterly Journal of Economics*, 12 (1989): 373–97.

Venn, John. *The Logic of Chance; An Essay on the Foundations and Province of the Theory of Probability with Especial Reference to Its Application to Moral and Social Science*. London: Macmillan, 1866.

Veysey, Laurence R. *The Emergence of the American University*. Chicago: University of Chicago Press, 1965.

von Frank, Albert J. *The Trials of Anthony Burns: Freedom and Slavery in Emerson's Boston*. Cambridge, Mass.: Harvard University Press, 1998.

V.X. "Mathematics in Court." *Nation*, 5 (1867): 238.

Ward, Lester F. *Glimpses of the Cosmos*. 6 vols. New York: Putnam, 1913–18.

Washington, Booker T. *The Booker T. Washington Papers*. Ed. Louis R. Harlan. 14 vols. Urbana: University of Illinois Press, 1972–89.

Weinberg, Julius. *Edward Alsworth Ross and the Sociology of Progressivism*. Madison: State Historical Society of Wisconsin, 1972.

Weiner, Jonathan. *The Beak of the Finch: A Story of Evolution in Real Time*. New York: Knopf, 1994.

Weiss, John. *The Life and Correspondence of Theodore Parker: Minister of the Twenty-Eighth Congregational Society, Boston*. 2 vols. New York: D. Appleton, 1864.

Weiss, Paul. "Charles Sanders Peirce." In *Dictionary of American Biography*. 26 vols. New York: Scribner, 1928–60.

Wenley, R. M. *The Life and Work of George Sylvester Morris: A Chapter in the History of American Thought in the Nineteenth Century*. New York: Macmillan, 1919.

Westbrook, Robert B. *John Dewey and American Democracy*. Ithaca, N.Y.: Cornell University Press, 1991.

Wheeler, John. *A Historical Discourse by Rev. John Wheeler, D.D., . . . Delivered on the Occasion of the Semi-Centennial Anniversary of the University of Vermont*. Burlington, Vt.: Free Press, 1854.

White, G. Edward. *Justice Oliver Wendell Holmes: Law and the Inner Self*. New York: Oxford University Press, 1993.

———. *Tort Law in America: An Intellectual History*. New York: Oxford University Press, 1980.

Wiebe, Robert H. *The Search for Order, 1877–1920*. New York: Hill and Wang, 1967.

Wiener, Philip P. *Evolution and the Founders of Pragmatism*. Cambridge, Mass.: Harvard University Press, 1949.

Wilson, Woodrow. *The Papers of Woodrow Wilson*. Ed. Arthur S. Link. 69 vols. Princeton: Princeton University Press, 1966–94.

Wise, M. Norton, ed. *The Values of Precision*. Princeton: Princeton University Press, 1995.

Woodward, C. Vann. *American Counterpoint: Slavery and Racism in the North-South Dialogue*. Boston: Little, Brown, 1971.

———. *The Burden of Southern History*. Baton Rouge: Louisiana State University Press, 1960.

———. *The Strange Career of Jim Crow*. 3rd rev. ed. New York: Oxford University Press, 1974.

Wright, Chauncey. "John W. Draper's Thoughts on the Future Civil Policy of America." *North American Review*, 101 (1865): 589–97.

———. *Letters of Chauncey Wright*. Ed. James Bradley Thayer. Cambridge, Mass.: privately printed by John Wilson, 1878.

———. "Mathematics in Court." *Nation*, 5 (September 19, 1867): 238.

———. "The Philosophy of Herbert Spencer." *North American Review*, 100 (1865): 423–76.

———. "A Physical Theory of the Universe." *North American Review*, 99 (1864): 1–33.

———. "Spencer's Biology." *Nation*, 2 (1866): 724–5.

———. "The Winds and the Weather." *Atlantic Monthly*, 1 (1858): 272–9.

Wundt, Wilhelm. *Grundzüge der physiologischen Psychologie*. 2 vols. Leipzig, 1873–74.

Young, Robert M. *Mind, Brain, and Adaptation in the Nineteenth Century: Cerebral Localization and Its Biological Context from Gall to Ferrier*. Oxford: Clarendon Press, 1970.

INDEX

Abbot, Francis Ellingwood, 201, 212–13, 215

Abbott, Caroline Livermore, 44

Abbott, Henry Livermore, 68; background and views, 40–41, 44; on O. W. Holmes, Sr., 40–41; and O. W. Holmes, Jr., 41–2, 44, 47, 60–61, 66–8; at Fredericksburg, 43, 68; death of, 53–4

Abbott, Josiah, 40–41

abolitionism, abolitionists, 9, 19, 20, 22, 25, 27, 29, 31, 39–40, 52–3, 64, 74, 80, 112, 145, 373–74, 401; and unionism, 4–6; origin and politics of, 13–16; R. W. Emerson and, 19–22; O. W. Holmes, Jr., and, 25–7, 31, 52, 62; James family and, 73–4; H. James, Sr., and, 87; L. Agassiz on, 105–6, 116; B. Peirce and, 160–62; Huxley and, 194

Abrams, Jacob, 428–9

Abrams v. United States, 65, 421, 428–31, 442

academic freedom, 411–17, 431; and Follen case, 12; and *Trustees of Dartmouth College v. Woodward*, 243, 417; in Germany, 256; J. Dewey and, 412–17, 419

Adams, Charles Francis, 13, 143

Adams, Henry, 140, 216; *Education of Henry Adams*, 140, 143; on Darwinism, 140–41, 143; and Civil War, 143, 146; and second law of thermodynamics, 198

Adams, Henry Carter, 303–4

Adams, John, 13

Adams, John Couch, 185

Adams, John Quincy, 168; and slavery, 13

Adams, John Quincy (grandson), 168

Adams, Marion Hooper, 205

Adams family, 13, 46

521

ILLUSTRATIONS AND TEXT CREDITS

Illustrations on pp. ii, 72, 78, 334: James Family Papers (pf bMS Am 1902, Portraits of William James), Houghton Library, Harvard University, by permission of the Houghton Library and Bay James; p. 2: Library of Congress, Prints and Photographs Division [LC-USZ62-106337]; p. 5: by permission of the Boston Medical Library in the Francis A. Countway Library of Medicine; pp. 24, 50, 432: courtesy of Art & Visual Materials, Special Collections Department, Harvard Law School Library; p. 96: by permission of the Harvard Medical Library in the Francis A. Countway Library of Medicine; p. 150: courtesy of the Massachusetts Historical Society; pp. 178, 254, 366: Tuttle Collection, Institute for Studies in Pragmaticism, Texas Tech University, by permission of the Harvard University Department of Philosophy; p. 202: Chauncey Wright Papers (B W933), by permission of the American Philosophical Society; p. 234: Hood Museum of Art, Dartmouth College, Hanover, New Hampshire, presented in memory of Francis Parkman (1898–1990) by his sons—Henry, Francis Jr., Theodore B., and Samuel—and by Edward Connery Latham in tribute to Elizabeth French Latham; p. 286: Jane Addams Collection, Swarthmore College Peace Collection; pp. 317, 444: John Dewey Photograph Collection (N3-1104, N3-1109), Special Collections, Morris Library, Southern Illinois University at

Carbondale; p. 374: Alain Locke Papers, Moorland-Spingarn Research Center, Howard University; p. 408: Eugene V. Debs Foundation, Terre Haute, Indiana.

Quotations from the James Family Papers and the William James Papers by permission of the Houghton Library, Harvard University and Bay James; from the Charles S. Peirce Papers by permission of the Houghton Library and the Harvard University Department of Philosophy; from the Barrett Wendell Papers, Wendell Phillips Papers, Charles Eliot Norton Papers, Emerson Papers, Abbott Brothers Civil War Letters, and Louis Agassiz Papers by permission of the Houghton Library; from the Oliver Wendell Holmes Papers, James Bradley Thayer Papers, and Learned Hand Papers by permission of the Harvard Law School Library; from the Chauncey Wright Papers and Franz Boas Papers by permission of the American Philosophical Society Library; from the Samuel Morton Papers by permission of the Historical Society of Pennsylvania; from the Daniel Coit Gilman Papers by permission of the Milton S. Eisenhower Library, Johns Hopkins University; from the William Rainey Harper Papers by permission of the Joseph Regenstein Library, University of Chicago; from the Alain Locke Papers by permission of the Manuscript Division, Moorland-Spingarn Research Center, Howard University; from the Wenley Collection by permission of the Bentley Historical Library, University of Michigan; from the E. R. A. Seligman Papers by permission of the Rare Book and Manuscript Library, Columbia University; from the letters of Horace Kallen by permission of David J. Kallen. All quotations from the letters of John Dewey are from *The Correspondence of John Dewey, Vol. 1: 1871–1918*, ed. Larry A. Hickman (Charlottesville, Virginia, InteLex Corporation, 1999) and are used by permission of the Center for Dewey Studies and the department of Special Collections, Morris Library, University of Southern Illinois at Carbondale. Quotations from *Touched with Fire: The Civil War Letters and Diary of Oliver Wendell Holmes, Jr., 1861–1864*, ed. Mark DeWolfe Howe, by permission of Harvard University Press. Quotations from *The Correspondence of William James*, volume 4, ed. Ignas K. Skrupskelis and Elizabeth M. Berkeley, by permission of the University Press of Virginia.

JOHN CARROLL UNIVERSITY

A Century of Service

Donald P. Gavin

The Kent State University Press

LD2601
J92
L38
1985

Library of Congress Cataloging in Publication Data

Gavin, Donald P.
  John Carroll University.

  Bibliography: p.   ·
  Includes index.
  1. John Carroll University—History. I. Title.
LD2601.J92G38 1985   378.711'32   84-20109
ISBN 0-87338-311-7

Contents

Preface

The centennial celebration by any institution of higher education provides an opportunity to pause momentarily and take stock of the past in the hope of profiting from experience and gaining insight into what the future may hold. One of the tasks of writing that history is to steer a steady course between the Scylla and Charybdis of recording institutional history. There is a strong temptation to dwell exclusively on the anecdotes and personalities of internal events as though the institution had no relation to the external world whose history it shares. In a similar manner the role of the external world can be emphasized to a point where the internal personalities are seen as mere puppets. Even the writer's best intentions to strike a balance are to a considerable degree affected by the relative availability of the sources, which in the present instance are more readily available than one might expect. As in every case, however, there are gaps in the evidence. What material is available has been provided freely and without restraint.

John Carroll University shares its history with the development of the Greater Cleveland area since the 1880s, the Cleveland Catholic Diocese, the life of the Catholic Church from that of the immigrant Church to the post-second Vatican Church, the growth of the Society of Jesus (Jesuits) in the United States, the impact of two World Wars, a major economic depression, and the current problems associated with higher education in general.

In the United States there is no uniformity of organization, administration, or support of institutions of higher education. The vast expanse of territory, the freedom to establish colleges, and the rivalries of local communities tended to provide considerable variation in the impulse to establish private colleges, which was in the beginning largely the result of religious motivation, Protestant as well as Catholic. Early private colleges considered religion as well as learning a proper motivation. Many of these colleges departed from their religious affiliations in the decades after the Civil War when the United States was becoming industrialized and urbanized.

Catholic colleges, in the period after the founding of Georgetown in 1789, shared many of the religious characteristics of the Protestant private colleges. However, in Catholic colleges it was often more difficult to distinguish between the work of the Church and the work of the college. Archbishop John Carroll, first Catholic bishop in the United States, set the tone in 1788 when he wrote to Cardinal Antonelli, Prefect of the Congregation of the Propagation of the Faith, as plans were being made for the establishment of Georgetown College:

> The *construction of a school* was begun a few days ago; however, that it may reach a happy conclusion is to be trusted principally, or rather entirely to the help of Divine providence. From this beginning, I think the preservation of Religion in these states depends entirely: for otherwise there will be neither a place for establishing an ecclesiastical seminary nor can pastors be provided in [illeg.] numbers to take care of the Faithful and to labor for the extension of religion.[1]

The basic problem, therefore, was that of training a native clergy; the college was thus not only a means of religious expansion but also the center of Catholic life.

As the number of Catholics grew, the bishops' leadership in establishing seminaries and founding colleges to prepare applicants for them strove to keep pace with the immigration of Catholics to the United States in the 1840s and 1850s. Without the help of the religious orders who established colleges as soon as they had the manpower, the bishops would have had a much more difficult task. Gradually, seminaries separated their activity from colleges. Of the approximately three hundred Catholic colleges at present, only about a dozen are diocesan colleges; the rest are staffed by various religious orders and congregations of men and women. The bishops came to confine their educational activities to the development of the parish elementary school and the high school, but this did not mean that they gave up all control of a Catholic college in their diocese even when it was operated by a religious order.

Although the canon law of the Church governed the relationship between the religious order and the bishop in his diocese, there was enough potential for conflict to cause more than occasional disputes. The bishop was the supreme head of the Church within his own diocese. The religious order, such as the Jesuits, was a hierarchical organization within the Church claiming by papal grant certain exemptions from episcopal control. The organization of the Jesuits was headed by a Father General in Rome assisted by representatives of the geographical areas known as Assistancies. Within the geographical area there were Provinces headed by a provincial who appointed the rectors and superiors of the various institutions within the province. No college could be established within a diocese without the bishop's permission. At a time in the early history of Catholic higher education when there was little, if any, distinction between the work of the college and that of the Church, it is easy to see how the bishop and the rector of a college run by a religious order could experience strong differences of opinion in the administration of the affairs of the college. The history of John Carroll University witnesses at least three such occasions of conflict. In the beginning, the Jesuits felt that they were forced by Bishop Richard Gilmour (1872–1891) to accept a West Side location in the city of Cleveland when they would have preferred one on the East Side. Bishop John P. Farrelly (1909–1921) thwarted efforts to establish a permanent location on the East Side and Bishop Joseph Schrembs (1921–1945) prevented the successful functioning of the Corporate College (1929–1933) experiment and the offering of an elementary education program by the university.

The history of John Carroll University, founded in 1886 as the nineteenth of the twenty-eight Jesuit colleges and universities in the United States, illustrates its relationship to the development of the Jesuit educational enterprise in this country. While there appears to be a lag between the development of John Carroll and that of Catholic higher education in general, there is a similar lag between the development of the University and that of Jesuit educational practices and programs in the United States. Jesuit colleges and universities in this country were, in their origin, the result of the missionary efforts of the various European Jesuit provinces. John Carroll owes its beginnings to the Buffalo Mission of the German province. Expelled from Germany under Bismarck's Kulturkampf, the German Jesuits established headquarters in Buffalo where a large German population gave hope for productive educational work. When they established St. Ignatius College in Cleveland as an offshoot of the Buffalo Mission, they brought with them the European six-year college course modelled on the *Ratio Studiorum* which did not differentiate between high school and college levels, as the American system would. The entire six-year course was considered preparatory to university work, and the term "college" had a different meaning in Europe from that normally understood in the United States; it was rather the equivalent of the European gymnasium.

By the time St. Ignatius College was founded, other Jesuit colleges were beginning to adjust to the American scheme of things. In the United States after World War I, American higher education began to change rapidly; the classical course was soon eroded by increased emphasis on the physical and social sciences, by the elective system, and by the developments in accreditation. Jesuit colleges could not remain unaffected by these changes if they were to survive in this country. Beginning with an interprovince committee in 1919, there was a change in some Jesuit educational policies; the aim was to make every Jesuit college conform to American educational standards in the field of higher education and to separate, even physically, the high school from the college. Development of Jesuit graduate and professional schools began to move at a faster pace. The changes were in a sense supervised and regulated to some degree by the Jesuit Educational Association, formed in 1935. Each province now had its prefect of studies to oversee the educational work of the province including the training and assignment of Jesuit teachers within the province.

When parochial schools became more numerous in the 1920s and 1930s, some diocesan clergy began to train for the task of preparing the nuns for teaching in those schools. In many of the larger cities the Jesuits were asked to assume the training task and did so without many objections. In some other cities, particularly those in Ohio, there was considerable controversy over the relative roles of Jesuits and the diocesan clergy in this enterprise. Diocesan control and coeducation were among the issues raised by the Ohio bishops in the 1930s.

This controversy, which was particularly bitter in the Cleveland diocese (1929–1934), hindered efforts at cooperation among the Catholic colleges of the diocese and left its mark on the rather serious efforts of the late 1960s to work out some form of institutional cooperation or merger. Characteristically, Catholic institutions of higher education have often operated in an atmosphere of fear, jealously, and competition with each other that has been destructive of too many cooperative efforts.

Perhaps one of the more traumatic experiences of Catholic colleges was the impact of the Second Vatican Council in the 1960s on the role and autonomy of the college. Ecclesiastical control was a major issue. Changes in the fields of theology and philosophy, two mainstays of the Jesuit college curriculum, added to the problem. The reassessment of the relationship between the religious order and the college or university it had controlled provided further internal controversy. All of these developments were complicated by the increasing necessity of hiring laymen, in the absence of sufficient religious vocations, to fill the need created by enrollment expansion of the 1950s and 1960s.

When the Buffalo Jesuits accepted Bishop Richard Gilmour's invitation to take over the administration of St. Mary of the Assumption German parish on the corner of Jersey and Carroll streets in August of 1880, they were beginning their work in a part of Cleveland on the west side of the Cuyahoga River formerly know as Brooklyn. This area was incorporated in 1836 as the City of Ohio and was annexed to Cleveland in 1854. The Jesuits were attracted to Cleveland because of the city's rapid commercial and industrial growth in the post–Civil War days; in 1880 Cleveland had just won the population race with Buffalo. A foreign-born population, composed chiefly of Irish and Germans, accounted for approximately

60,000 of Cleveland's total population of 160,146. Ethnic ties on the west side of the river continued with greater strength than on the east side where the city was more extensively developed. Transportation between the two sides of the city was exceedingly difficult because of the steep slopes to the river which separated the two sides and the lack of adequate bridges. The Jesuits would have preferred an East-Side location where the bulk of the population lived and where Euclid Avenue, proclaimed as the most beautiful street in the world, provided a great attraction for a choice site for a college and a parish; not until 1921 did the Jesuits receive permission from a bishop to select a permanent site, and not until 1935 did they actually begin classes on the east side.

To write the history of an institution such as a college or a university is in a certain sense to waltz through a minefield. Success depends to a great extent upon the cooperation of those who know where the mines have been laid and to what extent it is safe to set them off. Various groups—students, faculty, alumni, administrators, and others—have different levels of sensitivity and views of the institution's record. There are even those who would question the advisability of attempting to go through the minefield in the first place; it is a clash between the requirements of a proper history and the demands of those who would prefer to color the past for their own purposes. In the case of an institution which is church-related and run by a religious order these problems are magnified. There is also the problem of the availability and even the existence of some sources; the telephone and off-the-record conversations in the corridors and elsewhere cause further problems. Everyone concerned with the production of this volume has been willing to cooperate to the fullest extent possible in order to produce an acceptable record of the first century of the university's history which represents the sometimes painful transition of a traditional Jesuit college to a modern university.

Acknowledgments

The list of those to whom the author is indebted for assistance in preparing this history is long. To Father Henry F. Birkenhauer, president of John Carroll University when this project was begun, I owe a special debt of gratitude for his willingness to go out of his way to provide material assistance and to give of his time to read and discuss the manuscript. Dr. Arthur J. Noetzel, academic vice-president, was extremely helpful in the support of the project, and was always available for discussion of those parts of the history with which he was familiar.

John Piety, director of John Carroll University Library, and Archivist Charles Wood were most helpful not only in locating material but also in commenting on the manuscript. Brother William Balconi, S.J. of the John Carroll University Library Staff, and Virginia Krumholz and Chris Kroesel of the Diocesan Archives provided invaluable service. The staff of the Archives of Case Western Reserve University was especially helpful in finding material on the name changes in 1923.

Of all those who read the manuscript and offered advice, a special debt of gratitude must go to the Reverend Dr. Louis G. Pecek, dean of the Graduate School at John Carroll, who not only made useful criticisms of the final draft, but also together with Father Emmanuel Carreira, S.J. gave time and photographic talent to preparing numerous slides and pictures. Dr. Pecek was also willing to read the chapters as they were written and make valuable suggestions that undoubtedly improved the readability of the manuscript. The responsibility, however, for the final product is entirely the author's.

Father John F. Bannon, S.J. of St. Louis University was most gracious in giving his time to read the manuscript and to discuss matters pertaining to the history of the Jesuits in the United States. Special mention should be made of the late Father James A. Mackin, former director of the Grasselli Library of John Carroll University. He not only read and commented on an early portion of the manuscript, but also had done some research on the Buffalo Mission debt question which was of great assistance in writing the story of that problem. He was also instrumental in securing copies of some important letters from the archives of the Society of Jesus in Rome. Jesuit Fathers Aloysius Rieckus, S.J., late Archivist of the Missouri Province, and Charles Graf, S.J., Archivist of the Chicago Province, were extremely helpful in searching out material. Brother Michael Grace, S.J., Archivist of Loyola University in Chicago, was most generous with his assistance as was Father Robert Callan, S.J., Archivist at Marquette University.

Father J. Clayton Murray, S.J., Archivist at Canisius College, was most generous not only in providing material from the Buffalo Mission but also in locating pictures of some of the early Jesuits who served at John Carroll. He also read the manuscript and offered valuable suggestions. Among others who read the manuscript and offered comment were former president Joseph O. Schell, S.J., former rectors Joseph Zomber, S.J. and William Nichols, S.J., present rector, Frederick J. Benda, S.J., as well as faculty members Doctors William O'Hearn, Donald Poduska, David La Guardia, James Walsh, Joseph Miller, and Roger Welchans.

The capable and generous assistance of Mrs. Marie Geoghegan in typing the manuscript through its many revisions was invaluable. So also were her perceptive comments on the material in the manuscript. Mrs. Margie Wasdovich, faculty secretary, who typed some of the chapters, was also very helpful.

To all of those who helped, the author offers his sincere thanks, but especially to his wife, Mary, who put up with him during the research and writing of the history and was always ready with advice and comment when they were needed.

JOHN CARROLL UNIVERSITY
CHRONOLOGY

1847   Diocese of Cleveland founded. Amedeus Rappe, first bishop.

1862   First contact of Bishop Rappe with Father Arnold Damen, S.J., of the Missouri Province; effort to establish a college in the diocese.

1869   Buffalo Mission of the German Province of the Society of Jesus established. Bishop Rappe brings the Buffalo Jesuits to St. Mary Parish in Toledo.

1876   Bishop Rappe's successor, Bishop Richard Gilmour, invites the Buffalo Jesuits to establish a college in Cleveland.

1880   August 1, Bishop Gilmour places Buffalo Jesuits in charge of St. Mary of the Assumption German Parish on West 30th Street (Jersey Street). Father Michael Zoeller, S.J., appointed first Jesuit pastor.

1880–   Extended negotiations between Bishop Gilmour and the Buffalo Jesuits
1886   over establishing a college in Cleveland.

1886   April 19, formal agreement between Bishop Gilmour and Father Henry Behrens, S.J., Superior of the Buffalo Mission, to establish a college in Cleveland.

        May 1, Father John B. Neustich, S.J., appointed Vice-Rector and president of St. Ignatius College; also Pastor of St. Mary Parish.

        July 19, Father Neustich with the aid of some Jesuit Brothers begins construction of the two-story frame building on property opposite St. Mary Parish. The building served as the original classroom building of St. Ignatius College and later as a gymnasium.

1889   Northwest wing of the permanent five-story brick building on the corner of West 30th and Carroll Avenue completed.

1890   St. Ignatius College incorporated by the State of Ohio to grant degrees.

1891   Southwestern wing of the permanent building completed.

1892   Ignatius F. Horstmann succeeds Richard Gilmour as Bishop of Cleveland.

1903   Alumni Association formed.

1907   Father George J. Pickel, S.J., President 1906-1910, establishes Loyola High School on East 106th and Cedar Avenue.

        Buffalo Mission dissolved. St. Ignatius College becomes part of the Missouri Province.

1909   Bishop John P. Farrelly succeeds Bishop Horstmann. Bishop Farrelly opposed to the existence of Loyola High School and the Jesuits on the east side.

1914   New gymnasium built on Carroll Avenue; original temporary classroom building torn down.

1921   Joseph Schrembs succeeds John P. Farrelly as bishop of Cleveland; gives permission for the Jesuits to build a college and a parish on the east side.

1922   Loyola High School closed. First accreditation by the North Central Association of Schools and Colleges.

1923   March 19, purchase of present property in University Heights, then Idlewood Village.

        May 15, St. Ignatius College changes name to Cleveland University.

        September 10, Cleveland University forced to drop the name; the new name chosen: The John Carroll University

1925   John Carroll University becomes part of the newly created Ohio Vice-Province (Chicago Province, 1928). Gesu Parish established.

1928   Father Benedict J. Rodman, S.J., becomes President of John Carroll University, serves until 1937; Father Albert C. Fox, S.J., former President of Marquette University, becomes dean, serves until 1934.

1929   Campaign for buildings on the University Heights property.

        Corporate Colleges of John Carroll University established, continued until 1933.

1931   Construction begun on the new buildings; suspended in 1932, resumed in 1935.

1932   Charter revised to expand purpose.

1934   Department of Business Administration established.

1935   Classes open in October in the new buildings.

1943   Navy V-12 Program established, runs until 1945.

1945   School of Business, Economics, and Government opens.

1947   Temporary gymnasium erected on the original chapel foundation.

1949   Evening College established. Lay Advisory Board formed.

1950   Military Science Building.

1952   Pacelli Hall.

1955   Dolan Hall.

1956   Graduate Division becomes the Graduate School.

1957   New gymnasium.

1959   Student Activities Building.

1961   Grasselli Library.

1964   Murphy Hall.

1967   Bohannon Science Center.

1968   College of Arts and Sciences becomes officially coeducational.

1969   Laymen added to Board of Trustees; separate incorporation of the Jesuit Community.

1971   Fritzsche Religious Center (building constructed a year earlier).

1975   William H. Johnson Natatorium.

1979   North Hall, named Sutowski Hall in 1982.

1981   South Hall, named Millor Hall in 1982.

ARCHBISHOP JOHN CARROLL
CHRONOLOGY

1735	Born January 8 in Upper Marlboro, Maryland, of Daniel and Eleanor (Darnall) Carroll.
1746–1748	Attended Bohemia Manor Academy, Maryland.
1748	Went to St. Omer College in French Flanders.
1753	Jesuit Novitiate, Watten, Flanders.
1769	Ordination to the priesthood.
1770	Instructor in the Jesuit College at Bruges.
1773	Suppression of the Society of Jesus. College at Bruges closed; becomes chaplain of Lord Arundel of Wardour Castle, England.
1774	Returns to Rock Creek, Maryland.
1776	Member of the Continental Congress' Commission to Canada.
1783	Appointed to the Board of Directors of Washington College, Maryland.
1784	*Address to the Roman Catholics of the United States.* Appointed to the Board of Directors of St. John College, Annapolis. Placed in charge of the Missions in the United States.
1788	First Catholic diocese in the United States created; John Carroll named Bishop.
1789	Georgetown College founded.
1790	John Carroll consecrated Bishop by Bishop Charles Walmesley in Lulworth Castle, England.
1812	Declined position as Provost of the University of Maryland.
1814	Papal Bull restoring the Society of Jesus received in the United States.
1815	Death December 3.

Father John Carroll at about age forty. Painting attributed to Charles Willson Peale, c. 1776

Archbishop John Carroll at age seventy. Gilbert Stuart, 1803–5. Courtesy of Georgetown University Museum

Original location of St. Ignatius College marked on a map sent to the Provincial in 1909 by Father Pickel

St. Ignatius College

On 19 August 1886 there appeared on page eight of the *Catholic Universe,*
the Cleveland diocesan newspaper, tucked in among an assortment of notices about "Half Fare West via the Bee Line," "Notes from Cleveland,"
"Good Investments" mortgages, farm lands, and ads for a portrait of Cardinal Gibbons and for Lydia Pinkham's Compound, the following notice
in very small type:

St. Ignatius College
Cleveland, Ohio

The Educational Institution conducted by the Fathers of the Society of Jesus will be opened for the reception of students on the 6th of September, 1886.

The course of studies embraces the first year Christian Doctrine, the Latin,
English and German languages, Elocution, Arithmetic, Geography, and Penmanship. The college is intended for day scholars only.

For further information apply to

Rev. L. B. Neustich, S.J.
47 Jersey Street, West Side
632-44

This first announcement of the opening of St. Ignatius College, known
today as John Carroll University, appeared on successive Fridays from the
nineteenth of August through the twenty-first of October. Father Neustich's first initial was finally corrected to read "J" for John by the time of the
third appearance of the notice. This was the only announcement to the
diocese of yet another attempt to establish a Catholic college in the Diocese
of Cleveland. Considering the educational needs of the diocese one might
have assumed that it would have been a more newsworthy event. That it was
not was undoubtedly due in part to the failure of the many previous attempts
of the local bishops to establish and operate a college in the diocese. The six
years of negotiations which preceded the opening of St. Ignatius College, as
well as the often sharp and hostile tone surrounding them, probably convinced some that this latest effort would also fail and therefore was not
worth great interest. The German Jesuits' lack of interest in other than

Catholic students would explain why there were no notices in the Cleveland daily papers.

EARLY DIOCESAN EFFORTS TO ESTABLISH A COLLEGE

Many Catholic colleges had their origin in the efforts of the local bishop to establish a college where students could prepare for seminary training. In the Diocese of Cleveland, several unsuccessful efforts had been made during the tenure of the first bishop, Amedeus Rappe (1847–1870), and under his successor, Richard Gilmour (1872–1891). In two instances religious orders other than the Jesuits were involved. St. Louis College in Louisville, Ohio, some fifty miles southeast of Cleveland, had originally been established by the local pastor, Father Louis Hoffer, in 1866. In 1867, Bishop Rappe placed the college under the direction of the Basilian Fathers of Toronto, hoping that their success with St. Michael's College in Toronto could be duplicated in the Cleveland diocese.

The efforts of the Basilian Fathers at Louisville were no more successful than those to found and maintain a college in the Cleveland diocese. Survival on the basis of day scholars in such a location was impossible; boarding facilities were simply inadequate. After seven years of poor support the college was closed in 1873. Undismayed, Bishop Richard Gilmour was anxious to arrange some plan whereby a college opportunity could still be provided for young men in Cleveland. From the beginning, the Basilian Fathers were receptive to such an offer. Father Charles Vincent, Superior of St. Michael's College in Toronto, had in 1867 expressed the thought that Cleveland would be a "splendid opening for a college as it is a town of 80,000 and contains no college either Catholic or Protestant. But it is impossible to take one there on account of the high value of property and our scarcity of subjects."[1] Father Francis Hours, the man in charge of St. Louis College during the period of Basilian control, also had expressed similar thoughts. He and Bishop Rappe had at one time discussed the possibility of the Basilian Fathers taking over the Seminary as well as the preparatory college. If the offer were made, Father Hours thought, "we ought to make an effort to take it as I think it would be very successful."[2]

When the closing of St. Louis College was imminent, Bishop Gilmour again discussed with the Basilian Fathers the possibility of a move to Cleveland. In the spring of 1873, Father Charles Vincent came to Cleveland to discuss matters with the bishop. Although pleased with his reception, Father Vincent considered Bishop Gilmour to be a very decisive, impatient, and blunt man. There was talk of locating the college near the Seminary in Cleveland with the bishop defraying the expenses. There was talk also of a minor Seminary, but the real problem was the supplying of teaching personnel. Father Vincent would need help from his superiors, but Bishop Gilmour was not willing to wait long. In the end nothing came of the discussions.[3]

Even if the Basilian Fathers had been able to supply the necessary manpower immediately, serious financial problems would have prevented realization of the bishop's goal. In 1872, a year before St. Louis College closed, there was some $12,000 due on the college debt. Diocesan collections and scattered donations were the only sources of support. Other diocesan financial burdens were such that when Bishop Gilmour appealed to a diocesan synod for funds to pay the college debt, he was greeted with silence.[4]

Bishop Gilmour then turned to the Franciscans already located on the East Side of Cleveland at St. Joseph parish on Woodland Avenue. They agreed to open a college there which would be called St. Joseph College. Staffed by two Franciscan priests and one diocesan priest, the college opened in September 1875 with an enrollment of twenty-four in the newly erected building on the Woodland Avenue property. Increased enrollment forced the enlargement of the staff in 1876 to six, half of whom were Franciscans. In 1878 the college was chartered to offer degrees, by which time the students, mostly from neighboring parishes, had increased in number to eighty. Pressure on the Franciscans to staff their other college in Illinois forced the closing of St. Joseph's College to secular students in June 1879. The college was reopened in 1893 but as a college for Franciscans only.

When it became evident that the Franciscans would have to abandon their college in Cleveland, Bishop Gilmour turned to the Jesuits for assistance. The Jesuits were not unknown in the diocese since Jesuit missionary preachers from the Missouri Province of the Society had visited the diocese during Bishop Rappe's episcopacy. In 1862 a very popular preacher among English speaking people, Father Arnold Damen, preached in the cathedral. Bishop Rappe used the occasion in inquire about the possibility of establishing a Jesuit House in the diocese, preferably in Toledo, but there was not sufficient Jesuit manpower to comply with this and other requests the Jesuits were receiving from several bishops.[5] Bishop Rappe had another opportunity in 1868 when Father James Perron, Superior of the New York-Canada Jesuit Mission, suggested to Father General Peter Beckx that a German Mission be provided in the United States for German-speaking people. Father General sent a Visitor to Buffalo where some German Jesuits from the New York-Canada Province were already serving in a parish there.[6] Father Peter Spicher, the Visitor, traveled as far as Cleveland, where he met with Bishop Rappe. As a result, they reached an agreement to establish a Jesuit House in Toledo, and Jesuits from the newly created Buffalo Mission took over St. Mary parish there in 1869.[7] But there were no immediate plans for a college in Cleveland.

BISHOP GILMOUR: EARLY CONTACT WITH THE JESUITS

When Bishop Gilmour became head of the Cleveland diocese in 1872, there was some unfinished business in Toledo which gave the Bishop his first opportunity to deal with the Jesuits, who were pressing for legal title to the parish, much to Bishop Gilmour's irritation. Added displeasure arose closer at home, with the recall by his superior of a Jesuit who had been teaching in the seminary.[8] Meanwhile, the unsuccessful attempt of the Jesuits in Toledo to establish a high school and their request of the bishop to establish a college there added to the bishop's difficulties in dealing with the Jesuits.[9]

By 1876 the picture had changed a little. The Jesuits in Toledo now had legal title to their parish and the impending closing of the Franciscan college in Cleveland made Bishop Gilmour more inclined to see what the Jesuits could offer. He therefore invited the Buffalo Jesuits to accept a parish and open a college in Cleveland.[10]

Almost immediately the bishop asked that the Jesuits hold off on any plan for the Cleveland project. Somehow he had become aware that the Buffalo Jesuits were entertaining the idea of moving Canisius, their Buffalo college, to Cleveland; this he did not want because he felt that the college was too German in character. The idea of moving Canisius had apparently risen from the conclusion of Father Henry Behrens, Superior of the Buffalo Mission (1872–1876 and 1886–1892), that Canisius College would not succeed in Buffalo. Beset by the difficulty of trying to match the increasing number of English-speaking students with teachers who had not learned English, Father Behrens had complained frequently to Rome.[11] How a move to Cleveland would have solved this problem is not clear.

Father John B. Lessmann, who succeeded Father Behrens in 1876 as Superior of the Mission, made light of Father Behrens's fears for the success of Canisius and admitted that while his predecessor had entertained thoughts of moving to Cleveland, that surely was not the answer.[12] Father Lessmann soon came to the conclusion that the difficulty in dealing with Bishop Gilmour was a more cogent reason for not establishing a college in Cleveland.[13] Moreover, Father Lessmann was not entirely convinced that the reason for Bishop Gilmour's requested delay for the Cleveland college was entirely due to Canisuis College's German character. He suspected that the Franciscans did not want any competition in the city, especially on the East Side of town, where the Buffalo Jesuits preferred to locate.[14]

In spite of their mutual suspicion of each other, Father Lessmann and Bishop Gilmour met in Cleveland in January 1878. Bishop Gilmour agreed to ask the advice of the diocesan clergy on the establishment of a college in Cleveland and report back to Father Lessmann.[15] From the viewpoint of

Bishop Gilmour, the closing of the Franciscan college created some urgency to establish another college.

On 20 January 1878 Bishop Gilmour sent a "Circular Letter" to the clergy of the diocese. The successive failure of efforts to establish a college had convinced the bishop that more advice and support were needed. In the letter he reviewed the problem in an optimistic vein, speaking of the desire he had had for some time "to establish a college in Cleveland, in which boys and young men from the Diocese or elsewhere, could receive a good commercial or classical education."[16] He said he had "good reason to believe" that the college could be established "provided assurance of success can be given."[17] The bishop said he had been sounding out various religious orders and as a result, "I have offers made by some religious who, at their own risk, and without any burden to the Diocese by way of taxation or collection, agree to build a college and supply it with a first class corps of teachers and professors. Besides receiving day scholars they will also take boarders." What the bishop now needed was "the unbiased opinion" of the clergy of the diocese in answer to the following questions:

1. Do you think the establishment of such a college opportune?
2. Would such a college be a success?
3. Are there any families in your congregations likely to send their sons to it?[18]

An interesting aspect of the bishop's letter is that, although preparation for the Seminary was certainly the major objective, the need of an educational institution was put on a much broader basis to include a commercial course of study for young men not intending to study for the priesthood. It is also quite clear that such an institution as was proposed was not to put any financial strain on the dioceses; nor was it to involve diocesan clergy as teachers as had been the case in some previous attempts.

AN AMERICAN COLLEGE

Father Lessmann, anxious to hear the results of Bishop Gilmour's Circular Letter, kept in close touch with the bishop. Since he had offers from other bishops to consider, Father Lessmann asked for specific information from Bishop Gilmour on the "prospect we might take in view."[19] Anticipating Father Lessmann's interest in the results, the bishop wrote as soon as he could that there was "a good deal of variety of opinion about the proposed college. The principal objection of course, is the German character of the persons of the Buffalo Mission. All are satisfied if the college were to be conducted by the Americans."[20]

If Bishop Gilmour was worried about the German character of the proposed college, it was partly because the bishop was interested in speeding up the Americanization of a large non-English speaking immigrant Catholic population. In one of his many letters on the subject of Americanization of the immigrant, Bishop Gilmour expressed his interest in the process to Father William Tappert, a leader of the German Catholic cause, by saying, "let us work on the lines of our common Catholicism. As citizens let us be distinctly American, as Catholics distinctly Catholic."[21] Undoubtedly the bishop was also mindful that his predecessor had fallen victim of a nationality conflict, which was instrumental in forcing his resignation. Bishop Gilmour, having inherited a troubled diocese, wanted to put internal strife behind and move on. As a Scot and a convert from Presbyterianism, he may also have felt himself above this national strife and would do what he could to eliminate it.

The bishop also had less than fond memories of one of the German Jesuits, a missionary from the Missouri Province to German-speaking people, Father Francis X. Weninger, who had troubles with Bishop Rappe over nationality and language issues and was barred from the Cleveland Diocese as a *persona non grata.* Father Weninger had sought readmission to the diocese within a year of Bishop Gilmour's installation and wanted permission to continue his missionary efforts among the Germans. The bishop refused permission but when Father Weninger wrote again the bishop's reply was blunt and clear. Mindful that Father Weninger had complained to Rome about Bishop Rappe's closing German schools, and that Father Weninger's slogan, "the language is the faith," was a principal cause of trouble, Bishop Gilmour wished to put an end to any further entreaties.

> You asked to give missions in my diocese and because you had trouble with my predecessor, I refused. One would have thought this sufficient, but no, after six years you again ask, and for the same reasons and others you are refused, I am taken to task, . . . you say you have no mission to control the *private* life of a bishop? If not, might it not be wise to let Bishops control their own affairs and you will attend to yours? It is usually a thankless task to meddle in other people's business. . . . I will allow no man to come into this diocese to kick . . . This would be the case were I to admit you to the diocese of Cleveland. . . . I must be permitted to look through my own glasses.
>
> With this closes any future correspondence on my part of this subject. Rejoicing that at your age you are still able to work.[22]

Father Weninger was representative of the more active element among the German clergy interested in protecting the culture, language, and sense of community among the German Catholic immigrants in a hostile environment. The group was particularly strong in the Midwest in what was called the German triangle of the cities of Milwaukee, St. Louis, and Cincinnati. The goal was to establish independent German parishes and to obtain better representation of German bishops in the American hierarchy. Bishop Gilmour was one of a number of American bishops who strongly opposed such aims. He sought to follow the tradition of Archbishop John Carroll of Baltimore, first Catholic bishop of the United States, who wanted an American Catholic Church. Bishop Gilmour preferred attempting a fusion of the diverse groups and adapting them to American political and social customs without any compromise of doctrine. Of particular concern to Bishop Gilmour was the influence in Rome of German exiles from Bismarck's Kulturkampf who were likely to listen to the pleas from their brethren in the United States for support. Among these exiles in the Roman Curia were Paulus Cardinal Melchers, former Archbishop of Cologne and the Jesuit Cardinal, Johann Baptist Franzelin. There was also the fear that these German exiles would conclude from the pleas of their compatriots in the United States that the American bishops were neglecting the immigrants. How this issue could apply to the Cleveland diocese can be seen in the extended controversy over the successor to Bishop Gilmour on the latter's death in 1891. The appointment of Ignatius Horstmann as Bishop of Cleveland demonstrated the weight of the German influence. Bishop Horstmann was more of a German than an Americanizer, but the Cleveland Jesuits were to be happy with the choice.

Father Lessman, although aware of the bishop's strong feelings on nationality matters, expressed surprise in his reply to the charge of proposing a German college:

> I suspected that some difficulties against proposed College might have been moved in the consultation with your clergy about this matter; but I was hardly prepared to meet the objection regarding the German character of the said College. As your Lordship will remember, there was no question about a German College, but about a College like all other American Colleges, which should be conducted by the Fathers of the German province.[23]

Father Lessmann was willing to admit that Canisius College had been started as a college whose instruction was in German in order to serve German immigrants. He knew now that this was a "mistake of the Fathers, who at that time were not well acquainted with American affairs. We will not make again such a mistake."[24] The mistake had been corrected and "today our College is no longer a German College and I can say with confidence, that it is not in any way a failure."[25]

There were also other matters in the bishop's letter that worried Father Lessmann. The matter of the English language proficiency of the Fathers could be handled satisfactorily but "if your Lordship really desires, that the contemplated college should be American *quite from the beginning* 'in professors, tone, spirit,' I am unable to satisfy this request, of course as I told you openly, when I had the honor of a conversation with your Lordship the first time."[26] There was hope for the future because it was anticipated that there would be more American recruits for the Mission educated in the English language from early childhood. Some of these men were already studying in Europe. Bishop Gilmour apparently did not share Father Lessmann's hope for the future and advised him to take the Columbus, Ohio, bishop's invitation and locate a college there.[27]

Not until the end of the following year did the bishop resolve the problem of an American college. In a letter to Father Lessmann dated 12 November 1879, Bishop Gilmour informed him that "at a meeting of my council, held yesterday, your proposal to establish a college and boarding school in the city met with the unanimous approval of the members. I am, therefore, ready to enter into further and definite arrangements with you relative to the proposed college as you find it convenient."[28]

St. Mary Parish

The Jesuit proposal for the college in Cleveland included the administration of a parish, either an existing one or a new one. Consideration of this part of the proposal came just as the bishop was demanding that he be given the annual financial report of the Toledo parish. Father Lessmann contended that according to the contract made with Bishop Rappe the parish in Toledo was "given over" to the Society including the full administration of temporal affairs, which then belonged to the Superior of the Society. It was, according to Father Lessmann, common practice in the American provinces that bishops never asked for such a report "with the exception of one church where not our Society but the bishop himself is the proprietor, as I know positively."[29] Father Lessmann conceded that if the bishop "should commit to us the administration of St. Mary's parish in Cleveland for a limited time, it would be a different case and the annual report would be given just as from all other churches."[30] Bishop Gilmour did not argue the legal requirement in the Toledo case but said that if the people of the parish were given the report, which they were, he ought also to be given a copy. He didn't want to be the only person who did not know what was going on.[31] Father Lessmann complied with the bishop's wish.

Further delay in assigning a parish in Cleveland to the Jesuits occurred when Bishop Gilmour finally determined to give them St. Mary of the Assumption, a German parish on the West Side at the corner of Jersey and Carroll streets. St. Mary of the Assumption parish had been organized in 1863 by Bishop Rappe to serve the German population living west of the Cuyahoga River. Father Stephen Falk acted as both architect and pastor of the parish which had grown enough in 1869 to be divided, establishing a new parish, St. Stephen's. What the bishop had in mind was to give the administration of St. Mary's parish to the Jesuits if he could convince the pastor, Father Falk, to resign. Father Lessmann, unaware of the bishop's intention, was urging the bishop to act soon so that proper plans could be made.[32] Responding to the urging of Father Lessmann, the bishop wrote that Father Falk's illness had delayed the bishop from raising the question of the pastor's resignation, but Father Falk was "now up and I hope will be able to bear what I know will be a great pain to him, as he has been so long at St. Mary's and has everything in such nice order. I will let you know as soon as I can get the affairs arranged."[33] Not until June 1880 did Bishop Gilmour succeed; he informed Father Lessmann that he could "take possession of St. Mary's Cleveland on August 1st."[34] The bishop's immediate concern was that the

> Jesuits send such persons as with prudence and care will not touch the sensitiveness of all concerned. And I hope it is fully understood that for the present at least your Fathers take charge of the Congregation as Pastors thereof. The management and direction thereof being guided by and governed by the laws of the diocese. If the property is hereafter to be changed that would be a matter for future arrangement.[35]

On 10 July the bishop made a public announcement that the Jesuits would take charge of the congregation on 1 August.[36]

On that date, Father Michael Zoeller, a Jesuit from the Buffalo Mission, assumed the duties of pastor of St. Mary's congregation and remained in that post for the next six years. Father Zoeller was admirably suited to carry out Bishop Gilmour's wish that a man of great sensitivity fill the post. Father Zoeller was among those Jesuits who had been exiled from Germany in 1872 and had experience in parish work at Aix la Chapelle and Mainz in Germany. In the United States he had worked in parishes in St. Louis, Toledo, and Buffalo since 1875.

Meanwhile, Father Lessmann received orders from Rome in January 1880 to accept the Cleveland offer of a college as well as the one in Prairie du Chien, Wisconsin. A number of questions still remained; the matter of how the college was to be funded and where in the city it was to be located were still undecided.[37] Discussion of these matters by the Buffalo Mission consultors caused further delay.

PROLONGED NEGOTIATIONS

Not until May 1881 did Father Lessmann visit Bishop Gilmour to discuss the establishment of the college but he found the bishop away. The bishop

Above left, Richard Gilmour, Bishop of Cleveland, 1872–91; *right,* John Lessmann, S.J., Superior, Buffalo Mission, 1876–86; *Left,* Michael Zoeller, S.J., Chaplain, 1910–15, Pastor, St. Mary Parish, 1880–86

wrote and expressed regret at missing his visitor but hoped the college could be started soon and assured Father Lessmann that although there would be trials it would succeed.[38] By August, Bishop Gilmour was showing impatience and disappointment over continued delay. He was unhappy that there was "no apparent prospect as to when or the fact that you can ever have English Fathers. . . . The matter becomes very grave and somewhat compromises me the bishop and the diocese by the giving of St. Mary's to your Fathers and no college yet opened as expected."[39]

By November the problem of location became a major issue. Father Lessmann expressed a preference for an East Side location as offering a better chance for the success of the proposed college. This further irritated the bishop, who argued,

> I feel quite sure had you opened a school on the West Side it would have succeeded. So far no trial has been made so no result could be assumed. I wished you on the West Side so as not to have two male Religious orders on the East Side running counter to each other as they would necessarily do if each did pastoral duty. So I offered you a church and opening for a school thus leaving me free in time to open a school on the East Side, if in the future it would be found needed. My own opinion was, and is, all considered the West Side would succeed as a school and church combination and hence much desired it.[40]

Locating the college was not a simple issue. The kind of college-church proposed by Father Lessmann would, in Bishop Gilmour's judgment, "be an element of such disturbance as to debar its consideration *a principio.*"[41] Another of the bishop's reasons was that there was no place on the East Side suitable for both a church and college "where the church would not be in everybody's way" and thus "utterly unmanageable" because "two Religious orders on the East Side with churches . . . would never work"; such an arrangement as proposed might succeed in Europe, the bishop thought, but could never be adopted here.[42] As far as Bishop Gilmour was concerned the choice was either the parish and college arrangement which he proposed for the West Side, or a college alone on the East Side. "If neither can be accepted we must simply return to where we began and let me try elsewhere, as I must press this School-College [*sic*] question to a conclusion."[43] The bishop was not willing to place a collegiate church in Cleveland under the full control of the Jesuits on either side of the city.

In a letter of 10 February 1882 Bishop Gilmour charged the Jesuits with breaking faith with him in failing to establish a college. Father Lessmann in replying denied the charge and wished to "remove or prevent misunderstanding" by reviewing the course of events from the beginning. With regret to the issue of a parish, Father Lessmann said that the bishop was right in saying that the Jesuits neither asked for nor were desirous of taking a diocesan congregation. It was for this reason that Father Lessmann later asked "permission to build with the college a public chapel or church free from parish duties as well as parish rights."[44] The reason this request was not made in the beginning was that the bishop offered St. Mary's parish and there was hope that the Jesuits would find it convenient to build the college in connection with it. This offer was accepted with the consent of Father Peter Beckx, General of the Society, and only for that reason. At the time, Father Lessmann claimed that he "didn't fail to declare, that we would not bind ourselves already by this act of taking the administration of St. Mary's Church to build a College, but that our purpose was to have better opportunity to learn by experience in the city itself, *whether* or when, at what place, and under what conditions we might be able to do so."[45] Father Lissmann did not consider that establishing a college was a condition for having a parish.

Finding a convenient place for a college other than near St. Mary's parish was difficult. The Provincial of the German Province, Father Caspar Hoevel, approved, after "mature deliberation" the abandonment of the search for another site without giving up "at the same time the hope of starting the college on another spot."[46] It was then that Father Lessmann had asked to be allowed to have "*aequis et certis conditionibus ecclesiam propriam* with the College according to the custom and right of our Society."[47] The bishop, as was his right, rejected the petition and the Jesuits did not wish to dispute it. With this background Father Lessmann was at a total loss to understand why Bishop Gilmour was now saying that Jesuits wished him to hand over St. Mary's in fee simple. Father Lessmann could not understand how the Jesuits could be accused of breaking faith with the bishop in failing to start a college in Cleveland and hoped that the bishop would explain the matter in such a way that would "prevent a disagreement if we are compelled to do the same."[48] The Jesuits were willing, nevertheless, to continue to staff St. Mary's parish as a temporary measure under the condition that either the Jesuits or the bishop should give six months notice of termination of the arrangement.

Bishop Gilmour saw the problem in a totally different light. He referred to an earlier request of the Jesuits to build a college in Toledo with a public chapel attached, which he had refused. Bishop Gilmour believed the business of a public chapel was "never discussed" nor was the possibility of locating on the East Side really discussed.[49] The bishop claimed that they "did discuss quite seriously the opening of a college next to St. Mary's. Now all at once and as a finality your Superior says "that the college must have a church with all the rights of a parish."[50] As the bishop saw it the Jesuits had now injected "conditions never discussed, and distinctly refused."[51] The bishop complained that he had received unfair treatment at the hands of the Jesuits and said he "must so say in explaining your failure to the diocese."[52] It is not improbable that language problems contributed to the difference of opinion; neither man appeared to understand clearly what the other was saying.

There was a further exchange of correspondence between Bishop Gilmour and Father Lessmann a year later in March and April 1883. It was mostly a repetition of the earlier letters; the bishop was still convinced he had been let down.[53] The only point of some significance that the bishop made was the repetition of his contention that he left the Jesuit "free" to locate the college on the West or East Side, but suggested that the West Side was preferable for the future of the city. This certainly was not the view of Buffalo Mission Consultors, who considered the East Side more important in the development of the city.[54]

Meanwhile, the Jesuits in charge of St. Mary's parish were doing their best to serve that German congregation. Under the guidance of Father Zoeller the Jesuits attempted to steer an even course over a rather rough road. Many in the parish were not happy at losing Father Falk, with whom they had been associated for so many years. The parish trustees proved difficult through their exercise of considerable administrative control; Father Zoeller took heart in noting that as some of the older laymen were dying off, they were being replaced by better-minded persons.[55] On the other hand, a report to Rome said, "murmurings and complaints are heard and our whole manner of acting is unfavorably criticised."[56] Consolation was found in the fact that "we are on good terms with the secular clergy; in fact not a few among them showed themselves notably well disposed toward us."[57]

Although Bishop Gilmour was chiefly concerned with getting the college started he continued to keep the Jesuits under close scrutiny in the running of the parish. Father Zoeller apparently came to the conclusion that, because the matter of the college had been deferred, the Jesuits should have a contract with the bishop covering the parish and its boundaries. He was informed by Monsignor George Houck, chancellor of the Cleveland diocese, that the laws of the diocese were the sole guide to parish administration; "you need no such contract as you ask." The chancellor also reminded Father Zoeller that the condition on which the parish had been given, establishment of a college, had not been fulfilled.[58] Apparently Bishop Gilmour did not have a copy of the Toledo contract to which Father Zoeller had referred as a model, for Bishop Gilmour later wrote to Father William Kocherols, pastoral at St. Mary's, Toledo, asking for a copy of the contract for his files.[59]

Bishop Gilmour did not yet plan to remove the Jesuits from St. Mary's and he granted that the parish house at St. Mary's was not large enough to house the six Jesuits serving the parish in 1882. He sent his architect to draw up plans for a new house, the design of which was on such a grand scale that Father Zoeller felt that the architect "must have had in mind a palace for Nero . . . designed to exhaust our pocketbooks."[60] Consequently, Father Zoeller proposed a more modest plan to accommodate the four priests and two Brothers; the bishop approved.

Seeking Help Elsewhere

By mid-1883 Bishop Gilmour had given up hope of getting the Buffalo Mission Jesuits to open a college in Cleveland. St. Mary's congregation continued under Jesuit care in an uncertain and unspecified arrangement. Father Zoeller's attempt to get the bishop to give a contract for St. Mary's parish had probably been, at least in part, an attempt to provoke some kind of a solution to the stalemate. In any event, Father Zoeller remained the link between the bishop and the Buffalo Mission.

Determined to get a college established, the bishop again contacted some of those whose support he had failed to enlist earlier. Chief among these was Father Edward Sorin of the Holy Cross Fathers at Notre Dame, Indiana. In August 1883 there was correspondence between Bishop Gilmour and Father Sorin about the possibility of the Holy Cross Fathers opening a college in Cleveland. Again the bishop met with delay. Father Sorin was short of manpower but he promised Bishop Gilmour that the next college the Holy Cross Fathers opened would be in Cleveland, if the bishop had no success elsewhere.[61] Bishop Gilmour wrote Father Sorin that he would

vastly prefer that you should open a college here than any parties with whom I am acquainted. The Jesuits of this diocese are German and not ready for Cleveland. They seem to recognize this and have abandoned the idea. I do not care to get these sharply marked Germans when I would prefer an order like yours, American.[62]

The bishop wanted Father Sorin to be specific about the timing of the opening of a college because "it would do much to enable me to guide my actions in this matter. Success is sure."[63]

If the bishop's hopes had been raised by his initial contact with Father Sorin, they were dashed by the next reply. Father Sorin would be happy to come to Cleveland to discuss the kind of college that was contemplated, the time of opening, number of professors, and how long the bishop could wait. "You do not know how much I wish to oblige," but "there is no freedom for me in Indiana," said Father Sorin, spelling out a long list of the tasks that lay before him.[64] And so matters rested for a while.

Meanwhile, it became necessary for the bishop to ask Father Lessman for additional priests to care for some missions in Toledo because it would be many months before he himself could provide for those people and "it would be a great loss to let them be so long without a priest."[65] The Jesuits made a serious effort to accommodate the bishop in spite of a shortage of manpower.

In planning his attendance at the Third Plenary Council of Baltimore in November 1884 Bishop Gilmour considered it useful to seek the help of Father Lessmann, thus keeping up his contact with the Buffalo Jesuits. The plight of the Blacks in the post-Reconstruction period was a matter of common concern and Father Lessmann had already been involved in pertinent discussions on the subject. The Buffalo Mission Superior wrote the bishop:

> that it shall be my earnest endeavor to cooperate in the good works recommended by your Lordship Concerning [*sic*] the Negro, I have already tried to do something last winter, but the matter was postponed on account of difficulties which could not be removed at once. Afterwards it seemed to me advisable to do nothing until the next Plenary Council, hoping that the Negro question would be discussed there and practical instruction given by the Assembly of Bishops. But a little beginning perhaps may be made already before.[66]

The bishop, however, did not forget Father Sorin. While on a visit to Toledo, almost a year after the Plenary Council, Bishop Gilmour wrote to Father Sorin and said he would be "most glad to run down from Toledo to see you and all your good people. But I do not really see my [way] to it. Yet if I can do it at all, I will run down Saturday and return Monday."[67] After explaining how hard he was working, the bishop as a kind of afterthought wondered, "have you abandoned the idea of a college here? The offer is still open and I am quite sure it would succeed."[68] The bishop received no encouragement from Father Sorin.

In January 1886 the bishop's patience with the Jesuits ran out. Although it seemed clear that the matter was closed for some three years, the bishop, frustrated by failure to secure help elsewhere, now decided to make a formal and final break with the Jesuits, be relieving them of the administration of St. Mary's parish. In his usual direct manner when handling such matters, Bishop Gilmour informed Father Lessmann:

> in August, 1881 [*sic*], the pastoral administration of St. Mary's Church, Cleveland, was given to your Fathers on condition that your Society would open a college in the city of Cleveland.
>
> You have failed to open the college as agreed. Failing to open the college as agreed, the pastoral charge of St. Mary's has lapsed, you have failed to fulfill the

conditions on which it was given. Under these circumstances I hereby inform you that on Sunday, March 21st, prox. I will resume pastoral charge of St. Mary's Cleveland on that day your Fathers will cease to have pastoral charge of same.[69]

New Proposal for a College

Bishop Gilmour's letter formally ending ties with the Buffalo Jesuits was received just as Father Henry Behrens replaced Father Lessmann as Superior of the Mission on 2 February 1886. The Mission Consultors met on that same day to discuss the letter and unanimously agreed that it was "expedient and necessary" for the new Superior to meet with Bishop Gilmour in Cleveland and come to an agreement on the opening of a college.[70] Father Behrens set out immediately for Cleveland and met with the bishop. There appears to be no record of what went on at that meeting, but the Mission Consultors' minutes give some clues. It seems clear that the bishop insisted the college be started immediately or the residence of St. Mary's was to be given up on the date specified. The Mission Consultors appealed to the German Provincial to "at length bring this matter to an end and that he send some fitting teachers by whose help we can laudably open a college in that city." Each consultor was then urged to write to the Provincial and present the matter as the consultor viewed it.[71]

Everyone must have been anxious to establish the college, for by mid-April there was an agreement to begin preparations for the college. The bishop cooperated by allowing the Jesuits to retain the administration of St. Mary's parish beyond the stated deadline and informed Father Behrens on 19 April 1886:

> I hereby accept your offer to establish a college in this city, with the understanding, first—that the property bought and created for the college shall at all times be owned and controlled by the Jesuit Fathers; Second—that the control and management of said college shall be subject to the rules and manner of conducting colleges, as in force among the Jesuit Fathers; Third—that there shall be a chapel in connection with said college, with all the ordinary privileges of a chapel, but for the sole and exclusive use of those persons actually connected with said college, as professors, students, or servants.[72]

If there were additional points Father Behrens wanted included, the bishop was willing to consider them. For the day on which the arrangement was concluded, Bishop Gilmour put a single entry into his diary, "April 19, 1886. Rose tired. Arranged with Father Behrens for college to open September next."[73] Father Behrens, the hero of many legendary exploits in Europe and recipient of the Iron Cross of Germany for his work as chaplain in the Franco-Prussian War, was indeed a match for Bishop Gilmour. A tape recording of their conversation would make interesting listening. It seems doubtful whether Father Lessmann and the bishop could ever have come to any agreement.

St. Ignatius College Established

Father Behrens asked the bishop to bear with him while awaiting the formal approval from his Superiors of the bishop's offer. Father Behrens also informed Bishop Gilmour that "toward the end of May, I hope that everything shall be settled, at least not much later, so that I keep my promise to arrange matters in 3 or 4 months."[74] Father Behrens had one request to make. "I think it would be good that nothing may be known in Cleveland in order to avoid difficulties for buying a convenient place for the college."[75] There was no announcement in the diocesan or public press until Father Neustich's notice appeared in the *Catholic Universe* in the middle of August 1886. It may well be that Father Behrens's request was at least partly responsible for the lack of any advanced publicity.

In early June Father Behrens again visited Cleveland to complete arrangements for the college and to meet with the bishop. Since the bishop was absent from the city, Father Behrens wrote to him

> that everything regarding the college is settled. A few days ago I received the letters from my Superiors I was waiting for. We will begin the college next September with one class. The house for this purpose has been bought today.
>
> I am very glad that I have kept my promise that in 3 or 4 months everything would be settled.[76]

Father General Anton Anderledy was also pleased and later wrote to Father Behrens commending him on the establishment of a college in Cleveland.[77]

As soon as Father Behrens had completed the arrangements for the Cleveland college he named Father John B. Neustich Superior of the Cleveland Jesuit community. Father Neustich also became pastor of St. Mary's Congregation, replacing Father Zoeller, who was reassigned to the Jesuit parish in Toledo. Father Zoeller remained there until 1896 when he returned to St. Ignatius College as Spiritual Father to the Jesuit community until his death in 1919.

Father Neustich was born in Leiberg, Westphalia in 1840, and ordained a priest for the Paderborn diocese in Germany in 1865; he entered the Society of Jesus in 1869 and saw active service in the Franco-Prussian War as an army chaplain under Father Behrens, who was in charge of the Catholic chaplains. Exiled from Germany in 1872 with other Jesuit victims of Bismarck's Kulturkampf, he spent some time in England. From there he came to Buffalo to join the other Fathers at the Buffalo Mission. As the treasurer of Canisius College he had played an important role in the planning and building of that college and seemed an ideal choice for a similar task in Cleveland. As Father Neustich tells the story, Father Behrens told him to go to Cleveland, buy property, and Father Behrens would provide the money.[78] To preserve the silence Father Behrens had requested, Father Neustich was publicly announced, without any reference to a college, as Superior of the Jesuit Community at St. Mary parish on 24 May 1886. On 5 June Ascension Thursday, he was announced to the congregation of St. Mary's Church as its new pastor.[79] Public notice of the change of pastors appeared in the *Catholic Universe* of 3 June noting also that the appointment had the "approbation of Rt. Rev. Bishop Gilmour."[80] There was still no public indication of his role in beginning the college.

The house that Father Behrens said he had just purchased was on Jersey Street (West 30th Street) between Lorain Avenue and Carroll Street, across from the parish property. It would serve temporarily as headquarters for the new college until other arrangements could be made. By the ninth of June Father Neustich had purchased two adjacent fifty-foot lots on Jersey Street, each 239 feet deep. By the sixth of July he had succeeded in obtaining the lot on the corner of Jersey and Carroll streets adjacent to those already purchased. He now had obtained a total of 223 feet of frontage between Carroll and Lorain on the east side of Jersey Street. The total cost was $15,500; the money was supplied by the Buffalo Mission through Father Behrens.[81] An additional piece of property on Carroll Street next to the corner lot was purchased in early August at a cost of $3,500.[82] Within a year the remaining frontage on Carroll Street was acquired at an additional cost of $16,500, leaving only the property fronting on Lorain Avenue to be added at a cost of $11,760. All of the original lots were purchased in the name of Father Neustich and Father William Becker, first president of Canisius College, who now had been assigned to Cleveland.[83]

The name Carroll on the street on the northerly side of the newly acquired property seems prophetic since St. Ignatius College was to become John Carroll University in September 1923. Although the name Carroll appears on the Ohio City map of 1835, it is unlikely that the early settlers were that prophetic. More likely it was Charles Carroll of Carrollton, cousin of John Carroll and the last surviving signer of the Declaration of Independence, after whom the street was named. The death of Charles Carroll in 1832 was an occasion of national mourning, and a number of places such as Carroll County in Ohio were named in his honor.

Since the purchase of sufficient land was not completed before the middle of July, there was no time to build an elaborate classroom structure for the opening of classes in September. There also seems to have been some question as to exactly where the temporary building of the college should be located on the newly purchased property. Standing in the way of any construction were ten frame houses, four of which were soon removed; by 1896 except for the small structures on Riley Alley behind the property, all had been removed. One of the houses opposite St. Mary's parish house was to be used temporarily for two of the teachers; the third teacher was to live with the priests in the parish house.[84] Work on the stone foundation of the temporary structure, which was finally located two hundred feet to the rear of the two deep lots on Jersey Street, where no houses needed to be removed immediately, was begun on the nineteenth of July and finished just two days before classes were to begin on the sixth of September.[85] The classroom building was ninety feet by twenty-five feet with a height of thirty feet. A porch with a roof was added later to provide shelter for students between classes; a subsequent subdivision of one of the rooms provided a total of four classrooms. There was a two-hundred foot plank walk leading from the building to Jersey Street from where coal was hauled for the pot-bellied stoves in the classrooms. In August Father Behrens arrived in Cleveland to present three newly assigned Jesuits to Bishop Gilmour. They were Fathers Herman Kerckhoff, Joseph Gaechter, and a Scholastic, John Devlin. Together with Father Neustich they were the first faculty of St. Ignatius College.[86]

The location of the college on the West Side was not the result of any preference on the part of the Jesuits. They had accepted the administration of the parish in 1880, in the hope that it would give them a base from which they could operate temporarily while they sought a proper location for the college. They were aware of the eastward orientation of the city and the direction of its industrial and commercial growth. The East Side potential appeared far greater than that of the West Side and had it not been for Bishop Gilmour's insistence on the West Side location they certainly would not have established the college there. The immediate availability of the property across the street from St. Mary's parish determined the specific choice under the circumstances. The necessity of clearing the houses and sheds off that property was a minor matter.

On one issue, however, the Jesuits remained firm. In spite of Bishop Gilmour's insistence to the contrary, there would be no boarding school in that location. It was an area in which there were dwellings intermingled with stores of all sorts along with livery stables, a large brewery, and numerous saloons. It seemed hardly the atmosphere for a boarding school.

THE COLLEGE OPENS

A terse entry in the "House Diary" recorded the opening of classes on the sixth of September, stating simply, "Collegium St. Ignatii apertum est. 40

discipouli venerunt."[87] This is also the first recorded use of the name of the college. Within five days the number had risen to fifty-nine, and by 20 September, a total of sixty-five had enrolled. Students continued to enroll up to the middle of November when the total of seventy-six was reached. In their annual report to Superiors for this period the Jesuits commented on the prolonged enrollment process by saying that it seemed as if the students, not sure of what was in store for them, waited for those who showed up early to report what it was like.[88] Curiously, the Jesuits also commented on the great anticipation of the people which was to be found expressed in the newspapers.[89] The Jesuits must have been reading some German papers with very limited circulation, for none of the major newspapers carried any news of the opening of St. Ignatius College. It would seem Father Behrens's instruction to proceed in silence so as not to affect the price of the property they sought to purchase was carried out. Still, word of mouth was effective and a total of eighty-two students eventually registered, the last one registering on 28 February 1887.[90]

It is perhaps somewhat ironic that Bishop Gilmour had reluctantly arranged for the German Jesuits to open a college in Cleveland at a time when teachers of the German language were very much in demand in Cleveland. In the very week that St. Ignatius College opened, the local papers were complaining about the "lack of competent German teachers in the public schools."[91] Bishop Gilmour did not agree with those Cleveland citizens who saw military necessity requiring the teaching of German; he wanted nothing to interfere with the Americanization of immigrant Catholics; it was proceeding too slowly as it was.

Tradition and the only available written record of registration of the early students are in disagreement as to who was the first student registered. According to a long-standing story, Louis Litzler was the first student registered. Louis's mother is said to have heard early in 1886 that the Jesuits were to open a college soon. She immediately hurried to St. Mary Church rectory and enrolled Louis as the first student.

Father Neustich, who kept a written record of the first day's registration, lists the students, not alphabetically, but by numbers; Louis Litzler is number thirty-seven and a John Schilling is listed as number one. The difficulty with the traditional story lies in part with what is meant by "early" in the year 1886, for until late spring of that year it was not clear that the Jesuits would even remain in Cleveland. There is also the matter of silence enjoined on all concerned when arrangements for the college were finally made. Father Francis Haggeney, who joined the faculty six years after the opening of the college, further confuses the matter by contending that the given name of the first student was Ignatius as was also that of the student's father. A student, Ignatius Longtin, registered on that first day, fits the description but Father Neustich lists him as number ten.

Of the first class of students, slightly more than half were from the East Side of the city. Geographically, the students came from as far west as Lakewood and as far east as 79th Street, as far south as Newburgh. As one would expect from the location of the college, there were students from along Detroit, Madison, Lorain, and Pearl, major West Side streets. East Side students came from the downtown area and from parishes along Superior Avenue. One of the better-known names in the first class was that of Thomas Grasselli, son of Ceasar A. Grasselli, one of Cleveland's industrial leaders for some forty years. Young Thomas succeeded his father as president of the Gasselli Chemical Company in 1916 and later became a vice-president after the merger with E. I. duPont de Nemours and Company in 1928. Thomas Grasselli made the trip to St. Ignatius from East 55th Street, then known as Willson Avenue.

Nationality among the students of the first class was about evenly divided between Irish and German ancestry with little or no representation of those of other ancestry. About one fourth of the class had registered in the commercial course, and of these, twelve finished their course in 1890. Three fourths were registered in the classical course, and of these, eight finished the course on time in 1892. By that time, seventeen more had finished the commercial course. Only about half of the first class returned for the second year, a pattern too often repeated in the early years.

At the end of the first year on 27 June 1887 there was a convocation with a program and distribution of prizes for good work in the classroom. The program, intended as a demonstration of student accomplishment, emphasized two activities of the first year that were to become characteristic of the college in its early years, music and dramatics. At the beginning and end of the program the music and choral societies provided entertainment. The dramatic Society put on Cardinal H. E. Wiseman's two-act play, *The Hidden Gem*; some sixteen different students acted in the various roles. As one might expect, the awards for excellence in German language went to students of German ancestry but in the German Grammar Class the six awards went to students with Irish names; Matthew Lynch received the top award.[92]

EARLY TRIALS

The first year had more than its share of problems partly because of the short amount of time available to purchase land, construct the building, and get everything in readiness for a September opening, but Father Neustich and his staff of three could look back with some degree of satisfaction on their efforts. Father Neustich had a particularly difficult role since he was at first known only as pastor of St. Mary's congregation. Not until 14 September was he publicly announced as vice-rector of the new college.[93]

Priests of the diocese were understanding and appreciative of the work of the Jesuits; a number of priests loaned or contributed money over a long period of time to assist the development of the college. Monsignor Felix M. Boff, Vicar General of the Diocese and a frequent visitor to the Jesuit Community for dinner, lent several thousand dollars at a low rate of interest as did some other priests.[94] The Jesuits also helped out in the parishes on weekends, establishing further contact with the diocesan clergy and people on both the East and West sides of the city as well as in Youngstown, Ravenna, and other cities in the diocese.

Acceptance by the people of Cleveland and in particular by the clergy was of great concern to the Jesuits at St. Ignatius College. They felt that their association with a German parish on the West Side had not enhanced their appeal to East Side Catholics whom they were convinced were much more likely than those of the West Side to send their sons to college. Experience at Canisius College for the previous fifteen years had taught the Fathers that until they could overcome Irish opposition to things German they were unlikely to have success in Cleveland. This meant speaking English without an accent and providing Jesuits who had come from American backgrounds.

There were many painful memories of the Canisius experience and all of the Jesuits who were assigned to Cleveland had some taste of that experience. Acceptance even along purely German lines was also sometimes a problem; the German immigrants generally were lower middle class and had come to the United States often in protest of Prussia's domination of Germany. Most of the German Fathers had been brought up in an atmosphere of expectation for a new Germany and as exiles suffered from a sense of frustration.[95] The problem was further complicated by the different approaches of the younger and older Buffalo Jesuits. Father John La-Farge, who spent some time at Canisius and is perhaps best known as a pioneer American Jesuit for interracial justice, felt that he was somewhat of a moderator of the two groups because he had acquired German during his studies at Innsbruck and was familiar with German customs. One group was absolutely convinced that German must be the language of instruction as well as of study; preaching in English was to be discouraged. One of the arguments against the use of English was that once students learned it they tended to absorb "strange American ideas and depart from true orthodoxy."[96] Father LaFarge thought it was odd that during his stay at Canisius the reading at meals was done in German, some of it from material he had listened to at Innsbruck.[97] The dispute continued, according to Father La-Farge, until the dissolution of the Buffalo Mission in 1907, when the Mission was absorbed by the Missouri and the New York-Maryland Provinces.

The Irish, who were familiar with English and understood the American scene, were something of a mystery to the German Jesuits. Father Behrens was convinced that the emphasis on temperance by Irish bishops was fanaticism.[98] This background, which the Buffalo Jesuits brought with them to Cleveland, would for some time remain an obstacle to their becoming an integral part of the Cleveland scene. The report to Father General for 1886–1887, notes hopefully, but with caution, that the Jesuits' acceptance in Cleveland seemed somewhat improved by the end of the school year. More people were coming to the Jesuits, "Our [German] people because of the Sodalities, and the English speaking people on account of a better opinion of our abilities."[99] The Jesuits were in great demand to assist in the parishes with confession and Mass on weekends but this was not necessarily a sign of greater acceptance. "Is there, therefore, a great love of Ours everywhere?" the report continued. "Hardly, the dearth of priests, sickness, absences, fewer Franciscans, and possibly the newness and ease of obtaining our help have brought this about."[100] Perhaps the writer of the report described the situation best when he said,

> If you ask what is the attitude of the priests toward us, you will easily understand when I say that it is difficult to answer. We are German, we don't suddenly seem totally American. We speak German; the Irish do that as rarely as nightingales build their nests with eagles. We have learned English and if we have to give a sermon we are accustomed to have something prepared. . . . Germans do not seem to be sufficiently American! Are the Irish so? Germans do not detest beer, they do not think highly enough of the local drinks; they [Germans] think that lyric music and light songs are more appropriate for the theater than the Church; they are more frugal, industrious, even sometimes richer than the Irish brethren— for these reasons are they not sufficiently American? . . . It is true we do not make enemies, still on the other hand we are not overwhelmed by the gifts of friends nor hampered by their good will . . . this land does not produce better and stronger men because the primary interests of both people and priests is to look out for themselves and have little concern for others except for what they can do for you.[101]

An example of how the German Jesuits could complicate relations with Bishop Gilmour was their participation in a German Catholic Convention held in Cleveland in September 1889. Bishop Gilmour had learned early of the coming convention and wrote in the *Catholic Universe*,

> Last summer when the Chicago Convention of 'German Catholics' was on the boards, we took occasion to say: 'Such a convention of German Catholics has no raison d'etre in the United States; same applies to any religious denomination here save one—Catholic American. . . .

The convention is in error. It is a drive in the wrong direction. It perpetuates what we should seek to obliterate—European lines on American soil.

The highest interest of the Church and State demand that we Americanize our people.[102]

This did not stop the Cleveland Jesuits, who turned St. Ignatius College into a center for visiting conventioneers. "For these four days our house was like a hotel, where Bishops, secular priests and religious came and went."[103] Father Lessmann, assisted by Fathers Schulte and Boehmer, celebrated a solemn Mass for the delegates. There was a large procession with marching bands and various types of vehicles in which Fathers Lessmann, Neustich, and Boehmer took part. Bishop Gilmour probably thought he was right in the first place about these "sharply marked Germans."

Even the few satisfactions the Jesuits must have had in the beginning were hardly enough to offset the trials and hardships. A later rector in describing those first years observed,

our Fathers in coming to the city have certainly sown in tears and made astonishing sacrifices in money for the cause of higher education. The poverty of those early years was appalling; the income from tuition did not suffice for more than the midday meal even though it was frugal. To sustain themselves many had to go out every Saturday and Sunday; often not a Father was left to say Mass for the Scholastics and Brothers. The plainest rooms were theirs; no books, no library for years; stinting and saving was the order of the day.[104]

CURRICULUM

The first *Catalogue* of St Ignatius College did not go into any great detail on the course of study offered. It stated merely that "The Full Course of Studies embraces the Latin, Greek, English, German, and French Languages; Elocution, Poetry, Rhetoric, English Literature; History, Geography, a course of Mathematics, Natural Philosophy, Chemistry, Book-Keeping and Pennmanship [*sic*]."[105] Admission standards were briefly stated:

Candidates for Admissions will be examined and placed in that class to which they are entitled by their attainments. Every Candidate for Admission is required to furnish testimony of good moral character. Bad conduct, insubordination, or continued inapplication to studies are reasons for dismissal.[106]

Two hours of private study each evening were required and rules and regulations were "calculated to secure the order necessary for the effectual pursuit of studies, to develop and strengthen character, and to promote gentlemanly deportment and good manners."[107] The rules were to be "enforced with paternal gentleness, combined with energy and firmness. It is only when motives of honor, self-respect, conscience and religion fail, that punishment is resorted to."[108]

It would be a mistake to assume that the current elementary, high school, and college structure existed in 1886; the model of elementary school, junior high school, high school, and four years of college was not yet fully developed. Through almost the first quarter of the twentieth century the Jesuits preserved a continuity for the student through what would today be called secondary and collegiate levels. The high school and college were not thought of as distinct educational units. While a classical curriculum was not to be identified exclusively with Jesuit schools in the nineteenth century, it was the distinctive approach that was characteristic of Jesuit institutions. St. Ignatius College was no exception to the Jesuit pattern, but because of its stronger German ties it did bear a closer resemblance to the European application of the Jesuit *Ratio Studiorum* than some other Jesuit colleges longer established in the United States.

RATIO STUDIORUM

The *Ratio Studiorum* developed in the sixteenth century as an effort to give specific form to general rules on education contained in the Fourth Part of the Constitutions of the Society of Jesus. By 1580 the multiplication and popularity of the Jesuit colleges made it desirable to work out a general plan of studies for all the colleges. At the Fourth General Congregation of the Society in 1581, Father General Claudius Aquaviva took the matter into his own hands and summoned to Rome six Jesuits representing Spain, France, Portugal, Italy, Austria, and Germany, who had considerable experience in the colleges. This committee devoted nearly a year to the study of the customs and regulations of the colleges and received recommendations from all parts of the Society. A tentative plan was ready in 1585 and was submitted for further examination. A revision of this plan was then submitted to the provinces for experimentation in 1591. By 1599 the final plan, *Ratio atque Instituto Studiorum*, was approved.

The plan contained four sets of rules covering the roles of rectors, professors, superiors and a program of studies. Administration of the college was placed in the hands of the rector, who was to act with the advice of consultors and input from the professors. A prefect of studies was given the task of immediate supervision of the students and their work. Professors were given rules for methods of instruction; the rules for superiors made it clear that changes could be made if the local situation required it. In order to counteract what the Jesuits considered the deficiencies of the educational institutions of that day, the plan combined the best tradition of Christian humanism with the best secular thought of the day in an effort to educate the entire person.

The *Ratio* was formulated at a time when, for the Jesuits, "no speculative uncertainty clouded their vision of ultimate goals."[109] Learning was an instrument, not an end. The object of the course of studies was,

> to develop harmoniously all mental and moral faculties of the student, to combine erudition and logical accuracy, and to cultivate a sense for the beautiful in language. Such a course of studies gives the knowledge, refinement and culture which characterize true scholarship, and accustoms the student to serious application before he takes up professional branches.[110]

The classical course was considered the ideal instrument for the purpose of this education.

When the Society of Jesus was suppressed in 1773, its colleges were closed until after the restoration of the Society in 1814. There was a revision of the *Ratio* in 1832 but it did not have the same application and acceptance of the original because of the changed conditions in the nineteenth century. Nevertheless, the *Ratio* remained the bench mark for the college program even in the United States until after World War I.

The names of the various stages of progress through the classical course at St. Ignatius College are confusing to those unfamiliar with the traditional structure. The beginning class was called "Third Academic." It might be thought of as roughly comparable to the present ninth grade but there was nothing to prevent a capable sixth or seventh grader from entering. The student was considered to be a collegian once he enrolled in the beginning class; with ability and application he would progress through the "Second Academic" to the "First Academic." His task at the three years of the academic level was to acquire grammatical perfection in English, Latin, and Greek. "Humanities" was the next level and during this year, the student's fourth, he learned the beauty of literature; then on to a fifth year called "Poetry" where he studied the poetical masterpieces of ancient and modern languages. "Rhetoric," the sixth year, was devoted to expression and oratorical style; a seventh year, "Philosophy," finished the program. Philosophy included Logic, Ontology, Cosmology, Psychology, Natural Theology, and Ethics. The bachelor of arts degree was awarded on successful completion of the seven years. The student was then considered prepared for professional studies. Other subjects such as mathematics, chemistry, history, physics, astronomy, and geography were taught at the various levels but they were secondary to the classics.

THE COMMERCIAL COURSE

In the United States, as a concession to reality, Jesuit colleges maintained a commercial course designed to offer "the advantages of a thorough business education . . . intended for that class of youth, who, not wishing to follow the professions, stand in no need of a classical education."[111] There was also a Preparatory Class, another concession to reality, for those who were unable to begin in Third Academic. It was also possible for an exceptional student to advance rapidly by combining two of the academic courses.

The Jesuits feared that the commercial course, tolerated by necessity, would attract students of lesser ability and, although it might mean greater numbers of students, it would also mean lower quality and standards. At St. Ignatius College there was mixed opinion on the value of the commercial course and it is discussed in the Annual Letter to Rome of 1887 reviewing the first year's work. It was thought that a lower enrollment because of insistence on the classical course would tend to give the college more prestige and influence. While the necessity of offering the commercial course was obvious, it was hoped that in time the students could be lured into the classical course.[112]

FROM BUFFALO MISSION TO MISSOURI PROVINCE

When St. Ignatius College was founded it was of course part of the Buffalo Mission of the German Province. In 1907 the college became part of the Missouri Province with the dissolution of the Buffalo Mission thus affecting the program of studies at St. Ignatius. The Missouri Province had for some time attempted to provide for all of its colleges a uniform program more adapted to American custom and standards. In the colleges of the Missouri Province, prior to 1887, there had been considerable diversity. Some graduated students after six years, others after seven. Father Rudolph Meyer, Provincial of the Missouri Province, at the request of a provincial congregation in 1886, systematized and organized the programs of the colleges so that there would be uniformity in the Province.[113] Yet the Jesuit academy and the American high school were still organized differently, one on a three-year and the other on a four-year basis. Some Jesuit academies attempted to solve this problem by moving humanities to the academy level leaving only three years to the college course. The problem of synchronizing the Jesuit educational structure with that of development in American higher education as a whole remained an issue until 1912, when the eight-year program—four years of high school, four years of college—was prescribed for the Missouri Province. Adjustments continued to be made to retain the substance and spirit of the *Ratio* while conforming to the requirements of the American educational scene. One of the points at issue for some time was whether teachers should continue to take a class of students through the various subjects of the curriculum, a traditional Jesuit practice; not until 1915 did the practice change when the Missouri Province recognized the need of specialists. A further change came in 1919 when Greek was no longer required for the baccalaureate degree.[114] By 1921 the Province had decided they every Jesuit college should conform to American standards.[115]

MORE PERMANENT QUARTERS

The original wooden structure had been viewed as only a temporary affair; Jesuit living quarters in the parish were not conducive to community life and Father Behrens on his visitation had so noted.[116] When money was found to be available from the various societies in Germany that supported the Buffalo Mission, plans were made for a more permanent building which would include a residence for the Jesuits.

It seems that an unnamed Bohemian architect drew up the original plans for the new building but the estimated construction cost of the Jesuit residence part, the first of three parts, was too high. Father Behrens and Father Neustich agreed on what was to be changed to cut costs and abandoned original plans.[117] In order that the building have an architectural style more in conformity with other Jesuit colleges in the German Province, Father Behrens wrote to superiors in Holland and requested that Brother Frederick Wipfler, who had designed other Jesuit colleges, be sent to St. Ignatius. The Cleveland Jesuits argued, saying, "it is preferable in such an important affair to have the design meet our custom and needs than hurry into the plans drawn up by the Bohemian."[118] Brother Wipfler, an architect from Holland who had joined the Society in 1882 at the age of twenty-six, was assisted by a group of young but experienced Brothers, most of whom had joined the Society only recently. Among them were Brothers Christian Herzog, a carpenter, Aloysius Gastl, an engineer, and several others with skills in the various trades.[119] The building was constructed with metric measurement, a fact that later caused repair and replacement problems. The northeast wing was constructed first and completed in 1889. On 1 July of that year the Jesuits moved into their new living quarters.

Before the wing was completed, Father Neustich reported to Father General on the development at the college and was commended by him for securing the funds necessary for the new building; the General hoped that the college would be a credit to the Society through the quality of its stu-

Top, Original college, 1886, before porch was added; *Bottom,* Completed brick structure, 1891

dents. Father General was anxious that the Sodality be quickly established as a necessary instrument in the progress of the college.[120]

Pleased with progress thus far, Father General Anderledy sought to insure future success by relieving the president of the college of duties of pastor of the parish. Because it seemed wiser not to change pastors so soon, Father Neustich was to remain as pastor of St. Mary's congregation and a new president of the college was appointed, Father Henry Knappmeyer, who took office on 4 November 1888: Father Neustich remained as pastor of the parish until 1894, and at his departure was described by Bishop Ignatius Horstmann as one who "faithfully and successfully administered the affairs of the parish . . . an able and loving pastor" at whose loss the people felt a "deep affliction."[121] Father Neustich returned to St. Ignatius College in 1906 and became treasurer until 1922, when illness forced him to go to St. Stanislaus Jesuit House in Parma, where he died in 1924.

Father Knappmeyer came to St. Ignatius College from Sacred Heart College at Prairie du Chien where he had been since 1882. He was born in Munster, Germany in 1835 and entered the Society of Jesus in 1857. He taught in Austria but after his ordination came to Canisius College, where he was the first Prefect of Studies. Father Knappmeyer was a scholar in his own right; there was a feeling among his peers that had he engaged in literary pursuits, he would have been a distinguished writer.[122] Father Knappmeyer was considered to be a "firm disciplinarian, but . . . did not inspire fear, except where necessary."[123] Not surprisingly Father Knappmeyer later won the confidence of Bishop Ignatius Horstmann, who succeeded Bishop Gilmour in 1892, and who also had the reputation as a scholar of considerable merit. This friendship marked a new era in the relations between a Cleveland bishop and the Jesuits.

The students of St. Ignatius College appreciated Father Knappmeyer

on account of his prudent advice, eminently practical hints and exhortations, genial ways and ready wit. And, indeed, who could forget that merry twinkle of his eyes, that power of conviction which lay in his measured, quiet and kind way of speaking, those anecdotes which he used to tell either to illustrate the counsel or decision he was giving or to restore the good humor of one who was depressed and the course of another whose spirits were waning? No one of those who had any dealings with him will not recall that little man looking at him over spectacles resting on the tip of his nose and apparently in constant danger of falling off, now rubbing his hands, now shaking his finger, then again taking a pinch of snuff, and turning the box between his fingers.[124]

Father Knappmeyer arrived in November, three days before the presidential election of 1888. Arriving on Saturday, he was officially installed on Sunday. On Monday Father Joseph Gaechter, Prefect of Discipline, intro-

Above left, Henry Behrens, S.J., Superior, Buffalo Mission, 1872−76, 1886−92; *right,* John B. Neustich, S.J., President, St. Ignatius College, 1886−88, Treasurer, 1906−22; *Bottom,* Henry Knappmeyer, S.J., President, St. Ignatius College, 1888−93

duced Father Knappmeyer to the students to whom he immediately endeared himself by declaring the next day, which happened to be election day, a free day. The entry in the "House Diary" makes it clear that the free day was not because of the presidential election but because of the appointment of a new president of St. Ignatius College. [125] The new president, frequently described as "a kindly old gentleman, short and stout," displayed his good humor and further impressed the students when, on this occasion, he granted amnesty to a student who had been disciplined for leaving the college ahead of schedule by climbing out of a window.

The consultors of the Jesuit Community met on election day and decided unanimously that additional classroom space would be necessary for the expected increased enrollment. [126] Subsequent meetings confirmed this judgment. By spring of 1890 work was planned to continue with Brother Wipfler's design and add the northwest wing along Jersey or West 30th Street. [127] By 1891 the two wings running along Carroll and West 30th had been completed; a third part which was to extend further along West 30th, and include a chapel and a hall, was never built. For a while, at least, there was room in the five-story building for the expansion of classes through the college level as well as provision for the Jesuit Community. The beauty of the new structure caused the parishioners of St. Mary's parish across the street to think of renovating their church to match the splendor of the new college. [128]

In January 1889 Father Knappmeyer reported to Father General on the progress of the college. In his reply, Father General said he hoped for even better things in the future and cautioned Father Knappmeyer to observe the Rules of the Society and be sure that the students were instructed in Christian Doctrine. Father General took the occasion to express his gratitude for the work done by Father Neustich and said it would be necessary for Father Knappmeyer to keep to the course set by his predecessor in order to have continued success through the work of dedicated teachers. Father Knappmeyer was asked to be vigilant and report any problems he might have with teachers. The principle problem was still the need for teachers who could speak fluent English. [129]

INCORPORATION

In February 1889 St. Ignatius College began to acquire the remainder of the frontage along West 30th Street toward Lorain Avenue. Title to all the property acquired since 1886 was in the names of Fathers Neustich, Becker, or Knappmeyer because there was as yet no corporate entity known as St. Ignatius College to which title could be given. In order to correct this situation and to provide the necessary state authority to grant degrees, steps were taken to incorporate the college and to secure a charter from the state. On 29 December 1890 the charter was granted to "The St. Ignatius College of Cleveland, Ohio." The purpose clause in the Articles of Incorporation stated simply. "The purpose for which said corporation is formed is to enable the same to confer degrees on students attending same who will acquire therein sufficient of the learned languages and useful arts and sciences as well as of law and medicine entitling them thereto."[130] In July 1891 all the property that had been in individual names was transferred to St. Ignatius College.

Father Knappmeyer's health began to fail toward the latter part of 1892 and he was eventually replaced as rector and president by Father Joseph LeHalle on 22 June 1893. Father Knappmeyer went to St. Mary's, the Jesuit parish in Toledo, and remained there until his death on 4 January 1897. His term of office was relatively short but he left a marked impression on the students and saw the completion of the building plans he had supervised.

"The Iron Ages"
1886-1914

A student once referred to the early days of St. Ignatius College as the "Iron Ages." A former faculty member, Father Chester A. Burns, also commented on those years in somewhat the same vein:

> Novelties were ruthlessly ruled out, or rather never gained entrance. The classics and the sciences were taught with a systematic thoroughness of method that gives us pause, not to mention, reason for self-examination in these days of sipping and ladeling from the fountain of knowledge. Boys grew up under this influence with minds trained to quick and ready precision and with wills steeled to unhesitating act under stress of worthy motive. Infromation [*sic*] was not the sole object of these sturdy educators. They would have rejoiced over Professor John Dewey's dictum relative to the students: 'Make of their minds high powered rifles instead of wastebaskets.' There was little waste matter in their system, and minds were indeed taught to shoot as hard as rifles do.[1]

This atmosphere did not change very much until after World War I. As Father Chester Burns said:

> Quite simply the faculty of John Carroll (St. Ignatius College) kept them [modern methods] far from their door—wisely, no doubt, for the most part, a little unusually in smaller part. . . . The aim always was and still remained to educate the student's soul; to offer him the best that the dim past and the vivid present have to offer with the confiderice [*sic*] assurance that he will thus emerge a fine and fit instrument to put into the hands of the community to which he belongs.[2]

The benefit of some sixteen years of American experience at Canisius College did not convince most of the Cleveland Jesuits of any great need for major adaptations to the American scene. Most of the Jesuits who served at both colleges were convinced that what the Jesuits had to offer was needed in the United States.

CLASSICAL COURSE UNDER ATTACK

The moral and religious training of students was the objective for the Jesuits, who held that the "only really worthwhile pursuit is the realities of faith."[3] The classical course, considered the best instrument for attaining that end, was defended even when it was clear that it would not survive long in its original form. In Europe, where the classical program was offered in a college attached to a university, it was considered a preparation for entrance to the university. In America the early tendency was for the Catholic college to be associated in some way with the diocesan seminary; thus the classical program was preparation for professional theological study.[4]

As if to underscore the defense of the traditional curriculum at a time when it was under attack, an account of the college and the course of study appeared in a Sunday edition of the *Plain Dealer* in May 1900, together with a quarter-page picture of some students with the headline, "Students in the Classical Course of St. Ignatius College." The account under the picture made clear,

> The college adheres to the study of languages, based on the classics, not only furnishing unequaled mental training, but as forming the most solid basis for the future work of the student, whatever is to be his calling. The aim is to furnish a liberal education in the widest sense; to lay a firm foundation for future intellectual work and to avoid premature specialization.[5]

Even as this publicity appeared, changes in the classical course were already coming. As long as the purpose in attending a Catholic college was, for many boys, preparation for entering the seminary, the classical course could stand intact. At the same time, the rise of minor seminaries made less necessary the college's responsibility to prepare men for the priesthood.[6] The expansion of knowledge in the field of science and increasing interest in the world of business and commerce continued to press demands for the inclusion of subject matter from these areas. As a result the period from about 1870 to 1910 has been called the "heyday of curricular laissez faire."[7] Many of the Jesuit colleges did not begin to participate fully in these changes until after 1890; St. Ignatius College held off even longer. Not until the 1920s were there marked changes in the St. Ignatius College curriculum; at that point accreditation pressures played a major role.

Although resistance to change was strong, the gradual erosion of the classical course took place. Interest in so-called "practical" subjects could not be denied; it was no longer sufficient to list them as "extras" or "options" as had been done in many Jesuit colleges. By 1910 electives were accepted in practice although they were often denied in principle. At St. Ignatius College the only electives in the early days were German, French, drawing, shorthand, and vocal music.[8] Later, a limited choice was permitted from a host of electives in the fields of science, political economy, pedagogy, public speaking, and mechanical drawing.[9]

FACILITY IN THE USE OF ENGLISH

One change had already taken place in the recognition of English as a legitimate tool of study. English was not always looked upon as a language through which learning could take place.[10] Before a native American clergy could develop, it was considered more proper for the European clergy who staffed the early Jesuit colleges to use Latin in their instruction; it was, after all, the language of their seminary studies. Depending on which European province founded the college, French, Italian, or German priests who could hardly speak English were trying to use English. The German Jesuits at St. Ignatius College often found communication in English extremely difficult. Father Lessmann, mindful of Bishop Gilmour's wishes, had from the beginning instructed the Jesuits at St. Ignatius College to avoid the use of German in even their own communications with each other.[11] Again in 1890, Father Behrens, then Superior of the Buffalo Mission, repeated the admonition requesting that all of the Fathers use English in all their conversations; as he put it, "daily use of English is most desirable."[12] Another Superior, Father Theodore Van Rossum, found it necessary to repeat the advice in 1896.[13] Some Jesuits found it impossible to comply with their Superiors' instructions.

Later reports of Superiors' visitations no longer repeated the instruction but it should not be assumed that the admonition was no longer needed. Those Jesuits of the Buffalo Mission who could handle English well were particularly conscious of the continuing problem. Some, like the English-born Father James A. Rockliff, who succeeded Father Van Rossum as Superior of the Buffalo Mission in 1898, were especially blunt in their assessment of the issue. Father Rockliff thought that the answer was the establishment of a scholasticate and a theologate in the United States. It was not, he thought, merely a matter of speaking and understanding English well, it was a matter of understanding the literature and the culture also. He objected to scholastics coming from Europe for a year or so and then going back to Europe for studies. The German Fathers were trying to teach a language without knowing it; they were, he said, "unable to pronounce it correctly, or to speak or write it idiomatically."[14]

Father John Theis, who had attended Canisius College, became its ninth rector-president in 1898, and was later assigned to St. Ignatius College for a time, spoke in the same vein. The loss of some students was attributed to the teachers' lack of competence in the use of English. American-born Father John I. Zahm, also a president of both Canisius and St. Ignatius College, felt that the incompetence in English was also related to discipline problems. Dealing with American students was difficult enough without the added difficulty of a foreign accent.[15]

The reluctance of the early German Jesuits to use English was illustrated in an experiment between the Buffalo Mission and the New York-Maryland Province. English-speaking Jesuits were sent from the New York Province to Buffalo, but "they never stayed long and the Germans were glad to see them go. It was a matter of a reciprocal cross to be borne, as it were."[16]

While there are no available written records of specific problems of the early Cleveland Jesuits with the use of English or with discipline, it may be presumed that their experience did not differ much from that encountered at Canisius College, where some stories do endure. Such expressions as "Let me hear more silence," or "Leaf the room or get out," or "What can you do with a man you can't do anything with?" undoubtedly had their equivalents at St. Ignatius College. Cleveland Jesuits, however, were not faced with the problem, as were the Canisius Jesuits, of factory workers, mostly girls, visible from the windows of the factory across the street from the Canisius College, "putting up Lydia Pinkham Compound and Pierce Pink Pills for Pale People." More than once the Canisius students had to be admonished, "Don't be looking at dose Pierce girls."[17]

ADMISSION CRITERIA

In the early years requirements for admission to St. Ignatius College reflected those of other Jesuit colleges before the full development of the American secondary school. Taking students at whatever level they found them, the colleges remedied the deficiencies; the possibilities of articulation with either the public or Catholic high school was not considered.[18] Even after the administrative separation of the high school from the college in 1902, the continuity of the high school and college courses was expected to be maintained. "The object of the Collegiate Department, which leads to the degree of Bachelor of Arts is to broaden and deepen the classical knowledge gained in the Academic Department and to lay a suitable foundation for professional studies," according to the *Catalogue* of 1904–1905.

Admission criteria usually were not stated in exclusively intellectual terms. Standards of admission were as much moral as intellectual. The first *Catalogue* of St. Ignatius College made it clear that "Every Candidate for Admission will be required to furnish sufficient testimony of good moral character."[19] On the intellectual side, "Candidates for admission will be examined and placed in that class to which they are entitled by their attainments."[20] What might be called a strengthening of these requirements appeared in the 1903–1904 *Catalogue*: "Every candidate for admission, who is not personally acquainted with some member of the Faculty, must furnish testimonials of good moral character." The all-Jesuit faculty at that time numbered nineteen, and since the faculty did the recruiting for students, it may be that meeting the requirement was not that difficult. There is no way of knowing how many students came in on their own.

In the 1905–1906 *Catalogue*, transfer students were accepted on the basis of their record at their former institution. By 1910 the *Catalogue* was a little more specific about students entering from high schools other than St. Ignatius. If the work completed matched the course given at St. Ignatius the applicant was admitted without examination; otherwise an examination was given in Latin authors, grammar, and composition; Greek authors, grammar and composition; English, Rhetoric and Composition, Mathematics, History, and Civics. The 1915 *Catalogue* listed admission requirements in terms of the more commonly required sixteen units for high school diplomas. The personal attestation of good moral character was omitted, but "evidence of good moral character" was still required of new students.[21]

Early *Catalogues* made it clear: "Boarders are not admitted." The Fathers remained firm in their original refusal to have a boarding school at the West Side location and were unwilling to change in order to please the bishop.[22] A later *Catalogue* added, "But dinner can be provided daily at the college for those who wish at a charge of 20 cents;" a later charge was referred to as "moderate" without specifying the amount.[23] In the 1910–1911 *Catalogue*, although boarders were still not admitted, it was noted that, "Respectable boarding houses can be recommended by the college authorities to students not living in the city"; this was the first time that any official link was made between the college and the student for provision of living quarters. If is difficult to determine how many students actually took advantage of the college's offer but at the time of the purchase of the University Heights property in 1923 the student newspaper expressed the joy that many a student would experience at the propspect of a dormitory.[24]

The admission of non-Catholic students to the early Catholic colleges posed a problem. The colleges were acutely aware of their identity as Catholic colleges but would not put their charters in jeopardy by flatly stating that non-Catholics were not to be admitted. Precisely because of the Catholic colleges' strong moral commitment, many non-Catholics wished to send their sons to them. If the college had a professional school the problem was minimized; it was the undergraduate liberal arts college that faced the dilemma.[25] St. Ignatius College admission criteria seemed to assume that all students were Catholic. In the Annual Letter of St. Ignatius College to Rome for 1892–1893, the writer pointed out that "we take only Catholic students. A mixture of Catholic and non-Catholic breeds indifference."[26] As late as the 1909–1910 *Catalogue*, the statement in the general regulations of that year dealing with religious training said, "The Moral and Religious Training of the Scholars being the most important part of the education the students are required to be present at Mass every day, to make the Annual Retreat, and to go to the Sacraments at least once a month." In the 1910–1911 *Catalogue*, however, the same statement is expanded to say,

> In its moral training the college aims at building the conscience of its students for the right fulfillment of their civil, social, and religious duties. There is insistence on the cultivation of the Christian virtues which operate for this fulfillment; and, as the only solid basis of virtue and morality, thorough instruction in the principles of religion forms an essential part of the system.

There must, however, have been some non-Catholic students in the college because only Catholic students were now required to fulfill the mass and retreat obligations.

The admission of women in the early days was never a problem; it was simply a non-question. Bishop Gilmour's constant reference to a "college for men" made it clear that women were not considered, even from the bishop's point of view. There were colleges for women but coeducation was simply not possible; there is no evidence of a Catholic college for men considering it until the twentieth century.[27]

In part at least, the Jesuits blamed the slow growth of enrollment not on the curriculum and the admission requirements, but on the character of the American student, who badly needed what the college offered. The Annual Letter to Rome for 1892–1893 commented,

> boys born here rarely acquire that piety worthy of a vocation to the priesthood, nor are they moved by that nobler ambition that would strengthen them to take on the longer course of study with its labor and sweat. They first intend to make money as soon and as quickly as possible. As soon as the number of students have finished their studies at the college, and have improved their condition in society, the number (with nobler desires) will increase rapidly.[28]

FACULTY AND ADMINISTRATIVE STRUCTURE

One characteristic of the faculty of St. Ignatius College during this period was that with but few exceptions the staff was composed entirely of members of the Society of Jesus. A professor of vocal music in 1888, Henry J. Kroesen, was one exception; so also was a concertmaster Charles E. Murphy in 1898 and John Shea, concertmaster in that same year. The only other exception was Dr. B. F. Hambleton, a medical doctor who taught biology and physiology in 1905 and for three years thereafter.

At the head of the faculty was a Jesuit who served a twofold function. As rector, he was head of the religious community of Jesuits stationed at the college; as president, he was in charge of the college. It would not be quite correct to assume that the functions of this person were thought of in these separate categories. It was the rector-president who acted. Usually four Jesuits were appointed as consultors to assist him in his deliberations on a course of action. He could go against advice of his consultors or choose not to consult, but he then could be in trouble with his Provincial and with the community. These same consultors together with the president and usually two additional Jesuits formed the legal Board of Trustees of the Corporation which under the charter was required to meet to conduct the official business of the college. It was not until relatively recent times that the offices of rector and president were considered distinct, separate incorporation for the religious community provided, and provision made for the legal board of trustees to include lay persons.

Faculty concerns expressed in the regular "professors' meetings" and often referred to in the Superiors' "Memorials" were somewhat but not entirely different from those of later faculties. A major problem of the early days was that of outside parish work interfering with regular duties. Assisting in parishes both in the city and outside of it on weekends was the lot of most of the Jesuits attached to the college. It was a natural exercise of their priestly function but it also had its monetary aspect; without this work to supplement tuition income the institution probably would have had even greater difficulty in surviving. Nonetheless, Provincials were not happy with the situation; all through the early years they provided constant reminders of the dangers of the professors overextending themselves. Father Rudolph Meyer in 1909 and Father Alexander Burrowes in 1912 gave warnings especially against what they called "distant supply," the assisting at parishes which were a considerable distance from the city. [29]

The problem was not simply one of the necessity of providing income but also the fact that such assistance given to the parishes created a dependence on the Jesuits in many cases. The Annual Letter of 1889–1890 said,

> They are practically assistants in four parishes in the city, and in two outside the city they were practically pastors for some months. They were often called to give retreats in academies and convents, as well as to prepare boys in the parishes for first Holy Communion and to give sermons and hear confessions. [30]

For many years assistance to the parishes remained an issue. In 1915 Father Burrowes on his visitation to the college suggested that "prudence, and justice to the students should govern help in the parishes on Sunday."[31]

Building a library was another matter of concern discussed in "professors' meetings." There were splendid donations to the library from many sources; Bishop Horstmann was a principle contributor. There was, however, no plan or budget to permit systematic building of library holdings. By 1898 it was suggested that at least one hundred dollars per year be set aside for the purchase of new books.[32] With tuition at forty dollars and an enrollment of 195, this was a very meager amount, especially when it is remembered that not all students were paying full tuition.

The rector and his consultors were also occupied with management of the property of the college. By the end of the "Iron Ages" the property already acquired did not provide sufficient room either for current needs or for future expansion. The houses and stores on the Lorain Avenue property extended quite far into the yard area; eventually it was necessary to clear off the shacks and barns in the rear of these buildings to enlarge a playground area.[33]

The original wooden structure that served to house the first classes eventually became a victim of the attempt to provide more play area. When the permanent college building was finished in 1891, it provided living quarters for the Jesuit Community and additional classroom space. The wooden structure then was remodeled by removing some of the partitions so that it provided space for only four rooms. Two of these rooms were used for classes, one for a student recreation room, and one for a student chapel, thus permitting the students to attend daily Mass without interfering with the schedule in St. Mary's Church.[34] By 1914 the need for more space had become acute. A new gymnasium was built fronting on Carroll Street replacing the gymnasium to which the original wooden building had been converted. The continued need for space required the disposal of the original building. It was first thought it could be moved, but practical and legal difficulties ruled out that possibility. It was finally determined to remove the original building altogether along with two barns used by the tenants in Lorain Avenue houses. An offer of one hundred fifty dollars was accepted from a salvage company for the building. According to Father Francis Betten, the original college was finally razed by a wrecking crew for one hundred eighty dollars; that was thirty dollars more than the rector had intended to pay. He recounts this with some regret, not of a sentimental variety, but rather that the salvage company got a better deal than they should have even at the higher price. It seems that the building contained far more lumber than anyone had supposed.[35]

SPECIALIZATION UNDERMINES THE CLASSICAL COURSE

No account of the faculty and administrative structure of those years would be complete without pointing out that the concept of the seven-year course leading to the bachelor's degree usually assumed the assignment of faculty to a particular year of study. There was no departmentalization of subject matter. A professor of a particular year was supposed to teach whatever subject matter that year required.

This extensive personal contact of the professor with his class was of paramount importance. The efforts of the Jesuits were directed not to the subject matter but to the student,

> not to the class, not even to the college. St. Ignatius wished the educational process of his Society to reach down to every soul and fiber of the man; he emphasized the development of Christian manhood, rather than the formation of scientists and scholars. Jesuit education is intended to leave a definite impress on the youth; to give him a definite philosophy of life, to prepare him as far as possible to be a forceful leader of Catholic thought and action.[36]

In the Jesuit scheme of things the educational process was a totality; there was no intention of departing from that principle. Nevertheless for the Jesuits to have ignored the changing American educational structure would have been dangerous; in the long run specialization in subject matter and the distinction between secondary and higher education would have to be made. Adjustment to modern demands was especially difficult when the quality of the students produced by the traditional system was considered. Father Patrick Quigley, a diocesan priest commenting on the products of the classical course, said, "My experience for 20 years at St. Mary's seminary convinced me that students from Jesuit colleges as a rule excelled others in many things."[37]

At St. Ignatius College the year 1893 represents the transition from the earlier pattern to the departmental one; up to that time faculty assignments were professor of Poetry representing that particular year of study, or professor of Rhetoric or Humanities and so on. Other duties might also be assigned such as director of the Literary Society or Debating Society. It is true that some priests were assigned as professors of German, mathematics, and chemistry but these were not understood in the departmental sense. Even Father George J. Pickel, who is best known as a professor of chemistry in later years, first came in 1892 as professor of humanities, German, and shorthand; in addition he was director of the Literary Society.

Under the administration of Father Joseph LeHalle (1893–1897), the first steps in the change toward departmentalization were taken. The course of study was more strictly graded and standardized. A year in philosophy covering logic, epistemology, metaphysics, cosmology, and ethics was added; the first bachelor of arts degrees were granted in 1894 to Joseph Wennemann and Robert F. Fischer. In 1902 under the presidency of Father John L. Zahm (1902–1906), the high school department, although remaining in the same building, was administratively separated from the college department and a department of philosophy was added. With the growth of specialization and the establishment of the department of philosophy, departmentalization of subject matter would eventually work its way into the total structure. With the separation from the high school or Academic Department in 1902, the *Catalogue* of 1902–1903 listed the new organization of the college program. The freshman year now included not only the Latin and Greek but also English, mathematics, and history. The sophomore year included Latin, Greek, natural philosophy, chemistry, English, mathematics, and general physics. The junior year included Latin, Greek, English and American literatures, mathematics, chemistry, and history. The senior year included mental and moral philosophy, and mathematics, with choices of astronomy, political economy, biology, and aesthetics. If the student continued for another, or postgraduate, year the course of study was a continuation of ethics and political economy. In all years except the senior and postgraduate year there was a required course called "Evidences of Religion." Faculty listings were beginning to reflect specialization of subject matter and electives were beginning to edge their way further into the curriculum. The 1904–1905 *Catalogue* listed the course offerings by subject matter area rather than by the year of study such as was the practice under the traditional curriculum.

Father Frederick Odenbach, who joined the faculty in 1893, was perhaps the best early example of specialization. Even he had other duties besides instruction in physics and geography; he was prefect of discipline as well as professor of religious instruction. Not until 1910 was there more explicit recognition of a departmental structure. The *Catalogue* of that year spoke of "the departments of Philosophy, Language, Literature, History, Science, and Mathematics" as constituting the college course of four years.[38]

One subject matter area that presented a problem for departmentalization was that of instruction in religion. Since in the classical course religion was present without its being listed as an additional requirement, the problem was how to provide the newer nonclassical programs with an integrating religious component.[39] Teachers of a required course called "Evidences of Religion" were not necessarily specialists in the same way those in the sciences and other branches were; any ordained priest was presumed to be capable of teaching religion since it was viewed as a pastoral rather than academic matter. The requirement later came to be listed, but as late as 1922 there was no such department as Religion. An early solution of the problem can be seen in the "Memorial" of the Provincial, Father Rudolph Meyer, in 1908. He recommended strongly that one of the Fathers should give the weekly instruction to the students on a regular basis. He suggested that is should be the same Father in all instructions so that he could "act as a spiritual Father to them."[40] This office was in addition to the office of chaplain which had been instituted in 1902, with the appointment of Father Henry Boehmer who had been at the Jesuit parish of St. Ann in Buffalo.

In 1909 there was a significant change in the structure of the faculty. In that year the president relinquished a role he had held from the beginning of the college, that of prefect of studies and discipline. A vice-president, Father Louis Kellinger, was appointed to fill that role while Father Pickel remained as president and also as professor of chemistry and biology. In 1918 there was another change when Father Thomas J. Smith, who had been vice-president and prefect of studies and discipline, became dean of faculty. Until the late 1950s and early 1960s even though there were directors of departments, control of the department was in the hands of the dean, the lineal descendant of the prefect of studies and discipline.

ACADEMIC STANDARDS AND DISCIPLINE

Father LeHalle had the reputation of a scholar of considerable distinction, but he was also a disciplinarian, as the students soon discovered.

> But no one who knew him intimately would ever dream that under that stern exterior was hidden a most tender heart. He was a great disciplinarian as well as an efficient teacher and thus it came to pass that above all the younger students stood in mortal dread of the priest whose bushy eyebrows, blue spectacles, tall and majestic figure, and professional tone gave him the appearance of a severe and heartless man. But upon nearer acquaintance one discovered that a great part of this sternness was merely assumed to guard the wearer against overgreat mildness. That strong man actually had to make great efforts to check the flow of tears that would rise unbidden at the sight of suffering or other scenes apt to move the heart.[41]

During Father LeHalle's tenure the meteorological observatory was established but his chief concerns dealt with the upgrading of the program of studies and as one might expect, with disciplinary regulations. Urged to do so by Father Theodore Van Rossum, then Superior of the Buffalo Mission, Father LeHalle began immediately to demand a stricter grading of the classes so that passing to a higher class was more demanding.[42] Students were not to be promoted to the next year without passing all subjects of the previous year. Also, at Father Van Rossum's urging, there was to be an oral

Above left, Joseph P. Le Halle, S.J., 1892–97, President, St. Ignatius College, 1893–97; *right,* John Zahm, S.J., 1890–1906, President, St. Ignatius College, 1902–6; *Bottom,* Frederick Odenbach, S.J., 1893–1933

examination at the end of the classical course, at least in Latin and Greek; a written examination would be sufficient for the other subjects.[43]

For a number of years many students did not persevere to the end of the course. To keep up the enrollment many applicants were needed. Since applicants were sometimes admitted from the eighth grade and sometimes even from the sixth, disciplinary problems in the early years came from a group of students whose median age was probably about sixteen. Even when the administration of the college and high school programs was separated in 1902, disciplinary problems did not change much since both levels used the same building, the high school on the first two floors and the college on the upper three floors. The grounds were common property. Regulations as published in the *Catalogue* were simple enough; they concerned chiefly politeness and dress. The rules of politeness were considered almost as important as moral training and indeed were not to be considered out of the context of moral training:

> Whatever, therefore, is contrary to good breeding is out of place in College. Consequently, no boisterous conduct or rough play is tolerated on the premises, and silence is strictly enjoined in the class-rooms, and in the corridors or stairways leading thereto. Any ungentlemanly conduct among the students themselves, any disrespect or insubordination to a professor or officer of the college, shall be visited with dismissal, should the gravity of the offense require such a penalty. For faults committed outside the premises, the officers of the college are by no means responsible; should, however any serious charges be sufficiently proved, the guilty will be punished according to the gravity of the offense.[44]

So far as dress was concerned everyone was expected to be "clean and neat in person and apparel."[45]

How often the regulations had to be enforced with penalties the record does not reveal. According to the *Catalogue*, "The rules are enforced with firmness, and punishment is resorted to only when motives of honor, self-respect and religion fail."[46] What this meant in practice is hard to say but there is some evidence that an occasional pat on the back, low enough and hard enough, was administered. Father Van Rossum, in his visitation in 1897, repeated the admonition of the 1891 "Memorial" of Father Rathgeb to the effect that corporal punishment should not be administered without the special permission of the rector.[47]

Although corporal punishment had already been abolished in the Cleveland Public Schools in 1886 and strict orders against it were issued again in 1892,[48] the disciplinary regulations in the *Catalogue* in 1915 did not reflect any changes at St. Ignatius College. After 1915, the particular section dealing with such disciplinary regulations disappeared from the *Catalogue* and in its place were detailed academic admission requirements.

STUDENT ACTIVITIES

Two activities, drama and music, were particularly characteristic of the early years. Somewhat later, literary societies and debating activities were added to the list of student activities. Occasions for most such activities were the distribution of academic awards, oratorical contests, special holidays such as Washington's birthday, visitation of the Provincial and other dignitaries, special concerts, and the annual commencement exercises. Many of these affairs were held in the hall on St. Mary's Church property, others in the larger downtown halls such as the Lyceum and the Cleveland Theatre. Bishop Gilmour occasionally attended these events; when he was unable to attend, he was often represented by Father Thomas Thorpe, pastor of the Cathedral, or Monsignor Felix Boff.

The college orchestra was a main feature on many of these occasions, especially the awards exercises at the end of the school year. Father Godfrey J. Schulte, who became the third president in 1897, had been on the faculty since 1889 and on the faculty of Canisius College prior to that. He organized a college orchestra during the presidency of Father Knappmeyer and later when he became president used the opportunity to put his own talents to work by placing special emphasis on music.[49] In this he was ably assisted by two local musicians and friends, Professor Johannes Wolfram and Dr. M. Francisci, who undertook the task of developing the orchestra and remained for years as its director. Vocal music and a string quartet were major features of the music program. By 1915 the music department had acquired *Catalogue* status with emphasis on vocal and instrumental music. "Knowing the high value of music as an educational factor the college encourages the students in their musical effort."[50] In 1915 the college orchestra was discontinued temporarily until the arrival of Father Victor Winter who was assigned to continue its development.

Dramatic presentations, originally part of the awards exercises, were later put on independently and drew good-sized audiences. These presentations were often supplemented by oratorical contests and literary entertainments which combined music and poetry readings. Regularly scheduled concerts provided a full and active year for the students. There was a maximum effort to involve as many students as possible in these presentations. Among the names of the students who participated in these activities can be found many who later acquired prominence in law, medicine, and politics on the Cleveland scene as well as a number who became bishops, including Hubert LeBlond, James A. McFadden, and Joseph Koudelka, and many of seminary faculty.

The student activity with the longest continuity at St. Ignatius College was debating. The Jogues Debating Society put on the first public debate 1 February 1899 in honor of Bishop Ignatius Horstmann's feast day. The debate was on the topic "Resolved: That Imperialism be endorsed by the American people." James A. McFadden, later an auxilary bishop of Cleveland and bishop of Youngstown, and James McDonough, later rector of the diocesan seminary, were on the affirmative side.[51] The public debate became an annual affair during Bishop Horstmann's episcopacy, with timely topics selected for each occasion; among them were such subjects as arbitration, trade unions, women's suffrage, socialism, municipal ownership, initiative and referendum, restricting immigration, and limitation of the terms of the U.S. presidency. In order to provide better opportunity for more students to participate, the Jogues Debating Society soon became two separate debating societies under different moderators. The Senior Debating Society met weekly to "acquire skill in the art of speaking; and to read original essays and discuss debate subjects." The Junior Debating Society met every two weeks to "acquire ease and facility in composition and argumentative speaking"[52]

There was as yet no debating with students of other colleges. There was, however, intercollegiate competition in another area. The Jesuit Colleges of the Missouri Province competed each year in English and Latin contests. In the English contest a topic was chosen for all students of the Province to write on. The Latin contest combined translation with good English. In the 1914 contests St. Ignatius College won fourth and fifth place in the English and second, fifth, and eighth in the Latin. Public elocution contests also provided additional opportunities for student competition. These were held in the Public Library auditorium near the college.

As more students tended to remain longer and reach the philosophy course it was possible to hold public disputations on subjects in philosophy. Beginning in 1912, there were usually two disputations held each year. Each program consisted of two essays and two discussions.[53]

The student program of activities was concerned not only with the intellectual but also with the spiritual. The Sodalities of the Blessed Virgin were traditional in Jesuit colleges since the sixteenth century. The sodalities were to act as a kind of spiritual leaven and "to foster in the students an earnest religious spirit, and especially a tender devotion to the Mother of God."[54] There was one sodality for senior students and another for junior students. The purpose was "to put into practice the law of universal charity by mutual prayer for the intentions of all Associates."[55] It was customary for students to render service in the local charitable institutions and also in the local prison.

ENROLLMENT PROBLEMS

Recruiting students was not an easy matter; the Jesuits often blamed the lack of appreciation of higher education among Catholics as the principal reason for the difficulty.

> Out here in the West we may be glad if Catholic young men devote seven years to higher studies besides the time devoted strictly to professional studies, all the more so as the Catholics of Cleveland do not yet appreciate as they ought the advantages of a higher education.[56]

It may have been lack of appreciation for higher education, but it was also the difficulty the German Jesuits had in learning English that contributed to the problem of getting enough students to enroll and finish the course. It is also true that many of the students who did not continue their studies left primarily in order to support their families. Tuition of forty dollars a year, from 1886 to 1903, may not seem very much by today's standards but it was beyond the reach of many of that day, and students did not differ from those of today in the need for financial assistance. The generous tuition discounts noted on each student listed in the "Register of Students" still were not sufficient in many cases to help the student continue his studies. Scholarships, unofficially, had been available from the beginning; it was common practice to remit part or even all of the tuition of a student who was judged worthy. But the problem of the college meeting its expenses was constantly complicated by this practice.

There were no formal scholarships until Father Eugene M. O'Callaghan, pastor of St. Colman's parish, gave one in 1895 and added another in 1896 for poor boys studying for the priesthood. In 1896 three more temporary scholarships were added, given by Monsignor T. P. Thorpe, pastor of the Cathedral, Father T. Carroll, and Senator Marc A. Hanna. In 1889, an anonymous benefactor established five scholarships to be known as the St. Aloysius Scholarship.

Tuition costs rose to sixty dollars a year by 1915, in addition to an entrance fee of five dollars, a library fee of one dollar, and a laboratory fee of ten dollars for those taking physics, chemistry, or biology. There was also a diploma fee of five dollars. Student expenses were to remain at these levels through 1918 with the exception of a two-dollar gymnasium fee after 1915. By 1915 the amount of $1,250 was considered the necessary investment for a full scholarship. There were seventeen such scholarships in effect at that time, thirteen donated by diocesan clergy, the others donated by individual benefactors. Some scholarships of lesser value and competitive scholarships for the high school students only also were available.

In spite of financial assistance, students continued to leave before finishing their studies for a variety of reasons which were duly noted in the "Student Register." In a number of instances the father of the family had lost his job and the son had to go to work. In some cases widows simply could not afford to continue sending their sons to school; in others the son left school to assist in the family-owned business. Ill health was another major reason for leaving. Other students experienced academic difficulty due to infrequent attendance, lack of interest in study, and discouragement at inability to keep up with the pace. Some students, the Register noted, were "not worth wasting time on" and one student was dismissed because he was "almost an idiot." There were those who left without giving any reason and others for whom a simple "*Deo Gratias*" after their name sufficed. A few were listed as "thoroughly bad" and an occasional one was "not to be looked after if he stays away."[57] Even by modern standards the list of reasons is fairly representative.

Father General Anderledy took a positive attitude toward the problem of student retention. When Father Neustich made a report early in 1887 on the affairs of the college he received praise from Father General on the quality of the students who were retained. As for those who left for one reason or another, it was to be hoped that they were somehow better for having been exposed to religious influence.[58]

Because recruiting never quite kept pace with attrition, enrollment increases were sporadic. In 1895 there was a combined college and high school enrollment of 228. It rose to 292 in 1907 and then dropped to 209 in 1909, the last year for keeping combined enrollment figures. College enrollment was listed as 58 in 1910, and at 97 in 1916. Enrollment after World War I more than doubled in a relatively short time. The value of a college education was beginning to be appreciated.

By 1903 the number of graduates and former students was large enough to warrant the establishment of an alumni association. Eighty-five graduates had received certificates or diplomas in the classical course; of that number four had received the bachelor's degree and one a master's degree. Although Father Schulte had discontinued the commercial course in 1897, sixty-three students had received certificates in that course. The list of alumni officers was headed by the president, Father Thomas C. O'Reilly, who later became Bishop of Scranton. Two vice-presidents, a secretary, treasurer, historian, chaplain, and an executive committee of three rounded out the list. Among these officers were four clergy, including the president, one medical doctor, and four attorneys.

Not all student activity was devoted to intellectual pursuits even in the "Iron Ages." Physical exercise was recognized as not only appropriate but also necessary although for quite some time there was no formal exercise program. Competitive games were confined to interclass struggles; according to one graduate of those early years, "students and faculty constantly waged football war on campus."[59] A makeshift gymnasium in the former college building together with a lack of sufficient yard space and facilities as well as the menacing condition of the gravel and cinder yard combined to discourage any extensive formal athletic activities on the grounds.

The first evidence of any organized attempts to go beyond informal activities was in 1892, when in celebration of "Columbus Year" the college took part in a city-wide parade of all local organizations and institutions. In order to make a good showing in the college's first public appearance, the "students were trained for several days in marching by an expert."[60] According to Father Haggeney, "the students were drilled to the minute for that occasion and received the greatest applause for the wonderful execution they exhibited going through the various formations of military drill."[61] The report to Rome for that year said much the same thing, observing that, "during the entire parade, our group so conducted themselves among all the groups, that the public press, and this generally hostile, conceded them first place."[62] Wishing to compete academically also, the college, at the request of Bishop Horstmann, sent samples of the students' work in the classroom to Chicago and entered them in a Columbian year competition which was intended to illustrate the status of education in America. St. Ignatius's entries won four gold medals, one each in German, French, English, and Latin and Greek. Six judges rated the entries "carefully prepared and showing excellence."[63]

Not until 1904, when Father John B. Theis formed an athletic association known as the "Loyola Club," was there a serious attempt at organized sports. Father Theis was particularly interested in baseball as well as track and field events. A very large number of students responded to the call of Father Theis. The feeling was that up to now St. Ignatius College had furnished a good number of athletes to some of the big colleges and universities and that on its own it could be "relied upon to do some noteworthy work in the line of athletics in the future."[64]

A few years later, in 1907, the *Plain Dealer* carried an article noting

"Sport is being boosted at St. Ignatius College. An effort will be made to turn out athletic teams that will be able to compete with any college in the country."[65] The article was inspired by the work of Father J. O. Keller, who had made such an announcement at the Annual Field Day of the college. This field day had been held annually since 1904 as an effort to bring alumni, students, and friends together for food, games, and the awarding of prizes. Father Keller received an extensive write-up in the *Plain Dealer* as a man who was "an enthusiast in his work at the college" and who "believed that every student should be an athlete." He was praised for having "injected 'ginger' enough into the students at the college so that this has been the most successful year in the history of the institution."[66] Prospects for the future seemed bright because, "to keep the work going Father Keller himself jumps into the games and incites a desire on the part of the students to become strong, robust, healthy men. His work, clergymen say, is an innovation in his line."[67]

Class teams were formed in baseball and in track and field events, and awards were given at the end of the year to winning teams. The first evidence of competition with teams from other institutions and organizations appeared in 1904, when a new game called "roko" caught on in the area. There is very little information about the game but its object seems to have been to put a tethered ball into a suspended net. There could be as few as three players on a team and twenty points was the winning score. St. Ignatius not only played such other teams as University School but also local teams of various fraternal and industrial organizations. So successful was the St. Ignatius College team that in 1905, it claimed the division championship of Ohio.[68]

In 1907 over one hundred students, about a third of the student body, came out for track. The services of a former Lincoln High School coach, Clayton Townes, were secured and he expressed surprise at the "enthusiasm displayed by the men I am working with" and also the "huge store of the best sort of athletic apparatus" that was at his command.[69] Basketball was begun in 1905 on an interclass basis and eventually the teams played outside competition on a high school level although Baldwin and Oberlin colleges were also scheduled. Not until after the new gymnasium was completed in 1914 did the sport really develop. Baseball was by far the most popular sport of the early days. Interclass games were particularly popular; outside competition in the beginning was basically on the high school level. Baseball remained a strong sport until after World War I when football replaced it.

There was strong student sentiment for football in the early 1900s, but the faculty would not allow students to participate in what they considered a rough game. Strangely, the high school was finally allowed to play football while the college was permitted to play soccer, apparently on the assumption that soccer was not a rough sport. A class soccer league was formed in the fall of 1907 with the hope that a college team could be formed later. "Those who feared that socker [*sic*] would prove too tame and ladylike were sadly disappointed. Many of the scrimmages closely resembled a Rugby mixup, while three men were slightly injured in yesterday's battle."[70] With the assistance of Richard Milan, who had played the game in Ireland, and later a Mr. Wilson of the Cleveland Soccer League who changed to the English style, soccer became the most popular sport at St. Ignatius College. The hope that other schools in the same area would take up soccer was soon realized and although the preference still seemed to be for rugby football, the students were enthusiastic in their support of soccer teams. Teams in the Cleveland Soccer League were regular opponents.

The students of the "Iron Ages," undoubtedly under tighter disciplinary restrictions than their modern counterparts, were nevertheless capable of indulging in a normal penchant for getting into trouble or expressing themselves in unusual ways. Building a snowman on the teacher's desk was the extracurricular enterprise of one class. Graffiti on unwashed windows often had a touch of the classics. A student once wrote on one of the dirty windows, "I was once translucent, I am now opaque." On the other hand students quarrelled on Lorain Avenue with sufficient intensity and frequency to warrant on one occasion an investigation carried out by detectives. This action coincided with a decision in 1915, in an effort to keep out undesirables, to put a screen around the yard and a fence along Carroll Avenue in front of the new gymnasium.[71] This fence remained until 1927 when its removal caused some regrets among the students. The *Carroll News* bemoaned its demise because "to those who have known and loved it, who have sat or spat upon it, there can be no erasing of the memory it has left. Nor time nor new activities will ever rob us of its old memories."[72]

Unfortunately not many records of student escapades or achievements remain from the "Iron Ages." Occasionally one runs across such things as the mustache fad that hit the student body in 1915. A "Hirsute" club was formed; "a hispidulous upper lip being the only qualification necessary to join."[73] On the academic side, Justin W. Conkey, a graduate of 1908, took the Oxford examination given at Ohio State University and was one of four to qualify for a Rhodes Scholarship.

Sometimes it was a faculty member who made the news. Father Frederick Hillig, teaching chemistry in 1891, had a glass tube explode during a demonstration. Five of the students were close enough to be hit with flying glass, but all escaped serious injury. Grateful that the students had been spared their eyesight and serious injury, the students and faculty convened in the chapel the next day to sing a "*Te Deum*" and offer "special thanks to God for his protection in such an incident."[74]

Hubert Borling (Borlinghausen), who attended St. Ignatius College 1894–1898, was still living at the time of this writing. He was 104 years old at the time the author interviewed him but quite able to attest to the rigors of the "Iron Ages." He remembered the rigorous discipline of the German Jesuits against whom his only complaint was that they were not ecumenical. He recalled that Father Neustich not only had difficulty with English but that his German was "not very good." The rigid discipline of those years impressed him as did the willingness of the Jesuit teachers to give time after class hours to those students who wished extra help. His recollections of Bishop Gilmour were not as flattering as those of Bishop Horstmann.[75]

SOME JESUITS OF THE "IRON AGES"

The German Jesuits' efforts to build up the college cannot be minimized, but it was the American- and English-born Jesuits who provided the real impetus for forward movement. It will be recalled that one of the reasons for delay in opening the college was the lack of English-speaking Jesuits. Father Lessmann had promised Bishop Gilmour that this deficiency would be remedied; and so a beginning was made as early as 1887 with the assignment of Patrick Behan, a scholastic from Stonyhurst in England, to St. Ignatius. In 1890 another Englishman, James A. Rockliff, a native of Liverpool, England, also educated at Stonyhurst and a classmate of Sir Arthur Conan Doyle of Sherlock Holmes fame, was assigned to St. Ignatius. He attended the Jesuit college of Pildkirch, Germany, and joined the Jesuits in 1872, just in time to go into exile with other German Province Jesuits. After his studies he came to Buffalo in 1890 to be immediately assigned to Cleveland, where he remained until 1893, when he was reassigned to Canisius College. Urgent petitions from both students and faculty at St. Ignatius College brought about his return to Cleveland a year later, where he remained for two-and-a-half years until he was made president of Canisius College in 1897. In 1898 he became Superior of the Buffalo Mission and remained in that office until 1906, the year before its dissolution. He went on to become Superior of the new Japanese Mission in Tokyo, where he played a part in the founding of Sophia University. In 1910 he returned to the United States to become the Socius of the Provincial of the California Province.

Father Rockliff was a remarkable Jesuit. He came to St. Ignatius College at a time when, after four years of existence, it was not at all certain that the college would not close as had its predecessors in Cleveland. In Sep-

Above left, Godfrey Schulte, S.J., 1891–1902, President, St. Ignatius College, 1897–1902; *right,* James Rockliff, S.J., 1890–93, 1894–95; *Bottom,* Francis J. Haggeney, S.J., 1890–93, 1894–95, 1900–1927

tember 1891 the enrollment was 120 at the opening of class; within a month the enrollment rose to 158 largely because of the recruiting efforts of Father Rockliff. Twenty-three of the new students were from the Cathedral parish where Father Rockliff was in effect an assistant pastor.[76] He was an eloquent preacher, making friends easily, and he was chiefly responsible for bringing some stability to the college. Despite the transportation problem he managed to get an increased number of East Side students to attend, and laid the foundations for a later appeal for an East Side school.[77] Perhaps his excellent command of English had something to do with his success.

As Prefect of Discipline, Father Rockliff is remembered for carrying a

> little bell, with a little leather strap for a handle, that clanged with muffled protest in his pocket at every step he took; and when he unpocketed it, either to sound an armistice when vociferous youngsters protested an umpire [decision], or for cessation of play at the end of recess, shouts would die down and baseballs cease to fly.[78]

Since Father Rockliff was a born athlete he quickly endeared himself to the students:

> None could kick a football as high as or as far as he, none more adept at catching a baseball when 'shied' at him or at dodging the baseballs that flew around in all directions. It did not hurt either his authority or his shins to be in the midst of a melee at football as it was played in those days . . . he had played the game in England as a boy and his legs already looked like a hacksaw from kicks received in football matches.[79]

Father Rockliff was a "kind and sympathetic father to all the boys without exception, he was a veritable big brother to his charges . . . they brought their confidences to him, they found a priest who understood and sympathized perfectly" with them.[80] For a Jesuit who served at St. Ignatius a little less than four years he left a remarkable impression on the students, faculty, and people of Cleveland. The *Catholic Universe*, which was generally not particularly cognizant of activities at St. Ignatius College in those days, saw fit to mention his second transfer to Canisius College, noting that he had "made a host of friends throughout the city"; it praised his work in the parishes as well as at the school, his preaching and hearing confessions at the Cathedral, missions at St. Malachi's, and work at St. Patrick's parish.[81]

There were two outstanding American-born Jesuits who, although part of the "Iron Ages," were also forward-looking men who saw in the increasing interest in science a chance to capitalize on that interest. Father Freder-

Left, Frederick Odenbach, S.J., 1893–1933, on the University Heights Campus before its completion; *Right,* Odenbach and the searchlight

Aloisius Pfeil, S.J., 1896–99, 1905–6   John B. Theis, S.J., 1903–8

ick Odenbach, although a biologist, chose meteorology and seismology as his chief interests; Father George Pickel chose chemistry and had a strong side-interest in horticulture. Born in Rochester, New York, in 1857, Father Odenbach had graduated from Canisius College in 1881, and came to St. Ignatius in 1893 after completing his training as a Jesuit. His arrival was noted in the *Catholic Universe* where it was remembered that although he had been in the city only a few days, he had "made himself pretty well acquainted with the city and . . . expressed some ideas which, if carried out, will surely mean progress and growth for the institution he represents."[82] Father Odenbach was "an active man, slightly built, clear eyed, straight shouldered, and a rare good fellow."[83] Almost immediately after his arrival he set to work building a meteorological observatory on the fifth floor of the college building. A room about twenty by fifteen feet served as the observatory proper; a dark room for photographic developing, a battery room for the power source, and two smaller rooms for instruments, maps, and necessary tools made up the total complex. In the *Catalogue* of 1895–1896, a full report on the years's meteorological activity was given; similar reports continued to be a part of the *Catalogues* through 1910.

One very visible aspect of the Observatory was the array of weather flags, like those used by the United States Weather Bureau, flying from the roof of the college as weather signals. This aspect of the college's visibility was worthy of comment in the Annual Letter to Rome for the year 1895–1896:

> What most attracts the eyes of men to this seat of learning are the flags flying from the roof of the college, the rotating instruments and other apparatus which tell the changes of weather, speed and direction of the wind, and amount of rain.[84]

Father Odenbach is probably best known as a seismologist as was evident when he was introduced to Charles Brush, the Cleveland inventor, who is said to have remarked, "So you're the little man who makes earthquakes."[85] It was Father Odenbach's good fortune to live to see the many developments in science that came after World War I; wireless telegraphy was of particular interest to him. When the new buildings in University Heights were built he had great plans for them. When construction stopped in 1931, he moved into the tower of the unfinished buildings for a while with his dog, Hector, and two rifles probably for hunting pheasants which were numerous in the area. With a heater in the center of the room, on the top floor of the tower which he planned to use as an observatory, and with food stored on improvised shelving together with his instruments, he became a familiar figure in the neighborhood until shortly before his death in 1933.[86]

Father George J. Pickel was born in St. Louis, Missouri in 1867, graduated from Sacred Heart College (Campion) in Prairie du Chien, Wisconsin in 1888, and entered the Society of Jesus in the same year. He was first assigned to St. Ignatius College in 1892. Father Pickel, as was customary for the Jesuits of the Buffalo Mission, completed his studies in the Society at Valkenburg, Holland. He then received special studies in chemistry and physics at the University of Goettingen. He returned to St. Ignatius College in 1904, and became rector-president in 1906; his appointment to that post at the age of thirty-seven illustrates the need for American-born Jesuits in the Buffalo Mission. Illness forced him from office in 1910. Between 1911 and 1927 he taught at Campion College at Prairie du Chien, Wisconsin, at Spring Hill College in Mobile, Alabama, returning to St. Ignatius College in 1927, where he remained until his death in 1948. In 1937 he became acting president of John Carroll University following the departure of Father William Magee. Perhaps even more than Fathers Rockliffe and Odenbach he was able to influence the development of John Carroll University because of his abilities, vision, and many years of service to the institution. It was he who accomplished the first move to an East Side location in 1907, and played a major role in the design of the original science buildings on the Heights.

Father Pickel's progressiveness was illustrated when, in 1910, he thought he had an opportunity to attach a medical school to St. Ignatius College. The Cleveland College of Physicians and Surgeons, associated with Ohio Wesleyan University for over a half century, was in the process of being absorbed by Western Reserve University as part of a national effort to reduce the number of smaller medical schools. A committee from the College of Physicians and Surgeons approached Father Pickel in an attempt to get him to hold up the consummation of the merger, and to consider joining the college to St. Ignatius. Father Pickel, although interested, did not feel justified in pursuing the matter with his Provincial, saying,

> I could give no assurance of being able to take the proposition up definitely. However, I interviewed the bishop [John P. Farrelly, who had succeeded Bishop Horstmann in 1909] as to his position in the matter. He seemed to think our Superior, especially Father General would object to taking over a non-Catholic faculty that would probably be hard to control its teaching, [*sic*] etc. He said he would consult his consultors who were to meet soon. I have heard nothing from him since.[87]

There is no evidence that Bishop Farrelly ever formally brought the matter before his consultors. Father Pickel also needed to consult the Provincial on the taking over of the faculty before he could consider any further action. The need for a speedy decision, if the project was to be completed in time for the fall of 1910, prevented prolonged discussions. It was Father Pickel's understanding from his contacts with the doctors that the opportunity was there and so were the funds.[88] The acceptance by the College of Physicians and Surgeons of the Western Reserve offer precluded any further action.[89]

Prior to the request of the College of Physicians and Surgeons there had been an incident which probably encouraged Father Pickel to wish that St. Ignatius did have a medical school. Three graduates of St. Ignatius College had applied to the medical school of St. Louis University and had been accepted. Shortly thereafter Father Pickel discovered that the three students were going to enroll in the Western Reserve medical school. On looking into the matter and, with letters supplied by the students in question, Father Pickel learned that Western Reserve authorities had convinced the students that the St. Louis medical school was not a particularly good one. Father Pickel complained to the Provincial, Father Alexander Burrowes, that "the local Medical College has succeeded in getting all three graduates for itself. They had contemplated going to St. Louis University. We ought to protect ourselves against their discrimination."[90]

Quite apart from his work as a professor of chemistry or as president, Father Pickel was proud to be able to provide the English translation of a German text explaining the discovery in 1900 of the originals of two maps of the world as understood by cartographers in the early 1500s. One map of the world was produced in 1507, the other, known as the Carta Marina, in 1516. Both had been lost for centuries and known only through inaccurate copies and some literary references. They were discovered quite by accident by Father Joseph Fischer, a member of the Society of Jesus, while looking through the library in the castle of Prince Waldburg-Wolfegg. The maps were known to both Martin Waldseemuller and George Mercator. Father Pickel treasured his copies of the text and the maps. Shortly before he died he gave them to a former student whom he never forgave for pursuing the study of history rather than chemistry.

Several names could be added to the list of those Jesuits who helped shape the early days. At least three more can hardly be omitted: Father Francis J. Haggeney, who remained on the college faculty until 1926, as professor of philosophy and secretary of the Board of Trustees; Father Francis Betten, who joined the faculty in 1910, and whose textbooks in European history were used in schools throughout the country; and Father James A. Kleist, whose translations of scripture, the classics, and German textbooks gave him also something of a national reputation. That Father Betten joined the faculty in 1910, long after Bishop Gilmour's death, was probably fortunate for both Father Betten and the bishop. One of Father

Betten's first efforts was to form the St. Boniface Historical Society, whose purpose was "to win for the history of the German nation the place due it in English Catholic literature."[91]

Individual Jesuits could on occasion run afoul of Bishop's Gilmour's good will for reasons other than just being German. One such instance provided an opportunity for Bishop Gilmour to find fault with the teaching of Father Gustavus Ruebsaat, a professor of humanities, German, and Christian doctrine, who had come to St. Ignatius College from Canisius College. The bishop, who believed in the strict enforcement of ecclesiastical discipline, had raised questions about Father Ruebsaat's teaching that a Catholic's obligation to receive Communion during the Eastertime could be fulfilled in any parish. Failure to conform to the regulation that the obligation could be fulfilled only in one's own parish could result in denial of Christian burial. Father Knappmeyer, in a four-page letter, defended Father Ruebsaat, objecting to the bishop's taking things out of context. "I do not think it fair to take out of a discussion which lasted about three quarters of an hour, some single sentences, to connect them and to omit other ones which formed an essential part of the controversy."[92] If Father Ruebsaat had said what he was accused of saying, Father Knappmeyer would not have approved. The point at issue seems to have been the fact that in the United States, a mission country until 1908, the general law of the church was somewhat relaxed unless the local bishop had otherwise indicated. In this instance Bishop Gilmour had otherwise indicated.

There were two other Jesuits of the period who show the remarkable contrast between the traditional German character of those early years and the developing new American influence: Father Anthony Guggenberger, whose *History of the Christian Era* was a basic text, and a Cleveland native, Father Aloysius Pfeil, whose knowledge of things American served him well as Canisius's tenth president and as a member of the faculty at St. Ignatius College. Father Guggenberger, who also wrote many of the plays that were put on at both colleges, was known to have on occasion passed the snuff box around to the class to keep the students awake. He was said to have had the walls of his room covered with Latin grammar.[93]

Father Benedict Guldner was one of the Jesuits on loan to the Buffalo Mission from the New York Province. He was part of the experiment of bringing Jesuits who were reasonably fluent in English to Canisius and St. Ignatius colleges. At St. Ignatius in the 1890s, he taught English literature and debating. But the younger American Jesuits who began to come after the turn of the century were to lend a new look to the school. Jesuits like Fathers James Doyle, William Young, and Leo Vollmayer were among those whose presence marked the transition from the "Iron Ages."

The twenty-fifth anniversary of the opening of the college was an occasion to ignore, at least for a moment, the uncertainties, disappointments, and frustrations of the past while gaining some satisfaction in the college's accomplishments. The celebration opened with a Solemn Mass on 14 June 1911, with Bishop John P. Farrelly present. Father Godfrey Schulte was celebrant assisted by Father Neustich as Deacon and Father Haggeney as Sub-Deacon. Fathers Zahm and Furay were Deacons of Honor. Father James A. McFadden of the class of 1899 gave the sermon. On Thursday evening, 15 June, at the Commencement exercise in the Engineers Auditorium, twelve students were awarded degrees. On that occasion the address was given by Father Charles A. Martin of the class of 1894.

Speakers on both occasions recalled the uncertain beginnings and the accompanying hardships endured by the founding Jesuits. Enrollment problems, the speakers claimed, arose at least in part from the general lack of appreciation of the value of a higher education by the Catholic immigrants; nationality conflicts had also played their part as did competition from the growth of Catholic high schools. Inadequate means of transportation between the West Side and East Side made the appeal of the West Side school much less than it would otherwise have been. There had also been moments of tragedy. During the construction of the main building one of three workmen who fell from the fifth floor to the bottom of the elevator shaft died. Fire in St. Mary's church caused by lightning striking the steeple resulted in many anxious moments. There was also a student death by drowning during one of the summer vacations.

On the brighter side, the speakers recalled the solicitude of the early Jesuits, particularly Father William Becker, "the venerable gray haired figure" who was a friend and confidant of the students, and Father James Rockliff, who was credited with recruiting most of the East Side students. A "splendid science department" and an "artistic library," a seismological station and a body of devoted teachers, all came in for their share of praise.[94] The opening of Loyola High School on the East Side in 1907 was looked upon as the beginning of expansion to the East Side.

A student enrollment of 400 in 1910 indicated great promise. Noting that in its first quarter-century St. Ignatius College had sent 124 students on to the seminary, the speakers expressed the fear that the purpose of the college might be misunderstood. "There are many calls and various tasks in life and for all alike it is the purpose of the college to prepare her students. Her desire is to see in every avocation, in commerce, science and art, in literature and all the many professions, her graduates conspicuous."[95]

A survey in 1925 of the graduates since 1894 gave conclusive evidence that the majority of them entered the professions of medicine, law, and business. Over 70 percent entered those fields while slightly less than 18 percent entered the seminary. This survey, however, did not take into account the number of students who left St. Ignatius College after two years to enter the seminary or a religious order.[96]

Eastward Ho!

Not to be aware of the marked differences between the West Side and the East Side of Cleveland during the "Iron Ages" of St. Ignatius College is to fail to understand fully the almost constant efforts of the college to seek an East Side location. The city was in reality "two separate entities with only tenuous cultural and commercial connections and virtually no diplomatic relations."[1] The original plan of the city, which was founded in 1796, had an eastward orientation; Ontario Street was the official dividing line between east and west. The Cuyahoga River to the west of Ontario is the physical dividing line and served only to accentuate the official division. Indian claims to the west of the Cuyahoga River were not completely relinquished until 1805; subsequent rivalry between Cleveland and the developing community known as "Ohio City" to the west certainly did not ease tensions. Even after the annexation of "Ohio City" to Cleveland in 1854, the rivalry continued. Commercial contact between the two sections was hardly encouraged by inadequate float bridges, drawbridges, and viaducts. Not until the completion of the Detroit-Superior Avenue High Level Bridge in 1917, was there an efficient means of connecting the two sides of the river. Immigration, population growth, and industrialization affected the West Side and East Side differently. A transportation "system" in which the many competing lines allowed no transfers made it difficult for students from the East Side to attend St. Ignatius College. Not until 1910 under the Tayler Grant Plan were all lines consolidated and a regular fare system established.

Most important of all the differences between the two parts of the city was the growth of University Circle on the East Side near East 105th Street as the cultural center of the city. Both Case Institute of Technology and Western Reserve University located there in the 1880s just prior to the establishment of St. Ignatius College on the West Side. The Western Reserve Historical Society, Cleveland Museum of Art, the Cleveland Institute of Fine Arts, Institute of Music, University Hospitals, the Museum of Natural History, and Severance Hall were eventually to round out the group.

It is not surprising then that the Jesuit Fathers wished to be included in the area that appeared the most promising culturally and educationally. Although many sites were considered, East 105th Street, on the perimeter of the cultural center, seemed the most desirable and an affordable addition to or substitute for their West Side location. An anonymous two-page account of the founding of the college expressed the view that the Jesuits were forced to locate on the West Side in 1886, by the "chief advisor" of Bishop Gilmour, who later "used to express his regret for having forced the Fathers to build on the West Side." The advisor, Monsignor George F. Houck, later came to see that his advice "was against the best interests of the college in Cleveland."[2]

The Jesuits saw many disadvantages to the West Side location. The sons of the heavily immigrant West Side population were more likely to go to work than to college. The congregation of the German parish of St. Mary still felt considerable loyalty to their former pastor, Father Stephen Falk. Moreover, the congregation had a misconception that it was to bear the expenses of the college. There was also the popular myth that the college was only a preparatory school for the diocesan seminary and that all the courses were taught in German. The consequences of all these factors together with "a prejudice on the East Side against everything and everybody on the West Side" was that

> to be a member of the Cleveland Jesuit community meant to have to do hard work in the school during the week, work hard on Saturdays and Sundays in some church and to experience the effects of holy poverty on all sides. For the income was small, the debt incurred by purchasing the grounds in a downtown section and erecting a magnificent structure to please the bishop and people was hopelessly large and the outlook far from promising as long as the institution was confined to the West Side.[3]

"Long Looked For Agreement"

Bishop Ignatius F. Horstmann at first continued the policy of his predecessor, Bishop Gilmour, in limiting the Jesuits to the West Side of the city. Bishop Horstmann, unlike his predecessor, was a very frequent visitor to the Jesuit community and more sympathetic to the German Jesuits. Undoubtedly the Fathers talked with him about their desire for a place on the East Side as he joined them at dinner and recreation.

No direct action toward moving was made until early in 1907, less than a year before the bishop's death. Father George J. Pickel, now president of the college, called a meeting of the Board of Trustees on 7 January 1907 to discuss at length the advisability of seeking an East Side location. A majority "advocated the measure very strongly" and "empowered" Father Pickel "to investigate and open negotiations for the lease of a suitable building."[4]

On 1 July 1907 Father Pickel, in the name of the faculty, addressed a

George J. Pickel, S.J., 1892–1910,
1927–48, President, 1906–10, 1937

Ignatius F. Horstmann, Bishop of
Cleveland, 1892–1908

seven-page petition to Bishop Horstmann in which he requested permission "to open an Academic Department or High School on the East Side of the city of Cleveland." As if to forestall what might be an objection of the bishop, Father Pickel went on to disclaim seeking a college or new institution "but merely a branch of St. Ignatius College . . . to consist only of an Academic or High School department."[5] Among the reasons offered for presenting the petition was the insistence, particularly of late, by prominent Catholics who did not wish to send their sons over to the West Side.[6] Such a branch would also be a great "saving of carfare." Without such a branch the present buildings on the West Side could not handle an increased enrollment since they were already filled to capacity. The increasing demand for laboratory space was another reason for seeking a branch on the East Side; "we shall be able to offer a *scientific* course more easily to such as do not wish to pursue a strictly classical course as a preparation for technical training."[7]

The rest of the petition was devoted to a description of the course of studies at St. Ignatius: the Collegiate department of three years leading to the A. B. and an Academic department of four years which was "the equivalent of (and in many respects superior to) the regular Public High School course of four (4) years."[8] There was emphasis on the fact that completion of the eighth grade was necessary for admission to the Academic department in order to forestall criticism that some students who had not completed the eighth grade had sometimes been accepted. Father Pickel was careful to point out that in the few cases where this had happened the parent was faced with the choice of sending a son to work after six grades, since some parochial schools did not offer seventh and eighth grade work, or to a public high school. "We do not desire these pupils at all and have for years been trying to eliminate them altogether as this grade is not within our sphere of instruction and has been kept up only as a sort of necessary evil."[9] Father Pickel also remarked that "neither is there any intention on our part to interfere with those classes in so-called parochial high schools in which those boys, who desire only a preparation for business, are taught and who aspire to nothing higher."[10] Father Pickel used the occasion to express great concern for students who intended to take up preparation for college or technical school being held back in some of the "so-called parochial high schools and are caused to lose at least one year to little or no purpose if they are not estranged from higher pursuits altogether."[11]

Father Pickel saw St. Ignatius College addressing itself to the necessity of providing "truly representative Catholic laymen in all phases of professional and public life, who are able to lead and direct others and who will be the equals of the leading non-Catholic men. That such men must be possessed of a *solid liberal education* is self-evident."[12] The rapid growth of the city was making it necessary to expend every effort to help St. Ignatius College attain this end as its "sole object."[13] In offering support as to how much the college itself was contributing toward this end, Father Pickel pointed to a comparison of the amount of tuition charged and that actually received, which showed a considerable deficit caused by reduced rates to needy students and uncollectable accounts. A deficit in 1906 of $1500.00 did not really represent the full picture. In a total enrollment of 292, some 30 students were carried free. Tuition was fifty dollars a year, a figure that did "not suffice to cover running expenses."[14]

Father Pickel concluded his appeal by requesting that in fairness to the college, "no obstacle ought to be placed in the way of its legitimate expansion and due growth" and that his proposal "be considered with that largeness of view which the question at issue merits."[15] He felt that the college deserved the cooperation of all who claimed they were interested in Catholic higher education.

Since there was no immediate reply from the bishop, Father Pickel again wrote to Bishop Horstmann on 29 July. This time he merely recalled that he had submitted a request and was anxious for an answer.[16] On the third of September, the bishop, through his chancellor, sent the following reply: "Herewith I send you the long looked for 'agreement,' signed in duplicate copies by the Rt. Rev. Bishop. Kindly sign and seal both copies and return one of them to the chancery office, to be filed here 'in perpetuam rei memoriam.' "[17]

In view of the later controversy, which was so intense that it caused the Jesuits to consider leaving Cleveland altogether, it is well to observe what the agreement did and did not include. The parties to the agreement were the Bishop of Cleveland and St. Ignatius College. The college was "empowered by" the bishop "to open a *branch school*, comprising *High School* or *Academic* courses of study, on the so-called East Side of the city of Cleveland, Ohio: that in the chapel attached to the said High School no one except the students and inmates of the same shall be allowed to attend services."[18] While the contract was specific in indicating the type of school that was to be established it was indefinite as to where on the East Side the school could be located. Whether Bishop Horstmann would require another permission for the exact location of the high school, the agreement did not say. Bishop John P. Farrelly, Horstmann's successor, was to point out later the lack of a specific location as a defect in the contract as well as to note that the contract was never validated by permission from Rome called the *Beneplacitum Apostolicum*.[19] Moreover, according to Bishop Farrelly, the agreement did not reflect the full meaning of Bishop's Horstmann's intention as expressed in his instructions for drawing up the agreement. On the bottom of Father Pickel's twenty-ninth of July letter, Bishop

Location of Loyola High School and some of the properties considered in the University Circle area. Markings by Father Pickel in 1909

Horstmann had written the instructions, "Draw up an agreement confining the Academy on the East Side, absolutely to an Academy as a preparation for collegiate courses so that in future they will not expect another College."[20] The Jesuits were not aware of these instructions, which Bishop Farrelly used to support his position during the later controversy.[21]

Whatever may have been the limitations of the agreement, no questions about it were raised at the time. In fact almost three weeks before the agreement was actually received by the Jesuits, their Board of Trustees met to hear the results of Father Pickel's negotiations with a Colonel A. J. Barnitz "for the lease of his residence and the adjacent property of his wife on Cedar Avenue and East 106th Street.[22] It was deemed a suitable locality and the terms of the lease were thought fair. Questions of the duration of the lease and the price in case of subsequent purchase were still to be determined. The Board then authorized Father Pickel and Father Francis Haggeney, its secretary, to "finish the transaction according to their judgement."[23]

It may be that prior to this meeting of the Board there was some oral assurance of a forthcoming agreement, but the Fathers wasted no time in preparing for a September opening of the new branch; the decision to open the school in September was made at the August twelfth meeting of the Board. One class would be accepted for September and one more each successive year. During the month of August, St. Ignatius College ran a quarter-page ad in the *Catholic Universe* and on 23 August part of the ad was devoted to the announcement of Loyola High School, "the new branch of St. Ignatius College located on Cedar Avenue and 106th (one block beyond Doan Street) [East 105th]. A limited number of students will be received." This ad included a picture of St. Ignatius College together with a picture of the newly leased residence that was to serve as a classroom for the new Loyola High School. The ad ran for two successive weeks.

COLLISION COURSE

The opening of Loyola High School in 1907 marked the beginning of a series of events that put the Cleveland Jesuits and the diocesan authorities on a collision course. As long as Bishop Horstmann was in office there was no problem; his successor, however, had plans which prevented the Jesuits from succeeding in any expansion of the high school on the East Side.

The new bishop was quite a different person from Bishop Horstmann. John P. Farrelly, born in Memphis, Tennessee in 1856, had been received into the Catholic Church at an early age and had spent some time in Jesuit colleges both in this country and in Belgium. He completed his studies at the American College in Rome and was ordained a priest there in 1880. He returned to the United States after a trip to the Holy Land and became pastor of a Nashville parish in 1882. In 1887 he became secretary to Bishop Denis O'Connell, rector of the American College in Rome. He was consecrated bishop in Rome in 1909 and became Bishop of Cleveland in the same year. His long experience in Rome, where he was the confidant of many American bishops, gave him extensive knowledge of ecclesiastical affairs. He was in Rome at the time of an Irish dispute over the relation of the Jesuits to episcopal authority which resulted in Pope Leo XIII issuing a Constitution in 1881 setting out rules governing that relationship. The new bishop was not only a scholar but also a man of great personal dignity who came to Cleveland with considerable background in the relation of the Jesuits to episcopal authority.

One of the new bishop's plans was to move the cathedral from its downtown location to the University Circle area on the East Side. He also planned for a "free" high school staffed by diocesan priests and supported by parish funds. Loyola High School was located within sight of the planned diocesan center and Bishop Farrelly preferred that Loyola not be there nor any other place on the East Side. The Jesuits, unaware of the bishop's plans and dissatisfied from the beginning with the location of Loyola, sought to move closer to the center of University Circle. But the Jesuit plans were broader than just a better location for Loyola; they were now planning on a college, a Jesuit residence and a parish on the East Side. They were inclined to believe they could count on the continued support of the new bishop whom they assumed would be as friendly as his predecessor. Father Theodore Van Rossum, as Superior of the Buffalo Mission, once wrote to Bishop Horstmann, "we know that the bishop of Cleveland has a heart for the religious and in his diocese we feel like children in the house of their Father."[24] The Jesuits were soon to discover that they had miscalculated and were not perceptive enough to understand soon enough that Bishop Farrelly was using every opportunity to make clear that he considered the status of Loyola uncanonical and he wished the Jesuits to concentrate their efforts entirely on the West Side.

Bishop Farrelly contended that the permission to move to the East Side was not specific as to place and, therefore, the specific location had not been approved by the diocesan consultors and by Rome. He was also aware, although he never expressed it to the Jesuits, that Bishop Horstmann's instruction for drawing up the agreement of 1907 was a limiting one that precluded a residence, public chapel, and a college on the East Side. As to what Bishop Horstmann might have done at a later date, had he lived, there is one possible clue; it supports Bishop Farrelly's contention that the bishop's consultors' approval was needed. When the Jesuits wished to purchase property in Parma in 1897 for a Novitiate, they were not certain at first whether or not it would be a permanent location. When Father Van Rossum asked permission of Bishop Horstmann for a temporary location there, the bishop replied that "to have your novitiate temporarily at Brooklyn has my hearty approval. I thought you wished to locate it there permanently, and then it would be necessary to bring it before my consultors, was my first thought."[25] The bishop then added some fatherly advice on the wisdom of purchasing the property as soon as possible. That Loyola was located temporarily on its East Side site and that any move would have to go before diocesan consultors for approval was precisely Bishop Farrelly's point. Since lease on the Loyola property was to expire in 1916 at the same time the diocesan administration was contemplating the move of the cathedral and the establishment of a high school, conflict was inevitable. From the beginning of Father William B. Sommerhauser's term as president of St. Ignatius College in 1915 until the death of Bishop Farrelly in 1921, relations between the diocese and the Jesuits were strained to the breaking point in what Father Sommerhauser referred to as "this Cleveland Embroglio [*sic*]."[26]

"OUR BURNING QUESTION"

Shortly before Bishop Farrelly came to Cleveland, the Board of Trustees of St. Ignatius College met in order to make plans to secure a better site for Loyola High School. The Board listened to Father Pickel and to the principal of Loyola High School, Father Valentine J. Hormes, describe the benefits of securing a new piece of property on Euclid Avenue near the eastern end of University Circle. It was agreed that Father Pickel should make inquiry,[27] but nothing more came of the matter. This search for a new location for the high school after the opening of the new academy was not just an idle attempt to look around to see if there were any better properties; it was part of a long-entertained desire to move as close as possible to the University Circle area. The lease rather than the purchase of the Loyola site was one indication that the Jesuits were thinking of such a property search. Even Bishop Farrelly sensed this and expressed the view that, when the Jesuits couldn't get exactly what they wanted from Bishop Horstmann, a permanent location on the East Side, "they resolved to take what they could get, regretted their failure to get more, and planned to proceed piano, piano."[28]

After the failure of anything to develop from the inquiry into the Euclid Avenue property it did not take long to produce another prospective site to which much more serious attention was given. At a meeting of the Board of Trustees of the college in January 1909 Father Pickel, who must have been keeping a keen eye on real estate news in the local papers, reported on the availability of a thirteen-acre piece of property east of University Circle and warned that there was danger in delaying a decision to purchase the plot.[29] The Board voted, "after much discussion," to take out a thirty-day option at the cost of $500.[30] The property was located in East Cleveland on Euclid Heights Boulevard about one mile beyond the city limits, then at East 115th Street; the price was $5,000 per acre.[31] Not all of Father Pickel's consultors were willing to go so far out to find a "suitable location." Father Neustich, who had returned as treasurer in 1906, was of the opinion that the price was too high; because the entire property had to be purchased, and because "there are only a few houses" in the area, and "they say the nobler part of the City will never move that way," he felt the project should be dropped.[32] Father Neustich preferred "to buy a smaller plot within the City line where there are people living."[33] He was convinced that since there was permission for a high school only on the East Side and, since he considered St. Ignatius College "large enough" for Cleveland, property within the city limits would be adequate.[34]

Father Neustich understood that "our burning question is the purchase of property for our High School on the East Side,"[35] but some of the Fathers were also seeking to establish a boarding school on the East Side. If a boarding school and college were to be established, then Father Neustich was inclined to agree that the property should be beyond the city limits. "Yet even in this case I should not pay a price that was too high in itself and too high for me."[36] Father Neustich saw the neighborhood public schools as an example of how he thought the school should be located. With the Euclid Heights property, "all the boys whom we would expect would have to come from a great distance; we would accommodate no one. All would have to add some $25.00 street car fare to their Tuition."[37] To locate at an accessible place in the city would accommodate everyone with "no risk, no speculation."[38] In addition to the heavy financial burden that would be assumed, Father Neustich predicted that if the property was purchased, "people will wonder and say that the Jesuits must be enormously rich, if they can pay $65,000.00 for that place, and some will say they are foolish; many will laugh at us. And why should people be so anxious to pay what they owe if we be so rich, and how can we complain."[39] A second meeting of the Board of Trustees discussed the pros and cons of the purchase of the Euclid Heights property. Such was the persuasiveness of Father Neustich's arguments that, instead of pursuing the matter further, the Board agreed that "they could not in conscience agree to purchase it."[40]

In the spring of 1909 Father Pickel sought the advice of the Provincial as to his next move. Father Meyer was sympathetic and made it clear that he was as anxious as Father Pickel to secure a permanent place on the East Side, but the Provincial was concerned about where the money was coming from, and about the opinions of Father Pickel's consultors.[41] There was no chance of financial help from the Province, so an appeal would have to be made to Father General unless an unexpected source of funds turned up. It was on this last point that Father Meyer made a suggestion. "If you could combine . . . with some moneyed men, buy the tract in common, choose your part of it, and pay for it after you have chosen it, in that case the tract would not be ecclesiastical property—but only your part of it—and therefore there would be no need of asking the leave of the Holy See to dispose of the rest."[42] There is no evidence that Father Pickel took any immediate action on this advice. What he did do was to request the permission of Father General to borrow $100,000. Permission was granted to borrow the amount requested but not until 10 June 1910.[43] The permission did not designate any specific property; that was a matter for the Provincial.[44]

By midsummer of 1909, Father Pickel had decided that the bishop's understanding and cooperation were important enough to warrant a special effort to convey to the bishop an extensive analysis of the Jesuits' point of view. This he did in a four-and-one-half-page single-spaced typewritten "Memorial" to the bishop on 10 July.[45] In it he reviewed the accomplishments of St. Ignatius College in spite of the many hardships of the early years. Of special note was the account of finances showing the amount of scholarship money in the form of tuition discounts provided by the Jesuits. This sum showed that the Jesuit contribution to diocesan education was considerable. If one included the cost of buildings at $150,000, all of it funded by the Society of Jesus, the faculty of twenty Jesuits at a salary they could command at other schools, and the equipment required for the college, the total contribution of the Society of Jesus to higher education in Cleveland was, in Father Pickel's estimate, in the vicinity of one million dollars.

If that was the story of the past, what of the future, asked Father Pickel. For one thing, "it is a matter of almost daily experience that the college is very little known in the city due to its location."[46] It was this consideration that led to the establishment of Loyola High School. The place for the school "was chosen only tentatively, and it soon became evident that it would not serve its purpose more than a very few years."[47] This was why the search continued for a better location. "The problem is selecting a suitable site not too distant from the main arteries of travel, Euclid Avenue and East 105th Street," and one which would include a parish church.[48]

Father Pickel informed Bishop Farrelly that negotiations for the desired site had been going on for some time with the prospect of being able to secure one soon. It was, therefore, necessary to know the bishop's intentions. Travel from East Side to West Side was also a major issue. In Father Pickel's judgment, considering the growth of the city eastward, students cannot be expected to travel from the eastern confines of the city to the West Side and as a matter of fact will not do so. To propose to solve this question by opening another college under different management is to deal a severe blow to Catholic higher education. It means to attempt the maintenance of two rival institutions where one is encompassed by enough difficulties.[49]

The need, therefore, was the "upbuilding of one strong representative institution which can and will be on a par with the secular colleges of the city and a fit exponent of the importance of the Catholic community not only in religious matters but also in civil life."[50]

Father Pickel also called attention to the necessity of providing baccalaureate degrees for Catholic young men who wished to enter the professional schools of medicine and law. Otherwise, they were forced to finish their degrees at Western Reserve University or Baldwin University where they were exposed to Kantian Positivism and attacks on Thomistic philosophy.

> Partly to counteract these evil influences and partly to save our institution in the attack which Protestant Colleges and Universities make on the Catholic colleges through the legislature and other civil authorities, four years ago we opened a course of Philosophy which every college in good standing is supposed to give. Thus, Catholic students are enabled to obtain the degree of A.B. in our institutions.[51]

The problem was that there was not enough encouragement for students to finish the course; too many left after the second year of college. One of the reasons for this was that "prospective students as well as parents cannot be disadvised of the error that every young man who studies at St. Ignatius is expected to enter the priesthood."[52]

Illustrative of the seriousness of the situation was the fact that in the 1908–1909 academic year, only four students were in the graduation class, which contributed a total tuition income of $150.00. This small class took the time of four professors. If the college were to maintain its standing it could not give less than the seven-year course and unless there was a move to the East Side where the greater part of the Catholic population was, there could be no growth. If the bishop had thoughts of starting another college on the East Side he would be defeating his own purpose. It was the aim of St. Ignatius College "to unite all the Catholic forces of the city and its vicinity; to educate a thoroughly Catholic laity, who in every walk of life, professional and business, will be the equal of their non-Catholic fellow-citizens."[53]

There are several copies of Father Pickel's "Memorial" in the Archives of John Carroll University, all of which are identical except for one. On the back of the last page of this copy, which apparently was the one which was sent, there is, in Father Pickel's handwriting, a description of the site then being considered in Euclid Heights near Coventry Road and the Shaker Lakes. There is also the suggestion that Father Joseph F. Smith, pastor of St. Philomena's parish, was willing to give his parish to the Jesuits "if he were suitably provided for elsewhere."[54] Father Smith was willing to do this "in the interest of higher education in the diocese." The "Memorial" closed with Father Pickel begging the bishop's "kind indulgence for any seeming importunity in this matter."[55]

Father Pickel was a determined man and he was not willing to wait too long for the permission from Rome. In less than two weeks after he had sent the "Memorial" he had discovered one way to obtain some of the necessary money and was seeking the advice of the Provincial on how to proceed. Father Pickel, together with one of his consultors, visited Bishop Farrelly on the twenty-sixth of July in order to get the bishop's permission to borrow $10,000 from the Cemetery fund of St. Mary's parish. The bishop told Father Pickel that ever since his first visit a few days after the bishop had taken office, the entire educational question had been under consideration. The bishop made it clear that Father J. F. Smith would be left in his parish until his parish debt was cleared. Moreover, there was opposition from the clergy to having a Jesuit parish on the East Side. In any case there would be no immediate action by the bishop on the question.[56] "He gave us no encouragement whatever in regard to the East Side and said Bishop Horstmann had no right to allow us to start there without authorization from Rome," reported Father Pickel.[57] The rector's explanation that Bishop Horstmann and canonists for both the Jesuits and the diocese had looked into the matter at the time and agreed that permission from Rome was not needed, fell on deaf ears. The bishop's only reply to the news that the Jesuits were about to close the deal on the Euclid Heights property was that if they did, "it would be mere speculation."[58]

As far as the deal for the property on Euclid Heights Boulevard was concerned, Father Pickel had satisfied himself that the present owner's title was clear and the deed good. It was, therefore, safe to go ahead. He had also arranged with the Ursuline and Notre Dame Sisters to borrow $25,000 from them at four percent interest.[59] An additional $8,000 was to have come from the Cemetery Fund, but after the visit with the bishop, that was out of the question. At a meeting with his consultors on the same day he had visited the bishop, Father Pickel reported that he gave an account of that meeting to them; the judgment of the consultors was that the Jesuits could "not go on at the present East Side location for longer than one year without building and it was not the place to build."[60] Not all the consultors were convinced, however, that they should go ahead and purchase any property. Father Pickel's arguments eventually convinced them of the necessity of purchasing property. Then Father Pickel asked the Provincial whether he would agree, and whether it would be possible to secure a loan through a St. Louis bank. So anxious was Father Pickel for a reply that he asked Father Meyer to telegraph his answer. One of the reasons for the haste was that the deal had been arranged with two real estate men as a third party so that the college did not appear to be the ultimate buyer. Father Pickel sensed some suspicions on the part of the seller that the college was in on the deal. The papers were ready for closing and a quick "yes" from the Provincial would settle matters at once.[61]

Father Meyer was not to be rushed into an answer, nor did reply come by telegram.[62] He pointed out to Father Pickel that the Provincial consultors were not immediately available to discuss the matter, that Father Pickel did not have the wholehearted support of his own consultors, and that if the property were purchased it could be purchased only as an investment with some guarantee that it was a safe one.[63] Under the circumstances he advised Father Pickel to assemble his consultors, read them the Provincial's letter and, if all four agreed to the purchase, then Father Meyer would present the case to Rome. Father Meyer's own preference would have been to take over Father Smith's parish even with its debts. His advice to Father Pickel was "don't be discouraged; we can only do our best."[64]

There matters rested until October, when Father Pickel had an opportunity to call on Bishop Farrelly to introduce a newly assigned Jesuit. Father Pickel reported the bishop told him that he had been thinking about the Jesuits since two other religious orders were seeking admission to the diocese. Father Pickel summarized the meeting for the Provincial:

> He did not say for a college but I am sure that is what he meant from what he said afterwards. He added that he had not granted their petitions. I asked whether I might know who they were which he refused to answer. I think they are either the Holy Cross fathers of Notre Dame who have been catering to the clergy here in late years handing out degrees, and the Dominicans or Franciscans. On my remarking that it did not make much difference who they were as long as they were not admitted, he remarked that they might be admitted later unless we prayed for him. I said we would do that. Perhaps he meant that some of the priests were or would bring their influence to bear on the matter of admission of another college.[65]

Father Pickel concluded from this meeting that the move to a permanent site on the East Side was all the more urgent. "We must bestir ourselves and prevent another college from coming in. As I have said all along they will and must go to the East Side. We being on the West and then we will be—a very bad fix indeed."[66] Father Pickel thought that a visit to some of the bishop's consultors might bring further information. Meanwhile he wondered whether the Provincial might write the bishop. Some years later Father Sommerhauser, who became rector in 1915, was disturbed by a similar report of another religious order establishing a college in the city. Writing to the Provincial, Father Alexander Burrowes, he said, "Yesterday I learned for the first time of a rumor spread by the priests that the bishop would call the Dominicans to Cleveland to oppose the Jesuits. They are to be on the Heights, whether a chapel, a parish, or a college, I cannot ascertain."[67]

Before Father Pickel's health forced him to leave the presidency in 1910, several more pieces of property were considered. One that looked especially suitable was a twenty-seven-acre tract on Coventry Road, south of Cedar Avenue in what was then called Cleveland Heights Village; the price of this parcel was $75,000, a price considered too high and so nothing came of it.[68] Later, when Father Pickel was offered a thirteen-acre parcel about a half-mile east of the twenty-seven-acre tract, he had some second thoughts and said, "I wish I had those 27 acres on Coventry Road."[69]

Father Pickel had at one time spoken of a college on the East Side with lodging for students in the vicinity of the college as distinct from a boarding school. Father Meyer expressed complete disapproval of the idea because of experience with a similar arrangement at Creighton University in Omaha. Nor would Father Meyer approve a college located within the city on the East Side without a parish, if the college were to be a day school; tuition alone would not support it.[70] If the college were to have a boarding school then it should be located in the "country." Father Meyer cited the examples of St. Mary's, Kansas and Prairie du Chien, Wisconsin to illustrate what he meant by the proper boarding school location outside of the city.

In 1910 Father Pickel attempted to enlist the services of Caesar A. Grasselli of the Grasselli Chemical Company in discussing "certain matters of business in relation to the college and its future development"; Grasselli asked Father Pickel to give "an outline of the matter" in writing;[71] Father Pickel complied most willingly. The first item on which he sought help was the investment of some money to better advantage than at present. The second item, the future development of the college, Father Pickel explained at great length reviewing the past efforts at securing a permanent place on the East Side. Given the direction of the development of the city and the rapid growth of the Catholic population, the necessity of an East Side location seemed obvious to Father Pickel. The objectives could be achieved if Mr. Grasselli could "gain the cooperation of the Catholic body of the city."[72] Father Pickel, therefore, "planned to form an advisory board consisting of practical men of business whose function would be to lend their experience and counsel," and he hoped that Mr. Grasselli would be instrumental in forming such a body.[73] Mr. Grasselli regretted that he had not the time to develop an advisory board but he would give advice on investments.[74] Father Pickel had anticipated Father Frederick Welfle's action in forming a lay advisory board by thirty-nine years. Just as Father Pickel was about to leave the presidency, another property of considerable size, forty-eight acres, rather far out on Euclid Avenue well beyond the city limits, was offered to the Jesuits. It was located just to the east of what is now known as Nela Park. Father Meyer had been informed of this and had sent his representative, Father Francis Heiermann, to assist in making a judgment on the suitability of the property, referred to as the Ammon property.[75] It was left to Father Pickel's successor to deal with this matter.

THE "TRADITIONAL OBJECT"

Father John B. Furay, who became rector on 6 September 1910, was the first rector whose background was entirely in the Missouri Province. All previous rectors had been from the Buffalo Mission, part of which was joined to the Missouri Province in 1907. Since Jesuit community customs in the Missouri Province differed from those in the Buffalo Mission, one of Father Furay's tasks both at St. John's College, Toledo, where he was rector for two years, and at St. Ignatius was to adapt the Jesuit community to the traditions and customs of the Missouri Province. It was a task requiring the utmost prudence and charity. A story is told about how Father Furay took lessons in German in order to make one of the Jesuits at St. Ignatius College whose native language was German feel more at home talking to him. Father Furay later corresponded in German with his teacher.[76] Further testimony to the qualities of Father Furay can be found in his career after he left Cleveland in 1915 for the presidency of Loyola University in Chicago. He became a personal counselor of Cardinal Mundelein and was chosen by the Cardinal to head and personally select the Jesuit faculty for the Chicago diocesan seminary.[77]

One tradition of the Buffalo Mission at St. Ignatius College was unaffected by Father Furay's efforts to adapt the institution to the customs and traditions of the Missouri Province. That tradition was what Bishop Farrelly called the "traditional object . . . a college and parish on the East Side." As the bishop put it, "the Fathers aimed at this from the beginning and they have never ceased to aim at it."[78] As proof of the claim he cited Bishop Horstmann's directions in the Bishop's own handwriting for the drawing up of the Loyola agreement prohibiting a college and a parish. "Rectors changed—the traditions did not change," said Bishop Farrelly.[79]

The unfinished business of the Ammon property was now given serious

Above left, William B. Sommerhauser, S.J., President, 1915–19; *right,* John P. Farrelly, Bishop of Cleveland 1909–21; *Bottom,* John B. Furay, S.J., President, 1910–15

consideration. The options were three: buy the first plateau at a price almost equal to that for the entire piece; buy only the second ridge; buy the whole forty-eight acres at $100,000, "if we can get it."[80] The first two options were rejected immediately by the consultors and everyone opposed the third option because the site was too far out of the city. The bishop's anticipated refusal to approve any deal, and the likelihood of not being able to dispose of the land very easily, were other reasons for the consultors' disapproval. The consensus was that before any further attempts were considered some decision had to be arrived at as to whether property was being sought for a high school or a college with or without a parish. The final recommendation was that about ten or twelve acres on a side street near a main thoroughfare would be more desirable as well as "accessible and cheap."[81]

Father Furay reported to the Provincial the final results of his consultors' deliberations. The rector was content to abide by the views of his consultors and agreed that ten or twelve acres near the city would be adequate.[82] Father Furay anticipated no problem resulting from the rejection of the Ammon property; the "Consultors did not want to buy it and they are the best judges."[83]

When Father Furay heard that Father Francis Heiermann was still talking about a meeting of the Province Consultors to discuss the Ammon property he again wrote to Father Meyer repeating his reasons for wanting to reject the Ammon offer.[84] One of Father Furay's chief concerns was that the site eventually selected should be one within the means of St. Ignatius College, located in an area likely to maintain its desirability for years to come, easily accessible from the various parishes, and so placed as to control the East Side. For this reason the Ammon property offer would:

> place the college where it does not control the East Side. In fact, if another religious congregation opened a school in Cleveland, as they may within the next ten years, we have left room for them to settle 3 or 4 miles closer in—and open a School that will take the greater number of our boys. For they will be nearer the Catholic district and most of the boys will have to pass by or near their college and then go on 3 or 4 miles further to go to ours.[85]

Other properties closer in were available and the tentative offer of $100,000 for the Ammon property had been turned down by the owner.[86]

Father Heiermann, as the Provincial's representative, was discouraging attempts to look at properties other than the Ammon property. Father Furay was aware that Father Heiermann felt that "it is now or never,"[87] but the insistence of Father Heiermann on the "one place to the exclusion of every other will make this difficult matter still more difficult," Father

Furay informed his Provincial,[88] and also talked with the pastor of St. Philomena's parish, discovering that across Euclid Avenue from the parish property there were ten acres available for $40,000; it was worth investigating. The principal purpose of Father Furay's letter to the Provincial, however, was to let the Provincial know that Father Heiermann was not giving Father Furay's proposal its proper presentation. Father Furay also informed Father Meyer that he would in the future make his proposals directly to him.[89]

Even if agreement on an appropriate site were immediately possible, there was still the matter of the bishop's attitude. Father Furay was worried that because of all of the activity involved in the Ammon property matter the bishop must have some idea of what was going on. Father Furay had heard rumors about what the Jesuits were supposed to be doing from two independent sources; the bishop must have heard the same rumors. As a result "our independence or failure to take advice of him or acquaint him with our plans may be interpreted by him in a way that will hurt us when we come to him for permission to have a parish or open a college."[90] Father Furay had talked to many of the pastors of East Side parishes, all of whom he thought were friendly, "at least externally."[91] The thing to do, he thought, was to wait until these priests had some time to bring their influence to bear on the bishop; it was a time-consuming procedure but Father Furay recommended it.

Meanwhile, Father Heiermann continued to urge the purchase of the Ammon property. He wrote to the Provincial that the price was "not exorbitant," Father Furay's consultors were not in agreement, and the opinion of at least one of them who opposed the purchase did not count for much.[92] Father Furay's position was that even Father Pickel had opposed the purchase, and that until there were assurances from disinterested laymen to the contrary, he also would oppose the purchase; "it would seem not to be prudent at all to go against the overwhelming odds of those who are given to me to advise me."[93]

By the first of November Father Furay had investigated more thoroughly the suitability of the Ammon property. He consulted again with Mr. Fanning, president of the Standard Paving Company, Mr. Daly, president of East Ohio Gas Company, Mr. Madigan, former city treasurer, and Mr. Guilfoyle, a real estate man. All agreed that the flat area in the vicinity of the Ammon site eventually would be occupied by industry, that the price asked for the property was reasonable, but that the college would be better off located in the East 105th Street area. An even better place, it was suggested, would be the Heights area since it would remain residential for a considerable time.[94]

Father Furay continued his efforts to discover the attitudes of the diocesan consultors and of the East Side pastors. Of all the diocesan consultors, Father Gilbert Jennings, Pastor of St. Agnes Church on Euclid Avenue at 79th Street, was considered to be most favorable as far as a Jesuit college on the East Side was concerned; but he would oppose a Jesuit parish on the East Side. Probably two others could be counted on as favorable to the Jesuits. There was considerable doubt that one of the consultors, Father Thomas C. O'Reilly, a former St. Ignatius student, would favor the Jesuits; "he is scarcely in our favor." In a clear reference to the German flavor of the college, Father Furay wrote, "He is quite narrow and national and that has biased him in his dealings heretofore."[95] The German label of the institution was still an important factor in attitudes toward it. In the course of his contacts with the diocesan clergy, Father Furay had discovered that Bishop Farrelly was "somewhat hurt at the report that he is against religious orders, about which some (not ours) gave last year."[96] Pressure, meanwhile, was being brought by the Ammon property owner for a final decision on the deal. Father Furay attributed the delay of a final decision to his "imperfect acquaintance with the city."[97]

A couple of minor matters gave Father Furay an opportunity to visit the bishop and bring him up to date on the East Side problem. Father Furay reported that the bishop immediately raised the question of a parish, stating that "he could not allow us to open a public chapel or give us a parish. Father Jennings, he said had a debt of $85,000.00, Father Smith $52,000.00, and others in proportion."[98] The bishop's fear was that "if we were to come in, many people would come to our church or chapel and the consequence would be that he would be in difficulty with his own priests and the paying off the debts would be delayed."[99] Father Furay suggested that there were two possible alternatives; one, to locate beyond the city limits; or two, to establish a Jesuit community on the East Side without a parish. To the first the bishop thought any place too far out would be unsatisfactory for the Jesuits' purpose. With regard to the second, the bishop understood from friends in Rome that a college church was a necessity. However, the bishop was willing to "give permission for a community and a college if we waive a claim to a church; but this waiver must be a final act not for a period of years only."[100]

In spite of Bishop Farrelly's negative stand on an East Side location, other sites were proposed as alternatives to the Ammon property, including Luna Park, a competitor for the more popular Euclid Beach Park, which could be had for $75,000; a golf grounds off Cedar Avenue near the top of Cedar Hill; and property which was later to be occupied by the Baldwin Reservoir. By mid-November the many unsuccessful approaches to Bishop Farrelly had finally convinced the Jesuits that the bishop would not give them a parish in a desirable location such as East 105th Street. It was agreed now to explain to the Provincial that the bishop might accede to the request for an East Side college if the Jesuits would give up their request for a parish.[101]

In December the results of a meeting of the Provincial Consultors on the property question were made known to the consultors of St. Ignatius College. The Provincial Consultors recommended three options: select a site outside the present limits of city parishes for a college, securing the bishop's permission in writing for a parish when the neighborhood required one; take over St. Philomena's parish with its debts and buy property nearby; establish an academy only, located somewhat downtown and dependent on St. Ignatius College.[102] The Cleveland Jesuits immediately ruled out the second option since they were certain the bishop would never give permission for the Jesuits to take over Father Smith's parish. Their reaction to the first one is interesting since that one described the almost identical course to be followed thirteen years later in locating the present John Carroll University and Gesu parish. If the first option were chosen, however, the action, the Jesuits then felt, was the equivalent of "abandoning the city to any religious order that might come in."[103] Option number three was considered the best of a bad lot, but not acceptable as it stood. There was some agreement that a site of ten or twelve acres large enough to develop into a college, "should reason favor it," was perhaps all that could be hoped for. Their choice of location was still the University Circle area.

On 2 April 1911 the St. Ignatius Consultors met with the Provincial and agreed that it would be wise to continue to seek the bishop's permission for a community and to buy property of some ten to twelve acres in the vicinity of East 105th and Euclid Avenue where there was as yet no church.[104] Father Furay was to report the results of his efforts at a future meeting with the Provincial Consultors. There were no results. Father Furay had asked the bishop to permit a parochial residence on the East Side and the bishop and his Consultors simply said no.[105] Father Furay later admitted that if the Provincial's instructions had not been "explicit" he would not have asked for a parish.[106] The bishop had also refused a request to allow the Jesuits to have a residence at Loyola High School.

Father Furay tried again in January 1912. He wrote to the bishop reviewing his earlier request and emphasized the difficulties experienced by the Fathers in traveling daily back and forth from St. Ignatius College to Loyola High School. The loss of at least two hours each day so shortened the working day that at least one and probably two more teachers were needed than would be the case if the Fathers resided at Loyola. Sufficient manpower was not available, and the annual deficit incurred by Loyola each year was an additional problem; without the assurance of a permanent residence at the high school on the East Side, conditions would not improve. Moreover, the lack of a permanent site was holding up efforts at buying property and "arranging for an Academy that will be large enough and attractive enough to meet the requirements of the situation."[107] Aware of the many previous attempts to secure such permission, Father Furay concluded his letter by saying, "I do not wish to be nor to seem to be importunate or to press this matter unreasonably, but I feel that the interests of education justify me in laying this matter before you again in the hope of a favorable answer to my petition."[108] Bishop Farrelly saw matters in a much different light. Instead of being impressed by the plight of the traveling West Side Fathers, he claimed in a letter to Rome in defense of his position,

> Loyola has been a constant drag on St. Ignatius from many points of view, particularly according to the statement of Father Furay in his letter to me of January, 1912, because there was always a deficit there. Moreover, in order to secure students in sufficient numbers for Loyola, the Fathers each year must make a personal visitation of the East Side from house to house and as a matter of fact they have done so. It would be a greater clog still to St. Ignatius to try to make of Loyola what it ought to be, in order to serve properly as an Academic school. . . . For to do this would entail an enormous expense and the funds would have to come from St. Ignatius. It would be practically a repetition of the expense incurred during the first thirty years to bring St. Ignatius to its present point in efficiency and equipment. . . . And when finished, the only result could be to divide and weaken the educational efforts of the Jesuits in Cleveland.[109]

For the Jesuits to concentrate on further developing St. Ignatius College on the West Side seemed to Bishop Farrelly the wise and economical thing to do. Looking back at the issue from the standpoint of the present, the Jesuits should at least be thankful that Bishop Farrelly would not permit them to locate in some of the areas where they had intended.

TIME FOR DECISION

The Jesuits were still not willing to accept as final Bishop Farrelly's refusal of a residence and a parish on the East Side. At a consultors' meeting with Father Furay in February 1912 they agreed to wait patiently until such time as "Father Provincial can get an expression of the bishop's policy and in the event of a final and definite refusal to allow us on the East Side to build up our West Side College."[110] There is some evidence that the persistent efforts to secure the bishop's permission for a permanent East Side location finally caused second thoughts about the advisability of continuing to pursue this course. A communication from Father R. D. Stephen of the Jesuit Community in Cleveland to Father Alexander Burrowes, who became Provincial in January 1913, suggested the outright purchase of the Loyola property as a proper solution. Father Stephen was reporting that Father Furay had asked one of the older members of the community (probably Father Neustich or Father Haggeney) what he would think of the purchase of the Loyola property when the lease expired.[111] The basic argument for purchase was that there was too much opposition from the bishop and the clergy ever to expect a parish on the East Side; permission to move Loyola would probably be denied. All things considered, the present location of Loyola would be lost if the school were moved. The idea of moving the college to the East Side should be abandoned even if the bishop were to grant permission. The West Side was growing, too, and the center of the population could eventually be where St. Ignatius was located, especially with the completion of two new bridges, Lorain-Huron and Detroit-Superior. The better residential sections were on the West Side. The conclusion reached was that since the plans for St. Ignatius College called for a third wing which was never built, the building should be completed. There would be only college classes on the West Side and high school classes on the East Side. It was presumed that the bishop's permission would not be needed in this arrangement.[112] The Jesuit whose opinion was reported by Father Stephen felt that "a mistake was made some six or seven years ago in not purchasing the present site of Loyola Academy, . . . about as good a location as could be found."[113] It was clear that there was some urgency to come to a decision because, "something must be done now, both the college and Loyola are overcrowded and next year it will be impossible to take care of the normal increase."[114]

Nothing was done immediately to pursue this line of reasoning and matters remained pretty much at a standstill until the appointment of a new rector, Father William B. Sommerhauser, in August 1915. By this time the opinion of the consultors was unanimous that purchase of the Loyola site was the solution to the problem.[115] This involved also the purchase of adjacent lots in the block where the school was located. Both Father Sommerhauser and the consultors were convinced that for this purchase the bishop's permission was not needed. As Father Sommerhauser said:

> For although our right may not be canonical strictly speaking, still we are in 'possession'. We have the Rt. Rev. Bishop's permission where we are, we are established 7 or 8 years, the people are with us, and by buying we should give no occasion for complaint. Should there be any objection, nevertheless, on the part of the diocesan authorities, the odium would fall upon them which the Consultors think the said authorities will be slow to merit.[116]

Father Sommerhauser thought also that with land values rising the Loyola property could be easily sold if worst came to worst. Other sites were not worth wasting time on; they were not any better, "only a little more aristocratic."[117]

Father Sommerhauser in reporting his intentions to Father Burrowes listed several reasons for the purchase. Accessibility was a prime consideration, central location another, proper surroundings were in the University Circle area, the size and cost were right, and most important, an immediate solution was necessary. The recent city high school basketball championship won by Loyola in 1915 provided publicity upon which Father Sommerhauser wished to capitalize.[118] He also made it clear that he was taking seriously the Provincial recommendation on the occasion of his visit to St. Ignatius College that "it is high time to think about securing [property] on the East Side."[119]

Father Sommerhauser lost no time in arranging for the purchase of the Loyola site. Public announcement of the purchase appeared in the local newspapers in January 1916 with headlines such as "Loyola High School Plans a $200,000 Plant,"[120] and "College to erect East Side branch."[121] The story accompanying the latter headline said that the new plant would be "adequate to care for all of Cleveland's high school pupils residing on the East Side." In addition to classrooms the plant would "contain a large chapel, gymnasium, shower baths and recreation rooms for both sexes. Work is to be started this spring."[122]

This Cleveland Imbroglio

The 23 students on hand to greet the opening of Loyola High School in the fall of 1907 rose to 51 in two classes in 1908, 107 with all four classes in 1910 and 165 in 1915. As a feeder school for St. Ignatius College and as a foothold on the East Side, the school held out great promise which could not be fully realized until the thorny canon law questions of Loyola's status and location were settled.

A Present for the Diocese

Since Father Furay's prudence and patience had failed to produce an answer to the questions, Father Sommerhauser decided it was time for action. Bishop Farrelly was quick to recognize the change in attitude initiated by the new rector. Since the Jesuits had already completed the purchase of the Loyola High School property Father Sommerhauser announced to the bishop "with a voice and countenance, full of cheer" on Christmas Day 1915 that he "had a present for the diocese of Cleveland."[1] In a letter to the bishop a few days later, Father Sommerhauser said, "Agreeable to your Lordship's wish, expressed to me orally on Christmas Day, I hereby state to you in writing our recent purchase of the Loyola High School site. The Warranty Deed for the property was handed to me today."[2] It is no wonder that Bishop Farrelly described Father Sommerhauser as "a rector of a special type, evidently accustomed to face difficulties, ready to acknowledge (comprehend and appraise) a difficult undertaking, rather martial in his methods, and he employed the sword to cut the knot."[3] A similar estimate of this new rector was to come later from a Roman canonist, Monsignor Cerretti, who was trying to assist Father Sommerhauser in his efforts to validate the purchase of the Loyola site. Monsignor Cerretti wrote to a Jesuit advisor of Father Sommerhauser, Father Hector Papi, a canonist at Woodstock College, Maryland, and suggested that Father Papi write to Father Sommerhauser and "recommend to him (as nicely as you can) to keep in check his fiery spirit and put off to some other time the desired battle."[4]

It took almost a month for Bishop Farrelly to recover from his Christmas present. The bishop wrote to the rector on 23 January 1916, expressing surprise at Father Sommerhauser's purchase of the Loyola site, asking "upon whose authority you had made this purchase."[5] The bishop also repeated his refusal to allow a change of site, stating that he had "intimated" to Fathers Pickel, Furay, and Meyer his wish that the Jesuits concentrate on the West Side and was still of the same mind.[6] One day before the bishop wrote, Father Sommerhauser had written to the bishop that the Cleveland Street Railway Company had offered to buy the Loyola site. If the Bishop would give permission for the sale, then the Jesuits could move Loyola closer to the University Circle.[7] Father Sommerhauser wanted a reply within three days. Not receiving a reply within the specified time, and before he responded to the bishop's letter, Father Sommerhauser visited the bishop, and upon being informed that the bishop was not available and would be away the following week, wrote a brief note requesting a reply as soon as possible. Father Sommerhauser believed that "Doctor Scullen [William A. Scullen was Chancellor of the diocese] will be good enough to transmit your answer to me."[8] What the rector did receive from Doctor Scullen almost two months late in March, was a copy of the bishop's original letter of the twenty-third of January to which as yet there had been no response.[9]

Father Sommerhauser immediately replied to the bishop's second request by explaining that the "surprising nature of the questions raised" in the letter had necessitated extensive correspondence with previous rectors and Father General;[10] hence the delay. Father Sommerhauser felt that the bishop's desire to confine operations to the West Side as expressed in the January letter was "tantamount to closing our East-side High School 'Loyola' which means the ruin of St. Ignatius College."[11] This was an unsatisfactory answer for the bishop who, nevertheless, let matters rest until August, when he sent a blunt letter to the rector reminding him that it took two months for even an unsatisfactory reply to his January letter. It was now another two months later and there was still no satisfactory response. "As Bishop of this Diocese, I was and still am of the opinion that I was entitled to a frank reply from you. Were I to imagine that you thought for a moment that your letter of 23 March ult. was such a reply, I feel that would be making a very injurious reflection upon your perspicacity."[12] The bishop then contrasted Father Sommerhauser's action, or lack of it, with that of his predecessors who "saw fit to show their respect for the bishop of the Diocese by consulting with him."[13] The bishop ended the letter with the reminder "that I am in duty bound to rule this Diocese in accordance with the legislation of the Apostolic See, legislation which you seem to me to have ignored in your procedure."[14] Father Sommerhauser's reply was a simple statement that he needed no episcopal permission to buy the Loyola site and cited Father Edward Fine, "the official canonist of our Society" to support his contention.[15] Bishop Farrelly's response was that the citation from Father Fine was not pertinent to the case and cited the same Father Fine to support the bishop's contention that permission was needed for the final purchase of Loyola property.[16]

Father Sommerhauser's adamant defense of his position was undoubtedly bolstered by the responses he had received from both Father Pickel and Father Furay. Father Pickel said that there had never been any doubt in his mind about the proper canonical status of Loyola.

> Who says the grant was uncanonically made? Everyone concerned in the matter at the time certainly thought it was in every way authoritative . . . I am quite sure that we had no more, if as much, from Bishop Gilmour on our first coming to Cleveland. Was that uncanonical too? [Father Pickel was apparently unaware of the action of Bishop Gilmour and his consultors.]
>   And why did no one ever discover or affirm that our being at Loyola High was uncanonical until after a lapse of nearly ten years.[17]

Neither Father Pickel nor Father Sommerhauser saw a problem in buying the property that had already been leased. Bishop Farrelly saw quite a difference between a branch on a temporary site and a residence on a permanent one. Father Pickel mistakenly claimed in his letter that the original permission of Bishop Horstmann had been given by the bishop "after consultation with and approval by his consultors."[18] Bishop Farrelly was correct in denying that this was the case and added that not even the pastors in the vicinity had been consulted by Bishop Horstmann.[19] All the evidence shows that even Bishop Horstmann considered the Loyola site a temporary one.

The Jesuits resented the bishop's contention that they were trying to keep other religious orders out of the city. Yet, as if to prove the bishop's charge, Father Pickel recalled the occasion on which he had been told that other religious orders had asked to open an academy or college on the East Side. Father Pickel also recalled that he had "very strongly represented that this would mean disaster to St. Ignatius because by far the majority of the students always were from the East Side and that if another religious order were to open a school there we might as well close up St. Ignatius at once. These are the very words I used."[20]

On almost every point there was a sharp difference between Father Pickel's view of matters and that of the bishop. As evidence that it was understood that the Jesuits were to continue on the East Side, Father Pickel pointed to the renewal of the original short-term lease and to the building of the L-shaped classroom building "with full knowledge and at least the tacit consent of the bishop."[21] Bishop Farrelly contended that he gave permission to Father Furay "to erect a temporarily building . . . with the condition that structure be very cheap, in as much as it would be forfeited at the expiration of the lease. A glance at this building will convince you that Father Furay complied with my instructions."[22]

Father Pickel denied "flatly and absolutely" that Bishop Farrelly had intimated that he wished all students to attend St. Ignatius on the West Side. The bishop never made the "slightest suggestion or intimation to that effect." Father Pickel suggested that such intimations might have been made to Father Furay and projected back to Father Pickel. Father Furay did indicate in his letter to Father Sommerhauser that the bishop never said anything so direct as "that he did not wish us on the East Side . . . The nearest approach to it that I remember was that he said why don't you build up the West Side, whatever I can do for you there I will be pleased to do."[23] That Father Furay was not particularly alert to the bishop's thinking and manner of giving direction is clear from his reaction to the bishop's hint, "But there was nothing he could do for us there so I did not pursue that lead."[24] Bishop Farrelly said he never expressly ordered Loyola to be closed because "it was the part of prudence to let things stand. I tolerated a situation that was not of my making. I never expressly ordered Loyola to be closed, though it is plain that all my advice tended toward that consummation."[25] It was the bishop's conclusion that St. Ignatius, "independent of Loyola and unhampered by the Fathers' efforts to keep up Loyola, will always go forward in a steady career of success and progress, but cannot go backward."[26]

Father Pickel considered Bishop Farrelly's thinking as evidence that the

same old narrowminded and shortsighted opposition to the program and the development of the college is still at work instead of a large and constructive policy that would allow the college gradually to exert that influence in the city which is its due and which it will never have as long as it is forced to remain in an obscure corner of the West Side, where beside there is no possibility of expansion.[27]

Fathers Pickel and Furay did not agree in their advice on how to proceed now that the status of Loyola had been challenged. "The proper thing to do," in Father Pickel's opinion, "would to be to sell Loyola High School which you can do forthwith seeing that you are there uncanonically and also give up and dispose of St. Ignatius as soon as possible."[28] Father Furay urged caution and admitted that he had not understood the bishop's mind or he would not have tried to continue the search for another site for Loyola. He thought it unwise to deny what the bishop says he said to Father Meyer, Pickel, and himself, that "this would be a challenge of veracity. It may exculpate your action of buying without consulting him—but now that you know his mind and can sell and undo your action, it leaves you without ground to stand on if you don't follow his wishes."[29] Father Furay warned Father Sommerhauser to be "chary of advice—for you are on the ground and tell a hundred times better than I what is best to do or leave undone."[30] Father Sommerhauser needed little encouragement to follow his own inclinations.

Fathers Pickel's longer association with St. Ignatius College gave him perhaps a stronger attachment to the "traditional objective." He sympathized with Father Sommerhauser for having to work under discouraging circumstances and said,

> Cleveland under such conditions is about the last place I should care to be condemned in. I had rather go to India and work under the British Government which aids and assists our schools even though it is just now sending away our German brethen on account of the war.
>
> These are my sentiments and I don't care who knows them. You may make any use of this letter you see fit.[31]

BISHOP FARRELLY'S PLANS

Two diocesan projects in 1916, which Jesuits were soon to learn about, played important roles in the Loyola controversy. One was the perceived need by diocesan authorities to sell or lease the downtown cathedral property and move the cathedral to the East Side. An early step toward relocating the cathedral was taken when Bishop Horstmann purchased property adjacent to St. Agnes parish at East 79th and Euclid Avenue in 1900. As long as the site was intended for the new cathedral, St. Agnes was limited to a temporary church. By 1912 this sector of Euclid Avenue was deemed to be a developing business area and so the cathedral project for that site was abandoned. The rapid growth of the city was limiting the number of sites not likely to be business oriented, and so by 1915 the area at the entrance to Wade Park, where Severence Hall now stands, was considered to be about the only good location for the cathederal. Purchase of the property was not easily accomplished, but between August 1915 and June 1916, four parcels were acquired. A small parcel owned by people who would not sell remained to be acquired. Plans went ahead, however, and an architect's drawing of the new cathedral shown across the lagoon in front of the Art Museum was prepared.[32] For many reasons this project was never completed.

The other project was the opening of a free diocesan high school on the East Side in the vicinity of the proposed cathedral site and near Loyola

High School in September 1916. This project had been discussed at length by the bishop's consultors and, so the bishop claimed, "was not in opposition to the Jesuits" but was intended to be a further development of the parochial school system.[33] It was to provide an opportunity for the graduates of parochial schools to attend a Catholic high school when they "could not afford to pay tuition fees either at St. Ignatius or Loyola. It was to be a high school *for all rich and poor alike."* It was also intended to serve in the development of vocations. There is an ironic twist to this last purpose of the new school. Less than a year after the new high school, Cathedral Latin, opened, an article appeared in the *Catholic Universe* stating that "perhaps the most glorious chapter in the history of St. Ignatius is the record of vocations to the priesthood and religious fostered and matured in her hallowed halls."[34] It was claimed that over two hundred of its students had entered the diocesan seminary and thirty had entered religious orders. The majority of the junior clergy of the diocese were former St. Ignatius students.

The bishop's plans did not exclude concern for the graduates of the girls' parochial schools. At about the same time as the founding of Cathedral Latin a free high school for girls was established under the direction of Father William A. Kane, Superintendent of Parish Schools, in the cathedral parish school. It was staffed by nuns from several religious orders and had 34 graduates in 1920. In 1922 there were 410 enrolled, but the school was later discontinued; the building was needed for other purposes. [35] Both of these schools were to be funded by what in effect were taxes on the parish congregations for their members who attended the "free" schools. Cathedral Latin was temporarily housed in a building on the newly purchased cathedral property. Later, a more permanent place was purchased within two blocks of Loyola High School and the new building was dedicated and opened in 1918. The school started with 160 in two classes in 1916; in 1918, it enrolled 387 and in 1919, 740.[36]

The news of the intended "free" diocesan school did not take long to reach Father Sommerhauser's ears. Official announcement of the opening did not come before September 1916, but Father Sommerhauser in March had already informed his Provincial of the development. In reply Father Burrowes said, "I believe, as you say, that we now have the secret of the opposition to our academy on the East Side. The newspaper clipping explains it."[37] Father Burrowes agreed with the judgment of Father Hector Papi, the Woodstock College canonist, that the bishop's insistence on the *Beneplacitum Apostolicum* was a technicality, "but a serious one and according to it, our academies in St. Louis and Cincinnati (Avondale) might be closed. The bishop of Cleveland does not want us on the East Side and has recourse to this technicality."[38]

Father Burrowes's advice was to wait for Father General's judgment and "when we decide, we ought to act promptly. If we are to withdraw, let it be done promptly and the people will know conclusively without our saying it, why we gave up the East Side."[39] Two months earlier the Provincial had been more hopeful; he was not, however, surprised at the bishop's reaction to the purchase of the Loyola site, but felt there was the prospect of selling it and locating elsewhere in the same area. He also pointed out that unfavorable comment from Jesuit supporters in Cleveland was to be expected if the Jesuits were forced to settle for the Loyola site; yet he advised that the site should be retained for the present.[40] Father Burrowes was reasonably sure that since the "new place under consideration was not far from the present site, the bishop will not, I think, object."[41] He cautioned Father Sommerhauser, however, not to "let go of what you have until you have a place to jump to."[42] If permission were needed to sell the Loyola site he thought the permission of the Apostolic Delegate would be sufficient. Still in a hopeful mood, Father Burrowes subsequently referred to "a vague rumor" to the effect that Loyola's position was uncanonical during Father Furay's time but the bishop never made anything of it. Consequently, he saw no problem in demonstrating that the Jesuits were on the East Side "by some right."[43] Father Furay agreed the Jesuits not only had the permission for Loyola but had it in writing.[44] The Jesuits apparently could not or would not understand Bishop Farrelly's plans for an East Side diocesan school.

APPEAL TO ROME

Father Sommerhauser now decided on a course of action. The rector was convinced that the *"East Side is Cleveland"* and that without an East Side institution the Jesuits would never amount to anything in the city. He thought the original grant for Loyola to build on the East Side was given and received in good faith; it would not have been accepted if it had been thought that it might have been revoked at any time. The present attitude of the bishop together with continual excuses offered for not allowing a parish was simply another way of saying that the Jesuits were not wanted on the East Side.[45] He could not see nine years of work at Loyola without ever being aware of any difficulty wasted without a fight, especially against "what everybody here knows and speaks of as the 'Roman Clique' of the Bishop and his administration." Father Sommerhauser felt that "humbly bowing to every treatment received from the diocesan administration has put us in the condition of nobodies at Cleveland, not to say helots." It is an "open secret here, that we are victims of unfriendliness akin to unfairness."[46] It was time to act; "we as Jesuits have been taught to obey; but obedience need not stoop to weakness."[47] Confident then that "trials steel the warrior" and counting on the support of the clergy and laity, Father Sommerhauser sought to secure "prominence on the boulevard" for the East Side School. He considered his stand as "the first time that one of Ours has called a gentle halt on his Lordship."[48]

On 1 April 1916, Father Sommerhauser had written to Father Thomas Gannon, the Jesuits' American Assistant in Rome, explaining the problem in detail and asked two questions: was the permission secured by Father General in 1910 to incur a debt not to exceed $100,000 in the building of Loyola High School the equivalent of the *Beneplacitum Apostolicum*?; and could the equipping of two new classrooms and improving the gymnasium at Loyola be allowed as encouragement to the students and as a compromise to the already publicly announced plans for the new Loyola?[49] On this last point he thought that if the bishop objected, the Jesuits would be no worse off than they already were. He also had a third question which seemed more like a recommendation. The laity, he said, understood the problem and several prominent laymen had offered to purchase property and hold it until the matter was settled. "I encourage this step," said Father Sommerhauser.[50]

In July he sent a similar but even more detailed account of the problem and the history of the college to the Apostolic Delegate, noting that all attempts to deal with the bishop had failed, or as he put it, were "*sine fructu.*"[51] This letter followed a personal visit to the Apostolic Delegate in Washington, D.C. in the latter part of June. The written report to the Apostolic Delegate was five pages of single-spaced type in Latin with a one-page follow-up letter in English. The latter's purpose was to thank the Most Reverend Father John Bonzano, the Apostolic Delegate, and also to report rumors in the diocese of Loyola not opening in the fall of 1916, rumors which Father Sommerhauser was "not heeding." Father Sommerhauser remarked that while he was eager to place the matter in his Excellency's hands, he hoped "perchance the cognizance of this case by Dr. Phillipe Bernardine," a canonist at Catholic University, could be secured. He also hoped that notice would be taken of the situation by His Eminence, Diomede Cardinal Falconio, O.F.M., a former Apostolic Delegate in the United States, who would certainly "clear this matter up in a just and amicable way."[52] It was perhaps just coincidental that this follow-up letter was dated 14 July, Bastille Day.

The premature approach to the Apostolic Delegate resulted in an unsatisfactory reply to Father Sommerhauser. The Apostolic Delegate informed him that the document would be preserved together with the information therein. Father Sommerhauser then asked, "Are we to conclude from this that you do not find it expedient to send our petition to His Emminence, Cardinal Falconio?"[53] Suspecting that the Apostolic Delegate's reply hinted at some lack of proper procedure, the rector noted that he realized that such a petition should proceed from Father General. However, the European War and the exile of Father General in Switzerland extended the normal communication time considerably. He observed that he had written to Father General in March and received only an insufficient answer in July. Possible action by Bishop Farrelly could at any time further complicate matters. No immediate clarification or advice came from the Apostolic Delegate.

On 24 October 1916 Father Gannon sent a letter to Father Sommerhauser explaining proper procedure saying that Father General was pleased that the matter had not yet been referred to Rome and wished "now that we begin to proceed in this matter according to the way usual in our Society."[54] The rector was advised, therefore, to go through his Provincial, presenting the full case with its history, documents, arguements, and explanations to the best available canonists, who would then draw up the "Memorial" or *Supplica* to the Sacred Congregation of Religious. The *Supplica* would be sent by the Provincial directly to Rome. Father Sommerhauser was then to inform the Apostolic Delegate in Washington of the steps that had been taken. Further advice was given by Father Gannon on the points that would be useful in the presentation. The fact that Bishop Horstmann considered Loyola merely a branch of St. Ignatius College would be a good reason why he did not insist on getting the *Beneplacitum Apostolicum*. Father General at the time of the grant was Father Franz Wernz, a distinguished canonist in his own right; hence he probably had some explicit or implicit understanding with the Sacred Congregation. The explicit permission of the Congregation to borrow up to $100,000 for the school was considered a most important point.[55]

Before the end of 1916 nearly all of the necessary steps had been taken. Most of the early part of the following year was spent in reviewing drafts of the *Supplica* submitted by the canonist from Woodstock, Father Hector Papi. By August the work had been completed, Father General had received the necessary documents, and the Apostolic Delegate had been notified. The Apostolic Delegate seemed much more cooperative at this point and informed Father Sommerhauser that he had "requested Father Papi, who was recently in Washington, to write a friend in Rome and ask him to occupy himself with the affair."[56] Early 1918 was a time for waiting.

Meanwhile the rector had taken some steps to help enrollment at Loyola. Competitive scholarships for the high school were increased from two to five with one being for high school and college. The others were for four years of high school.[57] Within the Jesuit Community itself it was agreed not to talk to anyone about the problems of the East Side school, and to "speak well of His Lordship, also of the Free Diocesan High School," since the case was now in Rome and, therefore, should be left "entirely to Superiors."[58]

ROME'S ANSWER

Not until 10 December 1918 did the Sacred Congregation of Religious issue its finding. The decree permitted the Jesuits to retain Loyola in the place where it was located. It did not permit relocation elsewhere without the consent of the bishop because that was not within the Congregation's power.[59] Two identical copies of the decree were sent to Father Sommerhauser. One was addressed to Father Alfred Maertens, Procurator General of the Society, and Father Sommerhauser; the other was intended for Bishop Farrelly; Father Sommerhauser was asked to deliver it to the bishop. This he did and its receipt was acknowledged by the bishop through his Chancellor, Dr. William A. Scullen.[60]

What appeared at first to be a victory seemed upon further reflection to be something less than that. The original objective was really to have the right to move Loyola to a better site. That objective clearly was not included in the decree, and a reference to the original grant of Bishop Horstmann raised serious questions in Father Sommerhauser's mind. His canonist, Father Papi, confirmed his suspicions; Loyola could remain where it was but there was no right to locate elsewhere without the consent of the bishop. Because the decree itself did not explicitly state this, Father Sommerhauser had at first thought that relocaiton would be no problem. As Father Papi explained, the restriction was implicit in the decision and therefore it was not necessary to state it explicitly. The general permission given by Bishop Horstmann implies that its execution is not left entirely to the choice of the person or persons receiving it.[61] Bishop Farrelly put it a little differently. By not being specific as to location the original grant was defective and such defect made it necessary to consult the bishop when the grant was exercised and the site chosen.[62] It was Bishop Farrelly's contention that the location of Loyola at the time of its origin "was never presented to his (Horstmann's) judgment or at least was never ratified by him."[63] Bishop Horstmann approved only the lease and did not give a permanent location when it was in his power to do so. At best, Bishop Farrelly conceded, whatever permission the Jesuits had received they had already used; anything more was subject to his approval.

Father Papi's solution, which he proposed to Father Sommerhauser, was to select a proper place for Loyola and then approach Bishop Farrelly for his permission. Since Bishop Horstmann's general permission was for the East Side, Bishop Farrelly could object only to a specific place. If the bishop did object he would have to give specific reasons. If the reasons appear to be merely an excuse, then "we must ask Rome to devise some means of overcoming his opposition."[64] Father Papi also advised, in view of the bishop's position, that patience should be exercised.

Some three weeks before receiving Father Papi's advice, Father Sommerhauser had already gone to see Monsignor Cerretti in Washington on 22 February. Monsignor Cerretti, who as a Roman canon lawyer was very familiar with the case, had told Father Sommerhauser that he had been "granted all that Bishop Horstmann granted . . . and that in his opinion we could go ahead in Cleveland."[65] In writing to the new American Assistant to Father General, Father Joseph Hanselman, the rector was seeking some quick advice on how "to defend with all modesty and humility, but withal valiantly the rights of the Society in this stubborn persecution and most ignoble justice."[66] One piece of evidence that appeared to support the rector's description of conditions was a letter to the parish school principals from Father William A. Kane, Superintendent of Parish Schools, which prohibited the parish schools from giving a list of pupils "to anyone for any purpose," or distributing tickets for entertainment or attending entertainments without the pastor's permission; the new rule also prohibited parochial school students from taking "any examinations other than those given by the teachers of their respective classes, before the date of the Diocesan Examinations."[67] All of this seemed designed to interfere with Jesuit recruiting for Loyola High School and the presentation of plays and concerts.

Further support for the position that Bishop Farrelly's actions were nullifying the effect of the decree of the Congregation of Religious was contained in a letter dated 30 March 1919 and addressed to Father Sommerhauser, signed by a number of diocesan priests who had always given strong support to the Jesuits:

> We the undersigned pastors of the city of Cleveland, on our own initiative and moved solely by a deep appreciation of the noble work for higher education done by your community in this diocese, as also the willing and continued assistance constantly rendered us in parish work; hasten to assure you of our good will, and to enter our protest against the ingratitude and injustice which is now being shown toward you by our Ordinary.

> The erection of his Cathedral Latin School in its present location only two blocks away from your Loyola High School, and during your appeal to Rome, has nullified Rome's decision in your favor. Moreover his activities since the Roman decision make it practically impossible for candidates to enter your school, and thus destroy your work entirely and leave your community with a great debt, which was assumed for the benefit of our diocese.

> For us pastors to oppose the policy of our Ordinary would only emphasize the present scandal. We respectfully suggest that you petition the Holy See to instruct

the Apostolic Delegate that he use his kind office to bring peace. We are supremely confident that Mons. Bonzano's recognized wisdom and patient consideration will bring about an agreement which will protect the rights of both parties. Signed, N. Pfeil, rector, St. Peter, Joseph F. Smith, rector, St. Philomena, Francis T. Moran, rector, St. Patrick, William Kress, rector, St. Edward.[68]

This letter may have been prompted in part by meetings of diocesan pastors held at the new Cathedral Latin school on the fourth and twelfth of March at which the pastors were "practically urged to send their boys there, and to make their parishes pay $45 for every boy sent."[69] The consultors of St. Ignatius College saw that this action "logically leads to our own destruction; for we have no funds, and must needs charge tuition for our existence. Accordingly, it was the unanimous opinion of all CC [consultors] to take the necessary steps at Rome to save our existence."[70]

On 3 April 1919 Father Sommerhauser addressed a five-page single-spaced letter to Father General. Most of the letter was devoted to explaining how the bishop was seeking to nullify the decree's good effects by building the new Cathedral Latin School so near Loyola and generally creating or supporting an anti-Jesuit atmosphere in the city. The rector again pleaded for some speedy recourse to the Congregation of Religious, because "hinc ergo periculum in mora."[71] Whether this letter was the straw that broke the camel's back is hard to say, but it was another example of the rector, in his zeal and anxiety, failing to follow proper procedure. The response to this letter was a note from Father Hanselman saying that Father General had placed the Loyola matter in the hands of Father Francis X. McMenamy, the new Provincial of the Missouri Province. The Provincial was to confer with the bishop about a solution.[72] Father Sommerhauser then wrote to Father Hanselman on 12 June hoping that he or Father General would not think him "officious" for sending additional information on Loyola. The additional information turned out to be a restatement of what Father Sommerhauser had already reported about the bishop's attitude and the anti-Jesuit feeling in official diocesan circles, all of which amounted to a nullification of the good aspects of the Roman decree in spite of the support of certain diocesan priests.[73]

"On a one day notice, Father Sommerhauser was pulled out of Cleveland (2 July) by his Provincial, Father McMenamy, and sent to St. Charles, Missouri."[74] So wrote Father Thomas Jefferson Smith in his brief account of the next step in the Loyola High School situation. Father Sommerhauser's parting advice to Father Smith, who succeeded him, was to hold on to the property at Vermilion where the Jesuits had a villa with some 2000 feet frontage on Lake Erie.[75] As the only large piece of lake frontage, Father Sommerhauser thought it would become very valuable. Father Hanselman, apparently unaware of Father Sommerhauser's removal, wrote to him on 19 July acknowledging the 12 June letter and noting that Father General also saw it. He hoped that "sooner or later everything will right itself," and observed that "we can afford to be patient."[76]

Father Papi had been immediately informed by Father Sommerhauser of the events of 2 July and wrote to the former rector, "If for superiors it is always a relief to be honorably discharged," in Father Sommerhauser's case he had to "admire the wisdom of superiors who have chosen as your successor, one, who must be well acquainted with the college and its needs."[77] Father Sommerhauser must also have been pleased to receive a letter from Father General commending him for his zealous defense of the right of St. Ignatius College in the midst of many difficulties.[78] Father Sommerhauser's great fault was that he did not understand Rome's abhorrence of haste and its penchant for delay.

LOYOLA CLOSED

Some explanation of the diocesan position on the Loyola matter can be found in Bishop Farrelly's meeting with his consultors, Father's James O'Leary, George F. Murphy, Thomas F. Mahon, Francis J. Hroch, and William A. Scullen, about a year before the Roman decree was issued. The Loyola question was discussed and there was complete agreement that the canonical status of Loyola was at best "uncertain" because of the lack of the *Beneplacitum Apostolicum*; if such were granted it could only confirm the school in its present place. "By a solemn vote they declared their opinion that Bishop Farrelly should not permit the Fathers to move Loyola to another site on the East Side."[79] There was also absolute agreement with the bishop in his advice to the Jesuits to give up Loyola and concentrate on the West Side. There was complete approval for the establishment of Cathedral Latin School and the consultors "pledged their full support in the bishop's defense of the rights of parishes and the interests of the Diocesan Priests."[80]

The Loyola High School situation had reached an impasse. As far as the Jesuits were concerned the matter was now in the hands of the Provincial. The stand of the diocesan administration was unshaken by the decree in favor of the Jesuits' remaining at Loyola. There was little that the new rector, Father Smith, would be able to do. He recognized, as did his consultors, that, apart from the canonical issues, the need for new buildings and facilities was too urgent to be set aside without some attention. On this point there was agreement; even diocesan authorities spoke of the shabby buildings. Pending the results of the Provincial's conference with the bishop, if it were to occur, Father Smith and his consultors considered what their options might be. One of the consultors, Father James J. Doyle, proposed a unique plan; close Loyola, move the college farther west to Lakewood, and improve the high school on the present West Side location so that its excellence would be its best recommendation. An integral part of this proposal was to exchange St. Mary's German parish for an English-speaking one.[81] Another part of Father Doyle's plan was to sell the Vermilion property and use the proceeds to finance the proposal. He did not think competition from Cathedral Latin would be a factor because the irritation of pastors with the scheme of parish support would cause them to "direct secretly, if not openly the boys of their respective parishes to the Jesuits."[82] This plan might have met with the bishop's support since he was willing to allow the Jesuits some freedom on the West Side, but the proposal never passed the discussion stage. Interestingly enough, in the early months of 1922 occurred a discussion between Bishop Farrelly's successor, Bishop Joseph Schrembs, and his consultors over the advisability of asking the Jesuits to operate a free diocesan school on the West Side comparable to Cathedral Latin on the East Side, which had just been placed under the full direction of the Brothers of Mary. The consultors were unanimous in agreeing that if the bishop could accomplish this he should act at once.[83] No available evidence that this project ever came up in the Jesuit consultor's meetings survives, even though in 1922 both St. Ignatius and Cathedral Latin high schools turned away almost as many students as they enrolled.

As a result of further deliberations with his consultors, Father Smith prepared a list of pros and cons on the question of closing Loyola. Only three reasons could be advanced for giving up Loyola; a scandal would be removed; temporary relief from the "vexation by the Ordinary" would be achieved; the debt would be reduced by sale of the property. None of these reasons seemed compelling to Father Smith. In fact, the first one had no merit at all. The scandal was not of the Jesuits' making and there was no obligation to give up Loyola. Moreover,

> it would be rather strange to say that since the offender is an ecclesiastical dignity and attacks not an individual member, but the Society and the religious state in general, we ought to yield. Here a principle and a class are endangered, and, therefore, it behooves us not to yield.[84]

By far the greater weight was given to the reasons for not giving up Loyola. To give up Loyola would offend the Roman authorities who had been persuaded to work on behalf of the Jesuits. By giving in, the efforts of the Congregation and of "high personages in the immediate entourage of the Pope himself" would be rendered useless, "and we must expect nothing from them any more."[85] Friends at home would also be alienated and ridiculed. The best students would be lost as well as harm done to the classical course. Vocations would be lost to the Society as well as to the diocese. The

Society itself would be disgraced, for "unhappily, and without our fault, the East Side contention has become known throughout the whole country and is watched by many." To defend a right with extreme measures and then, after winning, give up, "on account of a merely temporary opposition of a man whose life cannot last long any more," would, Father Smith thought, show "fickleness."[86]

In the fall of 1920 Bishop Farrelly attended a meeting of bishops in Washington and was reported as not looking well. On 2 February 1921, he left Cleveland to spend some time with friends and relatives in Tennessee, where he contracted pneumonia and died on 12 February. In view of the Jesuits' inability or unwillingness to be alert to the numerous hints Bishop Farrelly gave in the Loyola controversy it is interesting to note the remarks of Father Thomas Mahon, one of the bishop's consultors and pastor of an East Side parish, St. Thomas Aquinas, on the occasion of a Month's Mind Mass for the bishop. Father Mahon said that the bishop's "reserved and apparent distant manner covered a gentle and forebearing disposition; he rarely gave commands, trusting that his confidence in them would produce the best results in clergy and people."[87]

Father Smith's recommendation even before the bishop's death was to "hold out in patience and trust in Divine Providence, . . . not to build unless it is absolutely necessary, . . . if building becomes a necessity, I would suggest putting up a modest structure which without much trouble and expense can be changed into an apartment house."[88]

The death of Bishop Farrelly meant that now both protagonists in the controversy had been removed from the scene. On 19 May Father McMenamy wrote to Father Smith saying that "in regard to your new Bishop, I believe that you are to be congratulated; so Father Busch thinks." Father Busch had been at St. John College, the Jesuit College in Toledo, and worked under Bishop Schrembs, whose transfer to Cleveland was not publicly announced until 16 June. But the Provincial had other news. He told Father Smith not to take any new students at Loyola in the fall. Plans were to be made only for the second, third, and fourth years. The problem had been the subject of discussions among the Province consultors and Father McMenamy said, "I should like to close the Academy entirely, but we cannot well do that as the boys who were with you last year could not be taken care of. We have not the men to provide two schools in Cleveland. The new Bishop may object, but I think that the matter can be explained to him. This has been in my mind and that of the consultors for the past two years."[89] A second letter dated the twenty-third of May repeated the decision to close Loyola, noting the lack of Jesuit manpower, the condition of the buildings, and the lack of funds for a new building as deterrents to its continuance.[90] The fall of 1921 saw only three classes at Loyola. Rather

Loyola High School,
barn used as a gym

Loyola High School,
Classroom Building

Loyola High School,
Faculty Building

than use the phase-out plan first suggested by the Provincial, it was decided to close the school in June 1922, and work the remaining students into classes at St. Ignatius High School in the fall of 1922.

Undisturbed and probably without much knowledge of the controversy, the students at Loyola gave eloquent testimony to their ability to carry on in spite of the controversy. The old barn which served as a gymnasium had produced a championship basketball team in 1915. The fact that the team practiced in the barn, which had its baskets flush against the wall, made the players a little more rugged in under-the-basket shots. A well-received theater presentation with perhaps a prophetic title, "The Triumph of Justice," was put on in 1916. The faculty was still urging students with high marks to do better. During the winter the wood-burning stove in the classroom building often contributed to air pollution when a student would put someone's galoshes in it. Undoubtedly the students heard rumors of impending closing but the only discordant note seemed to be the exodus of some students to the new Cathedral Latin High School.

While Father Smith was examining the pros and cons of closing the school prior to the Provincial's order, he argued that the strongest reason for keeping it open was the claim that the Loyola boys were "the best and most desirable students . . . both in character and manners, and in mental attainments and social position and, as a class, superior to the West Siders."[91] Their loss, Father Smith contended, would mean "irreparable harm to the college itself." While many of these students did later attend St. Ignatius College, they did so "only because we have them under our influence for four years. The prejudice against the West Side is now as strong as ever."[92]

Loyola was not the "drag" on the college that Bishop Farrelly claimed it was; Father Smith was right in saying that by far the school's greatest contribution was its students. Physical limitations of a remodeled residence, a barn used for a gymnasium and a cheaply constructed L-shaped brick classroom building were not obstacles either to the quality of the students or their spirit. Perhaps the facilities were an asset in producing a closeness among faculty and students that endured long after the school was closed.

The Move to the Heights

One of the more cogent reasons for retaining Loyola High School was the conviction of the Jesuits that there would never be another chance to locate on the East Side. Father T. J. Smith had expressed this clearly when he drew up his list of pros and cons on the retention of Loyola and must have felt keenly the order to close the school. He had been at St. Ignatius College as Prefect of Studies since 1916 and had experienced firsthand all of the problems connected with the controversy. He was "a leader by nature," a man of "a gentle simplicity which seems to be the very essence of his character."[1] Little did he realize that he was to be the one to establish a firm foothold on the East Side.

On 4 September 1921, four days before his installation as Bishop of Cleveland, Joseph Schrembs visited the Jesuit Community at St. Ignatius College. In 1911 he had become the first Bishop of the Diocese of Toledo, newly created out of the western counties of the Cleveland diocese. After ten years in Toledo Bishop Schrembs was no stranger to the Jesuits, who operated St. John College there. It is inconceivable that he was unaware of the various efforts made by the Cleveland Jesuits to establish a permanent East Side institution. Although there were to be times when the Jesuits did not think so, Bishop Schrembs was one of the most consistent supporters of the Society of Jesus. He never let problems with individual Jesuits interfere with that support.

On this first visit to the Cleveland Jesuit Community the bishop brought up the subject of the Jesuits establishing themselves on the East Side. Father Smith informed the bishop that the Jesuits were still interested. Bishop Schrembs then told Father Smith to find a location and that when he had, the bishop would give the Jesuits a parish in the area.[2] Such a simple solution to the years of controversy!

The Board of Trustees lost little time in taking action. On 11 September the Jesuits agreed to sell the Loyola property and find a "more favorable location on the East Side of the city" for the college. It was also agreed to sell the property at Vermilion since it was "not serving its purpose any longer"; the money would be used to purchase the new site for the college.[3] That sale never took place.

On the twenty-seventh of September the Mass of the Holy Ghost was celebrated in St. Mary's Church by Bishop Schrembs to open the 1921–1922 school year. It was the last year for Loyola High School but the first year the college could look forward with assurance to the fulfillment of its "traditional objective." The combined student bodies of Loyola High School, St. Ignatius High School, and St. Ignatius College, numbering nearly 700, attended, almost filling the church. The "occasion was one of considerable ceremony." A procession of acolytes and faculty preceded the bishop from the college across the street into the Church, returning after the ceremony to the college. The students recited the prayers and sang hymns. The bishop's sermon was delivered at the end of Mass; it stressed the tribute that was due to the teaching reputation of the Jesuits, the immense good coming from Catholic education, the necessity of having a purpose in life, and the necessity of using time efficiently and keeping one's nose to the grindstone.[4]

On 3 March 1922 the bishop's consultors considered a request from the Jesuit Provincial, Father McMenamy, to open a boarding school in the "vicinity of Cleveland. This school not to be a high school but with college departments only." The request was "favorably considered."[5] In 1924, after the college site had been purchased, the bishop approved the purchase of property for a parish.[6]

Father Smith had been in touch with the Van Sweringen Company, a real estate agency in the eastern suburbs, in an effort to sell the Vermilion property to secure funds to help purchase land on the East Side. In April 1922 George Arnold, a representative of the company, approached representatives of the Nickel Plate Railroad, whose tracks ran next to the Vermilion site. John J. Bernet, president of the railroad, when asked to purchase the property from the Jesuits responded that he did not believe that the railroad would be interested. If, at any time, the college or its successors would be interested in developing the property themselves, industrially or otherwise, the railroad would be happy to cooperate.[7]

Since the Jesuits still had the Loyola property to sell they were not without a source of funds and continued to look at East Side property. Interest soon centered on the Van Sweringen development of the former Shaker community on the East Side. The dissolution of the North Union Society Shaker settlement in 1889 was followed by the purchase of the abandoned Shaker Village by a group of Cleveland businessmen who formed the Shaker Heights Land Company. A real estate development was planned; North Park, South Park, and East Boulevard were laid out with the aid of some Rockefeller money. The new land company eventually sold to a Buffalo syndicate for some $316,000,[8] but the Buffalo syndicate had no better luck developing the area during the depression of the 1890s. Although prosperity returned, the value of the land declined. The Van Sweringen brothers, Oris Paxton, and Mantis James approached the Buffalo people and secured an option to sell some lots. When they had success in selling about 200 lots, the Van Sweringen brothers organized their own syndicate to sell the entire 1200 lots. A syndicate of bankers and businessmen provided the capital and the Van Sweringens the vision and ingenuity. The area was laid out with certain through streets running east and west as well as north and south. The intent was to avoid a pattern of streets running at right angles to each other and use instead a curving pattern. Success of the venture can be judged by the increase in population and property values. The Shaker population was about 200 in 1911, 1,600 in 1920, 1,800 by 1930. By 1923 property values had risen some 7,200 percent. Appraised value in 1910 was $2,526,800; in 1923, $29,282,000.[9] The Jesuits felt that this was the place to be, if they could afford it. The Van Sweringens, interested in educational institutions as an integral part of the new community, welcomed the Jesuit interest.

The first site looked at seriously was a twenty-nine-acre piece of land identified only as being "on a steep slope." There was the possibility that an additional ten acres could be secured. The only record that such a site was considered is to be found in Father Smith's notes made in his later years. It may have been in the North Park, Fairhill area. In any case after first deciding that it was the right place, Father Smith changed his mind, or as he said, "had second thoughts" and cancelled the deal.[10]

In July 1922 another location at the corner of South Park and Warrensville Center Road extending west to Courtland and north to the Park Strip was given even more serious consideration. This property is in the area where Hathaway Brown School is presently located.

The twenty-six-acre site that was offered to the Jesuits was to cost $225,000. The Van Sweringens, after some discussion, agreed to a $50,000 concession in price.[11] The concession involved the Van Sweringen Company agreeing to buy the Loyola High School property for that amount. The total price including taxes, improvements and interest at six percent came to approximately $260,000.[12]

Father Smith confirmed the agreement in a letter to George J. Arnold, vice-president and general manager of the Van Sweringen Company, with the Loyola property's transfer to the company as part of the deal. Father Smith thanked Mr. Arnold and the Van Sweringens "for the kindness and courtesy you have shown me on this and on former occasions when I had the pleasure to transact business with you."[13]

On 18 October 1922 an agreement embodying the details of the deal was presented to Father Smith. As a courtesy to Father Smith, the Van Sweringens did not charge for the option; Father Smith then applied for permission from Father General to conclude the deal. The permission from Rome to buy was received, but Father General did not approve the conditions of the agreement.

The agreement specified the most detailed requirements on buildings, grounds, and access roads, restrictions that were to bind for seventy-seven years, with the Van Sweringens retaining the sole and exclusive rights to make exceptions. Such things as "church bells, chimes, or other devices of a similar nature" were prohibited. No power plant could be erected unless it burned smokeless coal or unless it was "equipped with smoke prevention devices approved in writing by the Van Sweringen Company." Signs, billboards, bulletin boards, and the manufacture or sale of fermented liquors were not permitted. In effect, the Van Sweringens would have to approve everything from the architecture and plans to the operation of the university.[14]

Father Smith pondered the terms of the agreement, sought the advice of his consultors, and finally wrote to O. P. Van Sweringen:

> After much consultation I have determined not to sign the terms of the prepared agreement. While restrictions would protect and safeguard the owner, they would at the same time take away from him the independence which I deem necessary for myself and my successors. I have tried to recast the terms of number one in the agreement but without success. Whatever way it is put it would bind for a period of 77 years. During that long period such conditions and circumstances could arise which could make the conduct of the school difficult and embarrassing.
>
> While I regret that I have to decline the offer made by your company, I wish to thank you and Mr. Arnold for the kindness and courtesy extended to me while these negotiations were pending.[15]

According to Father Smith's "Notes" on the property deal, the Van Sweringens refused any concessions on the restrictions. Although there is no corroboration of the claim, Father Smith also said that the Van Sweringens were so irritated by his refusal that they said they would see to it that the Jesuits would never locate on the East Side.[16] The failure of the deal also meant failure to sell the Loyola property.

It was not long before one of the other real estate people with whom Father Smith had been dealing came across some property known as the "Wain Farm" which was not owned by the Van Sweringens. The property was next to Van Sweringen property but mostly in Idlewood Village (the name was changed to University Heights in 1925) rather than Shaker Heights. It was an eighty-acre tract and available at $5,000 per acre. The owner would not sell directly to the Van Sweringens but was willing to sell to St. Ignatius College through the Rapid Transit Land Sales Company.[17]

St. Ignatius agreed to purchase forty-five acres of the "Wain Farm" on 8 March 1923. The property had a 700-foot frontage on Fairmount Boulevard between Belvoir Boulevard and Warrensville Center Road and extended in a northerly direction to Washington Boulevard. The cost was $247,500 with $10,000 to be given as cash in hand, $50,000 within forty-five days and the rest financed over thirty-six months at six percent. The formal agreement was signed on 19 March and the deed was delivered on 30 March. Father Neustich, the only survivor of the founding Jesuits, must have rejoiced at attainment of the traditional objective.

As soon as the arrangements were completed, the Van Sweringen Company approached Father Smith and sought to exchange some adjacent property of theirs for some of Father Smith's purchase. The purpose of the exchange was "to obtain a better result architecturally and otherwise for the new university."[18] The intersection of Warrensville Road and Fairmount Boulevard at the time of the original purchase was a complicated intersection of four through streets and several adjoining streets. The Van Sweringens wanted to put a traffic circle at the intersection with several streets radiating from it. Approximately twenty acres of the frontage on Fairmount was to be given up by Father Smith for approximately the same acreage near Miramar Boulevard. The would have the effect of the university property facing the circle through the extension of North Park Boulevard. A similar arrangement was made with University School, a private high school, which had purchased the frontage opposite the St. Ignatius College on Fairmount after the college had completed its purchase. The exchange between the Van Sweringens and St. Ignatius College was agreed upon but not completed until a year later, 26 March 1924. According to Father Smith the reason for the delay was his insistence that the Van Sweringens' part of the exchange be free from all restrictions; Father Smith wanted this guarantee in writing. It took the Van Sweringens one year and cost them $25,000 to give the written assurance that Father Smith wanted.[19]

CLEVELAND UNIVERSITY

Concurrently with the negotiations for the new East Side site, St. Ignatius College underwent a name change. The movement to the East Side in 1923 was not to be just a change of geographical location but also a matter of providing the location and facilities for an institution that would "develop into the leading Catholic university of the midwest."[20] It was a step engineered to a considerable extent by Monsignor Joseph F. Smith, with the approval of Bishop Schrembs, in the hope of placing "Jesuit education in

Map showing the exchange of property after original purchase in 1923

this diocese on a footing comparable to that in other large cities."[21] Such a project was thought to deserve a name that would appropriately reflect its identity, ambitions, and geographical location.

The name Cleveland University was decided upon by Monsignor Smith and James F. MacGrath, the newly hired building fund campaign manager. The first use of the name of the city for a university was in 1850 when there had been an attempt to establish a university in Cleveland. Despite the support of prominent leaders including Asa Mahan, who left the presidency of Oberlin College to head up the new institution, the effort failed, chiefly because of inadequate financing. That first Cleveland University was, curiously enough, located in what was first called University Heights, then Lincoln Heights on the south side of the Cuyahoga River opposite Ontario Street. Its legacy lies chiefly in the names of some streets of the area, such as College Avenue, University Road, and Professor Street. The charter of St. Ignatius College was officially amended on 15 May 1923 to change the name to Cleveland University. One requirement stipulated by the State in acceding to the amendment was that within nine years one professional school was to be added. The liberal arts college of Cleveland University was to be known as St. Ignatius College of Cleveland University. In this way both the city in which the university was located and the founder of the Society of Jesus could be honored at the same time.[22]

Rumors of an impending name change were circulating prior to the official announcement by Father Smith on 29 May. This may have been due, in part at least, to an awareness that the deed delivered on 30 March for the new property was in the name of Cleveland University, although the agreement to purchase the Idlewood Village property on the nineteenth of March was in the name of St. Ignatius College. At a basketball banquet on 20 March over Western Reserve University in the first meeting ever of the two basketball teams, Father Smith noted the way the banquet tables were arranged and said they reminded him of the letter "C." He then said, "very soon followers of St. Ignatius will be called upon to lend their support in a new way. He hinted at a 'surprise' and a real one."[23] The *Cleveland Plain Dealer* report on the banquet was more specific. An article on the sports page with the headline, "Rumor of Enlargement Given Basis of Fact by Hints at Annual Basketball Banquet," claimed that recent persistent rumors that "St. Ignatius College might become a university under the title 'Cleveland University' culminated in a hint last night . . . that officials of the institution have such a vision in mind."[24]

With the name change official, the former St. Ignatius College was now ready to make reality out of a dream and finally accomplish its "traditional objective." The new name and the new location caused some later confusion. Not everyone understood the change and at least one person wondered what had happened to St. Ignatius College. Hardly any publicity was ever given to the retention of the name St. Ignatius College of Arts and Sciences. A researcher at Ohio State University in 1939 inquired of the bishop of Cleveland "what became of St. Ignatius College when it went out of existence."[25] At the time the question was asked, it should also have been, "what happened to Cleveland University," since that name lasted only five months.

The summer months of 1923 were months of preparation for the building fund drive announced for the fall. The entire project was conceived originally as a joint diocesan and a Jesuit project. If this arrangement seemed unusual after the events of 1916–1919, it was due in great measure to the influence of Monsignor Joseph F. Smith. A defender of the Jesuit's position in the Loyola controversy and *persona non grata* to Bishop Farrelly's administration, he was now one of Bishop Schrembs's consultors. His influence in the Cleveland community and his personal associations with the Rockefellers and most of the influential people in the city made him someone to be reckoned with. There were times when he, rather than Bishop Schrembs, appeared to be directing activities in the diocese. Although he used his influence on behalf of the Jesuits, there were also times when he seemed to be controlling them as well as working for them. In terms of personality he was almost the direct opposite of Father Thomas Jefferson Smith.

The joint drive was to be for six million dollars, to be split evenly between the Jesuits and the diocese. Plans for the drive were discussed early in June by the bishop and his consultors but no decision was reached on its precise details. The general plan was for the Jesuit half of the funds to be used to finance the new Cleveland University. The diocesan half was to be used to build a minor seminary in Cleveland, to pay the indebtedness of Cathedral Latin School, and to build a nurses' home and high school in the Youngstown district and high schools for the Akron, Canton, and Lorain districts. On 11 June Bishop Schrembs approved the plan, and also a meeting of his consultors with Father Smith to determine ways and means of organizing the campaign.[26]

Within a month Monsignor Smith announced that the bishop had changed his mind and it was now agreed that the Jesuits would start a single drive for three million dollars for Cleveland University.[27] Diocesan authorities preferred to wait until the cathedral plans were more fully developed.[28] All discussions seemed to take for granted that that amount of money could be raised among the Catholics of northeast Ohio.

Announcement of the Jesuits' campaign for Cleveland University was made by Monsignor Smith in July 1923. The campaign was to begin 30 September and run through 6 October with subscriptions expected from all

Above left, Joseph Schrembs, Bishop of Cleveland, 1921–45; *right,* Thomas J. Smith, S.J., 1916–25, 1927–28, President, John Carroll University, 1919–25; *Bottom left,* Proposed Administration Building, Cleveland University, 1923; *right,* Msgr. Joseph F. Smith counties in the diocese.[29] It was later decided not to limit the request for suppport only to Catholics, since the university was intended to serve non-Catholics as well.

A preliminary report on the design and location of the buildings for the new university described the site as "perfect, lying as it does, with its long axis north and south. The site is almost flat, rolling just enough to give character to the grouping of the various buildings."[30] The description of the plan of the buildings and the style of architecture is clear evidence of the grandiose plans and is worth quoting in its entirety.

> The Administration building and main entrance are on Fairmount Boulevard. Behind this is a quadrangle surrounded by the Library and Administration buildings on the south, and the chapel, flanked by two dormitories on the north. On the east and west are cloisters. Through the western one is an entrance way leading to the head Master's private residence. The Chapel is the center of the grouping and is raised probably eight feet from the ground so that it will dominate the entire group.
>
> On either side of the Chapel are gateways leading thru the cloister. On the west is a quadrangle enclosed by the Church, two dormitories and the faculty building. On the east is another quadrangle enclosed by the Chapel, two dormitories and, balancing the Faculty building, is the great Dining Hall.
>
> Connected with and surrounding the Dining Hall, and forming two more quadrangles, are future dormitories.
>
> Behind this group again, is the campus surrounded by the scholastic buildings such as class room buildings, science buildings, etc., and at the end of the campus, or the main axis of the entire college, is the Gymnasium.
>
> Behind the Gymnasium is a quarter mile stadium with bleachers, North, East and South and a grand stand on the West. The power house is placed behind the grand stand.
>
> The remainder of the property, northeast and northwest of the Stadium is used for practice grounds, tennis courts and similar athletic activities.
>
> In general, the buildings are to be Ohio sandstone in the mellow buff tones, warmed up by an antique appearing red brick, somewhat similar to "Harvard Brick." The style of Architecture followed, has been Scholastic Gothic of the type which reached its highest point of perfection in the English Universities of Oxford and Cambridge. This style was selected not only because of its quiet dignity, but also because of its livableness, as it has little of the cold austerity which is found in the majority of the French and Italian Universities. The buildings in general will be kept rather simple, relying on their mass, texture and design for their effect rather than upon their ornamentation. Rich, glowing spots, however, of symbolistic ornament will be used at the main focal points such as the Chapel, Main entrance gates, etc.
>
> The group is being laid out to adequately accommodate one thousand pupils with a possible increase to four thousand without sacrificing present design.[31]

The Rapid Transit Land Sales Company published a brochure entitled, *A Child's Birthright, A Home and Education*, intended for prospective homeowners in the area which stressed the education benefits to be provided in University Heights. The brochure stressed the fact that University Heights was to be an educational center "set in most attractive surroundings—on the hill-tops, on well wooded lands, enhanced by hills and dales."[32] The center pages of the brochure were devoted to a ground-level view of the proposed buildings of Cleveland University; a folding map insert in the back of the brochure contained an architect's aerial view of University Heights and surrounding territory.

THE CAMPAIGN OF 1923

An unsigned memorandum to Father Smith instructed him on how to proceed with the fund-raising campaign. Its contents and style suggest it probably was written by Monsignor Smith, who was constantly trying to guide the rector in the proper course of action. The basic point of the communication was the recommendation that the Jesuits dissociate themselves from the history and tradition of their West Side location. What started as a German Jesuit Community, said the memorandum, still remained a German community because of the personnel and its association with St. Mary's German parish. Clevelanders' knowledge of the Jesuits was limited to that background. It would be necessary to show people that the new community starting on the Heights was everything that the bishop and his friends knew the Jesuits to be, "masters of the language, identified in sympathy and character with the community into which they are entering."[33] The writer thought that,

> if you had a church built on the property turned over to the diocese, financed by the diocese and served by progressive and magnetic men, getting in touch with people of the new locality, attracting them to the little frame church, telling them of the work you had planned, you would get their minds centered on your new project.[34]

The writer also thought a frame church could be built in about a month and enough people could be attracted to more than pay for the services. The important thing was that such a church operating before the erection of the new university would center attention on that project. This was the "proper foundation that must be made, so that you will do your part in helping your friends to get from the community that which is your due and which will be necessary to establish a new college."[35] This advice may well be responsible for downplaying almost to the extent of denying the West Side origins of the institution after its move to University Heights.

In the absence of the bishop in Europe during July and August, some diocesan decisions were made by Monsignor Smith as Vicar General of the diocese. Before he left, Bishop Schrembs addressed a letter of support for the campaign to Father Smith giving his consent "to an intensive campaign for funds to be taken up in the near future in the entire diocese." The bishop also desired the "earnest and active co-operation on the part of all our pastors to help you in putting your appeal before the laity of this diocese."[36] A copy of this letter was sent to all pastors.

A professional fund-raiser from the Ward Systems of Chicago, James F. MacGrath, was hired as campaign director with campaign headquarters in a downtown office. One of MacGrath's first steps was to submit the names of a proposed executive committee to Monsignor Smith. W. G. Wilson, an Aetna Insurance Company executive, was suggested as a chairman who would be a "tower of strength to us all along the line."[37] Other prospective committee members were: William F. Lyon, head of the Catholic Charities Campaign; Newton D. Baker, former mayor of Cleveland and secretary of war during World War I; Richard F. Grant, president of the Chamber of Commerce; Paul Feiss, president of Mt. Sinai Hospital; Warren S. Hayden, an investment banker; and Charles Otis, a broker who because of his civic contributions acquired the name "Mr. Cleveland." MacGrath saw obvious strength in this mixture of Catholic and non-Catholic personnel, but none of these people had as yet been approached and had MacGrath thought the matter through he could have anticipated some problems.

MacGrath also gave his attention to the design of a seal for Cleveland University. He sent a description of a proposed seal to a Mr. Bloodgood Tuttle for him to prepare the proper sketch to go on the front page of the campaign booklet. Instead of the traditional overlapping shields representing the armorial bearings of the two families, Onaz and Loyola, there was developed a single shield divided in the middle with either family's arms on one side. Heraldry was certainly not one of MacGrath's strong points and it is evident that he made no attempt to correct his deficiency. In his effort to explain the traditional Jesuit seal to Mr. Tuttle he recognized the two animals on the left as wolves but the device of diagonal bars at the right

is something I cannot explain. It may be as skillet or a broiling pan or a broiler iron, or it may be a stringed musical instrument, or again it has been suggested that the cross sections represent degrees of Knighthood of the Loyola gentlemen. Whatever it may be, I would accept it as being anything that it may be named, so you see your latitude and opportunities of receiving credence from whatever you may designate, it is 100%.[38]

Some years later there was still confusion about the seal. In 1928 Father Murtha Boylan, then president of the college, wrote to Father Haggeney, who had been secretary of the college for many years, about the University Seal. Father Haggeney explained in reply that the official description of the Seal was in the book of "Minutes of the John Carroll University Corporation" as the last item of the constitution and by-laws. he also mentioned that a more detailed description written by Father Pickel could be found in one of the earlier catalogues. According to Father Haggeney the Seal must have "distinctive and different colors." Father Haggeney thought he had left an accurate copy at the college; he was

only obscurely aware of a small change to correct a heraldic mistake. That change was made by Father Tom Smith who mentioned it in recreation. . . . It certainly was done without any official action. In the days of the drive we were kept ignorant of things.[39]

NEW NAME CHALLENGED

During the month of July the major project was the organizing of the parish committees, a question of timely but not hasty action "lest public interest flag" before the campaign started in September.[40] In search of sponsors who would lend personal endorsement and such other help as they wished, Monsignor Smith drew up a list of over a hundred names of the most important people in the city. In early August each of these people received a personal request from the Monsignor. The response was mixed. Some were honored and agreed to help. Others were supportive but very busy. Dudley S. Blossom, an important civic leader, found it "impossible to accede to your request" and Newton Baker pointed out that he as a "trustee of Western Reserve, cannot, but will add my modest contribution of funds, when campaign is on."[41] Most were sympathetic but could not afford the time.

Two responses to Monsignor Smith's letter of a 4 August were particularly significant. One was from Frank A. Scott, president of The Warner & Swasey Co.; the other was from Henry Turner Bailey, Director of the Cleveland School of Art. Scott, a personal friend of Monsignor Smith's, regretted he could not follow his first impulse and respond favorably. Two reasons prevented him from doing so. Like Newton D. Baker he was a member of the Board of Trustees of Western Reserve University, and also a member of the corporation of Case School of Applied Science; both institutions were planning a combined appeal to the community for a considerable sum of money. The second reason was the name "Cleveland University." He felt there was "a good deal of argument in favor of reserving the name of the city as in 'University of Cleveland' for an institution which would be nonsectarian and which would thereby represent the entire population of the community."[42] Scott was somewhat apologetic for having to put the matter that way and denied that he made "this suggestion from any narrow point of view. I presume it has already been submitted to you by others to whom it would naturally occur."[43] Scott's reference to the use of the name University of Cleveland reflected a discussion that had been going on for some years about bringing all Cleveland institutions together under that title. As far back as 1912 Newton D. Baker had such a project in mind. At no time was St. Ignatius College considered as a potential member of the proposed University of Cleveland.

The response from Henry Turner Bailey also pointed out the name problem. He was a firm believer that

> the very life of the nation depends upon public education . . . but for five years, now, I have been an enthusiastic and outspoken advocate of the affiliation of all the institutions of higher learning in the vicinity of Wade Park, as the University of Cleveland. Therefore, I cannot now consistently allow the use of my name as Sponsor for your 'Cleveland University.'[44]

Bailey then went on to reprimand the institution for choosing the name Cleveland University "after all the public agitation concerning the University of Cleveland."[45] Such action was counterproductive and would "tend to alienate the interest of some of our first citizens—Catholic, non-Catholic and Jewish—whose goodwill support you affirm you are especially desirous of uniting in this great education movement."[46] Bailey also felt that his long residence in Boston had convinced him that two excellent institutions with similar names, Boston College and Boston University, "have brought much embarrassment to many, because of the similarity of their names."[47]

Meanwhile, efforts in preparation for the drive were directed toward securing newspaper support. On 14 August Monsignor Smith sent a letter to some forty newspapers in northern Ohio asking them to show their support by becoming a member of the Publicity Committee for Cleveland University during the period of the campaign.[48] The response was heartening; nearly all replied favorably. Organizing the parish teams was a different matter. In spite of the Monsignor's request not all pastors were willing to get involved. Of the 227 parishes contacted, only 44 sent in lists of prospective subscribers by the eighteenth of August.[49] One campaign worker reported to MacGrath that many of the priests he had met felt that Bishop Schrembs was asking too much of them.[50] There were indications from other campaign workers that organizing the parish campaign would not be easy.

Attempts to enlist the support of the Knights of Columbus in the drive did not meet with overwhelming success. That MacGrath was irritated by the failure of the Knights to give active support outside of the city was evident from a reply to the report of one Youngstown campaign worker. Acknowledging support by the Cleveland Knights of Columbus, Mac-Grath suggested that the workers, where there was reluctant support or none at all, should appeal to their sense of loyalty to Catholic education and suggest that their lack of support would not help the Catholic public image.[51]

In spite of the challenges to the new name and possible lack of support, a luncheon for the sponsors of the Cleveland University campaign was scheduled for the twenty-ninth of August. Invitations to some seventy-five persons were sent, signed by Monsignor Smith on the bishop's letterhead. The luncheon was to be purely an informal affair not lasting more than one hour. It was held in the Hotel Cleveland with appropriate signs in both lower and upper lobbies announcing the "Cleveland University Sponsors Luncheon, Assembly Room B on the Mezzanine Floor." Pictures of the proposed buildings, an organization chart, and campaign literature were also on display.

Monsignor Smith made the opening remarks. After recounting his efforts to chase a fly that had been bothering him all morning, he said that fat, bald-headed men are thus bothered according to God's design. In this way the flies "get after them to worry them and keep them thin."[52] Noting that the luncheon inaugurated the work of the campaign of Cleveland University he then said he wished

> to make a public announcement here that the name that we have chosen—the Cleveland University—we have found rather of such a nature that it doesn't express the work that we have on hand and doesn't do justice to the supporters that we are calling to our aid in putting over this great work of Cleveland University. We find that in our pride of Cleveland we have forgotten the sentiments of the other great centers of Youngstown, Canton, and Akron, and Lorain, and although they recognize our importance and the greatness of our community, at the same time there is a local pride there, and we feel as we are going out to the whole diocese embracing the twelve counties of the eastern section that we must expect to be subservient to the clientele of this university. . . . As soon as Father [T. J.] Smith can get the proper name he will announce the name later.[53]

The problem of the campaign literature already in circulation with the name Cleveland University could not be solved immediately since, as Monsignor Smith said, "we have made this change very suddenly." That problem would be solved as soon as the new name was chosen. Monsignor Smith went on to stress the broad appeal of the new university and therefore the logic of including all classes of citizens in the fund-raising appeal. He thought

> it would be best to approach the non-Catholics, and Protestants, if you will, through their corporations, therefore, avoiding the necessity of calling upon the individual executives, the officers of the corporations, both to save the embarrassment of calling upon those who are not directly interested, and because there is a stronger basis of appeal to the individuals . . . Now, we feel that there is an appeal to all the corporations of the city.[54]

The rest of Monsignor's remarks seemed to belabor points that he had not clearly thought out in advance and gave evidence that the decision to change the new name was indeed a sudden one. He attempted to justify the appeal to non-Catholics on the ground that Catholics had to support their own parochial schools and the majority of customers of the various business enterprises were Catholic. He pointed out that the majority of the immigrants were Catholic and could be reached only through the church. This made it worthwhile to support a Catholic educational institution. Monsignor Smith admitted that he started on the campaign "with a great deal of misgivings, fear, and timidity, wondering how the community would respond," but he was pleased with the reaction thus far.[55]

From the beginning of the move to University Heights, Monsignor Smith either made or strongly influenced practically all the major decisions; it was no less true in the dropping of the name Cleveland University. Father Smith testified to this in his remarks following those of Monsignor Smith:

> He has pushed the movement in every way. His word with me, from the very beginning, was law. And today, for the first time, when he brought the information to me that it was necessary to change the incorporated name that we now have of Cleveland University to another name, he gave me the reasons just as he gave them to you and I have said to him, 'Your word is law with me therefore, the change will be made.'[56]

Father Smith then reviewed briefly the history of St. Ignatius College and its present crisis of too little space for an expanding enrollment. He pointed to the plans for the new university as they appeared on the chart and hoped that within a few years the hope of a new university would be realized. Father Smith concluded his remarks by saying

> I am not here as a representative of St. Ignatius College; I am here as a citizen of Cleveland and of the state and of the United States to propose this campaign for education. This education will benefit, not only the Catholic community, but it

will be of benefit to the whole community. I think it is right, it is our right and our privilege to go out to the citizens of Cleveland, regardless of religion, and ask for funds for the beginning of this great undertaking.[57]

The third speaker, James F. MacGrath, used some of his more colorful language to describe the great advantage in dropping the name Cleveland University. He was also a little more explicit on the details of the meeting prior to the luncheon at which the change was agreed upon.

Up to twelve o'clock today we were about to hobble out on this campaign on one crutch. I felt that to go before the public with this appeal simply as a Catholic appeal, when in point of fact it meant a service to Catholic and non-Catholic, would be misvisioned and a mistake. I am very gald to learn that through the wonderful facile character of the Right Reverend Gentleman who presides, that today we have cast aside the crutch and are about to go forth, our spines stiffened, our shoulders straight, as a one hundred percent, American educational proposition.

After saying that the role of education was to "lift the savage out of the slime into the ethereal heights" he spoke of his discouragement caused by the many problems confronting the director of the campaign.

Of course, the Right Reverend Gentleman who presides has always the sunshine with him. He glows over the horizon morning after morning after morning like the rising sun. . . . So it was that the machinery today has functioned one hundred percent. He has done yeoman service, . . . we are going forth today, not simply as a Catholic movement, but we are going forth as a strictly American institution, . . . the scope of our enterprise today has broadened fifty percent, . . . and I believe sincerely that it will increase in return one hundred percent over what we anticipated.[58]

No longer would the campaign have to "hobble over the highway with a crutch and produce a passable campaign" that might have satisfied the modest needs of the Jesuits but would not satisfy Monsignor Smith. MacGrath referred then to the private meeting before the luncheon where business corporation support was promised in return for dropping the name Cleveland University; public explanation for dropping the name gave no hint of such a deal.

THE UNDERSTANDING

MacGrath wasted no time in getting even more details of the luncheon announcement to the campaign workers. Although he regretted that only forty-eight of the seventy-five invited attended the luncheon, those who were present included the "biggest men in Cleveland," among them the heads of seven banks and trust companies. In MacGrath's view this made it "one hundred percent successful."[59] He rejoiced that "at noon today an agreement was signed whereby the entire Western Reserve crowd will swing into line and will get after the big corporations throughout the fourteen counties."[60] He instructed his staff to read their local newspapers for the full story. He was certain that they would see the news in the papers before they received his memorandum. A week elapsed before the news appeared in the *Plain Dealer*; a brief article on page seven announced that the "New University to Drop Name as Too Limited." The story which followed was far from complete and merely repeated the remarks of Monsignor Smith dealing with the need of a name to include other cities in the diocese.[61]

MacGrath was explicit but somewhat inaccurate in describing the situation to his staff:

> This is the proposition. Western Reserve has had its heart so set upon having the name 'Cleveland University' [*sic*]; that the Catholics have graciously given them the opportunity of using it, but the campaign will be conducted along the same lines as hitherto conducted, except now and then a statement in the general publicity that will set things straight. . . . It means that the corporations are now likely to back the proposition one hundred percent where formerly they were in a state of mind regarding it and wondering if it was simply a one hundred percent Catholic appeal.[62]

The real issue, however, was the association of the name Cleveland with the Jesuit school.

In his letter to the staff MacGrath made statements that more than hinted that the problem of name was not as simple as the luncheon speakers pretended. Reaction to the Jesuit's "willingness" to give up the name Cleveland University was, he thought, "sure to be felt, because such news will travel by subterranean cable to Western Reserve and Case School of Applied Science, to every member of the faculty, the trustees and the incorporators."[63] He then disclosed that

> this result has been attained only through the most deft and facile diplomacy. . . . We have shown our American spirit in wishing to preserve amenities between all of our citizens and at the same time establishing an amity that is reasonable, understandable and highly efficient.[64]

It is clear that the most important results of the 29 August luncheon occurred at the noon meeting of a select few preceding the luncheon. It is also clear that Monsignor Smith and James MacGrath played principal roles in that pre-luncheon meeting. The 16 August letter of Frank Scott to Monsignor Smith certainly triggered the action that led to the name change. Yet, such a letter should not have been a complete surprise. Even at the time the name Cleveland University was acquired by St. Ignatius College there was opposition to this action which surely must have been known. The representatives of the proposed University of Cleveland held claim to that charter since 1912, although there was as yet no institution by that name, and objected to the acquisition of the name Cleveland University by St. Ignatius College. Since the amendment to the St. Ignatius Charter had already been granted, the Secretary of the State of Ohio would not revoke it.[65]

The written confirmation of the pre-luncheon understanding arrived at on 29 August was a single-paragraph letter typed on the bishop's official stationery, addressed to Frank A. Scott, bearing only two signatures, those of Monsignor Smith first and then Father T. J. Smith below the Monsignor's name. It contains no written confirmation of any promise that might have been made by anyone on behalf of Western Reserve; no one representing Western Reserve signed anything. The letter simply states

> that as soon as the necessary legal formalities can be accomplished to acquire a new charter for the movement now underway to establish the new University in the diocese of Cleveland, then the charter which we recently acquired and which covers Cleveland University, will be transferred to the following trustees: Samuel Mather, Warren S. Hayden, and Frank A. Scott.[66]

QUID PRO QUO?

The full story of the pressure brought to bear on Father Smith to relinquish the name Cleveland University was never made known. The explanation given to the public about the name being a limiting factor in the fund drive in other cities of the diocese was pure fiction. In fact so little was made public, that two of Father Smith's successors as president, Father Murtha Boylan (1925–1928), and Father Benedict J. Rodman (1928–1937), tried their best to find out from Father Smith what really happened; both of them assumed that there was a monetary consideration and wanted to know how much it was and where it was.

Father Boylan's inquiry of Father Smith was apparently prompted by a bill for campaign printing costs incurred by the university for reprinting literature after the name change. Father Smith did not think that an itemized bill of printing and miscellaneous costs would reach the $19,000 figure named by Father Boylan, but claimed that $100,000 "would not compensate us for the loss of the name."[67] Father Boylan was somewhat irked by the pressure Monsignor Smith brought to bear on him to present a bill to

Western Reserve University and wrote to his Provincial that he thought Monsignor Smith had been "playing politics some way or other in the matter."[68]

In 1928 Father Rodman also tried to learn what the University received in exchange for dropping the name Cleveland University. Monsignor Smith, however, was the first one to whom Father Rodman directed his query. Monsignor Smith first wrote to Frank Scott telling him that the new president had called upon him and asked,

> if I thought that Western Reserve University would still be willing to pay them for the change of their name from Cleveland University.
>
> I am sure you remember the incident quite well when Charley Adams and you called to see me in regard to the change of name.[69]

Monsignor Smith said that he thought the costs involved would come to around $50,000, covering printing bills, artists' fees and designs. "They had to reproduce all of that and they felt that their total loss in money was at the minimum, $50,000."[70] The Monsignor told Frank Scott that he had also spoken to Charles Adams "who would confirm the statement to you."[71]

Frank Scott appreciated hearing from his friend and immediately took the matter up with Dr. Robert Vinson, president of Western Reserve,

> to show him your letter and remind him of the fact that Mr. Andrew Squire was supposed to have drawn some kind of memorandum of contract which would indicate the nature of the transaction between the two universities and which would also recite whatever responsibility Western Reserve University was to bear. Dr. Vinson promised to get in touch with Mr. Squire immediately and discover whatever the files may contain.[72]

Scott confirmed that he did,

> of course, recall our conversation and the reference which was made to the preliminary campaign expense . . . and while I do not remember that we endeavored to fix any definite sum, . . . I am sure that the general fact was at that time brought to the attention of Mr. Squire. You may remember that Mr. Mather was away at the time and that I was leaving, either on the day on which I saw you and Father Smith of the college or on the next day, and it was on this account that Mr. Squire was brought in to handle the matter, so that he could present it to Mr. Mather on his return. I, of course, am expecting that the transaction can be washed out to the entire satisfaction of everyone involved.[73]

Mr. Scott's memory of the events is supported by all available evidence and adds some additional information regarding Andrew Squire. A letter of 30

August 1923 from Scott to Monsignor Smith confirms that Scott had indeed entrusted the completion of the "understanding" of 29 August to Andrew Squire and had also informed President Vinson:

> with respect to our conference yesterday, I am transmitting to you herein a copy of a letter today forwarded to Andrew Squire, Esq., and also one forwarded to President Robert E. Vinson of Western Reserve University.[74]

The letter to Andrew Squire explained the criticism of the Cleveland University charter and advised him to "trustee" the charter with certain men who were members of the Board of Trustees of Western Reserve University.[75] Scott requested Squire to draw up the necessary papers to make the formal transfer and explained that the "three trustees would be acting in an individual capacity and not in behalf of any institution, inasmuch as they are not authorized to act officially by anybody."[76] Scott then wrote to President Vinson and enclosed a copy of the letter to Andrew Squire noting that it was "self-explanatory."[77] The record does not show why no action was taken by Squire.

In November 1928 Monsignor Smith finally replied to Father Rodman's inquiry and mentioned the $50,000 figure. He concluded his letter indicating that even he was not certain of the amount, and it may be that "this amount is more than they expected. I would, therefore, ask you to look the matter up and see if you can make a bill of items that might cover this amount."[78] In a reply to Frank Scott, Monsignor Smith apologized for bothering him when he was in ill health and said he would "take the matter up with the Jesuits again."[79] It was this exchange of letters with Monsignor Smith that led Father Rodman to write to Father T. J. Smith only to discover that Father Smith had not been a full partner in the transaction.

Father Smith said he had been guided in the affair by Monsignors Smith and Francis T. Moran, and had yielded all claims to the name Cleveland University "graciously and unconditionally" to a group whom he thought were planning a civic university. Father Smith also had in mind the long fight of Dubuque College, 1914–1920, over the legal identity and different forms of the use of that city's name and wanted to avoid a similar situation. He had later discovered that the title of Cleveland University was not trusteed to the group with whom he thought he was dealing.[80] Father Smith was somewhat hurt by Father Rodman's implication that there was more to the story than he was willing to tell. In his reply, Father Smith indicates rather clearly that he was a follower, not a leader in the matter.

> I do not see what grounds you have for asking any reimbursement from Western Reserve University for the change of name. Others are free to state my opinion in this matter, but this is my statement and for this I am ready to stand

responsible. Dear Father I trust that this will remove any doubt in your mind that I am withholding any particulars in this transaction . . .

There was opposition to our campaign occasioned by the fact that we had chosen the name Cleveland University. After talking this matter over with Mr. Grant, the then President of the Chamber of Commerce, and again considering it with Mr. Charley Adams, Msgr. Smith and Msgr. Moran, concluded that the only way of removing the opposition and gaining the goodwill of the above mentioned influential men was to change the name. Through the kindness of Msgr. Smith a meeting was arranged with Mr. Frank S. [*sic*] Scott. In the presence of Msgr. Smith after discussing this opposition we came to an understanding of drawing up an agreement wherein I would relinquish the name and charter of Cleveland University to a board of Trustees composed of Messrs. Samuel Mather, Warren Hayden, and Frank S. [*sic*] Scott. In this understanding and written agreement there was no mention of a monetary reimbursement on the part of Western Reserve University for the change of name. [The reason is simple; it was not an agreement, it was signed only by Msgr. Smith and Father Smith, and merely said that the name of Cleveland University was being surrendered.] At the time I was accused of selling the name and I denied this charge for it was false and had no foundation. I never met Mr. Mather or Mr. Hayden or spoke to them in connection with this matter.[81]

Perhaps some of Father Rodman's frustration in trying to find out what happened stemmed from a reply he received from Joseph A. Schlitz in October 1928. Schlitz was then handling the University's legal affairs and had also been asked to find out what he could about the circumstances of the name change. After Schlitz had exhausted all the sources he thought would be productive, he came to the conclusion that no one other than MacGrath and Monsignor Smith knew the whole story. He thought that perhaps Mr. Richard Moriarty, an attorney and an alumnus of St. Ignatius College, came as close as anyone to knowing about the event although he had no part in it. Moriarty had been contacted by Father Smith when Richard Grant, President of the Cleveland Chamber of Commerce, had called upon the rector, protesting the use of the name Cleveland.[82] Mr. Moriarty did not recall all the details of his conversation with Father Smith but he did remember that the name Samuel Mather had come up in the conversation between Grant and Father Smith. He also surmised that the campaign manager MacGrath had engineered the name change from St. Ignatius College to Cleveland University.[83]

Apparently, Mr. Schlitz consulted only attorneys who in the past had handled the university's business. Had he consulted Monsignor Smith he might well have learned more. That contact, however, might have been fruitless since Monsignor Smith had left very few traces of his manifold activities.

Contacting sources connected with Western Reserve University might have been equally fruitless. In 1927, Harold T. Clark, an attorney with Squire, Saunders, and Dempsey, wrote to Sidney S. Wilson, treasurer of Western Reserve University, and said that Frank S. Whitcomb of the firm had been investigating and checking on the "situation relative to Cleveland University. It is rather difficult to cover the matter satisfactorily by letter. The next time you are near our office I think you might like to talk the situation over with Mr. Whitcomb."[84]

As late as 1943 Western Reserve administrators were continuing to keep alive the charter of Cleveland University which they had incorporated on 11 September 1923. The incorporators were not the ones named by Frank Scott but rather Messrs. Warren Bicknell, Andrew Squire, Harold T. Clark, F. S. Whitcomb, and Warren S. Hayden.[85] At a meeting of the Board of trustees of Cleveland University on 19 April 1943, "upon motion duly made, seconded, and carried W. G. Leutner, who is the president of Western Reserve University, was duly elected President of Cleveland University."[86]

Over the years those who remember that John Carroll University once had the name Cleveland University have speculated about why the name was dropped and what the Jesuits got in return. Such speculation always seemed to ignore the fact that Father Smith took direction from Monsignor Smith whose interests were broader than the single issue. At one point in the affair Monsignor Smith asked Father Smith to meet with President Vinson. Father Smith refused, saying,

I do not know what the Monsignor's intention was. But how could I ask for an appointment with the president of an institution that did not invite the president of John Carroll to attend the inauguration services of its President just a few months before![87]

As to any money involved in the transaction of the name change, there is evidence only for an amount to cover printing costs incurred because of the change.

There are stories about stocks given to the university by Samuel Mather. A list of such stocks is said to have existed.[88] These stocks were depreciated at the time of the supposed gift. In the renewed campaign of 1929 Mather is listed as donating $50,000 and there is a letter dated 6 February 1930 from Mather's secretary to Bishop Schrembs thanking the bishop for his letter which "Mr. Mather will much appreciate when he is here and has an opportunity of reading your letter."[89]

Whatever may be the uncertainties about the loss of the name Cleveland University, some things are reasonably clear. A very influential element in the city did not want the name of the city associated with the Jesuit university. Andrew Squire did nothing about drawing up a contract as he was instructed to do. All negotiations were carried on through the bishop's office rather than with the president of the university, Father Smith, who was influenced by Monsignor Smith and James MacGrath. Finally, there was no "quid pro quo."

Perhaps it was the events of 1923 that Father Patrick J. O'Connell, Chancellor of the diocese, had in mind when at Mass of the Holy Spirit in October 1924 he spoke of the need for the Catholic leaders in the city in civic and political fields. The editor of the college newspaper pointed out that "Father O'Connell certainly struck one of the most vital conditions in Cleveland affairs—the fact that Cleveland, the fifth largest city in the great American Republic, is one of the few places where a large assembly of Catholics have practically no voice in civic and political procedure. The reason for this is that few leaders among the laity have education enough to point out the way and persuade other people to follow it."[90]

JOHN CARROLL UNIVERSITY

For the second time within six months the Jesuits were faced with a name change for the college. The original choice of Cleveland University had been selected so that there would be available for Catholics a university of the "highest type" in their own city, bearing the name of that city.[91] Although the university was called St. Ignatius College in the period between the dropping of Cleveland University and the selection of a new name, there seems to have been no thought of simply calling it St. Ignatius University. One reason may have been that once the move to the East Side had been assured, the Jesuits were willing to follow the advice of Monsignor Smith and disassociate the East Side institution from its West Side beginnings. Constant references both before and during the fund drive spoke of "founding" an East Side university, a "new university," and similar expressions indicating a new beginning.

The first public hint of the choice of a new name came two days after the luncheon in a letter from MacGrath to John A. Dwan, a regional chairman for the drive. After complaining that the Jesuits are "slow in reaching a decision," MacGrath confided that the new name "may be Carroll University, after the famous Archbishop Carroll signer of the Declaration of Independence [*sic*] who was a Jesuit and one hundred percent American in that he was born and educated here."[92] MacGrath was never one to worry about facts; he persisted in giving out a number of less than accurate descriptions of John Carroll.

It would appear that although Father Smith had asked publicly for suggestions for a new name, a very early decision had been reached on the choice of John Carroll.[93] As was the custom in those days there was meal-time reading in the Jesuit refectory. Peter Guilday's recently published book (1922) on the life and times of John Carroll was being read during the period of the name controversy. As early 20 August the consultors were suggesting the change of name from Cleveland University to John Carroll as an answer to the opposition; there was unanimous agreement on the name, but not on making the change.[94] If the change were necessary the Jesuits were "willing to build with the ideals of John Carroll as their backgrounds; . . . willing to live in the light of that tradition, and more than willing to cast in their lot and to identify their cause with that of the great Churchman, Educator and Patriot."[95] Many of the Jesuits must have wondered why they had not long ago so honored their illustrious former member. Other names suggested but not chosen were, Cuyahoga University, Farrelly University and Gilmour University.

Henry Turner Bailey, who had complained about the Cleveland University name, returned from his vacation to rejoice at the turn of events. Informed that John Carroll was to be the new name, he exclaimed, "I cannot imagine a better title than John Carroll University. The person who thought of that title ought to have a special letter of congratulations from the bishop, together with his most potent blessing."[96]

Bailey's letter, addressed to Monsignor Smith, was sent on to MacGrath because the Monsignor was out of town. Instead of simply acknowledging receipt of the letter, MacGrath chose to instruct Bailey in the generosity, liberality, and neighborliness of the Jesuits. He assured Bailey that the Jesuits did not want to "make it appear that the acquisition of the name [Cleveland University] was a matter of pique or cleverness, but rather to show a neighborliness to those who felt that through the use of the name [University of Cleveland] unofficially it had more or less attached itself to Western Reserve in the larger program."[97]

Now that the name was to be John Carroll University the next step was to amend the Articles of Incorporation to secure the name. This action was taken by the Board of Trustees of Cleveland University on 10 September 1923, and approved by the Secretary of the State of Ohio on 12 September. The legal title thus became The John Carroll University. It was not until a later amendment in 1932 that the article "The" was dropped and the official name became simply John Carroll University.

Various assessments have been made of the results of the change of names in the midst of the fund drive. Father Smith saw no compensation adequate to make up for the loss of the name Cleveland University. MacGrath saw the news of the change "variously received, . . . but I think the general effect will be very wholesome."[98] Campaign workers, particularly in the Youngstown area, encountered clerical opposition to the name change. One parish priest was quoted as saying that the clergy had agreed among themselves "to do nothing for the Jesuits," because "the Jesuits had sold out the name Cleveland University without getting an actual quid pro quo in cash, from Mather, Otis and the others . . . promises [made by them] were salve to bunk the Jesuits and they would not do any actual giving of money."[99] Some knowledge of what actually happened had apparently filtered down to the clergy.

The students at St. Ignatius College saw the name change more positively. The student newspaper, *The Ignatian*, did not publish until 9 October when that issue carried the story of the new name with no reference to the problem involved in dropping the name Cleveland University. Two editorials devoted considerable space to the appropriateness of the new name, and the qualities of John Carroll as a man "whose character destroyed the basis of religious prejudice."[100] One editorial devoted its attention to the role of the freshman class of 1923 which was beginning "a new era in Cleveland's educational history, when the life of the new university is in its formative stages."[101] Reviewing the past, the editorial writer, a senior, described St. Ignatius College as a

shining light, a beacon of knowledge and right in Northern Ohio and the Diocese of Cleveland. John Carroll is now and will be in the future. St. Ignatius College led the way. She excelled in every mental attainment. Her students gained distinction and won honors in the Intercollegiate Latin and English contests. Her debating team, the first in the history of the college, swept every obstacle before it and won the sole right to be called the best debating team in twelve Jesuit colleges and universities in the Middle West after defeating them all. In sports her football and basketball teams earned for themselves an enviable niche in the Hall of College Fame. Socially, we yield to none. Our orchestra is the only Symphony College Orchestra in the United States. Our college prom every year was a greater success. So you see St. Ignatius was there. She was a leader in every worthwhile undertaking.

Now the question is, Will John Carroll University break the record of the past and achieve things in the future? The answer is YES.[102]

A later issue of *The Ignatian* reprinted an article from the *Cleveland Press* citing the appropriateness of the name as reason for supporting the fund drive. The article recounted John Carroll's role in the American Revolution and described him as

an American Revolutionist in the days when to be a revolutionist was an extremely hazardous adventure. . . . And so while some of us give to John Carroll University in the expectation that it will be a continuing influence for sober thought and respect for the institutions of the day, there may be others who will be glad to help blazon before the eyes of coming Cleveland generations the name of high courage who dared to rebel.[103]

It was not only the name that appealed to the students but also almost everything else about the new location and plans. When the purchase of the site had been first announced, the student newspaper not only referred to "beautiful Idlewood Village" as an excellent location but also pointed out that "a large commodious dormitory will supply a long felt want at the local school for numerous visitors who have been forced to board at private homes. They're all right—but!"[104] The new

> housing facilities for out-of-town students will strike a responsive chord in many a lad's heart, and will no doubt turn his eyes to the great Catholic educational center of Ohio, St. Ignatius, and soon the number of those enrolled from the surrounding cities of Northern Ohio will equal and perchance exceed the present enrollment in the college department.[105]

The idea of providing

> the new University—successor of St. Ignatius—with a spacious and beautiful home in the eastern Heights where college life can be lived with a maximum advantage and enjoyment and where students in Cleveland can spend their college days within easy reach of their homes[106]

seemed like the millenium to the students in the crowded quarters on the West Side.

CAMPAIGN FAILURE

The campaign of 1923 was a failure for many reasons. The delay in starting the drive caused by the unexpected change of name put the John Carroll campaign in direct conflict with a number of other locally significant fund-raising efforts. Organization and personnel problems also were serious obstacles to success. The original plan called for too heavy a dependence on the Catholics of Northeast Ohio with the parishes the operational base. It is questionable whether the amount of money needed could be found there and, if it could, it was more likely to be spent on parish projects. Pastors were naturally inclined to look to their own needs first.[107]

Competing campaigns such as the seminary drive ordered by Bishop Schrembs for October,[108] an Akron hospital drive of such great interest to Monsignor Smith that he was willing to have MacGrath run it as well as the John Carroll drive[109] and the Cleveland Community Fund drive forced the further postponement of the beginning of the John Carroll drive. The corporate gifts campaign never did get going even with the special efforts of Samuel Scovill, chairman of the Sponsor's Committee.

Toward the end of October, MacGrath discovered that he had not been kept accurately informed on the campaign's lack of progress. He complained to Father Smith of the situation in some detail.[110] MacGrath recommended that the campaign should be continued but that it would take much longer than had been anticipated to reach the goal. He also informed Father Smith that the Ward Systems and he himself would soon withdraw their services, leaving it to the Jesuits to continue on their own.

On the twenty-seventh of October Father Smith called a meeting of the Executive Committee to announce that the campaign would be temporarily discontinued.[111] It was probably just as well. Not only was there disorganization among the campaign workers, but it would take time to diminish the considerable amount of "animosity or heat . . . engendered in the course of the present campaign" as MacGrath remarked.[112]

THE YEAR 1923 IN RETROSPECT

The pivotal year in the history of John Carroll University was 1923. The dream of an East Side location was about to be fulfilled, the site had been selected and plans made, enrollment had never been larger, accomplishments in the scholastic and athletic areas were excellent. A name change forced upon the Jesuits, for which they got nothing in return and a campaign mismanaged and ultimately discontinued put an end to the dream, at least temporarily.

Reviewing the year in the annual letter sent to Father General in Rome, the writer, most probably Father Haggeney, dwelt chiefly on the failures and expressed his frustration in being unable to retain the name Cleveland University.[113] The whole purpose in acquiring university status and using the name of the city in the university title had been to fulfill promises to the bishop and to the Catholics of the city to give them an institution of higher education of superior quality. They would no longer be forced to seek an education in universities which were not Catholic. The condition of the charter requiring the addition of at least one professional school within nine years could easily be fulfilled. The name of St. Ignatius was to be preserved in the title of the college of liberal arts.

Problems arose, the writer felt, when those in the city who were not Catholic convinced friends of the Jesuits (most probably a reference to Monsignor Smith) that the name should be given up. The situation was attributed principally to one man who could not bear the disgrace of having the name of the city associated with a Catholic institution. The writer named no one in his report but he did refer to a person who was so powerful in his influence that his views had to be considered at all times. The description of this person and the circumstances that surrounded the transaction suggest that the writer referred to Samuel Mather. Mather, a descendant of one of the original Connecticut Land Company families, was known as the "First Citizen of Cleveland, first in business, first in philanthropy, and first as a patron of the arts and letters . . . his acceptance of service with any organization was a testimonial of his judgment of its worth."[114] Mather was a somewhat private person who prided himself on "discreetly saying little and being constantly on my guard against interviews on University matters."[115] Mather's role, if any, in the name change was not a visible one. There was concern that he be kept informed as is evidenced by MacGrath's effort to send him a telegram informing him that the problem had been solved.[116] It is quite probable that without the added pressure from Monsignor Smith and James MacGrath the Jesuits would not have given up the name.

The writer of the report also informed Father General of the failure of the fund drive. Even the support of the bishop did not produce success. The businessmen and industrialists did not expend any great effort. What was collected was something less than a seventh of the original goal and most of that was used for land purchase. Nothing was left for building. The future seemed far from promising. If, as seems quite likely, the actual writing of the letter was done by Father Haggeney, that does not mean that the sentiments expressed were not also those of Father Smith and most of the Jesuit Community. The annual letters for the early and mid 1920s were composed by Father Betten and Father Haggeney,[117] both of whom were representative of the sentiment of the Jesuit Community at the time.

Had the 1923 campaign gone off smoothly and successfully, the realization of the grandiose plans for building and expansion would have given quite a different direction to the university's history. It is most likely that professional schools would then have been established with all of the consequent advantages and problems.

REORGANIZATION OF THE CAMPAIGN

The withdrawal of James MacGrath as campaign manager did not end efforts to continue the drive. On 1 November 1923 a letter was sent to all parish chairmen by John A. Dwan, who had taken over direction of the campaign. The chairmen were informed that the campaign would be continued indefinitely until all efforts were exhausted.[118] The problem at this point was that many who were considered parish chairmen had long since bowed out; others were in the process of doing so and the parishes were simply not tuned in to any great need to support the drive.

By the beginning of 1924 it was clear that success was even farther away. In February the parish campaign was again reorganized and a campaign to solicit the large corporations was added.[119] This was the first time that the Committee on Corporations chaired by Samuel Scovill began to function.[120] Father Smith announced that the Ward Systems had now severed all connection with the campaign and that, in the future, members of the faculty with Father Bracken in charge would conduct the campaign.[121] Father Bracken was chosen to direct the campaign because of his experience, ironically, in athletics over the previous five years. Father Smith was optimistic because in his experience such campaigns usually took one to two years to reach their goal. The immediate aim was to get enough money to erect essential buildings—the administration building, science building, lecture hall, and dormitory. However, the attempt to continue the drive bogged down and in July 1925 the Jesuits still found themselves engaged in more discussion than action.[122] By this time the question of the location of the new parish and the choice of a pastor had become part of the discussion of the drive and ways to make it succeed.[123]

When Father Boylan became president in 1925, a new approach was tried in an effort to salvage something from the campaign. After receiving a letter from the Provincial urging him to take action, Father Boylan had a talk with Father Odenbach which resulted in a plan to build an observatory, and Father Boylan presented the plan to the Provincial for his approval.

> My idea was this, since the drive was a failure in many ways, and showed up the incapacity of the catholics [*sic*] of Cleveland at large to see our needs, it seems futile to me to look for any measure of success along those lines in the near future. Notably so, as the business men want to see the bishop at the head of a drive appealing to them. He too failed us in the last drive lamentably. So I thought to make an appeal to the business men of Cleveland, we must be able to show some guarantee of something already realized. The Observatory is a matter they understand. If this were there we could go ahead and make a new appeal to the business men.[124]

In order to build the Observatory at the new site, Father Boylan thought that Father Odenbach's friends in the local Knights of Columbus could help develop a national appeal for $100,000, a figure Father Boylan thought possible because the "Knights were our best donors in the late drive."[125]

Father Odenbach did talk to his friends but found that the local members of the Knights were not "well fixed" and the same was probably true of other locals. It was suggested to him that a private campaign might be useful; a public one would probably not please the bishop. A goal of

$50,000 seemed possible. Father Boylan felt that, if the permanence of the Observatory on the Heights could be assured, plans could be made for the future.[126]

The 3 December 1925 issue of the *Carroll News* carried headlines announcing that the Observatory would herald the start of the new university. In the article Father Odenbach explained his rather elaborate plans. "The observatory will be complete in every detail and will include not only an astronomical observatory but also accommodations for seismographical and meteorological apparatus, as well as quarters for a little colony of astronomers."[127] A two-story building would face north on Washington Boulevard where there was a terrace of some twenty-five feet to the street level. This building was to contain a laboratory, library, study, and living quarters for the astronomers. From the south side of this building a tunnel was to lead to an underground vault for the seismograph. To the East would be a one-story building, a continuation of the first floor of the main building. On the eastern end near Belvoir Boulevard would be a two-story building with a rotunda and dome.

Father Odenbach made it clear that the Observatory financing was to be "absolutely independent of the university fund," and said, "If you know of anybody who is more than anxious to contribute to the cause, tell him he can help us out in buying astronomical instruments, or I might even let him pay for the cement."[128] Financing for the project never materialized; it is interesting to contemplate what the present campus would look like if Father Odenbach had been successful in building the Observatory

Father Boylan made efforts in early 1926 to study the possibility of a loan but failed to accomplish anything along this line. The best that could be done seemed to be to continue the drive privately among a few friends and hope through them to reach some of the businessmen. For all practical purposes the drive activity was dead.

The Search for Recognition
1886–1928

While the long struggle for the location and name of John Carroll University was going on, St. Ignatius College was having its own problems. The first half century of its existence had been characterized by a struggle for recognition in the academic community and in the city, and the second half century was marked to a great extent by the same struggle. Although Father Benedict J. Rodman (1928–1937) made the first successful move for external recognition by the community and the academic world, it was really not until the presidencies of Father Frederick E. Welfle (1946–1956) and Father Hugh E. Dunn (1956–1967), that any marked success was achieved.

From the early days the German image and identification with the seminary were limiting factors. The desire for a new location on the East Side and the change of name to Cleveland University in 1923 were efforts to overcome those obstacles. The closing of Loyola High School after its amazing success during the brief period of its existence and the inability to retain the name Cleveland University were thus major frustrations.

Within the Society itself pressure to work with accrediting agencies was forcing a reconsideration of the traditional Jesuit college standards. The debt owed to the Buffalo Mission, which had been transferred to the Missouri Province in 1907, was becoming a matter of bitter dispute and still another frustration. There was a growing feeling that, somehow, the college was being discriminated against by the Province, because the leadership of the college was suffering from the lack of appropriate replacements for men like Fathers Pickel and Sommerhauser. There was, even in the mid-1920s, at least the beginning of a notion that the Jesuits ought to consider leaving Cleveland. From almost every angle the future did not look bright. But the outbreak of World War I acted to divert attention from all the frustrations that beset the Jesuits and forced them to concentrate on the more pressing matter of maintaining the college enrollment and contributing to the war effort.

STUDENTS' ARMY TRAINING CORPS

On the evening of 21 April 1917, within two weeks after the United States had formally declared war on Germany, a preparedness parade was held in Cleveland. Wishing to participate in this parade, St. Ignatius College immediately instituted marching drills for the students. The short preparation produced good results; the college magazine noted that, "It must have done the old grads good to see our delegates in line the night of the memorable patriotic demonstration. Those who witnessed the turnout could not miss us, for we made our presence known in no uncertain methods. And the old Blue and Gold floated proudly alongside the Red, White and Blue. It was 'some' night."[1]

The zeal and enthusiasm of the student body can be seen also in its participation in the second Liberty Loan drive toward the end of 1917. The colleges had been asked to help in the final stages of the drive by securing subscribers who would help put the drive over the top. The day after the invitation was received,

> a rally was held in the gymnasium amid scenes of wild enthusiasm. Numbers of students gave short addresses in which due significance and importance of the Liberty Loan were urged and various modes of approach examined. We felt the honor of our college was at stake and we burned with impatience until classes were dismissed for the day and we could go forth on our mission.[2]

The students were so successful in securing subscriptions that they gathered $8,000 the first day; by the final day they had secured $125,000. The total eventually reached $145,000 with the addition of $20,000 from Loyola. The student body of 335 had reason to rejoice that "the most significant feature of the whole thing is the fact that we surpassed Adelbert's (Reserve) total by almost half. And at that, they had a full week's start on us."[3] Further evidence of the rivalry involved in the venture can be found in the complaint that the Young Men's Christian Association was receiving all the praise for work in the army camps while the Knights of Columbus, which "is doing fully as much and even more, is calmly and totally ignored."[4]

As if to ward off any possible question of the college's patriotism, *Lumina*, the college magazine, commented that "as shown by her work in the loan campaign, and by the number of her boys who are in the service, St. Ignatius has no reason to fear that her escutcheon will ever bear the stain of unpatriotism."[5] Father James M. Hanley, the first Cleveland priest assigned to military camp work, was a St. Ignatius graduate. He served overseas with the 165th Infantry of the Rainbow Division, the sixty-ninth New York Regiment, and became known as the "fighting chaplain of the 69th" for his ministrations during the battles of St. Mihiel and the Argonne. He was gassed in the battle of Chateau-Thierry and never completely recovered; he died of pneumonia at the age of thirty-three.[6]

Catholic support of the war effort was singled out by the *Lumina* as evidence of the falsity of the still frequently heard claims about a Catholic's divided loyalty. Figures issued by Secretary of War Newton D. Baker in early 1918 showed that 40 percent of the Navy was Catholic, as was 50 percent of the Marines and 35 percent of the Army. These figures, said the *Lumina*, "will hardly afford little comfort or delectation to Guardians of Liberty and their ilk . . . the most eloquent testimony yet furnished of Catholic loyalty to the Flag, a testimony not of words, but of deeds—yea, of lives."[7]

A reduction of the minimum draft age to eighteen in the summer of 1918 prompted the government to establish the Students Army Training Corps to defer active military service for college students. Several hundred units were established throughout the country and St. Ignatius College acquired one of them. It was Father Sommerhauser's initiative that began negotiations for the unit. In fact, Father Sommerhauser had applied in 1917 for such a unit but could find none available.[8] The only conditions that he required were that morality be safeguarded and that the members of the unit "be allowed to enjoy the spiritual direction of their religious leaders."[9] If this were done, Father Sommerhauser felt that "the discipline received in military training, under experienced officers of the United States, would undoubtedly ne [*sic*] advantageous to the all around development of the youth of the country."[10]

When he applied for the unit, Father Sommerhauser was also concerned that the number of college students at St. Ignatius would be too small for the college to qualify. The seventy-five then enrolled in the college were of the "poor and middle classes, few indeed of the wealthy. If they were compelled to furnish, e.g., their uniforms, I fear it would provide a hardship to many of their parents. For the rest, they have shown themselves intensely patriotic."[11] As evidence of patriotism, some two hundred alumni had enlisted by early 1918, the students were gearing up for the third Liberty Loan drive, reading materials were being sent to the camps, and a night school run by volunteers enrolled 250 from the Naval Reserve station who were interested in higher mathematics.[12] In May 1918 a service flag with two hundred stars was blessed, and carried in procession down the aisle of the auditorium where exercises were held. The flag was then suspended over the college entrance.[13]

Since the minimum number required for the establishment of an SATC unit was a hundred, St. Ignatius College needed to acquire twenty-five more students to meet that number. Father Sommerhauser wrote to the

War Department's Committee on Education and Special Training and explained that reaching the required one hundred students was "particularly difficult because of the *Classical Course* only. There is, however, in the same building also a High School Department with some 250 students. If the Committee could see its way clear to allow us to add the High School students of physical quality and possibly even of sufficient age, we should have easily the required 100."[14] Approval of the War Department for use of high school students made it possible for the required number to be reached. Enlistment in the unit made the student a member of the armed forces liable to active duty; the student was on furloughed status until called.[15] The unit eventually enrolled 130 students. As part of the agreement between the college and the War Department, there was reimbursement for the actual costs of instruction, subsistence, and housing in addition to a tuition allowance. The government was to provide military instruction and uniforms. The college was to furnish academic instruction, housing, meals, and suitable grounds.

The program did not last long; the Armistice was signed before all of the uniforms arrived. The *Lumina* lamented that, although Father Smith, Prefect of Studies, and Father Sommerhauser "thrilled our hearts with patriotism—to get right up there in the first line trenches . . . the nearest we got to the battle front was E. 40th St. and that on the night of the Victory parade."[16]

The problem now was what to do with the SATC. Father Sommerhauser was for keeping the unit as were his consultors, at least until the end of the school year.[17] The difficulty was that, if the students had any say in the matter, probably half of them would leave college and return home.[18] As long as duty required, they had come and would remain, but since many had come from "non scholastic avocations," the signing of the Armistice had removed the duty.[19] The problem was solved when demobilization of the SATC was ordered by the government in December 1918.

In a full and rather lengthy report to the War Department, Father Sommerhauser summarized the impact of the SATC on St. Ignatius College. The effect on attendance was "appreciable." The reduction of the draft age limit to eighteen for 1918–1919 would have reduced classes "to practically nil." With demobilization the "lure of high wages" took its toll on enrollment. "Academic programs were interfered with by extra military duty during the influenza period." Grouping of students according to age caused problems with the normal grouping by intellectual ability although the "spirit of study was always good." The faculty approved "in the abstract, the combination of a degree of strictly military instruction with academic work"; although it is not possible for the military work to be "fully credited toward a degree." One interesting note, supporting the disciplinary reputation of the "Iron Ages," was that Father Sommerhauser considered "military supervision of study less strict than normally given by the college." Relations between the academic and military "could not have been more pleasant." As a final point, Father Sommerhauser wanted to "make clear that military discipline of itself will not produce character"; the training given by the college was superior.[20]

There were two legacies of the SATC program at St. Ignatius College; one was use of the evening hours for classes by the Knights of Columbus who from 1920–1922 sponsored classes intended for returning veterans. The veterans were admitted free to the classes conducted by K of C instructors. There were courses in French, Spanish, commercial law, salesmanship, accounting, shorthand, typing, and bookkeeping. The most popular courses by far were classes in auto repair, which were taught at 71st and Euclid Avenue. The college's agreement with the K of C involved only the rental of the facilities for five hundred dollars a month. It was agreed also that "Ours will not teach in these classes."[21] The classes in the evening averaged about four hundred-fifty students a year including some nonservice people who paid tuition.

The second legacy was the barracks building fronting on Lorain Avenue in the southeast corner of the yard. This building had provided housing for the SATC unit for the brief duration of the program. After the demobilization of the SATC unit the question arose as to what to do with this building as well as some others that had been used by the SATC unit. At a meeting of the consultors it was decided to tear down the small building that had served as a mess hall and kitchen; a similar fate awaited the house which had been the officers' quarters. The building that had served as an infirmary and canteen was also to be demolished. The result of this clearing away of buildings was the provision of space for two tennis courts. The barracks building was not torn down but put in condition for renting.[22]

The barracks legend began almost immediately with reminiscences in the college newspaper, *The Ignatian*, in its second issue in 1919. Eulogizing the barracks, the writer spoke of it in loving memory. "Sordid commercialism now claims you for her own. Where once we lay wrapt in the arms of soothing sleep lie bags of lifeless flour and where but a scant year ago, the reveille turned us out, now dusty denizens of toil are busy supplying the city of Cleveland with ice cream cones."[23] In the fall of 1920 the barracks was renovated and remodeled again to become the student library which had been housed in the first floor of the main building.[24] Two years later the library was moved once more, this time to the second floor of the barracks before being again moved back to the main building in 1927 and placed under the director of Father Louis J. Puhl as librarian. The barracks meanwhile was remodeled into four classrooms for the high school.[25] The

Top, SATC Drill, 1918; *Middle left,* Library, 1917; *right,* Barracks, 1918; *Bottom,* Fire in original college, 1914

total number of classrooms for the high school by this time was fourteen including those on the first and second floors of the main building. The college used the third, fourth, and fifth floors.

ENROLLMENT

The loss of students immediately after the demobilization of the SATC was temporary. The fear that the decrease would be permanent did not take into consideration the favorable impact of the war on the desirability of a college education. Part of the reason for the "back to college" movement could be found in the perception of many of the draftees that the difference in rank between a private and an officer was often education. St. Ignatius enrolled a reasonable share of the group interested in college, partly because of its "reputation for sound scholarship."[26] The largest attendance in history was enrolled in the fall of 1919 when 120 college students taxed the facilities to capacity. The large number of alumni and students in the armed forces had helped spread the word about St. Ignatius College. The record of the college in participating in various bond campaigns during the war had also helped to enhance its reputation. Until the SATC program raised the number of college students to 125 in 1918, the number of college students in the preceding years ranged from a low of 58 in 1910 to 97 in 1916. Between 1920 and 1928 the number rose from 146 in 1920 to 301 in the fall of 1928. In 1927 there were 165 enrolled in the first Saturday session and 222 in the first Summer session, composed largely of nuns of the various local religious congregations. If the 450 high school students are added to the college total, it is easy to understand the pressure on the use of the facilities. Loyola High School during the years of its existence also increased to the limits of its capacity. The increased enrollment encouraged thoughts of "A Greater St. Ignatius" and was largely responsible for the urgent need for expanded and separate facilities for high school and college.[27]

END OF CATHOLIC COLLEGE ISOLATION

It may be difficult to understand how St. Ignatius College could develop for so many years in at least partial isolation from the community in which it existed, an isolation which did not even permit the attendance of the Jesuits at Shakespearean plays in public theaters.[28] St. Ignatius was no different from most other Catholic colleges, including the Jesuit ones prior to World War I. Not only were Catholic colleges isolated from the world of higher education but they were also isolated from each other. The situation was caused in part by the dependence of Catholic colleges on first- or second-generation immigrants who had not yet acquired economic status. Most of the clergy in the religious orders which had founded these colleges or taught in them were in the process of learning English and separated to a considerable extent from the secular world. The European concept of the six-or seven-year college corresponding very roughly to the American junior college continued to World War I but it could hardly survive in the face of the development of American higher education. Even then, it took considerable effort on the part of forward-looking members of Catholic faculties to convince their colleagues of the necessity for change.

Father Samuel K. Wilson, at one time president of Loyola University in Chicago, cites an example of "two strikingly gifted men from a certain religious order sent to Johns Hopkins [in 1903] for the doctorate in classical languages and literature. They returned to their monastery in a few weeks with the explanation that Johns Hopkins had nothing to offer them."[29] Father Wilson describes the early period as one of "abysmal ignorance of contemporary achievement in general education . . . bolstered by pretense."[30]

As long as the Jesuits attempted to maintain the seven-year college program, the college remained in a position outside the developments in American higher education. It could even claim to be unaffected by all the changes that were going on. Yet the seven-year program simply did not fit the American educational ladder, on which the elementary school, a mixture of English and German precedents, was at the bottom. The secondary school, which had some roots in the English grammar school but had become the peculiarly American high school was next; then came the college of English origin, and the German graduate school was at the top.[31] The attempt of American educators to articulate these various levels and provide some measure of standardization during the 1890s and early years of the twentieth century made it necessary for the Jesuit college to work out its relations with this system if it was to achieve any measure of recognition.

The formation of accrediting associations, the various committees of the National Education Association, particularly the Committee of Ten of 1893, and the report of the Commission on Reorganization of Secondary Education in 1918 changed the picture for both high schools and colleges.[32] The development of the unit and the semester hour credit system of describing and counting courses in connection with college admission requirements made it easier for the student to transfer from one school to another and was bound to affect students from Jesuit schools who wished to pursue their studies in professional and graduate schools. If the Jesuits were to maintain status in education some changes had to be made.

Jesuits were getting pressure not only from the secular world but also from pastors in parishes where the Catholic parochial school was undergoing rapid development, particularly after 1890. Formerly many parochial schools went only as far as the sixth grade and Jesuit colleges often took in those who would have gone to the seventh and eighth grades.[33] St. Ignatius College had once been forced to take some students from the sixth grade during Father Pickel's presidency; their parents did not want to send them to the public school. Resentment that the Jesuits were picking off the best students even when the parochial school added the last two grades can be readily understood. By 1910 the Jesuit high school was distinct from the college and gave a standard four-year course, admission to which required the successful completion of the eighth grade. In spite of some resentment among conservative Jesuits, by 1917 all high schools in the Missouri Province had been directed to apply for admission to the North Central Association of Secondary Schools and Colleges. Although submitting to judgment by external standards, great effort was made to keep the Jesuit spirit and objectives.[34]

There were also efforts among the Catholic colleges of the country, including the Jesuit colleges, to set up their own standards and norms. This led to the formation of the Catholic Educational Association, which proposed to work out standards for all Catholic colleges at its meeting in St. Louis in 1904, an effort that met with opposition from the representatives of Jesuit colleges.[35] By 1915 the Missouri Province Jesuits had come to agree on the need for some kind of organization; the need to conform to the requirements of the American Medical Association for admission to medical schools provided some of the pressure to think more positively.[36] Few of the high schools of the Missouri Province were up to the standards now required of American high schools; St. Louis and Creighton Medical Schools were thus put in the position of jeopardizing their class A rating by admitting graduates of their own schools.[37] Thus the Jesuits of the Missouri Province now urged support of the Catholic Educational Association or some similar organization with standardization and accreditation as the desired ends. "The North Central Association had already (reputedly at the urging of B. J. Otting) [Father Bernard J. Otting, S. J. was president of St. Louis University, 1913–1920] consented to consider the contributed services of the S. J. staffs as the equivalent of endowment funds."[38] This would remove a major stumbling block to accreditation of Catholic colleges run by religious orders if the North Central would agree to this method of computing endowment.

In the Missouri Province a series of moves toward some kind of academic uniformity for all colleges of the Province and an attempt to be in contact with all of the secular schools were initiated. There was recognition that Latin and Greek were losing ground and the policy of adjusting to the new academic environment made a great deal of sense. Father Alexander Burrowes as Provincial, 1913 to 1919, encouraged these developments. Greek was eliminated as a requirement for the bachelor's degree in 1919 and at a meeting of Jesuit college deans of the Province at Prairie du Chien in 1921 the motto was, "every Jesuit college a standard college."[39]

By 1920 some improvements had been made but inadequate staffing, shaky financing, and administrative problems indicated that there would be difficulty in doing more. In 1921 the Jesuit Provincials of the American Assistancy set up an Inter-Province committee to consider what more should be done to bring Jesuit education to an acceptable level of recognition. Father Albert C. Fox became chairman of the committee. Father Fox, president of Campion College at the time, did not fit the traditional Jesuit mold; he never approved of Jesuit aloofness from the secular educational world.

Father Fox was perhaps the first Jesuit to participate actively and extensively in the affairs of the North Central Association. His interest most likely began when as Dean of Xavier College in 1913, he discovered in his desk an eighteen-year-old invitation to the college to become a charter member of the North Central Association. He is generally credited with a role in convincing the North Central to accept the concept of the "endowment of men" for religious institutions whose faculty of priests were paid no salary.

A fine orator whose main theme was teaching, Father Fox gained a national reputation as one who demanded the highest educational standards possible when he was president of Campion College from 1918 to 1922. Father Fox remained chairman of the Inter-Province Committee until 1931. He served as president of Marquette University from 1922 to 1928, and was largely responsible for the high place that institution came to hold in the academic world. His "rigorous" and "almost pitiless" demands for high academic standards resulted in one Milwaukee newspaper running a headline indicating that Marquette now "Breathes the Spirit of the Explorer" after whom the university was named.[40] Father Fox opposed what he called "half-educated" products of the "standardized and endowed mediocrity" of many public institutions.[41] He believed that a university owed public service to the community and he so acted during his presidency at Marquette that he convinced the city of Milwaukee that Marquette was the city's university. So well known had Father Fox become during his presidency at Marquette, that when he left office in 1928 to become dean of the college at John Carroll University, he was awarded an honorary degree by Columbia University. The citation praised "an earnest and devoted career of scholarship, religious teaching, and educational administration; exercising large influence in the movement to raise standards and the methods of college and university work throughout the United States, easily taking rank with the foremost educational leaders of the land, . . . "[42]

NEW STANDARDS AT JOHN CARROLL 1920–1928

Publication of the college *Catalogue* for 1920 was postponed until June of that year because the work of the Province Committee designing the new program was not completed in time for the usual publication date in February. The student newspaper greeted the changes in the curriculum as a "happy combination of the benefits of both the elective system and the prescribed system of studies."[43] The general plan was to confine fundamentals to the freshman and sophomore years leaving the junior and senior years to a major and minor together with the study of philosophy. "In this way," commented *The Ignatian*, "it is hoped that the demands of specialization will be met without in any way sacrificing the benefits which came from a prescribed course of fundamental branches."[44] For the first time the student was not required to take Greek for the bachelor's degree; it was replaced, if the student chose, in the freshman year by mathematics and in the sophomore year by history. Courses were structured on a credit hour basis and a major and correlated minors were to be chosen by the student at the end of the sophomore year. Electives appeared for the first time, not as additional courses, but as substitutes. A first-year course in a foreign language would not be accepted for credit towards a degree unless followed by a second-year course in the same language.

There were some things that did not change. The new *Catalogue* pointed out that

> The Jesuit system of education does not share the illusion of those who imagine that education while enriching and stimulating the intellectual faculties, also excercises a moral influence of human life. Experience proves that knowledge and intellectual development have of themselves no moral efficacy. This fact established, the Jesuit system aims at developing, side by side, the moral and intellectual faculties of the student and at sending forth to the world men of sound judgment, of acute and rounded intellect, of upright and manly conscience . . . In brief, the purpose of Jesuit teaching is to lay a solid substructure of science, professional and special, and to build up the moral life, civil and religious.[45]

Among other changes introduced by the new *Catalogue* were the spelling out of degree requirements in terms of the new credit hour structure, the classification of students according to the number of hours completed, and the course listings by department; in fact most of the things that are today found in a college catalogue were to be found for the first time in the new *Catalogue*. One interesting omission from the new *Catalogue* was the degree Bachelor of Music, which had been announced in the fall of 1919 before the new standards were adopted.[46] The only degrees listed were the Bachelor of Arts, Bachelor of Science, and a new Bachelor of Philosophy which was to be given for majors in philosophy, history, English, economics, political science, education, and sociology for those students who did not take Latin in their program.

Perhaps the most confusing part of the new arrangement for the student had to do with the choice of electives. *The Ignatian* attempted to solve the problem for the student by suggesting that "some opinions differ a little in the viewpoint [an elective versus a prescribed course] and explanation but they are all reducible to one single fact that the relative merits of the courses depend for the most part on the student himself."[47] It took some time to accustom both students and faculty to the new order. It was not until 1928 that some system of record keeping and counseling in the selection of courses was developed. By that time each student was given a personnel card by the registrar. The card was essentially an updated authentic transcript of the student's record to keep him informed of his status.[48]

The class schedule and calendar were also changed. Traditionally, Thursday had been the free day in the week; it was now replaced by Saturday as the free day. This change, not entirely due to the new standards, reflected more the increased interest in athletics, particularly football, and the difficulty of scheduling contests for Wednesday, which had been the usual practice.[49] It was also more convenient for students to find part-time work on Saturday than on Thursday. The question of religious holidays also came up for a review. The general, "good academic procedure not to multiply holidays," was to be followed.[50] This eliminated some holidays which had formerly been observed such as Pentecost Monday. The registration in the fall of 1920 gave the 140 college students, the largest number thus far in the history of the college, a chance to try out the new system.

A headline in *The Ignatian*, "'Tough Task' Wail of Ignatius Students Picking New Course," suggests that there were problems in the new freedom.[51] The responsibility suddenly cast upon the student left him in a quandary. Recourse to the *Catalogue*, "where all is set forth and intelligible to the initiated but sounds like Chinese to the novice," was not a great help.[52]

It was a very frequent occurrence during the days of registration at the college, for a student to journey thither, put in a mere matter of three or four hours trying to figure out just what he was going to do during the coming year, ask everybody from the Dean down to explain the problem, and finally give up in despair. The young man then went home and devoted a few more hours to a perusal of the catalogue.

'It's a tough task!' was the universal plaint at SIC.[53]

ACCREDITATION

Efforts to meet the standards of accreditation agencies soon began to have their effects. Students were impressed that "the strides taken by St. Ignatius College in the past few years have been anything but small. The school has progressed, yet this progression cannot afford to stop. To arrest and hamper its growth spells stagnation . . . but since it must continue to live, it must have the principal requirement for this evolution—NUMBERS."[54] Each student and alumnus was to make himself a recruiter by transforming "himself into a heart and soul BOOSTER"; the student or alumnus was to send names of prospective students to the college for follow-up by the college faculty.[55]

In March 1920 there was a visitation of the college by a committee from the Ohio College Association. Elias Compton, dean of Wooster College, and Winfred G. Leutner, dean of Adelbert College of Western Reserve University, composed the committee. St. Ignatius college was admitted to the Association as a result of their favorable report. Father Everard Beukers, Provincial of Holland, and Father M. J. O'Connor of St. Louis University as his assistant had been commissioned by Father General Wlodmir Ledochowski to visit the colleges of the Missouri Province. Father Beukers arrived at St. Ignatius College in March 1921, as part of his assignment "to look into the educational and religious work done by the Jesuits in the Middle West.[56]

In March 1922 a North Central Association inspector, W. W. Boyd, president of Western College for Women in Ohio and a member of the North Central commission on admissions, arrived at St. Ignatius College to make his inspection. Part of his report as quoted in *The Ignatian* made several points, "The esprit de corps of the student body, the earnestness and effort of the teachers, the splendid condition of the plant, the fine laboratory equipment, the fine student atmosphere, the ample provision of finances, and the evident policy of a purpose to maintain the high standard set up by the North Central Association would seem to warrant the accreditation of St. Ignatius College."[57] The report was accepted by the Association and St. Ignatius College was accredited. An explanation of the "ample provision of finances" was that in place of the $300,000 endowment required by the North Central, the annual contributed services of each Jesuit rated at

$2,500 per year gave an equivalent of an endowment of $500,000.[58] In 1928 the advantages of accreditation were evident when Father George Degleman, then dean of John Carroll University, received notice from the University of Illinois that the college had been placed on that university's accredited list with an "A" rating.[59]

The tradition of the classical course did not give way easily or rapidly to all of the new curriculum changes. Father Christopher Kohne, former dean of the college of St. Louis University, was at John Carroll in 1925 to give a retreat. In his remarks before leaving Cleveland he said that "Probably Carroll has the largest number of strictly classical students in Ohio or in the Missouri Province."[60]

There were still some Jesuits who were not always enthusiastic about belonging to the various educational associations. During the presidency of Father Murtha Boylan, 1925–1928, there seemed to be a pattern of inattention to the requirements of membership in these organizations and the legal requirements of being incorporated. Father Haggeney, who for many years was secretary of the Board of Trustees of the college, called Father Boylan's attention to the necessity of proper procedure in the Board's activities. Father Haggeney pointed out the distinction between a "special meeting" and an "extraordinary meeting." He feared that some "smart lawyer might use such irregularities to invalidate action," which almost happened under the presidency of Father T. J. Smith. "Those people go on the assumption that priests and religious are not observing the law. They may try to do it again," claimed Father Haggeney.[61]

Evidence of lack of support for the new openness can be found in Father Boylan's reluctance to pay dues to the Association of American Colleges in 1928 in spite of five requests by the dean, Father George Degleman, to do so.[62] Father Boylan's answer to the dean was that there was no money available and in any event he "did not care to have John Carroll in this association since he claimed it was fostered by Protestant Ministers"[63] Efforts to persuade Father Boylan that prestige and standing were involved were of no avail. Father Degleman had unhappy memories about a similar instance a year earlier when the triennial reports to the Ohio College Association were overdue, in spite of repeated requests by the dean to send them. Father Edward J. Bracken, dean of men at the time, finally managed diplomatically to get the reports sent.[64] Father Degleman considered

such reaction . . . strange to one who knows that if an institution is a member of any association, it is naturally expected and understood that the member complies with regulations and other matters concerning the association. It is impossible to explain and more than difficult to understand any other attitude. No constructive work is possible when attitudes interfere with building up efforts.[65]

Father Degleman's experience at Marquette University in setting up the college of business administration there in 1911, as dean of the graduate school there in 1922, and as professor of philosophy of education at St. Louis University from 1925 to 1927, had earned him the reputation as a "hard-nosed" administrator. It is not surprising that he felt his efforts to bring John Carroll University into the mainstream of higher education were hampered by inept administrators; he returned to St. Louis in 1928 to be succeeded as dean by Father Fox, who had been his president at Marquette and who was even more insistent on Jesuit colleges meeting the new standards.

DEAN OF MEN

Departmentalization and specialization had now replaced the traditional classical course and the academic dean replaced the prefect of studies. But what was to become of the former close teacher and student relationship during the college course? Was this also to be a casualty of the effort to meet new standards? As Father Boylan explained in the student newspaper,

> In former times students, especially those in high school, had the same prefect for all their studies. In this way the teachers were able to familiarize themselves with each student's character and understand his individual problems. The student in turn learned to confide in the teacher and a mutual bond of confidence resulted. With the change in the curriculum of the school, the professors specialized in certain subjects, and in this way the student had a different teacher for each subject. In order to have an advisor for both spiritual and temporal needs of the students, the office of Dean of Men was established at all Jesuit colleges and universities.[66]

The work of the dean of men was to be accomplished through confidential conferences in which he would counsel the student in his choice of a state in life and advise him in personal matters. Father Edward J. Bracken, who had been at the college since 1919, seemed to Father Boylan a logical choice as the first one to hold this position at John Carroll. Father Boylan himself had been dean of men at Xavier University before coming to John Carroll. According to Father Boylan, Father Bracken possessed the necessary qualities of being a person who knew the students and could direct them intelligently. "'In our universities,' said Father Boylan, 'where the Dean is always a priest his priestly character adds ground for additional confidence in his advice and direction.' "[67]

ACADEMIC STANDARDS AND PROCEDURES

Because Father Bracken had been the academic dean it was necessary to replace him when he took his new post, and Father Leonard Otting succeeded as academic dean in 1926. Father Otting is perhaps better known to many later John Carroll students as a professor of philosophy admired for his knowledge and teaching skill as well as feared as a disciplinarian; no student would attempt to enter his class without proper dress, including a tie. The halls between classes witnessed many a student trying to beg, borrow, or steal a tie so he would not be thrown out of class. At the time Father Otting became dean in 1926 he was thirty-eight years old and probably one of the youngest deans of any college. In an interview for the student newspaper shortly after taking office, Father Otting said, "What impressed me most of all was the manliness of the men. They did not hold back from me because I was a stranger. This was particularly true at the time of my visit to the football camp."[68] At the camp Father Otting said he had seen a lot of pep and spirit the Carroll team displayed.[69] He hoped the students would feel at home with him and come into his office and talk things over.

Father Otting returned in January 1927 from a meeting of Jesuit deans at Loyola University in Chicago with the news that there would be strict enforcement of the *Catalogue* requirements for graduation. One of the effects of this strict enforcement was to require non-Catholic students to complete 128 hours for graduation. Formerly they had been required to take only 120 excluding the eight hours of religion. They were not to be required to take the religion courses but could elect any eight hours. Father Otting announced that there would be further changes which he was not yet ready to make known.[70] Father Otting's career as dean was a short one; he was replaced in the fall of 1927 by Father T. J. Smith who had been at Xavier University for the previous two years. In December of that same year, Father George A. Degleman replaced Father Smith.

There had been increasing complaints from the faculty that the policy of dropping students for poor scholarship was inconsistently applied. The problem arose partly from allowing a student with an "E" grade (conditional) to take the conditional examination even if the student had been dropped, and partly from reducing grades because of absences; tardiness was counted as absence even for the 8:10 A.M. classes. The conclusion of Father Degleman was that "a good working policy which is effective seems better than one which is only a paper policy."[71] Father Degleman said that "To a stranger coming upon the situation, the inconsistency, uncertainty about regulations, the absence of any definite system and policy and a certain reluctance to establish any is very striking."[72] Full sympathy with and understanding of the new standards was slow to develop at John Carroll.

Father Degleman became concerned with the problem of providing a full

Top left, William J. Young, S.J., 1913–16; *center,* Leo J. Vollmayer, S.J., 1914–19, 1932–37; *right,* James J. Doyle, S.J., 1910–21; *Middle left,* James A. Kleist, S.J., 1897–98, 1916–28; *right,* Francis S. Betten, S.J., 1910–28; *Bottom,* Simon A. Blackmore, S.J., Literature, 1916–21

schedule for those who had failed a single course. The policy he found in existence when he came was that "here they make every effort to graduate the student in four years allowing programs up to twenty-one hours. That should not be done."[73] His solution was to organize a "class in Sociology in order to accommodate those who flunked."[74] This did not solve the schedule problem but it does explain why the sociology department was for years the *refugium peccatorum* in academic matters.

By Father Degleman's time the problem of athletes and their academic records had arisen. In 1920 such a problem was minimal. *The Ignatian* for 28 February 1920 reported that "athletics properly supervised are no detriment to one's studies was clearly demonstrated in the Mid-Year Exams. Of the eleven men that make up the college basketball squad, seven received an average of 85 percent or over and hence were entitled to first or second honors."[75] By 1928 there was concern that because of "emphasis on athletics" there were too many students uninterested in education; the solution suggested was simply to "flunk out those who do not pass semester exams."[76]

Not all of the dean's problems were with students. Father Degleman felt that he was often bypasssed by instructors who "have the habit of going to the president about matters which really belong to this office."[77] The dean also complained about the form, direction, and content of the thesis for the bachelor's degrees. What he saw in those that were submitted suggested that "some of the teaching staff do not understand what a thesis is—a definite something to be established and not a mere essay. Likewise some do not grasp the function of the adviser who should be ready to act by conferences, etc., and direct the progress of the thesis."[78] Father Degleman also thought it was time to issue sheepskin diplomas instead of the paper ones that had been used. The dean's point was that there was "scarcely a high school in the country which doesn't issue sheepskin. We should not humiliate our boys before others, especially the girls' colleges in the city. Besides, Colleges and Universities do not issue any diplomas except sheepskin . . . Let's get on the band wagon and study academic customs and traditions."[79] Father Degleman also pointed out that the ten-dollar diploma fee was not intended to make money but to defray expenses of the commencement exercises. The dean also made an attempt to correct irregularities connected with final examinations; all examinations would be duplicated and kept in the dean's office to prevent those who reproduced the examinations from selling copies.[80]

On the positive side, Father Degleman saw that considerable progress had been made in counseling the students on their academic programs; record keeping had been much improved. The dean also tried to interest seniors in going on to graduate school and in particular to think of teaching as a career. He sought to arrange assistantships in universities for those who could qualify.[81]

FACULTY EXPANSION: EMERGENCE OF LAYMEN

Pressures of expanding enrollment and the need for meeting qualifications of teachers under the new standards required more Jesuits than were available; lay teachers were needed to fill some of the new positions. It was perhaps with this thought in mind that Father Degleman began urging seniors to qualify for high school or college teaching. At St. Ignatius College laymen were hired for the high school before they were employed in the college; one exception was the musical director in the early years. As early as 1910 Father Pickel had been seeking "first class" teachers but the ones he sought would have had to fit into the classical program.[82]

In 1919–1920 the entire college staff of sixteen was made up of Jesuits but it was increasingly clear that laymen would be needed.[83] In 1920–1921 two laymen were added, George J. Conn, director of athletics, and William J. Dempsey, assistant director of athletics. The following year, Frank D. Burke, who had graduated from Catholic University, was hired as professor of chemistry and mathematics; Toby R. Erdman replaced George Conn as director of athletics. In 1922–1923 four laymen were on a faculty totaling twenty-one; Peter Small in Spanish and Samuel Avigdor in French had been added. No change occurred the following year but in 1924–1925 two student assistants in English were included in the faculty listing, Victor G. Eberhardt and Francis T. McDonough. In 1925–1926 there were ten lay persons on a faculty of twenty-eight; Aloysius A. Bungart in English, Clarence J. Haggerty in mathematics, James J. Harwood in sociology, A. I. O'Toole in mathematics, Ray C. Miller in English, and Miss Katherine Winters as assistant librarian were added to the staff. When Father Degleman became dean in the fall of 1927, the faculty had been reduced to twenty-one of whom nine were laymen. One of the nine was a medical doctor who taught the advanced courses in the biology department which now had seventy students using the improved laboratory facilities and new equipment.[84] The salary for the lay teachers was one hundred dollars a month for ten months.[85]

In 1917 an effort to provide the proper credentials for Jesuits was begun by St. Louis University. The policy announced by Father Bernard J. Otting, president of St. Louis University, 1913–1920, awarded doctoral degrees to those Jesuits who had taken their philosophy or theology at St. Louis University and whose publication record was acceptable in the judgment of a Committee on Degrees set up for that purpose. Father James Kleist's degree was of that type; Father George H. Mahowald, who taught

Latin and English, was the last to get such a degree in 1928 when the policy was discontinued.[86]

One of the reasons for the increasing need of teachers can be found in the development of summer, Saturday, and night classes in the late 1920s. Also there were occasions when some of the Jesuits taught courses for the nuns in the convents. As early as 1922, Father Haggeney taught at the Ursuline convent at a time when the idea of credits and semester hours was new to all concerned. Father Haggeney later wrote to Father Boylan of problems with these courses, which he felt were caused by Father Bracken, who was academic dean at the time. It seems the nuns had not properly registered for the courses and Father Bracken was not about to recognize the existence of the course, the teacher, or the students. Father Haggeney's response was that "as I was under higher orders, I did not mind him."[87] When the nuns wondered where their credits were after completing the course, a standoff between Father Bracken and Father Haggeney ensued. Father Haggeney did not think much of Father Bracken's record keeping since reports for the boys made out by the dean's office "were written so incorrectly that I had to get up in class and read the marks of every student in philosophy and Latin so that they might see to it that the mistakes might be corrected."[88]

Father Degleman's short term as dean brought order to many of the procedures necessary to meet a system of standards that was unfamiliar and befuddling to those who had had no experience with it. One practice that was introduced to help matters was the weekly dean's lecture period. Although it was designed to bring in speakers from the professional and business world as well as from the college and university world, it was often used to explain the procedures involved in the many academic regulations that affected the student. Father Albert C. Fox, when he became dean in 1928, continued these meetings and often used them to give students information that he admonished them to "put in the back of your head where it won't fall out."

The Public Image

The transition from the traditional Jesuit classical course to the more modern American college structure and program was not something that created any immediate change in the image the public had of St. Ignatius College; its image of a seminary preparatory school remained for many years. Participation in intercollegiate athletics, especially football, was seen by some Jesuits, especially Father Bracken, as a way of changing the public image. Lack of membership in the Ohio Conference for many years limited opponents to colleges outside the area and caused suspicion about the eligibility requirements of the college. Overlooked and not sufficiently capitalized on was the early fame the college had achieved in science and music. If the name of St. Ignatius College came up in public, two Jesuits were almost invariably identified with it, Father Frederick Odenbach and Father Victor Winter; each in his own way symbolized the institution for an interested part of the public.

From the moment he had joined the faculty in 1893, Father Odenbach was a public person; his meteorological apparatus on top of the college building had helped to keep the college in the public eye. In 1917, about the time of the entrance of the United States into World War I, Father Odenbach had become interested in wireless telegraphy. With the help of the Alumni Association a fund-raising drive was started to provide for the purchase of the necessary equipment for the operation of a station. The campaign was launched with a Smoker given by the Alumni Association. The speaker on that occasion was President Charles S. Howe of Case School of Applied Science, as it was then known. President Howe was a man of demanding standards of scholarship and not particularly fond of the liberal arts student.[89] He believed that "constant application of a man's talents is the foundation of all real progress and success.[90] His speech was so popular and so well given that those present hoped to hear him again and were grateful for the interest he aroused.

Interruptions and delays caused by the war postponed the purchase of the "singing arc" until 1920, when the very best instrument that could be bought was purchased by Father Odenbach himself. The new instrument, called an "audion," did away with the old style crystal and produced a continuous tone that was interrupted to form the dots and dashes. Complete with amplifier the "audion" had both telephone and telegraph connections.[91] Meanwhile, Father Odenbach had acquired four excellent seismographs, one of which he designed himself. Nearby street car traffic, trains, and waves on the lake created vibrations that made the instruments record more than earthquakes. Father Odenbach once said that the Calumet Copper Mines five thousand feet below the surface of Lake Superior was the only place he knew of where extraneous vibrations would not be recorded.[92]

Father Odenbach had become acquainted with Dr. Emmerick W. Ritter of the Southern Sulfur Company of Texas. Ritter was a former Clevelander whom Father Odenbach assisted in the process of producing pure sulfur crystals better adapted to the manufacture of rubber than any commercial product then available.[93] Father Odenbach was invited by Ritter to spend a month and a half in the Trans-Pecos region of Southern Texas as his guest. There Father Odenbach explored the area in search of mineral deposits. He also explored the insect world of the area, discovering some new species which he sent to the Smithsonian Institution. He brought home with him a couple of rattlesnakes which failed to endear him to anyone.[94]

He made another trip in 1922 to visit Ritter in Louisiana, where the latter was interested in materials for making silica-gel used in refining gasoline. Ritter was then a consulting chemist with the Union Sulfur Company and had succeeded in making the so-called German dyes.[95]

Perhaps one of Father Odenbach's more visible contributions to city life was giving Clevelanders an opportunity to set their watches daily to the correct time. An instrument relayed the exact time from the Observatory in Washington, D.C. to Father Odenbach's Observatory. The relayed time signal, connected to a huge searchlight perched on top of the college roof, turned the light on at exactly 7:55 P.M. every evening. The sky remained illuminated until 7:59 P.M., when the light began to flicker and went off altogether at 8:00 P.M. There may well have been times when the signal was not too helpful. "As Jack Raper of the Cleveland *Press* says in his daily 'Most Anything' column, 'Many people will be sitting up after 8 o'clock to set their watches by the St. Ignatius Flash.'"[96]

Sunspots and white ants also were given Father Odenbach's attention, the former when the sunspots began to interfere with telegraphic communications in the spring of 1921, the latter when a white ant invasion of Cleveland Heights in the spring of 1923 turned out to be termites, according to Father Odenbach's explanation of the "pestiferous invasion" to the newspapers.[97]

By 1923 Father Odenbach began to confine his activities to astronomy and meteorology. In 1929 he was the recipient of a complete weather instrument designed over thirty years before by a pioneer astrophysicist, Jesuit Father Pietro Secchi. The invention, a highlight of the 1878 Paris Exposition, was purchased by the United States government and put in the Smithsonian Institution. It was later decided to put it in a Jesuit institution because of its inventor: "John Carroll being somewhat inclined to the historic became the possessor."[98] Perhaps it was in part because of the publicity created for St. Ignatius College by Father Odenbach that the mayor of Cleveland was induced to address the commencement exercises on 17 June 1920. This was the first commencement in which there was an academic procession with cap and gown. There were only three bachelor's degrees, but St. Ignatius High Schol graduated thirty-eight and Loyola twenty-five.[99]

In a totally different way Father Victor Winter achieved recognition for St. Ignatius College. It was Father Winter's task to develop the college orchestra during and after World War I following its brief discontinuance in 1915. He achieved almost instant success in 1916 when a spring concert given at the Cleveland Theater evoked high praise from the critics. An overflow audience wondered how so much talent could be found in one college, and how Father Winter managed to organize so balanced and well-trained an orchestra. "At the rise of the curtain when the orchestra opened the program with an overture from 'Martha' many were under the impression that they were in the Hippodrome listening to a concert of the late Cleveland Symphony."[100] The Provincial added his measure of praise on his visit later that same year; the *Lumina* reported that he said there were few colleges in the country that could surpass St. Ignatius College when it came to musical talent.[101]

Encouraged by public acclaim, the Jesuit consultors thought "it was best not to restrict our Orchestra . . . for use of the college and Loyola only," but to consider possibly giving a performance for a public charity which would benefit from the proceeds.[102] In May 1918 the orchestra gave a concert at Grays Armory in the hope of raising three thousand dollars for the Knights of Columbus war effort. The goal was not quite reached but the concert was an artistic success, and in the opinion of many surpassed the concerts of the two previous years.[103] It was planned after the war to expand the music courses to allow for the conferring of the bachelor of music degree but the plans did not fully materialize, although there were courses in harmony and counterpoint listed in 1920.

The orchestra of ninety members continued its success before large audiences until in 1922 it gained some measure of wider recognition in *Musical America*, a national publication which praised the orchestra for "its extensive library all acquired through the efforts of the performers." The *Cleveland News Leader* noted that the "St. Ignatius Orchestra has reached a degree of musicianship rarely attained by amateur organizations." The *Cleveland Plain Dealer* also praised the orchestra, for it "can always be depended on to present a soloist of note."[104]

In 1924 the May issue of the *Dominant Orchestra Monthly* added its praise:

> The Symphony Orchestra of St. Ignatius College, Cleveland is claiming to be the only equipped student symphony orchestra in the country. Its past achievements represent a proud record, as is shown by the many favorable press notices commending its public concerts . . . its carefully prepared programs are played well nigh perfectly . . . imparting enjoyment totally impossible in the case of professional performers.[105]

The magazine also praised the unique character, youthful vigor, and love of music evident in the orchestra's performances.

COLLEGE FEDERATION PROPOSAL

Reference has already been made to the exclusion of St. Ignatius College from efforts to form a federated University of Cleveland in 1912 and again in the early 1920s. The concept, limited to institutions of University Circle and originally sponsored by Newton D. Baker, gave support to the early perception of the Jesuits that University Circle was the place to be. Yet even the work of the Zook Commission Report was not enough to accomplish the federation in 1924. The Jesuits were deprived of the name Cleveland for their university in 1923 but neither Case nor Western Reserve were interested in the name of the city. President Howe of Case felt that he could now do better at fund-raising on his own and he did not want to lose Case's identity in a federation that would have Western Reserve's name at the head of it. Western Reserve was unwilling to sacrifice its time-honored name in favor of the name of the city, which it felt had far less significance than that of Western Reserve.106

When the idea of a Case, Western Reserve merger was first brought up, the newspapers thought it would be a great idea for college football; the combined team would be stronger.107 The public press saw great academic advantages and the *Plain Dealer* regretted that Cleveland alone of all the major cities "has no great inclusive truly city-wide university."108 On 1 November 1924, the *Cleveland Times* suggested institutions other than those in University Circle institutions might be included.109 There was also a report in the *Plain Dealer* the next day that Western Reserve had issued an invitation to some sixteen institutions to meet and discuss incorporation into the proposed university. On 25 November 1924, President Vinson addressed the Cleveland Chamber of Commerce saying that what had been done in other cities "ought to be done in Cleveland."110

By this time the Van Sweringens had envisioned the possibility of John Carroll University's not being able to complete its move to the new site in University Heights successfully. In November 1924 the Van Sweringens offered to Case and Western Reserve a 300-acre site in Shaker Heights north of Shaker Boulevard along Courtland if the two institutions would merge and move to the site, which was just west of the property almost purchased by John Carroll.111 The offer was not enough to overcome the strong feeling of attachment of Case and Western Reserve to their own names, traditions, and location.

What John Carroll would have done had it been invited to join a University of Cleveland is not too difficult to guess; Father Boylan would not have been interested and he probably would have ignored the invitation. He might even have been pleased with the dissociation of John Carroll with the other institutions by its listing among "other" institutions in the appendix of the Zook Report. This listing noted that John Carroll was "formerly St. Ignatius College" but omitted any reference to the former name, Cleveland University.112 Baldwin-Wallace College, which in 1919 had been formed by the merger of Baldwin College and German Wallace College, was considered by the *Plain Dealer* as a possible member of the University of Cleveland since is was "on the western edge of the Cleveland Metropolitan district."[113] Not even the newspapers thought of including John Carroll which was certainly nowhere near the edge of the Cleveland Metropolitan District!

Although many people outside of Cleveland circles thought the proposed University of Cleveland was worthy of implementation, nothing was accomplished. The *Yale Alumni Weekly*, citing a long-time relationship between Yale and Western Reserve, "so close" since 1827, commended the proposal as a newcomer in higher education. "Does it hit the nail on the head? We think it does. Let's lead off."[114] The *Plain Dealer* felt that such a single large university "can knit itself more closely into the life of Northern Ohio than either Case or Reserve, or both of them operating as separate institutions."[115] The public discussion continued but although by 1926 the "consolidation of Cleveland's institutions of higher learning long proposed, has been found impossible, cooperation was urged . . . as the best and most feasible substitute for a dreamed of Greater Cleveland University."[116] A coordination plan which was then proposed appeared to the *Plain Dealer* "as neither fish, nor good red herring."[117]

CATHOLIC COLLEGE COOPERATION

While the proposed University of Cleveland was under discussion, there were also indications that the Catholic colleges and the Seminary were beginning to speak to each other. Writing to Father McMenamy in August 1923, Father T. J. Smith explained that Bishop Schrembs and Monsignor Smith had talked of a plan for the Jesuits to do some teaching in the seminary. "Since that time the present director of the Seminary and the Bishop took it for granted in a conversation I had with him that we were to teach the first year students of the Seminary beginning in September. . . . It was my conviction that the bishop expects us to teach in the Seminary and he will be greatly disappointed if we are not ready to assist him"; this was a different view from that which Father T. J. Smith had held earlier when he was under the impression that the Jesuits would have nothing to do with the Seminary until the college moved to the Heights.[118] Because the Provincial did not have enough manpower to spare, Father Smith had to refuse the bishop's request.

Two years later Father Smith was again writing to Father McMenamy about the bishop's latest request. Bishop Schrembs had brought up the matter of John Carroll's providing degrees for seminarians. Several priests, with the bishop's permission, had applied to Western Reserve University, where the authorities agreed that the Seminary requirements were sufficient for the bachelor's degree without any time in residence for a Western

Reserve degree.[119] At this point Father Smith said, "he called me and asked, in the presence of the young priest who had carried on the negotiations with Western Reserve, to take up the matter with our Committee on credits and offer the same opportunities as Western Reserve. I showed the bishop an excerpt from your letter to me concerning the matter of degrees. He read it but insisted that I should take up the matter again keeping in mind what W. R. has proposed"; the bishop was anxious for a quick decision.[120]

The priests were in need of the degrees because they had been asked to teach in the Catholic women's colleges. Reflecting the concern for standards in his reply, Father McMenamy warned, "I do not think that any institution in the country gives degrees to a candidate who has not spent the last year of his studies in that institution," and went on to suggest that "if priests in some way could be registered at Carroll and do the same work during the year before their A.B., then the difficulty would be obviated. The same holds true of M.A. degrees."[121] Father McMenamy was convinced that while some Catholic colleges may give degrees without work in residence, "we would lose cast if we did it. . . . I see your difficulty and hope that an arrangement can be made whereby the seminarians can keep their registration at John Carroll."[122]

Father John R. Hagan, superintendent of diocesan schools since 1922, the "young priest" referred to by Father Smith, confirms in essence the account of the conversation between Father Smith and Bishop Schrembs. He adds that Bishop Schrembs first approved of the priests going to Western Reserve and then changed his mind saying that for them to do so would be a reflection on John Carroll; when Carroll refused to make concessions the matter was dropped.[123]

There was a proposed affiliation of two women's colleges with John Carroll in the mid-1920s. In February 1925 Father Smith asked Father McMenamy for advice on "whether or not I should proceed to affiliate these girls' colleges now under the direction of the Ursuline and Notre Dame Sisterhoods. And if we can proceed what must be required of them? What should be done about the Seminary?"[124] This question continued to be discussed through the early part of 1926 without results.[125]

When Father Boylan succeeded to the presidency of John Carroll in August 1925, the issue of degrees for Seminarians came up again; there was still no solution to the problem of residency. Father Boylan said he would enable the seminarians to obtain a degree "but we should not lower our standards."[126] The residence problem seemed an insoluble one. Correspondence with Father Smith gave Father Boylan an account of the earlier discussions and the regret that conformity to North Central requirements was an obstacle to doing what Bishop Schrembs wanted.[127]

DARK DAYS

Father Boylan's presidency from 1925–1928 was a period when the frustrations and disappointments of the previous years almost brought about a departure of the Jesuits from Cleveland. The inclusion of John Carroll in a new province created out of the Missouri Province added further uncertainty to the situation. In 1925 the Missouri Province, now numbering 1,217 Jesuits, had become too large for proper management. A geographical range from Wyoming to Ohio further complicated the problem. On 8 September 1925, the states of Kentucky, Indiana, Ohio, Michigan, and part of Illinois were separated from the Missouri Province to become the Ohio Vice-Province, with temporary headquarters in Cincinnati. The Province was formally established as the Chicago Province on 15 August 1928, with headquarters in Chicago. Father Jeremias J. O'Callaghan, who had become vice-provincial in 1925, was named provincial in 1928.[128]

Father Haggeney, who had long been associated with John Carroll and was involved as an active participant in nearly all of the major decisions over the years, was perhaps the best spokesman for the views of the Cleveland Jesuits and often spoke of his "vivid" memory of events. Many of the *Litterae Annuae* for the early and mid-1920s were belatedly written by Father Haggeney while he was hospitalized in 1927 and had time to catch up on his chores. Father Haggeney complained to Father Boylan that it was not easy writing from a hospital bed, especially when nurses who know Latin are "awfully inquisitive."[129] A special burden that Father Haggeney had to bear was his feeling about the new Chicago Province: "Life is awfully hard for a German," he said, noting that his two meetings with Father O'Callaghan had been "rather painful."[130] When he was at the Milford Novitiate in the fall of 1927, Father Haggeney rejoiced that "novices of Irish and Italian extraction pick up on the German" to help take care of Brother Huhn who spoke only German.[131] He also rejoiced that "Brother Nussbaumer fires his German at anybody. If this goes on for a longer time Rev. Fr. Neenam will be a regular German farmer."[132]

Father Haggeney had advice for Father Boylan on how to conduct himself in troublesome times:

> I feel for you in all your troubles. I have been thinking these days how all these crosses are but a preparation for a great good you will accomplish at John Carroll. Fr. Pickel, Fr. Sommerhauser and you have to walk the same road. They brought the college forward, whilst under Fr. Furay and Fr. Smith no advance was made. I hope and pray you will be successful too. They had their troubles with the deans, so have you.[133]

The reference to deans reflects the dissatisfaction of many of the older Jesuits with the loss of the traditional Jesuit College structure in which appeal directly to the rector was often made.

Father Boylan's troubles were not only with deans, but also with the rather sad state of affairs at St. Mary's parish where the pastor, Father August M. Hackert, was considered to be doing less than a satisfactory job. There was bitterness, too, on the part of the people of the parish because the German language had been abolished in church services since the departure of Father Rudolph Meschenmoser.[134] The process of establishing a new parish on the Heights was to add to Father Boylan's difficulties. The fire that destroyed the St. Stanislaus Novitiate in Parma in April 1926 created still another problem for the Cleveland Jesuits. Only the first floor and side walls remained of the three-story structure that had been built in 1908. The estimated damage was put at $125,000.[135]

The visit of the American Assistant, Father Edward Mattern, accompanied by Father F. M. O'Connor, to Cleveland in July 1926 was the occasion of great concern even to Monsignor Smith. The visitation, which took place 13 July 1926, was followed five days later by a visit from the new vice-provincial, Father O'Callaghan. On 26 July Monsignor Smith wrote to Father Mattern expressing regret that he had not seen him when he was in Cleveland. Monsignor Smith said that Bishop Schrembs also wanted to speak to Father Mattern, but hesitated to do so for fear that he might be thought to be "seeking his own diocesan interests."[136] Monsignor Smith wrote to Father Mattern:

> I have a feeling of loyalty towards the Order and confidence in its officers that encourages me to tell just what is in my mind.
>
> In the first place, we are very much disappointed that there is a movement on hand to close out St. Stanislaus Novitiate at Parma. There was a fire at the place which destroyed much of building, but before that there was an inclination to take the novitiate out of our diocese.
>
> There is a great deal of hesitancy about building on the new site of John Carroll University. The diocese of Cleveland is willing to do its part financially and otherwise for the upbuilding of John Carroll University, and we are willing to appeal to the diocese to help build up a new St. Stanislaus Novitiate.
>
> We had considerable trouble during Bishop Farrelly's administration and the friends who stood loyally by the Jesuits are disheartened when they see the tendency on the part of your order to back out of the diocese.
>
> I have felt right along that when the German Mission of Cleveland was taken over by the St. Louis Province that, what I call prejudice existed on the part of that Province against the German Mission and that we in the diocese have suffered because of that attitude.
>
> I can assure you that it is with the deepest regret that we see the Jesuits hesitant in their development at the present time. They have not given us a fair show, and in a short time when conditions are ripe, we will put a campaign over for the

Jesuits that will prove our appreciation and will enable them to develop in the diocese in a way eminently satisfactory to them. . . .

I wish to emphasize here also a personal matter that Father Sommerhauser when he was rector had to suffer unjustly because of the unfortunate situation and from my knowledge of his ability and his wisdom and his administration that he would be able to work out this problem in the most satisfactory manner. I am making this statement in justice to him and with the feeling that I have been in the position to form the fairest and the justest [*sic*] judgment.[137]

Monsignor Smith told Father Mattern that he would not be disappointed if Father Mattern thought it "unwise" to answer; he offered to meet Father Mattern anywhere in the United States.[138]

After his visit to Cleveland, Father Mattern went to New Orleans, where he became ill and was hospitalized. Consequently he did not reply to the monsignor until September when he informed him that, "What you tell me about the situation of the Jesuit Fathers in Cleveland, will be of use to me when I get back to Rome and report to Father General. Some of this information I had already gathered during my visit to Cleveland. I can say that I was much impressed with the educational prospects of your big and beautiful city.[139] Monsignor Smith sent a copy of Father Mattern's reply to Bishop Schrembs with the suggestion that the bishop send a note to Father Mattern congratulating him on his recovery.

It is difficult to say how much influence, if any, the intervention of Monsignor Smith and Bishop Schrembs may have had on the future action of Jesuit Superiors. In the fall of 1928 Father Fox came from Marquette, where he had been president, to John Carroll as dean. Father Benedict J. Rodman became president at the same time and immediately began preparations to move the college to the new campus in University Heights. The assignment of two such capable men would seem to indicate some intention of assisting John Carroll in improving itself, even granting that Father Fox was not in good health.

Yet, there is evidence that anything that would be done would have to come from the initiative of the Jesuits at John Carroll without much help from the Province. Father Fox, writing to his friend Father Paul Blakely of the Jesuit magazine, *America*, said,

> When I came to Cleveland and faced the actual situation it was like running up a blind alley at midnight. John Carroll faced a crisis. It was clearly a case of getting large money or getting off the map. At the same time we were told that a campaign in view of the former fizzle was out of the question. Even the Provincial took this stand. I then urged that a local campaign manager be allowed to make a sixty day survey of possibilities. This was reluctantly granted as was the permission to attempt the campaign.[140]

Emergence from the "Iron Ages" 1915–1935

The paternalism and rigorous discipline of the "Iron Ages" slowly lost its grip on St. Ignatius during the years 1915 to 1935. Also changing was the cohesive student-teacher relationship of the early days and the general aloofness of the Jesuits from the public. Nationally, the period was one of transition for American higher education to a relaxation of former regulations and to the exercise of new freedom.[1] At St. Ignatius the change proceeded slowly and was often imperceptible. If changes were not necessary to meet accreditation standards those changes might have been even slower. Some students in the 1960s and 1970s felt that the change to a more modern style had never really been made. It might be said that St. Ignatius College's development was almost a generation behind that of many of the American colleges, including Catholic ones, a view that persisted even in later years.

The students in the years following World War I represented a broader spectrum of the community, were considerably more numerous, and were in many ways more independent than students of the prewar years. In 1915 69 students were enrolled in the college department; within ten years the number had risen to 346. In 1935 the number stood at 456, down from a peak of 517 in 1932. The postwar students, 70 percent of whom supported themselves, according to a survey in 1927,[2] were crowded into buildings which served both high school and college and a West Side campus that was far too small to allow proper space for recreation.

One of Father Sommerhauser's first moves in 1915 was to make better use of some of the buildings along Lorain Avenue. He hoped to provide space for a carpenter shop, printing shop, music rooms, and a scholastic's recreation room.[3] Tearing down some of the "shacks" that were behind the houses on Lorain Avenue did not materially help to enlarge the campus but it was a step in the right direction. The problem of how an increasing number of students in both high school and college could use the yard for recreation remained. A recurring issue was the complaint from the high school about college recreation periods disturbing high school classes. The solution suggested by the consultors was for mutual forebearance. "Why not divide the burden and have the high school bear it during the noon hour as we do." During other hours the college students were advised to play in the quadrangle just south of the building.[4]

Progress in breaking out of the mold of the "Iron Ages" was reported by the student newspaper in 1920. Comparing the past with 1920, the writer noted that:

> Last year when a fellow stopped you in the street and asked you what institution you attended, you told him St. Ignatius. You said it with pride and a sort of funny feeling around your heart. It was a good old College, none better. You for one were not staying awake nights wondering about the next pasture.
>
> That was last year.
>
> Well, now when anyone puts such a question to you, you rise joyously and smite him on the back, sock him in the eye, kick him in the shins and give a few hundred college yells, by all of which you convey the information that you are of St. Ignatius. Because, fellows, this is our big year.[5]

The cause of the change was attributed to the presence of a real football team, an excellent orchestra, oratorical and essay contest winners along with good teams in basketball, tennis, and track. The writer suggested a way to improve the college's image even further:

> Fellows, what do you think about making a new map and putting St. Ignatius on it in letters so large a fly will stock up with plenty of food and water before he attempts to cross them? . . .
>
> We have a start now, let's keep it up. [6]

There were signs, too, of more contact with the public. For an institution whose principal venture into the public eye had been participation in the Columbian Year competition and a parade in 1892, it was now time to put $140 into the *Plain Dealer's* jubilee section on education in 1916.[7] Participation in the St. Patrick's Day celebration was not to be passed up. Marching in the parade was only part of the celebration activity, for the "orchestra rendered their traditional soul-and-foot stirring lays in their usual creditable style and the Rev. Father rector (Sommerhauser) crowned the event with a pleasing address suitable to the occasion."[8] It may be presumed that the following comment in the student magazine was at least semi-deliberate. Referring to the remarks of several speakers of Irish ancestry, the writer commented that the speeches "threw a new light on the subject by showing how St. Patrick has become the inspiration of all Catholics, even Germans and he is no longer the exclusive Saint of Erin, shillelahs to the contrary notwithstanding."[9]

The postwar students didn't miss many opportunities to attract public attention. On one occasion the students staged a parade in preparation for a football game in such grand style that there was rejoicing in its results:

> Did we startle the natives?
> We'll say we did.
> In our humble opinion there was not a soul in the whole city of Cleveland who did not know something big was coming off after the Ignatius parade of last Friday.
> About 30 cars filled to the "gunnels" with vociferous Ignatians, a horse and wagon (the horse's name was Mary, by the way), banners, signs and paper streamers of blue and gold—just picture that aggregation coursing its way through the Public Square on its way to tour the East Side.
> Again, did we startle the natives?
> And echoes answer, "Yes"[10]

It was not only the new opportunities for exposure to the public that were bringing change to St. Ignatius College: it was also the personal interest and dynamism of Father Sommerhauser. Within a month after he had become president he reversed a recent decision of the consultors not to have a college magazine and ordered one established immediately; he also restored the college play and stressed the importance of the college orchestra.[11] Father Sommerhauser also made many changes in the general operating of the college. He changed from the Illuminating Company to Muny Light in 1916 when he discovered the differences in cost; he replaced the party line telephone service which he called a "nuisance" with a private line in 1917, and he installed oil-burning stoves at Loyola High School in 1918.[12] He passed up an opportunity to join with St. Vincent's Orphanage in seuring a special railroad siding for coal and market produce by carloads as "premature."[13] After the fire had destroyed the villa at Vermilion he thought the property ought to be sold since every year showed a deficit in its operation; he even received permission from Rome to sell it.[14] It was ironic that this was the time the diocese chose to sell the property on Carroll Avenue purchased to house seminarians who were to attend St. Ignatius College; the proceeds went to support the Cathedral Latin School Building Fund.[15] It is interesting to speculate on what Father Sommerhauser might have accomplished had he not been plagued during his entire presidency with the Loyola High School issue.

Significant changes in the spiritual life of the college also took place during the postwar years. The beginning of the school year was still marked by the celebration of the Mass of the Holy Spirit but the reading of the rules and regulations by the Prefect of Studies after Mass was eventually replaced by the issuance of a student handbook in 1930. This was intended to give the student a "detailed knowledge and understanding of all college regulations."[16] After the war years, the Sodality continued to flourish. Members of the catechetical section worked in the parishes on Sundays with the children of immigrant families. The members of the Charity Section collected and distributed clothing to the poor with the boys "nobly responding to the appeal."[17] In 1919 one traditional regulation was changed; college men were to be exempt from daily Mass.[18] As explained in the student newspaper, the change was the result of "a new stand which the faculty has taken," and it did not mean that daily Mass was not most desirable but that "the burden of forcing or dispensing with the observance" was left "to the students themselves."[19]

Less than ten years later the fewer number of students going to mass and confession caused Father Degleman to complain about a decline in the Christian tone of student life. He did not want to point a finger at anyone but he thought the dean of men and two associate spiritual directors seemed to be doing nothing beyond providing for a weekly chapel and annual retreat to keep a "high Christian tone." Father Degleman's "puzzling wonderment springing from the situation" caused him to comment, "nothing is done effectively to foster the spiritual life of the student."[20] Less than a month after those remarks, Father Degleman added,

It may also be noted for the record that the college Sodality, which functioned in a way during the first semester, was discontinued in February—just dropped. There is a difficulty, no doubt, in arranging for a suitable hour for meeting; but we cannot allow our Sodality to lapse. We also had no debate this year again. There undoubtedly is a reason. Yet, unless we keep up these student activities the college will suffer by it. It has suffered.[21]

Perhaps something of an answer to Father Degleman's observations could be found in a 1928 *Carroll News* article on student priorities which clearly stated that "standing before all others is sports," and urged those who couldn't participate to devote their energies to supporting the teams.[22] Following sports were "activities of social, religious and business nature, one just as important as the next to every student if he wishes to obtain all the benefits possible from his college career."[23]

One of the reasons for the change in priorities among student activities was that Father Bracken, who was dean of the college from 1919 to 1926, was also faculty director of athletics. He was credited by the student newspaper in 1920 with a large part in the "rejuvenation that made all student activities go forward with zest"; Father Bracken's priority was athletics.[24] A solution to the problem of scheduling activities was proposed by a committee set up by Father Fox in 1929 "to insure more satisfactory management of student activities to obviate difficulties of conflicting meetings and affairs."[25] The priority of athletics, particularly football, remained.

Whatever relaxation of the rules did develop, it was naturally not enough as far as students were concerned. The *Carroll News* was quick to point out that the statues of *Ora* and *Labora*, while representing the tradition of prayer and study, were "By standing at the second floor landing . . . loitering in the corridor during classes."[26] The statues were of course never in attendance at the not-so-popular weekly Dean's Lecture thus avoiding the particularly irritating method of checking attendance at the lecture. Each student was given a card as he entered; the card with the student's signature was collected as the students left. Anyone absent from the lecture was charged with an absence for each of his classes that day. The lecture period served two purposes; one was to bring in outside speakers, and the other was to deal with rules and regulations. Occasionally there would be admonitions such as one of Father Degleman's against "petty thieving among the students."[27]

Guest lecturers from outside usually talked about careers from the business or professional world. Occasionally one of them would dwell on related academic matters as did James J. McLaughlin in 1928 when he spoke to the students about looking on their graduation as the continuation of their "mental development."[28] Evidence that the elective system had opened up the need for counseling came when one of Father Degleman's lectures made the point "that there is not enough supervision over the student's progress by more monthly reports."[29] Henceforth there were to be weekly reports.

Famous lecturers were given a more public forum. Two of the more prominent were Edgar Guest, known as the "Poet of the Home," who addressed the college Literary Club in 1919 in St. Mary's Hall. The talk had been arranged by Leslie Raddatz, an alumnus and president of the Cleveland Advertising Club. Gilbert K. Chesterton addressed an audience of 1,500 in 1930, speaking on "What I Saw in Rome." Students also were part of the lecture circuit. The Little Flower Lecture Club gave illustrated lectures on a variety of topics before appreciative audiences.

The impact of the new curriculum and the problem of electives were felt in increasing intensity and demands upon the library presented a special difficulty. The library had a habit of changing location often enough to confuse even those students who thought of using it.[30] Originally there were two libraries, the professors' library and the students' library; by the end of the period, these two had become a single library. Moving back and forth between the main building and the one behind the "old stores" on Lorain, the 4500 volumes finally found a more permanent home in the main building in 1927. As a result of pressure from the North Central Association, the purchase of books was stepped up in 1931. It was estimated that to comply with North Central demands each college student would have to be assessed five dollars a term and each high school student one dollar for purchasing library books.[31] A four-dollar Library fee had been charged college students since 1925; the new arrangement was to charge a thirteen-dollar activity fee for all activities. By 1935 all activity fees were dropped and the tuition, which now included most fees, raised from seventy-five to one hundred twenty-five dollars a semester.

Of all the academic changes that were made, the end of the senior oral examination in philosophy was the most welcome. As late as 1918 seniors were still expressing fear of the ordeal. The *Lumina* asked,

> Why do they carry those black ominous binders under their arms? Why are they seen no more o'nights? Their oral exams are approaching and they are preparing to contradistinguish the minor and subdistinguish the "minorem subsumptam." Hence the worried looks. Hence the black binders. Hence, finally the midnight oil.[32]

The elimination of the conditional examination in 1932 was probably a mixed blessing; the risk of a failing grade was now greater.

A gold medal to the highest honors in each of the four classes was the only academic award. Efforts were revived in 1931 to establish an honor fraternity but with no success. Some students who thought that it was to be simply a reward for student activity felt that the "B" average requirement stipulated by the faculty would exclude too many.[33] Finally in October 1933 the Sigma Kappa Pi honor fraternity combining both scholarship and student activity was established with full faculty approval.[34] The organization, which had twenty-five members in 1934, was intended to serve as a bond between the more active students and the alumni. Among its activities was the sponsorship of a public debate in 1933 between John Carroll and Catholic University and the establishment of gold medal awards for the outstanding student each year in chemistry, biology, and sociology.

On the lighter side, what did the students do to let off steam or simply celebrate? The Loyola boys were inclined to celebrate the end of examinations with a banquet prepared by the Loyola chef. This may have been more daring than it seems in view of the reputation the chef had acquired through a creation of his known as the "Loyola bun." This delicacy appeared to some students to have an unappetizing green-looking exterior. One of these buns often found its way into the outstretched hands of the statue of St. Ignatius, signifying, perhaps, a burnt offering.[35] West Siders, too, were accustomed to buns, but theirs came from the nearby Kaase's bakery. A fire in the bakery cast gloom over the student body one day in

January 1920. *The Ignatian* recorded the "forlorn and hungry look" on most of the students' faces. Why the "sad and downcast look" the writer asked, "as we filed slowly down the corridor or labored slowly up the stairs? Alas, money we had but where were the buns?" The "blue and bunless" Monday was only a twenty-four-hour day and the hope was the bakery would be back in business, the writer assured the students.[36] Complaints about food are rather normal for college students. While there were no food riots in the St. Ignatius cafeteria, or at least no record of any, there were many complaints about the food. Many of these complaints were in the form of jokes in the humor column of the student publication.[37] The complaints were particularly numerous during the war years.

An organization of freshmen in 1918 known as the A.A.F., Amalgamated Association of Freshmen, had for one of its objectives, "dining exclusively in the college cafeteria."[38] It is not clear whether this was intended as some form of penance for the approaching Lenten season or whether it indicated improvement in the food. Evidence that it may have been the latter can be found in the holding of the first Freshman mixer in the cafeteria in 1917; all agreed that they had a "wonderful time! The Entertainment? Par Excellence; the luncheon—delicious."[39] Three scholastics were guests of the students, Lionel Carron, Leo Vollmayer, and Eugene Bork. According to the students, they "did not formally adjourn until they shook the downtown sky-scrapers with three vociferous cheers for the professors from the top of the High Level Bridge."[40]

Other classes celebrated events in different ways. The senior class of 1917 set "out to prove themselves regular fellows." The "weary, worrying grind of philosophy" had driven them to "forsake the din and fever heated industry of the first floor classroom," so that they might "conquer the world of pleasure."[41] Three members of the class met at six P.M. one day at the flagpole on the Square and "advanced toward the Opera House. Ah, what a beautiful sight to behold. Three blushing, blustering youths promenading the Avenue just as the shop girls poured out."[42] The account in the *Lumina* says that eventually they went to the Opera House and then they visited the "fruit salad sundaries and whistled themselves home."[43]

The freshman-sophomore "ball rush" conducted in the schoolyard tended at times to get out of hand. The year before Father Otting became dean witnessed one of those occasions that went considerably beyond the normal limits of such activity. Some fifty freshmen who had been victims of the sophomores' well-organized kidnapping activities managed to escape in time for the contest. The kidnapping activities were the "most colorful part of the affair," according to the student newspaper. Sophomores were better organized and seized freshmen as they arrived in the morning and hustled them off to the basement of the Smoke House. Some freshmen were captured as they emerged from street cars. Freshmen had an aptitude for breaking free, but were soon recaptured. "A chartered truck conveyed a batch of Freshmen to Shaker Lakes and abandoned them there sans a large percentage of their garments."[44] Even some of these returned. When the contest did start an "erratic barrage of 1904 eggs" along with similar vintage tomatoes and other ancient fruit was fired by each side as they rushed toward each other to be the first to get the huge ball over the goal. Some of the errant fruit and vegetables managed to splash on the front of the cassock of Father Bracken, who falsely presumed he was safe on the sidelines; he continued to watch unperturbed. The affair ended in a one-to-one tie after three exhausting periods.[45] This was a quite different competition from earlier years, when the two classes sought to hide a package containing a flag from each other.[46]

Father Boylan, as a result of previous "Ball Rush" activity, had expressly forbidden

> any kidnapping in connection with the annual rush. This order was either ignored by several sophomores or they were unaware of its existence when Monday morning October 11 [1926] they forcibly removed five Freshmen to an outlying district and abandoned them.
>
> This action occasioned the official ban on the ball rush, which was to have been held that Tuesday afternoon. Following the posting of the cancellation of kidnapping and egg throwing [some were kidnapped from the classrooms]. Several sophomores were thrown into the Public Square fountain following a clash between the two factions at noon Tuesday. Others were obliged to mount Tom Johnson's statue and address their captors and such outsiders as gathered to see the fun.[47]

Father Otting acted promptly, closing the university and suspending the two classes until each student came to his office to sign a statement to forego such combat and its accompanying disorders in the future. It was learned that the kidnapping activities ranged over a wider area than was at first suspected; many of the kidnapped students had been taken to several cities in northern Ohio. Even some high school students were accidental victims of the sophomores' activities. It was not exactly the kind of recognition and advertising the college was seeking.

One sure sign of the changing times was the development of a parking problem around the school by 1925. The student newspaper suggested a solution that would make John Carroll "look a little more decent." Members of the faculty were eligible to join in. The forward-looking proposal was as follows:

> It is a well known fact that college men have the corner on all movable junk in the U.S.A. About the stately porticos of John Carroll may be seen the replica of

E. 55th Street graveyards for slightly used automobiles. These sputtering gas chariots are cluttering up the highways and by-ways.

Now then, if the faculty would have the Traffic Commissioner prohibit parking within a radius of three blocks from John Carroll (between 8:10 A.M. and 6:00 P.M.) and then take over the forgotten walls of the brewery for a Garage-Storage, they could make it compulsory for those who motored to school to park at the Garage-Storage for a nominal fee.

In no time there would be accumulated enough Treasury Department samples to be able to give conditional exams and late registration free of charge (see your catalogue for full particulars).[48]

Organized student activities between 1915 and 1935 also underwent many changes. New ones were added and some old ones expanded to include what are now called extracurricular activities. Theater, debating, music, and science were emphases carried over from the early period. Competition in the Missouri and Chicago provinces' intercollegiate English and Latin essay contests was specially noteworthy, but another intercollegiate competition, football, came to dominate student interests. Other new activities led to a measure of student government in the development of the Student Union and the beginning of student publications.

STUDENT PUBLICATIONS

The *Lumina*, the answer to Father Sommerhauser's call for a student magazine, was published by the college and owned by the students of St. Ignatius College.[49] It was published five times a year, the first issue in October 1915, the last in June 1919; it was replaced by a newspaper, *The Ignatian*, in the fall of 1919. The first editor of the *Lumina* was Louis Litzler, who was assisted by Edward F. Madaras, managing editor, and Albert J. Murphy and John Kegg, business managers. All were of the class of 1915. Succeeding editors were Aloysius Bungart, '17, Raymond E. Craft, '18, and J. Harold Traverse, '19. The *Lumina* had a twofold purpose, "infusing a strong spirit into the students of the college, and the development of literary talent."[50] The first faculty moderator was Father William Young, who was a scholastic at the time. He was succeeded by Lionel V. Carron in 1917, who at that time was also a scholastic.

The class of 1915, which launched the *Lumina*, was undoubtedly one of the most remarkable classes of that era. As far as can be determined, every member of the class pursued a professional course of studies after graduating; careers in medicine, law, or the priesthood were their goals. Frank Doran and George Gaffney went on to St. Louis University Medical School, others to Western Reserve Medical School. James McLaughlin went on to Harvard Law School and Joseph Hurley to St. Mary's Seminary. There were four Gallaghers in the class, Farrell, Owen, and the brothers Jack and Al.

The makeup of the *Lumina*, which was to serve the college and both high schools, provided for a broad spectrum of interest with the emphasis on literary achievement. The magazine contained an editorial section, articles on various subjects, a scientific section, alumni notes, and news of high school and college activities. As testimony to the quality of the literary efforts one of the poems by Laurence Coughlin in the first issue was chosen for inclusion in the Schnittkind *College Anthology* for 1915.[51] The October 1917 issue was a special one dedicated to all the St. Ignatius College men in uniform. Another issue in April 1918, called a "Military Number," was devoted to the wartime activities of former students.

As early as the fall of 1918 consideration was given by the college board of trustees to letting a college newspaper take the place of the *Lumina*, but no action was taken.[52] One year later, in November 1919, when financial circumstances necessitated some kind of action, a newspaper did replace the *Lumina*. Walter J. Kiewel, '20, editor of the new publication, *The Ignatian*, said,

> It is with a certain feeling of sadness that we announce the suspension of the publication LUMINA. It was the prime venture of St. Ignatius in the literary field. . . .
> During its eventful career it set a standard for literary excellence which placed it at once among the finest college publications in the country. . . .
> No; it is not because of a paucity of poets, authors, or editors that the LUMINA will not grace your parlor table. The reason is merely this; a printer could not be found who did not demand, at least, a mortgage on the college in return for his work.[53]

It was Lionel V. Carron who proposed the newspaper as a replacement for the *Lumina*; the name *The Ignatian* was selected from among many suggested. The policy of *The Ignatian* was to be

> one of service, service in many ways. Through its news department we hope to keep our friends posted on all the activities of the college and the two High Schools. In its literary department, which will be a unique feature in itself, we think we will bring to light new Thackerays, new Shelleys. The Alumni section is intended to bind us closer to those who have left their Alma Mater in the last thirty years. It is the desire of the editors that the paper be considered not solely a college paper but also the organ of St. Ignatius and Loyola High.[54]

Students at Loyola High School were not taking any chances on their interests being fully served by *The Ignatian*. In December 1919 a senior paper called the "Weak Daily" circulated at the high school to publish articles which reflected their class activities.[55]

A number of circumstances threatened to cut short or make difficult the life of *The Ignatian*. In January 1920 the newspaper office escaped being burned out by an unfriendly wind from the fire in Kaase's bakery, which was three doors east of the building housing the editorial offices. The fire was so hot and wind so strong that the snow on the roof of the offices began to melt. Fortunately, the fire was brought under control before any damage was done.

What began as an eight-page paper was soon forced either to increase its pages or drop some of its features. The January 1920 issue chose to provide space for the expansion of college activities by dropping the Literary Supplement and devoting eight pages to news. Since the Literary Supplement was promised for the next issue, that issue had to be expanded to twelve pages with eight pages of news. By the fall of 1920 *The Ignatian* became a fortnightly; as time went on the literary and scientific sections began to shrink and finally disappear in favor of sport news.

Under Carron's direction a "Press Club" was formed to give experience in "literary journalism."[56] Benjamin Ling, '08, of the *Cleveland Press*, talked to the students about opportunities in the field of journalism.[57] After the renovation of the barracks the space needed for the expanding staff of *The Ignatian* was now available for the editorial and business offices. The second floor of the barracks was subdivided into four offices, *The Ignatian*, the college Union, the Athletic Association, and the head coach's office.[58]

One of the most well-known and popular students associated with *The Ignatian* was Raymond J. Gibbons of the class of 1924. He was the first junior ever to hold the post of editor-in-chief, a "living embodiment of Horatio Alger."[59] He was also a reporter with the *Cleveland News* and came to have his own by-line on the sports page of that paper. He was a product of Loyola High School and president of the class of 1924. He has an additional claim to remembrance by the students; it was he who christened the football team of 1924 the "Blue Streak."

Early in the newspaper's history a lengthy discussion ran through several issues on whether the paper contained enough humor. Gene Kelly, '23, published a humorous parody of the *The Ignatian* under the title *Stagnatian*. This name had faculty approval and was so successful that a second issue was distributed in 1924. It sold for one dollar. Unfortunately, no copies seem to have survived.

When the name John Carroll was adopted by the university in 1923 it seemed appropriate to change the name of the newspaper. With the first issue in October 1925, the *Carroll News* was found on the masthead. By this time Loyola High School had been closed so it was no longer necessary to include its news. Within two years, St. Ignatius High School issued its own newspaper, *The Eye*, thus leaving the *Carroll News* by 1927 strictly a college newspaper.

A new format was adopted for the *Carroll News* featuring a six-column size on a larger sheet with increased space for advertising. It was felt the "old *The Ignatian* afforded small chance for much variety because of its extremely limited space accommodations and while advertising had reached the saturation point it was not yielding sufficient returns to meet expenses."[60]

One new feature was added to university activities, a publicity department to facilitate contacts with the local newspapers by supplying articles and news about the university; it also provided contacts between the college newspaper and the local newspapers. The department developed into a news service bureau in 1932 and became a publicity bureau under the guidance of Mark Mulcahy in 1933.

The *Catholic Universe Bulletin*'s handling of John Carroll's news material did not always meet with the approval of the university. The new Catholic newspaper appeared in 1926 with Monsignor McFadden as president of its board as a result of the merger in 1926 of *Catholic Universe*, founded by Bishop Gilmour in 1874, and the *Catholic Bulletin*, started in 1911 as the newspaper for the German Catholic societies. The latter was linked with Father Betten's St. Boniface Historical Society.[61] The placement of Carroll news along with elementary and high school news on what was said to be largely a grade-school page soon became an issue. Father Murtha Boylan was particularly incensed when he received a letter addressed to him as "Sister Superior of John Carroll University."[62] Father Boylan might have considered that a letter so addressed could have been the result of his given name, Murtha; there were even letters addressed to Martha Boylan. In any case, Father Boylan suggested that college news should be put in a separate category. At a time when efforts were being made to improve the public image of the college one can understand his concern.

Monsignor McFadden's reply, dated 1 April, defended the arrangement of school news in the diocesan paper and claimed that Father Boylan was trying to impose on the Catholic newspaper something he was not imposing on other newspapers, namely, telling them where to put the news.[63] The Monsignor touched on a point that Father Boylan had perhaps not considered. The location of John Carroll news in a prominent place on the school page, said Monsignor McFadden, gave the younger and perhaps future students who would also read that page a better chance to notice the John Carroll stories. Therefore, asked Monsignor McFadden, "Why feel embarrassed because this younger generation learns about your University right on the school page of the diocesan paper."[64] Father Boylan was not impressed with that explanation. He was much more concerned with the salutation on the letter he had received from "some sarcastic person." He said he "saw the force of the insinuation" or he would not have mentioned it and still insisted John Carroll news should not be mixed "promiscuously" with "grade school news."[65]

THE COLLEGE UNION

The rapid multiplication of student activities created an immediate need for some kind of coordination but not until 1919 did there materialize any means for doing so. At that time a College Union was formed to take over the "coordination and promotion" of all college activities.[66] Its jurisdiction covered not only the college but also the two high schools; an executive council composed of three members of each class and a representative from each organization that was officially recognized worked with the faculty moderator. The Union selected its own officers. The college newspaper expressed the view that it was "a wonder . . . that this idea of a college union was never presented before."[67] The Union sought to preserve the identity of the various organizations and looked upon its function as similar to that of a rope; "a number of different organizations or strands, any one of which would break up under the least pressure. Yet bind them together with a common organization and you have a body that will last as long as there are students at St. Ignatius."[68]

The smoking room of the college department was the first item on the agenda of the new Union. A "few improvements" were made:

A hanging chalk apparatus now swings airily above the heads of our noon-day pipe dreamers. This does away with the necessity of chalking the cues with pieces of loose plaster in lieu of the missing chalk. Pictures, amazing works of art to our minds at least, adorn the hitherto barren walls. Furthermore, the pool table which gave every indication of becoming a wreck before its time by reason of the undivided attention lavished upon it by its devotees, has at last been repaired. Also a new cover for the table has been procurred. All's well now so on with the dance.[69]

Within a year the students' joy was somewhat dampened by the ban of cigarette smoking in the smoking room; cigars and pipes only were permitted. The objection of the students to the new regulation had both an olfactory and a financial basis.

The pipes are all right if your olfactory organs are in a dilapidated condition; but cigars presuppose that students are millionaires. No matter how they work it, students lose in the end.

A decent cigar costs at least 16 cents. Rather strenuous if they are bought two or three times a day. A cheap cigar means at least a day in bed hunting for the memorable knife of Tom Sawyer. A day off equals a few pounds off your class notes.

So what're ya gonna do?[70]

The students suffered another blow when they discovered that the college Union had appointed a "houseman" for the pool room, marking the end of free pool. "Heretofore games were played by practically the entire number of occupants of the room and they were played gratis. The reason was no houseman."[71] The "jitneys" collected were used to help provide better furnishings for the smoking room.

Not all of the Union's improvements had negative effects. A review of the first year's accomplishments showed that the Union

aided materially in putting Ignatius on the collegiate map. It resurrected a dormant pep. It awakened students to the fact that they really have an Alma Mater they can and should be proud of, if they only displayed a little zeal in promoting its interests, and it fostered every student activity designed to reflect to the credit of St. Ignatius College spirit.[72]

Smokers to which seniors from local Catholic high schools were invited were sponsored by the Union. Attendance at athletic contests was improved and the year's activities ended with a "college day" which had long been observed as a climax to the year's activities. Father Bracken played an active part in seeing that the spirit aroused in the first year of the Union's existence was fostered and increased in succeeding years.

In December 1920 the smoking room moved from the main building to a house in the southeast side of the yard next to the barracks. Increased enrollment necessitated the move, a move which left the editorial offices of the *The Ignatian* the exclusive use of the old smoking room. By 1926 the new smoking quarters were in need of renovation and the place was closed by the dean pending repairs. There were holes in the plaster in both walls and ceiling, egg stains and water marks, the evidence of skirmishes, and other signs of the place having been "lived in."[73] The number of pool sharks had apparently been diminishing for the suggestion was now made that the removal of the billiard table would give more floor space. The renovated "Smoke House" was opened in March 1926 as the "Union Club." It was hoped the new quarters would "revive the Carroll spirit of good fellowship."[74]

Pressures from increased high school enrollment began to complicate lunch hour scheduling. To help alleviate some of the difficulty, a furnished room which would double as a dining room and meeting room for college students was provided in the basement of the main building. The place, which was made ready by one of the scholastics, a Mr. Crowley, at a cost of five hundred dollars, was called the "College Inn."

In 1924 Roy Scott of Western Reserve University proposed a college league whose purpose was to establish and maintain a spirit of sociability among the various colleges of the city. Its social activities would include Saturday afternoon dances. The reaction of Carroll students to this bit of external recognition was expressed in a column called "Odds and Ends" in the student newspaper.

We hear Reserve wants us to join some kind of a league of colleges. That reminds us of a story Prendergast told us the other day. It seems that at the Junior Dance, although you really couldn't dance, somebody cut the "D" off a card marked 'Reserved,' decorated the card with red colors, and the result was the name and colors of our East Side contemporary. It also seems the young man who claimed reservation of the table on which the card rested was the same as he who appeared to be a delegate of the proposed union. Moreover it seems the gentleman came to Carroll only after the girls of Notre Dame College had refused to accept his kind offer of admission to the circle of real colleges, unless Carroll became a member. So the gentleman came to Carroll, remarking no doubt, like the miner who fell down the shaft, 'I guess I'll drop in on the boys.'[75]

Over the years, in addition to its many activities, the college Union found it necessary to revise its constitution almost annually. The first major revision came in 1925 in order to correct a defect in the original charter which did not properly bring out the absolute veto of the faculty moderator.[76] The next significant revision was made in 1930 for much the same reason, suggesting that the relationship of the faculty moderator to the Union was still not entirely clear. To provide more clarity it was stated that "The Union is organized each year to strike a happy medium between students and faculty. Before becoming official it must be approved by the faculty."[77]

THEATER

Putting on plays has a long tradition in Jesuit colleges and high schools. Theatrical presentations were part of Jesuit College activity in the sixteenth century and were aimed at giving the students a chance to demonstrate their skills and put across moral points. St. Ignatius College did its part to maintain that tradition. Part of the tradition was the choice of plays that had all-male casts or plays where it was possible for men to play women's roles. The play was usually an annual public presentation and the cast chosen, not from a dramatic club as such, but from the best actors in the shorter plays given by classes during the school year. Usually, these students were the same ones active in the literary and debating societies.

It has already been noted that at the time Father Sommerhauser was having his difficulties with Bishop Farrelly, the students at Loyola High School put on a play called "The Triumph of Justice." It played at the Duchess Theater and was called the "best play in years," a play where "The hero is dashing, the villain villainous."[78]

The college play, "For the King Eternal," in the same year, 1916, was described as "more than a success. It is a masterpiece."[79] People were turned away from the first performance at the Cleveland Theater and a second matinee performance had to be scheduled. Some sixty students participated in the play, directed by Father William F. Hendrix. The following year a two-act musical comedy based on Irish history was put on very successfully. This play was in addition to the annual play, "Greater than a King," which played to three packed houses with a total attendance of over five thousand.[80] Father Hendrix also directed this play. In 1918 "King Saul," one of the old standbys of the college repertoire, was put on. Roy Bourgeois, a principal actor, was called to military duty before the play could be performed; there was fear that no substitute could be found to "play the wicked, wiley role of the villain, but Harold Traverse took the part so successfully that many of the audience breathed a sigh of relief at the announcement of his death."[81] This particular play with a cast of fifty-five and two large choruses played at the local opera house.

In 1919 the decision was made to put on separate plays for the college and high school. The college play was to be scheduled for just after Christmas and the high school play just before Lent. There was also a departure from the Biblical or medieval drama in favor of modern comedy.[82] In 1920 the college play had to be cancelled because no theater was available at the time the play was scheduled.

By 1928 a declining interest in dramatics was awakened by Father Bracken, who saw an opportunity to support the athletic fund with the proceeds of the play, "The Blonde Heir." "The proceeds, whatever they were, were allowed to the athletic fund. The hope is that the reopening of dramatic interest may continue and that several plays may be given next year."[83] This was not the only time that funds from various activities went into the athletic fund.

In 1928 A. J. Friedle took charge of theater direction, succeeding Alfonso O'Toole, who had formed the Little Theater Society in 1927 but who now had too busy a schedule to continue his producing chores. Friedle had the reputation of being one of the best directors in the diocese of Cleveland.[84] The year 1935 marked the first time that women played women's roles in the plays; the consultors decided that Father William Murphy, now dean of men, could use those women registered in an evening speech class for that year's Little Theater Production.[85]

MUSIC

A well-established tradition of St. Ignatius College was its fine orchestra. It remained for Father Victor Winter to bring it to the peak of its perfection in the years he directed the orchestra between 1915 and 1929. The members of the orchestra increased from ten to ninety and in one season, 1925–1926, the orchestra gave seven concerts including one at the Public Auditorium. It was estimated that the total number of those who attended those performances was over twelve thousand. The old quarters of the orchestra on the second floor over the gymnasium were abandoned for better accommodations in the two-story house at 2901 Lorain Avenue, where a major portion of the work of remodeling was done by members of the orchestra. In February 1927 a recording of one of the selections of the orchestra's repertoire was made by the New York Phonographic Recording Company. All of the necessary equipment was transported from New York to Cleveland where the recording was made at the K of C Hall at 2612 Prospect Avenue.[86] Bishop Schrembs was particularly pleased with Father Winter's efforts and instructed Monsignor McFadden to write a letter to all pastors asking their support and encouragement for such efforts.[87]

The heyday of the St. Ignatius College orchestra coincided with the early development of the Cleveland Symphony Orchestra. The Musical Arts Association was organized in 1915 to promote the Cleveland Symphony Orchestra which also played at Grays Armory until it occupied its new quarters at Severance Hall in 1931. Between 1915 and 1929 both orchestras drew large audiences of many of the same people. As the fortunes of the Cleveland Orchestra rose, those of the St. Ignatius orchestra declined. Father Winter documented the lack of interest in 1928 by pointing to receipts of only $1,140 and expenses for the year of $1,984.[88] When Father Winter was reassigned to Rockhurst College in Kansas in 1929, the *Carroll News* regretted his leaving and regretted that his successor, Mr. Carl Firstos, a scholastic, was having little success in recruiting talent.

Week after week he patiently posted signs on various bulletin boards. Week after week his signs met with a cold indifference and lethargy that was surprising.

Surely old members will answer the call. Surely there is an embryo symphony orchestra of new men who are anxious to show their talent. Surely Carroll has

Lumina Staff, 1916. *Standing:* James Brennan, Edward McDonnell, Paul Murphy, Henry Smith, Cornelius McLaughlin, Arthur Brickel. *Seated:* Howard Smith, Dan Gallagher, Thomas Doran, Aloysius Bungart, Joseph Walsh, Julius Snyder, Raymond Craft, Eugene McCarthy

Above left, Ora and Labora, 1917; *right,* Victor Winter and "Fritz" in new Music Room, 1915; *Bottom,* Basketball Cartoon, 1915. Basketball replaces baseball after completion of new gym, 1914

not heard the last of the symphonies of Hayden, Beethoven, Dvorak, Wagner, and other great masters.

The orchestra must not die! Carroll wants it! Carroll needs it![89]

Carroll may have needed the orchestra but there was little evidence that the interest would ever reach the heights it once had. There was plenty of evidence that the interests of the students and administrators had changed considerably. Father Joseph Kiefer, who succeeded Firstos, continued to have difficulty in bringing the orchestra back to full strength. There was renewed interest in a glee club, which Father Kiefer also directed. Started in 1919, the glee club did not begin to develop until 1926. By 1930 the chorus included members from the Women's Colleges and Nursing Schools and hoped to go on tour.[90]

The competition of the new "Jazz" and the consuming interest in athletics undoubtedly had something to do with the demise of symphonic music. Although complaints about "Jazz" appeared in the student newspaper, the appearance by 1926 of "Jazz" groups to furnish music at basketball games and the use of a marching band at football games seemed to absorb whatever musical talent there was. A saxophone trio, The Tri C Club, began to play not only at athletic contests but even at affairs such as smokers where formerly members of the orchestra had performed.[91]

The anti-jazz movement of the early 1920s was so strong that the Federation of Catholic Societies in the United States endorsed it. The complaint against "jazz," or ragtime, was that it was tearing the "order and sense of rhythm to shreds."[92] The reason for its popularity, said an article in *The Ignatian*, was that "the money chasers among the composers" had catered to the public's abuse of good music.[93] Most of the new public taste was blamed on the war and there was hope that "jazz" was dying "a natural death"; it was noted that the pipe organ was replacing "jazz" in the theater and large orchestras seemed to be coming into favor.[94]

Interest in athletics not only gave impetus to the marching band but also provided unlimited opportunities for writing of fight songs, Alma Mater songs, and victory songs. In 1923 a contest was held for the composition of what would be the official song appropriate for "athletic triumphs" or "in fact wherever the sons of old Ignatius gather to honor their Alma Mater." The song was supposed to stir up memories of the old days, thrill students, and appeal to school spirit. Hundreds of entries were judged by Fathers Bracken, Charles McDevitt Ryan, and Edward Carrigan, a scholastic.[95] The winner was Edward M. Carney '24, the center on the football team. The winning verses were to be set to music for the graduation exercises for 1923 but by that time St. Ignatius College had become Cleveland University. Later a "fight song" was composed, but there were complaints that cheering at the football games left the spectators too hoarse to sing.[96] Another Alma Mater song made its appearance in 1928, this one chosen after considerable debate by the senior class. The words were written by Bob Hunt, a former student.[97] A new victory song appeared in 1929; this one was introduced to the public at Loew's State Theater.[98] The words to this one were suggested by Don Ranney and John Foy, both Carroll students; Bill Hope, another student, provided the music. Father Fox also got into the act, writing "Hail John Carroll U" and "Onward on John Carroll."[99]

In 1927 band music was provided at football games by the Parmadale Orphanage Band under the direction of Jack Hearns. A rift soon occurred when the Parmadale Band requested seventy-five dollars for its services at the games. Father Bracken refused and was upheld by the consultors.[100] In August 1931 Jack Hearns was hired to organize a John Carroll Band. He accomplished this in time for the band to perform at the fall football games.[101]

COMPETITION: FORENSIC AND LITERARY

The long-standing tradition in Jesuit education of the development of oral and written expression skills continued to be held in high esteem even in the postwar years. It was frequently overshadowed by the amount of attention given to athletics, but it remained a substantial element in the student life of John Carroll University; the principal characteristic of postwar years was the introduction of intercollegiate competition.

The literary society had been essentially a debating club out of which came an opportunity for students to discuss and attain skill in public speaking. Such a society went by many names, such as the Newman Literary Society at Loyola or the Senior Debating Society at St. Ignatius College, where it was "a scene of violent though friendly controversy, almost every meeting nowadays."[102]

Oratorical contests were an essential part of the program and in 1916 began to replace the public debates held previously. The first contest was held in April 1916, at a nearby library auditorium. John W. Kegg was the winner. The topic, "The Need of Social Activity," was evidence of the new interest in social problems. Kegg's talk dealt with sweat shops, slums, hunger, illness, drunkenness, victims of wife beating, and poverty, making the point that "The social problem today is a matter of the right of the needy and the duty of others, hence, becomes a moral issue, and as such demands an organization whose aim is the prevention rather than the alleviation of ills."[103]

The oratorical contests also served as a means of keeping contact with alumni by bringing back former students as judges and spectators. The contest in 1917 was attended by Father John R. Hagan and Paul J. Preusser and Charles Perrier, while Father Daniel Gallagher, Raymond Desson, and Dr. Alvin O. Sibila were the judges. That year's contest was won by Aloysius Bungart, who was president of a "half dozen college societies, and, as the results show, has never let slip an opportunity to speak in public. 'Verbum sat sapienti.' Second place was awarded to James P. Brennan."[104]

The subject matter of the speeches in the oratorical contests invariably tended to deal with social problems, a tendency which many parents found disturbing. The student newspaper in 1919 felt it necessary to allay the fears of parents regarding their sons' possible radical activities.

Be not alarmed fond parents if your sons have recently assumed an air of unwanted gravity. Don't become frightened or surprised if they go about the house muttering strange things about Social Unrest, Race Problems, Leagues of Nations, etc. They need no treatment other than silence and a chance to be by themselves. For the Oratorical Contest is in full swing.[105]

The Peace Treaty and League of Nations issues of the 1920s produced a great deal of oratorical activity and political interest. The St. Ignatius College students voted against a League of Nations in any form; forty-two students, twelve less than the majority, favored ratification of the Treaty by the Senate with reservation. Of the remaining votes, thirteen favored immediate compromise and five favored unqualified acceptance. Both Case and Western Reserve favored compromise as did also Marquette University.[106]

During the war years the Debating Society had been reorganized to give a more formal program of debates; such issues as universal military training and women's suffrage were popular topics. The formation of the college Union in 1919 brought another reorganization of the Debating Society to give it more leeway "to conduct debates on timely topics and to carry on discussions on literary subjects."[107] In the fall of 1920 there was still another change; the larger society was broken into smaller units "in which more individual training can be given and the student can advance and develop according to his ability and application."[108]

Intercollegiate debating began in 1922 with the opportunity afforded by the Missouri Province contest. Students were eager to compete because the athletic teams had shown themselves "aggressive and successful contenders for the honors of the diamond, the gridiron and the floor. Let the debating team show itself as redoubtable in the coming contest."[109] The intercollegiate debating team now became a reality and prepared to compete among the twelve colleges of the Missouri Province. The Province was divided into districts; St. Ignatius was in district two with St. John of Toledo and St. Xavier of Cincinnati. Winners of the districts were to meet in semifinals and then the two winners were to meet in a final debate. Father Charles McDevitt Ryan was the debate coach for the St. Ignatius team, which went on to win the Province title over Creighton University, Omaha. This was indeed a surprise for St. Ignatius College, which had never before engaged in such a contest. One editorial in *The Ignatian* attributed success to the work of Father Ryan and the experience of the students in *ex tempore* speaking.[110] Debating did not develop further until 1930, when Father Ryan returned to John Carroll after having spent five years at Creighton, where he coached debate. An Oratorical Society was founded in 1930 upon Father Ryan's return and within three years, debate had again established itself as a major activity.[111]

Debating was not the only academic venture into intercollegiate competition. The Missouri Province and later the Chicago Province also sponsored essay contests in English and Latin. Success in these contests had been attained so often that when in 1916 four places out of ten were won in the Latin Essay Contest, the *Lumina* complained that the announcement on the bulletin board met with "silence." "No handshakings, no congratulations. What's the matter? Have we grown so accustomed to places in the Latin contest that the record of winning four places of ten—almost half—cannot stir even a flutter of delight, even a momentary thrill of satisfaction?"[112] The following year, 1917, four places were again won in the Latin contest including first, second, third, and fifth. Much of the credit was given to Father James Doyle and a scholastic, Mr. William Young.[113] Even the war years did not interrupt winning places in the contest; at least two or three places in both Latin and English contests were annual awards in a competition numbering approximately a thousand students in the Province's colleges.

Perfection in English expression was so paramount that the college newspaper would call to the attention of its readers mistakes in the classroom and corridors. In 1921 it commented "We thought Ignatius a paradise of English idiomatic bliss until someone let slip to an appreciative audience the two words 'have sang.' After all our efforts this is what it has come to."[114] There was still hope, however, for in 1922, two articles by St. Ignatius students Frank J. Bitzan and John A. Weber appeared in Dr. Schnittkind's anthology. This was the first time in several years that any student had received such recognition. On the other hand, 1923 was the first time in years that no St. Ignatius student placed in the Province English Essay contest.